THE SOCIALITE
WHO KILLED A NAZI
WITH HER BARE HANDS

and 143 Other Fascinating People
Who Died This Past Year

AUGUST 2011 TO JULY 2012

D1051280

THE SOCIALITE WHO KILLED A NAZI WITH HER BARE HANDS

and 143 Other Fascinating People Who Died This Past Year

AUGUST 2011 TO JULY 2012

Edited and With an Introduction by William McDonald
Foreword by Tom Rachman

WORKMAN PUBLISHING • NEW YORK

Library of Congress Cataloging-in-Publication Data

The socialite who killed a Nazi with her bare hands : and 143 other fascinating people who died this past year : the best of the New York times obituaries, 2013 / edited by William McDonald.
    p. cm.
  ISBN 978-0-7611-7087-7 (alk. paper)
 1. Biography—20th century. 2. Biography—21st century. 3. Obituaries. 4. Obituaries—United States.
 5. United States—Biography. I. McDonald, William (Journalist) II. New York times.
  CT120.S63 2012
  920—dc23
                              2012021102

Design by Sarah Smith and Orlando Adiao

Workman books are available at special discounts when purchased in bulk for premiums and sales promotions as well as for fund-raising or educational use. Special editions or book excerpts can also be created to specification. For details, contact the Special Sales Director at the address below, or send an email to specialmarkets@workman.com.

Workman Publishing Company, Inc.
225 Varick Street, New York, NY 10014-4381
workman.com

WORKMAN is a registered trademark of Workman Publishing Company, Inc.

Printed in the United States of America
First printing October 2012

10 9 8 7 6 5 4 3 2 1

CONTENTS

FOREWORD

BY TOM RACHMAN

A N OBITUARY is the news column most brimming with life: full of endeavor, blunders, repentance and humor, and the industry of those you'll never meet but perhaps wish you had. Each obit records the intersection of a singular personality with an era shared by billions. In some cases, the epoch prevails; in others, the individual. Either way, the account humanizes history, recalling events long forgotten and animating decades that preceded our own.

Nearly unique in news, these are stories with endings. In the international section of a paper, wars conclude, but there's always a reconstruction ahead. In business articles, a bankrupt corporation is landscape in the saga of the economy. In sports, the championship team soon looks to next season.

But an obit is the completed story. After all that striving, this is what there was, flawed or inspirational, with no further outcomes. An ending defines one life, while a multitude of lives begins to define living, sketching out the range of human pursuits, the price of error, the weight of chance, and the disparate uses of time that, in the case of these subjects, ran out over a single year.

There are politicians in this volume, many musicians, a number of poets. There's an author of experimental fiction that some struggled to read; a writer of lurid novels that fans devoured; a children's author whose books were "roundly praised, intermittently censored and occasionally eaten." There are businessmen with vision enough to popularize the bagel, miniature golf and the Doritos corn chip. One inventor produced millions of couch potatoes with his wireless remote control, while another's shipping container, his obit states rather astonishingly, "is now acknowledged to have been the spark that touched off globalization."

There are Nobel Prize recipients, including one who passed away before hearing the good news. Several award-winning journalists died over the year, two of them while covering the violence in Syria. A third longtime correspondent earned renown for his retorts as much as his reports, savaging foes while enchanting allies with his champagne wit.

Several are profiled for their experiences during World War II, including those who survived the Holocaust and others who battled the Nazis, as well as a man convicted of complicity in the murder of thousands of Jews. A number of the subjects battled for equality during the postwar period, suffering and denouncing injustices based on race, gender and sexuality whose repercussions still roil contemporary society.

Other profiles record final connections to vanished worlds, such as the last veteran of World War I; or a man whose job — that of tummler — is now so obscure that it requires a definition; and a 111-year-old silent-movie scriptwriter whose obit contains this dynamite opening: "She told of Hollywood moguls chasing naked would-be starlets, the women shrieking with laughter."

Those who died young underscore current preoccupations: a conservative blogger, for example, and a tech innovator who named his company after a piece of fruit. There are coincidences, such as the deaths of three iconic TV music presenters; plus two dictators and the daughter of a third, who escaped her cruel father yet never escaped his shadow.

> The best way to contemplate what it is to possess a human life is to consider what others have done with theirs.

Some are included for their peculiarity, including an artist preoccupied with U.F.O.'s ("By his reckoning, 1 in 50 Americans has been abducted by an alien and simply does not know it"); an explorer who rowed across both the Atlantic and Pacific oceans; and a gambler who played poker with two presidents, a drug lord and a pornographer — though presumably not at the same time.

Most were public figures but some were private, and likely would have remained so had they not been profiled. There is a Coast Guard seaman who, patrolling a foggy Long Island beach in 1942, bumped into a bunch of German saboteurs. There's the owner of a Brooklyn dive bar who, after all the biographies of deceased laureates and powerbrokers, might seem an ordinary subject. Yet hers is a memorable and touching tale, and a reminder of something

familiar from experience but exceedingly hard to convey in news: how full are the lives around us, and how little we know of them.

That defunct lives regain vibrancy in this volume is credit to the superlative New York Times obituarists, who find what is noteworthy in the obscure and what is obscure in the noteworthy. Their accounts are not dry résumés of the eminent; they are what a famed British obituary editor once described as "biographical short stories."

Now, some readers may still be uneasy about the obit, touched as it is by the taboo of death. They might be reluctant even to open this book in public, wary of appearing ghoulish, especially if entries provoke a smile, as many should. But there is nothing macabre about this form. The obituary is only occasioned by death; it never dwells on that empty source. Readers ought never shrink from an interest in how others think and behave.

There may, of course, be egoistic motives for reading obits, too. What are the ways in which people die and which might be mine? What are the rewards and risks of living differently than I do? For what might I be remembered?

Such questions cannot be answered. After all, people will never know their own life story. The first years are lost to memory and the last may fade in clarity; or the end arrives abruptly, without the chance for a reckoning. If there is time for review, how accurate can it be, from a perspective that is simultaneously the most privileged and the least objective?

The best way to contemplate what it is to possess a human life is to consider what others have done with theirs. So, we listen to family lore, read literature and turn, with sympathy and curiosity, to the obits.

INTRODUCTION

BY WILLIAM McDONALD

A N OBITUARY IN THE GUARDIAN happened to catch the eye of a New York Times reporter in London one day, and she sent a Twitter message about it, telling her followers, You have to read this. So I did, and she was right: it was quite a story — precisely the kind that I and my colleagues on the New York Times obituary desk hope to come across every day (without wishing anyone's demise, of course). Devoted readers do, too, I suspect.

The obituary was about Count Robert de La Rochefoucauld, a dashing man with an elegant name, an illustrious lineage and a rather spectacular past. A descendant of one of France's oldest families, he was a saboteur in World War II, though that description alone doesn't do him justice. He was also a freedom fighter and an escape artist (not to mention a mayor in a later life), a man of bravery, cunning and ingenuity who had plenty of luck and no compunction about killing. Not surprisingly, The Times commissioned an obit of its own, and it can be read in full further on, but here is an excerpt to suggest why we couldn't resist writing it:

"His exploits were legend, involving an eclectic and decidedly resourceful collection of tools in the service of sabotage and escape, including loaves of bread, a stolen limousine, the leg of a table, a bicycle and a nun's habit — not to mention the more established accouterments of espionage like parachutes, explosives and a submarine."

It's fair to assume that few readers who came upon this obit had ever heard of Count de La Rochefoucauld. Certainly editors at The Times had not. But our lack of familiarity was no reason to disqualify him from a Times obit. Yes, great fame (or great infamy, for that matter) is a sure ticket to the Times obituary columns. (Turn to Andy Griffith and Col. Muammar el-Qaddafi, respectively.) So is great accomplishment, even if the name attached to it draws a blank from most readers. (Eugene Polley, inventor of the wireless television remote control.) But a third way into The Times is to have been, like the count, the protagonist in a story that even if dimly remembered will rightly cry out be told.

An obituary of this type often revolves around an event that attracted wide publicity at the time — that is, it was news. The obit presents an opportunity to recount the event in all its vivid detail through a biographical portrait of someone who was central to the story — that is, a newsmaker. John Fairfax falls into this group with great panache: an erstwhile pirate and lone-eagle adventurer who, in publicists' lingo, got a lot of press when he rowed across oceans. His story, too, can be found here.

And then there are the more anonymous souls who found themselves caught up in history and doing their small part to shape it. The last veteran of World War I. A homeless woman whose plight influenced housing law. A Hollywood love child who lived a lie.

That aforementioned bomb-planting aristocrat. They illuminate the past, and the likes of them populate much of this book as well.

This is the second annual compilation of selected obituaries from the pages of The Times, and if it carries a theme, it is the idea of story. Most of the obits here, a fraction of the total published over the course of a year, were chosen for their narrative pull. Some, to be sure, are about famous people, revealing sides to them that the spotlights may never have reached. But most are about the uncelebrated — people whose names may not register but whose lives nevertheless resonate.

Something in human nature requires a story — to be entertained, to be moved, to be edified, even to be given meaning. As children instinctively know, stories help us understand what it is to be alive in this world.

Obituaries perform the same function. They turn real lives into true stories. Indeed, more than any "story" in the newspaper, the obit, at its best, lives up to that billing: it is a rounded account whose arc has a clear beginning and end. That a certain artifice is involved in the writing is undeniable, and accepted by the reader. We know that no life reads like a novel or a script (although Count de La Rochefoucauld would make a smashing basis for either). But we grant the obituary writer a degree of literary license because we understand a life best when its various strands can be woven into a story, driven by events and moving in chapters to, in this case, an inevitable conclusion.

Where an obituary may differ from other forms is at the juncture of journalism. An obituary has news as well as a story to tell, and it tells it right at the top, under a headline. In an obituary, unlike a biography, The End comes first.

But that's an organizational matter, a journalistic convention that serves a newspaper's purpose and a reader's needs. With the news of the death duly reported, what draws the reader on is the promise of a story that made that death newsworthy in the first place — an account of a fascinating and consequential life. Many lie ahead in these pages.

THE BEST OF The New York Times OBITUARIES

AUGUST 2011
TO JULY 2012

RUDOLF BRAZDA

Branded in Pink at Buchenwald

JUNE 26, 1913 - AUG. 3, 2011

R UDOLF BRAZDA, who was believed to be the last surviving man to wear the pink triangle — the emblem sewn onto the striped uniforms of the thousands of homosexuals sent to Nazi concentration camps, most of them to their deaths — died on Aug. 3 in Bantzenheim, in Alsace, France. He was 98.

Mr. Brazda, who was born in Germany, had lived in France since the Buchenwald camp, near Weimar, Germany, was liberated by American forces in April 1945. He had been imprisoned there for three years.

It was only after May 27, 2008, when the German National Monument to the Homosexual Victims of the Nazi Regime was unveiled in Berlin's Tiergarten park — opposite the Memorial to the Murdered Jews of Europe — that Mr. Brazda became known as probably the last gay survivor of the camps. Until he notified German officials after the unveiling, the Lesbian and Gay Federation of Germany believed there were no other pink-triangle survivors.

A statement by Mémorial de la Déportation Homosexuelle, a French organization that commemorates the Nazi persecution of gay people, said that Mr. Brazda "was very likely

SURVIVING VICTIM: Rudolf Brazda, in 2008, in front of the German National Monument to Homosexual Victims of the Nazi Regime.

the last victim and the last witness" to the persecution.

"It will now be the task of historians to keep this memory alive," the statement said, "a task that they are just beginning to undertake."

One of those historians is Gerard Koskovich, curator of the Gay, Lesbian, Bisexual, Transgender History Museum in San Francisco and an author, with Roberto Malini and Steed Gamero, of "A Different Holocaust" (2006).

"The Nazi persecution represented the apogee of anti-gay persecution, the most extreme instance of state-sponsored homophobia in the 20th century," Mr. Koskovich said.

> "We know of instances where gay prisoners and their pink triangles were used for guards' target practice."

During the 12-year Nazi regime, he said, the police identified up to 100,000 men as homosexuals, about 50,000 of whom were convicted of violating Paragraph 175 of the German criminal code, which outlawed male homosexual acts.

There was no law forbidding female homosexual acts, he said, and only men were imprisoned. They totaled 5,000 to 15,000, according to research by Rüdiger Lautmann, a German sociologist, who found that about 60 percent of them died in the camps, most within a year.

"The experience of homosexual men under the Nazi regime was one of extreme persecution, but not genocide," Mr. Koskovich said, when compared with the "relentless effort to identify all Jewish people and ultimately exterminate them."

Still, the conditions in the camps were murderous, said Edward J. Phillips, the director of exhibitions at the United States Holocaust Memorial Museum.

"Men sent to the camps under Section 175 were usually put to forced labor under the cruelest conditions — underfed, long hours, exposure to the elements and brutal treatment by labor brigade leaders," Mr. Phillips said. "We know of instances where gay prisoners and their pink triangles were used for guards' target practices."

Two books have been written about Mr. Brazda. In one, "Itinerary of a Pink Triangle" (2010), by Jean-Luc Schwab, Mr. Brazda recalled how dehumanizing the incarceration was. "Seeing people die became such an everyday thing, it left you feeling practically indifferent," he is quoted as saying. "Now, every time I think back on those terrible times, I cry. But back then, just like everyone in the camps, I had hardened myself so I could survive."

Rudolf Brazda was born on June 26, 1913, in the eastern German town of Meuselwitz to a family of Czech origin. His parents, Emil and Anna Erneker Brazda, both worked in the coal mining industry. Rudolf became a roofer. Before he was sent to the camp, he was arrested twice for violations of Paragraph 175.

After the war, Mr. Brazda moved to Alsace. There he met Edouard Mayer, his partner until Mr. Mayer's death in 2003. He had no immediate survivors.

"Having emerged from anonymity," the book "Itinerary of a Pink Triangle" says of Mr. Brazda, "he looks at the social evolution for homosexuals over his nearly 100 years of life: 'I have known it all, from the basest repression to the grand emancipation of today.'"

— BY DENNIS HEVESI

BERNADINE P. HEALY

A Battler for Women's Health Undone by 9/11

AUG. 2, 1944 - AUG. 6, 2011

D R. BERNADINE P. HEALY, the first woman to lead the National Institutes of Health and the first physician to lead the American Red Cross until she was forced out in a storm of criticism over flawed responses to the Sept. 11 terrorist attacks, died on Aug. 6 at her home in Gates Mills, Ohio. She was 67.

The cause was recurring brain cancer, which she had battled for 13 years, her husband, Dr. Floyd D. Loop, said.

In a hybrid career in the largely male domains of medicine and government, Dr. Healy, a cardiologist and feminist, was a professor at Johns Hopkins University, dean of the Ohio State University medical school, a White House science adviser and president of the American Heart Association. She wrote scientific papers and magazine columns, and once ran for the United States Senate.

But she was best known as a tough, innovative administrator who, as director of the National Institutes of Health from 1991 to 1993, championed studies that overturned false assumptions about women's health. And as president of the American Red Cross from 1999 to 2001, she struggled to coordinate its complex, often contradictory missions of humanitarian disaster relief and the businesslike maintenance of blood supplies.

Dr. Healy's résumé was a compendium of academic and professional achievements that in its cold detail omitted a central fact: her relentless effort to counter the misperception that heart attacks were men's problems. Heart disease was by far the leading killer of American women,

who accounted for nearly 40 percent of its victims. Women's groups had long sought a greater focus on women's coronary health, cancers and the role of hormonal changes and therapy.

Dr. Healy, who had pushed similar concerns within cardiology, went to Washington and made the issue her own.

"The problem is to convince both the lay and medical sectors that coronary heart disease is also a women's disease, not a man's disease in disguise," Dr. Healy wrote in The New England Journal of Medicine in 1991. At the institutes of health, the country's largest medical research organization, Dr. Healy, a Republican appointed by President George H. W. Bush, inherited a sprawling agency of 15,000 people. It had gone without a director for two years and was beset by bureaucratic infighting, political interference and declining morale.

"I am willing to go out on a limb, shake the tree and even take a few bruises," she told reporters. "I'm not particularly concerned about being popular."

Dr. Healy cracked the whip on bureaucrats, recruited new talent, expanded the Human Genome Project and reversed policies that, like the medical establishment, had focused largely on men's health and virtually excluded women from clinical trials. She mandated the inclusion of women in trials wherever appropriate.

She began the Women's Health Initiative, a $625 million study of the causes, prevention and treatment of cardiovascular diseases, osteoporosis and cancer in middle-aged and older women. Long after her tenure, the initiative continued yielding important findings. In 2002, it found that prolonged estrogen-progestin hormone replacement therapy in postmenopausal women increased risks of breast cancer, stroke and heart attack.

DECISIVE ADMINISTRATOR:
Bernadine P. Healy led both the N.I.H. and the American Red Cross.

"Dr. Healy's stubborn insistence that the N.I.H. concern itself with women's health was not broadly supported at the time," Anne M. Dranginis, an associate professor of biological sciences at St. John's University, wrote in a 2002 Op-Ed article in The New York Times. "Had Dr. Healy not championed research on women's health, how much longer would healthy women have been encouraged to take hormone drugs?"

Dr. Healy stepped down when President Bill Clinton named a new N.I.H. director in 1993.

Six years later, Dr. Healy faced even more daunting challenges at the Red Cross. While it was widely seen as an icon of humanitarian work, the organization was an unwieldy behemoth with 1,000 chapters, 1.2 million volunteers, 3,000 staff members and a $3 billion budget. It was also a house divided, with nonprofit disaster-relief on one side and, on the other, a blood business run like a corporation.

Recovering from a brain tumor as she took over, Dr. Healy found what she called "turf battles, gossip and very little teamwork."

Her reform efforts stumbled in the face of resistant autonomous chapters, a staff that

chafed under her hard-driving style, cases of embezzlement and lax controls, which led to record fines for infected blood products. She made the safety of blood supplies a priority.

But she upset many by auditing local chapters' finances, overriding veteran administrators' decisions and strongly supporting Israel's Red Shield of David in its effort to join the international Red Cross and Red Crescent societies without having to accept a cross or crescent as its emblem. When the effort failed, she withheld dues from the international body in protest.

Missteps after the Sept. 11 terrorist attacks precipitated her downfall. Red Cross disaster-relief units responded poorly, especially at the Pentagon crash site, critics said. Later, her handling of blood donations for 9/11 victims came under fire. Collections far exceeded amounts needed. Some blood was kept for other users, but much of it expired and had to be discarded.

She was excoriated in Congress and by chapter leaders and donors over her Liberty Fund, established to aid victims of the terrorist attacks. It collected $564 million but kept $264 million for other uses, including aid in future attacks. She said it had never been intended just for Sept. 11 victims, but her critics insisted that the money had been raised under false pretenses. In response to the protests, the Red Cross redirected all the money to Sept. 11 relief.

Critics called Dr. Healy autocratic and said she had jeopardized the goodwill of a revered charity. Allies defended her as smartly decisive, even if she sometimes ignored political realities. She resigned under pressure, although one Red Cross director acknowledged, "We hired a change agent for a culture resistant to change."

Bernadine Patricia Healy was born in New York City on Aug. 2, 1944, one of four daughters of Michael and Violet McGrath Healy. Her parents ran a small perfume factory in Long Island City, Queens, where she grew up.

She graduated from Hunter High School in Manhattan in 1962, got through Vassar College in three years and graduated from Harvard Medical School in 1970. After postdoctoral work, she became a full professor at Johns Hopkins in 1982 and directed its cardiac care unit from 1976 to 1984.

Her first marriage, to Dr. George Bulkley, a surgeon she had met in medical school, ended in divorce in 1981. In 1985, Dr. Healy married Dr. Loop, a cardiac surgeon. Besides Dr. Loop, she is survived by a daughter from her first marriage and a daughter from her second.

Dr. Healy was President Ronald Reagan's deputy science adviser in 1984 and 1985, president of the American Heart Association in 1988 and 1989, and from 1985 to 1991 practiced cardiology and directed research at the Cleveland Clinic Foundation, which was operated by Dr. Loop.

She lost a Senate primary in Ohio in 1994, was a professor and dean at Ohio State from 1995 to 1999 and an adviser on bioterrorism to President George W. Bush.

— BY ROBERT D. MCFADDEN

\\\\\\\\\\\\\\\\\\\\\\\\\\\\\\

HUGH L. CAREY

Governor to City: I'm Here for You

APRIL 11, 1919 - AUG. 7, 2011

H UGH L. CAREY, the governor who helped rescue New York from the brink of financial collapse in the 1970s and tamed a culture of ever-growing spending, died on Aug. 7 at his summer home on Shelter Island, N.Y. He was 92.

From 1975 through 1982, as the state's 51st governor, Mr. Carey led a small group of public servants who vanquished the fiscal crisis that threatened New York City and State — the direst emergency a governor had faced since the Depression — by taking on powers over the city's finances that no governor had wielded before and none has wielded since.

A liberal Democrat, Mr. Carey reversed the upward spiral of borrowing, spending and entitlement under one of his predecessors, Nelson A. Rockefeller, a Republican who had presided in an era of seemingly limitless government promise. But even after eight years as governor, Mr. Carey remained an enigma. The witty storyteller who could charm an audience alternated with the irascible loner who alienated many of his allies. The brooding, private man, father of more than a dozen children, who mourned the deaths of his wife and, earlier, two sons killed in a car crash, gave way to a man who engaged in an exuberant, very public romance that led to a second marriage.

Hugh Carey rose to power as a Democrat outside his party's machine. He began the 1974 campaign for governor as a recently widowed congressman from Brooklyn, a long shot who was not taken seriously, then cruised to one of the most resounding victories in the state's history.

He spent his final years as governor frustrated, however. Absent an emergency, he often seemed bored with the job.

The political strategist David Garth, who was one of Mr. Carey's closest associates, once said of him: "Hugh Carey on the petty issues can be very petty. On the big stuff, he is terrific."

Mr. Carey's stature grew in his decades out of office, and he was hailed as a hero by Republicans and Democrats. As he acknowledged, his handling of government finances overshadowed all else he did. In an interview in 1982 in his last days in office, he said, "The objectives I set forth I've achieved in terms of a state that's respected fiscally, a city that's now well on its way back to concrete foundations."

In four terms as governor, Mr. Rockefeller had built a legacy of state universities and highways but also of much higher taxes and enormous debt. The pattern was repeated at the local level; under Mayor John V. Lindsay, a Republican turned Democrat, New York City had to borrow money for day-to-day operations. The 1974-75 recession opened yawning deficits and exposed years of unsound practices.

On Jan. 1, 1975, Mr. Carey declared in his inaugural address, "This government will begin today the painful, difficult, imperative process of learning to live within its means."

He immediately faced a cascade of emergencies, as New York City, Yonkers, various state authorities, several school districts and ultimately the state itself flirted with collapse.

New York City lay at the core of the crisis. Mr. Lindsay's successor as mayor, Abraham D. Beame, was taking drastic action, cutting tens of thousands of jobs, but a solution lay beyond the city's grasp. In May 1975, Wall Street firms refused to sell the city's bonds, threatening its ability to pay its bills.

Mr. Carey responded with a series of audacious moves to keep the city afloat. He created the Municipal Assistance Corporation to borrow money for the city. He created and headed the Emergency Financial Control Board, with the power to reject city budgets and labor contracts, giving him vast new authority at Mr. Beame's expense.

By seizing control of the city's finances, and then telling the mayor that he had to fire his closest aide to placate the bankers, Mr. Carey permanently soured his relationship with Mr. Beame, who had helped him get elected. But such tough measures were necessary to keep the enterprise from sinking. Felix G. Rohatyn, the investment banker whom the governor appointed to head the Municipal Assistance Corporation, later said of Mr. Carey, "He was the only one who had any credibility left."

The governor engineered more than $1 billion in state loans to the city and $200 million in new city taxes. He persuaded banks to refinance city debts and accept a moratorium on some debt payments, and he got municipal unions to invest their pension funds in Municipal Assistance Corporation bonds.

Despite those measures, New York City at one point came within hours of having to file for bankruptcy.

On Oct. 29, 1975, President Gerald R. Ford vowed that he would veto "any bill that has as its purpose a federal bailout of New York City." The next day, the front page of The Daily News famously proclaimed: "Ford to City: Drop Dead."

A fierce backlash ensued, and a chastened Ford was persuaded that the governor had the situation under control. The president agreed in early 1976 to $2.3 billion in federal loan guarantees to the city. The greatest peril had passed.

Outside the fiscal realm, Mr. Carey promised an era of openness and clean government. He mandated financial disclosure for top state officials, barred party leaders from holding major state posts, signed campaign finance laws that set limits and required disclosure and secured voter approval of a constitutional amendment providing for appointment, rather than election, of judges to the Court of Appeals, New York's highest court, a change that was viewed as insulating the court from politics.

A MATTER OF URGENCY: Hugh L. Carey, left, governor of New York, with Mayor Abraham D. Beame, right, and others during an Emergency Financial Control Board meeting in 1977. He rescued New York from fiscal ruin.

Like so many New York governors, Mr. Carey harbored presidential ambitions, but trouble at home doomed any hope he might have had. His austerity measures made him unpopular with many voters, and his support for Westway, a proposed highway along the West Side of Manhattan, made more enemies than friends.

In 1978, when Mr. Carey ran for a second term, he was challenged in the primary by his own lieutenant governor, Mary Anne Krupsak, an unheard-of affront to a sitting governor. But in the general election he managed a narrow victory over the Republican candidate, Perry B. Duryea, a former Assembly speaker.

Mr. Carey brought into government an impressive cadre of people. One was Mario M. Cuomo, his second lieutenant governor, who succeeded him as governor (and whose son Andrew was elected governor in 2010). Among the others were Mr. Rohatyn and Richard Ravitch, a lieutenant governor under Gov. David A. Paterson.

But Mr. Carey eventually feuded with nearly everyone around him, beginning with Ms. Krupsak, who felt ignored. In 1977, he helped orchestrate the downfall of his old ally, Mr. Beame, after one term as mayor. He encouraged Mario Cuomo's challenge of Mr. Beame's renomination, but Congressman Edward I. Koch defeated them both and became mayor.

Mr. Carey's relations with the Legislature turned rocky in his second term. The governor let legislators know that he considered them petty and parochial, while they accused him of being distant from the business at hand. In 1981 and 1982, the Legislature cut him out of the budget-making process; when he vetoed dozens of spending items, both houses overrode his vetoes. He was the first governor of New York in a century to see his veto overridden.

In 1982, the state approved the most significant legislation of his second term, an $8 billion package to restore New York City's crumbling transit system. But that was largely the doing of legislators and Mr. Ravitch, chairman of the Metropolitan Transportation Authority. The governor had been reduced to a bystander.

Mr. Carey acquired a reputation for erratic behavior. He created a furor by saying that one of New York's seats in the United States Senate had been and should remain "a Jewish seat." He offered to drink a glass of PCBs to allay fears of contamination at a state office building where an electrical transformer fire had spread soot laden with the toxic chemical.

BROOKLYN-BORN: Mr. Carey followed an educational path well worn by Irish-Catholic boys.

But it was his marriage to Evangeline Gouletas, a wealthy real estate investor, that made many people wonder about his judgment. They met at the inauguration of Ronald Reagan as president in January 1981 and married less than three months later. Ms. Gouletas said that she had been married twice before and that her first husband had died, but shortly after her wedding to Mr. Carey, reporters discovered that she had three former husbands, all quite alive.

To the dismay of his staff, the governor began dyeing his silver hair — not always quite the same shade — and including his wife in policy discussions. The newlyweds were often seen out dancing, and they turned up regularly at black-tie events; Mr. Carey suddenly seemed more bon vivant than sober executive.

Finally, it became clear that he would be challenged by other Democrats if he ran for a third term. Although Mr. Carey had been a prime sponsor of Mr. Cuomo's political career, their relationship had so deteriorated that Mr. Cuomo, as Ms. Krupsak had done, was considering running against him.

In January 1982, Governor Carey announced that at the end of his term later that year, at age 63, he would retire from politics. After leaving office, he practiced law and was an executive at the chemicals conglomerate W. R. Grace & Company. He and Ms. Gouletas divorced after several years. Mr. Carey quickly faded from the public eye, though he turned up occasionally at the Capitol in Albany to bask in encomiums for his handling of the fiscal crisis.

In 2010, the State Legislature voted to rename the Brooklyn-Battery Tunnel after Mr. Carey. Mr. Koch applauded the move, saying: "I have been trying for years to get something named for Hugh Carey. I think he's the greatest governor of the modern era."

Hugh Leo Carey was born on April 11, 1919, in Park Slope, Brooklyn, the fourth of five sons of Margaret and Denis J. Carey, both children of Irish immigrants. Denis Carey founded a successful business delivering fuel oil and kerosene, and the family lived comfortably.

Hugh Carey followed an educational path well worn by Brooklyn's Irish-Catholic sons: St. Augustine's Academy and High School, St. John's College. He left school to enlist in a National Guard cavalry unit in 1939 at Camp Drum, near Watertown.

He fought with the 104th Division in Europe, helping to capture Cologne and liberate prisoners at a concentration camp at Nordhausen. At his discharge in 1946, he was a lieutenant colonel.

In 1947 he married Helen Owen Twohy, the widow of a Navy flier killed in the war, and adopted her daughter. They had 13 more children together and divided their time between

Park Slope and Shelter Island, where their rambling white house with a wraparound porch became the family homestead.

Mr. Carey is survived by five daughters, six sons, three brothers, 25 grandchildren and six great-grandchildren.

After the war, Mr. Carey returned to St. John's, where he finished his undergraduate education and graduated from law school. He then entered the family oil business. His eldest brother, Edward, struck out on his own, creating the New England Petroleum Corporation and amassing a fortune that would help underwrite his brother's political career.

In 1960, Hugh Carey ran for Congress in a Brooklyn district that stretched from Park Slope to Bay Ridge, challenging a popular Republican incumbent. Running in a strongly Catholic district in a year when John F. Kennedy was pulling Catholics to the Democratic line, Mr. Carey squeezed out a 1,097-vote victory.

In seven terms in Congress, Mr. Carey ranked high on the scorecards of liberal groups and adhered to positions, like opposing the death penalty, even when they were unpopular. But he portrayed himself as a moderate, playing up his support for federal aid to parochial schools.

In Congress he became an influential member of the New York delegation. He sat on the House Education and Labor Committee, which handled most of the social welfare legislation enacted under Kennedy and President Lyndon B. Johnson, and later on the powerful Ways and Means Committee.

But Mr. Carey became restless. In 1969 he ran for mayor of New York as an independent, angering Democratic Party leaders and prompting predictions of his political demise. But he abandoned the race after his sons Peter and Hugh Jr., both teenagers, were killed in a car accident on Shelter Island. Another son, Paul,

died of cancer in 2001. After Helen Carey, who had been treated for cancer three years earlier, learned that the disease had returned, Mr. Carey decided to retire from politics.

Hailed for helping New York avert bankruptcy, then criticized for feuding and a bon vivant manner.

In December 1973, however, when Mr. Rockefeller resigned as governor, leaving Lt. Gov. Malcolm Wilson to serve the year remaining on his term, Mr. Carey saw an opening and began to prepare a run. Then, on March 8, 1974, Helen Carey died. Her husband, with seven school-age children still at home, was expected to bow out of the race. But on March 26, he announced his candidacy. Friends said he needed the challenge to distract him from his grief. After winning the Democratic nomination, he trounced Governor Wilson, 57 percent to 42 percent, in a national post-Watergate sweep by Democrats.

"All my life, people have been underestimating me," Mr. Carey often said. In rising to power, he repeatedly ignored the conventional wisdom and trusted his own judgment, and he would again as governor.

Years later, he told a reporter: "A mentor long departed told me that the greatest gift in political life, in any life, is to view yourself objectively, at arm's length, to make an assessment of yourself. So whom do I rely on? I rely on myself."

— BY RICHARD PÉREZ-PEÑA;
FRANK LYNN CONTRIBUTED REPORTING.

NANCY WAKE

A Belle of Paris, a Heroine of War

AUG. 30, 1912 - AUG. 7, 2011

NANCY WAKE DID NOT LIKE KILLING PEOPLE, but in wartime, she once told an interviewer, "I don't see why we women should just wave our men a proud goodbye and then knit them balaclavas."

Ms. Wake led a life that Hemingway might have sketched, rising from impoverished childhood in New Zealand to high-society hostess in the south of France, from freelance journalist to decorated heroine of the French Resistance during World War II. She was credited with saving the lives of hundreds of Allied soldiers and downed airmen between 1940 and 1943 by escorting them through occupied France to safety in Spain.

She helped establish communication lines between the British military and the French Resistance in 1944 that were deemed crucial to weakening German strength in France in advance of the Allied invasion.

By her own account, she once killed a German sentry with her bare hands and ordered the execution of a woman she believed to be a German spy.

"I was not a very nice person," Ms. Wake told an Australian newspaper in 2001. "And it didn't put me off my breakfast."

"THE WHITE MOUSE": Nancy Wake saved the lives of hundreds of Allied soldiers during World War II.

Ms. Wake, who died on Aug. 7 in London at the age of 98, received so many medals for her wartime service that she lived out her old age on the proceeds from their sale, she said. She was given the George Medal, Britain's second-highest civilian honor, and the Medal of Freedom, the United States' second-highest. France gave her the Legion of Honor, the highest military honor it bestows.

She once described herself — as a young woman — as someone who loved nothing more than "a good drink" and handsome men, "especially French men." The German military described her as "la souris blanche," or "the white mouse," for her ability to elude capture.

Between 1940 and 1944 she had close calls but always managed to give her pursuers the slip, her biographer, Peter FitzSimons, said in a radio interview in Australia after her death.

In film documentaries and in her 1985 autobiography, "The White Mouse," Ms. Wake said she underwent a metamorphosis during the war, from fun-loving girl to Resistance fighter.

It began, she said, with a visit to Vienna in the mid-1930s as a freelance journalist. There, she saw roving Nazi gangs randomly beating Jewish men and women in the streets. The attacks made her promise herself that "if ever the opportunity arose, I would do everything I could" to stop the Nazi movement, she said.

"My hatred of the Nazis was very, very deep."

The opportunity arose.

Nancy Grace Augusta Wake was born Aug. 30, 1912, in Wellington, New Zealand, the youngest of six children. Her father, a journalist, left the family shortly after moving them to Sydney, Australia.

Ms. Wake left home at 16, worked briefly as a nurse, and managed with the help of a small inheritance from an aunt to leave Australia at age 20. She traveled to London, New York and Paris, and decided Paris was the place that suited her best. While writing journalism she managed to live "Parisian nightlife to the full," according to Mr. FitzSimons.

In 1936, she met a Marseilles industrialist named Henri Fiocca, whom she married and settled with in Marseilles three years later.

With the German invasion of France, Ms. Wake's wealth and social standing gave her a certain cover as she began helping members of local Resistance groups.

She became a courier and then an escort for Allied soldiers and refugees trying to leave the country. "It was much easier for us, you know, to travel all over France," she told an interviewer for Australian television. "A woman could get out of a lot of trouble that a man could not."

In 1943, when occupation authorities became aware of her activities, she fled France.

Her husband, who stayed behind, was arrested and executed.

Ms. Wake found her way to England and was accepted for training by the British Special Operations Executive, or S.O.E., an intelligence group working with the French Resistance. In April 1944, when she was 31, she was among 39 women and 430 men who were parachuted into France to help with preparations for D-Day.

There she collected night parachute drops of weapons and ammunition and hid them in storage caches for the advancing Allied armies, set up wireless communication with England and harassed the enemy.

"I was never afraid," she said. "I was too busy to be afraid."

By most accounts, Ms. Wake never figured out what to do with her life after the war.

"It's dreadful because you've been so busy, and then it all just fizzles out," she told an Australian newspaper in 1983.

She worked briefly for the British government, then returned to Australia and ran unsuccessfully for public office in the early 1950s. She married a retired Royal Air Force pilot, John Forward, in 1957. He died in 1997.

Ms. Wake returned to London in 2001.

Film and television producers have used Ms. Wake's early life as the basis for various works, and she generally approved of them, except for those suggesting that she had love affairs during the war.

She did not have affairs, she insisted in a 1987 Australian documentary.

"And in my old age, I regret it," she said. "But you see, if I had accommodated one man, the word would have spread around, and I would have had to accommodate the whole damn lot!"

— BY PAUL VITELLO

MARK O. HATFIELD

A Liberal, Anti-War, No-Nukes Republican

JULY 12, 1922 · AUG. 7, 2011

MARK O. HATFIELD, a liberal Republican who challenged his party on the Vietnam War and on a balanced-budget amendment to the Constitution during his 30 years as a United States senator from Oregon, died on Aug. 7 in Portland, Ore. He was 89.

Mr. Hatfield served in the Senate from 1967 to 1997, spending eight years as the chairman of the Appropriations Committee. But he came out against the Vietnam War even earlier, during his second term as governor of Oregon.

At a meeting of the National Governors Association on July 28, 1965, as his colleagues rallied behind President Lyndon B. Johnson and his escalation of the war, Mr. Hatfield declared, "I cannot support the president on what he has done so far."

The American bombing campaign, he said, had resulted in "the deaths of noncombatant men, women and children" and "merits the general condemnation of mankind." American troops, he said, should not be shouldering South Vietnam's responsibility "to win or lose."

He was the first prominent Republican to come out against the war, joining only a few leading Democrats to have done so, among them Senator Wayne Morse, a fellow Oregonian.

By the time Mr. Hatfield reached the Senate, opposition to the war was growing. In 1970 and 1971, he worked with Senator George S.

BUCKING THE PARTY:
Mark O. Hatfield opposed the Vietnam War and budget cuts.

McGovern, Democrat of South Dakota, on unsuccessful efforts to set a deadline for withdrawing American troops. At a Washington prayer breakfast in 1973, he described the war as a "sin that scarred the national soul" and that demanded national repentance. President Richard M. Nixon, who was in attendance, had just signed a cease-fire that ended the combat role for American forces.

Mr. Hatfield was one of the most liberal Republicans in the Senate, averaging a 65 percent favorable rating from the liberal advocacy group Americans for Democratic Action.

Those stands often put him at odds with fellow Republicans. His most serious breach with the party's senators came in 1995, when he cast the only Republican vote against a constitutional amendment to require a balanced federal budget. His vote meant defeat for the measure, which had 66 votes, one short of the required two-thirds majority.

Mr. Hatfield had voted for a balanced-budget amendment in 1982, but changed his mind in 1986, saying the spending cuts necessary to achieve the amendment's requirement for ever-smaller deficits would cause serious harm to the country.

When he cast that decisive vote in 1995, young Republican senators demanded that he be stripped of his appropriations chairmanship. But senior Republicans blocked that effort.

"Oregon has always prized a flinty independence," said Norman J. Ornstein, a resident scholar at the American Enterprise Institute, and Mr. Hatfield's willingness to break with Republican orthodoxy, along with a courtly and unpretentious manner, appealed to Oregonians.

In 1982, Mr. Hatfield joined with Senator Edward M. Kennedy, Democrat of Massachusetts, to campaign for a mutual United States-Soviet freeze on nuclear weapons. "I see all life as a part of God's creation," Mr. Hatfield told The Christian Science Monitor, "and I think it's rather audacious and presumptuous of humankind to consider that it has the right to destroy creation, to destroy all life."

The Senate nevertheless rejected the freeze in 1983 and again the next year.

Mr. Hatfield's experience in World War II focused his thinking. A Navy lieutenant, he commanded amphibious landing craft that took Marines ashore at the battles of Iwo Jima and Okinawa and carried the wounded offshore.

When the war ended, he was sent to Vietnam to ferry Chinese Nationalist troops to fight the Communists. Writing to his parents, he told of observing squalor and people begging for food, conditions he attributed to French colonialism, not the Japanese. The experience influenced his views years later.

"It has remained my conclusion that the Vietnamese people have been fighting for over 20 years for the cause of nationalism," he wrote in a memoir, "Not Quite So Simple," published in 1968 at the height of the Vietnam War. "They are fighting in the name of social, political and economic justice, and although we may believe their view of 'justice' to be false and devilish, it is a vision for which they are prepared to die."

Before Vietnam he was sent to Japan in the wake of the atomic bomb attacks on Hiroshima and Nagasaki. "One month after the bomb, I walked through the streets of Hiroshima and I saw the utter devastation in every direction from nuclear power," he told Sojourners Magazine in 1996.

Mark Odom Hatfield was born in Dallas, Ore., on July 12, 1922. He graduated from Willamette University in Salem, Ore., in 1943, and taught political science there from 1949 to 1956. He began his political career in 1950, when he was elected to the State Legislature. He was elected secretary of state in 1956 and governor, for the first of two terms, in 1958.

Mr. Hatfield worked well with a Democratic-led Legislature, concentrating on economic development. He brought industry to the state and helped local companies, especially the timber industry, supporting its requests for increased logging. He took credit for an increase of 138,000 jobs in his eight years in office while taxes remained lower than in other West Coast states.

He also took leading roles in passing two state civil rights laws, drawing on an experience at Willamette, where he had the task of driving the singers Paul Robeson and Marian Anderson to Portland after performances because Salem hotels would not admit blacks. As a legislator in 1953, he managed the passage of a public-accommodations bill to bar such discrimination. As governor, he backed a fair housing law.

Mr. Hatfield was a strong advocate of federal spending on medical research, motivated in part by his father's Alzheimer's disease and other relatives' cancers. For his home state, he pushed for appropriations for the Oregon Health and Science University in Portland, and he backed bigger budgets for the National Institutes of Health and the creation of the institutes' Office for Rare Diseases Research. Medical research, he wrote in 2001, is one of the few things "the government does extremely well."

In March 1996, he told the Senate that with the end of the cold war, "the Russians are not coming," alluding to the 1960s film comedy "The Russians Are Coming, the Russians Are Coming." Instead, he said, "the greatest enemy we face today, externally, is the viruses that are coming, the viruses are coming." Money being spent on the military should be shifted to human needs, he argued.

After he retired from the Senate, he remained a vocal advocate of spending at the health institutes, which named a facility for him, the Mark O. Hatfield Clinical Research Center.

He is survived by his wife, the former Antoinette Kuzmanich, whom he married in 1958; two sons; two daughters; and seven grandchildren.

One blemish on his Senate career came in 1992, when the Ethics Committee rebuked him for failing to disclose gifts from a former university president who had sought his support for a government grant. But the committee found that there had been no "quid pro quo," and said his handling of the grant requests, from the University of South Carolina, had been routine.

Mr. Hatfield, a prominent Baptist layman, frequently spoke before church groups, and his liberal positions were often criticized by religious conservatives. He called the movement's growing role in the Republican Party an "embarrassment." Still, he said, its influence on the party was not what he was concerned about.

"What I'm really concerned about is the impact it's having on the cause of Christ," he said in the Sojourners interview, "that somehow I'm going to come into a relationship with Christ by agreeing to their political agenda. That is not the key to salvation from the biblical teaching."

— BY ADAM CLYMER

BUDD HOPKINS

From Abstract Art to Alien Abductions

JUNE 15, 1931 · AUG. 21, 2011

BUDD HOPKINS, a distinguished Abstract Expressionist artist who — after what he described as a chance sighting of something flat, silver, airborne and unfathomable — became the father of the alien-abduction movement, died on Aug. 21 at his home in Manhattan. He was 80.

A painter and sculptor, Mr. Hopkins was part of the circle of New York artists that in the 1950s and '60s included Mark Rothko, Robert Motherwell and Franz Kline.

His work — which by the late '60s included Mondrian-like paintings of huge geometric forms anointed with flat planes of color — is in the collections of the Metropolitan Museum of Art and the Museum of Modern Art in New York, the Corcoran Gallery of Art in Washington and the British Museum.

In later years Mr. Hopkins turned to large, quasi-architectural sculptures that seemed to spring from primordial myths. In 1985, reviewing one such piece, "Temple of Apollo With Guardian XXXXV" — it was part house of worship, part archaeological ruin, part sacrificial altar — Michael Brenson wrote in The New York Times:

"If the work is about sacrifice and violence, it is also about ecstasy and illumination. In the course of trying to re-establish the broadest meaning of the abstract geometry that has fascinated so many 20th-century artists, Hopkins makes us consider that ritual, worship, cruelty and superstition have always been inseparable."

Some articles about Mr. Hopkins made much of the relationship between these pieces and his fascination with otherworldly visitors, for by then his books, lectures and television appearances had made him well known as a U.F.O. investigator. Mr. Hopkins, however, disavowed a connection.

He was also quick to point out that he had never been abducted himself. But after what he described as his own U.F.O. sighting, on Cape Cod in 1964, he began gathering the stories of people who said they had not only seen space-ships but had also been spirited away in them on involuntary and unpleasant journeys.

As the first person to collect and publish such stories in quantity, Mr. Hopkins is widely

COLORFUL VISION: Before becoming the father of the alien-abduction movement, Budd Hopkins was part of a celebrated circle of abstract artists that included Mark Rothko.

credited with having begun the alien-abduction movement, a subgenre of U.F.O. studies. High-profile writers on the subject, including Whitley Strieber and the Harvard psychiatrist John Mack, said he had ignited their interest in the field.

In eliciting the narratives — many obtained under hypnosis — of people who said they had been abducted, Mr. Hopkins was struck by the recurrence of certain motifs: the lonely road, the dark of night, the burst of light, the sudden passage through the air and into a waiting craft, and above all the sense of time that could not be accounted for.

He went in search of that lost time. What he found, in story after story, was this: The aliens were technically sophisticated, and many spoke improbably good English. They were short, bug-eyed, thin-lipped and gray-skinned. They stripped their subjects naked and probed them with instruments, often removing sperm or eggs.

These narratives, Mr. Hopkins wrote, led him to a distasteful but inescapable conclusion: The aliens — or "visitors," as he preferred to call them — were practicing a form of extraterrestrial eugenics, aiming to shore up their declining race by crossbreeding with Homo sapiens.

In 1989 Mr. Hopkins founded the Intruders Foundation, based in Manhattan, to help sound the alarm.

He wrote four books on the subject, including "Intruders: The Incredible Visitations at Copley Woods" (1987), which spent four weeks on the New York Times best-seller list and was the basis of a 1992 TV movie starring Richard Crenna.

Mr. Hopkins's work drew inevitable fire; in interviews he sometimes likened his attackers to Holocaust deniers, an analogy that incurred further criticism.

Elliott Budd Hopkins was born on June 15, 1931, in Wheeling, W. Va., and at 2 survived polio. He earned a bachelor's degree in art history from Oberlin College in 1953 and afterward settled in New York, where he soon made his artistic reputation.

After the Cape Cod sighting he described — a silvery disc over Truro, Mass. — Mr. Hopkins began researching U.F.O.'s. In 1976 he published an article about abductions in The Village Voice, which led to an article in Cosmopolitan.

The exposure drew sacks of letters from readers wondering if they too had been abducted, and his second career was born. By the 1980s, it had eclipsed the first.

Mr. Hopkins's three marriages, to Joan Baer, April Kingsley and Carol Rainey, ended in divorce. He is survived by his companion, Leslie Kean; a daughter from his marriage to Ms. Kingsley; a sister; and a grandchild. He died of complications of cancer.

His memoir, "Art, Life and UFOs," was published in 2009 by Anomalist Books.

Unlike some writers in the genre who described their own abductions as spiritually transformative, Mr. Hopkins believed that no good could come of being the unwilling subject of a vast human genome project in the sky. He called his informants "victims" and ran group therapy sessions for them in New York.

Many who shared their stories with Mr. Hopkins had no conscious memory of their abductions at first. But they had lived for years, he said, with the nagging feeling that somewhere, something in their lives had gone horribly wrong.

Their condition, Mr. Hopkins said, was not as rare as one might suppose. By his reckoning, 1 in 50 Americans has been abducted by an alien and simply does not know it.

— By Margalit Fox

NICK ASHFORD

The Power Couple From Motown

MAY 4, 1941 - AUG. 22, 2011

Nick Ashford, who with Valerie Simpson, his songwriting partner and later his wife, wrote some of Motown's biggest hits, like "Ain't No Mountain High Enough" and "Ain't Nothing Like the Real Thing," before they remade their careers as a recording and touring duo, died

on Aug. 22 in a New York hospital. He was 70.

Mr. Ashford had throat cancer and was undergoing treatment at the hospital, the music publicist Liz Rosenberg said.

One of Motown's leading songwriting and producing teams, Ashford & Simpson specialized in romantic duets of the most dramatic kind, professing the power of true love and the comforts of sweet talk. In "Ain't No Mountain High Enough," from 1967, lovers in close harmony proclaim their determination that "no wind, no rain, no winter's cold, can stop me, baby," while also making cuter promises like "If you're ever in trouble, I'll be there on the double."

The song was their first of several hits for Marvin Gaye and Tammi Terrell, who also sang the Ashford & Simpson songs "Your Precious Love," "Ain't Nothing Like the Real Thing" and "You're All I Need to Get By." After leaving the Supremes in 1970, Diana Ross sang their "Reach Out and Touch Somebody's Hand," and later that year her version of "Ain't No Mountain High Enough" became her first No. 1 single as a solo artist.

"They had magic, and that's what creates those wonderful hits, that magic," Verdine White of Earth, Wind and Fire told The Associated Press after learning of his friend's death. "Without those songs, those artists wouldn't have been able to go to the next level."

Nickolas Ashford was born on May 4, 1941, in Fairfield, S.C., and grew up in Willow Run, Mich., where his father, Calvin, was a construction worker. He got his musical start at Willow Run Baptist Church, singing and writing songs for the gospel choir. After briefly attending Eastern Michigan University, in Ypsilanti, he headed to New York, where he tried but failed to find success as a dancer.

Mr. Ashford met Ms. Simpson in 1964 at White Rock Baptist Church in Harlem. He was homeless at the time; she was a 17-year-old recent high school graduate who was studying music. They began writing songs together, selling the first bunch for $64. In 1966, after Ray Charles sang "Let's Go Get Stoned," a song Ashford & Simpson wrote with Josephine Armstead, the duo signed on with Motown as writers and producers.

They wrote for virtually every major act on the label, including Gladys Knight and the Pips ("Didn't You Know You'd Have to Cry Sometime") and Smokey Robinson and the Miracles ("Who's Gonna Take the Blame").

While writing for Motown, Ashford & Simpson nursed a desire to perform, but Berry Gordy Jr., the founder of the label, discouraged it. They left the label in 1973 and married in 1974.

Ashford & Simpson's initial collaborations as recording artists sold poorly, but by the late '70s they had become fixtures on the upper rungs of the rhythm-and-blues charts with songs like "Don't Cost You Nothing," "It Seems to Hang On" and "Found a Cure." Their biggest success was "Solid," from 1984, a paean to enduring love ("Solid as a rock/And nothing's changed it/The thrill is still hot, hot, hot, hot, hot, hot, hot, hot").

MOTOWN HITMAKER: Nick Ashford and Valerie Simpson were one of the genre's leading songwriting and producing teams, creating hits for superstars like Marvin Gaye.

It went to No. 12 on the pop chart in the United States and in Britain climbed as high as No. 3.

They sang of monogamous devotion, and on their album covers the couple were usually pictured pulling each other close in various states of undress. But with his shock of slicked black hair, shirts open to the sternum and playful smile, Mr. Ashford also cut a perfect figure as a seducer for the swinging '70s.

They continued to write for other singers. "I'm Every Woman" was a hit for Chaka Khan in 1978, and later for Whitney Houston on the soundtrack to the 1992 film "The Bodyguard."

In 1996, they opened the Sugar Bar on West 72nd Street in Manhattan. In 2006 they received a credit on Amy Winehouse's song "Tears Dry on Their Own," which features a sample from "Ain't No Mountain High Enough."

Mr. Ashford, who lived in Manhattan, is survived by Ms. Simpson as well as two daughters, three brothers and his mother.

Ashford & Simpson toured throughout their career, their harmony and vocal interplay illustrating the passion of their lyrics and of their life together.

"When Ms. Simpson sits down at the piano and begins to sing in a bright pop-gospel voice, unchanged since the 1970s," Stephen Holden wrote in The New York Times in 2007, "she awakens the spirit and tosses it to Mr. Ashford, whose quirkier voice, with its airy falsetto, has gained in strength from the old days. Soon they are urging each other on. By the time their romantic relay winds to a close, both are sweating profusely, and the audience is delirious."

— BY BEN SISARIO

JERRY LEIBER

Wordsmith of Rock 'n' Roll

APRIL 25, 1933 - AUG. 22, 2011

J ERRY LEIBER, the lyricist who, with his partner, Mike Stoller, wrote some of the most enduring classics in the history of rock 'n' roll, including "Hound Dog," "Yakety Yak," "Stand By Me" and "On Broadway," died on Aug. 22 in Los Angeles. He was 78.

The team of Leiber and Stoller was formed in 1950, when Mr. Leiber was still a student at Fairfax High in Los Angeles and Mr. Stoller, a fellow rhythm-and-blues fanatic, was a freshman at Los Angeles City College. With Mr. Leiber contributing catchy, street-savvy lyrics and Mr. Stoller, a pianist, composing infectious,

bluesy tunes, they set about writing songs with black singers and groups in mind.

In 1952, they wrote "Hound Dog" for the blues singer Willie Mae Thornton, known as Big Mama. The song became an enormous hit for Elvis Presley in 1956 and made Leiber and Stoller the hottest songwriting team in rock 'n' roll, though they loathed Presley's interpretation of it. Still, they continued to write songs for him, including "Jailhouse Rock," "Loving You," "Don't," "Treat Me Nice" and "King Creole."

In the late 1950s, having relocated to New York and taken their place among the constellation of talents associated with the Brill Building, they emerged as perhaps the most potent songwriting team in the genre.

Their hits for the Drifters remain some of the most admired songs in the rock 'n' roll canon, notably "On Broadway," written with Barry Mann and Cynthia Weil. "Spanish Harlem," which Mr. Leiber wrote with Phil Spector, gave Ben E. King his first hit after leaving the Drifters. Mr. King's most famous recording, "Stand By Me," was a Leiber-Stoller song on which he collaborated.

They wrote a series of hits for the Coasters, including "Charlie Brown," "Young Blood" with Doc Pomus, "Searchin'," "Poison Ivy" and "Yakety Yak."

"Smokey Joe's Cafe," a 1954 hit written for the Robins, became the title of a Broadway musical based on the Leiber and Stoller songbook. In 1987, the partners were inducted into the Rock and Roll Hall of Fame.

"Jerry Leiber and Mike Stoller have written some of the most spirited and enduring rock 'n' roll songs," the hall said in a statement when they were inducted. "Leiber and Stoller advanced rock 'n' roll to new heights of wit and musical sophistication."

Jerome Leiber was born on April 25, 1933, in Baltimore, where his parents, Jewish immigrants from Poland, ran a general store. When Jerry was 5, his father died and his mother tried, with little success, to run a small store in one of the city's worst slums. When he was 12, she took him to Los Angeles.

It was while attending Fairfax High in Los Angeles and working in Norty's Record Shop

SPIRITED LYRICIST: Jerry Leiber, right, looking over the sheet music for "Jailhouse Rock" alongside his partner Mike Stoller and Elvis Presley in 1957.

that he met Lester Sill, a promoter for Modern Records, and confessed that he wanted to be a songwriter. After Sill urged him to find a pianist who could help him put his ideas onto sheet music, he met Mr. Stoller through a friend, and the two began writing together.

"Often I would have a start, two or four lines," Mr. Leiber told Robert Palmer, the author of "Baby, That Was Rock & Roll: The Legendary Leiber and Stoller" (1978). "Mike would sit at the piano and start to jam, just playing, fooling around, and I'd throw out a line. He'd accommodate the line — metrically, rhythmically."

Within a few years they had written modestly successful songs for several rhythm-and-blues singers: "K.C. Lovin'" for Little Willie Littlefield, which under the title "Kansas City" became a No. 1 hit for Wilbert Harrison in 1959.

In 1952, Sill arranged for Mr. Leiber and Mr. Stoller to visit the bandleader Johnny Otis (see page 186) and to listen to several of the rhythm-and-blues acts who worked with him, including Big Mama Thornton, who sang "Ball and Chain" for them. Inspired, the partners went back to Mr. Stoller's house and wrote "Hound Dog."

"I yelled, he played," Mr. Leiber told Josh Alan Friedman, the author of "Tell the Truth

Until They Bleed: Coming Clean in the Dirty World of Blues and Rock 'n' Roll" (2008). "The groove came together and we finished in 12 minutes flat. I work fast. We raced right back to lay the song on Big Mama."

In 1953 they formed Spark Records, an independent label, with Sill, but without national distribution it failed to score major hits. Atlantic Records, which had bought the Leiber and Stoller song "Ruby Baby" and "Fools Fall in Love" for the Drifters, signed them to an unusual agreement that allowed them to produce for other labels. The golden age of Leiber and Stoller began.

Their seemingly endless list of hit songs from this period included "Love Potion No. 9" for the Clovers (later a hit for the Searchers).

In the mid-1960s, Mr. Leiber and Mr. Stoller concentrated on production. They founded Red Bird Records, where they turned out hit records by girl groups like the Dixie Cups ("Chapel of Love") and the Shangri-Las ("Leader of the Pack," "Walking in the Sand").

They sold the label in 1966 and worked as independent producers and writers. Peggy Lee, who had recorded their song "I'm a Woman" in 1963, recorded "Is That All There Is?" in 1969.

Mr. Leiber, who died of cardio-pulmonary failure, is survived by three sons and two grandchildren. With Mr. Stoller and David Ritz, he wrote a 2009 memoir, "Hound Dog: The Leiber & Stoller Autobiography."

— BY WILLIAM GRIMES

\\\\\\\\\\\\\\\\\\\\\\\\\\

EUGENE A. NIDA

Bibles for a Babel-Like World

NOV. 11, 1914 · AUG. 25, 2011

THE REV. EUGENE A. NIDA, a linguist and Baptist minister who spurred a Babel of Bibles, recruiting and training native speakers to translate Scripture into a host of languages around the world, died on Aug. 25 at his home in Madrid. He was 96.

The American Bible Society, his longtime employer, announced the death. Mr. Nida, who also had a home in Brussels, had lived in Europe in retirement.

Widely considered the father of modern Bible translation, Mr. Nida (pronounced NYE-duh) was for four decades the head of the Bible society's translation program. He was known in particular for developing an approach to translation — and a method of training translators — that has influenced translators of religious and secular literature.

What defined Mr. Nida's work was his insistence that Bible translations be accessible to the people for whom they were intended. After joining the Bible society in 1943, he visited scores of countries, where he recruited native speakers and trained them as translators.

Previously, most Bible translations had been done by Western missionaries, who rarely had great familiarity with the local language. Not surprisingly, the word-for-word translations that resulted were often stiff, unpalatable and largely inaccessible.

"The genius of Nida was that he also developed a pedagogical approach," Philip C. Stine, the author of a biography, "Let the Words Be Written: The Lasting Influence of Eugene A. Nida," said in a telephone interview. "You could take people with very unsophisticated linguistic backgrounds and actually train them, using Nida's methods."

Drawing on linguistics, anthropology and communication science, Mr. Nida devised an approach to translation known as "dynamic equivalence." (It was later called "functional equivalence.")

Dynamic equivalence was intended to produce translations that read naturally, were rooted in the local idiom and yet retained fealty to the original Scripture. The approach, which took as its starting point Hebrew and Greek biblical texts, centered, quite literally, on the art of faithful adaptation.

Traversing the globe by plane, train and canoe, Mr. Nida set in motion the painstaking process of translating Scripture into more than 200 languages, among them Navajo; Tagalog and Ilocano, spoken in the Philippines; Quechua, an indigenous language of Peru; Hmong, spoken in Southeast Asia; and Inuktitut, an indigenous language of the Canadian Arctic.

Mr. Nida also played an active role in creating the Good News Bible, a colloquial English-language edition produced by the Bible society and published in two volumes — the New Testament in 1966, and the combined Old and New Testaments in 1976.

Sometimes criticized for its linguistic simplicity ("Behold the fowls of the air," for instance,

became "Look at the birds flying around"), the Good News Bible was originally intended for speakers of English as a second language. Embraced in unanticipated droves by native English speakers, it has sold millions of copies.

Eugene Albert Nida was born in Oklahoma City on Nov. 11, 1914. He earned a bachelor's degree in classics from the University of California, Los Angeles, followed by a master's in New Testament Greek from the University of Southern California. In 1943, he earned a doctorate in linguistics from the University of Michigan and was also ordained as a minister.

Traversing the globe by plane, train, and canoe.

One of his first tasks at the Bible society, as he recounted in a memoir, "Fascinated by Languages" (2003), was evaluating a translation of the Gospel of Mark into Yipounou, a language of Gabon, in West Africa.

In linguistics, Mr. Nida did important early work in morphology, which studies the internal architecture of words.

Mr. Nida's first wife, Althea Sprague, died before him. His survivors include his second wife, Elena Fernandez-Miranda, and stepchildren. Information on other survivors was not available.

Translated back into English, some of the Bible passages produced using Mr. Nida's method yield a resonant poetry. As The New York Times reported in a 1955 article about his work, "'I am sorrowful' gets a variety of translations for tribes within a small area of central Africa: 'My eye is black,' 'My heart is rotten,' 'My stomach is heavy' or 'My liver is sick.'"

— By MARGALIT FOX

STETSON KENNEDY

He Rode With the Klan, and Exposed It

OCT. 5, 1916 · AUG. 27, 2011

STETSON KENNEDY, a folklorist and social crusader who infiltrated the Ku Klux Klan in the 1940s and wrote a lurid exposé of its activities, "I Rode With the Ku Klux Klan," died on Aug. 27 in St. Augustine, Fla. He was 94.

Mr. Kennedy developed his sense of racial injustice early. A native of Jacksonville, Fla., he saw the hardships of black Floridians when he knocked on doors collecting payments for his father's furniture store. His social concerns developed further when he began collecting folklore data for the Federal Writers' Project in Key West, Tampa and camps for turpentine workers in north Florida, where conditions were close to slavery.

After being rejected by the Army because of a bad back, he threw himself into unmasking the Ku Klux Klan as well as the Columbians, a Georgia neo-Nazi group. He was inspired in part by a tale told by an interview subject whose friend had been the victim of a racial murder in Key West.

As an agent for the Georgia Bureau of Investigation, Mr. Kennedy, by his own account, infiltrated the Klavern in Stone Mountain and worked as a Klavalier, or Klan strong-arm man. He leaked his findings to, among others, the Washington Post columnist Drew Pearson, the Anti-Defamation League and the producers of the radio show "Superman," who used information about the Klan's rituals and code words in a multi-episode story titled "Clan of the Fiery Cross."

In a celebrated exploit, he stole financial information from a wastebasket outside the office of the Klan's Imperial Wizard, Sam Roper, in Atlanta.

The information led the Internal Revenue Service to challenge the group's status as a charitable organization and demand nearly $700,000 in back taxes. He helped draft the brief that Georgia used to revoke the Klan's national corporate charter in 1947.

After writing a series of articles on the Klan for the left-wing newspaper The Daily Compass

UNDERCOVER KLANSMAN: Stetson Kennedy's infiltration of the K.K.K. led to an investigation by the I.R.S. and a revocation of the Klan's national corporate charter.

— some with datelines like "Inside the Invisible Empire" and "Somewhere in Klan Territory" — he published "I Rode With the Ku Klux Klan" in 1954. It was republished in 1990 as "The Klan Unmasked."

In 2006, Stephen J. Dubner and Steven D. Levitt, the authors of "Freakonomics," reported in The New York Times that Mr. Kennedy had greatly exaggerated and dramatized his Klan-busting. The authors had interviewed Mr. Kennedy for their book and used his information about Klan symbolism, language and gestures to illustrate an economic point, but in telling Mr. Kennedy's story they elicited new interest in his claims, especially from a Florida writer, Ben Green.

Mr. Green, while researching the life of Harry T. Moore, a black civil rights advocate murdered in 1952, and collaborating for a time with Mr. Kennedy on the project, read Mr. Kennedy's archives in Atlanta and at the Schomburg Center for Research in Black Culture in Harlem.

Mr. Green concluded that Mr. Kennedy had relied heavily on the experiences of a man identified by the pseudonym John Brown, a union worker and former Klan official who had changed his ways and offered to infiltrate the Klan. Mr. Kennedy later confirmed that he had relied in part on an informant and that he had woven some of his testimony into his first-person account to make it more compelling. But he was unapologetic.

"I wanted to show what was happening at the time," he told The Florida Times-Union of Jacksonville in 2006. "Who gives a damn how it's written? It is the one and only document of the working Klan."

William Stetson Kennedy was born on Oct. 5, 1916, in Jacksonville, where he developed an interest in local turns of phrase and sayings that he called "folksays," jotting them down in notebooks.

While attending the University of Florida, where he took a writing course with Marjorie Kinnan Rawlings, he struck out on his own to do field work in Key West. There he married the first of his seven wives, a Cuban who gave him entree into the local émigré community for his folklore work. While gathering material for the Federal Writers' Project, he traveled across Florida with the writer Zora Neale Hurston.

His Florida research found its way into "Palmetto Country" (1942), a folkloric survey of territory from southern Alabama and Georgia down to Key West, and the series American Folkways, edited by Erskine Caldwell. In 1994 he returned to folklore in "South Florida Folklife," written with Peggy Bulger and Tina Bucuvalas, and "Grits and Grunts: Folkloric Key West" (2008).

Most of his writing was devoted to campaigns for social justice. A series on racial segregation written with Elizabeth Gardner for The Daily Compass in 1949 formed the basis of "Jim Crow Guide to the U.S.A." His other books included "Passage to Violence" (1954), a fictionalized version of his Klan experiences; "Southern Exposure" (1946); and "After Appomattox: How the South Won the War" (1995).

In addition to his wife, Sandra Parks, Mr. Kennedy is survived by a son, a grandson and several stepchildren.

Mr. Kennedy pursued the Klan and racist politicians through a variety of means. In 1950 he ran a write-in campaign for senator. Woody Guthrie, who lived on Mr. Kennedy's lakeside property near Jacksonville, writing 88 songs there, composed a campaign song for him, titled "Stetson Kennedy," declaring:

Stetson Kennedy, he's that man;
Walks and talks across our land;
Talkin' out against the Ku Klux Klan.
For every fiery cross and note;
I'll get Kennedy a hundred votes.

Ridicule, too, formed part of Mr. Kennedy's arsenal. In 1947 he tried, unsuccessfully, to incorporate his own shadow Klan so that he could sue the real Klan whenever it used the same name. He appointed himself Imperial Wizard and installed, as senior officers, an African-American, a Roman Catholic, a Jew, a Japanese-American and a Cherokee.

— By William Grimes

\\\\\\\\\\\\\\\\\\\\\\\\\\\

KEITH W. TANTLINGER

A Simple Invention, a Shipping Revolution

MARCH 22, 1919 - AUG. 27, 2011

N EARLY SIX DECADES AGO, Keith W. Tantlinger built a box — or, more accurately, the corners of a box. It was a seemingly small invention, but a vital one: it set in motion a chain of events that changed the way people buy and sell things, transformed the means by which nations do business and ultimately gave rise to the present-day global economy.

Mr. Tantlinger's box, large, heavy and metal, is known as the shipping container. Though he did not invent it (such containers had been in use at least since the 19th century to haul heavy cargo like coal), he is widely credited with having created, in the 1950s, the first commercially viable modern one.

The crucial refinements he made — including a corner mechanism that locks containers together — allowed them to be hefted by crane, stacked high in ships and transferred from shipboard to trucks and trains far more easily, and cheaply, than ever before.

Thus, without ever intending to, Mr. Tantlinger, an engineer who died at 92 on Aug. 27 and who had long worked out of the limelight, helped bring about the vast web of international trade that is a fact of 21st-century life. More than any other innovation, the modern shipping container — by turns venerated and castigated — is now acknowledged to have been the spark that touched off globalization.

As Marc Levinson, the author of "The Box: How the Shipping Container Made the World Smaller and the World Economy Bigger" (2006), said in a telephone interview after Mr. Tantlinger's death, "The scale of modern container shipping would not have been possible without Tantlinger's innovations."

He explained: "Most consumer goods, by a wide margin, come in by ship. Containerization made it possible to ship goods very long distances at very low costs. Globalization in the way we know it today just would not be possible without the container."

Mr. Tantlinger's work is everywhere. Thanks to the stacking and locking mechanisms he devised, a ship can now carry thousands of containers at once. Tens of millions of shipping containers roam the world today, filled with lumber, coal and hay, not to mention computers and cars. Refrigerated containers carry seafood, meat and other perishables across previously unimaginable distances.

Until the mid-1950s, however, seaborne cargo transport had changed little since the day man first lashed together a raft, stocked it with trade goods and set out for distant shores. For centuries, on waterfronts worldwide, goods as diverse as flour, coffee, whiskey and mail were literally manhandled — loaded by longshoremen onto ships in sacks and crates and barrels and, at the other end, loaded off again.

The method was expensive and took time. In 1954, Mr. Levinson's book reports, the cargo ship *Warrior* left Brooklyn for Germany carrying 194,582 separate items. These had arrived at the Brooklyn docks in 1,156 separate shipments.

Containerization unified the process, letting a single shipper move merchandise across land and sea. In 1958, The New York Times described the new technology this way: "A trailer is loaded, for example, in Springfield, Mo. It travels by road to New York or San Francisco, sealed, virtually damage-proof and theft-proof. By ship it goes to France or to Japan, eliminating warehousing, stacking and sorting. Each ship takes on her cargo with a few hundred lifts, compared to 5,000 individual lifts by the old method."

But designing a container 40 feet long and 8 or 9 feet tall that could be safely stacked six high on a rolling ship was no simple task. That was where Mr. Tantlinger came in.

The son of a citrus grower, Keith Walton Tantlinger was born in Orange, Calif., on March 22, 1919. (The family name is pronounced TANT-lin-gurr, with a hard "g.")

Mr. Tantlinger earned a bachelor's degree

in mechanical engineering from the University of California, Berkeley. During World War II he worked for the Douglas Aircraft Company, a precursor of McDonnell Douglas, where he designed tools used to produce the B-17 bomber.

In the mid-1950s, Mr. Tantlinger — then vice president of engineering at Brown Industries, a maker of truck trailers in Spokane, Wash. — took a call from the Pan-Atlantic Steamship Corporation. The company's owner, Malcolm P. McLean, wanted to devise a way to stack loaded trailers, minus the trucks, directly on ships.

OUTSIDE THE BOX: Keith W. Tantlinger created the first commercially viable modern shipping container.

Mr. McLean, who died in 2001 and is sometimes called the father of containerization, had been a trucking magnate. After buying Pan-Atlantic in 1955, he sought to make possible the seamless integration of land and sea transport for a wide range of cargo.

Intrigued by the challenge of making Mr. McLean's pipe dream a mechanical reality, Mr. Tantlinger joined Pan-Atlantic, later renamed Sea-Land Service. Among the foremost problems he would have to solve was devising a safe means of stacking shipping containers many layers high.

He designed a set of steel fittings, which were welded to each corner of a container. Each fitting contained a hole into which a lock he designed, called a twist-lock, could be dropped. A second container could then be stacked atop the first, a handle turned, and the two locked together. The process could be repeated, building a tall stack.

Cranes could latch directly onto Mr. Tantlinger's corner fittings, neatly lifting containers on and off ships. His twist-lock could also be used to secure a container to a truck chassis or a railroad car.

In the early 1960s, Mr. Tantlinger prevailed on Mr. McLean to relinquish the patents to the corner fittings and twist-lock, permitting them be used industrywide.

In later years, Mr. Tantlinger held executive positions with the Fruehauf Trailer Company and the Rohr Corporation, an aerospace manufacturer, before starting his own consulting concern.

Mr. Tantlinger died at his home in Escondido, Calif. His first marriage, to Marjorie Cunningham, ended in divorce. He is survived by his second wife, the former Wanda Gunnell Delinger, whom he married in 1981; a daughter from his first marriage; a stepson; and two grandchildren.

In 2009, he was awarded the Gibbs Brothers Medal, presented by the National Academy of Sciences for outstanding contributions in naval architecture and marine engineering.

Like many innovations, containerization has had its detractors. Longshoremen's unions worldwide vehemently opposed it at first, staging a series of bitter strikes. In the wake of the Sept. 11 attacks, United States officials have voiced concerns that terrorists, or the instruments of terror, might reach American shores inside shipping containers.

There is also a direct link between containerization and the decline of American manufacturing. "Manhattan used to be one of the great garment centers in the world," Mr. Levinson said. "That went away because of the container. It was cheaper to have apparel made in Asia and ship it to Macy's in Herald Square than to have apparel made in the Garment District."

On the other hand, Mr. Levinson said, containerization has made a profusion of low-cost goods available to consumers.

"Right now, shipping costs for most of the goods we import and export by sea are just an afterthought," he said. "They're not really a big part of the cost of your shoes, or your bottle of Australian wine, or that nice blouse you just got from China."

And all this sprang — improbably, unimaginably and indisputably — from a set of steel corners and a lock, conceived by a man who built a better box.

— By Margalit Fox

JOHN CULLEN

On a Foggy Night, War Came to Long Island

OCT. 2, 1920 - AUG. 29, 2011

IN THE SPRING OF 1942, Seaman John Cullen was assigned to one of the Coast Guard's less glamorous tasks in an America newly at war.

Seaman Cullen was a "sand pounder," the term for Coast Guardsmen who patrolled beaches looking for signs of lurking German submarines or perhaps someone or something suspicious on the sand.

"Once in a while you might run into somebody, but very rare," Mr. Cullen told a Coast Guard oral history interviewer in 2006, recalling his patrols on the eastern Long Island shore near his station at Amagansett.

On Saturday the 13th of June '42, Seaman Cullen was on patrol about a half-hour past midnight, when it was "so foggy that I couldn't see my shoes."

He spotted a figure in the mist and the outlines of three others behind him. "Who are you?" he called out, shining his flashlight at the group, his Coast Guard insignia visible.

The man closest to him said that he and his companions were fishermen who had run aground. He spoke English well enough, but one of the others, dragging a bag, shouted something in German.

Seaman Cullen, "armed" with only a flare gun for sending signals, figured they were surely German spies and fled, heading back to his station to sound an alarm. Later he led some fellow Coast Guardsmen to the spot where he had come across the four. They were long gone, but the Coast Guard dug up explosives they had buried.

Thus began a hunt for saboteurs who had been sent to the United States on U-boats by the German military spy service in a plot to blow up rail facilities and war-industry plants.

Eight men — the four who landed on Long Island and another four who arrived in Florida — were arrested before any sabotage could be carried out, and Seaman Cullen became a hero.

Mr. Cullen, who was 90, died of congestive heart failure on Aug. 29 in Chesapeake, Va. He had retired there with his wife, Alice, in the early 1990s after working as a dairy company sales representative on Long Island and living there in Westbury.

John Cornelius Cullen was born on Oct. 2, 1920, in Manhattan and grew up in Queens. He enlisted in the Coast Guard a few weeks after the Japanese attack on Pearl Harbor.

A few minutes after he discovered the supposed fishermen on that foggy night in 1942, the leader of the group, dropping all pretence, asked Seaman Cullen if he had a mother and father who would presumably grieve for him. The man did not display a weapon but said, "I wouldn't want to have to kill you."

Then the tone changed. The man offered Seaman Cullen what he said was $300 in American money. "Why don't you forget the whole thing?," the man said. Seeing a chance to escape, Seaman Cullen took the money, promised he would never identify the men and ran back to get help. (He then found he was shortchanged; he had been given $260.)

The four German agents, minus their explosives, took the Long Island Rail Road into Manhattan that morning, arriving at Pennsylvania Station. A week later, the group's leader, George Dasch, shaken by his encounter

'SAND POUNDING' HERO: John Cullen received the Legion of Merit after stumbling upon German spies on a Long Island beach during a late-night Coast Guard patrol.

with Seaman Cullen, traveled to Washington and surrendered to the F.B.I., hoping he would be regarded as a hero in America by exposing the plot.

That led to the roundup of his fellow conspirators in Operation Pastorius, named for Franz Pastorius, who in 1683 led the first German settlement in America.

At a secret military trial in Washington, Seaman Cullen identified Mr. Dasch as the man he had encountered on the beach. Six of the eight saboteurs were executed on Aug. 8, 1942. Mr. Dasch and another conspirator who cooperated were given prison terms and deported to West Germany after World War II.

Seaman Cullen became enveloped in the Coast Guard's publicity machine. He was presented at news conferences to tell of his adventure; appeared at parades, ship launchings and war-bond drives; and received the Legion of Merit. He remained stateside throughout the war as a driver for high-ranking Coast Guard officers, then left military service. He is survived by his wife, Alice; a son; a daughter; two sisters; five grandchildren; and six great-grandchildren.

During the hullaballoo over the spy story, a personnel employee at Macy's in Herald Square who had hired Mr. Cullen as a deliveryman's helper before his Coast Guard enlistment described him to The New Yorker as "a thoroughly wholesome, typically American boy" with "a modest demeanor."

Seaman Cullen played down the hero angle when he appeared at a Coast Guard news conference in 1942. "The German fellow was nervous," he said, "but I think I was more nervous."

— By Richard Goldstein

DAVID HONEYBOY EDWARDS

Up From the Delta, Singing the Blues

JUNE 28, 1915 · AUG. 29, 2011

D AVID HONEYBOY EDWARDS, who is believed to have been the last surviving member of the first generation of Delta blues singers, died on Aug. 29 at his home in Chicago. He was 96.

Mr. Edwards's career spanned nearly the entire recorded history of the blues, from its early years in the Mississippi Delta to its migration to the nightclubs of Chicago and its emergence as an international phenomenon.

Over eight decades Mr. Edwards knew or played his guitar with virtually every major figure who worked in the idiom, including Charley Patton, Muddy Waters and Howlin' Wolf. He was probably best known as the last living link to Robert Johnson, widely hailed as the King of the Delta Blues. The two traveled together, performing on street corners and at picnics, dances and fish fries during the 1930s.

"We would walk through the country with our guitars on our shoulders, stop at people's houses, play a little music, walk on," Mr. Edwards said in an interview with the blues historian Robert Palmer, recalling his peripatetic years with Johnson. "We could hitchhike, transfer from truck to truck, or, if we couldn't catch one of them, we'd go to the train yard, 'cause the railroad was all through that part of the country then." He added, "Man, we played for a lot of peoples."

PERENNIAL SIDEMAN: David Honeyboy Edwards played with everyone from Charley Patton to Muddy Waters. His career lasted over eight decades and took him across the country.

Mr. Edwards had earlier apprenticed with the country bluesman Big Joe Williams. Unlike Williams and many of his other peers, however, Mr. Edwards did not record commercially until after World War II. Field recordings he made for the Library of Congress under the supervision of the folklorist Alan Lomax in 1942 are the only documents of Mr. Edwards's music from his years in the Delta.

Citing the interplay between his coarse, keening vocals and his syncopated "talking" guitar on recordings like "Wind Howling Blues," many historians regard these performances as classic examples of the deep, down-home blues that shaped rhythm and blues and rock 'n' roll.

Mr. Edwards was especially renowned for his intricate fingerpicking and his slashing bottleneck-slide guitar work. Though he played in much the same traditional style throughout his career, he also had the distinction of being one of the first Delta blues musicians to perform with a saxophonist and drummer.

David Edwards was born June 28, 1915, in Shaw, Miss., in the Delta region. His parents, who worked as sharecroppers, gave him the nickname Honey, which later became Honeyboy. His mother played the guitar; his father, a fiddler and guitarist, performed at local social events. He also bought David his first guitar and taught him to play traditional folk ballads.

Mr. Edwards's first real exposure to the blues came in 1929, when the celebrated country bluesman Tommy Johnson came to pick cotton at Wildwood Plantation, the farm near Greenwood where the Edwards family lived at the time.

"They'd pick cotton all through the day, and at night they'd sit around and play the guitars," Mr. Edwards recalled in his autobiography, "The World Don't Owe Me Nothing" (1997). "Drinking that white whiskey, that moonshine, I'd just sit and look at them. I'd say, 'I wish I could play.'"

After spending the better part of two decades as an itinerant musician, Mr. Edwards made Chicago his permanent home in the 1950s. He performed frequently in its clubs and at the open-air market on Maxwell Street, but he recorded only sporadically during his first years there, notably for the independent Artist and Chess labels.

Mr. Edwards achieved new popularity during the blues revival of the 1960s. Near the end of the decade he appeared with

Willie Dixon and Buddy Guy on sessions that produced both volumes of the album "Blues Jam in Chicago" by the British rock band Fleetwood Mac.

In 1972 Mr. Edwards met Michael Frank, a blues aficionado and harmonica player, who would be his booking agent, manager and collaborator, on both stage and record, for the rest of his life.

Mr. Edwards was elected to the Blues Hall of Fame in 1996 and named a National Heritage Fellow by the National Endowment for the Arts in 2002. In 2007 he appeared as himself in the movie "Walk Hard: The Dewey Cox Story."

Survivors include a daughter, a stepdaughter and several grandchildren.

Mr. Edwards won a Grammy Award in 2008 for the album "Last of the Great Mississippi Delta Bluesmen: Live in Dallas," a collaboration with Henry Townsend, Pinetop Perkins (who died in March 2011) and Robert Lockwood Jr. He won a lifetime achievement Grammy in 2010.

He was still playing as many as 100 shows a year when he stopped touring, in 2008, though he continued to perform occasionally until this year. His last appearance was in April, at a blues festival in Clarksdale, Miss.

— BY BILL FRISKICS-WARREN

\\\\\\\\\\\\\\\\\\\\\\\\\\\\\\\\

BETTY SKELTON

Breaking Barriers With Wheels or Wings

JUNE 28, 1926 - AUG. 31, 2011

T HE "INVERTED RIBBON CUT" was one of her most daring maneuvers. In her single-seat, open-cockpit biplane, Betty Skelton would fly upside down at 150 miles per hour or so, maybe 10 feet above the ground, and slice through a ribbon stretched between two poles.

In a race car, she set women's land-speed records. In one 1956 event, she hit 145.044 m.p.h. in her Corvette on the sand flats of Daytona Beach, Fla. (The men's record at the time was just 3 m.p.h. faster.)

Whether in the air or on land, Ms. Skelton, who died on Aug. 31 at the age of 85, was a celebrated daredevil who shattered speed and altitude records. She was a three-time national aerobatic women's flight champion when she turned to race-car driving, then went on to

exceed 300 m.p.h. in a jet-powered car and cross the United States in under 57 hours, breaking a record each time.

"In an era when heroes were race pilots, jet jocks and movie stars, Betty Skelton was an aviation sweetheart, an international celebrity and a flying sensation," Henry Holden wrote in his 1994 biography, "Betty Skelton: The First Lady of Firsts." Her "enviable record is still recognized today by pilots and competitors."

She also broke gender barriers.

"Betty proved that women were capable of professional aerobatic flight competition," said Dorothy Cochrane, curator of general aviation at the National Air and Space Museum of the Smithsonian Institution in Washington, where Ms. Skelton's Pitts S-1C plane, Little Stinker, hangs near the entrance, upside down. "She paved the way for women like Betty Stewart, Mary Gaffney and Patty Wagstaff, who in 1991 became the first woman to win the national championship competing against both men and women."

In 1960, Ms. Skelton appeared on the cover of Look magazine, in an astronaut's flight suit. The headline asked, "Should a Girl Be First in Space?"

THE WORLD'S FASTEST WOMAN: Betty Skelton was a three-time national aerobatic flight champion and crossed the country in a Corvette in under 57 hours. She even flirted with space flight.

Ms. Skelton, who never grew beyond 5-foot-3 and about 100 pounds, acquired her passion for speed as an 8-year-old redhead sitting on her porch in Pensacola, Fla., finding herself riveted by the pilots from the nearby Navy base swooping overhead. Entering competitive flying, however, she was matched only against other women. She won the United States Feminine Aerobatic Championship in 1948, 1949 and 1950.

While the gender divide has disappeared — men and women both compete in what are now known as the United States National Aerobatic Championships — the maneuvers required to win the title are essentially the same as those in Ms. Skelton's day.

One is the hammerhead, in which the pilot soars vertically to a certain altitude, snaps the plane 180 degrees and roars straight down before pulling up. Judges also rate precision in the triple snap roll, which requires three horizontal 360-degree rolls while maintaining altitude. Another feat is the outside loop, a circle flown around a point in the sky with the cockpit facing outward.

"Difficult in an open-air cockpit like Betty's Pitts," Ms. Cochrane said.

Difficult, too, on the day in 1949 when Ms. Skelton became the first woman to perform the inverted ribbon cut at an airfield in Oshkosh, Wis. In an oral history for the National Aeronautics and Space Administration in 1999, she recalled how risky the maneuver was.

The first time she tried it, she said, "I misjudged slightly and flew underneath the ribbon, which put me even closer to the ground."

"I never made that mistake again."

In her six years as a competitive pilot, Ms. Skelton set women's records for light planes. In one, in 1951, she reached 29,050 feet in a Piper Cub at an airfield in Tampa, Fla. She traveled around the country in the air-show circuit, performing what she declined to call stunts.

"I considered it an art," she said, "and I spent a great deal of time trying to convince people that it was not simply diving to thrill a crowd, to make a lot of noise and to put out a lot of smoke. It was an art that took many thousands of hours to perfect."

By 1951, Ms. Skelton had become friends with Bill France Sr., a founder of Nascar. He had little difficulty persuading her to slip behind the wheel of a stock car during Speed Week at Daytona Beach. She went on to set a series of women's land-speed records.

Ms. Skelton appeared on the cover of Look magazine with the headline, "Should a Girl Be First in Space?"

In addition to the 145.044 m.p.h. she reached in her Corvette in 1956, she set a transcontinental speed record (for both sexes) that year, driving from New York to Los Angeles in 56 hours, 58 minutes. In 1965, on the Bonneville Salt Flats in Utah, she took a jet car, the Green Monster Cyclops, to a top speed of 315.74 m.p.h.

By then, she had also become the first woman to be hired as a test driver in the auto industry and a spokeswoman for Chevrolet, appearing at auto shows and in national print advertisements and television commercials.

At news conferences, she was often asked, "What makes you tick?"

"My heart makes me tick" was her ready response, she said in the 1999 interview, "and it's my heart that makes me do these things. I don't think I have any better answer than that, except that everyone is built a little differently, and my heart and my will and my desires are mixed up with challenge."

Born on June 28, 1926, in Pensacola, she took her first solo flight at 12, not old enough under the law. She was already enthralled by those overhead Navy flights (and model planes and aviation magazines) when her parents, David and Myrtle Skelton, began taking her to a local airport and allowing her to hop rides on private planes.

She soloed legally on her 16th birthday and soon after earned her license. An aerobatic pilot, Clem Whittenback, taught her how to do a loop and roll for a charity air show that her father was organizing.

Ms. Skelton was inducted into 10 halls of fame, including the International Aerobatic Hall of Fame in 1988 and the Corvette Hall of Fame in 2001. She died at her home in The Villages, Fla. Her first husband, Donald Frankman, died in 2001. She later married Allan Erde, her sole immediate survivor.

In 1991, when Patty Wagstaff became the first woman to win the American aerobatics championship in a competition with men, Ms. Skelton sent her a letter, at one point referring to the plane she had flown to fame. "Receiving my first Medicare card a few months ago was not much of a thrill," Ms. Skelton wrote. "I wanted to burn it immediately and go out and buy a Pitts!"

Well into her 80s, she continued to drive her Corvette.

— BY DENNIS HEVESI

RALPH J. LOMMA

Spouting Whales Were Par for the Course

MARCH 13, 1924 · SEPT. 12, 2011

RALPH J. LOMMA, who at midcentury helped set the static pastime of miniature golf in motion, letting players tilt at windmills, shoot across rising drawbridges and, at game's end, watch the ball vanish forever into the maw of a voracious clown, died on Sept. 12 in Scranton, Pa. He was 87.

Mr. Lomma (pronounced LOW-muh) did not invent miniature golf: the game, originally genteelly landscaped, has its roots in 19th-century Britain. Nor was he the first to seed the courses with whimsical figures like castles and gnomes.

But Mr. Lomma and his brother Alphonse are widely credited with having shaped the game's familiar postwar incarnation by giving those figures moving parts, a distinguishing feature of the first miniature golf course they opened, in Scranton, in the mid-1950s.

MINI-GOLF MOGUL: Ralph J. Lomma brought miniature golf to the masses in the mid-1950s.

They also were among the first people to mass-produce and sell its components (including artificial greens and obstacles like revolving wagon wheels and flashing traffic lights), which let operators install the courses relatively cheaply.

As a result, the Lomma brothers — responsible for thousands of miniature golf courses around the world — helped make the game a mass entertainment for the entire family on par with bowling or drive-in movies. Miniature golf's sheer ubiquity, enduring popularity and satisfyingly campy appearance are largely owed to them, historians of the game say.

During much of the early 20th century, miniature golf in the United States was simply a scaled-down version of the real thing. Early courses could be lavish, in their small way, with sand traps, water hazards and gracious shrubbery.

In the 1920s, when the game was intensely in vogue, its reach broadened, with simple courses found in suburban parks, on urban rooftops and in empty lots across America.

By the late '20s, some courses had begun to be adorned with sculptural figures like horses and whales. But for the most part, the figures just sat there, meant more to divert the eye than to challenge the players.

Ralph John Lomma was born in Scranton on March 13, 1924. He served in the Pacific with the Army Air Corps in World War II and afterward studied architecture at the University of Scranton.

The Lomma brothers opened their first miniature golf course after taking shrewd note of the fixed quality of existing courses. Ralph conceived many of the obstacles — his whale spouted water when a ball was hit through — and Alphonse did the mechanical engineering.

The moving figures were intended to catch the eye of passing motorists. They also made the game more involving, forcing players to time their swings, for instance, so that the ball might sail cleanly between a windmill's passing blades.

The brothers' company, Lomma Miniature Golf, has sold more than 5,000 indoor and outdoor courses in countries around the world, including Kenya, Vietnam and China.

Over the years, their work influenced that of other miniature golf course designers; the tens of thousands of courses in the world today, with their lavish designs and huge moving figures, are in a sense the Lomma brothers' cultural heirs.

Ralph Lomma's other ventures included the development of residential communities in Pennsylvania and Florida and the Elk Mountain Ski Resort in Union Dale, Pa.

Mr. Lomma's first marriage ended in divorce. He is survived by his second wife, the former Joyce Jean Hydeck; their son; and a grandchild.

Among the miniature golf innovations his father claimed with greatest pride, Jonathan Lomma said, was the insatiable clown at the end of the course.

— By Margalit Fox

RICHARD HAMILTON

A Pop Art Pioneer Hired by the Beatles

FEB. 24, 1922 - SEPT. 13, 2011

Richard Hamilton, a British painter and printmaker whose sly, trenchant take on consumer culture and advertising made him a pioneering figure in Pop Art and who found a bit of pop music fame by designing the cover of the Beatles' "White Album," died on Sept. 13 at his home near Oxford. He was 89.

In the grim, rationed Britain of the early 1950s, Mr. Hamilton joined a circle of fellow artists, critics and architects at the Institute of Contemporary Arts to discuss the place of new technology, advertising and mass culture in modern art.

When the Independent Group, as it was known, organized the groundbreaking exhibition "This Is Tomorrow" at the Whitechapel Gallery in 1956, Mr. Hamilton contributed a 10-inch-by-9-inch collage, "Just What Is It That Makes Today's Homes So Different, So Appealing?"

EVERYDAY OBJECTS: Richard Hamilton's art explored consumer culture (and wound up in stores as 'The White Album').

Using images cut from mass-circulation magazines, the collage depicted a nude bodybuilder and a nude woman, posing alluringly on a sofa with a lampshade on her head, in a living room stocked with the goods and emblems of the postwar good life, American-style. A canned ham sits on an end table. A cover of Young Romance magazine is framed on the wall. The man holds a giant Tootsie Pop, with the word "Pop" occupying the center of the collage at eye level.

It became his most famous work, often referred to as the first example of Pop Art.

"Such was the success of this tiny and painstaking collocation that many people are still stuck with the idea of Hamilton as the man who single-handedly laid down the terms within which Pop Art was to operate," the critic John Russell wrote in the catalog for a 1973 Hamilton retrospective at the Solomon R. Guggenheim Museum in New York.

With the stated mission of expressing, and critiquing, the essence of consumer culture, which he described as "popular, transient, expendable, low-cost, mass-produced, young, witty, sexy, gimmicky, glamorous and big business," Mr. Hamilton went on to create many of the paintings that defined first-generation British Pop Art.

Notable among these were "Hommage à Chrysler Corp.," in which the seductive curves of a car bumper and headlights blend with the ghostly image of a red-lipsticked Venus, and "She," in which a toaster, vacuum cleaner, refrigerator and breasts float in a consumer dreamspace that Mr. Hamilton regarded with a certain ambivalence.

"It looks as though the painting is a sardonic comment on our society," Mr. Hamilton wrote of "She" in Architectural Design. "But I would like to think of my purpose as a search for what is epic in everyday objects and attitudes."

Richard William Hamilton was born on Feb. 24, 1922, in London. After studying painting at Westminster Technical College and St. Martin's School of Art, he went to work for the advertising department of a commercial studio. During World War II he worked as a jig and tool designer.

After the war he returned to the Royal Academy, where he had studied briefly before the war, but he was expelled for "not profiting by instruction" and was drafted into the British

Army. On completing his military service, he studied for three years at the Slade School of Art.

Mr. Hamilton initially made his living by making models and designing art exhibitions. Later he taught design at the Central School of Arts and Crafts in London and the University of Durham in Newcastle-on-Tyne.

An exhibition he organized at the Institute of Contemporary Arts in 1955, "Man, Machine and Motion," signaled his fascination with modern technology and mass-produced images, toward which he adopted a critical but receptive stance.

"If the artist is not to lose much of his ancient purpose, he may have to plunder the popular arts to recover the imagery which is his rightful inheritance," he wrote in 1961.

Unusually for a Pop artist, Mr. Hamilton made an overtly political statement with "Hugh Gaitskell as a Famous Monster of Filmland" (1964), merging a photograph of Claude Rains as the Phantom of the Opera with a newspaper photograph of Hugh Gaitskell, leader of the Labour Party, who, when the work was begun, had refused to support nuclear disarmament.

Mr. Hamilton's veneration for Duchamp, and the concept of the ready-made, helped determine the course of his art after the 1960s. He manipulated found objects and photographs, putting his own spin on newspaper photographs, postcards and industrial objects — like the Braun electric toothbrush, which he topped with a set of candy teeth — as well as prints filtering the images of other artists.

He also produced a series of political paintings in the 1980s inspired by the troubles in Northern Ireland and the hunger strike of Bobby Sands.

His dealer in the 1960s, the ultrahip Robert Fraser (also known as Groovy Bob), drew him into the vortex of the British pop-music world, reflected in the silkscreen-on-canvas series "Swingeing London," depicting Mick Jagger and Mr. Fraser being driven away by the police after their 1967 drug arrest.

During this period he met Paul McCartney, who hired him to design the cover for the Beatles' next album. Surprisingly, Mr. Hamilton proposed an all-white jacket.

Drawn into swinging London by Groovy Bob.

"To avoid the issue of competing with the lavish design treatments of most jackets, I suggested a plain white cover so pure and reticent that it would seem to place it in the context of the most esoteric art publications," Mr. Hamilton told Rolling Stone in 1991.

To reinforce the idea of a small-press production, he embossed "The Beatles" in one corner almost haphazardly and numbered each copy in a style that suggested a hand-numbering machine. Inside, he included a collage poster of private Beatles photos.

In an interview with The Observer of London last year, he recalled that he had been paid 200 pounds for the assignment, adding, "I thought that was a bit mean."

Mr. Hamilton, who was the subject of retrospectives at the Tate Gallery in 1970 and 1992, worked intermittently for more than 50 years on a series of illustrations for James Joyce's "Ulysses." They were exhibited at the British Museum in 2002.

His first wife, Terry O'Reilly, died in a car accident in 1962. He is survived by their son and his wife, Rita Donagh.

At his death he was helping to organize a traveling exhibition of his work, which is scheduled to open at the Museum of Contemporary Art in Los Angeles in June 2013.

— BY WILLIAM GRIMES

\\\\\\\\\\\\\\\\\\\\\\\\\\

WALTER BONATTI

Incident in the Snow at 26,000 Feet

JUNE 22, 1930 - SEPT. 13, 2011

WALTER BONATTI, who was one of the world's greatest mountaineers, trailblazing some of the most difficult and breathtaking climbs on the earth's tallest mountains, often alone, died on Sept. 13 in Rome. He was 81, his name long associated with one of the bitterest episodes in mountain-climbing history.

Mr. Bonatti was a member of the Italian team that conquered K2 in northern Pakistan, the world's second-tallest mountain, on July 31, 1954. The ascent was a moment of glory for Italy, coming after its defeat in World War II less than a decade earlier and at a time of fierce international competition to lay claim to the Himalayas.

But the achievement was tarnished by controversy. Mr. Bonatti, at 24 the youngest member of the expedition, did not reach the summit and later accused two colleagues of denying him an opportunity to share the moment.

As he recounted the episode, he and a Hunza porter were carrying oxygen tanks to the highest camp, at 26,000 feet, to help the team in its final push. But arriving at the spot where the camp was supposed to be, there was no trace of it. Mr. Bonatti later accused his fellow climbers of moving the camp so that he would not be able to find them and join them in conquering the summit. Mr. Bonatti and the porter, Amir Mahdi, were forced to spend a terrifying night out in the open.

They barely survived. In the morning, Mr. Mahdi descended in a headlong rush, almost out of his mind, losing fingers and toes to frostbite afterward.

A few hours later, the other two men, Achille Compagnoni and Lino Lacedelli, emerged to retrieve the oxygen tanks that Mr. Bonatti and Mr. Mahdi had left in the snow and went on to reach the summit around 6 p.m.

The Italian climbing establishment sided with Mr. Compagnoni and Mr. Lacedelli, but the dispute left a bitter taste in the Italian climbing world and remained a subject of argument for the next 50 years.

Where the camp on K2 was supposed to be, there was no trace of it.

"The K2 story was a big thorn in his heart," Mr. Bonatti's companion, Rosella Podestà, 77, said in a telephone interview after his death while she and family members were taking his body from Rome to their home in Dubino, a village north of his birthplace, Bergamo, in northern Italy. "He could not believe that, even after all those many years, nobody had apologized or acknowledged the truth. This falseness has left a mark in his life."

Mr. Bonatti became known as an angry loner who shied away from the bigger expeditions to take on new routes and new peaks his own way, sometimes at great risk.

"Bonatti was just a boy from Bergamo who in a very few years became the best climber in the world," the mountaineer Reinhold Messner told the Italian newspaper La Repubblica after Mr. Bonatti's death. He said Mr. Bonatti had been envied around the world because he was "too ahead of the curve, too alone, too good."

David Roberts, a journalist who writes about mountaineering, said of Mr. Bonatti in an interview: "If you had a poll of the greatest mountaineers of all time, he might win it. It is that simple."

"Everything he did," he added, "was out there pushing a new frontier that no one else dared push."

Mr. Bonatti's greatest accomplishment came in 1955, when he took an untried route to make a solo ascent of the west face of the Petit Dru, a huge granite pinnacle hanging over Chamonix in the French Alps. A daunting section of rock he scaled there became known as the Bonatti Pillar.

Seven years later, alone in a Swiss Alps winter, he climbed a new route up the middle of the Matterhorn's north face. That was his last great climb. At 35, he more or less quit climbing to write books about mountaineering and work as a writer and photojournalist for magazines like Época in Brazil.

Besides Ms. Podestà, Mr. Bonatti, who was born on June 22, 1930, is survived by two stepsons from her previous marriage and nine stepgrandchildren. He had been divorced. He died in Gemelli Hospital in Rome, but neither the family nor the Alpine Club disclosed the cause.

In his later years he was a celebrated and honored adventurer who chronicled his career in an autobiography, "The Mountains of My Life." For all his many feats, however, the defining event of that life was what happened on K2, a colossus

COLD AND BITTER: Walter Bonatti, pictured here during his solo climb of Petit Dru, never reached the top of K2, accusing two fellow climbers of leaving him behind.

rising about 28,250 feet in the Karakoram range, surpassed in height only by Mount Everest (more than 29,000 feet). The name K2 was a designation in a 19th-century land survey.

After the expedition, Mr. Bonatti accused Mr. Compagnoni and Mr. Lacedelli of moving the final campsite to prevent him, a more able climber, from joining them in the summit attempt. "He got hung out to dry by Compagnoni and Lacedelli," Mr. Roberts said.

Mr. Compagnoni, in turn, accused Mr. Bonatti of siphoning off oxygen from the tanks to undermine the climb. In 1964, an Italian newspaper article accused Mr. Bonatti of trying to steal the summit by making false accusations. Mr. Bonatti sued for libel and won, and Nino Giglio, the journalist who wrote the article, testified that most of his information had come from Mr. Compagnoni.

The disputes dragged on as Mr. Compagnoni and Ardito Desio, the expedition's leader, traded attacks with Mr. Bonatti for years. Mr. Bonatti was vindicated in 2004, when Mr. Lacedelli, who had reached the summit with Mr. Compagnoni in 1954, broke his silence. In "K2: The Price of Conquest," a book he wrote with Giovanni Cenacchi, Mr. Lacedelli essentially supported Mr. Bonatti's version of events. The Italian Alpine Club soon followed suit.

"He carried the Italian flag in a moment when Italy was coming back to life after the tragedy of World War II," Umberto Martini, the club's president, said in a statement. "Walter Bonatti was an example of rigor and seriousness for us all."

Mr. Bonatti made plans to return to K2 and conquer it himself, but never did. Mr. Compagnoni and Mr. Lacedelli died in 2009, Mr. Desio in 2001.

Kurt Diemberger, a filmmaker who was also a climber in the Bonatti era, said that by the end of his life Mr. Bonatti had been fully accepted by his own countrymen. "He was a hero to the Italians," Mr. Diemberger said in an interview.

But Mr. Bonatti did not always feel that way, Mr. Roberts said. After receiving the French Legion of Honor for saving two climbers in the Alps, Mr. Bonatti complained that he was a hero in France but not in Italy.

"My disappointments," Mr. Bonatti wrote in his book, "came from people, not the mountains."

— BY GRAHAM BOWLEY; GAIA PIANIGIANI
CONTRIBUTED REPORTING FROM ROME.

TOM WILSON

Think of His Brainchild as Everyman

AUG. 1, 1931 - SEPT. 16, 2011

W HO IS THIS COMIC-STRIP CHARACTER NAMED ZIGGY? He can't be placed in time, location or economic status, and seems to be — but may not be — an adult male. It is known that he was created in 1969 by the cartoonist Tom Wilson, who suggested that Ziggy can be whatever you want him to be.

When asked by teenage girls if Ziggy had a girlfriend or family, Mr. Wilson had a ready answer: "He does have a girlfriend! His girlfriend is you!"

Short, bald, big-nosed, barefoot, Ziggy was actually meant to be all of us, as Ziggy might say (he likes to talk directly to the reader), as we stumble through the frustrations, ironies and disappointments of life. In newspapers across the country, in the single-panel strip that bears his name, he battles temperamental toasters and wicked A.T.M.s. He gets a ticket on the information superhighway. He is baffled by waitresses, clerks and fortunetellers. He has few human friends.

But his pets love him, including a cat named

Sid, who is afraid of mice, and a potato-shaped dog named Fuzz, who looks like him. Moreover, by talking to the reader rather than to other characters, he engenders the illusion of direct eye contact.

Ziggy and his tribulations emerged from Mr. Wilson's memories of childhood, which he called "a Ziggy experience." As he explained in 1996: "I think in our own heads we're never all that confident. I'm not."

So universal are Ziggy's troubles — not to mention his stubbornly innocent won- derment — that Mr. Wilson insisted he did not create him. "I simply acknowledged him," he said.

Mr. Wilson, who was 80, died of pneumonia on Sept. 16 in Cincinnati. His death was announced by Universal Uclick, the syndi- cate that distributes his strip to 500 daily and Sunday newspapers.

'LITTLE GUY IN A BIG WORLD': The cartoon character Ziggy emerged from Tom Wilson's childhood memories and became a pop-culture powerhouse.

Ziggy survives him, however. His son, Tom Jr., has been drawing the strip since 1987 and will continue to do so. Early on, Mr. Wilson trained his son to draw it. He himself would draw Ziggy stumbling into a manhole, say, and then hand the paper to the boy, asking him to draw a rescue. "Tommy, it's time for you to save Ziggy!" he would say.

Drawn by the younger Mr. Wilson, with occasional advice from his father, Ziggy became known to a new generation as the same old clumsy, wide-eyed, teddy-bear-shaped "little guy in a big world" even as he addressed new concerns like the environment.

Along the way Ziggy became something of a pop-culture juggernaut. He was the inspiration for uncountable calendars, cards, T-shirts and mugs as well as best-selling books of cartoons. His name was invoked in a hip-hop song and in television shows like "Cheers," "Seinfeld," "The Simpsons" and "30 Rock." In 1983, the Christmas special "Ziggy's Gift" won an Emmy for best animated program. In 2002, Ziggy was the official spokescharacter for the Leukemia and Lymphoma Society.

In addition to his son, Mr. Wilson is survived by his wife, the former Carol Sobble; two daughters; and five grandchildren.

Thomas Albert Wilson was born in Grant Town, W. Va., on Aug. 1, 1931. When his father could not find work as a stone- mason, he moved the family to Pennsylvania, where he worked as a coal miner.

Thomas developed an empathetic sense of humor watching Laurel and Hardy movies. He played bass in an Army band, graduated from the Art Institute of Pittsburgh and moved to Cleveland, where he got a job with the American Greetings Corporation. As an executive there, he helped develop humorous, photographic and roman- tic cards, as well as characters like Strawberry Shortcake and the Care Bears.

He also first drew Ziggy there, for a humor book. He liked the name because it meant the character would come last in the alphabetical order of life, a theme he illustrated — literally — in one memorable strip. In it, Ziggy is stranded on a rooftop during a flood as a rescue boat picks up people alphabetically.

— By Douglas Martin

\\\\\\\\\\\\\\\\\\\\\\\

CHARLES H. PERCY

The Makings of a President, Some Said

SEPT. 27, 1919 · SEPT. 17, 2011

C HARLES H. PERCY, a former United States senator from Illinois and a moderate Republican who clashed with President Richard M. Nixon over Watergate and whose own presidential ambitions were stymied by Nixon's resignation, died on Sept. 17 in Washington. He was 91.

His death was announced by the office of his son-in-law, Senator John D. Rockefeller IV of West Virginia.

A three-term senator, Mr. Percy went to Washington in 1967 after a strikingly successful career as a businessman. In 1949, at the age of 29, he was named president of Bell & Howell and then oversaw its rapid growth. He also arrived in the capital grief-stricken: one of his daughters had been murdered during his 1966 campaign.

Mr. Percy was talked about as presidential timber almost from the time he entered politics in 1964, when he ran for governor of Illinois; he narrowly lost to Otto Kerner Jr. The notion gained even wider currency in 1966, when, in an upset, he gained a Senate seat by defeating Paul H. Douglas, a respected three-term Democratic incumbent.

For many Republicans, Mr. Percy's business background, Midwestern roots and moderate views in the increasingly liberal political climate of the 1960s made him an attractive alternative to the hard-right conservatism that voters had rejected in 1964 in the landslide defeat of Senator Barry Goldwater.

His good looks and elegant manner enhanced his appeal; Republicans retained fresh memories of their narrow presidential loss to the handsome John F. Kennedy in 1960.

In 1967, only three months into his first Senate term, Chuck Percy, as he was familiarly known, drew attention when he proposed legislation to create a private foundation to finance low-cost housing and foster home ownership among low-income families. Though the measure did not pass, it drew strong support from Republicans in both the House and the Senate.

The New York Times columnist James B. Reston called him "the hottest political article in the Republican Party."

By the end of the year, he was considered a possible contender for the 1968 Republican presidential nomination; a Louis Harris poll in late 1967 put him ahead of President Lyndon B. Johnson in a head-to-head contest. But he declined to run and instead endorsed Gov. Nelson A. Rockefeller of New York, another moderate.

Mr. Percy became closely identified with the more liberal wing of the party known as Rockefeller Republicans, so much so that his name became attached to them as well — "decent Chuck Percy Republicans," as the writer Richard Ford described them in "The Lay of the Land," his novel of suburban New Jersey.

Mr. Percy's national stature was underlined when his endorsement of Rockefeller was treated as front-page news nationwide. The Times made the announcement its lead article on July 26, 1968, describing it as "counterbalancing" former President Dwight D. Eisenhower's endorsement of Nixon.

Mr. Percy was a handsome liberal Republican whom one poll showed beating Lyndon Johnson, but his presidential opportunities came and went.

Mr. Percy considered a bid for the White House only once. In June 1973, he formed an exploratory committee to look into a 1976 candidacy. But he closed it down after Nixon resigned in August 1974 and Vice President Gerald R. Ford became president. Within a week, Mr. Percy said Ford had gotten off to an excellent start and was likely to be nominated in 1976, as he was.

Mr. Percy's clash with Nixon came in the spring of 1973 as the president was trying to contain the Watergate scandal, set in motion by the break-in at the offices of the Democratic opposition by a White House team of burglars and aggravated by the administration's efforts to cover up the crime.

On May 1, the day after Nixon announced a staff shakeup and authorized a new attorney general to "make all decisions" relating to Watergate prosecutions, Mr. Percy proposed a Senate resolution demanding an independent prosecutor "of the highest character and integrity from outside the executive branch."

Mr. Percy told the Senate: "A simple and very basic question is at issue: Should the executive branch investigate itself? I do not think so."

His resolution was adopted without objection. Soon afterward, Nixon fumed to his cabinet that he would do all he could to make sure that Mr. Percy, who had already voted against two Nixon nominees for the Supreme Court, would never become president.

In 1977, after the election of President Jimmy Carter, Mr. Percy accused the White House budget director, Bert Lance, of backdating checks to gain tax deductions. Mr. Percy was the senior Republican on the Senate Governmental Affairs Committee, and he and Senator Abraham A. Ribicoff, Democrat of Connecticut, the chairman, demanded that Mr. Lance resign or be fired because of the checks as well as accusations of banking crimes.

Mr. Lance resigned but was acquitted of all charges arising from the Senate inquiry. Mr. Percy later apologized for the backdating accusation.

Mr. Percy was proud of his recommendations for judicial appointments, especially that of John Paul Stevens, a former college classmate. Mr. Percy had persuaded him to take a seat on a federal appeals court in 1970 and then backed his nomination when Ford named him to the Supreme Court in 1975. Mr. Percy consulted bar associations and lawyer friends about appointments and said he never chose a political supporter for the bench.

Over his 18 years in the Senate, Mr. Percy averaged a 52 percent rating from the liberal Americans for Democratic Action and only 30 percent from the American Conservative Union. With the party having moved steadily to the right since then, it was a rating few if any Republicans would receive today.

"Percy's passing reminds us that today's Republican Party is not your mother's Republican

Party," said Thomas C. Mann, a Congressional scholar at the Brookings Institution in Washington, adding that Mr. Percy had worked "comfortably" with Democrats.

"Perhaps the most significant change in American politics," Mr. Mann said, "which has picked up with the most intensity in recent years, is the disappearance of moderate, pragmatic Republicans like Percy."

Charles Harting Percy was born in Pensacola, Fla., on Sept. 27, 1919, the son of Edward Percy and the former Elizabeth Harting. He grew up in Chicago, where his father was a bank clerk. When the bank failed in the Depression and his father lost his job, the family went on relief, and Mr. Percy took several jobs as a child.

He graduated from the well-regarded New Trier High School in Winnetka, Ill., then received a scholarship to attend the University of Chicago. There he ran a cooperative that purchased services for fraternities, and sent money home to help his family. He was also the captain of the water polo team.

Mr. Percy was still a student when he began his association with Bell & Howell, taking summer jobs. The company hired him full time after he graduated in 1941. When war came later that year, he set up schools to teach military personnel how to use Bell & Howell movie cameras. He joined the Navy in 1943, training aviation personnel.

Rising quickly through the company's ranks, he was named president on Jan. 12, 1949, an appointment that drew wide attention not least because of his age. But the company, based near Chicago in Skokie, Ill., prospered under him as it extended its reach in the consumer electronics market and went beyond it, producing components for space photography. Annual sales were $13 million when he took over; when he left in 1963, they were more than $160 million.

Mr. Percy married Jeanne Valerie Dickerson in 1943. She died in 1947. In 1950 he married Loraine Diane Guyer, who survives him. He is also survived by a son and a daughter from his first marriage (that daughter, Sharon Percy Rockefeller, is married to Senator Rockefeller), as well as a son and daughter from his second marriage, nine grandchildren and six great-grandchildren.

Another daughter, Sharon's twin sister, Valerie, was bludgeoned to death in the family home in Kenilworth, Ill., during Mr. Percy's 1966 campaign. She was 21. The police kept the case alive for more than 20 years but never identified a suspect. They did rule out burglary, however, since nothing was stolen, and said the intensity of the attack suggested that the killing had been committed by someone who knew

ROCKEFELLER REPUBLICAN: Charles H. Percy in 1978, after claiming victory over his Democratic opponent. He was identified with the more liberal wing of his party.

Ms. Percy. Mr. Percy suspended his campaign for a couple of weeks but returned and won a solid victory over Mr. Douglas.

But just as Illinois voters had tired of Mr. Douglas by 1966, Mr. Percy was old goods by 1984. In a strong Republican year, with President Ronald Reagan campaigning for him, Mr. Percy could not overcome his Democratic opponent, Representative Paul M. Simon.

His position as chairman of the Foreign Relations Committee seemed remote to Illinois voters, as did his manner. The Chicago Tribune, The Washington Post and The Wall Street Journal all described him as "pompous."

Mr. Percy never persuaded conservatives to trust him, and some actually supported Mr. Simon in the hope that Senator Jesse Helms, Republican of North Carolina, would succeed him in the chairmanship. The Illinois economy was weak, and Mr. Simon won a narrow victory with 50.1 percent of the vote.

After his defeat, Mr. Percy lived in Washington and led a consulting firm that sought to help United States companies export their products. He was treated for Alzheimer's disease for many years.

Until the disease impaired him, Mr. Percy, a Christian Scientist, had read the Christian Science Bible Lessons every day.

— *By Adam Clymer*

\\\\\\\\\\\\\\\\\\\\\\\\\\\\\\\

ARCH WEST

On the Origin of Doritos

SEPT. 8, 1914 · SEPT. 20, 2011

S NACK-FOOD LOVERS PARTIAL TO DORITOS owe that pleasure, in large part, to Arch West.

Mr. West, who died on Sept. 20 at the age of 97, was at the forefront of the team at Frito-Lay that developed Doritos corn chips, a Southwestern-inspired alternative to the traditional salted potato or corn chip.

Though the company, Frito-Lay North America, declines to give Mr. West full credit for the chip — "as a company, there's never one person to invent or is the father or mother of a given product," said Aurora Gonzalez, a spokeswoman — others do.

"He widely gets the credit for Doritos," Andrew F. Smith, the author of the "Encyclopedia of Junk Food and Fast Food," published in 2006, said in an interview.

Today, Doritos are Frito-Lay's second-best seller, after Lays Potato Chips, both nationally and around the world, with total sales of nearly $5 billion a year.

Mr. West died at a hospital near his home in Dallas, his daughter, Jana Hacker, said. By her account, her father got the idea for Doritos in the early 1960s, when he was vice president of marketing for what was then the Frito Company. (It is now a division of PepsiCo.) While on vacation in San Diego, she said, the family stopped at "a little shack restaurant where these people were making a fried corn chip."

The chip's tangy taste captured her father's attention. Back in Dallas, after Frito merged with the H. W. Lay Company, he promoted the Doritos' production, which began in 1964, using corn tortillas cut into triangles and seasoned with cheese and chili flavorings.

"The '50s were very boring and bland in terms of snack foods, so this was a taste sensation," Mr. Smith said. "It came out at just the right time, when Mexican-American food was breaking out of the Southwest and increasingly becoming national cuisine." In 1962, Glen W. Bell Jr. had opened in Downey, Calif., the first of what would become an international chain of Taco Bell restaurants.

The flavorings associated with Doritos "were Mexican-ish," Mr. Smith said. "No one in Mexico would have consumed such a product, unless they were catering to American tourists." Still, he added, "Doritos have been popular for almost half a century, so it's been an incredible invention."

Archibald Clark West was born in Indianapolis on Sept. 8, 1914, to James and Jessie West. After graduating from Franklin College, near Indianapolis, he served as a gunnery officer in the Navy during World War II. Before joining Frito in 1960, he had worked in advertising in New York.

> In the "boring and bland" 1950s, Doritos "came out at just the right time, when Mexican-American food was breaking out of the Southwest."

Besides his daughter, Mr. West is survived by three sons, 12 grandchildren and six great-grandchildren. His wife of 50 years, the former Charlotte Thomson, died in 2010.

Their ashes were to be buried together. "We're going to let everyone toss in a Dorito," their daughter said.

— By Dennis Hevesi

EMANUEL LITVINOFF

A Poetic Rebuke, as Eliot Sat Listening

MAY 5, 1915 - SEPT. 24, 2011

EMANUEL LITVINOFF, an English-born Jewish poet known for his scathing verse indictment of T. S. Eliot's anti-Semitism — and for reading it before an audience that happened to include Eliot — died on Sept. 24 at his home in London. He was 96.

The author of several volumes of poetry, Mr. Litvinoff also wrote well-received novels centering on the struggles of Jews in the European diaspora. He was the author of "Journey Through a Small Planet" (1972), a highly praised memoir of the straitened yet vibrant Jewish community in London's prewar East End.

A seamstress's son, Mr. Litvinoff worked as a fur nailer's apprentice and often slept in doorways in the East End of London.

Mr. Litvinoff also advocated on behalf of the rights of Jews in the postwar East Bloc. He was the founder and editor of a newsletter originally titled Jews in Eastern Europe, which was published regularly from the late 1950s to the late '80s.

But it was for his poem "To T. S. Eliot" that he was best remembered. Written after World War II and widely anthologized, it was a response to the unapologetic anti-Semitic elements of Eliot's work. One Eliot poem, "Burbank With a Baedeker: Bleistein With a Cigar," included these lines:

> But this or such was Bleistein's way:
> A saggy bending of the knees
> And elbows, with the palms turned out,
> Chicago Semite Viennese.
> A lustreless protrusive eye
> Stares from the protozoic slime
> At a perspective of Canaletto.
> The smoky candle end of time
> Declines. On the Rialto once.
> The rats are underneath the piles.

> The jew is underneath the lot.
> Money in furs. The boatman smiles. . . .

The poem was first published in 1920. Before World War II, Mr. Litvinoff, who otherwise admired Eliot's work, was prepared to dismiss it as simply another link in the venerable chain of British literary anti-Semitism.

Eliot chose to reprint the poem in his anthology "Selected Poems," published in 1948. That, in the post-Holocaust world, struck Mr. Litvinoff as inexcusable.

He set to work and wrote "To T. S. Eliot." Addressed to the poet and invoking Shakespeare, the Nazi newspaper Der Stürmer and the Vistula River in Poland, it opens:

> Eminence becomes you. Now when the rock
>   is struck
> your young sardonic voice which broke on
>   beauty
> floats amid incense and speaks oracles
> as though a god
> utters from Russell Square and condescends,
> high in the solemn cathedral of the air,
> his holy octaves to a million radios.
> I am not one accepted in your parish.
> Bleistein is my relative and I share
> the protozoic slime of Shylock, a page
> in Stürmer, and, underneath the cities,
> a billet somewhat lower than the rats.
> Blood in the sewers. Pieces of our flesh
> float with the ordure on the Vistula.
> You had a sermon but it was not this. . . .

Mr. Litvinoff was by this time established himself. His published work included the volumes "The Untried Soldier" (1942) and "A Crown for Cain" (1948). In early 1951, he was invited to take part in an illustrious public poetry reading at the Institute of Contemporary Arts in London. He brought the poem with him.

He had no idea, though, that just before he began reading it aloud, its subject would walk through the door.

Emanuel Litvinoff was born on May 5, 1915, in the Whitechapel section of London, one of four children of parents who had fled czarist pogroms in Odessa, Ukraine. After the start of the Russian Revolution in 1917, Emanuel's father returned there to fight with the Bolsheviks and was never heard from again.

His mother supported the family as a seamstress. She remarried and had five more children. Emanuel was reared in the East End with his mother, stepfather and eight siblings in two tiny rooms.

So nervous that he could not hold a pencil when he sat for the entrance exam for academic secondary school, Emanuel was relegated to trade school, where he was trained as a shoemaker. The only Jewish boy there, he endured anti-Semitic baiting, and beatings, as he later wrote, at the hands of his schoolmates.

After leaving school, he held meager jobs, including fur nailer's apprentice, helping to stretch pelts on boards before they were cut and sewn. He could not always afford food and often slept in doorways.

During the war, Mr. Litvinoff served with the British Army in Northern Ireland, West Africa and the Middle East. He began writing poetry at this time.

Mr. Litvinoff was divorced from his first wife, Irene Maud Pearson, a celebrated British fashion model known professionally as Cherry Marshall. She was said to have had the smallest waist in London. He is survived by his second wife, Mary McClory, their son, two children from his first marriage, a half-brother, three grandchildren and two great-grandchildren. A daughter from his first marriage died in 2010.

His other books include the novels "The Lost Europeans" (1959), "The Man Next Door" (1968) and "Falls the Shadow" (1983), and "The Penguin Book of Jewish Short Stories" (1979), which he edited.

Before Mr. Litvinoff took the stage to read "To T. S. Eliot" that day in London, a murmur ran through the crowd, which included some of Britain's leading literary lights: Eliot, the 1948 Nobel laureate in literature, had just entered the room.

By the time it was Mr. Litvinoff's turn to read, he said afterward, he was keenly aware that

WRITER AND CRITIC: Emanuel Litvinoff, who wrote poems, novels and a memoir about the struggles of European Jews, criticized the poet T. S. Eliot for his unapologetic anti-Semitic work.

the target of the corrosive lines he was about to utter was sitting in the audience.

His voice shook, he recalled, giving his poem unintended force. After the opening stanzas, it continued:

Yet walking with Cohen when the sun
exploded
and darkness choked our nostrils,
and the smoke drifting over Treblinka
reeked of the smouldering ashes of children,
I thought what an angry poem
you would have made of it, given the pity. . . .
So shall I say it is not eminence chills
but the snigger from behind the covers of
history,
the sly words and the cold heart

and footprints made with blood upon a
continent?
Let your words
tread lightly on this earth of Europe
lest my people's bones protest.

When Mr. Litvinoff finished, as was widely reported, pandemonium ensued. The poet Stephen Spender stood up and denounced him for insulting Eliot, prompting others in the crowd to cry "Hear, hear!" in assent.

There was, however, a dissenting voice. Amid the tumult, a man in the back of the room was heard to mutter: "It's a good poem. It's a very good poem."

The man was Thomas Stearns Eliot.

— BY MARGALIT FOX

///////////////////////////

WANGARI MAATHAI

Tree by Tree, a Path to the Peace Prize

APRIL 1, 1940 · SEPT. 25, 2011

WANGARI MAATHAI, the Kenyan environmentalist who began a movement to reforest her country by paying poor women a few shillings to plant trees, died on Sept. 25 in Nairobi, Kenya. She was 71 and, for her efforts, became the first African woman to win a Nobel Peace Prize.

Dr. Maathai, one of the most widely respected women on the continent, played many roles — environmentalist, feminist, politician, professor, rabble-rouser, human rights advocate and head of the Green Belt Movement, which she founded in 1977. Its mission was to plant trees across Kenya to fight erosion and to create firewood for fuel and jobs for women.

Dr. Maathai was as comfortable in the crowded streets of Nairobi's slums and on the muddy hillsides of central Kenya as she was in the bastions of power, hobnobbing with heads of state, including Presidents Nicolas Sarkozy of France as well as Bill Clinton and Barack Obama. She won the Peace Prize in 2004 for what the Nobel committee called "her contribution to sustainable development, democracy and peace." It was a moment of immense pride in Kenya and across Africa.

Her Green Belt Movement has planted more than 30 million trees and has helped nearly 900,000 women, according to the United Nations, while inspiring similar efforts in other African countries.

"Wangari Maathai was a force of nature," said Achim Steiner, the executive director of the United Nations' environmental program. He likened her to Africa's ubiquitous acacia trees, "strong in character and able to survive sometimes the harshest of conditions."

Dr. Maathai toured the world, speaking out against environmental degradation and poverty, which she said early on were intimately connected. But she never lost focus on her native Kenya. She was a thorn in the side of Kenya's previous president, Daniel arap Moi, whose government labeled the Green Belt Movement "subversive" during the 1980s.

Mr. Moi was particularly scornful of her leading the charge against a government plan to build a huge skyscraper in one of central Nairobi's only parks. The proposal was eventually scrapped, though not long afterward, during a protest, Dr. Maathai was beaten unconscious by the police.

When Mr. Moi finally stepped down after 24 years in power, Dr. Maathai served as a member of Parliament and as an assistant minister on environmental issues until falling out of favor with Kenya's new leaders and losing her seat a few years later.

In 2008, after being pushed out of government, she was hit with tear gas by the police during a protest against the excesses of Kenya's entrenched political class.

Home life was not easy, either. Her husband, Mwangi, divorced her, saying, by her account, that she was too strong-minded for a woman.

FORCE OF NATURE: The environmentalist Wangari Maathai in the Newlands forest in Cape Town, South Africa, 2005. She was the first African woman to win a Nobel Peace Prize.

When she lost her divorce case and criticized the judge, she was thrown in jail.

"Wangari Maathai was known to speak truth to power," said John Githongo, an anticorruption campaigner in Kenya who was forced into exile for years for his own outspoken views. "She blazed a trail in whatever she did, whether it was in the environment, politics, whatever."

Wangari Muta Maathai was born on April 1, 1940, in Nyeri, Kenya, in the foothills of Mount Kenya. A star student, she won a scholarship to study biology at Mount St. Scholastica College in Atchison, Kan., receiving a degree in 1964. She earned a master of science degree from the University of Pittsburgh.

She went on to obtain a doctorate in veterinary anatomy at the University of Nairobi, becoming the first woman in East or Central Africa to hold such a degree, according to the Nobel Prize Web site. She also taught at the university as an associate professor and was chairwoman of its veterinary anatomy department in the 1970s.

A day before she was scheduled to receive the Nobel, Dr. Maathai was forced to respond to a report in The East African Standard, a daily newspaper in Nairobi, that she had likened AIDS to a "biological weapon," telling participants in an AIDS workshop in Nyeri that the disease was "a tool" to control Africans "designed by some evil-minded scientists."

She said her comments had been taken out of context. "It is therefore critical for me to state that I neither say nor believe that the virus was developed by white people or white powers in order to destroy the African people," she said in a statement released by the Nobel committee. "Such views are wicked and destructive."

In presenting her with the Peace Prize, the Nobel committee hailed her for taking "a holistic approach to sustainable development that embraces democracy, human rights and women's rights in particular" and for serving "as inspiration for many in the fight for democratic rights."

Dr. Maathai received many honorary degrees, including an honorary doctorate from the University of Pittsburgh in 2006, as well as numerous awards, including the French Legion of Honor and Japan's Grand Cordon of the Order of the Rising Sun. She was the author of several books, including "Unbowed: A Memoir," published in 2006.

Dr. Maathai died of cancer, the Green Belt Movement said. Kenyan news outlets said she had been treated for ovarian cancer and had been in a hospital for at least a week before she died. She is survived by three children and a granddaughter.

Former Vice President Al Gore, a fellow Peace Prize recipient for his environmental work, said in a statement, "Wangari overcame incredible obstacles to devote her life to service — service to her children, to her constituents, to the women, and indeed all the people of Kenya — and to the world as a whole."

In her Nobel Prize acceptance speech, Dr. Maathai said the inspiration for her work came from growing up in rural Kenya. She reminisced about a stream running next to her home — a stream that has since dried up — and drinking fresh, clear water.

"In the course of history, there comes a time when humanity is called to shift to a new level of consciousness," she said, "to reach a higher moral ground. A time when we have to shed our fear and give hope to each other. That time is now."

— BY JEFFREY GETTLEMAN

BOB CASSILLY

A Builder of Wonderlands

NOV. 9, 1949 - SEPT. 26, 2011

THE EPIPHANY FOR BOB CASSILLY came when he was building an underground city in the dirt beneath the porch of his family home. Eavesdropping on his parents' adult conversation, he thought, "What a shame not to be 11."

Mr. Cassilly held onto his sense of childlike wonder, shunning some of the usual trappings of adulthood. He never collected a regular wage, and insisted that his many occupations — sculptor, artist, businessman, landlord, real estate mogul and museum director — did not define him.

His imagination did. He created whimsical animal sculptures around the country, including hippopotamuses for children to play on in Riverside Park and Central Park in New York and a giraffe at the Dallas Zoo. It's the tallest sculpture in Texas if you count its outstretched tongue. In his native St. Louis he built a children's paradise of tree houses, caves, slides and odd treasures he found. He called it City Museum, and tourists flocked to it.

Perhaps his boldest vision was to create what he called Cementland, another tourist attraction, this one at the site of an abandoned cement factory in St. Louis next to the Mississippi River. He would go there alone sometimes on weekends to bulldoze dirt himself. He loved bulldozers.

On Monday, Sept. 26, a worker returning to the site after the weekend found Mr. Cassilly's body there, still behind the controls of the machine, at the foot of a monstrous pile of dirt. The bulldozer had apparently rolled over while he was pushing dirt and killed him before landing upright, the St. Louis authorities said. He had last been seen two days earlier, a Saturday. He was 61.

Mr. Cassilly had bought the site and was methodically turning it into a peculiar playground that illustrated, at least in his own idiosyncratic mind, the emergence of prehistoric life, the industrial revolution and the evanescence of time.

The attractions themselves were easier to grasp. Mr. Cassilly knew children of all ages would relish throwing rocks from the plant's 225-foot-high smokestack, or riding in a boat from the top of a silo along a winding water chute four-fifths of a mile long before dropping into a lake. There would be a castle, mazes of moats, tunnels and perhaps a pyramid. Rusted machinery scattered on the grounds would be set in motion for no apparent purpose.

"It will be a place where we can do things that are normally illegal," Mr. Cassilly said in a 2005 interview with The St. Louis Post-Dispatch.

After his body was found, Francis G. Slay, the mayor of St. Louis, said, "The city has lost some of its wonder."

Robert James Cassilly Jr. was born on Nov. 9, 1949, in St. Louis to a building contractor and a homemaker. At 7 years old, he recalled, he would lie in bed envisioning building things with no idea of their ultimate purpose. By 14 he was skipping classes to apprentice with a sculptor. He graduated from Fontbonne College (now Fontbonne University) in St. Louis.

Mr. Cassilly later built and operated a restaurant, for which he made fountains and sculptures. After selling the business, he moved to Hawaii to carve wood on a beach. Perfect days soon bored him, however, so he returned to St. Louis and Fontbonne to earn a master's degree. There, he met Gail Soliwoda, a fellow sculptor. He married her after divorcing his

DREAMER, CREATOR: Bob Cassilly at Cementland. He spent his days building imaginative parks and whimsical sculptures for the public to enjoy.

first wife, the former Cecilia Davidson. He and Ms. Soliwoda were also artistic and business partners until their divorce in 2002.

Mr. Cassilly married a third time and is survived by his wife, the former Melissa Giovanna Zompa. He is also survived by two children from his second marriage and two sons from his third.

In the mid-1970s Mr. Cassilly refurbished a house in a neglected St. Louis neighborhood, then followed up by building six new town houses. The architectural ornaments he designed led him to start a business making them, and that enterprise led to his animal sculptures. He made big ones for the St. Louis Zoo, including a 45-foot-long squid.

In 1983, he bought a 250,000-square-foot building complex housing a shoe factory in downtown St. Louis for 69 cents a square foot. He stuffed it with wonders like a five-story jungle gym partly built from the carcasses of two jet airplanes and a fire truck; a walk-through whale; a rooftop Ferris wheel; a circus; an aquarium; caves; a shoelace factory; what Mr. Cassilly said was the world's largest No. 2 pencil; and a collection of skateboard ramps where children could do everything but use skateboards. It opened as City Museum in 1997.

The Project for Public Spaces, a research and advocacy group, has listed City Museum as one of the "great public spaces in the world."

Mr. Cassilly began the museum as a nonprofit institution, but tired of formalities like a board of directors. He bought it in 2002 to run it as a business. A first step was charging for parking. He put up a sign, "Greedy Bob's Parking Lot." More than 600,000 people visit each year.

Mr. Cassilly, habitually clad in jeans and boots, called himself an anarchist. He often ignored building permits and once, using spray paint, defaced a family of concrete turtles he had made for a park after park workers changed their color when they applied a protective coating.

The do-it-yourself, trying-anything nature of the museum led, not surprisingly, to injuries and, also not surprisingly, to dozens of personal injury suits. Mr. Cassilly's response was to post telephone numbers of lawyers at the door.

When suits went to trial, he resented his time on the witness stand. "Jurors have no sense of irony," he said.

— By Douglas Martin

WILSON GREATBATCH

The Tinkerer and the Pacemaker

SEPT. 6, 1919 · SEPT. 27, 2011

Wilson Greatbatch, a professed "humble tinkerer" who, working in his barn in 1958, designed the first practical implantable pacemaker, a heart-rhythm device that has preserved millions of lives, died on Sept. 27 at his home in Williamsville, N.Y., outside Buffalo. He was 92.

Mr. Greatbatch patented more than 325 inventions, notably a long-life lithium battery used in a wide range of medical implants. He created tools used in AIDS research and a solar-powered canoe, which he took on a 160-mile voyage on the Finger Lakes in New York to celebrate his 72nd birthday.

In later years, he invested time and money in developing fuels from plants and supporting work at the University of Wisconsin in Madison on helium-based fusion reaction for power generation.

NO SMALL TASK: Wilson Greatbatch invented the first practical implantable pacemaker, saving millions of lives. He patented more than 325 inventions in his lifetime.

He also visited with thousands of schoolchildren to talk about invention, and when his eyesight became too poor for him to read in 2006, he continued to review papers by graduate engineering students on topics that interested him by having his secretary read them aloud.

"I'm beginning to think I may not change the world, but I'm still trying," Mr. Greatbatch said in a telephone interview in 2007.

He was best known for his pacemaker breakthrough, an example of Pasteur's observation that "chance favors the prepared mind."

Mr. Greatbatch's crucial insight came in 1956, when he was an assistant professor in electrical engineering at the University of Buffalo. While building a heart rhythm recording device for the Chronic Disease Research Institute there, he reached into a box of parts for a resistor to complete the circuitry. The one he pulled out was the wrong size, and when he installed it, the circuit it produced emitted intermittent electrical pulses.

Mr. Greatbatch immediately associated the timing and rhythm of the pulses with a human heartbeat, he wrote in a memoir, "The Making of the Pacemaker," published in 2000. That

brought to mind lunchtime chats he had had with researchers about the electrical activity of the heart while he was working at an animal behavior laboratory as an undergraduate at Cornell in 1951.

Back then, he had surmised that electrical stimulation could compensate for breakdowns in the heart's natural circuitry. But he did not believe the electronic gear of that era could be bundled into a stimulator for continuous use, much less into a device small and reliable enough to implant.

After the unintended circuit rekindled his interest, Mr. Greatbatch began experiments to shrink the equipment and shield it from body fluids. On May 7, 1958, doctors at the Veterans Administration hospital in Buffalo demonstrated that a version he had created, of just two cubic inches, could take control of a dog's heartbeat.

Mr. Greatbatch soon learned he was in a race with other researchers in the United States and Sweden to perfect a practical implant for humans. Relying on $2,000 in savings and a large vegetable garden to help feed his growing family, he went to work full time on the device in the barn behind his home in Clarence, N.Y., east of Buffalo. He was assisted by his wife, Eleanor, who administered shock tests for the pacemaker's transistors by first taping them to a bedroom wall.

His major collaborator was Dr. William C. Chardack, chief of surgery at the hospital where he had first tested the device on dogs. Mr. Greatbatch's device was implanted in 10 human patients in 1960, including two children. The device was licensed in 1961 to Medtronic, a Minneapolis company that had developed an external pacemaker. Buoyed by the new implanted devices, Medtronic went on to become the world leader in cardiac stimulation and defibrillation. The American Heart Association says that more than half a million pacemakers are now implanted every year.

Mr. Greatbatch profited handsomely from his invention and invested in other projects. In one, he adapted for human use equipment he had designed to monitor the health of test monkeys launched into space by the government. But he soon returned to address a crucial limitation in his pacemaker: its zinc-mercury batteries, which could drain in as little as two years.

Mr. Greatbatch acquired rights to a lithium iodine design invented in 1968 by researchers in Baltimore, and by 1972 he had re-engineered the device — it had been potentially explosive — into a compact sealed package that could be implanted in the body for a decade or more.

A company he founded in 1970 to make the batteries, today called Greatbatch Inc., became a leading power-component supplier for the entire medical device industry and later expanded into related businesses.

Mr. Greatbatch often told students that 9 out of 10 of his ideas failed, either technically or commercially. His last major interest, helium fusion experiments, may be the longest shot of all.

The reaction is theoretically attractive; unlike nuclear power generation, it produces no radioactive materials. But the raw material for it is an isotope of helium that exists only in trace amounts on earth. For the fusion to generate significant amounts of power, the isotope would have to be mined on the moon.

Wilson Greatbatch was born on Sept. 6, 1919, in Buffalo, the only child of Warren Greatbatch, a construction contractor who had immigrated from England, and the former Charlotte Recktenwalt, who worked as a secretary and named him in honor of Woodrow Wilson.

As a teenager, Mr. Greatbatch became fascinated with radio technology. He put his skills to use in the Navy during World War II working on shipboard communications and guidance systems before being assigned to fly combat missions. Mr. Greatbatch, a Presbyterian, cited the seeming randomness of death in wartime as the inspiration for his religious faith.

Returning from the war, Mr. Greatbatch married Eleanor Wright, his childhood sweetheart, and worked for a year as a telephone repairman before entering Cornell.

Nothing in Mr. Greatbatch's grades foretold success, but that was partly because he was also working at outside jobs to support his family. The jobs kept him abreast of developments in the electronics industry. After earning a master of science degree in electrical engineering at the University of Buffalo, he became manager of the electronics division of the Taber Instrument Corporation in Buffalo.

When Taber was unwilling to take on the risk of his pacemaker implant experiments, he began his life as an independent inventor and entrepreneur.

Eleanor Greatbatch died in January. Mr. Greatbatch is survived by a daughter, three sons, 12 grandchildren and eight great-grandchildren. Another son died in 1998.

Mr. Greatbatch saw a divine hand in much of what he did. When experiments bore no fruit, he wrote, it was impossible to know whether what looked like failure had not been intended by God as a contribution to success in the future. And he saw invention as an end in itself.

"To ask for a successful experiment, for professional stature, for financial reward or for peer approval," he wrote in his memoir, "is asking to be paid for what should be an act of love."

— BY BARNABY J. FEDER; DANIEL E. SLOTNIK
CONTRIBUTED REPORTING.

SYLVIA ROBINSON

"The Mother of Hip-Hop"

MARCH 6, 1936 - SEPT. 29, 2011

S YLVIA ROBINSON, a singer, songwriter and record producer who formed the pioneering hip-hop group Sugarhill Gang and made the first commercially successful rap recording with them, died on Sept. 29 in Edison, N.J. She was 75.

Ms. Robinson had a successful career as a rhythm and blues singer long before she and her husband, Joe Robinson, formed Sugar Hill Records in the 1970s and went on to foster a musical genre that came to dominate pop music.

She sang with Mickey Baker as part of the duo Mickey & Sylvia in the 1950s and had several hits, including "Love Is Strange," a No. 1 R&B song in 1957. She also had a solo hit, under the name Sylvia, in the spring of 1973 with her sultry and sexually charged song "Pillow Talk."

In the late 1960s, Ms. Robinson became one of the few women to produce records in any genre when she and her husband founded All Platinum Records. She played an important role in the career of The Moments, producing their 1970 hit single "Love on a Two-Way Street."

But she achieved her greatest renown for her decision in 1979 to record the nascent art form known

'RAPPER'S DELIGHT': Sylvia Robinson, a singer, songwriter and record producer, was the mastermind behind the first hip-hop single to become a commercial success.

as rapping, which had developed at clubs and dance parties in New York City in the 1970s. She was the mastermind behind the Sugarhill Gang's "Rapper's Delight," the first hip-hop single to become a commercial hit. Some called her "the mother of hip-hop."

"Back in the days when you couldn't find females behind the mixing board, Sylvia was there," said Dan Charnas, the author of "The Big Payback: The History of the Business of Hip-Hop" (2010). "It was Sylvia's genius that made 'Rapper's Delight' a hit."

At the time, the label the Robinsons had founded was awash in lawsuits and losing money. Facing financial ruin, Ms. Robinson got an inspiration when she heard Lovebug Starski rapping over the instrumental breaks in disco songs at the Harlem World nightclub.

"She saw where a D.J. was talking and the crowd was responding to what he was saying, and this was the first time she ever saw this before," her son, Joey Robinson, recalled in a 2000 interview with NPR. "And she said, 'Joey, wouldn't this be a great idea to make a rap record?'"

Using Joey Robinson as a talent scout, she found three young, unknown rappers in Englewood — Big Bank Hank, Wonder Mike and Master Gee — and persuaded them to record improvised rhymes as the Sugarhill Gang (sometimes rendered as Sugar Hill Gang) over a nearly 15-minute rhythm track adapted from Chic's "Good Times."

The song was "Rapper's Delight," and the Robinsons chartered a new label, Sugar Hill Records, to produce it. It sold more than 8 million copies, reached No. 4 on the R&B charts and No. 36 on Billboard's Hot 100, opening the gates for other hip-hop artists. (Sugar Hill is an area of Harlem.)

Ms. Robinson later signed Grandmaster Flash and the Furious Five, and in 1982 she was a producer of their seminal song, "The Message." It was groundbreaking rap about ghetto life that became one of the most powerful social commentaries of its time, laying the groundwork for the gangsta rap of the late 1980s.

Born Sylvia Vanderpool in New York City on March 6, 1936, Ms. Robinson made her recording debut at age 14 singing blues with the trumpet player Hot Lips Page on Columbia Records, while she was still a student at Washington Irving High School in lower Manhattan. She went on to make several other blues recordings for the label, including "Chocolate Candy Blues," before joining forces with Mr. Baker in 1956.

After several hits, Mickey & Sylvia broke up in 1962 when Mr. Baker moved to Paris. Two years later, Ms. Robinson married Joseph Robinson, a musician, and settled in Englewood, N.J., where the couple opened an eight-track recording studio, Soul Sound, and established the All Platinum label.

Ms. Robinson died of congestive heart failure at the New Jersey Institute of Neuroscience in Edison, where she had been in a coma, a family spokeswoman said. Besides her son Joey, she is survived by two other sons and 10 grandchildren. Her husband, Mr. Robinson, died of cancer in 2000.

— BY JAMES C. MCKINLEY JR.

RALPH M. STEINMAN

A Nobel Prize, Three Days Late

JAN. 14, 1943 - SEPT. 30, 2011

WHEN A REPRESENTATIVE of the Nobel Foundation could not reach Dr. Ralph M. Steinman by telephone on Oct. 3 to deliver the thrilling news that he had been awarded a Nobel Prize in Medicine for his breakthrough work in immunology, he sent him an e-mail.

But Dr. Steinman would never see the message nor learn of the prize. He had died of pancreatic cancer on Sept. 30, three days before the Nobel committee called. He was 68. He had been fighting the disease for more than four years, using a treatment he devised to try to prolong his life, essentially turning his body into an extension of his research.

Nobel Prizes cannot be awarded posthumously, however, and so the Nobel committee, which had believed Dr. Steinman to be alive, faced a quandary. As heartless as it might seem, would his prize have to be revoked?

"This is a unique situation — Steinman died hours before the decision was made," Goran Hansson, secretary of the Nobel committee for physiology and medicine, told Swedish Radio News after the situation came to light. "News of his death was not made public. We had no idea, nor did they know at his place of work."

After consulting its lawyers and the Nobel statutes, the foundation's board held that if a person who is announced as a prize winner dies before receiving it at the annual Nobel ceremonies on Dec. 10, the award remains valid.

And so Dr. Steinman became a Nobel laureate, sharing the prize with two other immunologists, Dr. Jules A. Hoffmann of France and Dr. Bruce A. Beutler of the University of Texas Southwestern Medical Center in Dallas and the Scripps Research Institute in San Diego. Dr. Steinman was the director of the Laboratory of Cellular Physiology and Immunology at Rockefeller University in Manhattan and a senior physician at the Rockefeller University Hospital.

All were honored for discoveries of essential steps in the immune system's response to infection. But it was Dr. Steinman who actually used his discoveries in the laboratory to try to save his own life. His career-long quest had been to develop a vaccine against cancer for humans,

POSTHUMOUS HONOR: Ralph M. Steinman never learned of his Nobel Prize. He had devised his own treatment for pancreatic cancer.

having shown 20 years ago that such a treatment could be effective in mice.

Four and a half years before his death, after he was found to be jaundiced from a spreading pancreatic cancer, he began tailoring an experimental vaccine against his own tumor. The idea was to use the principles learned in the experiments on mice and in the laboratory to produce immune cells derived from his dendritic cells, a class of cells that he and Dr. Zanvil A. Cohn had discovered in 1973.

After a piece of Dr. Steinman's cancer was removed, a colleague, Dr. Michel Nussenzweig, grew it in the laboratory to produce enough material to send to researchers at Rockefeller University and at least five other laboratories around the world to help develop the vaccine. Dr. Steinman organized the work among the researchers.

Once developed, the experimental vaccine was injected under Dr. Steinman's skin by doctors at Rockefeller. Its review board had approved the experiment. Dr. Steinman received standard chemotherapy as well.

"Ralph believed strongly that it would work," Dr. Nussenzweig said in an interview. "Obviously it did not work, or he would be here now, but possibly it prolonged his life." He said the research would continue.

Pancreatic cancer is among the most aggressive malignancies. It arises in a gland, deep in the abdomen, that is hard for doctors to feel with their hands, and it usually produces symptoms only after it has become advanced. About 20 percent of patients with pancreatic cancer survive one year after detection and 4 percent after five years, according to the American Cancer Society.

Dr. Nussenzweig and other doctors said it was impossible to determine whether Dr. Steinman would have survived as long without his self-tailored experimental treatment.

At his death, he was trying to develop a method for making a vaccine that could be used against cancer and certain infections but that would not need to be tailored to each patient. Provenge, a vaccine against advanced prostate cancer, was based on Dr. Steinman's work with dendritic cells. It was approved by the Food and Drug Administration in 2010 and is sold by the Dendreon Corporation of Seattle.

"Ralph's research has laid the foundation for numerous discoveries in the critically important field of immunology," Marc Tessier-Lavigne, the president of Rockefeller University, said in a statement, "and it has led to innovative new approaches in how we treat cancer, infectious diseases and disorders of the immune system."

Ralph Marvin Steinman was born on Jan. 14, 1943, in Montreal. He received a bachelor of science degree from McGill University in 1963 and a degree from Harvard Medical School in 1968.

After completing an internship and residency at Massachusetts General Hospital, he joined Rockefeller University in 1970 as a postdoctoral fellow in the Laboratory of Cellular Physiology and Immunology. Working with Dr. Cohn, he began researching the primary white cells of the immune system — the large macrophages and the highly specific lymphocytes — which operate in a variety of ways to spot, apprehend and destroy infectious microorganisms and tumor cells.

He later concentrated on the role of dendritic cells in the onset of several immune responses, including graft rejection, resistance to tumors, autoimmune diseases and infections, including AIDS. He and Dr. Cohn coined the term, whose Greek root, "dendron," or "tree," refers to the branched projections that the cells develop.

For sharing the Nobel, Dr. Steinman received $1.45 million.

Mr. Hansson, of the Nobel committee, said Nobel Prizes had been awarded posthumously twice before: in 1931, for literature, to the poet Erik Axel Karlfeldt; and, 30 years later, to Dag Hammarskjold, for peace.

"The situation was a little different then because the committee was aware that the recipients were dead," Mr. Hansson told Swedish radio. "The practice now is not to award the prize to someone who is deceased."

Dr. Steinman, who died in a Manhattan hospital, lived in Westport, Conn. He is survived by his wife, the former Claudia Hoeffelm; his mother; two daughters; two brothers; a sister; and three grandchildren.

One daughter, Lesley Steinman, said her father was determined to use his cancer to advance the cause of finding a cure. "He was very enthusiastic about the possibilities of immunotherapy," she said. "As soon as he was diagnosed, he said, 'I'm going to get right on this.'"

— BY LAWRENCE K. ALTMAN
AND NICHOLAS WADE;
WILLIAM GRIMES, CHRISTINA ANDERSON AND
MARIA V. ELKIN CONTRIBUTED REPORTING.

STEVEN P. JOBS

The Age of Apple

FEB. 24, 1955 · OCT. 5, 2011

S TEVEN P. JOBS, the visionary co-founder of Apple who helped usher in the era of personal computers and then led a cultural transformation in the way music, movies and mobile communications were experienced in the digital age, died on Oct. 5 at his home in Palo Alto, Calif. He was 56.

The death was announced by Apple, the company Mr. Jobs and his high school friend Stephen Wozniak started in 1976 in a suburban California garage. A friend of the family said the cause was complications of pancreatic cancer.

Mr. Jobs had waged a long and public struggle with the disease, remaining the face of the company even as he was being treated, introducing new products for a global market in his trademark blue jeans even as he grew gaunt and frail.

He underwent surgery in 2004, received a liver transplant in 2009 and took three medical leaves of absence as Apple's chief executive before stepping down in August 2011 and turning over the helm to Timothy D. Cook, the chief operating officer. When he left, he was still engaged in the company's affairs, negotiating with another Silicon Valley executive only weeks earlier.

"I have always said that if there ever came a day when I could no longer meet my duties and expectations as Apple's C.E.O., I would be the first to let you know," Mr. Jobs said in a letter released by the company at the time. "Unfortunately, that day has come."

By then, having mastered digital technology and capitalized on his intuitive marketing sense, Mr. Jobs had largely come to define the personal computer industry and an array of digital consumer and entertainment businesses centered on the Internet. He had also become a very rich man, worth an estimated $8.3 billion.

Tributes to Mr. Jobs flowed quickly on the evening of his death, in formal statements and in the flow of social networks, from President Obama, technology industry leaders and legions of Apple fans.

"For those of us lucky enough to get to work with Steve, it's been an insanely great honor," said Bill Gates, the Microsoft co-founder.

A Twitter user named Matt Galligan wrote: "R.I.P. Steve Jobs. You touched an ugly world of technology and made it beautiful."

Eight years after founding Apple, Mr. Jobs led the team that designed the Macintosh computer, a breakthrough in making personal computers easier to use. After a 12-year separation from the company, prompted by a bitter falling-out with his chief executive, John Sculley, he returned in 1997 to oversee the creation of one innovative digital device after another — the iPod, the iPhone and the iPad. They transformed not only product categories like music players and cell-phones but also entire industries, like music and mobile communications.

During his years outside Apple, he bought a tiny computer graphics spinoff from the movie director George Lucas and built a team of computer scientists, artists and animators that became Pixar Animation Studios.

Starting with "Toy Story" in 1995, Pixar produced a string of hit movies, won several Academy Awards for artistic and technological excellence, and made the full-length computer-animated film a mainstream art form enjoyed by children and adults worldwide.

Mr. Jobs was neither a hardware engineer nor a software programmer, nor did he think of himself as a manager. He considered himself a technology leader, choosing the best people possible, encouraging and prodding them, and

TECH (AND TASTE) LEADER: Steven P. Jobs unveiling the original iPad in 2010. He believed he was not just offering products but a lifestyle.

making the final call on product design.

It was an executive style that had evolved. In his early years at Apple, his meddling in tiny details maddened colleagues, and his criticism could be caustic and even humiliating. But he grew to elicit extraordinary loyalty.

"He was the most passionate leader one could hope for, a motivating force without parallel," wrote Steven Levy, author of the 1994 book "Insanely Great," which chronicles the creation of the Mac. "Tom Sawyer could have picked up tricks from Steve Jobs."

"Toy Story," for example, took four years to make while Pixar struggled, yet Mr. Jobs never let up on his colleagues. "'You need a lot more than vision — you need a stubbornness, tenacity, belief and patience to stay the course," said Edwin Catmull, a computer scientist and a co-founder of Pixar. "In Steve's case, he pushes right to the edge, to try to make the next big step forward."

Mr. Jobs was the ultimate arbiter of Apple products, and his standards were exacting. Over the course of a year he tossed out two iPhone prototypes, for example, before approving the third, and began shipping it in June 2007.

To his understanding of technology he brought an immersion in popular culture. In his 20s, he dated Joan Baez; Ella Fitzgerald sang at his 30th birthday party. His worldview was shaped by the '60s counterculture in the San Francisco Bay Area, where he had grown up, the adopted son of a Silicon Valley machinist. When he graduated from high school in Cupertino in 1972, he said, "the very strong scent of the 1960s was still there."

After dropping out of Reed College, a stronghold of liberal thought in Portland, Ore., in 1972, Mr. Jobs led a countercultural lifestyle himself. He told a reporter that taking LSD was one of the two or three most important things he had done in his life. He said there were things about him that people who had not tried psychedelics — even people who knew him well, including his wife — could never understand.

Decades later he flew around the world in his own corporate jet, but he maintained emotional ties to the period in which he grew up. He often felt like an outsider in the corporate world, he said. When discussing the Silicon Valley's lasting contributions to humanity, he mentioned in the same breath the invention of the microchip and "The Whole Earth Catalog," a 1960s counterculture publication.

Apple's very name reflected his unconventionality. In an era when engineers and hobbyists tended to describe their machines with model numbers, he chose the name of a fruit, supposedly because of his dietary habits at the time.

Coming on the scene just as computing began to move beyond the walls of research laboratories and corporations in the 1970s, Mr. Jobs saw that computing was becoming personal — that it could do more than crunch numbers and solve scientific and business problems — and that it could even be a force for social and economic change. And at a time when hobbyist computers were boxy wooden affairs with metal chassis, he designed the Apple II as a sleek, low-slung plastic package intended for the den or the kitchen. He was offering not just products but a digital lifestyle.

He put much stock in the notion of "taste," a word he used frequently. It was a sensibility that shone in products that looked like works of art and delighted users. Great products, he said, were a triumph of taste, of "trying to expose yourself to the best things humans have done and then trying to bring those things into what you are doing."

Regis McKenna, a longtime Silicon Valley marketing executive to whom Mr. Jobs turned in the late 1970s to help shape the Apple brand, said Mr. Jobs's genius lay in his ability to simplify complex, highly engineered products, "to strip away the excess layers of business, design and innovation until only the simple, elegant reality remained."

Mr. Jobs's own research and intuition, not focus groups, were his guide. When asked what market research went into the iPad, Mr. Jobs replied: "None. It's not the consumers' job to know what they want."

Steven Paul Jobs was born in San Francisco on Feb. 24, 1955, and surrendered for adoption by his biological parents, Joanne Carole Schieble and Abdulfattah Jandali, a graduate student from Syria who became a political science professor. He was adopted by Paul and Clara Jobs.

The elder Mr. Jobs, who worked in finance and real estate before returning to his original trade as a machinist, moved his family down the San Francisco Peninsula to Mountain View and then to Los Altos in the 1960s.

Mr. Jobs developed an early interest in electronics. He was mentored by a neighbor, an electronics hobbyist, who built Heathkit do-it-yourself electronics projects. He was brash from an early age. As an eighth grader, after discovering that a crucial part was missing from a frequency counter he was assembling, he telephoned William Hewlett, the co-founder of Hewlett-Packard. Mr. Hewlett spoke with the boy for 20 minutes, prepared a bag of parts for him to pick up and offered him a job as a summer intern.

Mr. Jobs met Mr. Wozniak while attending Homestead High School in neighboring

Cupertino. The two took an introductory electronics class there.

The spark that ignited their partnership was provided by Mr. Wozniak's mother. Mr. Wozniak had graduated from high school and enrolled at the University of California, Berkeley, when she sent him an article from the October 1971 issue of Esquire magazine. The article, "Secrets of the Little Blue Box," by Ron Rosenbaum, detailed an underground hobbyist culture of young men known as phone phreaks who were illicitly exploring the nation's phone system.

Mr. Wozniak shared the article with Mr. Jobs, and the two set out to track down an elusive figure identified in the article as Captain Crunch. The man had taken the name from his discovery that a whistle that came in boxes of Cap'n Crunch cereal was tuned to a frequency that made it possible to make free long-distance calls simply by blowing the whistle next to a phone handset.

Captain Crunch was John Draper, a former Air Force electronics technician, and finding him took several weeks. Learning that the two young hobbyists were searching for him, Mr. Draper arranged to come to Mr. Wozniak's Berkeley dormitory room. Mr. Jobs, who was still in high school, traveled to Berkeley for the meeting. When Mr. Draper arrived, he entered the room saying simply, "It is I!"

Mr. Jobs and Mr. Wozniak later used the information they had gleaned from Mr. Draper to collaborate on building and selling blue boxes, devices that were widely used for making free, and illegal, phone calls. They raised a total of $6,000 from the effort.

After enrolling at Reed College in 1972, Mr. Jobs left after one semester, but remained in Portland for another 18 months auditing classes. In a commencement address given at Stanford in 2005, he said he had decided to leave college because it was consuming all of his parents' savings.

Leaving school, however, also freed his curiosity to follow his interests. "I didn't have a dorm room," he said in his Stanford speech, "so I slept on the floor in friends' rooms. I returned Coke bottles for the 5-cent deposits to buy food with, and I would walk the seven miles across town every Sunday night to get one good meal a week at the Hare Krishna temple. I loved it. And much of what I stumbled into by following my curiosity and intuition turned out to be priceless."

He returned to Silicon Valley in 1974 and took a job there as a technician at Atari, the video game manufacturer. Still searching for his calling, he left after several months and traveled to India with a college friend, Daniel Kottke, who would later become an early Apple employee. Mr. Jobs returned to Atari that fall. In 1975, he and Mr. Wozniak, then working as an engineer at H.P., began attending meetings of the Homebrew Computer Club, a hobbyist group that met at the Stanford Linear Accelerator Center in Menlo Park, Calif. Personal computing had been pioneered at research laboratories adjacent to Stanford, and it was spreading to the outside world.

"What I remember is how intense he looked," said Lee Felsenstein, a computer designer who was a Homebrew member. "He was everywhere, and he seemed to be trying to hear everything people had to say."

Mr. Wozniak designed the original Apple I computer simply to show it off to his friends at the Homebrew. It was Mr. Jobs who had the inspiration that it could be a commercial product.

In early 1976, he and Mr. Wozniak, using their own money, began Apple with an initial investment of $1,300; they later gained the backing of a former Intel executive, A. C. Markkula, who lent them $250,000. Mr. Wozniak would be the technical half and Mr. Jobs the marketing half of the original Apple I Computer. Starting out in the Jobs family garage in Los Altos, they moved the company to a small office in Cupertino shortly thereafter.

In April 1977, Mr. Jobs and Mr. Wozniak introduced Apple II at the West Coast Computer Faire in San Francisco. It created a sensation. Faced with a gaggle of small and large competitors in the emerging computer market, Apple, with its Apple II, had figured out a way to straddle the business and consumer markets by building a computer that could be customized for specific applications.

GAME CHANGERS: Steven P. Jobs, left, with John Sculley, president and C.E.O. of Apple, and Steve Wozniak, right, in 1984. Mr. Jobs and Mr. Wozniak started Apple in 1976 in a suburban California garage.

Sales skyrocketed, from $2 million in 1977 to $600 million in 1981, the year the company went public. By 1983 Apple was in the Fortune 500. No company had ever joined the list so quickly.

The Apple III, introduced in May 1980, was intended to dominate the desktop computer market. I.B.M. would not introduce its original personal computer until 1981. But the Apple III had a host of technical problems, and Mr. Jobs shifted his focus to a new and ultimately short-lived project, an office workstation computer code-named Lisa.

By then Mr. Jobs had made his much-chronicled 1979 visit to Xerox's research center in Palo Alto, where he saw the Alto, an experimental personal computer system that foreshadowed modern desktop computing. The Alto, controlled by a mouse pointing device, was one of the first computers to employ a graphical video display, which presented the user with a view of documents and programs, adopting the metaphor of an office desktop.

"It was one of those sort of apocalyptic moments," Mr. Jobs said of his visit in a 1995 oral history interview for the Smithsonian Institution. "I remember within 10 minutes of seeing the graphical user interface stuff, just knowing that every computer would work this way someday. It was so obvious once you saw it. It didn't require tremendous intellect. It was so clear."

In 1981 he joined a small group of Apple engineers pursuing a separate project, a lower-cost system code-named Macintosh. The machine was introduced in January 1984 and trumpeted during the Super Bowl telecast by a 60-second commercial, directed by Ridley Scott, that linked I.B.M., then the dominant PC maker, with Orwell's Big Brother.

A year earlier Mr. Jobs had lured Mr. Sculley to Apple to be its chief executive. A former Pepsi-Cola chief executive, Mr. Sculley was impressed by Mr. Jobs's pitch: "Do you want to spend the rest of your life selling sugared water, or do you want a chance to change the world?"

He went on to help Mr. Jobs introduce a number of new computer models, including an advanced version of the Apple II and later the Lisa and Macintosh desktop computers. Through them Mr. Jobs popularized the graphical user interface, which, based on a mouse pointing device, would become the standard way to control computers.

But when the Lisa failed commercially and early Macintosh sales proved disappointing, the two men became estranged and a power struggle ensued. The board ultimately stripped Mr. Jobs of his operational role and with it his control of the Lisa project. As many as 1,200 Apple employees were laid off. He left Apple in 1985.

"I don't wear the right kind of pants to run this company," he told a small gathering of Apple employees before he left, according to a member of the original Macintosh development team. He was barefoot as he spoke, and wearing blue jeans.

That September he announced a new venture, NeXT Inc. The aim was to build a workstation computer for the higher-education market. The next year, the Texas industrialist H. Ross Perot invested $20 million in the effort. But it did not achieve Mr. Jobs's goals.

Mr. Jobs also established a personal philanthropic foundation after leaving Apple but soon had a change of heart, deciding instead to spend much of his fortune, $10 million, on acquiring Pixar, a struggling graphics supercomputing company owned by the filmmaker George Lucas.

The purchase was a significant gamble; there was little market at the time for computer-animated movies. But that changed in 1995, when the company, with Walt Disney Pictures, released "Toy Story." The film's box-office receipts reached $362 million, and when Pixar went public in a record-breaking offering, Mr. Jobs emerged a billionaire. In 2006, the Walt Disney Company agreed to purchase Pixar for $7.4 billion. The sale made Mr. Jobs Disney's largest single shareholder, with about 7 percent of the company's stock.

_____

When asked what market research went into the iPad, Mr. Jobs replied: "None. It's not the consumers' job to know what they want."

_____

His personal life also became more public. He had a number of well-publicized romantic relationships, including one with the folk singer Joan Baez, before marrying Laurene Powell. In 1996, his sister Mona Simpson, a novelist, threw a spotlight on her relationship with Mr. Jobs in the novel "A Regular Guy." The two did not meet until they were adults. The novel centered on a Silicon Valley entrepreneur who bore a close resemblance to Mr. Jobs. It was not an entirely flattering portrait. Mr. Jobs said about a quarter of it was accurate.

"We're family," he said of Ms. Simpson in an interview with The New York Times Magazine. "She's one of my best friends in the world. I call her and talk to her every couple of days."

His wife and Ms. Simpson survive him, as do two daughters and a son with Ms. Powell; another daughter from a relationship with Chrisann Brennan; and another sister.

Mr. Jobs went on to refocus NeXT, moving away from the education market to the business market and dropping the hardware part of the company; he decided to sell just an operating system. Although NeXT never became a significant computer industry player, it had a huge impact: a young programmer, Tim Berners-Lee, used a NeXT machine to develop the first version of the World Wide Web at the Swiss physics research center CERN in 1990.

In 1996, after unsuccessful efforts to develop next-generation operating systems, Apple, with Gilbert Amelio now in command, acquired NeXT for $430 million. The next year, Mr. Jobs returned to Apple as an adviser. He became chief executive again in 2000.

Shortly after returning, Mr. Jobs publicly ended Apple's long feud with its archrival Microsoft, which agreed to continue developing its Office software for the Macintosh and invested $150 million in Apple.

Once in control of Apple again, Mr. Jobs set out to reshape the consumer electronics industry. He pushed the company into the digital music business, introducing first iTunes and then the iPod MP3 player. The music arm grew rapidly, reaching almost 50 percent of the company's revenue by June 2008.

In 2005, Mr. Jobs announced that he would end Apple's business relationship with I.B.M. and Motorola and build Macintosh computers based on Intel microprocessors.

His fight with cancer was now publicly known. Apple had announced in 2004 that Mr. Jobs had a rare but curable form of pancreatic cancer and that he had undergone successful surgery. Four years later, questions about his health returned when he appeared at a company event looking gaunt. Afterward, he said he had suffered from a "common bug." Privately, he said his cancer surgery had created digestive problems but insisted they were not life-threatening.

Apple began selling the iPhone in June 2007. Mr. Jobs's goal was to sell 10 million of the handsets in 2008, equivalent to 1 percent of the global cell phone market. The company sold 11.6 million.

Although smartphones were already commonplace, the iPhone dispensed with a stylus and pioneered a touch-screen interface that quickly set the standard for the mobile computing market. Rolled out with much anticipation and fanfare, iPhone rocketed to popularity; by the end of 2010 the company had sold almost 90 million units.

Although Mr. Jobs took just a nominal $1 salary when he returned to Apple, his compensation became the source of a Silicon Valley scandal in 2006 over the backdating of millions of shares of stock options. But after a company investigation and one by the Securities and Exchange Commission, he was found not to have benefited financially from the backdating and no charges were brought.

The episode did little to taint Mr. Jobs's standing in the business and technology world. As the gravity of his illness became known, and particularly after he announced he was stepping down, he was increasingly hailed for his genius and true achievement: his ability to blend product design and business market innovation by integrating consumer-oriented software, microelectronic components, industrial design and new business strategies in a way that has not been matched.

If he had a motto, it may have come from "The Whole Earth Catalog," which he said had deeply influenced him as a young man. The book, he said in his commencement address at Stanford in 2005, ends with the admonition "Stay Hungry. Stay Foolish."

"I have always wished that for myself," he said.

— BY JOHN MARKOFF; STEVE LOHR
CONTRIBUTED REPORTING.

ANITA CASPARY

Leading 300 Nuns Out the Church Door

NOV. 4, 1915 - OCT. 5, 2011

A NITA CASPARY, the onetime mother superior who led the largest single exodus of nuns from the Roman Catholic Church in American history, died on Oct. 5 in Los Angeles. She was 95.

Her death was confirmed by the Immaculate Heart Community, a lay

Christian group that she and the 300 nuns who followed her established in 1970 after their break with the church. The news media called it the Immaculate Heart "rebellion."

The cause of the schism, though nominally about dress codes and bedtimes, was understood on both sides as a matter of church law. Dr. Caspary viewed the Vatican II reforms of the early 1960s as a mandate for nuns to assert more control over their own lives. Her boss, Archbishop James Francis McIntyre of Los Angeles, did not.

Dr. Caspary always contended that she and other

EXODUS: Anita Caspary established the Immaculate Heart Community after breaking with the Catholic Church.

a host of traditional regimens governing when they prayed, when they went to bed and what books were appropriate for nuns to read.

The cardinal cited pre-Vatican II law and centuries-old church tradition. In a letter to the Vatican, quoted in 1996 in his official biography, he wrote that to permit the changes proposed by the Sisters of the Immaculate Heart would in effect lead "our convents to become hotels or boarding houses for women." The conflict between Dr. Caspary and the cardinal lasted several years.

By her account, it proved to be her ultimate test of the spirit, since she had taken her vows in 1936 as Sister Humiliata, a religious title meaning humbled.

Convinced that they were being given no other options, and being asked to forsake the promise of Vatican II, Dr. Caspary and the other nuns broke away to establish the Immaculate Heart Community, an unofficial Christian

members of her order, the Sisters of the Immaculate Heart of Mary, never wanted to renounce their vows. They had been virtually forced into it, she said, by the intransigence of Cardinal McIntyre. In a 2003 memoir, "Witness to Integrity," she wrote that he had been adamant in refusing to let them teach in archdiocese schools unless they wore habits and adhered to communal organization that continues to provide services in the poorest neighborhoods of Los Angeles. Sandra M. Schneiders, a professor emeritus at the Jesuit School of Theology in Berkeley, Calif., said in an interview that the changes forbidden by Cardinal McIntyre were being widely adopted in other dioceses nationwide as a result of Vatican II reforms.

The Immaculate Heart of Mary nuns were ordered to wear habits in the classroom and told when to pray, what to read and when to go to bed.

"It's not like the Immaculate Heart women were doing anything outlandish," said Professor Schneiders, who has written about the episode. "All these changes were taking place without incident in the majority of dioceses around the country. Cardinal McIntyre simply was saying, 'Not in my diocese.'"

Cardinal McIntyre, a protégé of Cardinal Francis Spellman of New York, had been a vocal opponent of the reforms during the Vatican Council's meetings. "He has been described by more than one Vatican observer as the most reactionary prelate in the church, bar none — not even those of the Curia," an article in The New York Times said in 1964.

In her memoir, Dr. Caspary struggled for nunlike equanimity in writing about him. He was "stubborn, paternalistic, authoritative, frugal and puritanical," she said. "But he was also a hard-working, dedicated churchman who left monuments in his archdiocese in brick and mortar."

Anita Marie Caspary was born Nov. 4, 1915, in Herrick, S.D., the third of eight children of Jacob and Marie Caspary. The family moved to Los Angeles, where she received her bachelor's degree in English at Immaculate Heart College in 1936. She entered the convent the same year, and taught high school English while studying toward a master's degree at the University of Southern California. She received her Ph.D. from Stanford in 1948.

Dr. Caspary was president of Immaculate Heart College, which was operated by her order, from 1958 to 1963. (The school continued to operate until 1980.) After the break with the church, she taught at the Graduate Theological Union in Berkeley and served on the staff of the Peace and Justice Center of Southern California.

She wrote poetry throughout her life, and shortly before she died she had completed a volume she hoped to publish.

Her survivors include three sisters.

The Immaculate Heart Community was founded on democratic principles that are still observed. Its board directors are elected. Some members live together in a residence, but most live on their own. All contribute 20 percent of their wages to support what Dr. Caspary described as "a new way of people being together."

The community has not grown. It counts 160 members today.

In a 1972 interview with The Times, however, Dr. Caspary said she felt she was part of a cultural flourishing larger than a single enterprise.

"We've had an extraordinary experience for women," she said. "We've worked through the problem of liberation. We worked our way out of an oppressive situation."

—By Paul Vitello

\\\\\\\\\\\\\\\\\\\\\\\\\\\\\

DERRICK BELL

Challenging the Academy, and America, on Race

NOV. 6, 1930 - OCT. 5, 2011

DERRICK BELL, a legal scholar who saw persistent racism in America and sought to expose it through books, articles and provocative career moves — he gave up a Harvard Law School professorship to protest the school's hiring practices — died on Oct. 5 in Manhattan. He was 80.

Mr. Bell was the first tenured black professor at Harvard Law School and later one of the first black deans of a law school that was not historically black. But he was perhaps better known for resigning from prestigious jobs than for accepting them.

While he was working at the Civil Rights Division of the Justice Department in his 20s, his superiors told him to give up his membership in the N.A.A.C.P., believing it posed a conflict of interest. Instead he quit the department, ignoring the advice of friends to try to change it from within.

Thirty years later, when he left Harvard Law School, he rejected similar advice. At the time, he said, his first wife, Jewel Hairston Bell, had asked him, "Why does it always have to be you?" The question trailed him afterward, he wrote in a 2002 memoir, "Ethical Ambition," as did another posed by unsympathetic colleagues: "Who do you think you are?"

Professor Bell, soft-spoken and erudite, was "not confrontational by nature," he wrote. But he attacked both conservative and liberal beliefs. In 1992, he told The New York Times that black Americans were more subjugated than at any time since slavery. And he wrote that in light of the often violent struggle that resulted from the

Supreme Court's 1954 desegregation decision, Brown v. Board of Education, things might have worked out better if the court had instead ordered that both races be provided with truly equivalent schools.

He was a pioneer of critical race theory — a body of legal scholarship that explored how racism is embedded in laws and legal institutions, even many of those intended to redress past injustices. His 1973 book, "Race, Racism and American Law," became a staple in law schools and is now in its sixth edition.

Mr. Bell "set the agenda in many ways for scholarship on race in the academy, not just the legal academy," Lani Guinier, the first black woman hired to join Harvard Law School's tenured faculty, said in an interview after Professor Bell's death.

At a rally while a student at Harvard Law, Barack Obama compared Professor Bell to the civil rights hero Rosa Parks.

Professor Bell's core beliefs included what he called "the interest convergence dilemma" — the idea that whites would not support efforts to improve the position of blacks unless doing so was in their interest. Asked how the status of blacks could be improved, he said he generally supported civil rights litigation, but cautioned that even favorable rulings would probably yield disappointing results and that it was best to be prepared for that.

Much of Professor Bell's scholarship rejected dry legal analysis in favor of stories. In books and law review articles, he presented parables and allegories about race relations, then debated their meaning with a fictional alter ego, a professor named Geneva Crenshaw, who forced him to confront the truth about racism in America.

One of his best-known parables is "The Space Traders," which appeared in his 1992 book, "Faces at the Bottom of the Well: The Permanence of Racism." In the story, as Professor Bell later described it, creatures from another planet offer the United States "enough gold to retire the national debt, a magic chemical that will cleanse America's polluted skies and waters, and a limitless source of safe energy to replace our dwindling reserves." In exchange, the creatures ask for only one thing: America's black population, which they would take with them into outer space. The white population accepts the offer by an overwhelming margin. (In 1994 the story was adapted as one of three segments in a television movie titled "Cosmic Slop.")

Not everyone welcomed the move to storytelling in legal scholarship. In 1997 Richard Posner, the conservative law professor and appeals court judge, wrote in The New Republic that "by repudiating reasoned argumentation," scholars like Professor Bell "reinforce stereotypes about the intellectual capacities of nonwhites."

CAREER MOVE: Derrick Bell, the first tenured black professor at Harvard Law School, gave up his professorship in protest.

Professor Bell's narrative technique nonetheless became an accepted mode of legal scholarship, giving female, Latino and gay scholars a new way to introduce their experiences into legal discourse. Reviewing "Faces at the Bottom of the Well" in The Times, the Supreme Court reporter Linda Greenhouse wrote: "The stories challenge old assumptions and then linger in the mind in a way that a more conventionally scholarly treatment of the same themes would be unlikely to do."

Derrick Albert Bell Jr. was born on Nov. 6, 1930, in Pittsburgh to Derrick Albert and Ada Elizabeth Childress Bell. After graduating from Schenley High School near Pittsburgh's Hill District, he became the first member of his family to go to college, attending Duquesne University in Pittsburgh. He received his bachelor's degree in 1952.

A member of the R.O.T.C. at Duquesne, he was later an Air Force officer for two years, spending one of them in Korea. Afterward he attended the University of Pittsburgh Law School, where he was the only black student. He earned his degree in 1957.

After his stint at the Justice Department, he headed the Pittsburgh office of the N.A.A.C.P. Legal Defense and Educational Fund, leading efforts to integrate a public swimming pool and a skating rink. Later, assigned to Mississippi, he supervised more than 300 school desegregation cases.

In 1969, after teaching briefly at the University of Southern California, he was recruited and hired by Harvard Law School, where students were pressuring the administration to appoint a black professor. Mr. Bell conceded that he did not have the usual qualifications for a Harvard professorship, like a federal court clerkship or a degree from a top law school.

In 1980 he left Harvard to become dean of the University of Oregon School of Law, but he resigned in 1985 when the school did not offer a position to an Asian-American woman. After returning to Harvard in 1986, he staged a five-day sit-in in his office to protest the school's failure to grant tenure to two professors whose work involved critical race theory.

In 1990 he took an unpaid leave of absence, vowing not to return until the school hired, for the first time, a black woman to join its tenured faculty. His employment effectively ended when the school refused to extend his leave. By then, he was teaching at New York University School of Law, where he remained a visiting professor until his death. Harvard Law School hired Professor Guinier in 1998.

Professor Bell said his personal decisions took a toll on his first wife, Jewel, who had cancer when he left Harvard in 1990 and died that year.

In 1992 he began a correspondence with Janet Dewart, who was the communications director of the National Urban League. Ms. Dewart proposed marriage before the couple even met. A few months later, Professor Bell accepted.

Professor Bell, who lived on the Upper West Side of Manhattan, died of carcinoid cancer, his wife, Janet Dewart Bell, said. Besides her, he is survived by three sons from his first marriage, two sisters and a brother.

In "Ethical Ambition," Mr. Bell expressed doubts about his legacy: "It is not easy to look back over a long career and recognize with some pain that my efforts may have benefited my career more clearly than they helped those for whom I have worked."

But Professor Guinier, who continues to teach at Harvard, differed with that view. "Most people think of iconoclasts as lone rangers," she said. "But Derrick was both an iconoclast and a community builder. When he was opening up this path, it was not just for him. It was for all those who he knew would follow into the legal academy."

— BY FRED A. BERNSTEIN

FRED L. SHUTTLESWORTH

A Man of the Cloth Bloodied in Birmingham

MARCH 18, 1922 · OCT. 5, 2011

THE REV. FRED L. SHUTTLESWORTH, who survived beatings and bombings in Alabama a half century ago as he fought against racial injustice alongside the Rev. Dr. Martin Luther King Jr., died on Oct. 5 in Birmingham, Ala. He was 89.

It was in that city in the spring of 1963 that Mr. Shuttlesworth, an important ally of

Dr. King, organized two tumultuous weeks of daily demonstrations by black children, students, clergymen and others against a rigidly segregated society.

Graphic scenes of helmeted police officers and firefighters under the direction of T. Eugene (Bull) Connor, Birmingham's intransigent public safety commissioner, scattering peaceful marchers with fire hoses, police dogs and nightsticks, provoked a national outcry.

The brutality helped galvanize the nation's conscience, as did the Ku Klux Klan's bombing of a black church in Birmingham that summer that killed four

PUTTING HIS LIFE IN THE LINE OF FIRE: Fred L. Shuttlesworth outside his destroyed Montgomery, Ala., home in 1956. He helped organize the historic 1963 marches from Selma to Montgomery and was a founder of the Southern Christian Leadership Conference.

girls at Sunday school. Those events and the historic Alabama marches that year from Selma to Montgomery, which Mr. Shuttlesworth also helped organize, led to passage of the Civil Rights Act of 1964 and the Voting Rights Act of 1965, the bedrock of civil rights legislation.

"Without Fred Shuttlesworth laying the groundwork, those demonstrations in Birmingham would not have been as successful," said Andrew M. Manis, author of "A Fire You Can't Put Out," a biography of Mr. Shuttlesworth. "Birmingham led to Selma, and those two became the basis of the civil rights struggle." Mr. Shuttlesworth, he added, had "no equal in terms of courage and putting his life in the line of fire" to battle segregation.

With Dr. King, the Rev. Ralph David Abernathy and others, Mr. Shuttlesworth was a founder of the Southern Christian Leadership Conference, the engine of Dr. King's effort to unify the black clergy and their flocks to combat Jim Crow laws. At the time, 1957, Mr. Shuttlesworth was leader of the Alabama

Christian Movement for Human Rights, which he had helped form the year before to replace the Alabama offices of the N.A.A.C.P., which had been shut down for years by court injunction.

But for all their common ground as men of the cloth and fighters for civil rights, Mr. Shuttlesworth and Dr. King differed in background, personality and methods.

Dr. King was a polished product of Atlanta's black middle class. A graduate of Morehouse College, he held a Ph.D. in systematic theology from Boston University. Fred Shuttlesworth was a child of poor black Alabama whose ministerial degree was from an unaccredited black school. (He went on to earn a master's degree in education from Alabama State College.)

Where Dr. King could deliver thunderous oratory and move audiences by his reasoned convictions and faith, Mr. Shuttlesworth was fiery, whether preaching in the pulpit or standing up to Bull Connor, who dueled with him for years in street protests and boycotts leading up to their historic 1963 showdown.

Diane McWhorter, the author of "Carry Me Home," the Pulitzer Prize-winning 2001 book about the struggle in Birmingham, said Mr. Shuttlesworth was known among some civil rights activists as "the Wild Man from Birmingham."

"Among the youthful 'elders' of the movement," she wrote in an e-mail, "he was Martin Luther King's most effective and insistent foil: blunt where King was soothing, driven where King was leisurely, and most important, confrontational where King was conciliatory — meaning, critically, that he was more upsetting than King in the eyes of the white public."

Mr. Shuttlesworth was temperamental, even obstinate, and championed action and confrontation over words. He could antagonize segregationists and activists alike, quarreling with his allies behind closed doors.

But few doubted his courage. In the years before 1963 he was arrested time and again — 30 to 40 times by his count — and repeatedly jailed as the authorities tried to impede peaceful protests. He was twice the target of bombs.

In one instance, on Christmas night 1956, he survived an attack in which six sticks of dynamite were detonated outside his parsonage bedroom as he lay in bed. "The wall and the floor were blown out," Ms. McWhorter wrote, "and the mattress heaved into the air, supporting Shuttlesworth like a magic carpet."

When Mr. Shuttlesworth tried to enroll his children in an all-white school in 1957, Klansmen attacked him with bicycle chains and brass knuckles. When a doctor treating his head wounds marveled that he had not suffered a concussion, Mr. Shuttlesworth replied, "Doctor, the Lord knew I lived in a hard town, so he gave me a hard head."

Freddie Lee Robinson was born on March 18, 1922, in rural Mount Meigs, Ala., one of nine siblings. He took the surname Shuttlesworth from a man his mother, Alberta Robinson, later married. The family struggled against poverty by sharecropping and making moonshine liquor, an activity for which Mr. Shuttlesworth was sentenced to two years' probation in 1940. He became a truck driver.

Mr. Shuttlesworth was "confrontational where King was conciliatory."

Studying religion at night, he was drawn to the pulpit and became pastor of Bethel Baptist Church in Birmingham in 1953, then joined the Alabama chapter of the N.A.A.C.P. before the state outlawed it in 1956. He and others established the Alabama Christian Movement for Human Rights to carry on the chapter's work and to challenge the white power structure on many fronts.

By 1963, as a founder of the Southern Christian Leadership Conference, Mr. Shuttlesworth had become a force in the movement spearheaded by Dr. King. That year he welcomed Dr. King to Birmingham, where they planned a boycott of white merchants coupled with large marches that they expected would provoke an overreaction by city officials and show the world the depth of white resistance.

"We wanted confrontation, nonviolent confrontation, to see if it would work," Mr. Shuttlesworth later said. "Not just for Birmingham — for the nation. We were trying to launch a systematic, wholehearted battle against segregation, which would set the pace for the nation."

Mr. Shuttlesworth suffered chest injuries when the pummeling spray of fire hoses was turned on him. "I'm sorry I missed it," Mr.

Connor said when told of the injuries, The New York Times reported in 1963. "I wish they'd carried him away in a hearse."

After 1965, with the new civil rights legislation on the books and Dr. King turning his attention to poverty and black problems in the urban North, Mr. Shuttlesworth remained focused on local issues in Birmingham and Cincinnati, where he had moved to take the pulpit of a black church. He traveled frequently between Ohio and Alabama before returning permanently to Birmingham in 2008 for treatment after a stroke.

He died at Princeton Baptist Medical Center in Birmingham. He is survived by his wife, Sephira Bailey Shuttlesworth; four daughters; a son; a stepdaughter; five sisters; 14 grandchildren; 20 great-grandchildren; and one great-great-grandchild.

With the death of Dr. King, and later Dr. King's chief aide, Mr. Abernathy, Mr. Shuttlesworth became an elder statesman in the civil rights movement. In 2004 he was named president of the Southern Christian Leadership Conference, but he stepped down the same year, complaining that "deceit, mistrust and a lack of spiritual discipline and truth have eaten at the core of this once-hallowed organization."

He also came under criticism by gay rights advocates in 2004 when he lent his name to a campaign in Cincinnati to stop the city from passing a gay rights ordinance.

He remained an honored figure in Birmingham, however. In 2008, the city renamed its principal airport Birmingham-Shuttlesworth International Airport.

In 2009, in a wheelchair, he was front and center among other dignitaries in an audience of about 6,000 at the city's Boutwell Auditorium to watch a live broadcast as the nation's first black president, Barack Obama, was sworn in.

He had encountered Mr. Obama, then a senator from Illinois, two years earlier, along with former President Bill Clinton, during a commemoration in Selma of the Selma-to-Montgomery voting rights marches. As a crowd crossed the Edmund Pettus Bridge, where demonstrators were beaten and tear-gassed on "Bloody Sunday," March 7, 1965, Mr. Obama pushed Mr. Shuttlesworth's wheelchair.

— BY JON NORDHEIMER; DANIEL E. SLOTNIK
CONTRIBUTED REPORTING.

AL DAVIS

Football's Most Valuable Renegade

JULY 4, 1929 - OCT. 8, 2011

AL DAVIS, the irascible owner of the Oakland Raiders whose feuds with the National Football League reshaped professional football over the last half century and helped spur its rise to pre-eminence in American sports, died on Oct. 8 at his home in Oakland, Calif. He was 82.

Before there were sports franchise owners like George Steinbrenner, Jerry Jones or Mark Cuban, there was Al Davis, outspoken and brash. He was a central figure in the merger of the upstart American Football League with the established N.F.L., paved the way for the extravaganza known as the Super Bowl, and managed to win championships while irritating the rest of pro football.

Al Davis became the symbol of a Raiders franchise with a reputation for outlaw personalities.

He was a coach, general manager and owner of the Raiders for nearly 50 years. He left briefly, in 1966, to become the commissioner of the A.F.L., vowing to battle the older N.F.L. for the best players available. That attitude helped persuade the N.F.L. to play the A.F.L. in an annual championship game, which became the Super Bowl. In 1970, the leagues played a united schedule, creating the modern N.F.L.

Davis opposed the merger vehemently. And he feuded for decades with the former N.F.L. commissioner Pete Rozelle and sued the league in the early 1980s so that he could move the Raiders from Oakland to Los Angeles.

Thirteen years later, he moved them back.

"He is a true legend of the game whose impact and legacy will forever be part of the N.F.L.," Roger Goodell, the league's current commissioner, said in a statement.

Davis became the symbol of a franchise with a reputation for outlaw personalities and a counterculture sensibility. The Raiders were the first franchise in the modern era to have a Latino head coach (Tom Flores), a black head coach (Art

Shell) and a female chief executive (Amy Trask).

He was also one of a dwindling number of N.F.L. owners whose riches came primarily from the business of football. There were no hedge funds or shipping companies in Davis's background. He simply ran the Raiders, and his business model could be summed up by the phrase that became their motto: "Just win, baby!"

The Raiders did, appearing in five Super Bowls under his ownership, winning three.

Davis could inspire deep loyalty in his players, though he battled one of his stars, running back Marcus Allen. When he got along with his head coaches (not a given) — most notably John Madden, who led the Raiders from 1969 to 1978, perhaps their most successful decade — they spoke warmly of him. Wherever the team called home, Oakland or Los Angeles, Davis was a fan favorite — until he wasn't.

In league circles, he was not always viewed fondly. Known for, or at least suspected of, underhanded ploys like bugging the visiting team's clubhouse, he infuriated other owners with his relentless self-interest.

Dan Rooney of the Pittsburgh Steelers called him a "lying creep."

Don Shula, the Hall of Fame coach, said, "Al thought it was a compliment to be considered devious."

Davis said of his fellow owners, "Not all of them are the brightest of human beings."

But he knew football. A shrewd judge of talent, especially early in his career, he provided a home for gifted, wayward athletes, signing or trading for some who were undervalued or cast off by other teams, like quarterbacks Daryle Lamonica, George Blanda and Jim Plunkett, and running back Billy Cannon.

He rehabilitated others, like receiver Warren Wells, defensive linemen Lyle Alzado and John Matuszak, and quarterback Ken Stabler, whose reputations were sullied by allegations of criminal behavior, drug use, gambling or other transgressions.

Davis chose the Raiders' colors, silver and black, to intimidate. Their insignia is a shield bearing the image of a pirate in a football helmet in front of crossed sabers. He encouraged brutal physicality on defense and speed and long passing on offense.

But his allegiance to the so-called vertical passing game led to some ill-advised draft choices. One, late in his career, was JaMarcus Russell, a big-armed passer from Louisiana State who was the first pick in the 2007 draft. He was out of the game three years later.

On defense, Davis's Raiders were known for aggressiveness, meanness and borderline dirty play. The bump and run — a tactic in which a defensive back hits a wide receiver hard at the line of scrimmage to throw him off his route — was developed by Davis's Raiders, if not invented by them.

Their safeties and cornerbacks (most notably Lester Hayes) became known in the 1970s and '80s for smearing their hands with Stickum, not only to help them make fingertip interceptions but to make it tougher for the bumped receivers to tear away from coverage. Raiders players attracted nicknames like the Mad Bomber (Lamonica), the Snake (Stabler), Dr. Death (defensive back Skip Thomas) and the Assassin (safety Jack Tatum, whose hit in a 1978 preseason game broke the neck of New England Patriots receiver Darryl Stingley and paralyzed him).

"I don't want to be the most respected team in the league," Davis said in 1981. "I want to be the most feared."

When the Raiders hired him to be head coach and general manager in 1963, the team was playing in the A.F.L., the fledgling rival to the N.F.L. Until then the Raiders had won only 9 of 42 games. They went 10-4 in Davis's first season and 58-21-5 in the six after that, going to

SYMBOL OF A FRANCHISE: Al Davis with the Vince Lombardi Trophy, after the Oakland Raider's 1981 Super Bowl victory over the Philadelphia Eagles.

the second Super Bowl in January 1968 against Vince Lombardi's Green Bay Packers, who beat them.

The Raiders played in the A.F.L. championship game in 1967, 1968 and 1969, and when the A.F.L. and the N.F.L. merged in 1969, they went to the first of their 11 conference championship games in 1970. Davis's Raiders played in five Super Bowls, winning Super Bowls XI, against the Minnesota Vikings in 1977; XV, against the Philadelphia Eagles in 1981; and XVIII, against the Washington Redskins in 1984. From 1963 to 1985, the Raiders compiled an overall record of 229-91-11, the highest winning percentage of any team in professional sports during that time.

"Davis has become the iconoclast of American sports through four decades of inspiring hatred and love for a football team," The New York Times wrote in 2003, on the eve of the Raiders' most recent appearance in the Super Bowl, which they lost to the Tampa Bay Buccaneers. "He has been likened to Darth Vader, the dark lord of the 'Star Wars' movies. He has a story not unlike Frank Sinatra — East Coast reared, visionary talent who soars to the top, falls on hard times, and returns triumphant by trusting himself first, second and third. It has made Davis's team a target of derision and praise. It has left Davis a figure of scorn and respect."

Allen Davis was born in Brockton, Mass., on July 4, 1929, and grew up in Brooklyn, where his father, Louis, was a successful businessman. He often spoke of learning toughness on the city streets, but he came from a relatively affluent home and once confessed to a reporter: "I don't want this in the story. I wish you wouldn't print it. You follow me? But when I got out of public school, I won the American Legion medal for all-around kid."

He graduated from Erasmus Hall High School, then attended Wittenberg College in Ohio before transferring to Syracuse University, where he played junior varsity football and graduated with a degree in English. He coached at Adelphi University on Long Island and then in the Army, at Fort Belvoir, Va. His first job in pro football, when he was 24, was in the personnel department of the Baltimore Colts of the N.F.L. He was later an assistant at the Citadel and at Southern California, and from there returned to the pros in 1960, the inaugural season of the A.F.L., when his ambition to have the young league supersede its established rival took hold.

As a coach for the Los Angeles Chargers (they moved to San Diego in 1961), he was aggressive in recruiting college players, persuading many, including the great receiver Lance Alworth, to join the A.F.L. in general and the Chargers in particular. In 1962, the Chargers' head coach, Sid Gillman, said: "There isn't a doubt in Al Davis's mind that right now he's the smartest guy in the game. He isn't, but he will be pretty damned soon."

The Raiders hired Davis, then 33, the next year.

In April 1966, he left the Raiders to become the commissioner of the A.F.L., promising to wage war against the N.F.L. for top players, a move that many observers at the time believed

helped push the N.F.L. owners to agree to a merger of the two leagues only two months later.

When the owners agreed that Rozelle, the N.F.L. commissioner, would hold the same title in the merged league, Davis was further miffed, giving rise to their long, mutual enmity. Out of a job as A.F.L. commissioner, he returned to the Raiders as a part-owner, with the self-styled title of managing general partner. He became the principal owner in 2005.

Davis sued the N.F.L. several times. He once attacked the league as an unlawful cartel for forbidding him to move the Raiders from Oakland to Los Angeles to take advantage of a larger market. He accused Rozelle of standing in his way because Rozelle wanted to start a Los Angeles franchise himself. Davis won that fight, and the Raiders began play at the Los Angeles Coliseum in 1982.

By 1994, however, Davis was contending that the Coliseum was no longer an adequate stadium in an era of luxury boxes. The league gave him permission to move the franchise back to Oakland after the '94 season. (By then, Paul Tagliabue was commissioner. Rozelle, who died in 1996, had stepped down in 1989.) In a subsequent suit, Davis accused the league of having hampered the Raiders' effort to build a new stadium in Los Angeles; the league eventually won that suit in 2007.

In Davis's last 25 years with the Raiders, there were more feuds, not only with the league but also with his head coaches. Nine men have coached the Raiders since 1995, a period in which the team has made the postseason only three times.

One piece of Raiders lore has it that the team's fortunes declined after Davis began feuding with Marcus Allen, the team's career rushing leader, whose playing time was greatly curtailed in 1986, the season after he won the N.F.L. rushing title. The reasons for the dispute were never made public, but Allen said in a 1992 television interview that Davis had a vendetta against him, an accusation Davis denied. Signing with the Kansas City Chiefs as a free agent, Allen led the league in touchdowns and was named the comeback player of the year in 1993. On the final Sunday of the 1994 season, he gained 132 yards in 33 carries as the Chiefs beat the Raiders, 19-9, eliminating the Raiders from the playoffs and earning a postseason spot for themselves.

Davis's survivors include his wife, the former Carol Segal; and a son.

As self-interested and obdurate as he could be, Davis was also self-aware. He told People magazine that his focus on football was complete.

"It's tunnel vision, a tunnel life," he said. "I'm not really part of society."

— BY BRUCE WEBER

FRANKLIN KAMENY

His Firing Ignited a Gay-Rights Struggle

MAY 21, 1925 - OCT. 11, 2011

FRANKLIN E. KAMENY, who transformed his 1957 arrest as a "sexual pervert" and his subsequent firing from the Army Map Service into a powerful animating spark of the gay civil rights movement, died on Oct. 11 at his home in Washington. He was 86.

His death was confirmed by the United States Office of Personnel Management, which formally apologized in 2009 for his dismissal.

A half-century ago, Mr. Kameny was either first or foremost — often both — in publicly advocating the propositions that there were homosexuals throughout the population, that they were not mentally ill, and that there was neither reason nor justification for the many forms of discrimination prevalent against them.

Rather than accept his firing quietly, Mr. Kameny challenged his dismissal before the Civil Service Commission and then sued the government in federal court. That he lost was almost beside the point. The battle against discrimination now had a face, a name and a Ph.D. from Harvard.

Though he helped found the Mattachine Society of Washington, an early advocacy group, Mr. Kameny was not content to organize solely within the gay community. He welcomed and exploited the publicity that came from broader, if foredoomed, political efforts, like running in 1971 for the delegate seat representing the District of Columbia in the House of Representatives.

He also claimed authorship of the phrase "Gay is good" a year before the 1969 Stonewall uprising in New York, widely regarded as the first milestone in the gay rights movement. Many of the tributes that began to appear on the Web after his death noted that it coincided with National Coming Out Day.

Mr. Kameny has been likened both to Rosa Parks and to Gen. George Patton, two historical figures not frequently found in the same sentence. "Frank Kameny was our Rosa Parks, and more," Richard Socarides, the president of the advocacy group Equality Matters, said. During the Clinton administration, Mr. Socarides was the special assistant for gay rights in the White House, outside which Mr. Kameny and others had picketed in 1965 to protest their treatment by the government.

The Patton analogy was made by Dudley Clendinen and Adam Nagourney in their 1999 book "Out for Good: The Struggle to Build a Gay Rights Movement in America." (Mr. Nagourney is a reporter for The New York Times, and Mr. Clendinen, who died on May 30, 2012, was a former Times reporter.)

A MOVEMENT'S EARLY LEADER: Franklin Kameny, right, shaking hands with President Obama after the signing of a presidential memorandum on federal benefits and nondiscrimination, June 17, 2009.

"Franklin Kameny had the confidence of an intellectual autocrat, the manner of a snapping turtle, a voice like a foghorn, and the habit of expressing himself in thunderous bursts of precise and formal language," the authors wrote. "He talked in italics and exclamation points, and he cultivated the self-righteous arrogance of a visionary who knew his cause was just when no one else did."

Franklin Edward Kameny was born on May 21, 1925, in New York City. He entered Queens College, served in the Army in the Netherlands and Germany during World War II and was awarded his doctorate from Harvard in 1956. The Army Map Service hired him the next year as an astonomer but fired him five months later when it learned that the morals squad had arrested him in Lafayette Park, a gay cruising ground across from the White House.

At the time, under an executive order signed by President Dwight D. Eisenhower in 1953, "sexual perversion" was considered grounds for dismissal from government employment. Mr. Kameny contested his firing through level after level of legal appeal, until the United States Supreme Court declined to hear his case in 1961.

Unable to get another job in his field, he became radicalized, he told Eric Marcus, who interviewed him for the 1992 book "Making History: The Struggle for Gay and Lesbian Equal Rights, 1945-1990." Mr. Kameny said his personal manifesto emerged from the petition he prepared for the Supreme Court.

"The government put its disqualification of gays under the rubric of immoral conduct, which I objected to," Mr. Kameny said. "Because under our system, morality is a matter of personal opinion and individual belief on which any American citizen may hold any view he wishes and upon which the government has no power or authority to have any view at all. Besides which, in my view, homosexuality is not only not immoral, but is affirmatively moral.

"Up until that time, nobody else ever said this, as far as I know, in any kind of formal court pleading."

After this loss, Mr. Kameny recognized that

the American Psychiatric Association's classification of homosexuality as a sickness posed a high hurdle for the movement.

"An attribution of mental illness in our culture is devastating, and it's something which is virtually impossible to get beyond," he said to Charles Kaiser, who interviewed him in 1995 for his book "The Gay Metropolis: 1940-1996." He was among those who lobbied for its reversal.

In December 1973, the psychiatric association's board of trustees approved a resolution declaring that homosexuality, "by itself, does not necessarily constitute a psychiatric disorder."

Leading psychiatrists who believed otherwise, like Dr. Charles W. Socarides (the father of Richard Socarides), pushed for a membership-wide referendum in the hope of overturning the resolution. In April 1974, 5,854 of the association's roughly 20,000 members voted to support the trustees' position, 3,810 to oppose it. The result left Mr. Kameny "ecstatic," he said.

As for his firing, Mr. Kameny lived long enough to receive and accept an apology from John Berry, the director of the United States Office of Personnel Management, successor to the Civil Service Commission. Speaking of Mr. Kameny after his death, Mr. Berry said, "He helped make it possible for countless patriotic Americans to hold security clearances and high government positions, including me."

— By David W. Dunlap

LAURA POLLÁN TOLEDO

Ladies in White, Marching for the Jailed

FEB. 13, 1948 - OCT. 14, 2011

Laura Pollán Toledo, a former high school Spanish teacher who became one of Cuba's most public dissidents as she led other wives of political prisoners in protest every Sunday, died on Oct. 14 in a Havana hospital. She was 63.

The Cuban government gave rise to Ms. Pollán's crusade by arresting her husband, Héctor Maseda, an independent journalist, in March 2003 during a crackdown on political dissent known as the Black Spring.

In all, 75 men were arrested and sentenced after one-day trials to terms ranging from 6 to 28 years. Mr. Maseda was given a 20-year sentence for acting against "the territorial integrity of the state."

Encountering the wives of the other dissidents as she traveled from office to office seeking news of her husband, Ms. Pollán began organizing them to press for the men's release. She called the group the Ladies in White.

The women marched through the main streets of Havana after attending Mass, each dressed in white and holding a single gladiolus. They often faced down angry pro-government mobs, who surrounded them and screamed insults in what the Cuban government called "acts of repudiation."

In 2005, the European Parliament awarded the group the Sakharov Prize for Freedom of Thought, but Ms. Pollán was not permitted to travel to Europe to accept it.

Some of the prisoners were released over the years on medical grounds, but 50 were still in prison in 2010, when the Roman Catholic Church and the Spanish government succeeded in negotiating for their freedom with President Raúl Castro.

Most of the men were released on the condition that they fly into exile, but about a dozen refused to leave the island. Among those was Ms. Pollán's husband, who was not freed until February 2011.

SPREADING THE NEWS: Laura Pollán Toledo reporting a recent release of prisoners, July 2010.

While in prison, Mr. Maseda smuggled out his memoir, titled "Buried Alive." Ms. Pollán sent the book to Fidel Castro in 2008, according to the Committee to Protect Journalists.

The release and exile of the prisoners robbed the group of vigor as some of its members left the island with their husbands. But Ms. Pollán and other women continued to march every week.

"We are going to continue," she told The Associated Press a month before her death. "We are fighting for freedom and human rights. As long as this government is around there will be prisoners. Because while they've let some go, they've put others in jail. It is a never-ending story."

Ms. Pollán entered the hospital on Oct. 7 after she developed a respiratory illness. She died of cardiac arrest, her family said.

Just two weeks before she was hospitalized, a crowd gathered outside her house in Havana, jeering, jostling and shouting at the Ladies in White as they met to attend Mass.

"This fight will continue," Berta Soler, the group's spokeswoman, told the Spanish news agency EFE after Ms. Pollán's death. "Physically, Laura is no longer with us, but she is spiritually."

— BY ELISABETH MALKIN

PIRI THOMAS

'Mean Streets' Became Salvation Road

SEPT. 30, 1928 · OCT. 17, 2011

PIRI THOMAS, a writer and poet whose 1967 memoir, "Down These Mean Streets," chronicled his tough childhood in Spanish Harlem and the outlaw years that followed, and became a classic portrait of ghetto life, died on Oct. 17 at his home in El Cerrito, Calif. He was 83.

The memoir, a best seller and eventually a staple on high school and college reading lists, appeared as Americans seemed to be awakening to the rough cultures that poverty and racism were breeding in cities. A new literary genre had cropped up to explore those conditions, in books like "Manchild in the Promised Land," by Claude Brown, and "The Autobiography of Malcolm X."

NEW GENRE: Piri Thomas was one of the first authors to capture the cultures of racism and poverty in urban America.

"Down These Mean Streets" joined that list. The memoir, Mr. Thomas wrote on his Web site, had "exploded out of my guts in an outpouring of long suppressed hurts and angers that had boiled over into an ice-cold rage."

The novelist Daniel Stern, reviewing the book in The New York Times, called it "another stanza in the passionate poem of color and color-hatred being written today."

In the memoir, Mr. Thomas described how he was brought up as the only dark-skinned child among seven children, the son of a Puerto Rican mother, Dolores Montañez, and a Cuban father, Juan Tomás de la Cruz. His dark skin, Mr. Thomas recalled, made him feel like an outlier in his own family and neighborhood, where he was taunted about his looks. Even his father, he felt, preferred his lighter-skinned children.

He described the bravado, or "machismo," that he affected on the streets. Protecting his "rep" led him to "waste" people who insulted him, he wrote. He sniffed "horse" — heroin — even though he knew the consequences.

"The world of street belonged to the kid alone," he wrote. "There he could earn his own rights, prestige, his good-o stick of living. It was like being a knight of old, like being 10 feet tall."

As a merchant seaman in the Jim Crow South, he persuaded a white prostitute to sleep with him because, he told her, he was really Puerto Rican, not black. He then enjoyed stunning her by telling her she had just slept with a black man.

He returned home while his mother was dying in a poor people's ward at Metropolitan Hospital and resumed his old ways — selling and using drugs and robbing people. In one holdup he wounded a police officer and landed in prison for seven years, a harrowing time he vividly evoked. It was in prison that he finished high school and began thinking about writing. He found, he wrote, that words could be used as bullets or butterflies. He called writing "the Flow."

"It came very naturally," he told an interviewer. "I promised God that if he didn't let me die in prison, I would use the Flow."

The book, with its harsh language and scenes, was banned by some schools, but it soon became assigned reading in many others. The poet Martin Espada said its influence was enormous.

"Because he became a writer, many of us became writers," Mr. Espada said. "Before 'Down These Mean Streets,' we could not find a book by a Puerto Rican writer in the English language about the experience of that community, in that voice, with that tone and subject matter."

Carolina González, a professor of literature at Rutgers University, said her students continued to find the book "very immediate and descriptive of their lives."

After writing the memoir Mr. Thomas spent much of the rest of his life lecturing about it. He also wrote two novels, "Savior, Savior, Hold

My Hand" (1972) and "Seven Long Times" (1974), as well as several plays and the collection "Stories From El Barrio" (1979). He also set his poetry to music.

John Peter Thomas was born on Sept. 30, 1928, in Harlem Hospital, where he was given his Anglo-Saxon name. "They wanted to assimilate me," he said in an interview in 1995. "Whoever heard of a Puerto Rican named John Peter Thomas?" His mother called him Piri.

Mr. Thomas died of pneumonia. He is survived by his wife, Suzie Dod Thomas; two sons; four daughters; three stepchildren; seven grandchildren; and two stepgrandchildren.

Olga Luz Tirado, his onetime publicist, said that despite the hardships of his life, Mr. Thomas retained a sense of humor. She recalled taking him to a reading in Brooklyn in the 1990s. "On the way back I took a wrong turn and said to him, 'Piri, I think we're lost,'" she told a reporter. "He asked, 'We got gas?' I said, 'Yes.' And he said: 'We ain't lost. We just sightseeing!'"

— By Joseph Berger

JERZY BIELECKI

Love in the Shadow of Auschwitz

MARCH 28, 1921 - OCT. 20, 2011

Jerzy Bielecki was 19 years old, Roman Catholic and suspected of being a member of the Polish resistance when he was arrested by the Nazis in June 1940 and transported to Auschwitz. The number 243 was tattooed on his arm. Nearly three years later, Cyla Cybulska, her parents, her two brothers and

her younger sister were crammed into a train with thousands of other Polish Jews and shipped to Auschwitz. Only Cyla — No. 29558 — would survive. Because of Mr. Bielecki. Theirs was a tale of love and courage that would continue to resonate through almost 40 years of separation, each believing the other had died.

For his daring rescue of that one Jewish woman, Yad Vashem, Israel's center for Holocaust research and education, recognized Mr. Bielecki in 1985 as one of the so-called righteous gentiles. He died on Oct. 20 in Nowy Targ, Poland, at 90.

In the fall of 1943, Mr. Bielecki, known as Jurek, was in forced labor in a grain warehouse at the concentration camp when several young women were herded through the door. "It seemed to me that one of them, a pretty dark-haired one, winked at me," he said in an interview in 2010. "It was Cyla, who had just been assigned to repair grain sacks."

Over the next eight months, although able to exchange only a few furtive words each day, they fell in love. Mr. Bielecki began planning their escape. Aided by a fellow inmate working in a uniform warehouse, he began piecing together an SS guard's uniform.

On July 21, 1944, after obtaining a stolen pass, he put on the uniform and led Ms. Cybulska out of her barrack and onto a long path leading to a side gate. He had with him a forged document authorizing him to take a prisoner to a nearby farm. At the gate, a sleepy guard said "Ja" — yes — and let them pass.

Now free, they hid in the fields by day and walked by night, 10 nights altogether, until they reached the home of one of Mr. Bielecki's relatives. Though much in love, Mr. Bielecki decided that he had to join the Polish underground. He found a Polish family to take Ms. Cybulska in and hide her. He promised he would return, and they said their goodbyes. It was the last time they would see each other for 39 years. After the war, "through a variety of misunderstandings, each thought the other had died," said Stanlee J. Stahl, executive vice president of the Jewish Foundation for the Righteous, which assists non-Jews who risked their lives to save Jews.

Ms. Cybulska immigrated to the United States, married another Holocaust survivor, David Zacharowicz, and opened a jewelry business in Brooklyn. In Poland, Mr. Bielecki started a family of his own and became director of a school for car mechanics.

It was by pure chance that in 1983 they found each other again. By then, David Zacharowicz had died. "Cyla was at home talking to the Polish woman who cleaned for her, telling how this man had saved her and that she had been told he had died," Ms. Stahl said. "The cleaning lady said: 'I don't think he's dead. I saw a man telling the story on Polish television. He's alive.'"

A DARING RESCUE: Jerzy Bielecki, in 2010, with photos of himself and Cyla Cybulska. Escape from Auschwitz led to a 40-year separation.

Ms. Zacharowicz tracked down Mr. Bielecki's phone number in Nowy Targ and called him one morning in May 1983. Several weeks later she flew to Krakow to meet him. When she stepped off the plane, Mr. Bielecki, now 62, handed her 39 red roses, one for each of the years they had not seen each other.

"He and Cyla saw each other about another 15 times," Ms. Stahl said. "They were good friends for life."

Mr. Bielecki was born in Slaboszow, Poland, on March 28, 1921. Ms. Stahl said she did not have information about his survivors.

Interviewed by The Associated Press in 2011, Mr. Bielecki said he had been "very much in love with Cyla," who died in 2005.

"Sometimes I cried after the war, that she was not with me," he said. "Fate decided for us, but I would do the same again."

Cyla and David Zacharowicz had one child, Fay Roseman of Coral Springs, Fla. Without Mr. Bielecki, she said, "there wouldn't be this family."

— BY DENNIS HEVESI

MUAMMAR EL-QADDAFI

A Brutal Dictator, a Violent End

1942 - OCT. 20, 2011

Col. Muammar el-Qaddafi, the erratic, provocative dictator who ruled Libya for 42 years, crushing opponents at home while cultivating the wardrobe and looks befitting an aging rock star, met a violent and vengeful death on Oct. 20 in the hands of the Libyan forces that had driven him from power.

A small group of fighters from the rebel force attacking Colonel Qaddafi's former hometown and final hideout, the coastal town of Surt, said they had stumbled upon him hiding in a drainage pipe under a roadway. "Show me mercy!" he was said to have cried.

His last moments alive, captured in jerky video images, were shown worldwide. One clip showed him captured, bloody, disheveled and anguished; another showed his half-naked torso, his eyes staring vacantly, an apparent gunshot wound to the head, as jubilant fighters fired their weapons into the air. In a third video, posted on YouTube, his captors hovered around his lifeless-looking body, posing for photographs and yanking his limp head up and down by the hair. Later, more video showed his corpse being dragged through the streets of Surt.

"We can definitely say that the Qaddafi regime has come to an end," President Obama said. "The dark shadow of tyranny has been lifted, and with this enormous promise, the Libyan people now have a great responsibility to build an inclusive and tolerant and democratic Libya that stands as the ultimate rebuke to Qaddafi's dictatorship."

Throughout his rule, Colonel Qaddafi, 69, sanctioned spasms of grisly violence and frequent bedlam, even as he sought to leverage his nation's oil wealth into an outsize role for Libya on the world stage.

He embraced a string of titles: "the brother leader," "the guide to the era of the masses," "the king of kings of Africa" and, his most preferred, "the leader of the revolution."

But the labels pinned on him by others tended to stick the most. President Ronald Reagan called him "the mad dog of the Middle East." President Anwar el-Sadat of neighboring Egypt pronounced him "the crazy Libyan."

As his dominion over Libya crumbled, Colonel Qaddafi refused to countenance the fact that most Libyans despised him. He placed blame for the uprising against his rule on foreign intervention.

"I tell the coward crusaders: I live in a place where you can't get me," he taunted defiantly after the uprising against his rule started in February. "I live in the hearts of millions."

That defiance endured to the end. In one of his last speeches, made as a fugitive weeks after Tripoli, the capital, fell, he exhorted Libyans to defeat the uprising.

"The people of Libya, the true Libyans, will never accept invasion and colonization," he said on Syrian television after he had lost control of Libya's airwaves. "We will fight for our freedom, and we are ready to sacrifice ourselves."

Colonel Qaddafi was a 27-year-old junior officer when he led the bloodless coup that deposed Libya's monarch in 1969. Soon afterward he began styling himself a desert nomad philosopher. He received dignitaries in his sprawling white tent, which he erected wherever he went: Rome, Paris and, after much controversy, New York, on a Westchester County estate in 2009. Inside, its quilted walls might be printed with motifs like palm trees and camels, or embroidered with his sayings.

Colonel Qaddafi declared that his political system of permanent revolution would sweep away capitalism and socialism. But he hedged his bets by financing and arming a cornucopia of violent organizations, including the Irish Republican Army and African guerrilla groups. He became an international pariah after his government was linked to terrorist attacks, particularly the 1988 bombing of a Pan Am jet over Lockerbie, Scotland, killing 270 people.

After the American-led invasion of Iraq, however, Colonel Qaddafi seemed to usher in a new era of relations with the West when he announced that Libya was abandoning its pursuit of unconventional weapons and canceling a covert nascent nuclear program. At home, though, he ruled through an ever-smaller circle of advisers, among them his sons, and destroyed any institution that might challenge him.

By the time he was done, Libya had no parliament, no unified military command, no political parties, no unions, no civil society and no nongovernmental organizations. His ministries were hollow, with the notable exception of the state oil company.

'I Am a Glory'

Eight years into his rule, he renamed the country the Great Socialist People's Libyan Jamahiriya. (Jamahiriya was his Arabic translation for a state of the masses.) "In the era of the masses, power is in the hands of the people themselves, and leaders disappear forever," he wrote in The Green Book, a three-volume political tract that was required reading in every school.

For decades, Libyans noted dryly that he did not seem to be disappearing any time soon; he became the longest-serving Arab or African leader. Yet he always presented himself as beloved guide and chief clairvoyant rather than ruler. He seethed when a popular uprising inspired by similar revolutions next door in Tunisia and Egypt first sought to drive him from power.

"I am a glory that Libya cannot forgo and the Libyan people cannot forgo, nor the Arab nation, nor the Islamic nation, nor Africa, nor Latin America, nor all the nations that desire freedom and human dignity and resist tyranny!" Colonel Qaddafi shouted in February. "Muammar Qaddafi is history, resistance, liberty, glory, revolution!"

It was a typically belligerent and rambling harangue. He vowed to fight to his last drop of blood.

A STRONGMAN EMERGES: Muammar El-Qaddafi, then a 27-year-old junior officer, addressing a crowd of supporters after leading the 1969 bloodless coup that deposed Libya's monarchy.

"This is my country!" he roared as he shook his fist and pounded the lectern. "Muammar is not a president to quit his post. Muammar is the leader of the revolution until the end of time!"

He blamed all manner of bogeymen: the United States, Al Qaeda operatives, even youths "fueled by milk and Nescafé spiked with hallucinogenic drugs." But he also made it clear that he was ready to hunt down and eliminate any "rat" who challenged his rule.

In the 1990s, faced with growing Islamist opposition, Colonel Qaddafi bombed towns in eastern Libya, and his henchmen were widely believed to have opened fire on prisoners in Tripoli's Abu Salim prison, killing about 1,200. He survived countless coup and assassination attempts and cracked down afterward, alienating important Libyan tribes. He imported soldiers from his misadventures in Sudan, Chad and Liberia, transforming Libya's ragtag militias into what he styled as his African or Islamic legions.

At least once a decade, Colonel Qaddafi fomented shocking violence that terrorized Libyans. In the late 1970s and early '80s, he eliminated even mild critics through public trials and executions. Kangaroo courts were staged on soccer fields or basketball courts, where the accused were interrogated, some urinating in fear as they begged for their lives. The events were televised to make sure that no Libyan missed the point.

The bodies of one group of students hanged in downtown Tripoli's main square were left there to rot for a week, opposition figures said. Traffic was rerouted to force cars to pass by.

Muammar el-Qaddafi was born to illiterate Bédouin parents in a tent just inland from the coastal town of Surt in 1942. (Some sources give the date as June 7.) His father herded camels and sheep. One grandfather was killed in the 1911 Italian invasion to colonize Libya. His parents scrimped for his education. He grew to idolize

President Gamal Abdel Nasser of Egypt, who preached Arab unity and socialism after deposing the king in a 1952 coup. He showed enough promise to enter the Royal Military Academy at Benghazi, in eastern Libya, and in 1966 was sent to England for a course on military communications. He learned English.

On Sept. 1, 1969, he led young officers in seizing the government while King Idris was abroad. They dissolved Parliament and set up a 12-member Revolutionary Command Council to rule Libya, mirroring Mr. Nasser's Egypt. He was promoted to colonel and armed forces commander. Egypt was his blueprint, and he proclaimed that the newly named Libyan Arab Republic would advance under the Arab nationalist slogan "Socialism, unity and freedom."

Yet in a country where the deposed king, Idris, had come from a long line of religious figures, Colonel Qaddafi felt compelled to shore up his Islamic credentials. He banned alcohol and closed bars, nightclubs and casinos. He outlawed teaching English in public schools. Traffic signs and advertisements not in Arabic were painted over.

Decades later, only one nightclub had opened in Tripoli, in a nondescript building plastered with revolutionary slogans and displaying the mandatory picture of the leader, who seemed to stare down from every wall in Libya.

Colonel Qaddafi claimed that Mr. Nasser had declared him his son, and in the early years of his rule, he set about trying to win his idol's approval by modernizing Libya and trying, in vain, to unite it with other Arab countries. He expelled American and British military bases, then nationalized the property of Italian settlers and a small Jewish community. He railed against Israel.

He also vowed to eliminate Libya's tribes, worried that they were too powerful, even though Libya's urbanizing population had been moving away from them for some time.

Libya had been desperately poor until oil was discovered in 1959. A decade later, Libyans had touched little of their wealth.

The 1969 coup changed that. The new Libyan government forced the major oil companies to cede majority stakes in exchange for continued access to the country's oil fields, and it demanded a greater share of the profits. The pattern was emulated across the oil-producing states, profoundly changing their relationship with the oil giants.

With the increased revenue, Colonel Qaddafi set about building roads, hospitals, schools and housing. And Libyans, who had suffered during the Italian occupation before World War II, were allowed to celebrate an anticolonial, Arab-nationalist sentiment that had been bottled up under the monarchy. Life expectancy, which averaged 51 years in 1969, is now over 74. Literacy leapt to 88 percent. Per capita annual income grew to above $12,000, though the figure is markedly lower than that found in many oil-rich countries. Yet Colonel Qaddafi warned his people that the oil would not last.

"Petroleum societies are lazy everywhere," he observed. "People are used to having more money and want everything available. This revolution wants to change this life and to promote production and work, to produce everything by our hands. But the people are lazy."

A CHICKEN IN EVERY APARTMENT
The mercurial changes in policy and personality that kept Libyans off balance began in earnest with the three volumes of his Green Book, published from 1976 to 1979. (Green, he explained, was for both Islam and agriculture.) The book offered his "third universal theory" to improve on capitalism and socialism, and elevated the mundane to the allegedly profound, condemning sports like boxing as barbarism and pointing out that men and women are different because women menstruate.

Colonel Qaddafi also introduced Orwellian revolutionary committees in every neighborhood to purge the country of the ideologically unsound, calling it "people power." He began foisting social experiments on Libyans.

> His death, captured on video, was as bloody as his 42-year rule.

Once he demanded that all Libyans raise chickens to promote self-sufficiency and deducted the costs of cages from their wages. "It made no sense to raise chickens in apartments," said Mansour O. El-Kikhia, a Qaddafi biographer at the University of Texas and a member of an opposition family. "People slaughtered the chickens, ate them and used the cages as dish racks."

Colonel Qaddafi said women were not equal to men, but he exhibited them as a symbol of the success of the Libyan revolution. None had a higher profile than his phalanx of female bodyguards, who wore camouflage fatigues, red nail polish and high-heeled sandals and carried submachine guns.

To consolidate his power, Colonel Qaddafi tried to eliminate or isolate all of the 11 other members of the original Revolutionary Command Council. Strikes or unauthorized news reports resulted in prison sentences; illegal political activity was punishable by death. Western books were burned, and private enterprise was banned. Libyan intelligence agents engaged in all manner of skulduggery, reaching overseas to kidnap and assassinate opponents.

He vowed to turn Libya into an agriculture powerhouse through the Great Man-Made River, a grandiose $20 billion project to pump water from aquifers underneath the Sahara and send it over 1,200 miles to the coast through a gargantuan pipeline.

He also invaded Chad during the 1980s after encroaching on its border for years, only to be defeated by it in 1987 with French and American military aid.

Meanwhile he was cementing Libya's rogue-state status by bankrolling terrorist and guerrilla organizations, including Abu Nidal, the radical Palestinian organization, and the violent Red Army Faction in Europe. At least a dozen coups or coup attempts in Africa were traced to his backing. That set him on a collision course with the West.

In the early 1980s, President Reagan closed the Libyan Embassy in Washington, suspended oil imports and shot down two Libyan fighters after Colonel Qaddafi tried to extend Libya's territorial waters across the Gulf of Sidra.

In London in 1984, gunshots from the Libyan Embassy killed a police officer and wounded 11 demonstrators. In 1986, Libyan agents were linked to the bombing of a disco in West Berlin, killing two American service members and a Turkish woman and wounding 200 people.

President Reagan retaliated 10 days later by bombing targets in Libya, including Colonel Qaddafi's residence in his compound at the Bab al-Aziziya barracks in Tripoli.

He preserved the wreckage of the house as a symbol of American treachery and, in front of it, installed a sculpture of a giant fist crushing an American jet fighter. It became his preferred stage for major events; his major speech during the 2011 uprising was delivered from the first floor.

LOCKERBIE

In 1988, in the deadliest terrorist act linked to Libya, 259 people aboard Pan Am Flight 103 died when the plane exploded in midair over Lockerbie. The falling wreckage killed 11 people on the ground. Libyan agents were also believed to have been behind the explosion of a French passenger jet over Niger in 1989, killing 170 people.

Nearly a decade of international isolation started in 1992, after Libya refused to hand over two suspects indicted by the United States and Britain in the Lockerbie bombing. France also sought four suspects in the Niger bombing, among them Abdullah Senussi, a brother-in-law of Colonel Qaddafi's and the head of external intelligence. He was convicted in absentia.

Colonel Qaddafi bankrolled terrorist groups and was accused in the heinous bombing of a jetliner over Lockerbie, Scotland.

The United Nations imposed economic sanctions, and when his fellow Arabs enforced them, Colonel Qaddafi turned away from the Arab world. He began his quest to become leader of Africa, coming closest in title, at least, in 2009, when he was named the chairman of the African Union for a year.

In 1999, Libya finally handed over two Lockerbie suspects for trial in The Hague under Scottish law and reached a financial settlement with the French. One suspect was acquitted but another, Abdel Basset al-Megrahi, was convicted and sentenced to 27 years in a Scottish jail. When the government released him in 2009, on the grounds that he was terminally ill, the outcry was swift. The British were accused of trying to curry favor with Tripoli for oil and arms deals. (Mr. al-Megrahi died in Libya in May 2012.)

The international sanctions against Libya were lifted in 2003 after it accepted responsibility for the bombing and agreed to pay $2.7 billion to the families of victims in the Lockerbie bombing and in other attacks.

The Libyans did not admit guilt, however. They said they were simply acting to restore ties with the West. But when Judge Mustafa Abdel-Jalil, the justice minister, defected during the uprising in February 2011, he told a Swedish newspaper that he had proof that Colonel Qaddafi had ordered the operation.

Tripoli truly began to emerge from the cold after the September 2001 attacks against the United States. Colonel Qaddafi condemned them and shared Libya's intelligence on Al Qaeda with Washington. Libya had been the first country to demand an international arrest warrant for Osama bin Laden.

Colonel Qaddafi also said he would destroy his weapons stockpile. President George W. Bush said Libya's decision demonstrated the success of the invasion of Iraq, in that it had persuaded a rogue state to abandon its menacing ways, although Libya had made a similar overture years before and many experts did not consider its programs threatening.

Nevertheless, Britain and the United States reestablished diplomatic relations. Prime Minister Tony Blair and Secretary of State Condoleezza Rice led a parade of world leaders to Colonel Qaddafi's tent seeking trade deals. Ms. Rice was the first American secretary of state to visit since 1953.

Before the visit, Colonel Qaddafi was effusive about Ms. Rice. "I support my darling black African woman," he said on the network Al Jazeera, adding: "I admire and am very proud of the way she leans back and gives orders to the Arab leaders. Yes, Leezza, Leezza, Leezza — I love her very much."

State Department cables released by WikiLeaks suggested that there was another woman who had won Colonel Qaddafi's affection, and confidence — a "voluptuous blonde" Ukrainian nurse, described as the senior member of a posse of nurses around him.

The cables described him as a hypochondriac who feared flying over water and who often fasted twice a week. He followed horse racing, loved flamenco dancing and added "king of culture" to his myriad titles, the cables said.

Around 1995 he published a collection of short stories and essays called "The Village, the City, the Suicide of the Astronaut and Other Stories." It later came out in Britain as "Escape to Hell and Other Stories." As a reviewer in the British newspaper The Guardian put it: "There are no characters, no twists, no subtle illuminations; indeed, there is precious little narrative. Instead, you get surreal rants and bizarre streams of consciousness obviously unmolested by the hand of any editor."

Colonel Qaddafi married at least twice. His oldest son, Mohammed, from his first marriage, became a businessman and the agent for foreign companies working in Libya.

Seven other children — six sons and a daughter — came from his marriage to Safia Farkash, a former nurse. Seif al-Islam, the oldest son, had been the face of modern Libya, establishing an international charity and forever pledging that political reform was just around the corner. His moderate reputation evaporated with the uprising after he vowed that Libya would flow with blood. He was indicted by the International Criminal Court, accused of crimes against humanity during the uprising.

Libyan militia fighters said they captured Seif al-Islam and a small entourage on Nov. 19 in the southwestern desert. The news set off nationwide celebrations.

Among Seif's brothers, Muatassim, Khamis and Hannibal were military officers who commanded their own brigades. Muatassim headed the National Security Council but was also known for carousing in hot spots like the Caribbean island of St. Bart's, where he was reported to have paid singers, including Mariah Carey, $1 million each for appearing at his holiday parties. He was killed along with his father, and Libyan television showed what it called his lifeless body on a gurney.

The anti-Qaddafi forces said they killed Khamis, once head of the feared Khamis Brigade guarding Tripoli, as he and his bodyguards tried to break through a rebel checkpoint in August.

Hannibal gained notoriety for beating his wife and servants in luxurious European hotels. After he was arrested in Switzerland in 2008, Colonel Qaddafi broke off diplomatic relations and held two Swiss businessmen hostage.

Hannibal, Mohammed and their sister, Aisha, who gained attention as a lawyer after she offered to join Saddam Hussein's legal defense team in Iraq, all fled to neighboring Algeria. Another son, Saadi, a military officer, had been a professional soccer player who was allowed onto Italian teams more for the publicity than for his skills. He was given refuge in Niger, on Libya's southern border.

The seventh son, Seif al-Arab, was believed killed in an air raid during the uprising. Colonel Qaddafi was also believed to have adopted two children, including a nephew.

As the circle around Colonel Qaddafi shrank, his sons increasingly became his advisers, but it was never clear if he had anointed any of them as his successor. He was believed to play one off against the other, granting and then withholding favor.

FLAMBOYANT AND CAPRICIOUS

As Colonel Qaddafi grew older, the trim, handsome officer with short black hair gave way to someone more flamboyant. Brocade and medals festooned his military uniforms, as if he were some Gilbert & Sullivan admiral, while his black curls grew long and unruly. After he adopted Africa as his cause, he favored African robes in a riot of colors.

He was "notoriously mercurial," a cable obtained through WikiLeaks said, a man who "avoids making eye contact" during meetings and thinks nothing of "long, uncomfortable periods of silence." He would sometimes show up hours late for a state banquet honoring an African head of state, then sit in a far corner before bolting away. African leaders accepted this in exchange for a check for a million dollars or two, diplomats said.

After he put his worst years of sponsoring terrorism behind him, the West and the rest of the Arab world tended to treat him as comic opera, though he could still outrage, as he did in 2009, when, appearing for the first time before the United Nations General Assembly, he spoke for some 90 minutes instead of his allotted 15 and seemed to tear a copy of the charter, condemning the Security Council as a feudal organization.

When scores of children in a Benghazi hospital developed AIDS, most likely because of unsanitary conditions, Colonel Qaddafi accused the C.I.A. of developing the virus that caused it and of sending a group of Bulgarian nurses to spread it in Libya. The nurses were arrested, tortured, tried and sentenced to death before they were eventually freed.

He never tired of pushing his idea for an Israeli-Palestinian solution, a unified country called "Isratine" in which both Jews and Arabs would enjoy equal rights as soon as all Palestinian refugees were allowed to return. Other Arab leaders derided the proposal.

At home, though, Libyans suffered under his dictates. He switched from the standard

Muslim calendar to one marking the years since the Prophet Muhammad's death, only to decide later that the birth year was a more auspicious place to start. Event organizers threw up their hands and reverted to the Western calendar. He also decided to rename the months. February was Lights. August was Hannibal.

Given the conceit that "popular committees" — and not Colonel Qaddafi himself — ran the country, everyone was required to attend committee sessions called at random once or twice a year to discuss an agenda "suggested" by the grand guide. Every single office — schools, government ministries, airlines, shops — had to shut for days, sometimes weeks. Scofflaws risked fines.

Colonel Qaddafi once declared that any money over $3,000 in anyone's bank account was excessive and should revert to the state. Another time he lifted a ban on sport utility vehicles, then changed his mind a few months later, forcing everyone who had bought one to hide it.

His long effort to eliminate the government left Libya in shambles, its sagging infrastructure belying its oil wealth. Libyans grumbled that they had no idea what had happened to their oil money; the official news agency said the country earned $32 billion in 2010 alone. When prices were low or Libya was under sanctions during most of the 1980s and '90s, the nearly one million people on the public payroll never got a pay raise; experts calculated that most lived on $300 to $400 per month.

The general disarray was another way of ensuring that no one developed the confidence

THE DICTATOR: Muammar El-Qaddafi survived multiple coups and assassination attempts and became one of the world's longest-ruling leaders.

and connections to try to overthrow him. Libyans lived constantly on edge. "It is an awful feeling when you don't know what tomorrow is going to bring," said Dr. Kikhia, the biographer. "People don't work — they cannot make a decision at any level."

When revolutions succeeded in two Arab neighbors, deposing the presidents of Tunisia and Egypt, Colonel Qaddafi was among the only leaders in the region to speak out publicly. The people had been swayed by foreign plots, he maintained. He tried to warn his people that Tunisians now lived in fear of being killed at home or on the streets. But few Tunisians died.

His first speech after the Libyan uprising erupted proved a classic Qaddafi moment, mocked by the outside world while accompanying a grueling civil war at home. He vowed to hunt down the insurgents "house by house and alley by alley." The unusual Libyan word for alley — "zenga zenga" — was turned into a jingle, with various young women belly dancing to it in YouTube videos.

Even as Libyans died, Colonel Qaddafi demanded recognition that he alone had made them relevant.

"In the past, Libyans lacked an identity," Colonel Qaddafi roared in the February speech. "When you said Libyan, they would tell you Libya, Liberia, Lebanon — they didn't know Libya! But today you say Libya, they say Libya — Qaddafi, Libya — the revolution!"

— By Neil MacFarquhar

ELIZABETH WINSHIP

But to Her Young, Unsure Readers, Just 'Beth'

MAY 17, 1921 - OCT. 23, 2011

O NE LETTER, signed Tinsel Teeth, asked, "How can a boy kiss a girl who wears braces?"

Another, signed Dumbo, said: "I have enormous ears. Kids say I look like a car with both doors left open. Is there an operation to whittle them down to size?"

And over the years there were too many like the one that said: "I am in terrible trouble and I don't know where to turn. I'm 14 and I'm pregnant."

Thousands of youngsters — and sometimes their befuddled parents — sent letters on flowery stationery or notebook paper and, more recently, by e-mail to Elizabeth Winship, seeking her solid, sympathetic and often witty advice. And for 35 years she could be relied on to offer it in her column "Ask Beth," which she wrote for The Boston Globe and which appeared in 70 other newspapers across the country.

Mrs. Winship died on Oct. 23 in Roseville, Minn. She was 90.

"Should I sleep with my boyfriend?" a 10-year-old girl once asked. That was among the simpler questions Mrs. Winship dealt with.

With more complex issues, like clashes with parents, she could be blunt and hardly prudish. A 16-year-old boy once wrote that his mother was disgusted by masturbation. Beth suggested that the boy's father could enlighten his wife and "tell her, while he's at it, that masturbation is no longer considered disgusting."

"If they awarded Pulitzers for good sense and stable judgment," William McKibben wrote of Mrs. Winship in a 1985 profile of her in The

New Yorker, "she would win one every year."

Mrs. Winship, whose husband, Thomas Winship, was editor of The Globe from 1965 until 1984, was not always unreserved. She was 14 before she applied lipstick or kissed a boy, she once said. She was a junior at Radcliffe and her future husband a senior at Harvard when they went on their first date. "I made my brother come with me," she said.

Elizabeth Coolidge was born in Pittsfield, Mass., on May 17, 1921, to Albert and Margaret Coolidge. Her father was a chemistry professor at Harvard. Known to her friends as Liebe, not Beth, she graduated from Radcliffe in 1943 with a degree in psychology. She married Mr. Winship in 1942. He died in 2002. Her daughter Peg took over the column when her mother retired in 1998 and continued writing it until five years ago. She, another daughter, two sons, a sister, eight grandchildren and one great-granddaughter survive.

Mrs. Winship began reviewing books for The Globe in the early 1950s and later became its children's-book review editor. In 1963, editors asked her to write a column that would connect with young readers.

It quickly caught on, and the letters started pouring in. In 1973, responding to a girl wondering about how to get to know a boy she liked, Beth said simply, "Flirt!"

"Look at all the things animals do to attract attention to mate," she added. "The penguin, for example, lays a stone at his beloved's feet. Don't bring stones. But go ahead and be gay. Life without gaiety is as bland as a boiled egg without salt."

By the time Mrs. Winship retired in 1998,

the word "gay" had certainly evolved. By then, one young adult had written her: "I grew up in a small town as a gay teen. Reading the letters in your column from other gay teens, along with your reassurance and frank and honest information, helped me realize that I was not some freak of nature, helped me through one more day, and I believe, may have saved my life."

— DENNIS HEVESI

YVONNE McCAIN

A Home of Her Own Was Her Victory

OCT. 25, 1948 - OCT. 29, 2011

YVONNE McCAIN, a once-homeless mother of four whose years of living in a fetid, ramshackle welfare hotel in Manhattan led to a landmark court ruling requiring New York City to provide decent shelter for homeless families, died on Oct. 29. She was 63 and, at her death, living in a rent-subsidized, two-bedroom,

middle-income apartment on Staten Island.

Ms. McCain was the lead plaintiff in a lawsuit originally called McCain v. Koch. Except for hers, the names on the class-action suit changed three times as new mayors took office. The case, filed in 1983, was finally settled by the city and the Legal Aid Society in 2008.

But the primary issue was settled in 1986, when the Appellate Division of the State Supreme Court in Manhattan ruled that the city could not deny emergency shelter for homeless families with children. Previous cases had established the right of single homeless men and women to shelter.

The appellate court ruled that thousands of children had been subjected "to inevitable

emotional scarring because of the failure of city and state officials to provide emergency shelter."

Nearly 40 more proceedings were held as the suit wound through trial and appeals courts for the next 22 years as the parties wrestled over many issues, including whether the city was meeting basic standards of habitability. When the final settlement was reached, Mayor Michael R. Bloomberg said it marked "the beginning of a new era." Now, he said, "we can all move forward in our shared commitment to effectively meet the needs of homeless families."

Steven Banks, the chief lawyer of the Legal Aid Society, led the McCain case. After her death, he said, "The import of the settlement, and in a sense Ms. McCain's life, is that no matter who the mayor is now or in the future, tens of thousands of homeless children and their families are entitled to a roof over their heads."

That was not always so for Ms. McCain.

She and her children were evicted from their Brooklyn apartment in 1982 after she withheld rent because her landlord refused to make repairs. They ended up in a filthy, dilapidated hotel in Herald Square.

"They put us in a room on the 11th floor," she said in 1992. Both sides of the mattresses were stained with urine. "I remember calling my mother and asking if she could bring me newspapers to put over the mattresses," she said. "I stayed up worrying that the kids didn't climb out the windows, because there were no bars."

Ms. McCain, a battered woman, spent four years in that hotel. As the case crawled through the courts, she bounced from shelter to city-supported apartment and back. Her estranged husband once found her and broke her nose.

She and the children moved into the Staten Island apartment in 1996.

LANDMARK RULING:
Yvonne McCain's case led to city-provided shelter for homeless families.

Ms. McCain went on to work as a nurse's aide. In 2005, she received an associate's degree in human services from Borough of Manhattan Community College. In recent years, she worked in the college's health service office.

The success of her case surprised her. When the lawsuit was first filed, Ms. McCain recalled in 2003, "I thought we were going to get new mattresses and guardrails on the windows and that's it."

"I never imagined that this suit would end up being so helpful to so many people."

Born in Harlem on Oct. 25, 1948, Ms. McCain was the only child of Lillie McCain and John Henry Bonds. She died of cancer and is survived by two daughters, four sons, 19 grandchildren and three great-grandchildren.

One of her daughters, Tameika McCain, said her mother had found peace on Staten Island.

"My mom loved this apartment," she said. "She said she was never going to leave it, never going to be homeless again."

— By Dennis Hevesi

JIMMY SAVILE

A Blooming TV Eccentric, He Was

OCT. 31, 1926 - OCT. 29, 2011

Jimmy Savile, a celebrated English television host whose dress, hair and verbal flummery made all other comers in a nation renowned for eccentrics look like Puritans, was found dead on Oct. 29 at his home in Leeds, in the north of England. He was 84.

A puckish man, he years ago erected a memorial bench to himself in Scarborough, also in the north, bearing a plaque reading "Sir Jimmy Savile (but Not Just Yet)."

That eventuality came when the West Yorkshire Police were called to Mr. Savile's home and found his body. The death appeared to be of natural causes.

Mr. Savile was the longest-serving host of "Top of the Pops," broadcast on the BBC from 1964 to 2006 and featuring the chart-topping singles of the week. He was seen regularly from its debut until 1984 and returned for the valedictory episode after it was cancelled.

Artists appearing on the show included the Beatles, the Rolling Stones, Chubby Checker, Barry Manilow, Green Day and thousands of other marquee names.

Early on, the show relied on lip-syncing, though the practice was later abandoned.

A blunt if hyperbolic Yorkshireman, Mr. Savile (the name rhymes with "gravel") was simultaneously revered and ridiculed. On the air he served up patter that in its manic opacity verged on Dada. He also yodeled — often.

To Britons, though, Mr. Savile was ultimately better known for "Jim'll Fix It," a BBC television show broadcast from 1975 to 1994. On the show he granted supplicants (usually children) their dearest wish: to tame lions, to fly the Concorde, etc.

This despite the fact that by his own account, he did not care for children. "I couldn't eat a whole one . . . I hate them," he once said.

Mr. Savile came from a threadbare background but seemed to have transcended his roots, even those on his head. His hair was often a bright cascade of platinum, though as a young man, according to many news items, he once dyed it tartan plaid. No details are available about which clan's tartan he chose.

JIM'LL FIX IT: Jimmy Savile was the colorful host of two celebrated BBC television shows and counted Prince Charles and Diana, Princess of Wales, as friends.

His default outfit was a shiny tracksuit, though at least once, it was reported, he hosted "Top of the Pops" in a banana suit of some kind. Immense sunglasses, often with rose-colored lenses, were a frequent accessory.

Mr. Savile's signature embellishment was a tangle of gold: medallions, chains and rings. His head-to-toe ensemble, including his ever-present cigar, can be bought as a costume, authorized by him and in its way remarkably true to life.

Mr. Savile was also widely known for charity work, and was reported to have raised more than £30 million (about $48 million) for hospitals and other causes. This, apparently, gave Queen Elizabeth II plausible deniability for knighting him in 1990. He also belonged to Mensa and the Knights of Malta.

Throughout his career Mr. Savile was a Zelig — or maybe a Walter Mitty — in gold lamé. Interviews he gave contained a torrent of claims, some true, some false and others occupying the vast limbo of credibility in between. Among them:

• He was the first D.J. to use a double turntable, for continuous play. (Doubtful: Advertisements for such turntables date to at least the early 1930s.)

• He ran more than 200 marathons, the last when he was 78 (true), and was once a professional wrestler (true: won-lost record 7-100).

• He played marriage counselor to Prince Charles and Diana, Princess of Wales, as their relationship waned. (Dubious, though he did count them as coveted acquaintances. In a statement, Prince Charles expressed sorrow at Mr. Savile's death but made no mention of counseling.)

• He spent 11 Christmases as Margaret Thatcher's guest. (Hugely false, her daughter, Carol, told The Daily Mail of London in 2008.)

• He lived with his mother, Agnes, from his father's death in the early 1950s to hers in 1972; for years they occupied his suede-walled flat in Scarborough. After she died he kept her body tenderly in the flat for five days and maintained her bedroom with curatorial rectitude ever after. (All true.)

The youngest of seven children, James Wilson Vincent Savile was born in Leeds on Oct. 31, 1926. His father, Vincent, was a miserably paid bookmaker's clerk. At Christmastime the children's present was a trip to a department store to see the toys.

Jimmy left school at 14 and during World War II was conscripted to work in British coal mines. A few years later he suffered severe spinal injuries in a mine explosion. After a grueling recuperation he began managing dance halls and was later a radio disc jockey.

"Top of the Pops" was first broadcast on Jan. 1, 1964; that episode, which included four sleek-haired Liverpool lads singing "I Want to Hold Your Hand," was presented by Mr. Savile and the D.J. Alan Freeman.

Mr. Freeman was one of a rotating cast of co-hosts and guest hosts that over time included Davy Jones of the Monkees and Elton John. This arrangement, Mr. Savile often said, was to avoid overexposing himself.

Mr. Savile never married, though in talking of women he often described himself as a Lothario who could never be trapped into staying all night. "Good heavens," he said in a 2000 BBC television profile, "anything more than two hours — brain damage!"

> The host of "Top of the Pops," Mr. Savile had transcended his threadbare roots, even those on his head.

Information on survivors was unavailable.

The day before his funeral in Leeds, Mr. Savile lay in repose in his favorite local hotel inside a gold-lacquered metal coffin next to a table holding two unfinished cigars. The coffin, on view to mourners trooping by, was raised on a platform in the bar "in the manner of a dead monarch lying in state," as The Daily Mail of London put it.

He was reported to have been dressed in a tracksuit, but that could not be confirmed.

The coffin, alas, was closed.

— BY MARGALIT FOX

DOROTHY RODHAM

What She Never Had, She Gave Her Daughter

JUNE 4, 1919 · NOV. 1, 2011

Dorothy Rodham, who overcame years of struggle to become a powerful influence on the life and career of her daughter, Hillary Rodham Clinton, the former first lady who became a senator from New York, a presidential candidate and the secretary of state, died on Nov. 1 in Washington. She was 92.

Mrs. Clinton had canceled a trip to London and Istanbul to be at her mother's side.

As her daughter rose to prominence, Mrs. Rodham stayed mostly in the background, appearing only occasionally in public and rarely giving interviews. But Mrs. Clinton credited her mother with giving her a love of the higher learning that Mrs. Rodham never had, a curiosity about a larger world that Mrs. Rodham had not seen, and a will to persevere — about which Mrs. Rodham knew a great deal.

Her childhood had been Dickensian. She was abandoned by dysfunctional, divorced parents at the age of 8 in Chicago, sent unsupervised on a cross-country train with a younger sister to live with unwelcoming grandparents in California and, at 14, escaped into the adult world of the Depression as a $3-a-week nanny.

On her own, she attended high school and became a good student, though her job left little time for other activities. Her employers were kind to her, however, and she had two influential teachers. College proved to be out of the question, but she got a job as a secretary in Chicago, and after years of lonely toil she married a gruff traveling salesman and settled into a life of cooking, cleaning and raising three children.

In her autobiography, "Living History" (2003), Mrs. Clinton recalled her mother's hardships: "I thought often of my own mother's neglect and mistreatment at the hands of her parents and grandparents, and how other caring adults filled the emotional void to help her."

Mrs. Clinton portrayed her mother as a caring beacon of strength in the family, offering intellectual stimulation and teaching her children to be calm and resolute. "I'm still amazed at how my mother emerged from her lonely early life as such an affectionate and levelheaded woman," she wrote.

Dorothy Emma Howell was born on June 4, 1919, in Chicago, the oldest of two children of Edwin John Howell Jr., a firefighter, and the former Della Murray. Her sister, Isabelle, was born in 1924. They lived as boarders in a house with four other families. The parents fought often and sometimes violently, according to Cook County records of the time.

Mr. Howell sued for divorce, accusing his wife of abandonment and abuse of the children. She did not show up in court; her sister, Frances Czeslawski, testified against her, and Mr. Howell was granted the divorce and custody of the children in 1927. But unwilling or unable to care for them, he put them on a train to Alhambra, Calif., where his parents, Edwin Sr. and Emma, lived.

The grandparents were ill-prepared to raise the girls. Mr. Howell, a laborer for the city, left the task to his wife, whom Mrs. Rodham recalled as a strict woman in black dresses who discouraged visitors and parties and berated and punished them for small infractions. When she discovered that Dorothy had gone trick-or-treating one Halloween, she ordered her confined to her room for a year, except to go to school.

In 1934 Dorothy moved out and became a housekeeper, cook and nanny for a family in San Gabriel. Her employers gave her a room, board and $3 a week and encouraged her to read and go to school. Dorothy enrolled at Alhambra High School, where she joined the Scholarship Club and the Spanish Club.

Years later, Mrs. Rodham recalled two teachers: Miss Drake, who taught speech and drama, and Miss Zellhoefer, who taught her to write. "She taught English and was very strict," Mrs. Rodham wrote in a book marking the school's centennial in 1998. "We came from her

A POWERFUL INFLUENCE: Hillary Rodham Clinton, right, with Dorothy Rodham, center, and Chelsea Clinton. Mrs. Clinton credited much of her success to her mother.

class with respect for her and a solid ground in English. What made her special was her desire that we develop critical thinking."

After graduating in 1937, Dorothy returned to Chicago at the request of her mother, Della, who had remarried. The girl was told that her mother's new husband had offered to help pay her college expenses, and Dorothy hoped to enroll at Northwestern University. But when she got to Chicago, she discovered that the offer had evaporated, and that her mother actually wanted her to work as her housekeeper.

"I'd hoped so hard that my mother would love me that I had to take the chance and find out," Mrs. Rodham said long after that wrenching, sentimental journey. "When she didn't, I had nowhere else to go."

She found secretarial work in Chicago. In 1942 she married Hugh Ellsworth Rodham, eight years her senior, who became the owner of a small drapery-fabric business. They moved to suburban Park Ridge, where their children — Hillary, Hugh and Tony — were born and reared. They survive her, as do four grandchildren.

Mrs. Rodham pushed her children to stand up for themselves, Mrs. Clinton said. Once, when she was 4, she went home in tears after a neighborhood girl had bullied her. "You have to face things and show them you're not afraid," her mother told her. If she was hit again, Mrs. Rodham advised, "hit her back."

"She later told me she watched from behind the curtain as I squared my shoulders and marched across the street," Mrs. Clinton wrote. "I returned a few minutes later, glowing with victory."

As a freshman at Wellesley College in Massachusetts, Hillary called home to express doubts about her ability to stay on and compete. "You can't quit," Mrs. Clinton quoted her mother as telling her. "You've got to see through what you've started."

Mr. and Mrs. Rodham moved to Little Rock, Ark., in 1987, to be near Mrs. Clinton, whose husband, Bill, was then governor of Arkansas, and their granddaughter Chelsea. Mrs. Rodham took college courses in psychology and other subjects. She kept her home in Little Rock after Mr. Clinton became president. Mr. Rodham died in 1993.

In 1996, at the Democratic National Convention in Chicago, Mrs. Rodham was featured in a film shown before Mr. Clinton made his acceptance speech as he began his bid for re-election. "Everybody knows," she said, "there is only one person in the world who can really tell the truth about a man, and that's his mother-in-law."

Mrs. Rodham, who had done little traveling abroad, accompanied Chelsea on a trip to Jodhpur, India, in 2000. After Mrs. Clinton joined the Senate in 2001, Mrs. Rodham spent time at her Washington home. The Clintons bought her a condominium near their home in Chappaqua, N.Y., in 2003. After 2006, she lived mostly at Mrs. Clinton's home in Washington.

She was in the Senate gallery when Mrs. Clinton took the oath for her second term in January 2007, and appeared in Iowa and New Hampshire early in Mrs. Clinton's 2008 campaign for the Democratic presidential nomination. And when she quit the race in June 2008, Mrs. Clinton stood with her mother and her daughter at the National Building Museum in Washington, their hands raised together in a memorable three-generation tableau.

— BY ROBERT D. MCFADDEN

ANDY ROONEY

America's Front-Porch Philosopher

JAN. 14, 1919 · NOV. 4, 2011

ANDY ROONEY, whose prickly wit was long a mainstay of CBS News and whose homespun commentary on "60 Minutes," delivered every week from 1978 until 2011, made him a household name, died on Nov. 4 in New York City.

He was 92 and lived in Manhattan, though he kept a family vacation home

in Rensselaerville, N.Y., and the first home he ever bought, in Rowayton, Conn. CBS News said in a statement that Mr. Rooney died after complications following minor surgery.

In late September, CBS announced that Mr. Rooney would be making his last regular weekly appearance on "60 Minutes" on Oct. 2. After that, said Jeff Fager, the chairman of CBS News and the program's executive producer, he would "always have the ability to speak his mind on '60 Minutes' when the urge hits him."

But a little more than three weeks after that appearance, CBS announced that Mr. Rooney had been hospitalized after developing "serious complications" from an unspecified operation.

Mr. Rooney entered television shortly after World War II, writing material for entertainers like Arthur Godfrey, Victor Borge, Herb Shriner, Sam Levenson and Garry Moore. Beginning in 1962, he had a six-year association with the CBS News correspondent Harry Reasoner, who narrated a series of Everyman "essays" written by Mr. Rooney.

But it was "A Few Minutes With Andy Rooney," his weekly segment on "60 Minutes," that made him one of the most popular broadcast figures in the country. With his jowls, bushy eyebrows, deeply circled eyes and advancing years, he seemed every inch the front-porch philosopher as he addressed mostly mundane subjects with varying degrees of befuddlement, vexation and sometimes pleasure.

He admitted to loving football, Christmas, tennis, woodworking and Dwight D. Eisenhower, one of the few politicians who won his approval because, as an Army general during World War II, he had refused to censor Stars and Stripes, the G.I. newspaper for which Mr. Rooney worked. He also claimed to like shined shoes and properly pressed pants and had machines in his office to take care of those functions, although somehow he always managed to look rumpled.

But he was better known for the things he did not like. He railed against "two-prong plugs in a three-prong society," the incomprehensibility of road maps, wash-and-wear shirts "that you can wash but not wear," the uselessness of keys and locks, and outsize cereal boxes that contained very little cereal.

"I don't like any music I can't hum," he grumbled.

He observed that "there are more beauty parlors than there are beauties" and that "if dogs could talk, it would take a lot of the fun out of owning one."

He made clear that he thought Gen. George S. Patton and Ernest Hemingway, both of whom he had known personally, were gasbags. He disliked New Year's Eve, waiting in line for any reason and the bursars at whatever colleges his children attended.

He once concluded that "it is possible to be dumb and be a college president," but he acknowledged that "most college students are not as smart as most college presidents."

On the subject of higher education, he declared that most college catalogs "rank among the great works of fiction of all time," and that a student of lackluster intellect who could raise tuition money would find it "almost impossible to flunk out."

Time magazine once called him "the most felicitous nonfiction writer in television." But Mr. Rooney was decidedly not everyone's cup of tea.

The New York Times columnist Anna Quindlen, for example, took strong issue with Mr. Rooney's dismissive comments after Kurt Cobain of the band Nirvana committed suicide in 1994. It was not surprising, she wrote, that Mr. Rooney "brought to the issue of youthful despair a mixture of sarcasm and contempt," but it was "worth noting because in 1994 that sort of attitude is as dated and foolish as believing that cancer is contagious."

Mr. Rooney's opinions sometimes landed him in trouble. In 1990, CBS News suspended him without pay in response to complaints that he had made remarks offensive to black and gay people.

The trigger was a December 1989 special, "A Year With Andy Rooney," in which he said: "There was some recognition in 1989 of the fact that many of the ills which kill us are self-induced. Too much alcohol, too much food, drugs, homosexual unions, cigarettes. They're all known to lead quite often to premature death." He later apologized for the statement.

But the gay newspaper The Advocate subsequently quoted him as saying in an interview: "I've believed all along that most people are born with equal intelligence, but blacks have watered down their genes because the less intelligent ones are the ones that have the most children. They drop out of school early, do drugs and get pregnant."

Mr. Rooney denied that he had made such a statement, and because the interview had apparently not been taped, the reporter was unable to prove that he had. "It is a know-nothing statement, which I abhor," Mr. Rooney said.

Still, he was suspended for three months, though brought back after only one. He said he had accepted the suspension rather than end his relationship with CBS News. And he insisted that he was not a prejudiced man. When he was an Army trainee, he said, he had been arrested in the South because he insisted on riding in the back of a bus with some black soldiers who were friends of his.

Many of his colleagues stepped forward to defend him. "I know he is not a racist," Walter Cronkite said.

During Mr. Rooney's monthlong absence, the ratings for "60 Minutes" declined by 20 percent, and the network received thousands of letters and telephone calls from viewers who missed his commentaries.

Mr. Rooney aroused more criticism in 2002, when he said in an interview on a cable sports

SPEAKING HIS MIND: Andy Rooney in his New York office, 1978. He appeared weekly on "60 Minutes" from 1978 to 2011, with the exception of a few suspensions.

show that women had "no business" being sideline television reporters at football games because they did not understand football.

He did it again in 2007, with a newspaper column complaining about the current state of baseball. "I know all about Babe Ruth and Lou Gehrig, but today's baseball stars are all guys named Rodriguez to me," he wrote.

He subsequently acknowledged that he "probably shouldn't have said it," but denied that his intent had been to denigrate Latin American players.

Andrew Aitken Rooney was born on Jan. 14, 1919, in Albany, the son of Walter and Ellinor Rooney. His father was in the paper business. After his graduation from Albany Academy, he worked as a copy boy for The Knickerbocker News before attending Colgate University in Hamilton, N.Y., where he played left guard on the football team (even though he was only 5-foot-9 and 185 pounds) and worked for the weekly newspaper, The Colgate Maroon.

In 1941, three months before Pearl Harbor, he was drafted into the Army and used his powers of persuasion to get himself assigned to Stars and Stripes. He did not know much about reporting, but he learned his craft by working with journalists like Homer Bigart, Ernie Pyle and Mr. Cronkite.

He became a sergeant, flew on some bombing missions, covered the invasion of France in 1944 and won a Bronze Star for reporting under fire during the battle of Saint-Lô in Normandy. A year later, he was among the first Americans to enter the concentration camps at Buchenwald and Thekla, Germany.

In collaboration with Bud Hutton, a Stars and Stripes colleague, Mr. Rooney wrote two books: "Air Gunner" (1944), a collection of sketches of Americans who had been stationed in Britain, and "The Story of the Stars and Stripes" (1946).

On "60 Minutes,"
Mr. Rooney railed
against "two-prong plugs
in a three-prong society,"
road maps, wash-and-wear
shirts and cereal boxes that
contained little cereal.

After his discharge, Mr. Rooney returned to Albany and worked as a freelance writer.

By 1949, he had persuaded Mr. Godfrey to hire him as a writer. He continued writing for several entertainers, but also became involved in news and public affairs when he was asked to write scripts for "The Twentieth Century," a documentary series narrated by Mr. Cronkite. That led to his long-term association with Mr. Reasoner, which led to his involvement with "60 Minutes," initially as a writer.

In the early 1970s, after briefly working for PBS, Mr. Rooney returned to CBS and began appearing on camera in a series of specials, one of which, "Mr. Rooney Goes to Washington," won a Peabody Award.

Mr. Rooney was as outspoken about CBS, his longtime employer, as he was about everything else. He made no secret of his dislike for Laurence A. Tisch, the network's chief executive from 1986 to 1995. Protesting Mr. Tisch's cost efficiencies and job cuts in 1987, Mr. Rooney said CBS News had been "turned into primarily a business enterprise, and the moral enterprise has been lost." He threatened to quit if a writers strike against CBS News was not settled.

Although his commentary was mostly written for CBS News, he also had a syndicated newspaper column for more than 30 years, beginning in 1979. In 2003 he was given a lifetime achievement award by the National Society of Newspaper Columnists. (That same year he received a similar award from the Academy of Television Arts and Sciences.) He published a number of books, primarily collections of his commentaries, most recently "Out of My Mind" (2006), "And More by Andy Rooney" (2008) and "Andy Rooney: 60 Years of Wisdom and Wit" (2010).

His wife of 62 years, Marguerite Howard, died in 2004. Mr. Rooney is survived by their three daughters and son, five grandchildren, and two great-grandchildren.

Mr. Rooney said he considered himself "one of the least important producers on television" because his specialty was light pieces. "I just wish insignificance had more stature," he said.

But he put things in perspective in his last regularly scheduled "60 Minutes" appearance — his 1,097th.

"I've done a lot of complaining here," he said before signing off, "but of all the things I've complained about, I can't complain about my life."

— BY RICHARD SEVERO AND PETER KEEPNEWS

JOE FRAZIER

An Everlasting Link to His Rival, Ali

JAN. 12, 1944 · NOV. 7, 2011

J OE FRAZIER, the former heavyweight champion whose furious and intensely personal fights with a taunting Muhammad Ali endure as an epic rivalry in boxing history, died on Nov. 7 at his home in Philadelphia. He was 67.

His death, on a Monday night, came after a spokesman announced over the weekend that Frazier had liver cancer — a diagnosis he received four or five weeks earlier — and that he had been moved to hospice care. The news prompted an outpouring of tributes and messages of support.

Known as Smokin' Joe, Frazier stalked his opponents around the ring with a crouching, relentless attack — his head low and bobbing, his broad, powerful shoulders hunched — as he bore down on them with an onslaught of withering jabs and crushing body blows, setting them up for his devastating left hook.

It was an overpowering modus operandi that brought him versions of the heavyweight crown from 1968 to 1973. Frazier won 32 fights in all, 27 by knockouts, losing four times, twice to Ali in furious bouts and twice to George Foreman. He also recorded one draw.

A slugger who weathered repeated blows to the head while he delivered punishment, Frazier proved a formidable figure. But his career was defined by his rivalry with Ali, who ridiculed him as a black man in the guise of a Great White Hope. Frazier detested him.

Ali vs. Frazier was a study in contrasts. Ali: tall and handsome, a wit given to spouting poetry, a magnetic figure who drew adulation and denigration alike, the one for his prowess and outsize personality, the other for his anti-war views and Black Power embrace of Islam. Frazier: a bull-like man of few words with a blue-collar image and a glowering visage who in so many ways could be on an equal footing with his rival only in the ring.

Ali proclaimed, "I am the greatest" and he preened how he could "float like a butterfly, sting like a bee." Frazier had no inclination for oratorical bravado. "Work is the only meanin' I've ever known," he told Playboy in 1973. "Like the man in the song says, I just gotta keep on keepin' on."

Frazier won the undisputed heavyweight title with a 15-round decision over Ali at Madison Square Garden in March 1971, in an extravaganza known as the Fight of the Century. Ali scored a 12-round decision over Frazier at the Garden in a nontitle bout in January 1974. Then came the Thrilla in Manila championship bout, in October 1975, regarded as one of the greatest fights in boxing history. It ended when a battered Frazier, one eye swollen shut, did not come out to face Ali for the 15th round.

The Ali-Frazier battles played out at a time when the heavyweight boxing champion was far more celebrated than he is today, a figure who could stand alone in the spotlight a decade before an alphabet soup of boxing sanctioning bodies arose, making it difficult for the average fan to figure out just who held what title.

The rivalry was also given a political and social cast. Many viewed the Ali-Frazier matches as a snapshot of the struggles of the 1960s. Ali, an adherent of the Nation of Islam who had changed his name from Cassius Clay, came to represent rising black anger in America and opposition to the Vietnam War. Frazier voiced no political views, but he was nonetheless depicted, to his consternation, as the favorite of the establishment. Ali called him ignorant, likened him to a gorilla and said his black supporters were Uncle Toms.

SHOWDOWN: Joe Frazier, left, taking on Muhammad Ali, right, during their heavyweight fight in Madison Square Garden on March 8, 1971. Frazier would win the so-called Fight of the Century with a 15-round decision.

"Frazier had become the white man's fighter, Mr. Charley was rooting for Frazier, and that meant blacks were boycotting him in their heart," Norman Mailer wrote in Life magazine after the first Ali-Frazier bout.

Frazier, wrote Mailer, was "twice as black as Clay and half as handsome," with "the rugged decent life-worked face of a man who had labored in the pits all his life."

Frazier could never match Ali's charisma or his gift for the provocative quote. He was essentially a man devoted to a brutal craft, willing to give countless hours to his spartan training-camp routine and unsparing of his body inside the ring.

"The way I fight, it's not me beatin' the man: I make the man whip himself," Frazier told Playboy. "Because I stay close to him. He can't get out the way." He added: "Before he knows

it — whew! — he's tired. And he can't pick up his second wind because I'm right back on him again."

In his autobiography, "Smokin' Joe," written with Phil Berger, Frazier said his first trainer, Yank Durham, had given him his nickname. It was, he said, "a name that had come from what Yank used to say in the dressing room before sending me out to fight: 'Go out there, goddammit, and make smoke come from those gloves.'"

Foreman knocked out Frazier twice but said he had never lost his respect for him. "Joe Frazier would come out smoking," Foreman told ESPN. "If you hit him, he liked it. If you knocked him down, you only made him mad."

Durham said he saw a fire always smoldering in Frazier. "I've had plenty of other boxers with more raw talent," he told The New York Times Magazine in 1970, "but none with more dedication and strength."

Ali himself was conciliatory when Frazier's battle with cancer became publicly known. "My family and I are keeping Joe and his family in our daily prayers," Ali said in a statement. "Joe has a lot of friends pulling for him, and I'm one of them."

And when word reached him that Frazier had died, Ali, in another statement, said: "The world has lost a great champion. I will always remember Joe with respect and admiration."

A Son of Field Hands

Billy Joe Frazier was born on Jan. 12, 1944, in Laurel Bay, S.C., the youngest of 12 children. His father, Rubin, and his mother, Dolly, worked in the fields, and the youngster known as Billy Boy dropped out of school at 13. He dreamed of becoming a boxing champion, throwing his first punches at burlap sacks he stuffed with moss and leaves, pretending to be Joe Louis or Ezzard Charles or Archie Moore.

At 15, Frazier went to New York to live with a brother. A year later he moved to Philadelphia, taking a job in a slaughterhouse. At times he battered sides of beef, using them as a punching bag to work out, the kind of scene used by Sylvester Stallone in the film "Rocky." (Stallone said he drew on the life of the heavyweight contender Chuck Wepner in developing the Rocky Balboa character.)

Durham discovered Frazier boxing to lose weight at a Police Athletic League gym in Philadelphia. Under Durham's guidance, Frazier captured a Golden Gloves championship and won the heavyweight gold medal at the 1964 Tokyo Olympics.

He turned pro in August 1965, with financial backing from businessmen calling themselves the Cloverlay Group (from cloverleaf, for good luck, and overlay, a betting term signifying good odds). He won his first 11 bouts by knockouts. By winter 1968, his record was 21-0.

A year before Frazier's pro debut, Cassius Clay won the heavyweight championship in a huge upset of Sonny Liston. Soon afterward,

affirming his rumored membership in the Nation of Islam, he became Muhammad Ali. In April 1967, having proclaimed, "I ain't got nothing against them Vietcong," Ali refused to be drafted, claiming conscientious objector status. Boxing commissions stripped him of his title, and he was convicted of evading the draft.

An eight-man elimination tournament was held to determine a World Boxing Association champion to replace Ali. Frazier refused to participate when his financial backers objected to the contract terms for the tournament, and Jimmy Ellis took the crown.

"Frazier would come out smoking," George Foreman said. "If you hit him, he liked it."

But in March 1968, Frazier won the version of the heavyweight title recognized by New York and a few other states, defeating Buster Mathis with an 11th-round technical knockout. He took the W.B.A. title in February 1970, stopping Ellis, who did not come out for the fifth round.

In the summer of 1970, Ali won a court battle to regain his boxing license, then knocked out the contenders Jerry Quarry and Oscar Bonavena. The stage was set for an Ali-Frazier showdown, a matchup of unbeaten fighters, on March 8, 1971, at Madison Square Garden.

Each man was guaranteed $2.5 million, the biggest boxing payday ever. Frank Sinatra was at ringside taking photos for Life magazine. The former heavyweight champion Joe Louis received a huge ovation. Hubert H. Humphrey, back in the Senate after serving as vice president, sat two rows in front of the Irish political activist Bernadette Devlin, who shouted, "Ali, Ali," her left fist held high. An estimated 300 million watched on television worldwide, and the gate of $1.35 million set a record for an indoor bout.

Frazier, at 5 feet 11½ inches and 205 pounds, gave up three inches in height and nearly seven inches in reach to Ali, but he was a 6-to-5 betting favorite. Just before the fighters received their instructions from the referee, Ali, displaying his arrogance of old, twice touched Frazier's shoulders as he whirled around the ring. Frazier just glared at him.

Frazier wore Ali down with blows to the body while moving underneath Ali's jabs. In the 15th round, Frazier unleashed his famed left hook, catching Ali on the jaw and flooring him for a count of 4. It was only the third time Ali had been knocked down. Ali held on, but Frazier won a unanimous decision.

Frazier declared, "I always knew who the champ was."

Frazier continued to bristle over Ali's taunting. "I've seen pictures of him in cars with white guys, huggin' 'em and havin' fun," Frazier told Sport magazine two months after the fight. "Then he go call me an Uncle Tom. Don't say, 'I hate the white man,' then go to the white man for help."

For Frazier, 1971 was truly triumphant. He bought a 368-acre estate called Brewton Plantation near his boyhood home and became the first black man since Reconstruction to address the South Carolina Legislature. Ali gained vindication in June 1971 when the United States Supreme Court overturned his conviction for draft evasion.

Frazier defended his title against two journeymen, Terry Daniels and Ron Stander, but Foreman took his championship away on Jan. 22, 1973, knocking him down six times in their bout in Kingston, Jamaica, before the referee stopped the fight in the second round.

'THRILLA IN MANILA'

Frazier met Ali again in a nontitle bout at the Garden on Jan. 28, 1974. Frazier kept boring in and complained that Ali was holding in the clinches, but Ali scored with flurries of punches and won a unanimous 12-round decision.

Ali won back the heavyweight title in October 1974, knocking out Foreman in Kinshasa, Zaire — the celebrated Rumble in the Jungle. Frazier went on to knock out Quarry and Ellis, setting up his third match, and second title fight, with Ali: the Thrilla in Manila, on Oct. 1, 1975.

In what became the most brutal Ali-Frazier battle, the fight was held at the Philippine Coliseum at Quezon City, outside the country's capital, Manila. The conditions were sweltering; hot lights overpowered the air-conditioning.

Ali, almost a 2-to-1 betting favorite in the United States, won the early rounds, largely remaining flat-footed in place of his familiar dancing style. Before Round 3 he blew kisses to President Ferdinand Marcos and his wife, Imelda, in the crowd of about 25,000.

But in the fourth round, Ali's pace slowed while Frazier began to gain momentum. Chants of "Frazier! Frazier!" filled the arena by the fifth round, and the crowd seemed to favor him as the fight moved along, a contrast to Ali's usually enjoying the fans' plaudits.

Frazier took command in the middle rounds. Then Ali came back on weary legs, unleashing a flurry of punches to Frazier's face in the 12th round. He knocked out Frazier's mouthpiece in the 13th round, then sent him stumbling backward with a straight right hand.

Ali jolted Frazier with left-right combinations late in the 14th round. Frazier had already lost most of the vision in his left eye from a cataract, and his right eye was puffed and shut from Ali's blows.

Eddie Futch, a renowned trainer working Frazier's corner, asked the referee to end the

SMOKIN' JOE: During his boxing career, Joe Frazier won 32 fights and an Olympic gold medal. He announced his retirement in 1976.

bout. When it was stopped, Ali was ahead on the scorecards of the referee and two judges. "It's the closest I've come to death," Ali said.

Frazier returned to the ring nine months later, in June 1976, to face Foreman at Nassau Coliseum on Long Island. Foreman stopped him on a technical knockout in the fifth round. Frazier then announced his retirement. He was 32.

He later managed his eldest son, Marvis, a heavyweight. In December 1981 he returned to the ring to fight a journeyman named Jumbo Cummings, fought to a draw, then retired for good, tending to investments from his home in Philadelphia.

Both Frazier and Ali had daughters who took up boxing, and in June 2001 it was Ali-Frazier IV when Frazier's daughter Jacqui Frazier-Lyde fought Ali's daughter Laila Ali at a casino in Vernon, N.Y. Like their fathers in their first fight, both were unbeaten. Laila Ali won on a decision. Joe Frazier was in the crowd of 6,500, but Muhammad Ali, impaired by Parkinson's syndrome, was not.

In addition to his son Marvis and his daughter Jacqui, Frazier is survived by five other sons, four other daughters and a sister. He and his wife, Florence, had divorced.

Long after his fighting days were over, Frazier retained his enmity for Ali. But in March 2001, the 30th anniversary of the first Ali-Frazier bout, Ali told The New York Times: "I said a lot of things in the heat of the moment that I shouldn't have said. Called him names I shouldn't have called him. I apologize for that. I'm sorry. It was all meant to promote the fight."

Asked for a response, Frazier said: "We have to embrace each other. It's time to talk and get together. Life's too short."

Fascination with the Ali-Frazier saga has endured.

After a 2008 presidential debate between Barack Obama and John McCain, the Republican media consultant Stuart Stevens said that McCain should concentrate on selling himself to America rather than criticizing Obama. Stevens's prescription: "More Ali and less Joe Frazier."

Frazier's true feelings toward Ali in his final years seemed murky.

The 2009 British documentary "Thrilla in Manila," shown in the United States on HBO, depicted Frazier watching a film of the fight from his apartment above the gym he ran in Philadelphia.

"He's a good-time guy," John Dower, the director of "Thrilla in Manila," told The Times. "But he's angry about Ali."

In March 2011, however, on the eve of the 40th anniversary of the first Ali-Frazier fight, Frazier said he was willing to put the enmity behind him.

"I forgave him for all the accusations he made over the years," The Daily News quoted Frazier as saying. "I hope he's doing fine. I'd love to see him."

Frazier once told The Times: "Ali always said I would be nothing without him. But who would he have been without me?"

— By Richard Goldstein

JAMIE PIERRE

Daring Young Man on His Flying Skis

FEB. 22, 1973 · NOV. 13, 2011

N 2006, JAMIE PIERRE skied off a 255-foot cliff in the backcountry of Grand Targhee, Wyo., plummeting nearly headfirst and without a helmet for more than four seconds. He struck the deep powder at the base of the cliff with such force that friends had to dig him out.

The jump was intentional. Pierre was a professional big-mountain skier, and his monumental leap in the Teton Mountains was considered to have set the world height record for a cliff jump on skis. Except for a bloody lip, he emerged unscathed that day, as he had often done in his career as an extreme skier.

On Nov. 13, Pierre was on a more routine snowboard trip at Snowbird Resort in the Wasatch Range of Utah when an avalanche carried him about 800 feet over rocky terrain and a small cliff. He came to a stop partly buried and died of trauma, a representative of the Utah Avalanche Center said. Pierre was 38 and lived in Big Sky, Mont.

Pierre and a friend — Jack Pilot, according to the ski photographer Pete O'Brien — had hiked out to ride an area of Snowbird called the South Chute when the avalanche occurred. The avalanche center said the area was off-limits at the time; the resort had not yet opened for the season and avalanche-control measures had not yet been taken. Pilot, who was at a higher

THRILL SEEKER: Jamie Pierre's adventurous pursuits on the slopes made him a famous extreme skier.

elevation, called for a rescue after watching the avalanche sweep Pierre away.

Pierre was a free skier known for his daring, tackling dizzying drops in dangerous terrain. Surviving plunges of more than 100 feet requires technical prowess, near-perfect snow and weather conditions and careful planning.

In 2003, Pierre was the first to leap off a 165-foot cliff at Wolverine Cirque near Alta, Utah. The next year, he landed on his back in shallow snow amid rocks after skiing off a 185-foot cliff in Switzerland. In 2005, he launched himself off an eight-foot-tall snow ramp and sailed over an Oregon highway, soaring more than 40 feet into the air and traveling about 110. The Norwegian skier Fred Syversen eclipsed Pierre's cliff-jump record with a drop of more than 350 feet.

In a profile of Pierre in Skiing magazine, the renowned extreme skier Scot Schmidt likened Pierre to "a test dummy."

"I've seen a lot of crazy stuff over the years, but he goes beyond that," Schmidt said. "You just can't anticipate when the wind might grab your skis and flip you upside down. There's no room for error."

Pierre was frequently photographed for ski magazines like Powder and Freeze and appeared in some of Warren Miller's acclaimed ski films, among them "Cold Fusion" (2001) and "Children of Winter" (2008).

In another Miller film, "Off the Grid" (2006), Pierre spoke of slowing down in his 30s.

"Well, you know, now I can retire," he said, over footage of his record-breaking jump. "I just wanted to hold the record for it, even if it's only for one day."

Matthew Jamison Pierre was born in Minnesota on February 22, 1973, according to O'Brien, a longtime friend. He grew up in Minnetonka, Minn., with seven siblings and started skiing at Buck Hill in Burnsville in the early 1980s. He moved to Utah in the early 1990s and worked odd jobs there while developing his skiing skills.

He is survived by his wife, Amee, as well as a daughter, a son, his parents, five brothers and two sisters.

Pierre had many concussions over the years but refused to wear a helmet.

"If something's so dangerous it requires a helmet," he said, "then maybe I shouldn't be doing it."

— BY DANIEL E. SLOTNIK

RENÉ MOREL

Restoring Violins to Pitch-Perfect Health

MARCH 11, 1932 - NOV. 16, 2011

RENÉ A. MOREL, a world-renowned surgeon whose clients had names like Perlman, Zukerman and Ma and whose patients had names like Stradivari, Guarneri and Amati, died on Nov. 16 in Wayne, N.J. He was 79.

For decades, Mr. Morel reigned as one of the world's master luthiers. The word,

pronounced loo-TYEY, is from the Old French for "lute-maker." It now denotes a maker or restorer of stringed instruments in general and of bowed string instruments in particular.

Mr. Morel, who specialized in restoration, was among the finest violin restorers, perhaps the very finest, of his day, a calling that requires the skills of a diagnostician, acoustician and microsurgeon in equal measure.

At his death, he presided over René A. Morel Adjustments, on West 54th Street in Manhattan, whose very name testifies to the precise, incremental nature of his art. There, at his previous shops and in hotel rooms and concert halls around the world, he was consulted, often in panic, by some of the brightest luminaries ever to hold a bow.

Among them were the violinists Isaac Stern, Itzhak Perlman and Pinchas Zukerman and the cellists Pablo Casals, Yo-Yo Ma and Bernard Greenhouse. (Mr. Morel's two-year restoration of Mr. Greenhouse's 1707 Stradivarius is the subject of a 2001 book, "The Countess of Stanlein Restored," by Nicholas Delbanco, Mr. Greenhouse's son-in-law.)

"Basically, he was 'my guy' as far as adjusting the violin went," Mr. Perlman said in a telephone interview. He had entrusted his instruments, a Stradivarius and a Guarnerius, to Mr. Morel's ministrations for decades.

Violins, and their siblings, violas and cellos, are temperamental creatures. With tops of spruce and backs and sides of harder wood — often maple — they are fundamentally trees, reconfigured in strange and glorious ways that nature never intended.

For these instruments, every bump and jostle, every change in temperature or humidity, is occasion for protest. Wood shrinks and swells and strains against itself. Cracks can appear. Their sonorous voices can be reduced to growls and grumbles.

Enter Mr. Morel.

"René was really committed to the instrument as a musician's tool," said Sam Zygmuntowicz, a prominent New York violinmaker who trained under Mr. Morel. "He was not trying to stabilize something to sit in a museum: he was trying to make something that could really be taken on the road and put through its paces in the most demanding of settings."

René Alfred Morel was born in Mattaincourt, in northeast France, on March 11, 1932. His father was a violinmaker, as was his maternal grandfather. At 12, René began his training nearby in Mirecourt, a renowned French violinmaking center.

Dexterous, technically minded and a keen pilot, he also built an airplane as a youth. It

MASTER LUTHIER: René Morel was one the world's most renowned restorers of stringed instruments.

was by all accounts a luthier's airplane, made principally of wood. Whether it was actually flyable is unknown.

After serving in the French Air Force as a young man, Mr. Morel moved to the United States. In 1955, he joined the Rembert Wurlitzer Company, a distinguished New York violin dealer. He later spent 30 years as a partner in Jacques Français Rare Violins in Manhattan.

To legions of musicians, Mr. Morel, attired unvaryingly for work in a blue smock, was a comforting constant. For some, like Mr. Greenhouse, he did major surgery, which could entail an instrument's lying in pieces on the workbench for months or more.

But his work also encompassed far less invasive, though no less crucial, adjustments. These involved the ear as much as the hand and, as Mr. Perlman described the process, typically went like this:

A player would enter the shop, instrument in hand. Mr. Morel would ask how it was sounding, and the player demonstrated.

"Aha! Very interesting," Mr. Morel would say. Then, with a slender tool, he might reach inside the instrument and, almost imperceptibly, move one of its vital internal organs, the soundpost, the wooden dowel that fits between the top and the back and transmits vibrations from one to the other.

The player played some more, and the process was repeated until the sound was sublime. Mr. Morel, a nonplayer himself, had a failsafe way of knowing precisely when that was.

"He would put up his sleeve and say, 'You see the goose bumps,'" Mr. Perlman recalled.

"He said as long as he didn't get the goose bumps, it was not properly adjusted."

Mr. Morel died of cancer, according to Tarisio Fine Instruments and Bows, the New York auction house at which he maintained his shop. He lived in Rutherford, N.J., and was divorced. He is survived by Christa Nagy, his companion, as well as three children, a brother, a sister and grandchildren.

He is also survived by a generation of string players, now at loose ends.

"I was talking to my wife today, and I said, 'What am I going to do now?'" Mr. Perlman said. "I'm going to have to find somebody that can produce goose bumps."

— BY MARGALIT FOX

BASIL D'OLIVEIRA

An Athlete's Toughest Opponent Was Racism

OCT. 4, 1931 [Unconfirmed] · NOV. 19, 2011

JUST AS JESSE OWENS AND JACKIE ROBINSON pursued their athletic dreams and developed superlative skills before altering history, Basil D'Oliveira, who was classified as colored under South African apartheid, wanted only to play at the highest levels of his sport, cricket. His struggle to do that in a

country of government-enforced racial segregation became a powerful symbol in the ultimately successful fight against apartheid.

D'Oliveira had to move far from South Africa before his experience could shine a light on its system of racial injustice. Unable to perform there in competition commensurate with his skills, he moved to England, became a British citizen and joined England's national cricket team. He rose to international prominence in 1968, when South Africa canceled a much-anticipated visit by the English team because England wanted to include him in the contests, against whites.

Because of its refusal, South Africa, long a cricket power, did not play another international cricket match until 1991. Nelson Mandela called the D'Oliveira episode decisive in the antiapartheid movement's eventual triumph.

D'Oliveira, who had Parkinson's disease, died on Nov. 19 in England. He was believed to be 80, but the governing organization Cricket South Africa said he may have been as many as three or four years older, allowing that he may have lied about his age in his playing days.

D'Oliveira was an accomplished player for England, participating in 44 major international competitions, or test matches. A powerful, focused batsman, he scored 19,490 runs in the top English cricket league and 1,859 in test matches. The numbers are considered impressive, but experts reckon that he could have doubled them had he immigrated to England sooner.

Paul Yule, who made a 2006 documentary about the D'Oliveira episode, "Not Cricket," said in an interview on D'Oliveira's Web site that his significance came from his role in "a pivotal point in 20th-century politics," not from his sporting skills, though they were indisputable.

"Here was a man who didn't look particularly dark-skinned," Yule said, "but the inequality of the South African system meant you were classified either white or nonwhite, and since he was classified as nonwhite, he could play no part in the national sporting life of his country."

D'Oliveira, who was of Indian-Portuguese heritage, was easily classified as colored. Many other nonwhite cricketers were subjected to what was called the pencil test to determine which segregated league they would play in. A pencil was placed in a player's hair, and if the pencil fell out, the player was called colored and placed in the colored league. If it stayed put, he was judged black and placed in the black league.

South Africa was ostracized in global sports beginning in the 1950s with table tennis. By 1964 antiapartheid organizers had succeeded in getting the country barred from that year's Olympics, and in 1970 the International Olympic Committee expelled the country from the Olympic movement.

The country's absence from international sports rankled South Africans; by 1977 they listed it in a poll as one of the three most damaging consequences of apartheid.

South Africa had been selecting exclusively white cricket teams for test matches since 1889. As the game blossomed in places like the Caribbean, India and Pakistan, South Africa found itself playing only all-white teams from England, Australia and New Zealand. Peter Osborne, in the 2004 book "Basil D'Oliveira, Cricket and Conspiracy: The Untold Story," said the cricket authorities justified this by saying that cricket was a sport for whites, arguing that if blacks or coloreds did take it up they "played at an abysmally low level."

Basil Lewis D'Oliveira, a tailor's son, disproved this by excelling on the cricket fields around Cape Town, where he was most often said to have been born on Oct. 4, 1931. He went on to become a star performer on nonwhite teams; in one year he captained a black team on a trip to Kenya.

But he was in his late 20s when he realized that he had no hope of taking part in top competition in South Africa. A vaunted West Indian team was scheduled to tour the country in matches against a team composed of blacks and coloreds, of which D'Oliveira was captain, but when antiapartheid forces protested that such a high-profile sports event might give credibility to the regime, the trip was canceled.

Deciding to leave the country, D'Oliveira wrote to John Arlott, a prominent cricket commentator in England, asking for help. Arlott got

BATTING FOR A NEW HOME TEAM: Basil D'Oliveira playing for England's national team, 1968. He became an English citizen and was honored by Queen Elizabeth.

him a contract with a minor league team in the Lancashire League.

D'Oliveira was lonely and poverty-stricken at first. Having lived so long under apartheid, he found himself looking for playing-field entrances and facilities for nonwhites. After a slow start his play picked up, and his wife and son, who survive him, joined him. He eventually earned a spot on England's national team.

When he sought to join the squad for the trip to South Africa, however, the sport's governing body in England, the Marylebone Cricket Club, turned him down. Its officials said he had been passed over for athletic reasons, an assertion British newspapers called outlandish. It later emerged that the president of South Africa, John Vorster, had threatened to cancel the event if D'Oliveira was part of the team.

Still, when another player was injured, the cricket club had a change of heart and named D'Oliveira to replace him. D'Oliveira said the South African government offered him a sizable bribe and a coaching job in South Africa if he would withdraw. When he refused, it terminated the competition rather than accept him.

Queen Elizabeth made D'Oliveira an officer of the Order of the British Empire in 1969 and promoted him to a commander in 2005. In 2000 he was named one of the 10 South African cricketers of the century, despite not having played for South Africa. The trophy for the test series between England and South Africa is named for him.

D'Oliveira played in the top division of English cricket into his late 40s; most cricketers retire in their early 30s. His major regret was that he did not hit the big stage sooner, say in his 20s.

"I was some player then," he said in 1980. "I was over the hill when I came to England."

— BY DOUGLAS MARTIN

RUTH STONE

Acclaim Finally Knocked on the Farmhouse Door

JUNE 8, 1915 - NOV. 19, 2011

R
UTH STONE, a poet who wrote in relative obscurity until receiving the National Book Award at the age of 87 for her collection "In the Next Galaxy," died on Nov. 19 at her home in Ripton, Vt. She was 96.

A quietly respected poet who wrote in rural solitude, Ms. Stone became something of a public figure after the news accounts of her winning the award in November 2002 drew attention to her unusual life story of struggle and belated acclaim, shadowed by the suicide of her poet husband in 1959.

New readers discovered a poet of varied and uncommon gifts, fierce and funny, by turns elegiac, scathing, lyric and colloquial.

"Things will be different," she wrote in the title poem of "In the Next Galaxy," continuing:

No one will lose their sight,
their hearing, their gallbladder.
It will be all Catskills with brand
new wrap-around verandas.

Ms. Stone often took as a starting point the natural world she observed from a farmhouse in Goshen, Vt., where she lived and wrote for more than 50 years. Though her verses were compact, her themes were broad, embracing love and loss, the struggle of women to find a voice and the emotional intricacies of family living. The oddities of everyday life, too, served as springboards into distant imaginative territory.

UNDER THE RADAR: At 87, the poet Ruth Stone went from relative anonymity to literary celebrity.

The poet Frances Leviston, reviewing Ms. Stone's 2008 collection "What Love Comes To" in The Guardian of London, defined her scale of preoccupations as extreme: "at one end, something as tangible as a spider's web; at the other, the entire cosmos."

Ms. Stone had particular insight on the subject of loss and grief. In 1959 she and her husband, Walter Stone, a promising poet, were living in Britain on a year's sabbatical from Vassar, where he taught in the English department. She was on the verge of publishing her first poetry collection, "In an Iridescent Time," when he committed suicide, leaving her to raise their three daughters in poverty.

His death inspired some of her most harrowing, emotionally naked verse. "Serial-killer of my days," she wrote of her husband's suicide in the poem "March 15, 1998." She described the death itself unflinchingly:

Tied a silk cord around his meat neck
and hung his meat body, loved though it was,
in order to insure absolute quiet,
on the back of a rented door in Soho.

Often, though, she spoke of the joyful urgency of seeing the world and racing to translate her impressions into poetry.

"I was hanging laundry out and I saw all these ants crawling along the clothes line," she told The Paterson Literary Review in 2001. "Well, I just dropped whatever I was hanging and ran upstairs in the house to get a book and write it down." She continued, "Never keep a poem waiting; it might be a really good one, and if you don't get it down, it's lost."

Ruth Swan Perkins was born on June 8, 1915, in Roanoke, Va. Her father was a drummer and a heavy gambler. Her mother read Tennyson to her when she was an infant and paid her a penny for each poem she recited as a child.

She grew up in Indianapolis with her paternal grandparents. Soon after graduating from high school, she married a man she later described as a "boring chemist."

When her husband pursued graduate work at the University of Illinois, she enrolled as a student. They divorced after she fell in love with Walter Stone, then a graduate student at the university and an aspiring poet and novelist. They had two daughters, who survive her, as does another daughter from her first marriage, seven grandchildren and four great-grandchildren.

To earn a living after her husband's death, Ms. Stone became an academic itinerant, writing poetry and short stories at her Vermont farmhouse and wandering the United States to teach at a long list of campuses before receiving tenure at the State University of New York in Binghamton in 1990.

Her 13 poetry collections include "Topography and Other Poems" (1971); "Cheap: New Poems and Ballads" (1975), "Who Is the Widow's Muse?" (1991), "Simplicity" (1995) and "In the Dark" (2004).

She began to gain a wider audience when her collection "Ordinary Words" (1999) won the National Book Critics Circle Award in 2000. With the publication of "In the Next Galaxy," by Copper Canyon Press, her ascent to the front rank of American poets was confirmed. In 2007 she was named to a four-year term as Vermont's state poet.

Inevitably, in her later years, the poetry took on a more somber tone. Age, with its ravages and regrets, became a constant theme. Her husband's suicide and the long decades of widowhood continued to haunt her verse. In "Getting to Know You," she wrote:

In my 30 years of knowing you
cell by cell in my widow's shawl,
We have lived together longer
in the discontinuous films of my sleep
than we did in our warm parasitical bodies.

The mood could shift abruptly, from the cuttingly satirical mode of "Male Gorillas" ("At the doughnut shop/twenty-three silverbacks/ are lined up at the bar,/sitting on the stools") to the comic exuberance of "Relatives," a rollicking song of praise to grandmothers of every stripe:

It's grandma you have to contend with.
She's here — she's there!
She works in the fast food hangout.
She's doing school lunches.
She's the crossing guard at the school corner.
She's the librarian's assistant.
She's part-time in the real estate office.
She's stuffing envelopes.

Ms. Stone once called poetry "emotional opinion." It coursed through her life, she said in her acceptance speech at the National Book Awards ceremony, a verbal stream heard above the thrum and buzz of everyday existence. "It just talked to me, and I wrote it down," she said. "So I can't even take much credit for it."

— By WILLIAM GRIMES

JOHN G. LAWRENCE

After an Arrest, a Gay Rights Hero

AUG. 2, 1943 - NOV. 20, 2011

JOHN G. LAWRENCE, whose bedroom encounter with the police in Texas led to one of the gay rights movement's signal triumphs, the Supreme Court's 2003 decision in Lawrence v. Texas, died at his home in Houston on Nov. 20. He was 68.

The cause was complications of a heart ailment, his partner, Jose Garcia, said in an interview on Dec. 23 in which he confirmed the death. Aside from a posting on a funeral home's Web site that did not mention the Supreme Court decision, Mr. Lawrence's death apparently received no immediate publicity. It came to light when a lawyer in the case, Mitchell

Katine, sought to reach Mr. Lawrence with an invitation to an event commemorating the ruling.

The Lawrence decision struck down a Texas law that made gay sex a crime and swept away sodomy laws in a dozen other states. The decision reversed a 17-year-old precedent, Bowers v. Hardwick, which had ruled that there was nothing in the Constitution to stop states from making it a crime for gay men to have consensual sex at home.

But Justice Anthony M. Kennedy, writing for five justices in the 6-to-3 Lawrence decision, said, "The petitioners are entitled to respect for their private lives."

"The state," he wrote, "cannot demean their existence or control their destiny by making their private sexual conduct a crime."

Paul M. Smith, who argued in the Supreme Court on behalf of Mr. Lawrence, said the decision "laid the foundation for all the good things that have happened since," including decisions from state courts endorsing same-sex marriage and the repeal of the military's policy forbidding gay men and lesbians from serving openly.

The logic of the Lawrence decision, Justice Antonin Scalia wrote in dissent, supported a constitutional right to same-sex marriage.

The case began on Sept. 17, 1998, when police investigating a report of a "weapons disturbance" entered Mr. Lawrence's apartment. They said they saw Mr. Lawrence and Tyron Garner having sex and arrested them for violating a Texas law prohibiting "deviate sexual intercourse with another individual of the same sex."

The two men were held overnight and each fined $200. Texas courts rejected their constitutional challenges to the state law, relying on the Bowers decision.

In a new book, "Flagrant Conduct: The Story of Lawrence v. Texas," which was published in March by W. W. Norton & Company, Dale

LAWRENCE V. TEXAS: John G. Lawrence, left, and Tyron Garner at a Houston courthouse to face charges of homosexual conduct under Texas' sodomy law in 1998.

Carpenter, a law professor at the University of Minnesota, writes that the conventional understanding of what happened that night is flawed.

In interviews for the book, police officers gave contradictory accounts of the sex act they saw. Mr. Lawrence, for his part, told Professor Carpenter that he and Mr. Garner, who died in 2006, had not had sex, then or ever, and were seated perhaps 15 feet apart when the police arrived.

"If the police did not observe any sex," Professor Carpenter wrote, "the whole case is built on law enforcement misconduct that makes it an even more egregious abuse of liberty than the Supreme Court knew."

What is clear is that the arrest infuriated Mr. Lawrence.

"I don't think he appreciated the constitutional issues," said Mr. Katine, a Houston lawyer who represented Mr. Lawrence. "He was upset about how he was treated, physically and personally, that night. The fire stayed in him. When he was vindicated in the Supreme Court, he felt he got justice."

Suzanne B. Goldberg, who represented Mr. Lawrence as part of her work at Lambda Legal, a national gay rights advocacy group, said Mr. Lawrence "was not your typical test-case plaintiff."

"He had not been active in the gay rights movement or even out as a gay man to all of his co-workers and family," said Professor Goldberg, who now teaches at Columbia Law School. "Instead, this was something that happened to him. The police came into his bedroom and put him into the middle of one of the most significant gay rights cases in our time."

John Geddes Lawrence Jr. was born on Aug. 2, 1943, in Beaumont, Tex. He served four years in the Navy and worked as a medical technician until his retirement in 2009. In addition to Mr. Garcia, he is survived by a brother and a sister.

Mr. Lawrence attended the Supreme Court argument in his case, his lawyers recalled, mingling with the people who had waited in line all night to see it, alive with excitement, pride and a sense of history. "He was willing to be the real-life face of injustice," Mr. Katine said.

Mr. Lawrence reflected on his case years later in an interview with Professor Carpenter. "Why should there be a law passed that only prosecutes certain people?" he asked. "Why build a law that only says, 'Because you're a gay man you can't do this. But because you're a heterosexual, you can do the same thing'"

— By ADAM LIPTAK

DANIELLE MITTERRAND

The First Lady Refused to Play Hostess

OCT. 29, 1924 · NOV. 22, 2011

DANIELLE MITTERRAND, the widow of former President François Mitterrand of France, who pushed beyond stereotypical notions of a first lady to champion leftist causes — she once kissed Fidel Castro on the steps of the Élysée Palace — died on Nov. 22 in Paris. She was 87.

When Mr. Mitterrand, a Socialist, became president in 1981, Mrs. Mitterrand made it clear that she had no enthusiasm for the traditional first-lady roles of hostess, decorator and good-will ambassador. During her husband's 14-year incumbency, the longest of any French president, Mrs. Mitterrand spoke up for ethnic Kurds, criticized President Ronald Reagan's Central American policies and started a foundation to promote human rights.

After her husband left office she continued to press her concerns, including drinking-water shortages in developing countries.

"I have no power," she told The Washington Post in 1989. "I have only my power of indignation, my power of conviction."

She also had the ear of the most powerful politician in France. "François would tell the complainers: 'Her causes are just, I can't stop defending them,'" she told Le Journal du Dimanche, a French weekly newspaper, in October.

Mrs. Mitterrand was regarded as more leftist than her husband, who was elected leader of the Socialist Party in 1971 and invited Communists into his government in 1981. Catherine Nay, in her 1984 biography, "The Black and the Red: François Mitterrand, the Story of an Ambition," quoted him as saying, "She considers me much too moderate in my political life."

It was she who invited Mr. Castro to Paris in 1995; her husband's government emphasized that it was not a state visit.

Mrs. Mitterrand made a large international impression at her husband's funeral in 1996. At the grave site, along with two of her sons with Mr. Mitterrand, she stood near his longtime mistress, Anne Pingeot, a museum curator, and his long-secret daughter with Ms. Pingeot, Mazarine Pingeot. She was photographed consoling the daughter. "It was instinct," Mrs. Mitterrand said.

In her 1996 memoir, "En Toute Liberté" ("In All Liberty"), she wrote that she had known about the daughter since her birth in 1974. Mr. Mitterrand, she said, "excelled in the art of seducing."

"I had to make the best of it," she wrote.

She more than forgave him; she defended him, saying his puritanical critics exhibited "this hypocrisy of conformity."

Danielle Gouze was born on Oct. 29, 1924, in Verdun in eastern France, site of the horrific World War I battle. During World War II her father lost his job as a school principal after refusing to identify Jews in the school, as ordered by France's collaborationist Vichy government.

CANDID: Danielle Mitterrand was the outspoken wife of France's first Socialist president.

She joined the underground resistance as a nurse at 17 in Burgundy and won the Medal of Resistance.

The story goes that Mr. Mitterrand, also a resistance fighter, first saw Danielle in a photograph at her sister's home. "She's quite ravishing," he said. "I'll marry her."

They married on her 20th birthday. The war accelerated their courtship. "When death hovers above you, your feelings multiply quickly," she recalled in Franz-Oliver Geisbert's authorized biography, "François Mitterrand."

Mrs. Mitterrand, a petite brunette with striking eyes, characterized her appearance as "simple." Unlike her predecessors, she did not frequent the haute couture. As a hobby she became an accomplished bookbinder.

She is survived by two sons. Her third son died very young.

Mrs. Mitterrand's political involvement accelerated after her husband left office in 1995. In 2005, she urged a "no" vote in the French referendum on a European Union constitution, saying it valued the economy more than people. It was soundly rejected. She also campaigned for the release of Mumia Abu-Jamal, a former Black Panther who had been on death row in the killing of a white police officer in Philadelphia. (He was released from death row 15 days after Mrs. Mitterrand's death and ordered to serve the rest of his life in prison.)

In a message on the Web site of her foundation, France Fondation Danielle Mitterrand, she explained why she never lost her strong public voice. "After a certain age," she said, "people go to sleep. As for me, I have no intention of dying by inches."

— BY DOUGLAS MARTIN

LANA PETERS

The Strange Odyssey of Stalin's Daughter

FEB. 28, 1926 - NOV. 22, 2011

HER THREE SUCCESSIVE NAMES WERE SIGNPOSTS on a twisted, bewildering road that took her from Stalin's Kremlin, where she was the "little princess," to the West in a celebrated defection, then back to the Soviet Union in a puzzling homecoming, and finally to decades of obscurity, wandering and poverty.

At her birth, on Feb. 28, 1926, she was named Svetlana Stalina, the only daughter and last surviving child of the Soviet tyrant Josef Stalin. After her father died in 1953, she took her mother's last name, Alliluyeva. And in 1970, having defected and married an American, she became and remained Lana Peters. She died of colon cancer on Nov. 22 in Richland County, Wis., at the age of 85.

Her death, like the last years of her life, occurred away from public view. There were hints of it online and in Richland Center, the Wisconsin town in which she lived, though a local funeral home said to be handling the burial would not confirm the death. A county official in Wisconsin thought she might have died several months ago. Phone calls seeking information from a surviving daughter, Olga Peters, who now goes by the name Chrese Evans, were rebuffed, as were efforts to speak to her in person in Portland, Ore., where she lives and works. Not until Nov. 28 could her death be confirmed, by Richland County's corporation counsel.

Ms. Peters's prominence came only from being Stalin's daughter, a distinction that fed public curiosity about her life across three continents and many decades. She said she hated her past and felt like a slave to extraordinary circumstances. Yet she drew on that past, and the infamous Stalin name, in writing two best-selling autobiographies.

> "You can't regret your fate, although I do regret my mother didn't marry a carpenter."

Long after fleeing her homeland, she seemed to be still searching for something — sampling religions, from Hinduism to Christian Science, falling in love and constantly moving. Her defection took her from India, through Europe and on to the United States. After she had moved back to Moscow in 1984, and from there to Soviet Georgia, friends told of her returning to America, then departing for England, then to France, then back to America, then to England again, and on and on. All the while she faded from the public eye.

Ms. Peters was said to have lived in a cabin with no electricity in northern Wisconsin; another time, in a Roman Catholic convent in

Switzerland. In 1992, she was reported to be living in a shabby part of West London in a home for elderly people with emotional problems.

"You can't regret your fate," Ms. Peters once said, "although I do regret my mother didn't marry a carpenter."

Her life was worthy of a Russian novel. It began with a loving relationship with Stalin, who had taken the name, meaning "man of steel," as a young man. (He was born Ioseb Besarionis dze Jughashvili.) Millions died under his brutally repressive rule, but at home he called his daughter "little sparrow," cuddled and kissed her, showered her with presents, and entertained her with American movies.

She became a celebrity in her country, compared to Shirley Temple in the United States. Thousands of babies were named Svetlana. So was a perfume.

At 18, she was setting the table in a Kremlin dining room when Churchill happened upon her. They had a spirited conversation. But all was not perfect even then. The darkest moment of her childhood came in 1932, when her mother, Nadezhda Alliluyeva, Stalin's second wife, committed suicide. Svetlana was 6. Her mother had died of appendicitis, she was told. She did not learn the truth for a decade.

In her teenage years, her father was consumed by the war with Germany and grew distant and sometimes abusive. One of her brothers, Yakov, was captured by the Nazis, who offered to exchange him for a German general. Stalin refused. Yakov was killed.

In her memoirs she told of how Stalin had sent her first love, a Jewish filmmaker, to Siberia for 10 years. She wanted to study literature at Moscow University, but Stalin demanded that she study history. She did. After graduation, again following her father's wishes, she became a teacher, teaching Soviet literature and the

English language. She then worked as a literary translator.

A year after her father broke up her first romance, she told him she wanted to marry another Jewish man, Grigory Morozov, a fellow student. Stalin slapped her and refused to meet him. This time, however, she had her way. She married Mr. Morozov in 1945. They had one child, Iosif, before divorcing in 1947.

Her second marriage, in 1949, was more to Stalin's liking. The groom, Yuri Zhdanov, was the son of Stalin's right-hand man, Andrei Zhdanov. The couple had a daughter, Yekaterina, the next year. But they, too, divorced soon afterward.

Her world grew darker in her father's last years. Nikita S. Khrushchev, Stalin's successor, wrote in his memoirs about the New Year's party in 1952 when Stalin grabbed Svetlana by the hair and forced her to dance.

After Stalin died in 1953, his legacy was challenged, and the new leaders were eager to put his more egregious policies behind them. Svetlana lost many of her privileges. In the 1960s, when she fell in love with Brijesh Singh, an Indian Communist who was visiting Moscow, Soviet officials refused to let her marry him. After he became ill and died, they only reluctantly gave her permission, in early 1967, to take his ashes home to India.

Once in India, Ms. Alliluyeva, as she was known now, evaded Soviet agents in the K.G.B. and showed up at the United States Embassy in New Delhi seeking political asylum. The world watched in amazement as Stalin's daughter, granted protection, became the most high-profile Soviet exile since the ballet virtuoso Rudolf Nureyev defected in 1961. The United States quickly dispatched a C.I.A. officer to help her travel through Italy to neutral Switzerland, but American officials worried that accepting her into the United States could damage its improving relations with Moscow. Finally,

President Lyndon B. Johnson, on humanitarian grounds, agreed to admit her but asked that there be as little fanfare as possible.

Unknown to Washington at the time, the K.G.B. was discussing plans to assassinate Ms. Alliluyeva, according to former agency officials who were quoted by The Washington Times in 1992. But, they said, the K.G.B. backed off for fear that an assassination would be traced back to it too easily.

Her arrival in New York, in April 1967, was more triumphant than low-key. Reporters and photographers were waiting at the airport, and she held a news conference in which she denounced the Soviet regime. Her autobiography, "Twenty Letters to a Friend," was published later that year, bringing her more than $2.5 million. In 1969 she recounted her journey from the Soviet Union in a second memoir, "Only One Year."

Settling in Princeton, N.J., Ms. Alliluyeva made a public show of burning her Soviet passport, saying she would never return to the Soviet Union. She denounced her father as "a moral and spiritual monster," called the Soviet system "profoundly corrupt" and likened the K.G.B. to the Gestapo.

Writing in Esquire magazine, Garry Wills and Ovid Demaris — under the headline "How the Daughter of Stalin Denounced Communism and Embraced God, America and Apple Pie" — said the Svetlana Alliluyeva saga added up to "the Reader's Digest ultimate story."

As the Kremlin feared, Ms. Alliluyeva became a weapon in the cold war. In 1968 she denounced the trial of four Soviet dissidents as "a mockery of justice." On Voice of America radio, Soviet citizens heard her declare that life in the United States was "free, gay and full of bright colors."

In truth she was lonely, as she acknowledged in interviews. She missed her son, Iosif, who was 22 when she left Russia, and her daughter,

Yekaterina, who was then 17. But she seemed to find new vibrancy in 1970, when she married William Wesley Peters. Mr. Peters had been chief apprentice to the architect Frank Lloyd Wright and, for a time, the husband of Wright's adopted daughter, also named Svetlana. She and her son were killed in a car crash in 1946.

Wright's widow, Olgivanna Wright, encouraged the Peters-Alliluyeva marriage, even though the adopted daughter who had died was Mrs. Wright's biological daughter from a previous marriage. Because her daughter and Ms. Peters were both named Svetlana, Mrs. Wright saw mystical meaning in the match.

The couple lived with Mrs. Wright and others at Taliesin West, the architect's famous desert compound in Scottsdale, Ariz. There, Ms. Peters began chafing at the strict communal lifestyle Mrs. Wright enforced, finding her

COLD WAR WEAPON?: Lana Peters, then Svetlana Alliluyeva, on "Meet the Press" in 1969. After defecting to the United States, she denounced the Soviet Union and her father, Josef Stalin.

as authoritarian as her father. Mr. Peters, meanwhile, objected to his wife's buying a house in a resort area nearby, declaring he didn't want "a two-bit suburban life."

Within two years, they separated. Ms. Peters was granted custody of their 8-month-old daughter, Olga. They divorced in 1973.

Information about the next few years is sketchier. Ms. Peters became a United States citizen in 1978 and later told The Trenton Times that she had registered as a Republican and donated $500 to the conservative magazine National Review, saying it was her favorite publication.

She and Olga moved to California, living there in several places before uprooting themselves again in 1982, this time for England so that Olga could enroll in an English boarding school. She also began to speak more favorably of her father. Perhaps she felt she had betrayed him. "My father would have shot me for what I have done," she said in 1983.

At the same time, Stalin's name was undergoing something of a rehabilitation in the Soviet Union. Soviet officials who had blocked Ms. Peters's attempts to communicate with her children in Russia now relaxed their grip. Iosif, then 38 and practicing as a physician, began calling. He said he would try to come to England to see her.

"For this desperate woman, seeing Iosif appeared to herald a new beginning," Time magazine said in 1983.

But hopes were dashed when Iosif was abruptly refused permission to travel. Ms. Peters decided she had one option. In November 1984 she and Olga, now 13, went to Moscow and asked to be taken back. Olga was distraught; she had not been consulted about the move.

Allowed to return to her homeland, Lana Peters now denounced the West. She had not known "one single day" of freedom in the West, she told reporters. She was quoted as saying

that she had been a pet of the C.I.A. Any conservative views she had expressed in the United States, if they still existed, went unexpressed. When an ABC correspondent in Moscow tried to question her a few days later, she exploded in anger, exclaiming: "You are savages! You are uncivilized people! Goodbye to you all."

Ms. Peters and Olga were given Soviet citizenship, but soon their lives worsened. The son and daughter who lived in Russia began shunning her and Olga. Defying the official atheism of the state, Olga insisted on wearing a crucifix. They moved to Tbilisi, Georgia, but it was no better there.

In April 1986, they returned to the United States, with no opposition by the Soviet authorities. Settling at first in Wisconsin, Ms. Peters disavowed the anti-Western things she had said upon her arrival in Moscow, saying she had been mistranslated, particularly the statement about being a pet of the C.I.A. Olga returned to school in England.

Ms. Peters said she was now impoverished. She had given much of her book profits to charity, she said, and was saddled with debt and failed investments. An odd, formless odyssey began. Friends said she appeared unable to live anywhere for more than two years.

Mr. Peters died in 1991. Ms. Peters's son, Iosif Morozov, died in November 2008. Besides her daughter Olga, now Ms. Evans, Ms. Peters is survived by her daughter Yekaterina Zhdanov, a scientist who goes by Katya and was living on the Kamchatka Peninsula in Eastern Siberia studying a volcano. Reached later on Nov. 28 by e-mail, Ms. Evans told The Associated Press that her mother had died in a nursing home in Richland Center, where she had lived for three years. "Please respect my privacy during this sad time," The A.P. quoted her as saying.

Ms. Peters was said to enjoy sewing and reading, mainly nonfiction. She chose not to own a television set. In an interview with The Wisconsin State Journal in 2010, she was asked if her father had loved her. She thought he did, she said, because she had red hair and freckles, like his mother.

But she could not forgive his cruelty to her. "He broke my life," she said. "I want to explain to you. He broke my life."

He left a shadow from which she could never emerge. "Wherever I go," she said, "here, or Switzerland, or India, or wherever. Australia. Some island. I will always be a political prisoner of my father's name."

— By Douglas Martin;
Elizabeth A. Harris and Lee van der Voo
contributed reporting.

OSCAR GRIFFIN JR.

David and Goliath in West Texas

APRIL 28, 1933 · NOV. 23, 2011

JUDGE Roy Bean, the 19th-century Texas justice of the peace and saloonkeeper, called himself "the law west of the Pecos." Not until the 1960s was Judge Bean's legend challenged — by Billy Sol Estes.

Mr. Estes was a glad-handing West Texas wheeler-dealer who used cash from his $100 million agricultural empire to practically purchase the town of Pecos, buying up businesses ranging from a tractor dealership to a funeral home.

Mr. Estes had two planes, a barbecue pit big enough for 10 sizzling steers and decidedly nonindigenous palm trees in his front yard. A monkey climbed the trees until he got mumps.

Mr. Estes was also well connected politically, boasting that the president of the United States took his calls. On his wall at the time were autographed pictures of President John F. Kennedy and a longtime friend, Vice President Lyndon B. Johnson.

In Pecos, population 12,728 then, Mr. Estes essentially ruled — until a 29-year-old journalist named Oscar Griffin Jr. toppled him.

Mr. Griffin, who died on Nov. 23 at 78, was the city editor of a semiweekly Pecos newspaper that competed fiercely with a daily paper owned by none other than Mr. Estes. On a five-person news staff, Mr. Griffin was by necessity a jack of all trades, as much reporter as editor. And it was as a reporter that he brought down Mr. Estes, unraveling an elaborate fraud scheme in four articles that earned Mr. Griffin and his little newspaper, The Pecos Independent and Enterprise, a Pulitzer Prize in 1963 for distinguished local reporting.

The series, which was as understated and meticulous as Mr. Griffin and took months to prepare, caused no fuss or fanfare in Pecos at first. The articles carried no byline, ran under headlines smaller than those for the major articles and did not even mention Mr. Estes by name.

But their description of how he master-minded a byzantine scheme to borrow money using nonexistent fertilizer storage tanks as collateral caught the attention of the F.B.I. Congressional hearings into this and other Estes flimflams led to the highest levels of the Kennedy administration, particularly Johnson, who had been a business associate of Mr. Estes's in several ventures.

Some histories say the vice president tried to help Mr. Estes in questionable dealings with the Agriculture Department that emerged after Mr. Griffin had exposed the tank fraud. Some say Kennedy may have considered dropping Johnson from his ticket in 1964, partly because of the Johnson-Estes connection.

SMALL-TOWN HERO: Oscar Griffin Jr. in 1962, the year his series appeared in The Independent.

In 1963, Mr. Estes was convicted of a battery of fraud charges by federal and state courts and was sentenced to 24 years in prison. (The United States Supreme Court overturned the state conviction on the ground that television and radio coverage of his pretrial hearing had violated his rights.)

After six years in prison, Mr. Estes was released on parole in 1971. Eight years later, he was convicted of other fraud charges and served four more years.

As the Estes story unfolded and the national news media picked up on it, Mr. Estes's supporters outnumbered his detractors in Pecos, nestled at the juncture of the Pecos River and the old Comanche Trail.

"You have to remember that Billy Sol was like God in this town," one man told The New York Times in 1962, adding, "Anyone opposed to him might just as well pack up their bags and leave town."

The episode began in 1961, when Dr. John Dunn, a physician who bought The Independent the year before with three partners, grew suspicious of Mr. Estes's maneuvers. Dr. Dunn's mother, who ran a retail credit shop, had told him of the unusual number of mortgages being carried by farmers dealing with Mr. Estes.

Dr. Dunn soon discovered that Mr. Estes had borrowed $24 million — $180 million in today's dollars — using as collateral fertilizer tanks that turned out not to exist. Mr. Estes had persuaded farmers in a cotton-growing area to pretend to buy tanks by taking out mortgages on them. He offered the farmers 10 percent of the purchase price — in effect, something for nothing.

Dr. Dunn told the F.B.I., but federal agents found no violation of banking laws. Before long Dr. Dunn sold his interest in the paper and turned over his material on the Estes case to The Independent.

Mr. Griffin said he first became suspicious of Mr. Estes's easy-money scheme when he overheard farmers talking in a small cafe. "It's like pennies from heaven," he quoted one as saying.

In pursuing the story, Mr. Griffin was taking on a competitor. Mr. Estes started his newspaper in August 1961 after The Independent refused to back him as a candidate for the local school board. Mr. Estes's paper slashed advertising rates to try to force The Independent out of business and warned advertisers to avoid it.

The strategy appeared to be working. The Independent cut its editorial staff from five to two.

The Independent's trump card was Mr. Griffin's investigative series, which came out in February and March 1962. Mr. Estes was arrested on March 29. In addition to the fertilizer tank scam, he was convicted of defrauding the federal government's grain storage program in a scheme that in one instance involved taking three federal agriculture officials on a shopping spree at the Neiman Marcus store in Dallas.

The day before Mr. Estes was arrested, Mr. Griffin said he went to see him and asked him "point blank" if the fertilizer tanks existed. "He told me that there weren't as many tanks as the mortgages showed," Mr. Griffin wrote. "That sure was the understatement of the year."

Oscar O'Neal Griffin Jr. was born in Daisetta, Tex., on April 28, 1933. He served in the Army in the 1950s, graduated from the University of Texas in 1958, and worked at several other small Texas papers before joining The Independent.

After his series appeared, he joined The Houston Chronicle in 1962 and covered both the Kennedy and Johnson administrations. He was later a spokesman for the federal Transportation Department, worked at small Texas oil companies and earned an M.B.A. from Harvard Business School.

His family said he died of cancer in New Waverly, Tex., where he lived.

Mr. Griffin is survived by his wife of 56 years, the former Patricia Lamb, as well as three daughters, a son, a brother, a sister and seven grandchildren.

The Independent not only got the goods on Mr. Estes; it also defeated his newspaper, The Pecos Daily News, which Mr. Estes had started in the hope of grinding The Independent out of existence. After the scandal broke, The Daily News went into receivership. The Independent survives as The Pecos Enterprise.

Mr. Estes, now 86, still lives in Texas, in Granbury, and still nurses hard feelings about Mr. Griffin, the reporter who helped put him in jail.

"It's a good riddance that he left this world," Mr. Estes said in a brief telephone interview. "The son of a bitch was no damn good."

— By Douglas Martin

JUDY LEWIS

A Child of Hollywood Kept in the Dark

NOV. 6, 1935 - NOV. 25, 2011

H ER MOTHER WAS LORETTA YOUNG. HER FATHER WAS CLARK GABLE. Yet Judy Lewis spent her first 19 months in hideaways and orphanages, and the rest of her early life untangling a web of lies spun by a young mother hungry for stardom but unwilling to end her unwed pregnancy.

Loretta Young's deception was contrived to protect her budding movie career and the box-office power of the matinee idol Gable, who was married to someone else when they conceived their child in snowed-in Washington State. They were on location, shooting the 1935 film "The Call of the Wild," fictional lovers in front of the camera and actual lovers outside its range.

Ms. Lewis, a former actress who died on Nov. 25 at the age of 76, was 31 before she discerned the scope of the falsehoods that cast her, a daughter of Hollywood royalty, into what she later described as a Cinderella-like childhood. Confronted by Ms. Lewis, Young finally made a tearful confession in 1966 at her sprawling home in Palm Springs, Calif.

Young was 22 and unmarried when she had her brief affair with Gable, who was 34 and married to Maria Langham. Young spent most of her pregnancy in Europe to avoid Hollywood gossip. Ms. Lewis was born on Nov. 6, 1935, in a rented house in Venice, Calif. Soon she was turned over to a series of caretakers, including St. Elizabeth's Infants Hospital in San Francisco, so that Young could return to stardom.

When Ms. Lewis was 19 months old, her mother brought her back home and announced through the gossip columnist Louella Parsons that she had adopted the child.

Ms. Lewis grew up in Los Angeles, cushioned in the luxury of her mother's movie-star lifestyle even as she endured what she later described as an outsider's isolation within her family and the teasing of children at school.

They teased her about her ears: they stuck out like Dumbo's. Or, as Hollywood rumors had it, they stuck out like Clark Gable's. Ms. Lewis's mother dressed her in bonnets to hide them. When Ms. Lewis was 7 her ears were surgically altered to make them less prominent.

Until Ms. Lewis, as an adult, confronted her years later, Young did not acknowledge that Ms. Lewis was her biological daughter, or that Gable was Ms. Lewis's father. When Young married and had two children with Tom Lewis, a radio producer, Judy took his name but remained the family's "adopted" daughter.

And though conceding the story privately to her daughter — and later to the rest of her family — Young remained mum publicly all her life, agreeing to acknowledge the facts only in her authorized biography, "Forever Young," and only on the condition that it be published after her death. She died in 2000.

But Ms. Lewis revealed the story of her parentage in her own memoir, "Uncommon Knowledge," in 1994. She described feeling a powerful sense of alienation as a child. In an interview that year, she said, "It was very difficult for me as a little girl not to be accepted or acknowledged by my mother, who, to this day, will not publicly acknowledge that I am her biological child."

After Ms. Lewis released the memoir, her mother refused to speak to her for three years.

The lightning bolt that gave Ms. Lewis the first hint about her parentage came in 1958 during an identity crisis two weeks before her wedding day. Confiding in her fiancé, Tom Tinney, she told him that she did not understand her confusing relationship with her mother and that she did not know who her father was. "I can't marry you," she told him. "I don't know anything about myself."

Mr. Tinney could offer little guidance about her mother, she wrote, but about her father's identity he was clear.

"It's common knowledge, Judy," he said. "Your father is Clark Gable."

She had no inkling, she wrote.

In interviews after her book was published, Ms. Lewis was philosophical about the secrecy in which she grew up. If Young and Gable had acknowledged her in 1935, she said, "both of them would have lost their careers."

Much of Ms. Lewis's account was painful to recall, she said. She quoted Young as saying, "And why shouldn't I be unhappy?" explaining her decision to give birth. "Wouldn't you be if you were a movie star and the father of your child was a movie star and you couldn't have an abortion because it was a mortal sin?"

Young was a Roman Catholic.

After graduating from Marymount, a girls' Catholic school, Ms. Lewis left Los Angeles to pursue acting in New York. She was a regular on one soap opera, "The Secret Storm," from 1964 to 1971, and had featured parts on numerous others. She appeared in several Broadway plays, produced television shows and in her mid-40s decided to return to school. She earned a bachelor's degree and a master's degree in clinical psychology from Antioch University in Los Angeles, and became a licensed family and child counselor in 1992.

LOVE CHILD: Judy Lewis, the daughter of the Hollywood stars Loretta Young and Clark Gable, circa 1966.

Ms. Lewis, who was a clinical psychologist specializing in foster care and marriage therapy, died of lymphoma at her home in Gladwyne, Pa., her daughter, Maria Tinney Dagit, said.

Besides her daughter, Ms. Lewis is survived by two grandsons and two half-brothers. Her marriage to Mr. Tinney ended in divorce.

In a 2001 interview on CNN with Larry King, Ms. Lewis recalled speaking to her mother about her early life.

"I was also asking her about being adopted," she said, "as adopted children do. They say, 'Where are my . . .'"

Mr. King interjected, "'Who's my mother?'"

"Yes," Ms. Lewis said. "'Who's my mother? Who's my father?' And she would answer it very easily by saying, 'I couldn't love you any more than if you were my own child,' which, of course, didn't answer the question, but it said, 'Don't ask the question.'"

But at that point Ms. Lewis was wistful about her past. "Call of the Wild" was one of her favorite movies, she said, and the love scenes between her parents "show the love they feel for each other."

Mr. King asked if she ever fantasized about the life she might have had if her parents had married and brought her up.

"I would have liked them to have," she replied. "But that is just my dream, you know. Life is very strange. Doesn't give us what we want."

— BY PAUL VITELLO

TOM WICKER

A Must-Read on American Politics

JUNE 18, 1926 - NOV. 25, 2011

TOM WICKER, who covered the assassination of President John F. Kennedy for The New York Times, became the paper's Washington bureau chief and wrote an iconoclastic political column for 25 years, becoming one of postwar America's most distinguished journalists, died on Nov. 25

at his home near Rochester, Vt., at the age of 85.

On Nov. 22, 1963, Mr. Wicker, a brilliant but relatively unknown White House correspondent who had worked at four smaller papers, written several novels under a pen name and, at 37, had established himself as a workhorse of The Times's Washington bureau, was riding in the presidential motorcade as it wound through downtown Dallas, the lone Times reporter on a routine political trip to Texas.

The searing images of that day — the rifleman's shots cracking across Dealey Plaza, the wounded president lurching forward in the open limousine, the blur of speed to Parkland Memorial Hospital, and the nation's anguish as the doctors gave way to the priests and a new era — were dictated by Mr. Wicker from a phone booth in stark, detailed prose drawn from notes scribbled on a White House itinerary sheet. It filled two front-page columns and the entire second page, and vaulted the writer to journalistic prominence overnight.

Nine months later, Mr. Wicker, the son of a small-town North Carolina railroad conductor, succeeded the legendary James B. Reston as chief of The Times's 48-member Washington bureau, and two years later he inherited the column, although hardly the mantle, of the retiring Arthur Krock, the dean of Washington pundits, who had covered every president since Calvin Coolidge.

In contrast to the conservative pontificating of Mr. Krock and the genteel journalism of Mr. Reston, Mr. Wicker brought a hard-hitting Southern liberal/civil libertarian's perspective to his column, "In the Nation," which appeared on the editorial page and then on the Op-Ed Page two or three times a week from 1966 until his retirement in 1991. It was also syndicated to scores of newspapers.

Riding waves of change as the effects of the divisive war in Vietnam and America's civil rights struggle swept the country, Mr. Wicker applauded President Lyndon B. Johnson and Congress for passage of the Civil Rights Act of 1964 and the Voting Rights Act of 1965, but took the president to task for deepening the American involvement in Southeast Asia.

"The gravest threat to freedom of the press," Mr. Wicker wrote, "comes from the press itself."

He denounced President Richard M. Nixon for covertly bombing Cambodia, and in the Watergate scandal accused him of creating the "beginnings of a police state." Nixon put Mr. Wicker on his "enemies list," but resigned in disgrace over the Watergate cover-up. Vice President Spiro T. Agnew upbraided Mr. Wicker for "irresponsibility and thoughtlessness," but he, too, resigned, after pleading no contest to evading taxes on bribes he had taken while he was governor of Maryland.

The Wicker judgments fell like a hard rain upon all the presidents: Gerald R. Ford, for continuing the war in Vietnam; Jimmy Carter, for "temporizing" in the face of soaring inflation and the Iranian hostage crisis; Ronald Reagan, for dozing through the Iran-contra scandal; and the elder George Bush, for letting the Persian Gulf war outweigh educational and health care needs at home. Mr. Wicker's targets also included members of Congress, government secrecy, big business, corrupt labor leaders, racial bigots, prison conditions, television and the news media.

In the 1970s, Mr. Wicker, whose status as a columnist put him outside the customary journalistic restrictions on advocacy, became a fixture on current-events television shows and on college campuses. Speaking at a 1971 "teach-in" at Harvard, he urged students to "engage in civil disobedience" in protesting the war in Vietnam. "We got one president out," he told the cheering crowd, "and perhaps we can do it again."

Mr. Wicker was attacked by conservatives and liberals, by politicians high and low, by business interests and labor leaders, and for a time his activism — crossing the line from observer to participant in news events — put him in disfavor with many mainstream journalists. But his speeches and columns continued unabated.

His most notable involvement took place during the uprising by 1,300 inmates who seized 38 guards and workers at the Attica prison in upstate New York in September 1971. Having written a sympathetic column on the death of the black militant George Jackson at San Quentin, Mr. Wicker was asked by Attica's rebels to join a group of outsiders to inspect prison conditions and monitor negotiations between inmates and officials. The radical lawyer William M. Kunstler and Bobby Seale, chairman of the Black Panther Party, also went in, and the observers took on the role of mediators.

Mr. Wicker, in a column, described a night in the yard with the rebels: flickering oil-drum fires, bull-necked convicts armed with bats and iron pipes, faceless men in hoods or football helmets huddled on mattresses behind wooden barricades. He wrote: "This is another world — terrifying to the outsider, yet imposing in its strangeness — behind those massive walls, in this murmurous darkness, within the temporary but real power of desperate men."

After a four-day standoff, troopers and guards stormed the prison. Ten hostages and 29 inmates were killed in what witnesses called a turkey shoot; three inmates were killed by other convicts, who also beat a guard to death.

Afterward, many prisoners were beaten and abused in reprisals.

Mr. Wicker wrote a book about the uprising, "A Time to Die" (1975), and George Grizzard portrayed him in a 1980 television movie, "Attica."

Mr. Wicker produced a shelf of books: 10 novels, ranging from potboilers under the pen name Paul Connolly to political thrillers; and 10 nonfiction books that re-examined the legacies of ex-presidents, race relations in America, the press and other subjects.

Mr. Wicker's first nonfiction book was "Kennedy Without Tears: The Man Beneath the Myth" (1964), a 61-page look back that some critics said did not in fact penetrate the armor of sentiment growing over the dead president.

"JFK and LBJ: The Influence of Personality Upon Politics" (1968), was better received. It analyzed the two presidents' character to explain why Kennedy had been unable to push many programs through Congress and why Johnson's credibility had been a casualty of the Vietnam conflict.

Published shortly before Mr. Wicker retired, "One of Us: Richard Nixon and the American Dream" (1991) offered a surprising reassessment of the president he had scorned 20 years earlier. Nixon, credited with high marks in foreign policy, mainly for opening doors to China, actually deserved more notice for domestic achievements, Mr. Wicker argued, especially in desegregating Southern schools.

His political novel "Facing the Lions" (1973) and his Civil War story "Unto This Hour" (1984) were both best-sellers.

Mr. Wicker was a hefty man, 6 feet 2 inches tall, with a ruddy face, petulant lips and a lock of unruly hair that dangled boyishly on a high forehead. He toiled in tweeds in pinstriped Washington, but seemed more suited to a hammock and straw hat on a lazy summer day. Yet the easygoing manner and the down-home drawl masked a fiery temperament, a tigerish competitiveness and a stubborn idealism that infused his observations of the American scene for more than a half century.

Thomas Grey Wicker was born on June 18, 1926, in Hamlet, N.C., the son of Delancey Wicker, a railroad freight conductor, and the former Esta Cameron. He worked on his high school newspaper.

After Navy service in World War II, he studied journalism at the University of North Carolina at Chapel Hill, graduating in 1948. He was an editor and reporter at several newspapers in North Carolina, including The Winston-Salem Journal, eventually becoming its Washington correspondent.

Mr. Wicker married the former Neva Jewett McLean in 1949. The couple had two children and were divorced in 1973. In 1974, he married Pamela Hill, a producer of television documentaries. She survives him, as do a daughter and son, two stepdaughters and a stepson. He died apparently of a heart attack, his wife said.

Mr. Wicker had briefly been associate editor of The Nashville Tennessean when Mr. Reston hired him for The Times's Washington bureau in 1960, making him one of "Scotty's boys," a cadre of protégés that included Max Frankel, Anthony Lewis and Russell Baker. Mr. Wicker covered Congress and the Kennedy White House, the 1960 political campaigns and presidential trips abroad. His output was prodigious — 700 articles in his first few years.

His work was often entertaining as well as informative. "The most familiar voice in Ameriker lahst yeeah warz that of a Boston Irishman with Harvard overtones who sounded vaguely like an old recording of Franklin D. Roosevelt speeded up to 90 r.p.m.'s," Mr. Wicker wrote for the magazine, summing up 241 Kennedy speeches in his first year in the

EYEWITNESS REPORT: What was meant to be a routine political trip to Dallas, Tex., on Nov. 22, 1963, became a defining moment for Tom Wicker's career.

presidency. "Nor will the Beacon Street 'a' and the Bunker Hill 'r' fall any less frequently on the American eeah in the coming yeeah."

Mr. Wicker was named chief of the Washington bureau on Sept. 1, 1964, at the insistence of his mentor, Mr. Reston, who had asked to be relieved. Mr. Wicker was an indifferent administrator. He continued to cover Washington and national news and write news analyses. In 1966, he took on Mr. Krock's column, adding to his workload.

In 1968, after complaints by Times editors in New York that Mr. Wicker was devoting too much attention to his writing, The Times announced that James Greenfield, a former Time magazine reporter and State Department official, would replace him as bureau chief.

Mr. Wicker and some of his colleagues opposed the appointment, seeing it as an effort to rein in the relative independence the bureau had enjoyed under Mr. Reston. The publisher, Arthur Ochs Sulzberger, withdrew Mr. Greenfield's name and named Mr. Frankel as bureau chief. Mr. Wicker became associate editor, a title he retained until his retirement, and after 1972 wrote his column from New York.

The vitality of the American press remained a central concern, the fullest expression of which came in 1978 in his book "On Press." There he had enlarged on complaints he had made for years: the myth of objectivity, reliance on official and anonymous sources. Far from being robust and uninhibited, he wrote, the press was often a toady to government and business.

"The gravest threat to freedom of the press," he wrote, "is not necessarily from public animosity or mistrust, legislative action or court decision." The threat, he said, "comes from the press itself — in its longing for a respectable place in the established political and economic order, in its fear of the reaction that boldness and independence will always evoke."

He added, "My life in journalism has persuaded me that the press too often tries to guard its freedom by shirking its responsibility, and that this leads to default on both. What the press in America needs is less inhibition, not more restraint."

— BY ROBERT D. MCFADDEN

ODUMEGWU OJUKWU

From the Fields of Oxford to Bloody Nigeria

NOV. 4, 1933 - NOV. 26, 2011

O DUMEGWU OJUKWU, an Oxford-educated Nigerian colonel who proclaimed the Republic of Biafra in 1967 and led his Ibo people into a secessionist war that cost more than a million lives, many of them starved children whose skeletal images shocked the world, died at a hospital in London. He was 78.

The date of death was not clear. The Associated Press said he died on Nov. 26; Bloomberg News said the death occurred the day before. Mr. Ojukwu had a stroke at his home in Enugu, Nigeria, in December 2010, and had since been under treatment in London, but no cause of death was given.

Mr. Ojukwu was an unlikely militarist and a reluctant rebel: the sports-car-driving son of one of Nigeria's richest men, an urbane student of history and Shakespeare who read voraciously, wrote poetry, played tennis and, with his wealth and connections, might have been a business mogul or a worldly rouge-et-noir playboy.

But he spurned his father's offer of a business partnership and instead joined Nigeria's civil service and then its army in the turbulent last years of British colonial rule. And as maps of Africa were redrawn by forces of national and tribal self-determination, he became military governor of the Ibo homeland, one of three tribal regions, at a historic juncture.

At 33, he found himself at the vortex of simmering ethnic rivalries among Nigeria's

Hausas in the north, Yorubas in the southwest and Ibos in the southeast. The largely Christian Ibos were envied as one of Africa's best-educated and most industrious peoples and possessed of much of Nigeria's oil wealth. Tensions finally exploded into assassinations, coups and a massacre of 30,000 Ibos by Hausas and federal troops.

While he denounced the massacre and cited other Ibo grievances, Colonel Ojukwu for months resisted rising Ibo pressure for secession. He proposed a weak federation to separate Nigeria's three tribal regions politically. But Col. Yakubu Gowon, leader of the military government in Lagos, rejected the idea. A clash over federal taxation of the Ibo region's oil and coal industries precipitated the final break.

"Long live the Republic of Biafra," Colonel Ojukwu proclaimed on May 30, 1967.

Five weeks later, civil war began when Nigerian military forces invaded the breakaway province. It was a lopsided war, with other nations supporting federal forces seeking to unify the country and Biafra standing virtually alone. Nigeria was Africa's most populous nation, with 57 million people, of which 8 million to 10 million were Ibos.

Poorly equipped and outnumbered four to one, Biafra's 25,000-member army held its own for months, supported by a citizenry that donated food, clothing and supplies. Colonel Ojukwu ran Biafra as a wartime democracy, fought alongside his troops and was said to be revered by his people.

He gave orders in a slow, deliberate baritone: native Igbo with an Oxford accent. Fond of Sibelius, he chose "Finlandia" as Biafra's national anthem. And he read Shakespeare. "Hamlet was my favorite," he told The New York Times. "I wonder what the psychiatrists will make of that."

Over a battle map he looked like a brooding Othello, with solemn eyes and a luxuriantly bearded countenance. He slept irregularly, sometimes working nonstop for days, taking a meal now and then, rarely touching alcohol but chain-smoking English cigarettes.

Tanzania, Zambia, the Ivory Coast and Gabon recognized Biafra, and France and other nations provided covert aid. But the Soviet Union, Egypt and even Britain, after a period of neutrality, supplied weapons and advisers to Nigeria. The United States, officially neutral, provided diplomatic and relief coordination aid. But after 15 months of war, Biafra's 29,000 square miles had been reduced to 5,000, and deaths had soared.

As crops burned and refugees streamed away from advancing federal forces, much of the population was cut off from food supplies. As the 30-month civil war moved onto the world stage as one of the first televised wars, millions around the globe were stunned by pictures of Biafran babies with distended bellies and skeletal children who were succumbing to famine by the thousands daily in the war's final stages.

Colonel Ojukwu appealed to the world to save his people. International relief agencies responded, and scores of cargo planes ferried food in to the encircled Biafrans, but airlifts were woefully inadequate. Deaths from starvation were estimated at more than 6,000 a day, and postwar studies suggested that a third of Biafra's surviving preschoolers — nearly 500,000 — were malnourished at war's end.

In January 1970, secessionist resistance was crushed and its leader, by then a general, fled into exile in Ivory Coast and London. Granted a presidential pardon after 13 years, he returned to Nigeria in 1982 and was welcomed by enormous crowds. He became a Lagos businessman and ran unsuccessfully for president several times, but remained a hero in the eyes of many of his countrymen.

The legacies of the war were terrible. Deaths from fighting, disease and starvation were estimated by international relief agencies at one million to three million. Besides widespread destruction of hospitals, schools, homes and businesses, Ibos faced discrimination in employment, housing and political rights. Nigeria reabsorbed Biafra, however, and the region was rebuilt over 20 years as its oil-based economy prospered anew.

Chukwuemeka Odumegwu Ojukwu (pronounced chuk-woo-MA-ka oh-doo-MAG-woo oh-JU-kwoo) was born on Nov. 4, 1933, in Zungeru, Nigeria. From modest beginnings, his father, Sir Louis Phillipe Odumegwu Ojukwu, had made fortunes in transportation and real estate, and was Nigeria's wealthiest entrepreneur when he died in 1966.

The boy, nicknamed Emeka, attended Kings College in Lagos, Nigeria's most prestigious secondary school; Epsom College, a boys' prep school in Surrey, and Lincoln College, Oxford, where he graduated with honors in history in 1955. Classmates said he was popular, dressed stylishly, drove a bright red MG sports car and loved discussions of Machiavelli, Hobbes, Louis XIV and Shakespeare.

He had three wives. His first, Njideka, a law student he met at Oxford and wed in 1962, died in 2010. His second, Stella Onyeador, died in 2009. He married Bianca Odinaka Onoh, a former beauty queen and businesswoman 34 years his junior, in 1994. Returning to Nigeria in 1956, he rejected his father's business overtures, worked on development in remote villages, and in 1957 joined the army. He called himself an amateur soldier, but rose rapidly in the ranks

A COUNTRY OF HIS OWN: Odumegwu Ojukwu holding up the new currency and postage stamps for the Republic of Biafra, which seceded from Nigeria in 1967.

after Nigeria gained independence in 1960. In 1966, he became military governor of the Ibo region, and declared Biafran independence after repression enveloped his people.

He sometimes compared Biafrans to Israelis. "The Israelis are hard-working, enterprising people," he told a visitor to his besieged field headquarters in 1969. "So are we. They've suffered from pogroms. So have we. In many ways, we share the same promise and the same problems."

— BY ROBERT D. McFADDEN

ALAN SUES

A 'Laugh-In' Regular Was Hiding Something

MARCH 7, 1926 - DEC. 1, 2011

ALAN SUES, an actor whose loud, clownish comedic style made him an invaluable cast member on "Rowan & Martin's Laugh-In," one of the top-rated shows on television in the late 1960s, died on Dec. 1 at his home in Los Angeles. He was 85.

On "Laugh-In," Mr. Sues was part of an ensemble cast in a comedy-sketch show that prefigured "Saturday Night Live" and helped jumpstart the careers of stars like Goldie Hawn, Lily Tomlin and Flip Wilson.

Mr. Sues played Uncle Al the Kiddies' Pal, a consistently hung-over children's entertainer; Big Al, an effeminate sportscaster more obsessed with ringing a bell than announcing the day's action; and a drag imitation of the cast member Jo Anne Worley. He first performed on the show in 1968 as a manic fan who accosts Rowan and Martin with a 30-second recap of a "Laugh-In" episode.

Mr. Sues tended to perform with over-the-top flamboyance on the show, displaying stereotypically gay mannerisms. What he did not disclose was that he was gay, fearing that to tell the truth about his sexual orientation would have ended his career, his friend and administrator Michael Michaud said.

"It wasn't because he was ashamed of being gay; it was because he was surviving as a performer," Mr. Michaud said. Mr. Sues, he said, was actually an inspiration to many gay viewers. "Many gay men came up to him and said how important he was when they were young because he was the only gay man they could see on television."

"Laugh-In" combined vaudeville routines, topical and physical humor and jokes in a rapid, stream-of-consciousness format. Episodes began with banter by the hosts, the comedy team of Dan Rowan and Dick Martin, then quickly devolved into a cavalcade of psychedelic sight gags, sketches and bikini-clad dancers punctuated by catchphrases like "Sock it to me!" and "You bet your sweet bippy."

The show, which first appeared as a special in 1967 and ran until 1973, satirized the counterculture and featured show-business guests like Diana Ross as well as public figures like the Rev. Billy Graham and Richard M. Nixon. Nixon, appearing while running for president and trying to shed a stiff image, drew laughs and a few gasps when he asked, "Sock it to me?"

Mr. Sues, who left the show before its last season, said his success on "Laugh-In" had left him typecast as a wacky comedian.

"When I first started out," he told The Los Angeles Times in 1993, "I did a lot of straight dramatic roles, but after 'Laugh-In,' audiences wouldn't accept me in anything but a comedy."

Alan Grigsby Sues was born on March 7, 1926, in Ross, Calif., to Peter and Alice Murray Sues. His father raised racehorses, requiring him to move the family frequently, uprooting Alan and his brother, John, from one school after another. Alan Sues served in the Army in Europe during World War II.

After the war he used veterans' benefits to pay for acting lessons at the Pasadena Playhouse, where he performed before moving to New York in 1952. He made his Broadway debut in 1953 in Elia Kazan's "Tea and Sympathy." While the play was running he met and married Phyllis Gehrig, a dancer and actress.

When the production ended in 1955, he and his wife started a vaudevillian nightclub act in Manhattan, then took it on the road across the country. Characters he developed for the act would appear in "Laugh-In."

After they divorced in the late 1950s, Mr. Sues settled in California, where he appeared in films, among them "The Americanization of Emily"

A THIN VEIL: Although he kept his sexuality secret, Alan Sues played many gay characters on TV.

in 1964, and on television shows. In one, "The Twilight Zone," he appeared in "The Masks," a 1964 episode in which a wealthy man insists that family members gathered at his deathbed wear masks reflecting their true natures.

Later in the '60s Mr. Sues joined Ms. Worley in the Off Broadway musical comedy revue "The Mad Show."

After "Laugh-In," Mr. Sues appeared in an original one-man play, "No Flies on Me," in 1993; television shows like "Punky Brewster" and "Sabrina, the Teenage Witch"; and a popular commercial for Peter Pan peanut butter in the early 1970s.

Returning to Broadway in 1975, he had a successful dramatic turn playing Moriarty in the Royal Shakespeare Company's revival of William Gillette's "Sherlock Holmes."

Mr. Sues, who lived in West Hollywood, appeared to have died of a heart attack, Mr. Michaud said. Survivors include a sister-in-law. His brother, John, died several years ago.

Mr. Sues's road to "Laugh-In" began Off Broadway when his performance in "The Mad Show" caught the attention of the producer George Schlatter. Mr. Schlatter soon cast him in Edie Adams's Las Vegas act and later "Laugh-In," which he was also producing.

Mr. Sues was in New York when he learned that Mr. Schlatter wanted to work with him.

"When I heard that he wanted to talk to me, I called him in Los Angeles," Mr. Sues was quoted as saying in "From Beautiful Downtown Burbank: A Critical History of Rowan & Martin's Laugh-In, 1968-1973," by Hal Erickson. "His secretary said he was on the other line, so I said, 'Well, tell him I'm in a phone booth and it's filling with water.'"

— BY DANIEL E. SLOTNIK

BILL TAPIA

The 'Duke of Uke'

JAN. 1, 1908 - DEC. 2, 2011

N 2001, BILL TAPIA took one of his guitars to a Southern California music shop to get it fixed. A woman was buying a ukulele, and Mr. Tapia asked to see it. He began playing it, masterfully, with a distinctive jazz inflection.

"Hey, who are you?" the store's owner asked.

If Mr. Tapia could have seen the future, he might have answered, the "Duke of Uke," the title of an album he recorded in 2005 at the age of 97. But at the time, he knew only that he was sad that his daughter and wife had recently died in quick succession, and that playing the ukulele felt good.

Mr. Tapia, who died on Dec. 2 at the age of 103, first played the instrument as an 8-year-old street musician, then went on to become one of Hawaii's premier young ukulele players in the 1920s and '30s. But after World War II he switched to the guitar to get jobs playing jazz, his favorite kind of music, gave away his ukuleles and for a half-century had almost nothing to do with the instrument that had defined his youth and middle age.

Then something astonishing happened: Mr. Tapia was "discovered" as a ukulele virtuoso at a time when the instrument was riding a resurgence of popularity. He became a ukulele star, twice making the Top 10 on the jazz charts, wowing concertgoers by playing the ukulele behind his head à la Jimi Hendrix, and making three albums, one of which honored his 100th birth-

COMEBACK AT 96: Bill Tapia quit playing the ukulele after World War II, but found fame again.

day. He was elected to the Ukulele Hall of Fame.

"Bill Tapia has been involved with the ukulele, jazz and Hawaiian music perhaps longer than any other living person," the Hall of Fame said when it inducted him.

His daughter and his wife, Barbie, died in 2001. He is survived by grandchildren, great-grandchildren and great-great-grandchildren.

William Tapia was born in Honolulu on New Year's Day 1908. He fell in love with Hawaiian music listening to sugarcane workers play it. He bought his first ukulele when he was 7 years old, paying 75 cents. The seller was one of the first men to make them commercially.

After his father abandoned the family the next year, young Bill dropped out of school to collect tips as a street musician.

At 10 he came up with his own version of "Stars and Stripes Forever," which he played for troops headed for duty in the last months of World War I. At 12 he played vaudeville. At 16 he worked on luxury liners. At 19 he performed at nightclubs and speakeasies in Hollywood and at parties at the home of Charlie

Chaplin. At 21 he sat in with Louis Armstrong's band at a Los Angeles nightclub. By this time he was playing the banjo and guitar in addition to the ukulele, and was moving between Hawaii and the mainland.

When the Royal Hawaiian Hotel staged its grand opening in 1927, Mr. Tapia played ukulele in the orchestra. He was the only one of the original musicians to return for the hotel's 75th anniversary — and its 80th. The second two times were better, he said: he got fed.

In 1933, the Royal Hawaiian hired him to drive one of its touring cars — a yellow-and-blue seven-passenger Packard — to ferry the wealthy and famous to scenic spots. He played the ukulele for his passengers and threw in a lesson for anyone interested. His pupils included Jimmy Durante, Shirley Temple and the stars of the "Our Gang" comedies.

He even claimed to have taught a lick or two to Arthur Godfrey, whose ukulele playing on television sparked the instrument's popularity in the 1950s.

During World War II, Mr. Tapia organized entertainment for servicemen in Honolulu. After the war, he moved to the San Francisco area and devoted himself to the guitar, and to jazz. The big bands and combos with which he played had no use for ukuleles.

More than 55 years later, Alyssa Archambault was researching the background of her great-great-grandfather, a steel guitar player in Hawaii, and approached Mr. Tapia. A former disc jockey and promoter, she was captivated by Mr. Tapia's music, and his story. She put him in touch with professional ukulele players. They thought he had died years ago. When they heard him play, they were awed.

He released his first album, "Tropical Swing," in 2004, when he was 96, and "Duke of Uke" the next year, both on the small Moon Room label. A live recording of his 100th-birthday concert at the historic Warner Grand Theater in San Pedro, Calif., was released in June.

Mr. Tapia played concerts regularly, delighting audiences with songs like "Little Grass Shack." The most recent was on Feb. 11, 2011 — not counting his regular gig at a local senior center, the last of which was only weeks before his death.

Mr. Tapia had a line that never failed to impress audiences: "Here's a song I performed during World War I."

— BY DOUGLAS MARTIN

CHRISTOPHER LOGUE

Achilles With an Uzi: Updating the 'Iliad'

NOV. 1926 - DEC. 2, 2011

CHRISTOPHER LOGUE, an English poet acclaimed for his multivolume modernization of the "Iliad" — a literary endeavor noteworthy for lasting four times as long as the Trojan War itself; even more noteworthy for its use of evocative anachronisms like Uzis, helicopters and aircraft carriers to conjure the world of Homer's Bronze Age warriors; and still more noteworthy for having been accomplished without his knowing a word of Greek — died on Dec. 2 at his home in London.

Mr. Logue, whose life was a fittingly picaresque epic that also included being imprisoned in a Crusader castle, writing a pornographic novel, acting in films by the director Ken Russell and committing a modest armed robbery at the age of 8, was 85.

Though he wrote more than two dozen well-received volumes of original Modernist poetry, Mr. Logue remained best known for his English-language "Iliad," a project on which he embarked in 1959 and worked in intense fits and starts for more than 40 years.

He would come nowhere near to reworking the 24 books and more than 15,000 lines of Homer's epic, for, as the British newspaper The Independent pointed out in 1991, Mr. Logue "has accounted for one line every three days on average; at this rate he should be through by about 2080."

The sections of the "Iliad" he did complete were published as "War Music" (1981), which reworked Books 16 to 19; "Kings" (1991; Books 1 and 2); "The Husbands" (1995; Books 3 and 4); "All Day Permanent Red" (2003), which centers on the poem's first battle scenes and whose title Mr. Logue took from an advertisement for lipstick; and "Cold Calls" (2005), winner of the Whitbread Poetry Award, which continues the battle.

Mr. Logue, who used earlier English translations as points of departure and consulted frequently with scholars of Homeric Greek, took pains to stress that his "Iliad" was not a translation but an adaptation.

Wanting it to stand or fall on its merits as English poetry, he reordered and invented scenes, created new characters and modernized language and imagery: his text includes references to Shakespeare, Venetian blinds and World War II. In "Kings," he writes:

> *Nine days of this,*
> *And on the tenth, Ajax,*
> *Grim underneath his tan as Rommel after*
> *   'Alamein,*
> *Summoned the army to the common sand. . . .*

Not surprisingly, Mr. Logue's Homer loosed the wrath of scholastic purists and some critics. But it was overwhelmingly lauded, even by classicists, for the combined power of its luminous language, cinematic imagery and hurtling pace. These things, reviewers said, lent his account of the decade-long conflict between Greece and Troy in the 12th century B.C. a force heard in few other English versions.

As a result, Mr. Logue's "Iliad" seemed to capture truly the swift-footed immediacy of the original, which was composed and transmitted by generations of oral bards starting in the ninth or eighth century B.C.

Named a Commander of the British Empire in 2007, Mr. Logue had been described by The Independent two years earlier as "the greatest war poet in England."

Here he is, in "All Day Permanent Red," showing Greek troops rising for battle:

> *Think of a raked sky-wide Venetian blind.*
> *Add the receding traction of its slats*
> *Of its slats of its slats as a hand draws it up.*
> *Hear the Greek army getting to its feet.*
> *Then of a stadium when many boards are*
> *   raised*
> *And many faces change to one vast face.*
> *So, where there were so many masks,*
> *Now one Greek mask glittered from strip to*
> *   ridge.*

By his own account, John Christopher Logue was born a rogue — in Portsmouth, on England's south coast, in November 1926.

His father, a postal clerk, and his mother, a homemaker, were inclined to indulge his youthful high spirits, as when, at 8, he trained a pistol on a girl in the street and made off with her ice cream. That it was a toy pistol was at least partly mitigating.

The young Mr. Logue, whose formal education ended when he was 17, served with the British Army during World War II.

While stationed in Palestine, he helped himself to six blank Army pay books — official documents used to record a soldier's pay and establish his identity. After boasting idly that he planned to sell them, he was court-martialed and served about a year and a half in Acre Central Prison, a 12th-century fortress built by Crusaders in western Galilee.

BRONZE AGE TO MODERN AGE: Christopher Logue was best known for his adaption of the "Iliad."

"It wasn't so different from being at boarding school," Mr. Logue told the newspaper The Scotsman in 1996. "In other words, it was bloody awful. It was during that time, though, that I got properly interested in poetry. So it was quite useful in the end."

In London in the 1950s, Mr. Logue resorted to a time-honored refuge of impecunious writers by composing a pornographic novel, "Lust." Written under the name Count Palmiro Vicarion, it was published in Paris in 1959 by Maurice Girodias, whose other titles included Vladimir Nabokov's "Lolita."

He wrote the screenplay for Mr. Russell's "Savage Messiah," a film about the life of the French primitive sculptor Henri Gaudier-Brzeska. Vincent Canby, writing in The New York Times, called the movie one of the 10 worst of 1972. Mr. Russell died in November at 84.

Mr. Logue had on-screen roles in Mr. Russell's television movie "Dante's Inferno" (1967) and his feature film "The Devils" (1971), in which he played Cardinal Richelieu. His other acting credits include small parts in "Jabberwocky" (1977), directed by Terry Gilliam, and "The Affair of the Necklace" (2001), starring Hilary Swank.

Mr. Logue's survivors include his wife, Rosemary Hill, who is a historian and biographer. His publisher, Faber & Faber, announced his death but did not give a cause.

His other work includes children's picture books; a memoir, "Prince Charming" (1999); and "Selected Poems" (1996).

In 1959, Mr. Logue, already an established poet, was asked by the BBC to adapt a section of the "Iliad" for broadcast; his lack of Greek did not deter them. Four decades later, he found himself still embedded with Ajax, Achilles and their lot.

Long active in progressive politics, Mr. Logue was an original signatory of the Committee of 100, the British antiwar group founded in 1960 by the philosopher Bertrand Russell and others.

He often said he considered his sanguinary, loud-thundering retelling of the "Iliad" to be his deepest antiwar statement of all.

— By Margalit Fox

SÓCRATES

Much More Than a Soccer Star

FEB. 19, 1954 - DEC. 4, 2011

SÓCRATES, the soccer great and medical doctor who transcended the sport through his involvement in Brazil's pro-democracy movement and his outspoken defense of his own bohemian excesses, died on Dec. 4 in São Paulo, Brazil. He was 57.

The cause was septic shock from an intestinal infection, according to Hospital Israelita Albert Einstein, where he was admitted the day before.

Sócrates, the captain of Brazil's team in the 1982 World Cup, had been hospitalized three times in the previous four months. In interviews he described liver problems related to decades of heavy drinking, for which he was pilloried.

"This country drinks more cachaça than any other in the world, and it seems like I myself drink it all," he said, referring to the popular Brazilian spirit made from fermented sugar cane. "They don't want me to drink, smoke or think?

"Well," he said, "I drink, smoke and think."

His exuberant style reflected an expansive and multifaceted career. In addition to playing soccer, he practiced medicine and dabbled in coaching and painting. He also wrote newspaper columns, delving into subjects as varied as politics and economics, and made forays into writing fiction and acting on the stage.

Sócrates Brasileiro Sampaio de Souza Vieira de Oliveira was born on Feb. 19, 1954, in the Amazonian city of Belém do Pará, Brazil. His upbringing was more privileged than that of many Brazilian professional soccer players, who often rise from abject poverty.

Emerging in the 1970s as a promising young player in Ribeirão Preto, in the interior of São Paulo State, he studied medicine while playing for provincial teams before attaining his medical degree at 24. After that, he moved to Corinthians, the famous São Paulo club with a big following among Brazil's poor.

MANY-SIDED MAN: A football champion, medical doctor and political activist, Sócrates lived a bohemian lifestyle and struggled publicly with his demons.

Known to his fans as Doctor and Big Skinny, a reference to his spindly 6-foot-4-inch frame, Sócrates arrived at Corinthians at a time of intense political activity in São Paulo, when anger and resistance were coalescing against Brazil's military dictatorship.

In addition to organizing a movement advocating greater rights for Corinthians players, Sócrates spoke at street protests in the 1980s calling for an end to authoritarian rule. The movement helped usher in a transition to democracy.

"Dr. Sócrates was a star on the field and a great friend," said former President Luiz Inácio Lula da Silva, a Corinthians fan who was being treated for throat cancer at the hospital where Sócrates died. "He was an example of citizenship, intelligence and political consciousness."

On the field, Sócrates was known as a wily strategist who could elegantly employ his signature move, a back-heel pass. At a time when many players maintained a clean-cut appearance, Sócrates had a beard and sometimes appeared with his long hair held back in a headband, like the tennis star Bjorn Borg.

Fans of Sócrates mention his name in the same breath as Brazilian soccer greats like Pelé, Ronaldo and Romário. But unlike those players, he was never part of a World Cup championship team.

The team he captained in 1982 was considered among the best to play the game, but it lost to Italy, 3-2, in the second round. In the 1986 World Cup, Sócrates missed a penalty kick in a quarterfinal loss to France.

Revered for his rebellious irreverence and his "heel of gold," he deplored the way Brazilian soccer had evolved in recent years, criticizing the new playing styles as "bureaucratic" and "conservative."

"Being sensible isn't always the best thing," Sócrates told The Guardian in 2010.

He is survived by his wife and six children.

While Sócrates often defended his nonconformist style, he struggled publicly with his demons, too. In televised comments this year, he described his struggle with alcoholism, leading to a broader debate in Brazil over the country's drinking habits. In August he said he had stopped drinking.

— BY SIMON ROMERO

MURIEL PETIONI

Harlem's Family Doctor

JAN. 1, 1914 - DEC. 6, 2011

IN HER LAST DAYS, DR. MURIEL PETIONI summoned to her bedside many of the colleagues, protégés and political allies she had amassed during a lifetime as a Harlem physician and community activist. She gave them marching orders: make sure the new geriatric center at the hospital has the homey atmosphere we agreed on. Have you recruited new volunteers for the Harlem Elders program, as we discussed? The new clinic on 146th Street — let's make sure it has the equipment it needs.

"She's pointing a finger at me," said Representative Charles B. Rangel, the veteran Harlem congressman, who was among the dozens she summoned. "She's saying, 'Do you understand?'"

Dr. Petioni, who died on Dec. 6 in Manhattan at 97, was prominent in Harlem the way doctors were once prominent in every small town in the country. She was the family physician to Harlem's political elite, the Rangels and the Percy Suttons, among them. But she also treated so many thousands of others that she often identified public health issues before they hit the epidemiologists' radar.

She was preaching against sugar, junk food and obesity in the early 1950s, when she first hung her shingle at 114 West 131st Street (charging $2 for an office visit and $3 for house calls). Her dietary warning — "You're digging your grave with your fork" — became her signature, as did the motherly finger-pointing that usually accompanied it.

The heroin epidemic in the 1960s and '70s, and the crack and AIDS epidemics of the 1980s, came early to her door — whether directly in the blood work of her patients or indirectly in the stress-related health problems she saw in patients who were grandparents raising addicts' children.

Gunmen came, too. Dr. Petioni was held up a number of times for cash, drugs or prescription pads. She was never harmed and never considered leaving Harlem.

Until her retirement as a physician in the late 1990s, Dr. Petioni maintained her practice on the ground floor of the house on 131st Street where she and her family had lived, and where she had grown up.

SHE MADE HOUSE CALLS: Muriel Petioni was physician to both Harlem's elite and its underprivileged and identified public health issues early.

Her ties to Harlem ran deep. She was the daughter of one of Harlem's first black physicians. She was among the first generation of black M.D.'s given staff privileges at Harlem Hospital in the 1950s, when most hospitals in the country still made black physicians refer their patients to white doctors before admitting the patients to the hospital.

"Harlem is the black capital of the world, and Harlem Hospital is the black hospital of the world," she told The New York Times in 2001.

In an interview this year with The New York Amsterdam News, Dr. Petioni gave a modest assessment of her career. "I would give people as much time as they needed," she said. "If you had your heart and mind bursting and needed to talk to someone who was a physician, not bleeding in the body but bleeding in mind and soul, I would listen. I wasn't brilliant. I wasn't the best physician in the world, but I was nice enough to make people feel good."

The Amsterdam News called her "the mother of medicine in Harlem."

Muriel Marjorie Petioni was born on Jan. 1, 1914, in Trinidad to Charles and Rosa Petioni. Her father was a journalist whose advocacy for an end to colonial rule led to his expulsion in 1917. He arrived in New York, took pre-med classes at City College while working as a porter and brought his family to join him in 1919.

After being admitted to Howard University's medical school in Washington, he studied there full time while Muriel's mother remained in Harlem, supporting her and another daughter. Mr. Petioni, who was 40 when he became a doctor in 1925, settled his family and medical practice at the 131st Street house a few years later.

Muriel Petioni followed her father's path, graduating from Howard University Medical School in 1937, the only woman in her class. In 1942, she married Mallalieu S. Woolfolk, a Tuskegee Airman, who later became an influential lawyer in Harlem serving many of its political leaders. They divorced in the 1970s.

Dr. Petioni is survived by a son and two granddaughters.

In a career of more than half a century, Dr. Petioni worked as a school physician for the city's health department, maintained her private practice, and was a founder or leader of many community organizations promoting health care, housing development and education in Harlem. She mentored dozens of black medical students, went to public schools to tell young people to think about becoming doctors, and founded the Friends of Harlem Hospital, an organization that remains a bulwark against budget-cutting threats to that city-run hospital's existence.

Late in life, she became interested in the needs of the elderly. She helped plan a new geriatric wing at Harlem Hospital and marshaled support to expand and improve the Greater Harlem Nursing Home.

"I think she was about 89 when she began to focus on the lack of geriatric services," her son, Charles Woolfolk, said. "She said, 'You know, I'm starting to understand those old people.'"

— BY PAUL VITELLO

BONNIE PRUDDEN

Personal Trainer for a Flabby America

JAN. 29, 1914 - DEC. 11, 2011

B ONNIE PRUDDEN, whose alarm over the flabbiness of American children propelled her to become one of the most visible postwar champions of physical fitness, died on Dec. 11 at her home in Tucson. She was 97.

Ms. Prudden (pronounced PROO-den) appeared on the cover of Sports Illustrated in 1957 wearing a full-length leotard and a giant smile even as she contorted her body in a way that appeared painfully ambitious. She was one of the first fitness instructors to appear regularly on national television, as she did on the "Today" show in the 1950s. She wrote fitness books for babies, the elderly and people eager to enliven their sex lives. She carried her message to schools, hospitals and prisons, where she advocated sit-ups as a riot-prevention measure.

She entered the national spotlight in 1955 as an author of a report to President Dwight D. Eisenhower that revealed that 56 percent of American school children had failed at least one of a battery of fitness measures, including leg lifts and toe touches. In Europe, the figure was 8 percent.

The study came to be referred to as "the report that shocked the president." As a result, Eisenhower, worried that slack American youth would make less-than-intimidating soldiers, created the President's Council on Youth Fitness, now the President's Council on Fitness, Sports and Nutrition.

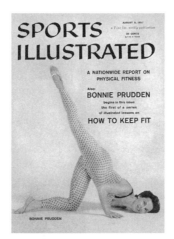

SPORTS ILLUSTRATED

A NATIONWIDE REPORT ON PHYSICAL FITNESS

BONNIE PRUDDEN
begins in this issue
the first of a series
of illustrated lessons on
HOW TO KEEP FIT

BONNIE PRUDDEN

NATIONAL PROFILE: Bonnie Prudden gained renown with a report on fitness to President Eisenhower.

instructor, and might have garnered even more fame, like Jane Fonda, had home video existed at the time.

In later years, Ms. Prudden came up with a way to eliminate the pain caused by exercising. It involved applying pressure with an elbow or thumb on what she called "trigger points," immediately followed by remedial exercise. She trademarked the name Myotherapy and opened a clinic in Tucson, where she and a half-dozen employees administered it.

Ms. Prudden believed American children were lollygagging in front of the television and not walking to school or performing chores. Her response was to gather her daughters, then 4 and 8, and 10 friends of each in a fitness class she taught herself.

It was the beginning of a lifelong campaign in which she would devise some of the first exercise and swim classes for infants and toddlers, exercises for the blind, and even "toilet training" for adults wanting to build muscle while attending to necessary business. She invented exercise equipment and one of the first climbing walls.

She also became one of the first exercise instructors on television, appearing as a guest on the "Home" and "Today" shows on NBC in the 1950s, and then on a syndicated show named for her in the 1960s. She wrote fitness articles for Sports Illustrated. She recorded a half-dozen records and wrote 15 books. She shared the television spotlight with Debbie Drake, another fitness

Ruth Alice Prudden was born in Manhattan on Jan. 29, 1914. She acquired the nickname Bonnie, she said, from people who deemed her a "bonnie lass." She grew up in Mount Vernon, N.Y., where, around age 3, she began to climb out her bedroom window to wander the neighborhood. Her parents' doctor thought she might stop if she got sufficiently tired, so they enrolled her in a rigorous ballet school. By the time she was 20, she was dancing on Broadway.

In 1936 she married Richard S. Hirschland, a wealthy metal container manufacturer who would have rather been an artist. She abandoned her dancing career to be a homemaker in Westchester County, where she did volunteer work for charities before starting the fitness sessions for her daughters and their friends in the mid-1940s at the Pleasant Ridge Elementary School in Harrison, N.Y. As the program grew it eventually moved to a Knights of Columbus hall. In 1954, she named the program the Institute for Physical Fitness. Enrollment inexplicably spurted when she began to charge a fee.

She and Mr. Hirschland climbed the Matterhorn on their honeymoon and became avid climbers in the Shawangunk Mountains in New York State. They often climbed with Dr. Hans Kraus, the professor of physical medicine and rehabilitation with whom Ms. Prudden wrote the report that influenced President Eisenhower.

In her 20s, Ms. Prudden had a skiing accident and broke her pelvis in five places, putting her in traction for three months. She was told that she would never ski, climb or have children. None of that turned out to be true. But the injury most likely did contribute years later to two total hip replacements, in 1970 and 1980.

She never stopped exercising, however. Even triple bypass heart surgery at 92 did not hinder her daily routine, by then largely done in the swimming pool or in bed, for which she had devised a set of rigorous exercises.

Ms. Prudden's marriage ended in divorce in the mid-1950s. She is survived by two daughters, four grandchildren and five great-grandchildren. One daughter, Suzy Prudden, is an author and motivational speaker. Her mother had motivational messages of her own. "You can't run back the clock," she liked to say, "but you can wind it up again."

— By Douglas Martin

\\\\\\\\\\\\\\\\\\\\\\\\\\\

ERICA WILSON

A World Watched Her Every Stitch

OCT. 8, 1928 - DEC. 13, 2011

Erica Wilson, the Julia Child of needlework, who brought the gentle art of crewel — as well as cross-stitch, needlepoint and other traditional embroidery techniques — to an international audience through her books, television shows, correspondence courses, syndicated column and retail shops,

died on Dec. 13 in Manhattan. She was 83.

British by birth, Ms. Wilson had lived in New York since arriving in the United States in 1954 for what was supposed to be a yearlong teaching assignment. Since then, without ever really intending to, she built a public career as a teacher of the domestic arts that paralleled Ms. Child's and in many respects anticipated Martha Stewart's.

Ms. Wilson, who wrote more than a dozen instructional books, was the host of "Erica," a public-television program produced by WGBH in Boston in the early 1970s and broadcast nationally.

Her Upper East Side flagship store, Erica Wilson Needle Works, offered classes in a range of needle arts and sold kits designed by Ms. Wilson for needlepoint pillows and the like. (Her best-known kits include a series based on the Unicorn Tapestries in the Metropolitan Museum of Art.)

The store, on Madison Avenue at 63rd Street, was a neighborhood fixture for decades until it closed in 2006, a casualty of rising commercial rents and the urban knitting boom. Ms. Wilson also had shops on Nantucket; in Palm

Beach; and in Southampton, on Long Island. The Nantucket shop remains in business.

Trained in London at the Royal School of Needlework, Ms. Wilson arrived in the United States at a propitious moment. American women, flush with postwar prosperity but without careers of their own, had time and disposable income on their hands.

Ms. Wilson put those hands to work. As a result, she was largely responsible for the midcentury American renaissance of hand embroidery, a traditional art that had waned in the 20th century amid the rise of machine sewing.

Under her guidance, women (and some men) learned centuries-old needle arts like cross-stitch, a technique, often seen on American Colonial samplers, in which patterns are formed by arrangements of embroidered X's; crewel embroidery, in which floral or other motifs are filled in with wool, leaving the background bare; and needlepoint, in which stitches fill the entire canvas, giving the look of tapestry.

Erica Moira Susan Wilson was born on Oct. 8, 1928, in Tidworth, England, near Stonehenge. Her father was a colonel in the British Army, and she spent her first five years in Bermuda. Returning to Britain with her mother after her parents divorced, she was reared in England and Scotland.

THE JULIA CHILD OF NEEDLEWORK: Erica Wilson wrote dozens of books and articles on knitting and was the host of a syndicated television program.

Ms. Wilson, who had done needlework as a child, found her vocation almost by default. "She was going to make a lousy secretary, and she wasn't very keen on mathematics," her husband, the prominent furniture designer Vladimir Kagan, said in an interview hours after his wife died.

Her mother solved the problem, he said, by suggesting the Royal School. After graduating, Ms. Wilson taught there for several years. In 1954, she was recruited by a visiting American, a well-to-do woman who wanted to start a needlework school in Millbrook, N.Y.

Ms. Wilson set out bravely for her American adventure, suitably armed.

"I brought a big trunk of my own wool, thinking I was going to Indian Country, where such things wouldn't be available," she told The News and Courier of Charleston, S.C., in 1973.

Before long, she had settled in Manhattan, where she taught at the Cooper Union. She also held workshops in her apartment, and the mimeographed handouts she gave her students soon blossomed into a full-fledged correspondence course. Enrolling thousands of students, it led to her books and the television show, which was filmed in the studio next to Ms. Child's.

Ms. Wilson also appeared on television in Britain and Australia. Her syndicated column, "Needleplay," appeared in American newspapers in the 1980s. Her books include "Crewel Embroidery" (1962), "Erica Wilson's Embroidery Book" (1973) and "Erica Wilson's Knitting Book" (1988).

Ms. Wilson died of a stroke. She had homes in Manhattan and Palm Beach and on Nantucket. Besides her husband, whom she married in 1957, she is survived by two daughters, a son and six grandchildren.

All of the above grew skilled at holding their hands aloft for long periods, letting Ms. Wilson wind all the wool she needed in a single sitting.

— BY MARGALIT FOX

ANTHONY AMATO

Opera Impresario of the Lower East Side

JULY 21, 1920 - DEC. 13, 2011

A NTHONY AMATO, the founder and artistic director of the Amato Opera Theater, a scrappy, often threadbare and very rarely dull chamber opera company on the Lower East Side of Manhattan that was a mainstay of New York's cultural life for 61 years, died on Dec. 13 at his home on City Island, in the Bronx.

Mr. Amato, who was also the company's stage director, music director, prompter, vocal coach, diction coach, caterer, broom pusher and emergency tenor, among other things, was 91.

Founded in 1948 by Mr. Amato and his wife, Sally, Amato Opera was long the brightest star in the constellation of semiprofessional opera companies spread over the city — the Off Broadway of the opera world.

> Snowstorms were created with cascades of oatmeal, to the satisfaction of resident mice.

From its repertory of more than 60 productions, it staged a half-dozen each season, including old reliables like Puccini's "Bohème" and rarely heard works like "Lo Schiavo," an 1889 opera by the Brazilian composer Carlos Gomes.

In Amato's first decades, when opera training programs were less ubiquitous, it was known as a proving ground for talented young singers. Many alumni went on to sing with major companies, including the Metropolitan Opera; among them are the tenors George Shirley and Neil Shicoff and the mezzo-soprano Mignon Dunn.

Critics routinely praised Amato's dramatic snap and sparkle, if not always its singing. But if the company's later productions were often cast with singer-doctors, singer-lawyers and singer-dog groomers, that did nothing to dim the ardor of Amato's perennially devoted audience.

It was not only the ticket prices that drew them, though that was a consideration: Tickets cost $1.80 early on; in 2009, the year the company was disbanded, they were still only $35. (Nowadays, tickets for the Met normally cost $100 or more.)

For the faithful, who returned year after year to the 107-seat theater at 319 Bowery, near Bond Street, a night at the Amato also offered the chance — a rare thing in this city — to witness grand opera as participatory democracy.

Operagoers were greeted by Mrs. Amato, who, when not taking tickets, making costumes, running the lights or selling coffee and cookies at intermission, sang many of the company's leading roles under her given name, Serafina Bellantone.

On some nights the overture wafted through the theater on record, spun by Mr. Amato.

(At first the orchestra pit had room for a piano or a pianist, but not both comfortably at once; it later accommodated a keyboard and a few woodwinds.)

Costumes were rehabilitated until they fell to dust; many a wig began life as a mop. And if that wig sometimes became entangled with the scenery, the show went on.

Onstage, snowstorms were accomplished with cascades of raw oatmeal, to the great satisfaction of the theater's resident mice.

Antonio Amato was born on July 21, 1920, in Minori, on the Amalfi Coast of Italy. At 7, he moved with his family to New Haven. He left high school amid the Depression to become a butcher, honest work that pleased his father. But young Mr. Amato, called Anthony or Tony, adored opera. He eventually prevailed, appearing as a tenor with regional companies and in summer stock.

Mr. Amato met his wife in 1943 at the Paper Mill Playhouse in Millburn, N.J., where they were performing in Rudolf Friml's operetta "The Vagabond King." Every night onstage he knocked her down, as called for, and every night offstage he apologized so profusely that she took pity on him and married him, in 1945.

Afterward, Mr. Amato ran an opera workshop at the American Theater Wing in New York. Many of his students were returned servicemen, and he conceived Amato Opera to give them a place to perform. (Mr. Amato, who sang till the end of his life, was the company's default understudy for all male roles.)

The Amato's first production, Rossini's "Barber of Seville," opened on Sept. 12, 1948, in the basement of Our Lady of Pompeii Church in Greenwich Village.

For many years, singers were paid in meatballs, tenderly cooked by Mr. Amato and consumed family-style by the company. In later years singers got a stipend: $10 a performance.

MUSIC DIRECTOR AND BROOM PUSHER: Anthony Amato in the Lower East Side opera house he founded in 1948. The 107-seat theater could hardly accommodate an orchestra pit.

After playing in various spots around town — the church had commandeered its space for bingo — the company moved in 1964 to its Bowery home, near the punk-rock club CBGB.

Mr. Amato died of cancer, said Rochelle Mancini, an editor and former principal singer with the company. She helped Mr. Amato write a memoir, "The Smallest Grand Opera in the World," published in 2011 by iUniverse. His survivors include a brother. Mrs. Amato died in 2000 at age 82.

Reviewers often called the Amatos' theater "intimate," but the word scarcely did justice to its confines. The stage was just 18 feet wide, with negligible wings. Singers sometimes had to exit through the theater's back door, then re-enter by running through the parking lot, around the corner, through the front door, down the aisle and onto the stage.

The parking-lot sprint entailed rubbing elbows with the neighborhood's skid-row denizens. As one singer later recalled, he once made the dash costumed in tie and tails. Several men, thinking fortune had sent them a millionaire at last, touched him for money on his way through.

— By Margalit Fox

\\\\\\\\\\\\\\\\\\\\\\\\\\\\\\\\\\\\\

GEORGE WHITMAN

Bookseller on the Seine

DEC. 12, 1913 - DEC. 14, 2011

G EORGE WHITMAN, the American-born owner of Shakespeare & Company, a fabled English-language bookstore on the Left Bank in Paris and a magnet for writers, poets and tourists for close to 60 years, died on Dec. 14 in his apartment above the store. He was 98.

More than a distributor of books, Mr. Whitman saw himself as patron of a literary haven and the heir to Sylvia Beach, the founder of the original Shakespeare & Company, the celebrated haunt of Hemingway and James Joyce.

As Mr. Whitman put it, "I wanted a bookstore because the book business is the business of life."

Overlooking the Seine and facing the Cathedral of Notre-Dame, the store, looking somewhat beat-up behind a Dickensian facade and spread over three floors, has been an offbeat mix of open house and literary commune. For decades Mr. Whitman provided food and makeshift beds to young aspiring novelists or writing nomads, often letting them spend a night, a week, or even months living among the crowded shelves and alcoves.

He welcomed visitors with large-print messages on the walls. "Be not inhospitable to strangers, lest they be angels in disguise," was one, quoting Yeats. Next to a wishing well at the center of the store, a sign said: "Give what you can, take what you need. George." By his own estimate, he lodged some 40,000 people.

Mr. Whitman's store, founded in 1951, has also been a favorite stopover for established authors and poets to read from their work and sign their books. Its visitors list reads like a Who's Who of American, English, French and Latin American literature: Henry Miller, Anaïs Nin, Samuel Beckett and James Baldwin were frequent callers in the early days; Lawrence Durrell and the Beat writers William Burroughs, Allen Ginsberg and Gregory Corso were regulars, too, all of them Mr. Whitman's friends.

Another was the Beat poet Lawrence Ferlinghetti. The two met in Paris in the late 1940s and discussed the importance of free-thinking bookstores. Mr. Ferlinghetti went on to found what became a landmark bookshop in its own right, City Lights, in San Francisco. Their bookstores would be sister shops, the two men agreed.

Mr. Whitman's beacon and enduring influence was Walt Whitman (no relation), who also ran a bookstore, more than a century ago. In a pamphlet, Mr. Whitman wrote that he felt a kinship with the poet. "Perhaps no man liked so many things and disliked so few as Walt Whitman," he wrote, "and I at least aspire to the same modest attainment."

George Whitman was born on Dec. 12, 1913, in East Orange, N.J., and grew up in Salem, Mass. His thirst for travel was awakened when his father, a physics teacher, took the family to China for a sabbatical year at Nanking

University. After majoring in journalism at Boston University and graduating in 1935, Mr. Whitman began traveling in earnest, taking extended walking trips across North America and through Central America while writing and exploring, coming home from the latter after getting bogged down in a swamp in Panama.

After enrolling at Harvard, he enlisted in the Army in 1941, serving as a medic for several months at an outpost in Greenland.

With the end of the war he resumed his travels, exploring Europe before settling in Paris in 1946. There he used his G.I. Bill benefits to start a small lending library in his windowless room in the Hotel de Suez near the Sorbonne, where he studied for a time.

After moving his English language books to a kiosk, he opened his store, first calling it Le Mistral. It was said to be named after the Chilean poet Gabriella Mistral, whose work Mr. Whitman admired.

Mr. Whitman, who had called himself a frustrated novelist, poured his energy into

A FABLED LITERARY HAUNT: George Whitman's celebrated Left Bank bookstore became a magnet for readers, writers and tourists.

selling and lending books and moving in literary circles.

How Le Mistral became Shakespeare & Company has been a matter of debate. Some accused Mr. Whitman of pilfering the name. But Clive Hart, a Joyce scholar, wrote in a recent e-mail that he attended a gathering in 1958 in which Sylvia Beach "announced that she would like to offer George the old name of Shakespeare & Company."

"George was of course delighted," Mr. Hart wrote.

Mr. Whitman adopted the name in 1964, to honor Ms. Beach on the 400th anniversary of Shakespeare's birth, the bookstore said. He named his daughter, Sylvia Beach Whitman, born in 1981, after her.

Ms. Whitman, who now runs the store, is Mr. Whitman's only child. She said that while he had many romantic attachments, he was married only once, and briefly, to her mother, Felicity Leng. He is also survived by a younger brother.

For all the romanticism surrounding the bookstore, Mr. Whitman went through difficult times. The shop was closed for a year, in 1967, for lack of a proper license, but with the support of friends he continued lending books and published the first issue of The Paris Magazine, which he called "the poor man's Paris Review," a reference to the literary journal founded in 1953 by George Plimpton and others. Mr. Whitman's magazine carried work by Durrell, Ginsberg, Jean Paul Sartre, and Marguerite Duras.

It has come out only sporadically since then. A fire once destroyed almost 5,000 volumes in the library above the store.

Mr. Whitman was famously frugal and expected the bibliophiles residing in his store to work a few hours every day sorting and selling books. Yet he also invited uncounted numbers of people for weekly tea parties to his own apartment, or for late-night readings enriched with dumplings or pots of Irish stew.

Some guests later described him as a kind and magnetic father figure to needy souls but also as a man who could throw tantrums and preside over the store's residents, sometimes up to 20 people, like a moody and unpredictable dictator.

Mr. Whitman had variously called himself a communist, a utopian and a humanist. But he may have also been a romantic himself, at least concerning his life's work. "I may disappear leaving behind me no worldly possessions — just a few old socks and love letters, " he wrote in his last years. Paraphrasing a line from Yeats, he added, "and my little Rag and Bone Shop of the Heart."

— BY MARLISE SIMONS

CHRISTOPHER HITCHENS

A Quiver Full of Arguments, Laced With Wit

APRIL 13, 1949 - DEC. 15, 2011

C HRISTOPHER HITCHENS, a slashing polemicist in the tradition of Thomas Paine and George Orwell who trained his sights on targets as various as Henry Kissinger, the British monarchy and Mother Teresa, wrote a bestseller attacking religious belief, and dismayed his former comrades on the left

by enthusiastically supporting the American-led war in Iraq, died on Dec. 15 in Houston. He was 62.

His death, at the M. D. Anderson Cancer Center, was caused by pneumonia, a complication of esophageal cancer, which he learned he had while on a publicity tour in 2010 for his memoir, "Hitch-22." He lived in Washington.

Mr. Hitchens wrote and spoke about his illness frequently. "In whatever kind of a 'race' life may be, I have very abruptly become a finalist," he wrote in Vanity Fair magazine, for which he was a contributing editor.

He took pains to emphasize that he had not revised his position on atheism, articulated in his best-selling 2007 book, "God Is Not Great:

How Religion Poisons Everything," although he did express amused appreciation at the hope among some concerned Christians that he might undergo a late-life conversion.

Mr. Hitchens also professed to have no regrets for a lifetime of heavy smoking and drinking. "Writing is what's important to me, and anything that helps me do that — or enhances and prolongs and deepens and sometimes intensifies argument and conversation — is worth it to me," he told Charlie Rose in a television interview in 2010, adding that it was "impossible for me to imagine having my life without going to those parties, without having those late nights, without that second bottle."

Armed with a quick wit and a keen appetite for combat, Mr. Hitchens was in constant

demand as a speaker on television, radio and the debating
platform, where he held forth in
a sonorous, plummily accented
voice that seemed at odds with
his disheveled appearance. He
was a master of the extended per-
oration, peppered with literary
allusions, and of the bright, off-
the-cuff remark.

In 2007, when the interviewer
Sean Hannity tried to make the
case for an all-seeing God, Mr.
Hitchens dismissed the idea
with contempt. "It would be like
living in North Korea," he said.

Mr. Hitchens, a British
Trotskyite who had lost faith in the Socialist
movement, spent much of his life wandering
the globe and reporting on the world's trouble
spots for The Nation magazine, the British
newsmagazine The New Statesman and other
publications.

His work took him to Northern Ireland,
Greece, Cyprus, Portugal, Spain and Argentina
in the 1970s, generally to shine a light on the evil
practices of entrenched dictators or the imperial
machinations of the great powers.

After moving to the United States in 1981,
he added American politics to his beat, writing
a biweekly Minority Report for The Nation. He
wrote a monthly review-essay for The Atlantic
and, as a carte-blanche columnist at Vanity Fair,
filed essays on topics as various as getting a
Brazilian bikini wax and the experience of being
waterboarded, a volunteer assignment that he
called "very much more frightening though less
painful than the bikini wax." He was also a columnist for the online magazine Slate.

His support for the Iraq war sprang from a
growing conviction that radical elements in the
Islamic world posed a mortal danger to Western

UNAPOLOGETIC CRITIC:
A prodigious journalist,
Christopher Hitchens befriended
writers like Martin Amis and
made enemies of power players
like Henry Kissinger.

principles of political liberty and
freedom of conscience. The first
stirrings of that view came in
1989 with the Ayatollah Ruhollah
Khomeini's fatwah against the
novelist Salman Rushdie for his
supposedly blasphemous words
in "The Satanic Verses." To Mr.
Hitchens, the terrorist attacks
of Sept. 11, 2001, confirmed the
threat.

In a political shift that shocked
many of his friends and readers,
he cut his ties to The Nation and
became an outspoken advocate
of the American-led invasion of
Iraq in 2003 and a ferocious critic
of what he called "Islamofascism." Although he
denied coining the word, he popularized it.

He remained unapologetic about the war.
In 2006 he told the British newspaper The
Guardian: "There are a lot of people who will
not be happy, it seems to me, until I am compelled to write a letter to these comrades in Iraq
and say: 'Look, guys, it's been real, but I'm
going to have to drop you now. The political
cost to me is just too high.' Do I see myself doing
this? No, I do not!"

Christopher Eric Hitchens was born on
April 13, 1949, in Portsmouth, England. His
father was a career officer in the Royal Navy and
later earned a modest living as a bookkeeper.

Though it strained the family budget,
Christopher was sent to private schools in
Tavistock and Cambridge, at the insistence of
his mother. "If there is going to be an upper
class in this country, then Christopher is going
to be in it," he overheard his mother saying to his
father, clinching a spirited argument.

He was politically attuned even as a
7-year-old. "I was precocious enough to
watch the news and read the papers, and I can

remember October 1956, the simultaneous crisis in Hungary and Suez, very well," he told the magazine The Progressive in 1997. "And getting a sense that the world was dangerous, a sense that the game was up, that the Empire was over."

Even before arriving at Balliol College, Oxford, Mr. Hitchens had been drawn into left-wing politics, primarily out of opposition to the Vietnam War. After heckling a Maoist speaker at a political meeting, he was invited to join the International Socialists, a Trotskyite party. Thus began a dual career as political agitator and upper-crust sybarite. He arranged a packed schedule of antiwar demonstrations by day and Champagne-flooded parties with Oxford's elite at night. Spare time was devoted to the study of philosophy, politics and economics.

After graduating from Oxford in 1970, he spent a year traveling across the United States. He then tried his luck as a journalist in London, where he contributed reviews, columns and editorials to The New Statesman, The Daily Express and The Evening Standard.

"I would do my day jobs at various mainstream papers and magazines and TV stations, where my title was 'Christopher Hitchens,'" he wrote in "Hitch-22," "and then sneak down to the East End, where I was variously features editor of Socialist Worker and book review editor of the theoretical monthly International Socialism."

He became a staff writer and editor for The New Statesman in the late 1970s and fell in with a literary clique that included Martin Amis, Julian Barnes, James Fenton, Clive James and Ian McEwan. The group liked to play a game in which members came up with the sentence least likely to be uttered by one of their number. Mr. Hitchens's was "I don't care how rich you are, I'm not coming to your party."

After collaborating on a 1976 biography of James Callaghan, the Labour leader, he published his first book, "Cyprus," in 1984 to commemorate Turkey's invasion of Cyprus a decade earlier. A longer version was published in 1989 as "Hostage to History: Cyprus From the Ottomans to Kissinger."

His interest in the region led to another book, "Imperial Spoils: The Curious Case of the Elgin Marbles" (1987), in which he argued that Britain should return the Elgin marbles to Greece.

In 1981 he married a Greek Cypriot, Eleni Meleagrou. The marriage ended in divorce. He is survived by their two children; his wife, Carol Blue; their daughter; and a brother.

Mr. Hitchens's reporting on Greece came through unusual circumstances. He was summoned to Athens in 1973 because his mother, after leaving his father, had committed suicide there with her new partner. After his father's death in 1987, he learned that his mother was Jewish, a fact she had concealed from her husband and her children.

After moving to the United States, where he eventually became a citizen, Mr. Hitchens became a fixture on television, in print and at the lectern. Many of his essays for The Nation and other magazines were collected in "Prepared for the Worst" (1988).

He also threw himself into the defense of his friend Mr. Rushdie. "It was, if I can phrase it like this, a matter of everything I hated versus everything I loved," he wrote in his memoir. "In the hate column: dictatorship, religion, stupidity, demagogy, censorship, bullying and intimidation. In the love column: literature, irony, humor, the individual and the defense of free expression."

To help rally public support, Mr. Hitchens arranged for Mr. Rushdie to be received at the White House by President Bill Clinton, one of Mr. Hitchens's least favorite politicians and the subject of his book "No One Left to Lie To: The Triangulations of William Jefferson Clinton" (1999).

He regarded the response of left-wing intellectuals to Mr. Rushdie's predicament as feeble, and he soon began to question many of his cherished political assumptions. He had already broken with the International Socialists when, in 1982, he astonished some of his brethren by supporting Britain's short-lived war with Argentina over the Falkland Islands.

The drift was reflected in books devoted to heroes like George Orwell ("Why Orwell Matters," 2002), Thomas Paine ("Thomas Paine's 'Rights of Man': A Biography," 2006) and Thomas Jefferson ("Thomas Jefferson: Author of America," 2005).

His polemical urges found other outlets. In 2001 he excoriated Mr. Kissinger, the secretary of state in the Nixon administration, as a war criminal in the book "The Trial of Henry Kissinger." He helped write a 2002 documentary film of the same title, based on the book.

Mr. Hitchens became a campaigner against religious belief, most notably in his screed against Mother Teresa, "The Missionary Position: Mother Teresa in Theory and Practice" (1995), and "God Is Not Great." He regarded Mother Teresa as a proselytizer for a retrograde version of Roman Catholicism rather than as a saintly charity worker.

"I don't quite see Christopher as a 'man of action,'" the writer Ian Buruma told The New Yorker in 2006, "but he's always looking for the defining moment — as it were, our Spanish Civil War, where you put yourself on the right side, and stand up to the enemy."

One stand distressed many of his friends. In 1999, Sidney Blumenthal, an aide to Mr. Clinton and a friend of Mr. Hitchens's, testified before a grand jury that he was not the source of damaging comments made to reporters about Monica Lewinsky, whose supposed affair with the president was under investigation by the House of Representatives.

Contacted by House investigators, Mr. Hitchens supplied information in an affidavit that, in effect, accused Mr. Blumenthal of perjury and put him in danger of being indicted.

At a lunch in 1998, Mr. Hitchens wrote, Mr. Blumenthal had characterized Ms. Lewinsky as "a stalker" and said the president was the victim of a predatory and unstable woman. Overnight, Mr. Hitchens — now called "Hitch the Snitch" by Blumenthal partisans — became persona non grata in living rooms all over Washington. In a review of "Hitch-22" in The New York Review of Books, Mr. Buruma criticized Mr. Hitchens for making politics personal.

In Mr. Hitchens's view, he wrote, "politics is essentially a matter of character."

"Politicians do bad things," Mr. Buruma continued, "because they are bad men. The idea that good men can do terrible things (even for good reasons), and bad men good things, does not enter into this particular moral universe."

Mr. Hitchens's latest collection of writings, "Arguably: Essays," published in 2011, was a best-seller and ranked among the top 10 books of the year by The New York Times Book Review.

Mr. Hitchens discussed the possibility of a deathbed conversion, insisting that the odds were slim that he would admit the existence of God.

"The entity making such a remark might be a raving, terrified person whose cancer has spread to the brain," he told The Atlantic in August 2010. "I can't guarantee that such an entity wouldn't make such a ridiculous remark, but no one recognizable as myself would ever make such a remark."

Readers of "Hitch-22" already knew his feelings about the end. "I personally want to 'do' death in the active and not the passive," he wrote, "and to be there to look it in the eye and be doing something when it comes for me."

— By WILLIAM GRIMES

KIM JONG-IL

The Unknowable 'Dear Leader'

UNKNOWN · DEC. 17, 2011

K IM JONG-IL, the reclusive dictator who kept North Korea at the edge of starvation and collapse, banished to gulags citizens deemed disloyal, and turned the country into a nuclear weapons state, died on Dec. 17, the country's official news media announced on Dec. 19. He was reported to be 69.

He had been in ill health since a reported stroke in 2008.

Called the "Dear Leader" by his people, Mr. Kim, the son of North Korea's founder, remained an unknowable figure. Everything about him was guesswork, from the exact date and place of his birth to the mythologized events of his rise in a country formed by the hasty division of the Korean Peninsula at the end of World War II.

CULT FIGURE: Kim Jong-il was mythologized in an isolated North Korea.

North Koreans heard about him only as their "peerless leader" and "the great successor to the revolutionary cause." Yet he fostered what was perhaps the last personality cult in the Communist world. His portrait hangs beside that of his father, Kim Il-sung, in nearly every North Korean household and building. Towers, banners and even rock faces across the country bear slogans praising him.

Mr. Kim was a source of fascination inside the Central Intelligence Agency, which interviewed his mistresses, tried to track his whereabouts and sought to psychoanalyze his motives. And he was an object of parody in American culture.

Short and round, he wore elevator shoes, oversize sunglasses and a bouffant hairdo — a Hollywood stereotype of the wacky post-cold-war dictator. Mr. Kim was fascinated by film. He orchestrated the kidnapping of an actress and a director, both of them South Koreans, in an effort to build a domestic movie industry. He was said to keep a personal library of 20,000 foreign films, including the complete James Bond series, his favorite. But he rarely saw the outside world, save from the windows of his luxury train, which occasionally took him to China.

He was derided and denounced. President George W. Bush called him a "pygmy" and included his country in the "axis of evil." Children's books in South Korea depicted him as a red devil with horns and fangs. Yet those who met him were surprised by his serious demeanor and his knowledge of events beyond the hermit kingdom he controlled.

"He was a very outspoken person," said Roh Moo-hyun, who as South Korea's president met Mr. Kim in Pyongyang, the North's capital, in 2007. "He was the most flexible man in North Korea."

Wendy Sherman, now the No. 3 official in the State Department, who was counselor to Secretary of State Madeleine K. Albright and accompanied her to North Korea, said in 2008, "He was smart, engaged, knowledgeable, self-confident, sort of the master-director of all he surveyed."

Ms. Albright met Mr. Kim in October 2000 in what turned out to be a futile effort to strike a deal with North Korea over limiting its missile program before President Bill Clinton left office.

There were tales of a playboy lifestyle, and with a bouffant hairdo, oversize sunglasses and elevator shoes, he fit the Hollywood stereotype of a wacky dictator.

"There was no denying the dictatorial state that he ruled," Ms. Sherman said. "There was no denying the freedoms that didn't exist. But at the time, there were a lot of questions in the U.S. about whether he was really in control, and we left with no doubt that he was."

When Ms. Albright and Ms. Sherman sat down with him to talk through a 14-point list of concerns about North Korea's missile program, "he didn't know the answers to every question, but he knew a lot more than most leaders would — and he was a conceptual thinker," Ms. Sherman said.

And though he presided over a country that was starving and broke, he played his one card, his nuclear weapons program, brilliantly,

first defying the Bush administration's efforts to push his country over the brink, then exploiting America's distraction with the war in Iraq to harvest enough nuclear fuel from his main nuclear reactor at Yongbyon to produce the fuel for six to eight weapons.

A DEAL WITH WASHINGTON

Mr. Bush said during his first term in office that he would never tolerate a nuclear North Korea, but as his presidency wound down, many White House aides believed that he did exactly that.

It was not until the spring of 2007 that Mr. Bush was told by the Israelis that North Korea was helping Syria build a nuclear reactor; before the Syrians or the North Koreans were confronted with that evidence, Israel sent bombers on a secret mission to destroy the Syrian plant. The North Koreans have never explained their role.

By the time Mr. Bush left office in 2009, the administration had moved from four years of confrontation with the North to three years of halting negotiations. Led by Christopher R. Hill, a veteran American diplomat, the negotiations resulted in a deal that hawks hated: the United States agreed to supply North Korea with large amounts of fuel oil in return for the dismantlement of the aging Yongbyon plant, described by inspectors as a radioactive accident waiting to happen.

Mr. Kim played a weak hand very well. He succeeded in fending off pressure from Washington and Beijing, and in forcing Washington to talk and ultimately haggle with him. He dragged out negotiations, holding on to his nuclear fuel and whatever weapons he had produced, giving him continued leverage. It is that arsenal that continues to worry American and Asian officials.

"When the history of this era is written," said Graham Allison, a Harvard professor and expert on nuclear proliferation, "the scorecard will be Kim 8, Bush 0."

But if "he was the greatest master of survival, against all odds," said Andrei Lankov, a North Korea expert at Kookmin University in Seoul, South Korea, "it was his own people who paid the price, and the price was pretty high."

Mr. Kim's policy of songun, or "army first," lavished the country's scarce resources on the military, at 1.1 million-strong the world's fifth largest. During his rule, the North expanded its ballistic missile arsenal and, in October 2006, became the eighth country in the world to conduct a nuclear test.

But as the North's economy shrank, its isolation deepened. Possibly as many as two million people — almost 10 percent of the population — died in a famine in the mid- to late 1990s brought on by incompetence and natural disasters.

"Do not expect me to change!" is a popular catchphrase credited to Mr. Kim and used to exhort his people to remain loyal to his socialist ways.

Mr. Kim is believed to have been born in Siberia in 1941, when his father, Kim Il-sung, was in exile in the Soviet Union. But in North Korea's official accounts, he was born in 1942, in a cabin, Abe Lincoln–like. The cabin was in a secret camp of anti-Japanese guerrillas his father commanded on Mount Paektu, a holy piece of land in Korean mythology. The event, the official Korean Central News Agency would often say, was accompanied by the appearance of a bright star in the sky and a double-rainbow that touched the earth.

Little is known of his upbringing, apart from the official statement that he graduated in 1964 from Kim Il-sung University, one of the country's many monuments to his father. At the time, North Korea was enmeshed in the cold war, and the younger Kim watched many crises unfold from close up, including North Korea's seizure

UNCERTAIN FUTURE: Kim Jong-il, left, with his father, North Korea's founder, Kim Il-Sung, and his mother. The younger Mr. Kim wasn't always heir apparent.

of the Pueblo, an American spy ship, in 1968. He appeared episodically at state events, rarely speaking. When he did, he revealed a high-pitched voice and little of his father's easygoing charisma.

In his youth and middle age, there were stories about his playboy lifestyle, like hosting extravagant meals at a time when his country was starving. (His cook wrote a book after leaving the country.) His wavy hair and lifted heels, along with a passion for top-label liquor, made him the butt of jokes.

There was also speculation that he was involved in the 1983 bombing of a South Korean political delegation in Burma, now known as Myanmar, and that he had known of the kidnapping of Japanese citizens and perhaps had ordered it. Nothing was proved.

Washington put North Korea on its list of state sponsors of terrorism after North Korean agents planted a bomb that blew up a South Korean passenger jet in 1987 — under instructions from Mr. Kim, according to one of the agents, who was caught alive.

Mr. Kim campaigned for power relentlessly. He bowed to his father at the front porch each morning and offered to put the shoes on the father's feet long before he was elected to the Politburo, at age 32, in 1974, said Hwang Jang-yop, a former North Korean Workers' Party secretary who had been a key aide for the Kim regime before his defection to Seoul in 1997.

"At an early age, Kim Jong-il mastered the mechanics of power," Mr. Hwang said.

It was not until 1993, as the existence of the Yongbyon nuclear plant and North Korea's nuclear weapons ambitions became publicly known, that Mr. Kim appeared to be his father's undisputed successor. That year, he became head of the National Defense Commission, the North's most powerful agency, in charge of the military.

In 1994, in a showdown with the United States, North Korea threatened to turn its stockpile of nuclear fuel into bombs. It was the closest the two countries came to war since the armistice that ended the Korean War in 1953. The standoff was defused when Kim Il-sung welcomed former President Jimmy Carter, who pushed Mr. Clinton and Mr. Kim into a deal.

Within a month, however, the country's founder and "Great Leader" was dead. Many doubted at the time that the younger Kim would take over. There were rumors of a military coup, and theories that he would be allowed to keep his fast cars and to consort with visiting European "entertainers" as long as he did not try to run the country. Like much intelligence about North Korea, that turned out to be wrong.

Though his home life was a mystery, it is known that Mr. Kim had three sons, any one of whom could potentially have succeeded him.

His oldest son, Kim Jong-nam, would have been the natural choice, but he had a handicap: his mother never married Mr. Kim. Since his health crisis in 2008, Mr. Kim had been grooming his third son, Kim Jong-un, to be his successor. The son is believed to be in his late 20s. Less than two weeks after Mr. Kim's death, Kim Jong-un was declared the country's "supreme leader" by the president of its parliament.

Mr. Kim consolidated power in the late 1990s, flexing his muscle by testing a North Korean missile over Japan and sending Japan, a much larger and more powerful nation, into a panic. It was through episodes like this that Mr. Kim learned true power: that he could blackmail his way to survival.

But he could not learn to feed his own people, and his country became even more dependent on China for food and fuel and on "humanitarian" donations from South Korea and the United States. In June 2000, Mr. Kim played host in Pyongyang to the first summit meeting with a South Korean president, Kim Dae-jung, since the peninsula was divided more than five decades before.

NUCLEAR NORTH KOREA: Kim Jong-il used his country's limited money and resources to create the world's fifth-largest army and conduct alarming nuclear tests.

PRESSURING PYONGYANG

The South Korean leader received the Nobel Peace Prize later that year, though his reputation was soon tainted by revelations that a South Korean company had paid off the North Koreans, and presumably their leader, to arrange the trip.

Once President Bush took office in January 2001, all cooperation between Washington and Seoul over how to deal with the North came to a crashing halt. Mr. Bush rejected the South's "sunshine policy" of engagement with North Korea and ended Clinton-era talks that he viewed as dangerous appeasement.

A concerted effort to push North Korea over the brink began, setting off an uprising against Kim Jong-il's leadership. To the degree Washington could, it cut off North Korean trade, its access to cash and its ability to export weapons and drugs. Mr. Bush called Mr. Kim a "tyrant" who "starves his own people."

In October 2002, the administration presented North Korea with evidence that Pyongyang had secretly tried to evade the 1994 nuclear agreement with the United States by purchasing equipment to enrich uranium from Abdul Qadeer Khan, a founder of Pakistan's nuclear weapons program. The evidence was strong — the United States had tracked the shipments with spy satellites — but the C.I.A. overstated its confidence that the North was building separate, secret nuclear facilities.

That led to a confrontation that changed the nature of the North Korean threat. Mr. Kim ordered the ouster of United Nations inspectors who had been stationed at Yongbyon. The United States pressed for an end to fuel shipments to the North. In retaliation, from January through March 2003, just as the United States military was barreling toward the invasion of Iraq, Mr. Kim did what his father had come so very close to doing nine years before: he announced that he was reprocessing spent fuel rods into bomb fuel.

After the invasion of Iraq, Mr. Kim was not seen for nearly two months; there were reports that he had gone into hiding, thinking he was Mr. Bush's next target. He emerged only to start another confrontation in 2006, first with a series of missile tests, then, in October, with the North's first nuclear test.

Some Asian and American officials interpreted Mr. Kim's decision as a fit of pique because "six-party talks" — negotiations among North Korea, China, South Korea, Russia, the United States and Japan — were moving so slowly. Others said Mr. Kim had simply learned from Saddam Hussein's mistakes and determined that he would never face the United States without a nuclear weapon.

The test itself was something of a fizzle; it ended with a sub-kiloton explosion, less than a tenth of the power of the bomb the United States dropped on Hiroshima, Japan, in 1945. But Mr. Kim had made his point. He was condemned in the United Nations, and China briefly cut off oil and other trade. But within months the United States agreed on a new series of negotiations.

While there were many starts and stops, and disagreements over what it means to dismantle a nuclear program fully, Mr. Kim agreed in the summer of 2007 to stop the production of new nuclear fuel at Yongbyon. By then he presumably had all the weapons he needed.

The plant began to be dismantled, and in the summer of 2008 the Bush administration talked about starting on the hardest negotiations of all, over the price of giving up North Korea's nuclear arsenal. Mr. Kim died before serious talks could begin.

As soon as President Barack Obama took office, Mr. Kim ordered a second nuclear test, this one more successful than the first. And he waited out the predictable hail of international condemnation. The move aborted any efforts by Mr. Obama to engage with the North Koreans. And the next three years were spent with the United States and South Korea demanding that the North live up to the denuclearization pledges it had made during the Bush administration.

Instead, it did the opposite. In November 2010, the North Koreans showed a visiting American scientist from Stanford University, Siegfried Hecker, an apparently working uranium enrichment plant that the country had been building for years and that the C.I.A. had missed, though the agency had been right about other secret facilities. The plant gave North Korea a new way to produce nuclear weapons, even as its people fell into another food shortage.

The same year, the North made two attacks against the South Korean military, sinking a ship and later shelling an island near Northern waters. The episodes caused the United States and South Korea to conduct new joint exercises, even while the Chinese, apparently fearing a complete collapse of the North Korean regime, increased its economic aid.

Despite his ill health, Mr. Kim was reported to have visited one of the units that attacked the South, to hand out medals, and recently managed one last visit to his benefactors in China. It was unclear whether Kim Jong-un had accompanied him.

— BY DAVID E. SANGER; CHOE SANG-HUN
CONTRIBUTED REPORTING.

DOE AVEDON

A Photographer's 'Pygmalion'

APRIL 7, 1925 · DEC. 18, 2011

D OE AVEDON, a bookish beauty reluctantly transformed into a high-fashion model at the hands of a visionary photographer, Richard Avedon — a story that inspired the 1957 musical "Funny Face," about a bookish beauty (Audrey Hepburn) reluctantly transformed into a high-fashion model

at the hands of a visionary photographer (Fred Astaire) — died on Dec. 18 in Los Angeles. She was 86.

Ms. Avedon's career has a "Pygmalion" aspect that befits midcentury Hollywood, the milieu into which her dark good looks eventually propelled her. For after meeting her by chance in the 1940s, Mr. Avedon set about transforming her, changing not only her profession (she had

worked in uninspiring office jobs that gave her time to read) but also her name.

He changed her first name to Doe because of her soft wide eyes — and because it made up in glamour what her given name, Dorcas, seemed to lack. He changed her last name by marrying her.

Although the marriage lasted just five years, her work as his muse and frequent subject led

Ms. Avedon into a career, equally unanticipated, as a stage, film and television actress.

Ms. Avedon, who later married the director Don Siegel and was known in private life as Doe Avedon Siegel, had roles in a handful of pictures, including "The High and the Mighty" (1954), starring John Wayne, and "Deep in My Heart" (1954), starring José Ferrer. She returned to the screen in 1984 in "Love Streams," directed by John Cassavetes.

On television, she had a recurring role in "Big Town," a noirish newspaper drama broadcast from 1950 to 1956.

On Broadway, she won a Theater World Award in 1949 for "The Young and Fair," a drama by N. Richard Nash, in which she played the mean girl at a college for young ladies. She also appeared that year in the short-lived comedy "My Name Is Aquilon."

BOOKISH BEAUTY: Doe Avedon's love affair with a visionary photographer inspired the 1957 musical "Funny Face."

If Ms. Avedon's career was modest, that by all accounts was fine with her. An orphan at 12, she wanted nothing more, her daughter Anney Siegel-Wamsat said, than to be a wife and mother.

Dorcas Marie Nowell was born on April 7, 1925, in Old Westbury, N.Y., on Long Island, where her father was butler to a wealthy lawyer. Her mother died when she was 3, her father when she was 12, and she was reared by his employer's family.

As a young woman in New York, she held various jobs, including working in a bank. The precise circumstances of her meeting Mr. Avedon varied in the telling, her daughter said:

in one version, he walked into the bank, took one look at her and the plot flowed cinematically from there.

They married in 1944, and Ms. Avedon was soon posing for other major photographers, including Karl Bissinger, and rubbing elbows with Noël Coward and his glittering ilk. Through her friendship with Leonard Gershe, who would write the screenplay for "Funny Face," the film was conceived.

In 1949 she divorced Mr. Avedon to marry an actor, Dan Mathews. "I would have crawled to the Bronx on my knees to bring Doe back," Mr. Avedon told ABC News in 1993.

Mr. Mathews died in an automobile accident in the early 1950s; in 1957, Ms. Avedon married Mr. Siegel. They divorced in the mid-1970s; Mr. Siegel, the director of "Dirty Harry" and other films, died in 1991.

Besides Ms. Siegel-Wamsat, Ms. Avedon, who lived in Los Angeles, is survived by another daughter, two sons, a stepson, seven grandchildren, five great-grandchildren and her longtime companion, Michael Liscio. Richard Avedon died in 2004.

Though she chose to pass her later life in domestic pursuits, for a moment Ms. Avedon's flame burned so brightly that it illuminated a path to her door thousands of miles long.

As Ms. Siegel-Wamsat recounted, her mother once received a letter from an overseas admirer. The envelope was addressed with a single word: "Doe."

— BY MARGALIT FOX

VACLAV HAVEL

The Playwright in Prague Castle

OCT. 5, 1936 - DEC. 18, 2011

V ACLAV HAVEL, the Czech writer and dissident whose eloquent dissections of Communist rule helped to destroy it in revolutions that brought down the Berlin Wall and swept Mr. Havel himself into power, died on Dec. 18 at his country house in northern Bohemia. He was 75.

The Czech Embassy in Paris said Mr. Havel, a heavy smoker who almost died during treatment for lung cancer in 1996, had been having severe respiratory problems since the spring.

Mr. Havel was a shy yet resilient man, unfailingly polite but dogged in his ambition to articulate "the power of the powerless," as he put it. He spent five years in and out of Communist prisons, lived for two decades under secret-police surveillance and endured the suppression of his plays and essays. He wrote 19 plays, inspired a film and a rap song and remained one of his generation's most seductively nonconformist writers. And for 14 years he was his country's president.

Mr. Havel came to personify the soul of the Czech nation. His moral authority and his moving use of the Czech language cast him as the dominant figure during Prague street demonstrations in 1989 and as the chief behind-the-scenes negotiator who brought about the end of more than 40 years of Communist rule and the peaceful transfer of power known as the Velvet Revolution. It was a revolt so smooth that it took just weeks to complete, without a single shot fired.

He was chosen to be post-Communist Czechoslovakia's first president, accepting the office more out of duty, he said, than aspiration. And after the country split in January 1993, he became president of the Czech Republic, elected by its parliament. As president he bound the country tightly to the West, clearing the way for the Czech Republic to join the North Atlantic Treaty Organization in 1999 and the European Union five years later.

Both as a dissident and as a national leader, Mr. Havel (pronounced VAHTS-lahv HAH-vell) impressed the West as one of the most important political thinkers in Central Europe. Reform-minded Communist leaders like Alexander Dubcek in his own country and, years later, Mikhail S. Gorbachev in the Soviet Union posited that Communist rule could be made more humane. Mr. Havel rejected that notion.

His star power and multilayered personality drew world leaders to Prague, including the Dalai Lama, with whom Mr. Havel meditated for hours, and President Bill Clinton, who joined a saxophone jam session at Mr. Havel's favorite jazz club during a state visit in 1994.

Even after Mr. Havel retired in 2003, leaders sought him out, including President Barack Obama. At their meeting in March 2009, Mr. Havel warned of the perils of limitless hope being projected onto a leader. Disappointment, he said, could boil over into anger and resentment. Mr. Obama replied that he was becoming acutely aware of the possibility.

Mr. Obama said he was saddened by Mr. Havel's death. "His peaceful resistance shook the foundations of an empire," the president said in a statement, "exposed the emptiness of a repressive ideology and proved that moral leadership is more powerful than any weapon."

IDEALISM AND DISCONTENT

It was as a dissident that Mr. Havel most clearly championed the ideals of a civil society. He helped found Charter 77, the longest enduring human rights movement in the former Soviet bloc, and articulated the humiliations that Communism imposed on the individual.

In his now classic 1978 essay "The Power of the Powerless," which circulated in underground editions in Czechoslovakia and was smuggled to other Warsaw Pact countries and to the West, Mr. Havel foresaw that the opposition could eventually prevail against the totalitarian state.

MORAL AUTHORITY: Vaclav Havel went from imprisoned playwright and dissident leader to Czech president.

Mr. Havel, a child of bourgeois privilege whose family lost its wealth when the Communists came to power in 1948, became active in the Writers Union in Czechoslovakia in the mid-1960s, when his chief target was not Communism so much as it was the "reform Communism" that many were seeking.

During the Prague Spring of 1968, the brief period when reform Communists, led by Mr. Dubcek, believed that "socialism with a human face" was possible, Mr. Havel argued that Communism could never be tamed. In an article titled "On the Theme of an Opposition," he advocated the end of single-party rule, a bold idea at the time. In May 1968, he was invited by the American theater producer Joseph Papp to see the New York Shakespeare Festival's production of Mr. Havel's second play, "The Memorandum."

It was the last time Mr. Havel was allowed out of the country under Communist rule; the visit contributed to an abiding affection for New York.

After the Soviets sent tanks to suppress the Prague reforms in August 1968, Mr. Havel persisted in the fight for political freedom. In August 1969 he organized a petition that repudiated, in 10 points, the politics of "normalization" with the Soviet Union. He was accused of subversion, and in 1970 was vilified on state television and banned as a writer.

At the time, the Czechoslovak leader Gustav Husak was reversing the Dubcek reforms, and tens of thousands of Communists deemed too sympathetic to them were expelled from the party. Mr. Havel nonetheless kept writing. In 1975, in an open letter to Mr. Husak (whom he eventually replaced), he attacked the regime, arguing that Czechoslovakia operated under "political apartheid" in which rulers were separated from the ruled.

The government, Mr. Havel wrote, had chosen "the most dangerous road for society: the path of inner decay for the sake of outward appearances; of deadening life for the sake of increasing uniformity."

In 1977, Mr. Havel was one of three leading organizers of Charter 77, a group of 242 signers who called for the human rights guaranteed under the 1975 Helsinki accords. Mr. Havel was arrested, tried and convicted of subversion; he served three months in prison. He was arrested again in May 1979 on a charge of subversion and was sentenced to four and a half years.

The severity of this sentence elicited protests from the Communist parties in France, Italy and Spain, but Mr. Havel remained in prison until February 1983, when he was released suffering from pneumonia.

In prison, he was prohibited from writing anything but letters to his wife about "family matters." But written more as essays — and later published to acclaim as the collection "Letters to Olga" — they enabled him to make some sense of his incarceration. One theme was that by repressing human freedom, his persecutors were undercutting themselves and inviting their own demise.

His refusal to break with Charter 77 led to other, briefer periods of detention as his celebrity status grew abroad. In January 1989, he was detained and tried after defying police orders to stay away from a demonstration.

His release in May that year represented the beginning of the end for Czechoslovakia's Communist government, which was far out of step with reforms under way in neighboring Poland and Hungary and in the Soviet Union itself, under Mr. Gorbachev.

Mr. Havel resisted government pressure to emigrate, and though not widely known at home outside dissident and intellectual circles in Prague, he was sought out by Western diplomats and visitors, who would tramp up to the top-floor apartment of a six-story house that his father had built and converse with him. Visible from his window, across the Vltava River, was the labyrinthine Prague Castle, long the country's seat of power.

He was forced to take a menial, low-paying job at a brewery, but royalties he received from the publication of his work outside Czechoslovakia allowed him to live comfortably. He bought a Mercedes-Benz and decorated his book-crammed apartment with abstract paintings. He also owned the cottage at Hradecek, where he died.

VELVET REVOLUTION

Mr. Havel's chance at power came in November 1989, eight days after the Berlin Wall fell. A tentative dialogue had already started when the police broke up an officially sanctioned student demonstration on Nov. 17, beating many demonstrators and arresting others.

Two days later, Mr. Havel convened a meeting of dissidents in the Magic Lantern, a Prague theater. They established what they called the Civic Forum and emerged calling for the resignation of the leading Communists, an investigation of the police action and the release of all political prisoners.

The next day, about 200,000 people took to the streets in Prague in the first of several demonstrations that would end Communist domination.

It was Mr. Havel, huddled with the others in the theater's smoke-filled rooms, who had mapped out the strategy and shaped the proclamations that finally undermined Communist rule. "It was extraordinary the degree to which everything ultimately revolved around this one man," wrote the historian Timothy Garton Ash, who was at the meetings. "In almost all the forum's major decisions and statements, he was the final arbiter, the one person who could somehow balance the very different tendencies and interests in the movement."

Once installed at the Castle as president, Mr. Havel discarded faded jeans and rumpled sweaters for crisp shirts and somber suits. They appeared to be an uncomfortable fit, however; he seemed more at home among writers and

A BLOODLESS REVOLUTION: Vaclav Havel waving to supporters on Human Rights Day, Dec. 10, 1989. Communist rule would topple days later.

that had allowed neighbors to send one another to labor camps.

In July 1992, as Czechoslovakia began to break up, Mr. Havel resigned rather than preside over the split. He now spoke of his misgivings about achieving power. For a philosopher to become a politician, he said, was a difficult metamorphosis.

"Putting into practice the ideals to which I have adhered all my life, which guided me in the dissident years, becomes much more difficult in practical politics," he said.

Even so, he did not abandon politics. He would go on to be elected president of the new Czech Republic.

As soon as he came to power, Mr. Havel steered his country toward the West. On his first visit to the United States as president, in February 1990, he stressed that American financial aid was not as important as technical assistance to help his country, historically an industrial power, compete again in the international marketplace.

Days later, he met Mr. Gorbachev in Moscow and negotiated the withdrawal of 70,000 Soviet troops stationed in Czechoslovakia.

At home, Mr. Havel's role evolved into one of educator and moral persuader. In weekly radio talks, he often addressed human rights, touching on delicate issues in Czech society. He championed, for instance, the rights of Gypsies, or Roma, despite surveys showing that most Czechs would not want a Gypsy as a neighbor.

Early in his presidency, he also went against popular sentiment when he formed a commission to inquire into the expulsion of three million Sudeten Germans after World War II.

artists and musicians. On a trip abroad in 1995, he ignored waiting dignitaries and lingered on an airport tarmac to chat with Mick Jagger. Indeed, the Rolling Stones and Frank Zappa were among his first visitors to the Castle. Mr. Havel covered a side of the building with a large neon-red heart and careered along the corridors on a child's scooter.

"Initially, he had difficulty changing his mentality from being a dissident to a politician," said Jiri Pehe, who was his chief political adviser from 1997 to 1999. But Mr. Pehe argued that Mr. Havel became a better president than many had expected.

"Because of his moral authority, he was able to stretch a weak presidency beyond what was written in the Constitution," Mr. Pehe said.

Mr. Havel's critics said that for a self-professed reluctant leader, he learned to like power a little too much. Many Czechs were disappointed that he had refused to outlaw the Communist Party or to put on trial the system

Political ideas, not economics, interested him. His country, widely considered to have made a smooth transition from Communism to market democracy, came in for a devastating critique in December 1997, when he attacked corruption and the sell-off of government-run industries in a thinly veiled barb at his political nemesis, the longtime prime minister, and now president, Vaclav Klaus.

> Though worshiped in the West, Mr. Havel, an idealistic son of wealth, was often mocked at home as naïve.

Expressing disdain for what had happened to Czech society under Mr. Klaus, Mr. Havel told Parliament that a "post-Communist morass" had allowed "the most immoral people" to achieve financial success at the expense of others.

Mr. Klaus, a right-wing maverick who espoused the untrammeled capitalism that Mr. Havel disliked, succeeded Mr. Havel as president in 2003.

While many in the West worshiped Mr. Havel, many in his native country expressed ambivalence, even scorn. His slogan during the revolution, that truth and love must prevail over lies and hatred, was mocked as naïve. But he never lost his childlike idealism: he continued to sign his name with a small heart, and even his critics regarded him with affection.

Mr. Havel's standing with Czechs slipped a bit in 1997 when, only a year after the death of his much-admired wife of 31 years, Olga,

he surprised everyone by marrying Dagmar Veskrnova, a flamboyant and outspoken actress who had once played a topless vampire in a film. Soon his behavior with his new wife was criticized as arrogant. They were accused of meddling in political affairs. In January 1998 Parliament elected him to a second presidential term, but by only one vote.

Erik Tabery, a Czech journalist and the author of a book on the Czech presidency, said some Czechs resented Mr. Havel for holding up a mirror to their history of passivity. "While the Communists ruled for 40 years, most Czechs stayed at home and did nothing," Mr. Tabery said. "Havel did something."

Mr. Havel had his own theory — that he had unwittingly become a character from a fairy tale whom he himself did not recognize.

A CHILD CHAUFFEURED

Born on Oct. 5, 1936, Mr. Havel was one of two sons of Bozena and Vaclav Havel. His father, a civil engineer, was a major commercial real estate developer who acquired important property. When the Communists took power three years after World War II, they seized the family holdings. After their rule ended, Mr. Havel and his brother, Ivan, won back much of the property.

Mr. Havel wrote that his privileged upbringing had heightened his sensitivity to inequality: "I was different from my schoolmates whose families did not have domestics, nurses or chauffeurs. But I experienced these differences as a disadvantage; I felt excluded from the company of my peers."

He started writing, he said, to overcome this feeling of being an outsider. Because of his upper-class background, the Communists blocked him from going to college, and at age 15 he started work as a technician in a chemistry lab.

Mr. Havel was called up for military service in 1957, and wrote a satirical play while in the army. In 1960, he joined the Theater on the Balustrade as a stagehand. In 1963 he wrote his first publicly performed play, "The Garden Party," about a person who has lost his sense of identity.

In 1956 Mr. Havel met Olga Splichalova, a lively, dashing actress, whom he married in 1964. A working-class heroine for many Czechs, she helped inspire the essays published as "Letters to Olga." And though Mr. Havel was a celebrated womanizer, his wife neverthe-less fiercely defended him, though when he was in prison, friends said, she gained a measure of reassurance. "At least she knew where he was," one said.

When Mr. Havel became president, his wife seldom took part in formal events but used her new platform to campaign for the handicapped. She died of cancer in January 1996. They had no children. Mr. Havel is survived by his second wife, Dagmar; and his brother, Ivan.

After stepping down as president in 2003, Mr. Havel, ailing and tired, returned to writing, insisting he was happy with a peaceful life. In his memoir, "To the Castle and Back," published in 2007, he called his political rise an accident of history. Post-Communist society disappointed him, he said.

In 2008, Mr. Havel re-emerged as a play-wright with a new absurdist tragic-comedy, "Leaving," depicting a womanizing former political leader who grudgingly confronts life outside of politics.

He never stopped preaching that the fight for political freedom needed to outlive the end of the cold war. He praised the American inva-sion of Iraq for deposing a dictator, Saddam Hussein. And he continued to worry about what he called "the old European disease" — "the tendency to make compromises with evil, to close one's eyes to dictatorship, to practice a politics of appeasement."

— BY DAN BILEFSKY AND JANE PERLEZ; ALISON SMALE CONTRIBUTED REPORTING.

LYNN SAMUELS

On Talk Radio, Not One of the Guys

SEPT. 2, 1942 - DEC. 24, 2011

L YNN SAMUELS, whose brash political opinions and unrestrained New York accent made her an unmistakable voice in the male-dominated world of political talk radio, died on Dec. 24 at her apartment in Woodside, Queens. She was 69.

Ms. Samuels, one of the first women to host a political radio show, was found dead by the police. They investigated after she had failed to

show up for a scheduled 10 a.m. show on Sirius XM Satellite Radio, a company spokesman said. No cause of death was announced. Friends said she had seemed well the night before, when they exchanged e-mails with her. The medical examiner later attributed her death to heart disease and hypertension.

Ms. Samuels made her name on WABC radio in the 1980s and '90s as the voice of liberalism in a lineup composed mainly of right-wing men, including Rush Limbaugh. For several years, Mr. Limbaugh took over Ms. Samuels's chair and microphone at the end of her shift. They got along fine, she once said, by chatting about television shows and movies.

She received most of the hate mail sent to WABC in those years for her defense of President Bill Clinton, environmentalists, gun-control advocates, the Democratic Party and Tinky Winky's right to his sexual identity, whatever it was. (She brought it up mainly to mock the Rev. Jerry Falwell's claim that Tinky Winky, a character of indiscernible gender from the children's television show "Teletubbies," was "role modeling" a gay lifestyle.)

Unlike many radio hosts, Ms. Samuels was adept at holding an audience's attention with intimate, personal commentary. She talked about members of her family, old boyfriends, her phobias and how she spent her time off the air. "To tell you the truth," she once said, "I don't like talking too much once I leave this booth. I'm talked out."

Michael Harrison, publisher of Talkers, the trade journal of the talk radio industry, called Ms. Samuels "a pioneer for women in the modern talk radio era, and for liberal talk radio."

"But also she was a master of a kind of radio that many people look back on wistfully," he said, "when radio was about spending a few hours with an interesting human being, hearing their take on life."

Her take was often gloomy. A favorite word was "doomed." Being contrary sometimes seemed as important to her as being right. When

THEY COULDN'T STOP LISTENING: A pioneer for female radio hosts, Lynn Samuels didn't shy away from voicing her candid political opinions on the air.

she worked at the ultra-liberal, listener-supported radio station WBAI, she was considered something of a right-wing nut by some staff members — against whom she conducted on-air, internecine warfare over control of station programming in the 1980s.

At WABC, she was fired three times (and rehired twice) for comments the station deemed subversive.

On Sirius XM Satellite Left, a subscriber-based channel for a left-of-center audience, where she began working eight years ago, she inveighed against illegal immigrants and turned viciously critical of President Barack Obama.

"She could be very hard to deal with; she wouldn't listen to reason," said John Mainelli, a longtime friend who, as program director at WABC, hired her. "But she did her homework, she was funny, compulsively candid, and you just couldn't help listening to her."

For years, Mr. Mainelli said, he tried to convince Ms. Samuels that she could become a national talk radio star if she damped down her accent. "I said, 'The syndicators like you, but they say you're just too New York.'"

"I know what that means," he recalled her

telling him. "That means I'm too Jewish." Then she said what she thought of people who used phrases like "too New York."

Lynn Margaret Samuels was born in Queens on Sept. 2, 1942. Her mother was a schoolteacher. Her father worked in the entertainment business, though several people who knew her for years said Ms. Samuels had been extremely private and almost never spoke of her family. They said a sister and two nephews were her only survivors. She moved to Queens after living in Greenwich Village for decades.

Bob Grant, the talk radio host, who was a colleague at WABC, said Ms. Samuels was "funny, smart and original."

"What I admired about her was, she wasn't afraid. With all these right-wingers around," he said, referring to her view of him as well, "she just said what she had to."

— BY PAUL VITELLO

HELEN FRANKENTHALER

Stained Canvas and a New School of Art

DEC. 12, 1928 - DEC. 27, 2011

HELEN FRANKENTHALER, the lyrically abstract painter whose technique of staining pigment into raw canvas helped shape an influential art movement in the mid-20th century, died on Dec. 27 at her home in Darien, Conn. She was 83.

Known as a second-generation Abstract Expressionist, Ms. Frankenthaler was married during the movement's heyday to the painter Robert Motherwell, a leading first-generation member of the group. But she departed from her predecessors' romantic search for the "sublime" to pursue her own path.

Refining a technique, developed by Jackson Pollock, of pouring pigment directly onto canvas laid on the floor, Ms. Frankenthaler developed a method of painting best known as Color Field, heavily influencing the colorists Morris Louis and Kenneth Noland. (Clement Greenberg, the critic most identified with the genre, called it Post-Painterly Abstraction.)

Where Pollock had used enamel that rested on raw canvas like skin, Ms. Frankenthaler poured turpentine-thinned paint in watery washes onto the raw canvas so that it soaked into the fabric weave, becoming one with it.

Her staining method emphasized the flat surface over illusory depth, and it called attention to the very nature of paint on canvas, a concern of artists and critics at the time. It also brought a new, open airiness to the painted surface and was credited with releasing color from the gestural approach and romantic rhetoric of Abstract Expressionism.

Ms. Frankenthaler said she more or less stumbled on her stain technique, first using it in creating "Mountains and Sea" (1952). Produced on her return to New York from a trip to Nova Scotia, the painting is a light-struck, diaphanous evocation of hills, rocks and water. Its delicate balance of drawing and painting, fresh washes of color (predominantly blues and pinks) and breakthrough technique have made it one of her best-known works.

"The landscapes were in my arms as I did it," Ms. Frankenthaler told an interviewer. "I didn't realize all that I was doing. I was trying to get at something — I didn't know what until it was manifest."

She later described the seemingly unfinished painting — which is on long-term loan to the National Gallery of Art in Washington — as "looking to many people like a large paint rag, casually accidental and incomplete."

Unlike many of her painter colleagues at the time, Ms. Frankenthaler, born in New York City on Dec. 12, 1928, came from a prosperous Manhattan family. She was one of three daughters of Alfred Frankenthaler, a New York State Supreme Court judge, and the former Martha Lowenstein, an immigrant from Germany. Helen, their youngest, was interested in art from early childhood, when she would dribble nail polish into a sink full of water to watch the color flow.

After graduation from the Dalton School in Manhattan, where she had studied art with the Mexican painter Rufino Tamayo, she entered Bennington College in 1946. There, in Vermont, the painter Paul Feeley, a thoroughgoing taskmaster, taught her "everything I know about Cubism," she said. The intellectual atmosphere at Bennington was heady, with instructors like Kenneth Burke, Erich Fromm and Ralph Ellison setting the pace.

As a self-described "saddle-shoed girl a year out of Bennington," Ms. Frankenthaler made her way into the burgeoning New York art world

with a boost from Mr. Greenberg, whom she met in 1950 and with whom she had a five-year relationship. Through him she met crucial players like David Smith, Jackson Pollock, Willem and Elaine de Kooning and Franz Kline.

In 1951, at Mr. Greenberg's prompting, she joined the new Tibor de Nagy gallery, run by the ebullient aesthete John B. Myers. She had her first solo show there that year. She spent summers visiting museums in Europe, pursuing an interest in quattrocento and old master painting.

Her marriage to Mr. Motherwell in 1958 gave the couple an art-world aura. Like her, he came from a well-to-do family, and "the golden

STRAYING FROM HER PREDECESSORS: Helen Frankenthaler developed her own method of painting and became one half of Abstract Expressionism's "golden couple."

couple," as they were known in the cash-poor and backbiting art world of the time, spent several leisurely months honeymooning in Spain and France.

In Manhattan, they removed themselves from the downtown scene and established themselves in a house on East 94th Street, where they developed a reputation for lavish entertaining. The British sculptor Anthony Caro recalled a dinner party they gave for him and his wife on their first trip to New York, in 1959. It was attended by some 100 guests, and he was seated between David Smith and the actress Hedy Lamarr.

"Helen loved to entertain," said Ann Freedman, the former president of Knoedler & Company, Ms. Frankenthaler's dealer until its recent closing. "She enjoyed feeding people and engaging in lively conversation. And she liked to dance. In fact, you could see it in her movements as she worked on her paintings."

Ms. Frankenthaler's passion for dancing was more than fulfilled in 1985 when, at a White House dinner to honor the Prince and Princess of Wales, she was partnered with a fast stepper who had been twirling the princess.

"I'd waited a lifetime for a dance like this," she wrote in an Op-Ed article for The New York Times in 1977. "He was great!"

His name meant nothing to her until, on returning to her New York studio, she showed her assistant and a friend his card. "John Travolta," it read.

Despite the early acknowledgment of Ms. Frankenthaler's achievement by Mr. Greenberg and her fellow artists, wider recognition took some time. Her first major museum show, a retrospective of her 1950s work with a catalog by the poet and critic Frank O'Hara, a curator at the Museum of Modern Art, was at the Jewish Museum in 1960. But she became better known to the art-going public after a major retrospective

organized by the Whitney Museum of American Art in 1969.

Although Ms. Frankenthaler rarely discussed the sources of her abstract imagery, it reflected her impressions of landscape, her meditations on personal experience and the

---

With washes of color, Ms. Frankenthaler broke with the romantic rhetoric of Abstract Expressionism.

---

pleasures of dealing with paint. Visually diverse, her paintings were never produced in "serial" themes like those of her Abstract Expressionist predecessors or her Color Field colleagues like Noland and Louis. She looked on each of her works as a separate exploration.

But "Mountains and Sea" did establish many of the traits that have informed her art from the beginning, the art historian E. A. Carmean Jr. has suggested. In the catalog for his 1989-90 Frankenthaler retrospective at the Modern Art Museum of Fort Worth, he cited the color washes, the dialogue between drawing and painting, the seemingly raw, unfinished look, and the "general theme of place" as characteristic of her work.

Besides her paintings, Ms. Frankenthaler is known for her inventive lithographs, etchings and screen prints she produced since 1961, but critics have suggested that her woodcuts have made the most original contribution to printmaking.

In making her first woodcut, "East and Beyond," in 1973, Ms. Frankenthaler wanted to make the grainy, unforgiving wood block receptive to the vibrant color and organic, amorphous forms of her own painting. By dint of trial and error, with technical help from printmaking studios, she succeeded.

For "East and Beyond," which depicts a radiant open space above a graceful mountain-like divide, she used a jigsaw to cut separate shapes, then printed the whole by a specially devised method to eliminate the white lines between them when put together. The result was a taut but fluid composition so refreshingly removed from traditional woodblock technique

---

Ms. Frankenthaler and her first husband, the painter Robert Motherwell, both from well-to-do families, were known as "the golden couple" in the cash-poor art world of the time.

---

that it has had a deep influence on the medium ever since. "East and Beyond" became to contemporary printmaking in the 1970s what Ms. Frankenthaler's paint staining in "Mountains and Sea" had been to the development of Color Field painting 20 years earlier.

In 1972, Ms. Frankenthaler made a less successful foray into sculpture, spending two weeks at Mr. Caro's London studio. With no experience in the medium but aided by a skilled assistant, she welded together found steel parts in a way that evoked the work of David Smith.

Although she enjoyed the experience, she did not repeat it. Knoedler gave the work its first public showing in 2006.

Critics have not unanimously praised Ms. Frankenthaler's art. Some have seen it as thin in substance, uncontrolled in method, too sweet in color and too "poetic." But it has been far more apt to garner admirers like the critic Barbara Rose, who wrote in 1972 of Ms. Frankenthaler's gift for "the freedom, spontaneity, openness and complexity of an image, not exclusively of the studio or the mind, but explicitly and intimately tied to nature and human emotions."

Ms. Frankenthaler and Mr. Motherwell were divorced in 1971. In 1994 she married Stephen M. DuBrul Jr., an investment banker who had headed the Export-Import Bank during President Gerald R. Ford's administration. Her husband survives her, as do two stepdaughters and six nieces and nephews. Her two sisters died before her. Her longtime assistant, Maureen St. Onge, said Ms. Frankenthaler died after a long illness but gave no other details.

In 1999, Ms. Frankenthaler and Mr. DuBrul bought a house in Darien, on Long Island Sound. Water, sky and their shifting light are often reflected in her later imagery.

As the years passed, her paintings seemed to make more direct references to the visible world. But they sometimes harked back to the more spontaneous, exuberant and less referential work of her earlier career.

There is "no formula," she said in an interview in The Times in 2003. "There are no rules. Let the picture lead you where it must go."

She never aligned herself with the feminist movement in art that began to surface in the 1970s. "For me, being a 'lady painter' was never an issue," Ms. Frankenthaler was quoted as saying in John Gruen's book "The Party's Over Now" (1972). "I don't resent being a female painter. I don't exploit it. I paint."

— By Grace Glueck

EVA ZEISEL

High Art Next to the Knife and Fork

NOV. 13, 1906 - DEC. 30, 2011

E VA ZEISEL, a ceramic artist whose elegant, eccentric designs for dinnerware in the 1940s and '50s helped revolutionize the way Americans set their tables, died on Dec. 30 in New City, N.Y. She was 105, her work having spanned nine decades.

Ms. Zeisel (pronounced ZY-sel), along with designers like Mary and Russel Wright and Charles and Ray Eames, brought the clean, casual shapes of modernist design into middle-class American homes with furnishings that encouraged a postwar desire for fresh, less formal styles of living.

"Museum," the porcelain table service that brought Ms. Zeisel national notice, was commissioned by its manufacturer, Castleton China, in conjunction with the Museum of Modern Art in New York. The museum introduced the service in an exhibition of her work in 1946, its first devoted to a female designer.

Ms. Zeisel's creations were at the heart of what the museum promoted as "good design": domestic objects that were beautiful as well as useful and whose beauty lent pleasure to daily life.

"She brought form to the organicism and elegance and fluidity that we expect of ceramics today, reaching as many people as possible," said Paola Antonelli, a curator of architecture and design at the Modern. "It's easy to do something stunning that stays in a collector's cabinet. But her designs reached people at the table."

Born Eva Amalia Striker in Budapest on Nov. 13, 1906, Ms. Zeisel was the daughter of Laura Polanyi Striker and Alexander Striker.

Her father owned a textile factory. Her mother was a historian, feminist and political activist.

In 1923, Ms. Zeisel entered the Royal Academy of Fine Arts in Budapest to study painting. She withdrew three semesters later, inspired to become a ceramist by an aunt's Hungarian peasant pottery collection. She apprenticed to Jakob Karapancsik, a member of the guild of chimney sweepers, oven makers, roof tilers, well diggers and potters, and graduated as a journeyman.

During a summer trip to Paris in 1925, she visited the Exposition Internationale des Arts Décoratifs et Industriels Modernes — the source of the term Art Deco — which exhibited work by leading new designers like Le Corbusier. The show introduced Ms. Zeisel to modern movements like the Bauhaus and the International style. She later wrote that she thought modernist design "too cold," an aspect she tried to keep out of her work with humane, humorous versions of it.

Back in Budapest, Ms. Zeisel's exhibition at trade fairs brought her to the attention of Hungarian ceramic manufacturers, who commissioned several collections. In 1926 her work was displayed at the Philadelphia Sesquicentennial.

Two years later a ceramics manufacturer in Schramberg, Germany, hired her to design tableware. The job transformed her from a studio artist who threw pots on a wheel into an industrial designer. Now she drafted designs whose success would be based not only on their aesthetic appeal but also on their capacity to be manufactured and merchandised on a mass scale.

Ms. Zeisel moved to Berlin in 1930, immersing herself in the vibrant cafe society of the Weimar Republic. A visit to Ukraine in 1932 opened her eyes to new possibilities as a designer.

Taking work at the former imperial porcelain factory in Leningrad, she realized through exposure to its archives of 18th-century tableware that "the clean lines of modern design could be successfully combined with sensuous, classic shapes," she later wrote. Ms. Zeisel's signature became just that: forms that were at once contemporary and lyrical.

LEADING A TABLEWARE REVOLUTION: In the 1940s and '50s, Eva Zeisel brought the clean, casual shapes of modernist design into the homes of middle-class Americans.

By 1935, she was working in Moscow as the artistic director of the Russian republic's china and glass industry. There, a colleague falsely accused her of conspiring to assassinate Stalin, and on May 28, 1936, she was arrested. She was imprisoned for 16 months, mostly in solitary confinement, an experience that Arthur Koestler, a childhood friend, drew on in writing his celebrated 1941 novel, "Darkness at Noon."

Again, Ms. Zeisel's eyes were opened, this time by the deprivations of prison. "You feel the difference first in the way you see colors," she wrote.

Released from prison in 1937 without explanation, Ms. Zeisel traveled to Vienna but left on March 12, 1938, when the Nazis entered Austria. Arriving in Britain, she was reunited with Hans Zeisel, a lawyer and sociologist whom she had met in Berlin. They were married and emigrated to the United States that year.

In New York Ms. Zeisel immediately put herself in touch with American ceramics manufacturers by looking up the addresses of trade publications at the public library. She began teaching at Pratt Institute in Brooklyn, where she presented ceramics not as craft, as it was traditionally taught, but as industrial design.

In 1940, Castleton China, a Pennsylvania company, was looking for a designer to create a modernist porcelain table service and asked the Museum of Modern Art to recommend one. Eliot Noyes, director of the design department, suggested Ms. Zeisel. The design was completed in 1943, but the war delayed production until 1946.

Though critically acclaimed, her "Museum" table service was commercially controversial. Formal china was expected to look fancy. But the publicity brought Ms. Zeisel more commissions and hefty sales, encouraging her to develop a sense of play in her designs.

Motherhood opened her eyes once more; a daughter was born in 1940 and a son in 1944. Dinner services now took on familial relationships, their shapes complementing one another rather than repeating themselves. "Town & Country," designed in the 1940s, has salt and pepper shakers that nestle, one into the other, like a mother and child.

"Men have no concept of how to design things for the home," Ms. Zeisel was quoted as saying. "Women should design the things they use."

Still, after leaving Pratt in 1954, Ms. Zeisel returned less and less frequently to commercial design over the next 20 years. In 1964 she exhibited a metal chair at the Milan Triennale and received a mechanical patent for it. Small collections of ceramics, glass and metal appeared in the 1980s and '90s, as well as reissues of earlier work, which had become prized by collectors. She was the subject of a retrospective, "Eva Zeisel: Designer for Industry," organized in 1984 by the Montreal Museum of Decorative Arts.

In 1999 Ms. Zeisel collaborated on a collection of vases with two young ceramists in Brooklyn, James Klein and David Reid. She continued to work almost until the end of her life. She had homes in New City and Manhattan.

She is survived by her daughter and son as well as three grandchildren. Her husband, Hans Zeisel, a professor of sociology at the University of Chicago, died in 1992.

Ms. Zeisel's work can still be found in the marketplace. Crate and Barrel sells an updated version of her Hallcraft dinner service, and recent rug and furniture designs of hers are being sold. A line of lighting fixtures was being released in 2012.

Her book "Eva Zeisel on Design" was published by Overlook Press in 2004, and a memoir of her time in prison was to be published online in 2012.

"She's a conduit to pure things," Mr. Klein said in 2007. She once told him never to *try* to create anything new, he said. When he asked her how to make something beautiful, she replied, "You just have to get out of the way."

— *By William L. Hamilton*

GORDON HIRABAYASHI

A World War II Battle Belatedly Won

APRIL 23, 1918 - JAN. 2, 2012

Gordon Hirabayashi, who was imprisoned for defying the federal government's internment of Japanese-Americans during World War II, then vindicated 45 years later when his conviction was overturned, died on Jan. 2 in Edmonton, Alberta. He was 93.

When Mr. Hirabayashi challenged the wartime removal of more than 100,000 Japanese-Americans and Japanese immigrants from the West Coast to inland detention centers, he became a central figure in a controversy that resonated long after the war's end.

Mr. Hirabayashi and his fellow Japanese-Americans Fred Korematsu and Minoru Yasui, who all brought lawsuits before the United States Supreme Court, emerged as symbols of protest against unchecked governmental powers in a time of war.

"I want vindication not only for myself," Mr. Hirabayashi told The New York Times in 1985 as he was fighting to have his conviction vacated. "I also want the cloud removed from over the heads of 120,000 others. My citizenship didn't protect me one bit. Our Constitution was reduced to a scrap of paper."

In February 1942, two months after the Japanese attacked Pearl Harbor, President Franklin D. Roosevelt, in the name of protecting the nation against espionage and sabotage, authorized the designation of areas from which anyone could be excluded. One month later, a curfew was imposed along the West Coast on people of Japanese ancestry, and in May 1942, the West Coast military command ordered their removal to inland camps in harsh and isolated terrain.

Mr. Hirabayashi, a son of Japanese immigrants, was a senior at the University of Washington when the United States entered World War II. He adhered to the pacifist principles of his parents, who had once belonged to a Japanese religious sect similar to the Quakers.

When the West Coast curfew was imposed, ordering people of Japanese background to be home by 8 p.m., Mr. Hirabayashi ignored it. When the internment directive was put in place, he refused to register at a processing center and was jailed.

Contending that the government's actions were racially discriminatory, Mr. Hirabayashi would not yield. He refused to post $500 bail because had he done so he would have been transferred to an internment camp while awaiting trial. He remained in jail from May 1942 until October of that year, when his case was heard before a federal jury in Seattle.

Found guilty of violating both the curfew and internment orders, he was sentenced to concurrent three-month prison terms. While his appeal was pending, he remained at the local jail for four more months before being released and sent to Spokane, Wash., to work on plans to relocate internees when they were finally released.

His appeal, along with one by Mr. Yasui, a lawyer from Hood River, Ore., who had been jailed for nine months for curfew defiance, made its way to the Supreme Court. In 1943, ruling unanimously, the court upheld the curfew as a constitutional exercise of the government's war powers. Mr. Hirabayashi served out his three-month prison term at a work camp near Tucson.

The Supreme Court declined to rule at the time on Mr. Hirabayashi's challenge to internment as well. (Mr. Yasui had contested only the curfew.) But in December 1944, in a case brought by Mr. Korematsu, a welder from Oakland, Calif., the court upheld the constitutionality of internment in a 6-to-3 vote.

Mr. Hirabayashi later spent a year in federal prison for refusing induction into the armed forces. He contended that a questionnaire sent to Japanese-Americans by draft officials demanding that they renounce any allegiance to the emperor of Japan was racially discriminatory because other ethnic groups were not asked about adherence to foreign leaders.

The Hirabayashi, Yasui and Korematsu cases were revisited in the 1980s after Peter Irons, a professor of political science at the University of California, San Diego, found documents indicating that the federal government, in coming before the Supreme Court, had suppressed its own finding that Japanese-Americans on the West Coast were not, in fact, threats to national security.

Interning Japanese-Americans, "the Constitution was reduced to a scrap of paper," Mr. Hirabayashi said.

In September 1987, a three-member panel of a federal appeals court in San Francisco unanimously overturned Mr. Hirabayashi's conviction on charges of failing to register for evacuation to an internment camp and of ignoring a curfew. The convictions of Mr. Korematsu and Mr. Yasui had been overturned earlier.

Federal legislation in 1988 provided for payments and apologies to Japanese-Americans who were interned during World War II.

Gordon Kiyoshi Hirabayashi was born on April 23, 1918, in Seattle. His father operated a fruit and vegetable stand.

After the war, Mr. Hirabayashi graduated from the University of Washington and received a master's degree and a doctorate there in sociology. He taught at the American University of Beirut, the American University in Cairo and in Canada at the University of Alberta in Edmonton, where he lived.

Mr. Hirabayashi, who had Alzheimer's disease, is survived by his wife, Susan Carnahan, as well as two daughters and a son from a previous marriage that ended in divorce, a sister, a brother, nine grandchildren and nine great-grandchildren.

Mr. Yasui died in 1986 and Mr. Korematsu in 2005.

"When my case was before the Supreme Court in 1943, I fully expected that as a citizen the Constitution would protect me," Mr. Hirabayashi told Professor Irons in "The Courage of Their Convictions: Sixteen Americans Who Fought Their Way to the Supreme Court" (1988).

"Surprisingly, even though I lost, I did not abandon my beliefs and my values," he said. "And I never look at my case as just my own, or just as a Japanese-American case. It is an American case, with principles that affect the fundamental human rights of all Americans."

— BY RICHARD GOLDSTEIN

\\\\\\\\\\\\\\\\\\\\\\\\\\\\\\

EVE ARNOLD

Glimpses of Unscripted Hollywood

APRIL 21, 1912 - JAN. 4, 2012

Eve Arnold, who fell in love with photography after a boyfriend gave her a camera and who came to be regarded as a grande dame of postwar photojournalism for her bold, revealing images of subjects as diverse as Marilyn Monroe and migratory potato pickers, died on Jan. 4 in London. She was 99.

American-born, Ms. Arnold had lived in Britain since 1961.

Her death was announced by Magnum Photos, the photography cooperative to which she belonged for more than 50 years. She was among the first women it hired to make pictures.

Ms. Arnold was a leading light in what is considered the golden age of news photography, when magazines like Life and Look commanded attention with big, arresting pictures supplied by adventurous photographers like Henri Cartier-Bresson, Gordon Parks, Robert Capa and Margaret Bourke-White.

Acclaimed for capturing celebrities in intimate moments after winning their trust, Ms. Arnold developed a particular rapport with Marilyn Monroe, the subject of a book of Arnold photographs. One image showed Monroe emerging from the black of a nightclub into the white glare of a spotlight with a smiling Arthur Miller, her husband at the time. Another showed her pensively studying her lines on location in the vast Western setting for the 1961 film "The Misfits."

Foreshadowing the celebrity portfolios of photographers like Annie Leibovitz, Ms. Arnold captured Joan Crawford squirming into a girdle and James Cagney and his wife doing an impromptu dance in a barn.

But other pictures, just as memorable, were of the unfamous. Among the more than 750,000 Ms. Arnold made was one taken in 1963 showing an English curate mowing a lawn, his robes tied up to keep them clear of the blades. She took pictures in a South African shantytown, a Havana brothel and a Moscow psychiatric hospital. She documented a Long Island hamlet, Miller Place, and the first minutes of a baby's life. She was an official photographer on 40 movie sets.

After waiting 10 years for a visa, she visited China twice in 1979. Traveling 40,000 miles, she photographed Communist officials, Mongolian horsemen and oil drillers. The trip was chronicled in an exhibit at the Brooklyn Museum and a book, one of dozens she wrote and photographed.

THE GRANDE DAME: Eve Arnold, here on the set of "Becket" in 1963, captured intimate portraits of celebrities like Marilyn Monroe and Joan Crawford.

In 1985, Mary Blume of The International Herald Tribune wrote, "In a distinguished career, Eve Arnold has photographed Everyone with a capital 'E' and also everyone."

Eve Cohen was born in Philadelphia on April 21, 1912, one of nine children of immigrants from Ukraine. Her father was a rabbi. At 28, she abandoned ambitions of becoming a doctor to move to New York. "That's where the boys are," she told The New York Times in 2002.

She did find a boyfriend, and he gave her a camera, insisting she learn how to use it. It was a $40 Rolleicord, the cheaper version of the Rolleiflex. Her first picture was of a bum on the New York waterfront. The boyfriend was gone in a couple of years.

Ms. Cohen got a job in a photofinishing plant, where she rose to manager. In 1948 she married Arnold Arnold, an industrial designer; later that year she gave birth to a son, who survives her.

Enrolling at the New School, she studied photography under Alexey Brodovitch, the renowned art director for Harper's Bazaar magazine. One day he assigned his students to photograph a fashion story, and Ms. Arnold decided on an unconventional approach. She

found it when she learned from her babysitter that fashion shows were held in Harlem — in churches, bars and other places there. Mr. Brodovitch liked her pictures so much that he suggested she return to Harlem to create a portfolio. The British journal Picture Post bought her Harlem work.

Ms. Arnold and her family moved to England in 1961. Her marriage ended in divorce. In addition to her son, she is survived by three grandchildren.

Her honors include the Order of the British Empire and the lifetime achievement award of the American Society of Magazine Photographers. She was a fellow of the Royal Photographic Society and named a "master photographer" by the International Center of Photography in New York, considered by many to be the world's most prestigious photographic honor.

Ms. Arnold joined Magnum in 1951 on an informal basis and became a member of the cooperative in 1957. In an interview after she died, John G. Morris, who was Magnum's executive editor and a creative force in postwar photojournalism, remembered her work as "offbeat" and praised her photos of Monroe and Malcolm X. Perhaps her most famous picture of Malcolm shows him collecting fistfuls of dollars at a rally in Washington.

Ms. Arnold covered politics, including the Republican National Convention in 1952 and Senator Joseph R. McCarthy's investigation of suspected Communist subversion in 1954. But she earned wider note for her celebrity photos, starting in 1952 with Marlene Dietrich and her legendary legs, immortalized in a striking Arnold picture.

She won the trust of stars by treating them with unusual courtesy. In the 1950s she was hired to photograph Joan Crawford, who wanted to promote her new movie, "Autumn Leaves." By Ms. Arnold's account, Ms. Crawford arrived spectacularly inebriated, kissed her on the mouth, stripped naked and demanded to be photographed. Ms. Arnold demurred at first, then took the pictures.

A few days later, over lunch, Ms. Arnold handed the negatives to Ms. Crawford, assuring her that they would never be published. Ms. Crawford thanked her by allowing her to do a day-in-the-life photo feature about her. The pictures, which appeared in Life, are an up-close study of an aging star coping with her fading beauty — applying makeup, for instance, and struggling with that girdle.

In an interview with the London newspaper The Independent, Ms. Arnold said she had never been tempted to make the nude photos public, not so much out of concern for Ms. Crawford's image as for her own.

"I didn't think they would do me credit," she said. "I had in mind a long career."

— By Douglas Martin

FREDERICA SAGOR MAAS

A Last Link to the Silent Movies

JULY 6, 1900 - JAN. 5, 2012

S HE TOLD OF HOLLYWOOD MOGULS chasing naked would-be starlets, the women shrieking with laughter. She recounted how Joan Crawford, new to the movies, relied on her to pick clothes. She complained, constantly, about how many of her story ideas and scripts were stolen and credited to others.

Frederica Sagor Maas told all — and maybe more — in interviews and in her memoirs, which she published in 1999 at the age of 99. Before dying on Jan. 5 in La Mesa, Calif., at 111, Mrs. Maas was one of the last living links to cinema's silent era. She wrote dozens of stories and scripts, sat with Greta Garbo at the famed long table in MGM's commissary, and adapted to sound in the movies and then to color.

Perhaps most satisfying, Mrs. Maas outlived pretty much anybody who might have disagreed with her version of things. "I can get my payback now," she told the online magazine Salon.com in 1999. "I'm alive and thriving, and, well, you S.O.B.'s are all below."

She was also the 44th-oldest person in the world, according to the Gerontology Research Group, which keeps records of such things and which announced her death.

Mrs. Maas's life was like the plot of an old-fashioned movie. She dropped out of college to scout Broadway for movie ideas. She moved to Hollywood, rejected encouragement to be an actress and wrote for the Universal, MGM, Paramount and Fox studios. After the industry had no further use for her work, she almost committed suicide.

Much later, after giving up on Hollywood, Mrs. Maas said she would have preferred to be a "wash lady."

Still, Hollywood gave her stories to tell: about meeting Crawford, whom she called "a gum-chewing dame," and helping her find the sort of tailored clothes she herself favored; about seeing Clara Bow dancing naked on a table at a Jazz Age blowout. Sex, she wrote, became as "humdrum as washing your face or cleansing your teeth."

Frederica Sagor, one of four daughters, was born on July 6, 1900, in a cold-water railroad flat at 101st Street near Madison Avenue in Manhattan. Her parents, Jewish immigrants from Russia, shortened their name from Zagosky. Frederica gave up plans to be a doctor and studied journalism at Columbia. She worked a summer as a copy girl for The New York Globe.

She joined the movie industry, and left school, after answering a want ad for an assistant to the story editor at Universal Pictures in New York. Getting the job, she learned about movies

INTIMATE KNOWLEDGE:
Frederica Sagor Maas, a silent era screenwriter, knew old Hollywood's secrets.

by seeing ones she liked three or four times, studying them frame by frame.

"I was fierce in my passion for this new medium," she wrote in her memoir, "The Shocking Miss Pilgrim: A Writer in Early Hollywood," the title taken from a film she helped write.

In 1924, Frederica Sagor moved to Hollywood to write for Preferred Pictures. She helped adapt "The Plastic Age," a popular novel about collegiate life, for a 1925 movie that was a hit for Clara Bow. (Five years older than Bow, she outlived her by more than 46.) After that success, she signed with MGM, where, she said, others took credit for her work. In a studio system with armies of writers, she added, that was not unusual.

"Unless you wanted to quit the business, you just kept your mouth shut," she wrote.

She moved on to Tiffany Productions, where she got credit for the flapper comedies "That Model From Paris" (1926) and "The First Night" (1927).

She married a screenwriter, Ernest Maas, in 1927, and went on to write scripts both with him and by herself. For her story for "Rolled Stockings" (1927), starring Louise Brooks, she was credited not only on the screen but on the poster as well, a rarity then.

The couple's lives began a downward spiral when they lost $10,000 in the 1929 stock market crash. They survived by writing movie reviews and turned out screenplays, but all but one were rejected. The exception was "The Shocking Miss Pilgrim," a joint effort released in 1947. The film was about a young stenographer who becomes the first woman ever hired by a Boston shipping office, but even that was twisted by the

Hollywood homogenizers. Written as a study of a woman's empowerment, "Miss Pilgrim" was turned into a frothy musical starring Betty Grable.

Impoverished and disillusioned, the couple drove to an isolated hilltop at sunset in 1950 with the intention of asphyxiating themselves. But they could not go through with it, Mrs. Maas said. Suddenly clutching each other, they cried and turned off the ignition.

"We had each other and we were alive," Mrs. Maas told the online magazine Salon.

The couple had no children, and Mrs. Maas left no immediate survivors. Mr. Maas died in 1986 at 94.

Neither of the two returned to the industry. To get a job as a typist in an insurance agency, Mrs. Maas lied about her age, saying she was 40 when she was actually 50. She advanced to adjuster.

As for movies, Mrs. Maas stopped going. "I think the product they're making today," she said in 1999, "is even worse than the product we made in the early days."

— By Douglas Martin

ROGER BOISJOLY

Before Disaster in the Sky, a Warning

APRIL 25, 1938 - JAN. 6, 2012

S IX MONTHS BEFORE THE SPACE SHUTTLE CHALLENGER exploded over Florida on Jan. 28, 1986, Roger Boisjoly wrote a portentous memo. He warned that if the weather was too cold, seals connecting sections of the shuttle's huge rocket boosters could fail.

"The result could be a catastrophe of the highest order, loss of human life," he wrote.

The memo was meant to jolt Morton Thiokol, the company that made the boosters and employed Mr. Boisjoly. In July 1985, a task force had been formed, partly on Mr. Boisjoly's recommendation, to examine the effect of cold on the boosters. But the effort had become mired in paperwork, procurement delays and a rush to launch the shuttle, according to later investigations.

Meanwhile, his apprehensions only grew. The night before the Challenger's liftoff, the temperature dipped below freezing. Unusual for Florida, the cold was unprecedented for a shuttle launching, and it prompted Mr. Boisjoly and other engineers to plead that the flight be postponed. Their bosses, under pressure from NASA, rejected the advice.

The shuttle exploded 73 seconds after launching, killing its seven crew members, including Christa McAuliffe, a high school teacher from Concord, N.H.

Mr. Boisjoly's memo was soon made public. In a federal investigation of the disaster, he became widely known as a whistle-blower. And though he was hailed for his action by many, he was also made to suffer for it.

Mr. Boisjoly (pronounced like Beaujolais wine) died in Nephi, Utah, near Provo, on Jan. 6. He was 73 and lived in southwest Utah, in St. George. His wife, Roberta, said he had only recently learned that he had cancer in his colon, kidneys and liver.

Until the Challenger disaster, Mr. Boisjoly was known in his field as a crackerjack troubleshooter who had worked for companies in California on lunar module life-support systems and the moon vehicle. In 1980, he accepted a cut in pay to move with his family to Utah to deepen his involvement in the Mormon religion and to join Morton Thiokol.

After the Challenger explosion, Mr. Boisjoly gave a presidential commission investigating the disaster internal corporate documents. His disclosure of the internal memo he had written six months before the disaster was a bombshell.

Mr. Boisjoly was awarded the Prize for Scientific Freedom and Responsibility by the American Association for the Advancement of Science, and spoke to more than 300 universities and civic groups about corporate ethics. He became sought after as an expert in forensic engineering.

But he had also paid the stiff price often exacted of whistle-blowers. Thiokol cut him off from space work. He was shunned by colleagues and managers. A former friend warned him, "If you wreck this company, I'm going to put my kids on your doorstep," Mr. Boisjoly told The Los Angeles Times in 1987.

He had headaches, double-vision and depression, he said. He yelled at his dog and his daughters and skipped church to avoid people. He filed two suits against Thiokol; both were dismissed.

He later said he was sustained by a single gesture of support. Sally Ride, the first American woman in space, hugged him after his appearance before the commission.

"She was the only one," he said in a whisper to a Newsday reporter in 1988. "The only one."

Roger Mark Boisjoly was born in Lowell, Mass., on April 25, 1938, and earned a mechanical engineering degree from the University of Massachusetts at Lowell.

Besides his wife, the former Roberta Malcolm, he is survived by two daughters, three brothers and eight grandchildren.

Mr. Boisjoly worked for 27 years in the aerospace industry. But it was one moment that stood out. On the night of Jan. 27, 1986, Mr. Boisjoly and four other Thiokol engineers used a teleconference with NASA to press the case for delaying the next day's launching because of the cold. Makers of critical shuttle components had the power to postpone flights. At one point, Mr. Boisjoly said, he slapped some photos on the table showing the damage cold temperatures had caused to an earlier shuttle. It had lifted off on a cold day, but not this cold.

"How the hell can you ignore this?" he demanded.

He seemed persuasive at first, according to commission testimony later. The Thiokol engineers — four of them were vice presidents

COLD-WEATHER PERIL: Roger Boisjoly examining a model of the O-rings used to take the Challenger into orbit. His warning to delay the launch was ignored.

— went offline to huddle. Finally, Jerry Mason, Thiokol's general manager, told them to take off their engineering hats and put on management hats.

It was a go, NASA was told.

Later, in explaining the decision, Morton Thiokol executives said the data had not been conclusive — and not persuasive enough to stop a launching that had already been postponed twice. They thought the naysayers might be operating on gut reaction, not science.

The next morning Mr. Boisjoly watched the launching. If there was going to be a problem, it would come at liftoff, he thought. As the shuttle cleared the tower, his prayers seemed answered.

"Thirteen seconds later," Mr. Boisjoly said, "we saw it blow up."

— By Douglas Martin

PILAR MONTERO

When the Ships Came In, the Bar Got Busy

DEC. 2, 1921 - JAN. 14, 2012

P ILAR MONTERO spent most of her life in the little bar she owned near the waterfront in Brooklyn with her husband, or around the corner in the apartment where they reared their children. But Mrs. Montero saw the world. It came through the front door of Montero's Bar and Grill in waves — first

in the tide of seafarers who used to pile in, drinking and fighting in a dozen languages; then in the neighborhood regulars who knitted the place into their lives; and finally in the crowds of new Brooklynites who took to Montero's for what they considered its dive chic.

Mrs. Montero, who died on Jan. 14 at 90, presided as grande dame of the establishment and came to embody a sort of Brooklyn bridge between the old and new versions of the borough's salty character. "She is a human time machine," The New York Times wrote in 2006.

Montero's was one of a dozen similar bars along Atlantic Avenue near the Red Hook section when Mrs. Montero and her husband, Joseph, opened for business in 1945. Like the others, Montero's was open from 8 a.m., when

HOLDING COURT: Pilar Montero, in 2006, at her usual spot at Montero's Bar and Grill. She opened the Atlantic Avenue landmark with her husband in 1945.

longshoremen's midnight shift ended, until 4 a.m., when the law required bars to close.

Unlike the others, which shuttered or upgraded to suit a more genteel clientele when dock traffic declined in the 1970s, Montero's kept its character as a seafarers' place after the seafarers had left. Later it attracted artists, writers and Hollywood location scouts.

Scenes from the 1989 film "Last Exit to Brooklyn" were shot there. Fashion photographers used it as a backdrop. (Twiggy, who spent a day in the '60s posing along Montero's curving, glass-brick bar, struck Mrs. Montero as more fetching than she had appeared in the newspapers. "She was a beautiful girl," family members recalled her saying.)

Frank McCourt, the teacher and author who lived in an apartment upstairs in the early 1980s, liked the noirish authenticity of the place, with its blinking neon sign "turning my front room from scarlet to black to scarlet," he wrote in "Teacher Man," his 2005 memoir.

Mrs. Montero was a businesswoman first, her family said, and valued all her customers. But when she reminisced in later years, it was usually to tell stories about the era of the mariners: about how the Swedes and the Danes would fight, and then stand each other rounds; about the parrot named Poncho, Montero's mascot; about how every barmaid she hired had to have a good head, fast hands and nice legs.

"She read the shipping news very closely, and she had contacts down at the union hall who told her when a ship was coming in," her son Frank said. And if a ship was coming, he said, "we'd hear my mom and dad: 'There's a Swedish ship coming in Thursday. We're going to need a couple of extra barmaids. Check this, check that.'" It was like readying for a show, he said.

Mrs. Montero, whose husband died in 1999, remained active in operating the bar into her 80s. Her son Joseph, known as Pepe, now runs it with his wife, Linda. After retiring, Mrs. Montero became a regular visitor and could usually be found in the corner near the front where the red-topped bar meets the wall, sitting on the perch she called her throne, holding court.

Maria Pilar Rivas was born in Manhattan on Dec. 2, 1921, one of three children of Francisco and Rita Rivas. Her father, who worked on ferries and tugboats, left when she was young; her mother supported the children as the proprietor of a boarding house in Greenwich Village.

In 1943 Pilar married Joseph Montero, a merchant seaman from Spain. Besides their sons Joseph and Frank, she is survived by another son, a daughter, seven grandchildren and six great-grandchildren.

"The bar, and the family, that was her life," Frank Montero said. As she was the daughter and the wife of boatmen, her empathy for seamen came with the package, he added. "Especially a lot of guys who ended up alone, never married."

For them, he said, "she always bought the first drink."

In return for the welcome, many seamen gave the Monteros nautical models and novelties they had built themselves during their long voyages. Model-building was a common pastime at sea in the days before video games and satellite TV. Montero's is decorated from stem to stern with such work, including 34 handmade model ships and a working, miniature steam engine, greasy and covered with dust, on a shelf above the spot where the cigarette machine used to be.

A voluble talker and acute observer, Mrs. Montero once told an interviewer that she might have liked to have been a lawyer, though she had no regrets about her life in the saloon business.

"I didn't have no college, but I made it," she said, punctuating her words with an index-finger salute.

The little salute was one of her trademarks.

— BY PAUL VITELLO

JOHNNY OTIS

'The Godfather of Rhythm and Blues'

DEC. 28, 1921 - JAN. 17, 2012

J OHNNY OTIS, the musician, bandleader, songwriter, impresario, disc jockey and talent scout who was often called "the godfather of rhythm and blues," died on Jan. 17 at his home in Altadena, Calif. He was 90.

His death was confirmed by his manager, Terry Gould.

Leading a band in the late 1940s that combined the high musical standards of big band jazz with the raw urgency of gospel music and the blues, Mr. Otis played an important role in creating a new sound for a new audience of young urban blacks. Within a few years it would form the foundation of rock 'n' roll.

With a keen ear for talent, he helped steer a long list of performers to stardom, among them Etta James, Jackie Wilson, Esther Phillips and Big Mama Thornton — whose hit recording of "Hound Dog," made in 1952, four years before Elvis Presley's, was produced by Mr. Otis and featured him on drums.

At Mr. Otis's induction into the Rock and Roll Hall of Fame in 1994, Ms. James referred to him as her "guru." (He received similar honors from the Rhythm & Blues Foundation and the Blues Foundation.)

Mr. Otis was also a political activist, a preacher, an artist, an author and even, late in life, an organic farmer. But it was in music that he left his most lasting mark.

Despite being a mover and shaker in the world of black music, Mr. Otis was not black, which as far as he was concerned was simply an accident of birth. He was immersed in African-American culture from an early age and said he considered himself "black by persuasion."

"Genetically, I'm pure Greek," he told The San Jose Mercury News in 1994. "Psychologically, environmentally, culturally, by choice, I'm a member of the black community."

As a musician — he played piano and vibraphone in addition to drums — Mr. Otis can be heard on Johnny Ace's "Pledging My Love," Charles Brown's "Drifting Blues" and other seminal rhythm and blues records, as well as on jazz recordings by Lester Young and Illinois Jacquet. As a bandleader and occasional vocalist, he had a string of rhythm and blues hits in the early 1950s and a Top 10 pop hit in 1958 with his composition "Willie and the Hand Jive," later covered by Eric Clapton and others. His many other compositions included "Every Beat of My Heart," a Top 10 hit for Gladys Knight and the Pips in 1961.

As a disc jockey (he was on the radio for decades starting in the 1950s and had his own Los Angeles television show from 1954 to 1961) he helped bring black vernacular music into the American mainstream.

Johnny Otis was born John Alexander Veliotes — some sources give his first name as Ioannis — on Dec. 28, 1921, in Vallejo, Calif., the son of Greek immigrants who ran a grocery.

He grew up in a predominantly black area of Berkeley. Mr. Otis began his career as a drummer in 1939. In 1945 he formed a 16-piece band and recorded his first hit, "Harlem Nocturne."

As big bands fell out of fashion, Mr. Otis stripped the ensemble down to just a few horns and a rhythm section and stepped to the forefront of the emerging rhythm and blues scene. In 1948 he and a partner opened a nightclub, the Barrelhouse, in the Watts section of Los Angeles.

From 1950 to 1952 Mr. Otis had 15 singles on Billboard's rhythm and blues Top 40, including "Double Crossing Blues," which was No. 1 for nine weeks. On the strength of that success he crisscrossed the country with his California Rhythm and Blues Caravan, featuring singers like Ms. Phillips, billed as Little Esther — whom he had discovered at a talent contest at his nightclub — and Hank Ballard, who a decade later would record the original version of "The Twist," the song that ushered in a national dance craze.

Around this time Mr. Otis became a D.J. on the Los Angeles-area radio station KFOX. He was an immediate success, and soon had his own local television show as well. He had a weekly program on the Pacifica Radio Network in California from the 1970s until 2005.

Hundreds of Mr. Otis's radio and television shows are archived at Indiana University. In addition, he is the subject of a coming documentary film, "Every Beat of My Heart: The Johnny Otis Story," directed by Bruce Schmiechen, and a biography, "Midnight at the Barrelhouse," by George Lipsitz, published by the University of Minnesota Press in 2010.

While he never stopped making music as long as his health allowed, Mr. Otis focused much of his attention in the 1960s on politics and the civil rights movement. He ran unsuccessfully for a seat in the California State Assembly and served on the staff of Mervyn M. Dymally, a Democratic assemblyman who later became a United States representative and California's first black lieutenant governor.

Mr. Otis's first book, "Listen to the Lambs" (1968), was largely a reflection on the political and social significance of the 1965 Watts riots.

In the mid-1970s Mr. Otis branched out further when he was ordained as a minister and opened the nondenominational Landmark Community Church in Los Angeles. While he acknowledged that some people attended just "to see what Reverend Hand Jive was talking about," he took his position seriously and in his decade as pastor was involved in charitable work including feeding the homeless.

A NEW SOUND: Johnny Otis, center foreground, with his band circa 1957. Mr. Otis combined big band jazz with gospel music and the blues, forming the foundation of rock 'n' roll.

In the early 1990s he moved to Sebastopol, an agricultural town in northern California, and became an organic farmer, a career detour that he said was motivated by his concern for the environment. For several years he made and sold his own brand of apple juice in a store he opened to sell the produce he grew with his son Nick. The store doubled as a nightclub where Mr. Otis and his band performed.

Later that decade he published three more books: "Upside Your Head!: Rhythm and Blues on Central Avenue" (1993), a memoir of his musical life; "Colors and Chords" (1995), a collection of his paintings, sculptures, wood carvings and cartoons (his interest in art had begun when he started sketching cartoons on his tour bus in the 1950s to amuse his band); and "Red Beans & Rice and Other Rock 'n' Roll Recipes" (1997), a cookbook.

Mr. Otis continued to record and perform into the 21st century. His bands often included family members: his son John Jr., known as Shuggie, is a celebrated guitarist who played with him for many years, and Nick was his long-time drummer. Two grandsons, Lucky and Eric Otis, also played guitar with him.

In addition to his sons, he is survived by his wife of 70 years, the former Phyllis Walker; two daughters; nine grandchildren; eight great-grandchildren; and a great-great-grandchild.

Long after he was a force on the rhythm and blues charts, Mr. Otis was a familiar presence at blues and even jazz festivals. What people wanted to call his music, he said, was of no concern to him.

"Society wants to categorize everything, but to me it's all African-American music," he told The San Francisco Chronicle in 1993. "The music isn't just the notes, it's the culture — the way Grandma cooked, the way Grandpa told stories, the way the kids walked and talked."

— BY IHSAN TAYLOR; PETER KEEPNEWS
CONTRIBUTED REPORTING.

ETTA JAMES

'At Last' Will Always Be Hers

JAN. 25, 1938 - JAN. 20, 2012

ETTA JAMES, whose powerful, versatile and emotionally direct voice could enliven the raunchiest blues as well as the subtlest love songs, most indelibly in her signature hit, "At Last," died on Jan. 20 in Riverside, Calif. She was 73. Her manager, Lupe De Leon, said that the cause was complications of

leukemia. Ms. James, who died at Riverside Community Hospital, had been undergoing treatment for some time for a number of conditions, including leukemia and dementia. She lived in Riverside.

Ms. James was not easy to pigeonhole. She is most often referred to as a rhythm and blues singer, and that is how she made her name in the 1950s with records like "Good Rockin' Daddy." She is in both the Rock and

Roll Hall of Fame and the Blues Hall of Fame.

She was also comfortable, and convincing, singing pop standards, as she did in 1961 with "At Last," which was written in 1941 and originally recorded by Glenn Miller's orchestra. And among her four Grammy Awards (including a lifetime-achievement honor in 2003) was one for best jazz vocal performance, which she won in 1995 for the album "Mystery Lady: Songs of Billie Holiday."

Regardless of how she was categorized, Ms. James was admired. Expressing a common sentiment, Jon Pareles of The New York Times wrote in 1990 that she had "one of the great voices in American popular music, with a huge range, a multiplicity of tones and vast reserves of volume."

For all her accomplishments, Ms. James had an up-and-down career, partly because of changing audience tastes but largely because of drug problems. She developed a heroin habit in the 1960s; after she overcame it in the 1970s, she began using cocaine. She candidly described her struggles with addiction and her many trips to rehab in her autobiography, "Rage to Survive," written with David Ritz (1995).

Etta James was born Jamesetta Hawkins in Los Angeles on Jan. 25, 1938. Her mother, Dorothy Hawkins, was 14 at the time; her father was long gone, and Ms. James never knew for sure who he was, although she recalled her mother telling her that he was the celebrated pool player Rudolf Wanderone, better known as Minnesota Fats. She was reared by foster parents and moved to San Francisco with her mother when she was 12.

MORE THAN THE BLUES: Etta James wanted her music to rise above sadness.

She began singing at the St. Paul Baptist Church in Los Angeles at 5 and turned to secular music as a teenager, forming a vocal group with two friends. She was 15 when she made her first record, "Roll With Me Henry," which set her own lyrics to the tune of Hank Ballard and the Midnighters' recent hit "Work With Me Annie." When some disc jockeys complained that the title was too suggestive, it was changed to "The Wallflower," although the record itself was not.

"The Wallflower" rose to No. 2 on the rhythm-and-blues charts in 1954. As was often the case in those days with records by black performers, a toned-down version was soon recorded by a white singer and found a wider audience: Georgia Gibbs's version, with the title and lyric changed to "Dance With Me, Henry," was a No. 1 pop hit in 1955. Its success was not entirely bad news for Ms. James. She shared the songwriting royalties with Mr. Ballard and the bandleader and talent scout Johnny Otis, who had arranged for her recording session. Mr. Otis died three days before Ms. James did. (See page 186.)

In 1960 Ms. James was signed by Chess Records, the Chicago label that was home to Chuck Berry, Muddy Waters and other leading lights of black music. She quickly had a string of hits, including "All I Could Do Was Cry," "Trust in Me" and "At Last," which established her as Chess's first major female star.

She remained with Chess well into the 1970s, reappearing on the charts after a long absence in 1967 with the funky and high-spirited "Tell

Mama." In the late '70s and early '80s she was an opening act for the Rolling Stones.

After decades of touring, recording for various labels and drifting in and out of the public eye, Ms. James found herself in the news in 2009 after Beyoncé Knowles recorded a version of "At Last" closely modeled on hers. (Ms. Knowles played Ms. James in the 2008 movie "Cadillac Records," a fictionalized account of the rise and fall of Chess.) Ms. Knowles also performed "At Last" at an inaugural ball for President Barack Obama in Washington.

When the movie was released, Ms. James had kind words for Ms. Knowles's portrayal. But in February 2009, referring specifically to the Washington performance, she told an audience, "I can't stand Beyoncé," and threatened to "whip" the younger singer for doing "At Last." She later said she had been joking, but she did add that she wished she had been invited to sing the song herself for the new president.

Ms. James's survivors include her husband of 42 years, Artis Mills, as well as two sons and four grandchildren.

Though her life had its share of troubles to the end — her husband and sons were locked in a long-running battle over control of her estate, which was resolved in her husband's favor only weeks before her death — Ms. James said she wanted her music to transcend unhappiness rather than reflect it.

"A lot of people think the blues is depressing," she told The Los Angeles Times in 1992, "but that's not the blues I'm singing. When I'm singing blues, I'm singing life. People that can't stand to listen to the blues, they've got to be phonies."

— BY PETER KEEPNEWS

\\\\\\\\\\\\\\\\\\\\\\\\\\\\\\\\

EIKO ISHIOKA

In Surreal Designs, East Met West

JULY 12, 1938 - JAN. 21, 2012

EIKO ISHIOKA, a designer who brought an eerie, sensual surrealism to film and theater, album covers, the Olympics and Cirque du Soleil, in the process earning an Oscar, a Grammy and a string of other honors, died on Jan. 21 in Tokyo. She was 73.

Trained as a graphic designer, Ms. Ishioka was for decades considered the foremost art director in Japan and later one of the foremost in the world.

She received an Academy Award for costume design in 1992 for "Bram Stoker's 'Dracula,'" directed by Francis Ford Coppola. One outfit for the film was a suit of full body armor for the title character (played by Gary Oldman), whose glistening red color and all-over corrugation made it look like exposed musculature. Another creation was a voluminous wedding dress worn by the actress Sadie Frost, with a stiff, round, aggressive lace collar inspired by the ruffs of frill-necked lizards. These typified Ms. Ishioka's aesthetic. A deliberate marriage of East and West — she had lived in Manhattan for many years — it simultaneously embraced the gothic, the otherworldly, the dramatic and the unsettling and was suffused with a powerful, dark eroticism. Her work, whose outsize stylization dazzled some critics and discomforted others, was provocative in every possible sense of the word, and it was meant to be.

Ms. Ishioka was closely associated with the director Tarsem Singh, for whom she designed costumes for four films. In the first, "The Cell" (2000), she conceived for Jennifer Lopez, who plays a psychologist trapped by a serial killer, an encasing headpiece resembling a cross between a rigid neck brace and a forbidding bird cage.

"Jennifer asked me if I could make it more comfortable," Ms. Ishioka told The Ottawa Citizen in 2000, "but I said, 'No, you're supposed to be tortured.'"

For Mr. Singh, she also costumed "The Fall" (2006), an adventure fantasy, and "Immortals," a violent tale of ancient Greece released in 2011. Their fourth collaboration, "Mirror Mirror," an adaptation of "Snow White," was released in March.

Ms. Ishioka's other film work includes the production design of "Mishima: A Life in Four Chapters," Paul Schrader's 1985 film about the doomed writer Yukio Mishima. That year the Cannes Film Festival jury awarded her — along with the film's cinematographer, John Bailey, and its composer, Philip Glass — a special prize for "artistic contribution."

A DRAMATIC AND POWERFUL AESTHETIC: Sadie Frost in a costume designed by Eiko Ishioka for "Bram Stoker's Dracula." Ms. Ishioka, one of the leading art directors in the world, won an Oscar for the 1992 film.

For the Broadway stage, Ms. Ishioka designed sets and costumes for David Henry Hwang's 1988 drama "M. Butterfly," for which she earned two Tony nominations, and, most recently, costumes for the musical "Spider-Man: Turn Off the Dark."

She won a Grammy Award in 1986 for her design of Miles Davis's album "Tutu," whose cover is dominated by an Irving Penn photograph of Mr. Davis, shot in extreme close-up and starkly lighted.

Eiko Ishioka was born in Tokyo on July 12, 1938. Her artistic pursuits were encouraged by her parents: her father was a graphic designer, her mother a homemaker who, in accordance with the social norms of the day, had forsaken literary ambitions to marry and raise children.

But when Eiko, as an undergraduate at the Tokyo National University of Fine Arts and Music, announced that she planned to be a graphic artist, even her father warned that she would have a much easier life designing things like shoes or dolls. Graphic design in Japan, with its close connection to the sharp-elbowed world of advertising, was every inch a man's game then.

The young Ms. Ishioka persevered, graduating in 1961 and joining the advertising division of the cosmetics giant Shiseido. She opened her own design concern in the early 1970s; among her chief clients was Parco, a chain of boutique shopping complexes for which she created advertising and promotional materials for more than a decade.

Ms. Ishioka's work extended to TV commercials, "M. Butterfly," Miles Davis, Jennifer Lopez, the Olympics, and Cirque du Soleil.

Ms. Ishioka's work for Parco, which embodied an eclectic, avant-garde internationalism rarely seen in Japanese advertisements of the period, helped cement her reputation. Her print ads, for instance, sometimes showed models who were naked or nearly so, a rarity in Japanese advertising then.

"You've seen a kimono: they're not big into full-on nudes," Maggie Kinser Hohle, a writer on Japanese design, said earlier in January in an interview for this obituary. (As Maggie Kinser Saiki, she is the author of "12 Japanese Masters," a book about design that features Ms. Ishioka.) "That's extremely shocking. And yet she did it in a way that made you drawn to the beauty of it, and then you realize you're looking at nipples."

Perhaps the most striking thing about Ms. Ishioka's ads was that they rarely depicted any actual item sold at Parco. For Japanese television, she created a Parco commercial in which, over the course of a minute and a half, the actress Faye Dunaway, black-clad against a black background, slowly and wordlessly peels and eats a hard-boiled egg.

In other work, Ms. Ishioka designed uniforms and outerwear for selected members of the Swiss, Canadian, Japanese and Spanish teams at the 2002 Winter Olympics in Salt Lake City. She was also the director of costume design for the opening ceremony of the 2008 Summer Olympics in Beijing.

Ms. Ishioka's portfolio extended to the circus and a magic show. She designed costumes for Cirque du Soleil's "Varekai" (2002) and was the visual artistic director of the illusionist David Copperfield's 1996 Broadway show, "Dreams and Nightmares."

She also designed costumes for the singer Grace Jones's "Hurricane" tour in 2009 (they were noteworthy even by Ms. Jones's lofty standards for the outré) and directed Bjork's music video "Cocoon." Her books include "Eiko by Eiko" (1983) and "Eiko on Stage" (2000), both available in English.

Ms. Ishioka, who died of pancreatic cancer, is survived by her husband, Nicholas Soultanakis, whom she married last year, as well as her mother, two brothers and a sister.

Though she was known in particular for the form of her designs, Ms. Ishioka did not neglect function. For some athletes at the 2002 Winter Games, she created what she called the Concentration Coat, a full-length cocoon of foamlike fabric into which wearers could withdraw from the press scrum around them, podlike studies in portable solitude.

— By Margalit Fox

JOE PATERNO

He Was Penn State, in Glory and Disgrace

DEC. 21, 1926 - JAN. 22, 2012

JOE PATERNO had won more games than any other major-college football coach. For almost half a century he was the face of Pennsylvania State University and a symbol of integrity in collegiate athletics. But a child sexual-abuse scandal that shocked the nation undid all that.

When told that his former defensive coordinator Jerry Sandusky had been observed molesting children, Paterno did nothing, and for that failure he was fired during the 2011 season. His reputation unraveling, it would get worse: Sandusky's trial and conviction, a damning report arising from a seven-month investigation, and blunt N.C.A.A. sanctions would leave Paterno's reputation in tatters.

But he did not live to see the fallout, to see his own statue removed from outside Beaver Stadium. Paterno died on Jan. 22 in State College, Pa., at 85, having learned he had lung cancer — the listed cause of death — in mid-November as the scandal unfolded.

During his 46 years as head coach, as he paced the sideline in his thick tinted glasses, white athletic socks and rolled-up baggy khaki pants, Paterno seemed as much a part of the Penn State landscape as Mount Nittany, overlooking the central Pennsylvania campus known as Happy Valley.

When Penn State defeated Illinois, 10-7, on Oct. 29, 2011, the victory was Paterno's 409th, and he surpassed Eddie Robinson of Grambling for most career victories among N.C.A.A. Division I coaches. Penn State's president at the time, Graham B. Spanier, presented Paterno with a commemorative plaque in a postgame ceremony.

It would be Paterno's last game. Within days his former defensive coordinator Jerry Sandusky was indicted and arrested on multiple charges of sexually abusing young boys extending back to his time on Paterno's staff. On Nov. 9, Paterno and Spanier were fired by the university's board of trustees because of their failure to go to the police after they were told of an accusation against Sandusky in 2002.

The following June Sandusky was convicted of 45 counts of sexually assaulting 10 boys. And the following month, Louis J. Freeh, the former judge and director of the F.B.I., concluded in his report to the trustees that Paterno and other Penn State officials were aware in 1998 that the university police were investigating child-abuse accusations against Sandusky but that they did nothing. They did not even speak to Sandusky.

Further, the report made it clear that Paterno had persuaded Spanier and others not to report Sandusky to the authorities in 2001 after he had violently assaulted another boy in the football building's showers.

The officials, the report said, had shown a "total and consistent disregard" for the welfare of children, had worked together to conceal Sandusky's assaults and had done so for one central reason: fear of bad publicity, which would have harmed the university's nationally ranked football program, Paterno's reputation, the Penn State "brand" and the university's ability to raise money.

Paterno, Freeh said, "made perhaps the worst mistake of his life."

On July 22, the Paterno statue was removed, and the next day the N.C.A.A. fined the university $60 million, restricted its ability to offer scholarships to players and vacated all of the team's victories from 1998 to 2001. Paterno was no longer the major-college career leader in football wins.

His fall from grace hardly could have been imagined. He had held himself to a high standard with what he called his "grand experiment": fielding outstanding teams with disciplined players whose graduation rate far exceeded that at most football powers. His program had never been tainted by a recruiting scandal. Alongside his statue was the legend "Educator, Coach, Humanitarian." Former players who succeeded in professional life far beyond the football field had told of their debt to him.

"Look how many go to medical school or law school," said Bill Lenkaitis, a dentist in Foxborough, Mass., who played for Paterno in the 1960s and who became a longtime center for the New England Patriots. "Look how many become heads of corporations."

Many a Pennsylvania home was stocked with Paterno knickknacks: Cup of Joe coffee mugs, Stand-up Joe life-size cutouts, JoePa golf balls bearing his likeness.

During his years as head coach, donors gave hundreds of millions of dollars to the university, helping to make it a major research institution. Paterno and his wife, Sue, gave more than $4 million. He was a five-time national coach of the year. He had five unbeaten and untied teams, and he coached Penn State to the No. 1 ranking in 1982 and 1986. He took his Nittany Lions to

37 bowl games, winning 24 of them, and turned out dozens of first-team all-Americans.

On Saturdays at Beaver Stadium, crowds of 100,000 cheered on players recruited by Paterno largely from Pennsylvania and nearby states. Many went on to stellar professional careers, among them running backs Franco Harris and Lydell Mitchell and linebacker Jack Ham.

Before many of his victories were taken away, Paterno had 409, along with 136 defeats and 3 ties. He was surpassed only by John Gagliardi, who has won 484 games at Carroll College in Montana and St. John's of Minnesota, coaching below the major-college level.

"Joe Paterno, to me, is maybe the greatest coach ever," Bobby Bowden, the former Florida State coach, who is No. 3 in major-college coaching victories, said in 2006. "I mean that truly, and I said that 10 years ago."

Penn State hired Bill O'Brien, the 42-year-old offensive coordinator for the New England Patriots, to replace Paterno.

After the accusations against Sandusky surfaced, the university's athletic director and the official who supervised the campus police were arrested on charges including perjury before a grand jury. They pleaded not guilty.

Sandusky had retired after the 1999 season but had retained access to the Penn State football facilities, where he escorted disadvantaged boys being helped by a foundation he created. In the most notorious episode, a graduate assistant said he had tried to explain to Paterno that he saw Sandusky sexually abusing a boy in a team locker room late one night in March 2002. Paterno reported a version of the story to two superiors, saying he had set up a meeting between the graduate assistant and the athletic director and university vice president. He evidently never followed up.

Paterno's firing came hours after he said he would retire, although he had planned to coach the final three games of the season after compiling an 8-1 record.

When word came of Paterno's ouster, thousands of Penn State students rampaged through the downtown area near the university in support of him. And at Penn State's next game, against Nebraska, many students in the crowd came dressed as Paterno, with pants legs rolled up, white socks and thick-framed black eyeglasses. Hundreds wore T-shirts reading "Joe Knows Football."

Rather than sprinting onto the field, the Penn State players walked from an end-zone tunnel hand in hand, and a moment of silence was dedicated to victims of child abuse. Paterno had remained at his ranch in State College, less than a mile from the campus, and when his son Jay, the quarterbacks coach, arrived at his parents' home after the game — a 17-14 Nebraska victory — he pumped his fist in the air and chanted "We are . . . "

"Penn State!" some two dozen cheering students responded, completing the traditional campus chant.

Joseph Vincent Paterno was born on Dec. 21, 1926, and grew up in the Flatbush section of Brooklyn. His father, Angelo, obtained a law degree after working as a court clerk and encouraged his children to pursue education.

Joe Paterno played football and basketball at Brooklyn Prep, a Jesuit-run high school, and studied the classics, which he said had taught him the importance of being committed to an ideal. He entered Brown University in 1946, played quarterback and defensive back, and majored in English. A younger brother, George, was a teammate, as he had been in high school.

Paterno planned to attend Boston University Law School, but when Rip Engle, Brown's head football coach, left to coach Penn State in 1950, Paterno went with him to coach the quarterbacks.

Paterno proved intense, brash and ambitious, and in June 1964 he was named Penn State's associate football coach. He then succeeded Engle when he retired in 1966.

Engle never had a losing season at Penn State, but his teams had never made it to a high-profile bowl game. His last squad had a 5-5 record.

Paterno was 5-5 as well in his first season as the head coach, but his team went 8-2-1 the next year, when he designed a new defensive system meant to confuse opposing offenses with shifts after the ball was snapped.

Then came the team's breakout on the national football scene. Penn State went 10-0 in 1968 and in '69 before victories in the Orange Bowl each season. It was unbeaten for 31 straight games before losing to Colorado in September 1970.

Early in 1973, Paterno turned down an offer to become the head coach of the New England Patriots. That June, he became the first Penn

THE FACE OF PENN STATE: Joe Paterno in 1965. He would go on to win more games than any other major-college football coach and become a legend at the university.

State football coach to deliver the university's commencement address.

But Paterno was long stymied in his bid for a No. 1 ranking. His 1973 team, starring John Cappelletti in his Heisman Trophy season, was 12-0 without a top ranking. His 1978 squad was unbeaten in the regular season but lost to Alabama in the Sugar Bowl in the battle for the No. 1 spot. Paterno finally reached the top ranking with his 1982 and 1986 teams.

Paterno seemed indestructible, but in November 2006, he sustained a broken leg and a severe knee injury in a sideline collision during a game. He had surgery and did not return for the rest of the season. But he went onto the field for Penn State's 2007 opener, beginning his 42nd season there as the head coach and surpassing the major-college longevity record at one program set by Amos Alonzo Stagg at the University of Chicago from 1892 to 1932.

Paterno was walking with a cane early in the 2008 season, in pain from leg and hip problems. He began coaching from the press box in October, then had hip-replacement surgery. Penn State nonetheless made it to the Rose Bowl, with a No. 6 national ranking, and Paterno coached his team, again from a press box, in a loss to Southern California.

His 2009 team was 11-2 and beat Louisiana State in the Capital One Bowl, but his 2010 squad was 7-6 and lost in the Outback Bowl to Florida. Then came his final season, when Penn State had lost only once when he was fired.

Usually preferring a conservative ground game, Paterno was best known as a strategist for his defensive units. Penn State was known

SEEMINGLY INDESTRUCTIBLE:
Joe Paterno's reputation was untarnished until the Sandusky scandal.

as Linebacker U. He was also demanding at practice, where little escaped his notice. He was devoid of flourishes. His players wore high-top black shoes and white helmets with a simple blue stripe, and their blue and white jerseys were unadorned by names on the back, all to project toughness and a selfless attitude.

"He's a tremendous motivator," said Kenny Jackson, who was a wide receiver on Paterno's 1982 national championship team and who later coached under him.

In 2007, Paterno became the third active coach inducted into the College Football Hall of Fame.

But as Paterno coached on into his 70s, his teams faltered. He had only one winning season from 2000 to 2004 and seemed overmatched in the Big Ten, which Penn State had joined in 1993 after years of success as an independent. There were several off-the-field incidents as his teams struggled: one quarterback needed stitches after a fight at an ice rink, and a center was held out of games for damaging an apartment wall by firing a bow and arrow. The episodes added to the air of disappointment surrounding Paterno, who prided himself on his athletes' character.

Some critics also complained that Paterno's run-oriented offense remained too conservative. High school stars were said to be looking elsewhere.

On the Sunday before Thanksgiving Day in 2004, Spanier, the Penn State president, and three top university administrators went to Paterno's home and suggested he retire, although he had been given a four-year contract extension the previous spring.

"Relax. Get off my backside," Paterno told them. They did.

Paterno's team lost only one game in 2005 and captured the Big Ten championship before defeating Florida State in the Orange Bowl in 2006.

"You guys think that you write something and all of a sudden I'm bothered?" Paterno told The Associated Press at the outset of the 2007 season. "I don't read it."

In addition to his wife and his son Joseph Jr., known as Jay, Paterno is survived by two other sons, two daughters and many grandchildren. His brother George died in 2002. Joe Paterno's wife and five children were Penn State graduates.

For all his achievements, Paterno insisted that there was more to college football than results on the scoreboard. As he wrote in The New York Times in 1989:

"A hard-fought, well-fought, hairline-close game is as classical in sports as tragedy in theater. A tragedy usually ends with the stage strewn with bodies from both sides of a struggle, and you can't tell who won and who lost.

Victory is contained within defeat, and defeat is contained within victory. That's the way it is in the best of games. What counts in sports is not the victory but the magnificence of the struggle."

> They sold Cup of Joe mugs and JoePa golf balls, but all his renown, influence and victories couldn't save him from a final, crushing defeat.

Paterno said he was disappointed by the trustees' decision to fire him after he announced he would retire at the end of the 2011 season. But in a statement just before the board acted, he expressed remorse over his failing.

"This is a tragedy," he said. "It is one of the great sorrows of my life. With the benefit of hindsight, I wish I had done more."

— BY RICHARD GOLDSTEIN

CAMILLA WILLIAMS

Opera History Made, Then Forgotten

OCT. 18, 1919 - JAN. 29, 2012

O N MAY 15, 1946, an unknown singer named Camilla Williams took the stage at City Center in Manhattan as Cio-Cio-San, the doomed heroine of Puccini's "Madama Butterfly." Her performance would be the capstone of a night of glorious firsts.

Miss Williams, a lyric soprano who began her career as a concert singer, had never been in an opera. The New York City Opera, the young upstart company with which she was making her debut, had never before staged "Madama Butterfly."

But there was another, far more important first, though its significance has been largely forgotten over time:

As Cio-Cio-San, Miss Williams, the daughter of a chauffeur and a domestic in the Jim Crow South, was the first black woman to secure a contract with a major United States opera company — a distinction widely ascribed in the public memory to the contralto Marian Anderson.

Miss Williams's performance that night, to rave reviews, came nearly a decade before Miss Anderson first sang at the Metropolitan Opera. As Miss Williams, who died on Jan. 29 at 92, well knew, it was a beacon that lighted the way to American opera houses for other black women, Miss Anderson included.

That Miss Williams's historic role is scarcely remembered today is rooted in both the rarefied world of opera-house politics and the ubiquitous racial anxiety of midcentury America. And though she was far too well mannered to trumpet her rightful place in history, her relegation to its margins caused her great private anguish.

"The lack of recognition for my accomplishments used to bother me, but you cannot cry over those things," Miss Williams said in a 1995 interview with the opera scholar Elizabeth Nash. "There is no place for bitterness in singing. It works on the cords and ruins the voice. In his own good time, God brings everything right."

Miss Williams's hiring by City Opera was of a piece with the tentative first stabs by postwar America at integrating the worlds of culture and entertainment.

In 1945, the year before she first sang there, the baritone Todd Duncan, who in 1935 had created the part of Porgy in the original Broadway production of "Porgy and Bess," made his City Opera debut as Tonio in "Pagliacci." In so doing, he became the first black man to sing a featured role with a prominent company.

The year after Miss Williams's City Opera debut, Jackie Robinson integrated major league baseball.

The daughter of Cornelius Booker Williams and the former Fannie Carey, Camilla Ella Williams was born on Oct. 18, 1919, in Danville, Va. Theirs was a singing family, and Camilla, the youngest of four siblings, first sang in church at 8. At 12 she took lessons from Raymond Aubrey, a Welsh singer teaching at local white colleges. Amid Jim Crow, he had to teach his few black students, including Camilla, in a private home.

The young Miss Williams earned a bachelor's degree in music education in 1941 from the Virginia State College for Negroes, now Virginia State University. After graduating, she taught third grade and music at a black school in Danville, though she hoped to become a singer.

The next year, a group of Virginia State alumni paid her way to Philadelphia for study with the distinguished voice teacher Marion Szekely-Freschl. There, Miss Williams supported herself by working as an usherette in a movie house.

Miss Williams won a Marian Anderson Award, a vocal scholarship established by Miss Anderson, in 1943 and again the next season. Soon afterward, she embarked on a concert career.

In 1944 she gave a recital in Stamford, Conn. In the audience was the soprano Geraldine Farrar. One of the most renowned singers of the first half of the 20th century, Miss Farrar had been the Met's first Madam Butterfly in 1907.

Captivated by Miss Williams's voice, she became her mentor, helping her secure a recording contract with RCA Victor and writing to the impresario Arthur Judson with the suggestion that he manage her. On receiving the letter, as Miss Williams recalled in the 1995 interview, a suspicious Mr. Judson telephoned Miss Farrar.

"He didn't believe the great Farrar would take time to write a letter about an unknown little colored girl," she said. "When Judson confirmed it really was Miss Farrar, he was dumbfounded."

Miss Farrar also arranged for an audition with Laszlo Halasz, City Opera's director, who had founded the company in 1943. It went well enough that had there not been a war on, Miss Williams might have sung Cio-Cio-San even sooner than she did.

"Since Miss Farrar had been one of the greatest interpreters of 'Madama Butterfly,' they had thought of that role for me," Miss Williams said in the same interview. "The war with Japan was on, however, and it was forbidden to perform that opera. 'If I ever give this opera,' Mr. Halasz said, 'call this young girl in to sing for me.'"

The call came in 1946, and she learned the part of Cio-Cio-San in two months. Reviewing Miss Williams's debut in The New York Times, Noel Straus wrote, "There was a warmth and intensity in her singing that lent dramatic force of no mean order to the climactic episodes, and something profoundly human and touching in her delivery of all of the music assigned her."

At City Opera, with which she performed regularly until 1954, Miss Williams also sang Nedda in Leoncavallo's "Pagliacci," Mimi in Puccini's "Bohème" and the title role in Verdi's "Aïda."

But even there, she said afterward, she was primarily confined to playing "exotic" heroines like Aïda and Cio-Cio-San. European characters largely eluded her.

A BREAKTHROUGH PERFORMANCE: Camilla Williams, the first black woman to secure a contract with a major American opera company, made her debut in "Madama Butterfly" in 1946.

"I would have loved to sing the Countess and Susanna in 'Le Nozze di Figaro,'" Miss Williams said in 1995. "Mozart was so right for my voice. But they were afraid to put me in a white wig and whiter makeup."

Miss Williams also appeared with the Boston Lyric Opera and the Vienna State Opera, among other companies. She was a soloist with some of the world's leading orchestras, including the Philadelphia Orchestra and the New York Philharmonic, and sang at the White House.

She toured worldwide as a recitalist, though her concerts tended to be less well reviewed than her opera work, at least by New York critics.

Miss Williams sang Bess in what was then the most complete recording of "Porgy and Bess," released by Columbia Records in 1951 and featuring Lawrence Winters as Porgy. Her other recordings include "A Camilla

Williams Recital" and "Camilla Williams Sings Spirituals."

In 1977, Miss Williams became the first black person appointed to the voice faculty at Indiana University in Bloomington, where she taught until her retirement in 1997. Her death, at her home in Bloomington, was announced by the university, where she was an emeritus professor of voice.

Miss Williams's path crossed Miss Anderson's many times. At the 1963 March on Washington, she substituted for Miss Anderson, who was stuck in traffic, before the Rev. Dr. Martin Luther King Jr.'s "I Have a Dream" speech, racing up the steps of the Lincoln Memorial to sing "The Star-Spangled Banner." By all accounts, the two women maintained a warm, enduring friendship.

Why, then, is Miss Williams's name not uttered in the same breath as Miss Anderson's?

For one thing, Miss Anderson (1897-1993) spent far longer in the public eye. She had been a cause célèbre since 1939, when she was denied permission to sing at Constitution Hall in Washington, owned by the Daughters of the American Revolution.

The first lady, Eleanor Roosevelt, resigned from the D.A.R. in protest and helped arrange a concert by Miss Anderson at the Lincoln Memorial, a landmark event that drew 75,000 people and was heard by many more on the radio.

For another, the longstanding David-and-Goliath relationship between the scrappy City Opera and the august Met inevitably came into play.

"Camilla never did sing at the Met," Stephanie Shonekan, the co-author of her memoir, "The Life of Camilla Williams" (2011), said in a telephone interview after Miss Williams' death. "And that's something that sort of haunted her all her life. The Met, in many

people's minds, was superior to the New York City Opera. So there's that tendency, then, to discount what happened at the New York City Opera and count only what happened at the Met."

A third reason, said Professor Shonekan, who teaches ethnomusicology and black studies at the University of Missouri, was rooted in the fact that Miss Williams happened to come of age as a singer toward the start of the civil rights movement, timing that seemed to make her managers wary.

"She signed with Columbia Artists, and as we moved into the '50s, Camilla's feeling was that Columbia Artists did not want to put her 'out there' too much, because they didn't want her to deal with the race issue," she said. "And she wouldn't have anyway: her personality is not to be 'out there' with an Afro, holding up her fist. But I think that there was a fear from her management that she would deal with the race issue as other artists were doing at that time."

Miss Williams's husband of 19 years, Charles T. Beavers, a civil rights lawyer who was the court-appointed defense counsel for Thomas 15X Johnson, one of three men convicted of murdering Malcolm X in 1965, died in 1969. No immediate family members survive.

On Jan. 7, 1955, when Miss Anderson made her Met debut as Ulrica in Verdi's "Ballo in Maschera," Miss Williams was in the audience as her invited guest. Both women were keenly aware of the significance of the evening, but both, Miss Williams recalled, were also mindful of a night in May nine years earlier.

"As the first African-American woman to appear with a major American opera company," Miss Williams said in 1995, "I had opened the door for Miss Anderson."

— BY MARGALIT FOX

ANGELO DUNDEE

And in This Corner, Behind the Champion . . .

AUG. 30, 1921 - FEB. 1, 2012

A NGELO DUNDEE, the renowned trainer who guided Muhammad Ali and Sugar Ray Leonard to boxing glory, died on Feb. 1 in Clearwater, Fla. He was 90.

In more than 60 years in professional boxing, Dundee was acclaimed as a brilliant cornerman, whether adjusting strategy between rounds to counter an opponent's style, healing cuts or inspiring his fighters to battle on when they seemed to be reeling.

"You come back to the corner and he'll say, 'The guy's open for a hook,' or this or that," Ali told The New York Times in 1981. "If he tells you something during a fight, you can believe it. As a cornerman, Angelo is the best in the world."

When Thomas Hearns was rallying against Leonard in their welterweight championship unification fight in September 1981, Dundee got Leonard going again after the 12th-round bell, telling him, "You're blowing it, son, you're blowing it." Leonard knocked Hearns down in the 13th round and won the bout when the referee stopped it in the 14th.

Dundee "knew precisely how to get through to me at the most pivotal moments, and no moment in the fight, or in my career, was as pivotal as this," Leonard recalled in his memoir "The Big Fight" (2011), written with Michael Arkush.

Dundee's first champion was Carmen Basilio, the welterweight and middleweight titleholder of the 1950s from upstate New York. Although best remembered for Ali and Leonard, Dundee also trained the light-heavyweight champion Willie Pastrano, the heavyweight titleholder Jimmy Ellis and the welterweight champion Luis Rodriguez. Dundee advised George Foreman when he regained the heavyweight title at age 45. He was inducted into the International Boxing Hall of Fame in 1992.

He was born Angelo Mirena in Philadelphia, the son of a railroad worker. He became Angelo Dundee after his brother, Joe, fought professionally under the name Johnny Dundee, in tribute to a former featherweight champion; another brother, Chris, also adopted the Dundee name.

After working as a cornerman at military boxing tournaments in England while in the Army Air Forces during World War II, Dundee served an apprenticeship at Stillman's Gym near the old Madison Square Garden on Eighth Avenue at 49th Street, learning his craft from veteran trainers like Ray Arcel, Charley Goldman and Chickie Ferrara. In the early 1950s he teamed with his brother Chris to open the Fifth Street gym in Miami Beach. It became their longtime base, Angelo as a trainer and Chris as a promoter.

60 YEARS AND COUNTLESS ROUNDS: During his career, Angelo Dundee trained two of professional boxing's greatest champions, Muhammad Ali and Sugar Ray Leonard.

In the late 1950s, Dundee gave some tips to a promising amateur named Cassius Clay, and in December 1960, after Clay's first pro bout, Dundee became his trainer, working with him in Miami Beach. He guided him to the heavyweight title with a technical knockout of Sonny Liston in February 1964.

Dundee avoided the temptation to tamper with the brilliance of his young and charismatic fighter, and he used a bit of psychology in honing his talents.

"I never touched that natural stuff with him," Dundee recalled in his memoir, "My View From the Corner" (2008), written with Bert Sugar, who died in March. He added: "So every now and then I'd subtly suggest some move or other to him, couching it as if it were something he was already doing. I'd say something like: 'You're getting that jab down real good. You're bending your knees now, and you're putting a lot of snap into it.' Now, he had never thrown a jab, but it was a way of letting him think it was his idea, his innovation."

When Cassius Clay became Muhammad Ali after winning the heavyweight title, his boxing management and financial affairs were handled by the Nation of Islam. Dundee was the only white man in his camp, and he grew disturbed over references to that fact.

In his memoir, Dundee said that he and Ali "had this special thing, a unique blend, a chemistry."

"I never heard anything resembling a racist comment leave his mouth," he said. "There was never a black-white divide."

Dundee knew all the tricks in the boxing trade, and then some.

When Ali — or Clay, as he was still known — sought to regain his senses after being knocked down by Henry Cooper in the fourth round of their June 1963 bout, Dundee stuck his finger in a small slit that had opened in one of Ali's gloves, making the damage worse. Then he brought the badly damaged glove to the referee's attention. Dundee was told that a substitute glove wasn't available, and the few seconds of delay helped Clay recover. He knocked Cooper out in the fifth round.

In the hours before Ali fought Foreman in Zaire in 1974 — the Rumble in the Jungle —

Dundee noticed that the ring ropes were sagging in the high humidity. He used a razor blade to cut and refit them so that they were tight, enabling Ali to bounce off them when Foreman let go his "anywhere" punches from all angles. Ali wore Foreman out, hanging back with the "rope a dope" strategy Ali undertook on his own, and he went on to win the bout.

Dundee became Sugar Ray Leonard's manager and cornerman in 1977, when Leonard turned pro. He taught him to snap his left jab rather than paw with it, and guided him to the welterweight championship with a knockout of Wilfred Benitez in 1979.

Roberto Duran captured Leonard's title on a decision in June 1980, but Leonard won the rematch in November when Dundee persuaded him to avoid a slugfest and instead keep Duran turning while slipping his jabs. A thoroughly beaten Duran quit in the eighth round, uttering his inglorious "no mas."

In talking about his boxing savvy, Dundee liked to say, "When I see things through my eyes, I see things."

"When Dundee speaks, traditional English usage is, to say the least, stretched and malapropisms abound," Ronald K. Fried wrote in "Cornermen: Great Boxing Trainers."

"Yet the language is utterly original and Dundee's own — and it conveys exactly what Dundee knows in his heart."

After retiring from full-time training, Dundee had stints in boxing broadcasting. He taught boxing technique to Russell Crowe for his role as the 1930s heavyweight champion Jimmy Braddock in the 2005 movie "Cinderella Man."

In the month before he died, he flew to Louisville for a celebration of Ali's 70th birthday.

Dundee had been living in Palm Harbor, Fla., and treated for blood clots recently. His survivors include a daughter, a son, six grandchildren and one great-grandchild. His wife, Helen, died in 2010.

"I'm not star quality," Dundee once remarked. "The fighter is the star."

But he took pride in his craft. As he put it: "You've got to combine certain qualities belonging to a doctor, an engineer, a psychologist and sometimes an actor, in addition to knowing your specific art well. There are more sides to being a trainer than those found on a Rubik's Cube."

— By Richard Goldstein

DON CORNELIUS

Every Saturday Morning, Soul Music for All

SEPT. 27, 1936 - FEB. 1, 2012

DON CORNELIUS, the smooth-voiced television host who brought black music and culture into America's living rooms when he created the dance show "Soul Train," was found dead on Feb. 1 at his home in Los Angeles. He was 75.

Police officers responding to a report of a shooting found Mr. Cornelius's body at 4 a.m. on the floor of his house on Mulholland Drive with a gunshot wound to the head. The Los Angeles coroner's office said the death was a suicide.

"Soul Train," one of the longest-running syndicated shows in television history, played a critical role in spreading the music of black America to the world, offering wide exposure to musicians like James Brown, Aretha Franklin, Marvin Gaye and Michael Jackson in the 1970s and '80s.

> "Soul Train" showcased dances and clothing styles that were popular among young blacks and was soon imitated across the country.

"'Soul Train' created an outlet for black artists that never would have been if it hadn't been for Cornelius," said Kenny Gamble, who with his partner, Leon Huff, created the Philly soul sound and wrote the theme song for the show. "It was a tremendous export from America to the world that showed African-American life and the joy of music and dance, and it brought people together."

News of Mr. Cornelius's death prompted an outpouring of tributes from civil rights leaders, musicians, entrepreneurs, academics and writers. Lonnie G. Bunch III, the director of the Smithsonian's National Museum of African American History and Culture, said Mr. Cornelius offered the country a window on black culture and music.

"For young black teenagers like myself," he said, "it gave a sense of pride and a sense that the culture we loved could be shared and appreciated nationally."

Mr. Cornelius, a former disc jockey, created "Soul Train" in 1970 for the Chicago television station WCIU and was its writer, producer and host. When the show became a local sensation, he moved it to Los Angeles, where he began what would be a 35-year nationally syndicated broadcast.

In its heyday, "Soul Train" gave young people of all backgrounds a formative experience every Saturday morning. It gave some of the most important soul and R&B acts their first national television exposure. And it gave white rock musicians like Elton John and David Bowie a stage from which to reach black audiences.

Even more, "Soul Train" showcased dances and clothing styles that were popular among young blacks and that were soon imitated across the country. Later dance programs like Fox's "So You Think You Can Dance" and MTV's "America's Best Dance Crew" built on the "Soul Train" model.

Born on Chicago's South Side on Sept. 27, 1936, Mr. Cornelius graduated from DuSable High School in 1954, did a stint in the Marine Corps and then returned to Chicago to marry a childhood sweetheart, Delores Harrison. They had two sons, who are among his survivors.

Mr. Cornelius had ambitions to go into broadcasting from an early age but had put them aside, taking jobs selling insurance and cars instead. In 1966, however, he decided finally to pursue the dream. Quitting his job, he enrolled in a three-month broadcast course despite having young children to feed.

With his deep baritone, he landed a job as a substitute disc jockey at WVON in Chicago and later as a sports anchor on the television program "A Black's View of the News." He produced the "Soul Train" pilot with $400 of his own money, taking the title from a road show he had created for local high schools.

"'Soul Train' was developed as a radio show on television," Mr. Cornelius told The New York Times in 1995. "It was the radio show that I always wanted and never had. I selected the music, and still do, by simply seeing what had chart success."

He said the show had originally been patterned on Dick Clark's "American Bandstand," but with a focus on black music, fashion and dance. "There was no programming that targeted any particular ethnicity," he told The Associated Press in 2006. "I'm trying to use euphemisms here, trying to avoid saying there was no television for black folks, which they knew was for them."

The formula for the show did not change much over the years, though the sets were updated and the music evolved from Motown to funk and eventually to rap. As the host every week, Mr. Cornelius, tall and powerfully built, would play the hottest songs and corral a few performers to be interviewed. They would do a song or two, sometimes live, sometimes lip-syncing. He signed off each show by intoning "Love, peace and soul."

Mr. Cornelius stepped down as host in 1993, handing the reins to a series of actors, comedians and other guest hosts. "I took myself off because I just felt that 22 years was enough and that the audience was changing and I wasn't," he said.

It was not until 2006, however, that he stopped producing new shows. He sold the franchise and the archives two years later to a subsidiary of Vibe Holdings LLC.

In recent years he went through a bitter divorce from his second wife, Viktoria Chapman-Cornelius, a Russian model. In 2008, after what the police called a domestic dispute with his wife in their home, he was arrested

SOUL MAN: Don Cornelius was the creator of one of TV's longest-running syndicated shows.

and charged with spousal battery, assault with a deadly weapon and dissuading a witness from making a police report, all misdemeanors.

A year later he was sentenced to three years' probation after pleading no contest to misdemeanor charges of spousal battery in a plea bargain. During divorce proceedings later that year, he mentioned having "significant health problems" but did not elaborate.

Clarence Avant, a former chairman of Motown Records, said the suggestion that Mr. Cornelius had committed suicide surprised his friends. He did not appear despondent or upset when the two men met for lunch the week before, Mr. Avant said, though Mr. Cornelius did mention that he had had seizures recently and had avoided driving.

"He was very private," Mr. Avant said.

— *By James C. McKinley Jr.*

\\\\\\\\\\\\\\\\\\\\\\\

DOROTHY GILMAN

Her Spy Came in From the Garden

JUNE 25, 1923 · FEB. 2, 2012

DOROTHY GILMAN, an espionage writer whose best-known heroine, Mrs. Pollifax, is very likely the only spy in literature to belong simultaneously to the Central Intelligence Agency and the local garden club, died on Feb. 2 at her home in Rye Brook, N.Y. She was 88.

In "The Unexpected Mrs. Pollifax" (1966), the first novel in what would be a 14-book series, Mrs. Gilman introduces Emily Pollifax, a 60-ish New Jersey widow bored by the compulsory round of tea and good works.

In search of adventure, she offers her services to the C.IA. — who, after all, is going to peg a suburban grandmother as a cold war secret agent? — and adventure she finds. In the course of the series, which concluded in 2000 with "Mrs. Pollifax Unveiled," she fetches up in Mexico, Turkey, Thailand, China, Morocco, Sicily and elsewhere.

Clever, lucky and naïvely intrepid, Mrs. Pollifax employs common sense and a little karate to rescue the kidnapped; aid the resistance (when you are a suburban lady spy, a fashionable hat is ideal for concealing forged passports); and engage in all manner of cheery deception (when doing business with a malefactor who is expecting a can of plutonium, a can of peaches makes an excellent if short-term substitute).

Reviewers sometimes quibbled about the improbability of the novels' basic premise. But the books proved popular with readers: in a genre in which women had long been young and sultry, Mrs. Pollifax, with her peril and petunias, made an irresistible, early feminist heroine.

The series was the basis of two movies, the feature film "Mrs. Pollifax — Spy" (1971), starring Rosalind Russell, and the telefilm "The Unexpected Mrs. Pollifax" (1999), starring Angela Lansbury.

A series of popular novels about an intrepid, slightly naïve suburban grandmother who finds adventure with the C.I.A. Who would have guessed they'd be a success?

The Mystery Writers of America named Mrs. Gilman its 2010 Grand Master.

Dorothy Edith Gilman was born in New Brunswick, N.J., on June 25, 1923; she decided on a writing career when she was still a child. Planning to write and illustrate books for children, she studied at the Pennsylvania Academy of the Fine Arts. Under her married name, Dorothy Gilman Butters, she began publishing children's books in the late 1940s.

Her marriage to Edgar A. Butters Jr. ended in divorce. She died of complications of Alzheimer's disease and is survived by two sons and two grandchildren.

Mrs. Gilman was also the author of several nonseries novels for adults, among them "The Clairvoyant Countess" (1975), "Incident at Badamya" (1989) and "Kaleidoscope" (2002); and novels for young people including "Enchanted Caravan" (1949) and "The Bells of Freedom" (1963).

By the seventh Mrs. Pollifax novel, "Mrs. Pollifax and the Hong Kong Buddha," published in 1985, Mrs. Gilman's heroine has remarried. But for the most part, she is quite content to leave her husband at home for the duration of the series as she gads about the world, a paladin packing peaches.

— By Margalit Fox

FLORENCE GREEN

The Last Veteran of World War I

FEB. 19, 1901 - FEB. 4, 2012

THE LAST VETERAN OF WORLD WAR I was a waitress, and for 90 years no one knew her name.

Florence Green, a member of Britain's Royal Air Force who was afraid of flying, died in England on Feb. 4, two weeks shy of her 111th birthday. She was believed to have been the war's last living veteran — the last anywhere of the tens of millions who served.

Mrs. Green, who joined the R.A.F. as a teenager shortly before war's end, worked in an officer's mess on the home front. Her service was officially recognized only in 2010, after a researcher unearthed her records in Britain's National Archives.

That Mrs. Green went unrecognized for so long owes partly to the fact that she served under her maiden name, Florence Patterson, and partly to the fact that she conducted herself, by all accounts, with proper British restraint, rarely if ever flaunting her service.

It also owes to the fact that her life followed the prescribed trajectory for women of her era: by the time the 20th century had run its course, Mrs. Green had long since disappeared into marriage, motherhood and contented anonymity.

With the death in May of Claude Stanley Choules, an Englishman who served aboard a Royal Navy battleship, Mrs. Green became the last known person, male or female, to have served in the war on either side.

Her death, at a nursing home in King's Lynn, in eastern England, was announced on the Web site of the Order of the First World War, an organization based in Florida that keeps track of veterans.

In the spate of interviews she gave after her existence was discovered, Mrs. Green expressed quiet pride in her service. She also recalled approvingly the courtly behavior of the officers she served.

"It was very pleasant, and they were lovely," she once told an interviewer. "Not a bit of bother."

But though she was aware of her historical position as the war's last veteran, Mrs. Green was philosophical about the war itself, one of the defining events of modern history, in which more than 20 million people died. Speaking of it on the occasion of her 110th birthday, she told The Independent, "It seems like such a long time ago now."

The daughter of Frederick Patterson and the former Sarah Neal, Florence Beatrice Patterson was born in London on Feb. 19, 1901, and moved to King's Lynn as a child.

In September 1918, two months before the war ended, Florence, then 17, joined the Women's Royal Air Force. An auxiliary branch of the R.A.F., it had been created not long before to help free men for combat duty by recruiting women to work as mechanics and drivers and in other noncombat jobs.

Made a steward in the officers' mess, she was assigned first to the Narborough Aerodrome and later to the R.A.F. base at Marham, both in England's Norfolk region.

She served the officers meals and tea, and in free moments she would roam the base, admiring the men. "I met dozens of pilots and would go on dates," Mrs. Green told The Daily Mail in 2010.

But when they offered to take her aloft in their craft — Sopwith Camels and other biplanes — she demurred. She was afraid to fly.

At Marham, Mrs. Green witnessed what was undoubtedly the most benign bombing of the war. On Nov. 11, 1918, when armistice was declared, the Marham fliers celebrated by swooping down on the Narborough airfield, a few miles away, and letting loose bags of flour. The Narborough boys quickly retaliated by pelting Marham with bags of soot.

Mrs. Green, who remained in the Women's R.A.F. until July 1919, married Walter Green in 1920. Mr. Green, a railway porter, died in the 1970s.

Mrs. Green's wartime experience, as a British Royal Air Force waitress, remained unsung until 2009. The war, she said at 110, "seems like such a long time ago now."

Her survivors include two daughters, a son, four grandchildren and seven great-grandchildren.

Mrs. Green's wartime experience remained unsung until 2009, when an English newspaper, The Lynn News and Advertiser, wrote about her 108th birthday. Andrew Holmes, a British researcher for the Gerontology Research Group, an American organization that keeps statistics on people who live well past 100, then located her service records in the National Archives, resulting in Mrs. Green's recognition as a veteran the next year.

For her funeral, the R.A.F. sent personnel from the Marham base to join an honor guard, and the Union Jack draped the coffin.

— By Margalit Fox; Richard Goldstein
CONTRIBUTED REPORTING.

JOHN FAIRFAX

Bored With Piracy, He Rowed the Oceans

MAY 21, 1937 - FEB. 8, 2012

H E CROSSED THE ATLANTIC because it was there, and the Pacific because it was also there.

He made both crossings in a rowboat because it, too, was there, and because the lure of sea, spray and sinew, and the history-making chance to traverse two oceans without steam or sail, proved irresistible.

In 1969, after six months alone on the Atlantic battling storms, sharks and encroaching madness, John Fairfax, who died this month at 74, became the first lone oarsman in recorded history to traverse any ocean.

In 1972, he and his girlfriend, Sylvia Cook, sharing a boat, became the first people to row across the Pacific, a yearlong ordeal during which their craft was thought lost. (The couple survived the voyage, and so, for quite some time, did their romance.)

Both journeys were the subject of fevered coverage by the news media. They inspired two memoirs by Mr. Fairfax, "Britannia: Rowing Alone Across the Atlantic" and, with Ms. Cook, "Oars Across the Pacific," both published in the early 1970s.

Mr. Fairfax died on Feb. 8 at his home in Henderson, Nev., near Las Vegas. The apparent cause was a heart attack, said his wife, Tiffany. A professional astrologer, she is his only immediate survivor. Ms. Cook, who became an upholsterer and spent the rest of her life quietly on dry land (though she remained a close friend of Mr. Fairfax), lives outside London.

For all its bravura, Mr. Fairfax's seafaring almost pales beside his earlier ventures. Footloose and handsome, he was a flesh-and-blood character out of Graham Greene, with more than a dash of Hemingway and Ian Fleming shaken in.

At 9, he settled a dispute with a pistol. At 13, he lit out for the Amazon jungle.

At 20, he attempted suicide-by-jaguar. Afterward he was apprenticed to a pirate. To please his mother, who did not take kindly to his being a pirate, he briefly managed a mink farm, one of the few truly dull entries on his otherwise crackling résumé, which lately included a career as a professional gambler.

Mr. Fairfax was among the last avatars of a centuries-old figure: the lone-wolf explorer, whose exploits are conceived to satisfy few but himself. His was a solitary, contemplative art that has been all but lost amid the contrived derring-do of adventure-based reality television.

The only child of an English father and a Bulgarian mother, John Fairfax was born on May 21, 1937, in Rome, where his mother had family; he scarcely knew his father, who worked in London for the BBC.

Seeking to give her son structure, his mother enrolled him at 6 in an Italian scouting organization. It was there, Mr. Fairfax said, that he acquired his love of nature — and his determination to bend it to his will.

On a camping trip when he was 9, John concluded a fight with another boy by filching the scoutmaster's pistol and shooting up the campsite. No one was injured, but his scouting career was over.

His parents' marriage dissolved soon afterward, and he moved with his mother to Buenos Aires. A bright, impassioned dreamer, he devoured tales of adventure, including an account of the voyage of Frank Samuelsen and George Harbo, Norwegians who in 1896 were the first to row across the Atlantic. John vowed that he would one day make the crossing alone.

At 13, in thrall to Tarzan, he ran away from home to live in the jungle. He survived there as a trapper with the aid of local peasants, returning to town periodically to sell the jaguar and ocelot skins he had collected.

He later studied literature and philosophy at a university in Buenos Aires and at 20, despondent over a failed love affair, by his account, resolved to kill himself by letting a jaguar attack him. When the planned confrontation ensued, however, reason prevailed — as did the gun he had with him.

In Panama, he met a pirate, applied for a job as a pirate's apprentice and was taken on. He

WITHOUT STEAM OR SAIL: John Fairfax in the 22-foot boat he rowed across the Atlantic in 1969. Mr. Fairfax battled storms and sharks and made the trip in six months.

spent three years smuggling guns, liquor and cigarettes around the world, becoming captain of one of his boss's boats, work that gave him superb navigational skills.

When piracy lost its luster, he gave his boss the slip and ended up in 1960s London, at loose ends. He revived his boyhood dream of crossing the ocean and, since his pirate duties had entailed no rowing, he began to train.

He rowed daily on the Serpentine, the lake in Hyde Park. Barely more than half a mile long, it was about one eight-thousandth the width of the Atlantic, but it would do.

On Jan. 20, 1969, Mr. Fairfax pushed off from the Canary Islands, bound for Florida. His 22-foot craft, the Britannia, was the Rolls-Royce of rowboats: made of mahogany, it had been created for the voyage by the eminent English boat designer Uffa Fox. It was self-righting, self-bailing and partly covered.

Aboard were provisions (Spam, oatmeal, brandy); water; and a temperamental radio. There was no support boat and no chase plane — only Mr. Fairfax and the sea. He caught fish and sometimes boarded passing ships to cadge food, water and showers.

The long, empty days spawned a temporary madness. Desperate for female company, he talked ardently to the planet Venus.

On July 19, 1969 — Day 180 — Mr. Fairfax, tanned, tired and about 20 pounds lighter, made landfall at Hollywood, Fla. "This is bloody stupid," he said as he came ashore. Two years later, he was at it again.

This time Ms. Cook, a secretary and competitive rower he had met in London, was aboard. Their new boat, the Britannia II, also a Fox design, was about 36 feet long, large enough for two though still little more than a toy on the Pacific.

"He's always been a gambler," Ms. Cook, 73, recalled by telephone. "He was going to the casino every night when I met him — it was craps in those days. And at the end of the day, adventures are a kind of gamble, aren't they?"

Their crossing, from San Francisco to Hayman Island, Australia, took 361 days — from April 26, 1971, to April 22, 1972 — and was an 8,000-mile cornucopia of disaster.

"It was very, very rough, and our rudder got snapped clean off," Ms. Cook said. "We were frequently swamped, and at night you didn't know if the boat was the right way up or the wrong way up."

Mr. Fairfax was bitten on the arm by a shark, and he and Ms. Cook became trapped in a cyclone, lashing themselves to the boat until it subsided. Unreachable by radio for a time, they were presumed lost.

For all that, Ms. Cook said, there were abundant pleasures. "The nights not too hot, sunny days when you could just row," she recalled. "You just hear the clunking of the rowlocks, and you stop rowing and hear little splashings of the sea."

Mr. Fairfax was often asked why he chose a rowboat to beard two roiling oceans. "Almost anybody with a little bit of know-how can sail," he said in a profile on the Web site of the Ocean Rowing Society International, which adjudicates ocean rowing records. "I'm after a battle with nature, primitive and raw."

Such battles are a young man's game. With Ms. Cook, Mr. Fairfax went back to the Pacific in the mid-'70s to try to salvage a cache of lead ingots from a downed ship they had spied on their crossing. But the plan proved unworkable, and he never returned to sea.

In recent years, Mr. Fairfax made his living playing baccarat, the card game also favored by James Bond.

Baccarat is equal parts skill and chance. It lets the player wield consummate mastery while consigning him simultaneously to the caprices of fate.

— *By Margalit Fox*

WHITNEY HOUSTON

Soaring Star, Fallen Idol

AUG. 9, 1963 - FEB. 11, 2012

Whitney Houston, the multimillion-selling singer who emerged in the 1980s as one of her generation's greatest R&B voices only to deteriorate through years of cocaine use and an abusive marriage, died on Feb. 11 in Beverly Hills, Calif. She was 48.

Her death came as the music industry descended on Los Angeles for the annual celebration of the Grammy Awards. She was to have attended a pre-Grammy party that night being hosted by her pop mentor,

Clive Davis, the founder of Arista Records.

Ms. Houston was found underwater in the bathtub of her room at the Beverly Hilton hotel, and paramedics were unable to revive her, the authorities said. She was pronounced dead at

3:55 p.m The Los Angeles County coroner said in March that she had accidentally drowned and that a host of prescription and illegal drugs, including cocaine, were found in her system.

From the start of her career more than 20 years ago, Ms. Houston had the talent, looks and pedigree of a pop superstar. She was the daughter of Cissy Houston, a gospel and pop singer who had backed up Aretha Franklin, and the cousin of Dionne Warwick. (Ms. Franklin is Ms. Houston's godmother.)

Ms. Houston's voice was an instrument of power and purity: plush, vibrant and often spectacular. With a range spanning three octaves, she could pour on the exuberant flourishes of gospel or peal a simple pop chorus; she could sing sweetly or slide into a sultry rasp. And in her triumphal years her songs were full of positive spirit, exulting in love and insisting on dignity.

POP STAR PEDIGREE: Whitney Houston signing her first contract with the Arista Records founder Clive Davis in 1983. Ms. Houston was a cousin of Dionne Warwick and a goddaughter of Aretha Franklin.

Whether wearing a formal gown or a T-shirt, she cultivated the image of a fun-loving but passionate good girl with songs as perky as "I Wanna Dance With Somebody (Who Loves Me)" and as torchy as Dolly Parton's "I Will Always Love You," which Ms. Houston made her signature song.

But by the mid-1990s, even as she was moving into acting with films like "The Bodyguard" and "The Preacher's Wife," she became, as she told Oprah Winfrey in 2009, a "heavy" user of marijuana and cocaine. By the 2000s she was struggling, her voice smaller, scratchier and less secure, her performances increasingly erratic.

All of Ms. Houston's studio albums were million-sellers, and two — her 1985 debut album and the 1992 soundtrack to "The Bodyguard," which includes "I Will Always Love You" — have sold more than 10 million copies in the

United States alone. She sold more than 55 million albums in the United States, and tens of millions more abroad. The Recording Industry Association of America ranked her as the best-selling female R&B singer of the 20th century.

But her marriage to Bobby Brown, the former frontman for the New Edition, grew miserable, at one point becoming the subject of "Being Bobby Brown," a short-lived reality television series on Bravo. In the 2000s her singles slipped from the Top 10. She became a tabloid subject. The National Enquirer published a photograph of her bathroom showing drug paraphernalia. And each new album — "Just Whitney" in 2002 and "I Look to You" in 2009 — became a comeback.

At Central Park in 2009, singing for the ABC television program "Good Morning America," her voice was frayed, and on the international tour that followed the release that year of the album "I Look to You," she was often shaky, no longer the invincible performer the world had known.

Whitney Houston was born on Aug. 9, 1963, in Newark, N.J. She sang in church. As a teenager in the 1970s and early '80s, she did some modeling and worked as a backup studio singer and featured vocalist with Chaka Khan, the Neville Brothers and Bill Laswell's Material.

Mr. Davis signed her after hearing her perform in a New York City nightclub and spent two years supervising production of the album "Whitney Houston," which was released in 1985. It placed her remarkable voice in polished, catchy songs that straddled pop and R&B, including three No. 1 singles: "Saving All My Love for You," "How Will I Know" and "The Greatest Love of All."

Despite the success of her debut album, Ms. Houston was ruled ineligible for the best new artist category of the Grammy Awards because she had been credited on previous recordings, including a 1984 duet with Teddy Pendergrass. But with "Saving All My Love for You," she won her first Grammy, for best female pop vocal performance, an award she would win twice more.

Her popularity soared for the next decade. Her second album, "Whitney," in 1987, became the first album by a woman to enter the Billboard charts at No. 1, and it included four No. 1 singles. In 1990 she shifted her pop slightly toward R&B on her third album, "I'm Your Baby Tonight," which had three more No. 1 singles.

For much of the 1990s she turned to acting, bolstered by her music. In 1992 she played a pop diva opposite Kevin Costner in "The Bodyguard." Its soundtrack album included the hits "I'm Every Woman," "I Have Nothing" and "Run to You" in addition to "I Will Always Love You" and sold 17 million copies in the United States. It won the Grammy for album of the year, and "I Will Always Love You" won record of the year for a single.

She went on to make "Waiting to Exhale," a 1995 film with Angela Bassett based on a Terry McMillan novel, followed by "The Preacher's Wife" (1996), a family Christmas film with Denzel Washington that gave her the occasion to make a gospel album. She resumed her pop career with "My Love Is Your Love" in 1998.

Ms. Houston married Mr. Brown in 1992, and in 1993 they had a daughter, who survives her, as does her mother.

Ms. Houston's 2009 interview with Ms. Winfrey portrayed the marriage as passionate and then turbulent, marred by drug use and by Mr. Brown's professional jealousy, psychological abuse and physical confrontations. They divorced in 2007.

"I think somewhere inside, something happens to a man when a woman has that much control or has that much fame," Ms. Houston said.

Her albums in the 2000s presented a tougher, angrier side.

"Just Whitney," in 2002, was defensive and scrappy, lashing out at the media and insisting on her loyalty to her man. Her most recent studio album, "I Look to You," appeared in 2009, and it, too, reached No. 1. The album included a hard-headed breakup song, "Salute," and a hymnlike anthem, "I Didn't Know My Own Strength." Ms. Houston sang, "I crashed down and I tumbled, but I did not crumble/I got through all the pain." Her voice did not hide its scars.

Her death came on another Grammy weekend. Lt. Mark Rosen, a spokesman for the Beverly Hills Police Department, said that emergency workers responded to a 911 call from security at the Beverly Hilton hotel on Wilshire Boulevard saying that Ms. Houston was unconscious in her fourth-floor suite. Fire Department personnel were already on the scene to help prepare for a pre-Grammy party, he said.

Ms. Houston had arrived at the hotel with what Lieutenant Rosen described as an entourage of friends and family, some of whom were in the hotel suite at her death. Later reports said an assistant who had run out to do an errand returned to discover Ms. Houston submerged in the bathtub.

In a preliminary autopsy report released in March, the county coroner said multiple drugs were found in Ms. Houston's system, including cocaine and marijuana; Xanax, which is usually prescribed for anxiety; Flexeril, a muscle relaxant; and Benadryl, an over-the-counter antihistamine. A final autopsy report in April said she had been found face-down in "extremely hot water" and that the "effects of atherosclerotic heart disease and cocaine use" were contributing factors in her death.

The streets in front of the Beverly Hilton, already crowded because of the Grammy Awards party there, swarmed with fans drawn by the news, many in shock. Onlookers brandishing cellphones took pictures of a police crime laboratory van.

Inside, Mr. Davis's party went on as scheduled. (Ms. Houston had been a regular

AN INSTRUMENT OF POWER:
Whitney Houston was one of her generation's greatest voices.

guest and performer there in past years.) The glamour of the event seemed undiminished, even if Ms Houston's name was on everyone's lips. Neil R. Portnow, president of the National Academy of Recording Arts and Sciences, which bestows the Grammys, called her "one of the world's greatest pop singers of all time."

Outside, saddened fans milled about. "I was in utter, total disbelief," said one of them, Lavetris Singleton. "Who was not a fan of Whitney Houston at some point?"

"I want to show support because she inspired a lot of people and nobody's perfect," she said. "But if we're not out here, then she'll be forgotten. We are her legacy."

— BY JON PARELES AND ADAM NAGOURNEY; IAN LOVETT, JENNIFER MEDINA, BEN SISARIO, CHANNING JOSEPH AND JAMES C. MCKINLEY JR. CONTRIBUTED REPORTING.

LILLIAN BASSMAN

Rediscovered Negatives and a Career Renewed

JUNE 15, 1917 - FEB. 13, 2012

LILLIAN BASSMAN, a magazine art director and fashion photographer who achieved renown in the 1940s and '50s with high-contrast, dreamy portraits of sylphlike models, then re-emerged in the 1990s as a fine-art photographer after a cache of lost negatives resurfaced, died on

Feb. 13 at her home in Manhattan. She was 94.

Ms. Bassman entered the world of magazine editing and fashion photography as a protégée of Alexey Brodovitch, the renowned art director of Harper's Bazaar. In late 1945, when the magazine generated a spinoff called Junior Bazaar, aimed at teenage girls, she was asked to be its art director, a title she shared with Mr. Brodovitch, at his insistence.

In addition to providing innovative graphic design, Ms. Bassman gave prominent display to future photographic stars like Richard Avedon, Robert Frank and Louis Faurer, whose work whetted her appetite to become a photographer herself.

At Harper's Bazaar, she had already begun frequenting the darkroom on her lunch hours to develop images by the great fashion photographer George Hoyningen-Huene, using tissues and gauzes to bring selected areas of a picture into focus and applying bleach to manipulate tone.

"I was interested in developing a method of printing on my own, even before I took photographs," Ms. Bassman told B&W magazine in 1994. "I wanted everything soft edges and cropped." She was interested, she said, in "creating a new kind of vision aside from what the camera saw."

When Mr. Avedon went off to photograph fashion collections in Paris in 1947, he lent her his studio and an assistant. She continued her self-education and in short order landed an important account with a lingerie company. In its last issue, in May 1948, Junior Bazaar ran a seven-page portfolio of wedding photographs she had taken, titled "Happily Ever After."

Ms. Bassman became sought after for her expressive portraits of slender, long-necked models advertising lingerie, cosmetics and fabrics. Her lingerie work in particular brought lightness and glamour to an arena previously known for heavy, middle-aged women posing in industrial-strength corsets.

"I had a terrific commercial life," Ms. Bassman told The New York Times in 1997. "I did everything that could be photographed: children, food, liquor, cigarettes, lingerie, beauty products."

Lillian Violet Bassman was born on June 15, 1917, in Brooklyn and grew up in the Bronx. Her parents, Jewish émigrés from Russia, allowed her a bohemian style of life, even letting her move in, at 15, with the man she would later marry, the documentary photographer Paul Himmel.

Ms. Bassman studied fabric design at Textile High School, a vocational school in the Chelsea section of Manhattan. After modeling for artists employed by the Works Progress Administration's Federal Art Project and working as a muralist's assistant, she took a night course in fashion illustration at Pratt Institute in Brooklyn.

She soon showed her work to Mr. Brodovitch, who was impressed. Waiving tuition, he accepted her into his Design Laboratory at the New School for Social Research, where she changed her emphasis from fashion illustration to graphic design.

Mr. Brodovitch took her on as his unpaid apprentice at Harper's Bazaar in 1941, but, desperate to earn money, she left to become an assistant to the art director at Elizabeth Arden. To get her back, Mr. Brodovitch soon anointed her his first paid assistant. Like her mentor, she was artistically daring. At Junior Bazaar, she experimented with abandon, treating fashion in a bold, graphic style and floating images in space. "One week we decided that we were going to do all green vegetables, so we had the designers make all green clothing, green lipstick, green hair, green everything," she told Print magazine in 2006.

Her nonadvertising work appeared frequently in Harper's Bazaar, and she developed close relationships with a long list of the era's top models, including Barbara Mullen (her muse), Dovima and Suzy Parker.

The stylistic changes of the 1960s, however, left her cold. The models, too. "I got sick of them," she told The Times in 2009. "They were becoming superstars. They were not my kind of models. They were dictating rather than taking direction."

In 1969, disappointed with the photographic profession and her prospects, she destroyed most of her commercial negatives. She dumped more than 100 editorial negatives in trash bags, putting them aside in her converted carriage house on the Upper East Side. Before long she forgot all about them.

By the mid-1970s, she was out of the fashion world entirely and had begun focusing on her own work, taking large-format Cibachrome photographs of glistening fruits, vegetables and flowers, pictures of cracks in the city streets, and distorted male torsos based on photographs in bodybuilding magazines.

It was not until the early 1990s that Martin

Harrison, a fashion curator and historian who was staying at her house, found the long-forgotten negatives. He encouraged her to take a fresh look at them. She did, and had an inspiration. She began reprinting them, applying some of the bleaching techniques and other toning agents with which she had first experimented in the 1940s, creating more abstract, mysterious prints.

"In looking at them I got a little intrigued, and I took them into the darkroom, and I started to do my own thing on them," she told The Times. "I was able to make my own choices, other than what Brodovitch or the editors had made."

Her reinterpretations, as she called them, found a new generation of admirers. A full-fledged revival of her career ensued, with gallery shows and international exhibitions, including a joint retrospective at the Deichtorhallen museum in Hamburg with her husband and a series of monographs devoted to her photography.

A one-woman show at the Hamiltons Gallery in London, organized by Mr. Harrison in 1993, was followed by exhibitions at the Carrousel du Louvre in Paris and an assignment from The New York Times Magazine to cover the haute couture collections in Paris in 1996. She completed her last fashion assignment for German Vogue in 2004.

Mr. Himmel died in 2009, having abandoned photography in his late 50s to become a psychiatric caregiver in the city's hospitals and later a psychotherapist in private practice. She is survived by a son, Eric Himmel, the editor in chief of Abrams Books, as well as a daughter, two grandchildren and a stepgrandchild.

Ms. Bassman's work has been published in "Lillian Bassman" (1997), "Lillian Bassman: Women" (2009) and "Lillian Bassman: Lingerie" (2012).

— By WILLIAM GRIMES

FROM FASHION TO FINE ART: Lillian Bassman's rediscovered negatives reinvigorated her long-abandoned photography career and introduced her work to a new generation of admirers outside of the fashion world.

DORY PREVIN

Wounds Dressed in Song

OCT. 22, 1925 - FEB. 14, 2012

ORY PREVIN, an Oscar-nominated lyricist who as a composer and performer mined her difficult childhood, bouts of mental illness and a very public divorce to create a potent and influential personal songbook, died on Feb. 14 at her home in Southfield, Mass. She was 86.

Ms. Previn was one of a number of women who rose to prominence as singer-songwriters in the early 1970s, joining the likes of Joni Mitchell, Carole King and Laura Nyro. But she never achieved their degree of popularity, partly because her voice was never as big as theirs, and partly because her lyrics — frank and dark, even when tinged with humor, and often wincingly confessional — were not the stuff of pop radio.

In "With My Daddy in the Attic," Ms. Previn wrote of her complicated relationship with her disturbed father. "Esther's First Communion" was about a girl's indoctrination into religious ritual and her revulsion at it. "Yada Yada La Scala" told of women in a mental hospital. In "Lemon Haired Ladies," an older woman pines for a younger man:

Whatever you give me
I'll take as it comes
Discarding self-pity
I'll manage with crumbs.

Unusual for a pop singer of the day, Ms. Previn's background was in neither folk nor rock but in Hollywood, writing songs for the movies, mostly as a lyricist working with her husband, the composer and later conductor André Previn. Their songs were recorded by Frank Sinatra,

Rosemary Clooney, Bobby Darin, Sammy Davis Jr. and Nancy Wilson, among others.

Together they were nominated for two Academy Awards: in 1960 for the song "Faraway Part of Town," from "Pepe," and in 1962 for "Second Chance," from "Two for the Seesaw." Their best-known collaboration was the theme from the 1967 film version of Jacqueline Susann's drug-soaked show-business novel "Valley of the Dolls." It begins:

Gotta get off, gonna get
Have to get off from this ride
Gotta get hold, gonna get
Need to get hold of my pride.

The halting, almost stammering progression of laments, Ms. Previn said, came from her experience of relying on pills. (The song was later recorded by Dionne Warwick.)

In 1969, working with the composer Fred Karlin, Ms. Previn earned a third Oscar nomination, for "Come Saturday Morning," from "The Sterile Cuckoo." The song became a hit for the Sandpipers.

By then the Previn marriage was in a shambles. The year before, Mr. Previn had begun an affair in London with the actress Mia Farrow — she was 24 and he was approaching 40 — and

Ms. Previn, who had a history of emotional fragility and mental illness, fell apart. Fearful of flying, she had a breakdown on an airplane that was waiting to take off, shouting unintelligibly and tearing at her clothes. She spent several months in a psychiatric hospital.

The episode proved to be a turning point. Her first album afterward, "On My Way to Where" — the title was a reference to the airplane incident — was released in 1970, the year of her divorce and of Mr. Previn's marriage to Ms. Farrow, and it included perhaps her most famous song, "Beware of Young Girls." The song, about Ms. Farrow, who had been a guest in the Previn home, expresses feelings of betrayal. ("We were friends," Ms. Previn sang.) It begins:

A PERSONAL SONGBOOK: Dory Previn's hit songs were based on the more painful parts of her life, including her public divorce from the conductor and composer André Previn.

> Beware of young girls
> Who come to the door
> Wistful and pale
> Of twenty and four.

In "Mythical Kings and Iguanas" (1971), Ms. Previn's subsequent album, many critics heard a growing self-confidence that became even more pronounced later that year in the album "Reflections in a Mud Puddle/Taps Tremors and Time Steps," which included a song about her father's death.

"Ms. Previn is no great singer, her guitar playing is only adequate, and her melodies sometimes have an uncomfortable tendency to move in too-familiar directions," the critic Don Heckman wrote about "Reflections" in The New York Times. "But her message is stated so brilliantly in her lyrics, and the tales she has to tell are so important, that they make occasional musical inadequacies fade away."

Dorothy Veronica Langan was born in New Jersey — sources differ on the town, Rahway or Woodbridge — on Oct. 22, 1925. She grew up in Woodbridge. Her father, Michael, was a laborer and a frustrated musician who pushed her toward music and dance. In a 1976 memoir, Ms. Previn wrote that he had been left deranged by the gassing he endured during his military service in Europe in World War I. He was convinced that it had made him sterile, she wrote, and that therefore she could not be his daughter. For a while he locked himself in the attic.

Ms. Previn left home as a teenager and worked in summer stock theater and in radio commercials and sang in small clubs, writing new verses to popular songs. Her work came to the attention of Arthur Freed, the producer of the MGM movie musicals "An American in Paris" and "Singin' in the Rain," and he hired her. It was at MGM that she met Mr. Previn. In 1958, Mr. Previn, on piano, and the jazz guitarist Kenny Burrell accompanied her when, as Dory Langdon, she recorded an album of her songs, "The Leprechauns Are Upon Me." She and Mr. Previn married in 1959. A brief, earlier marriage of hers had ended in divorce.

The Previns separated in 1969 after Ms. Previn learned that Ms. Farrow was pregnant with a child by her husband. The divorce was finalized in 1970. Later in the '70s Ms. Previn met Joby Baker, a Canadian-born actor and painter almost nine years her junior. They married in 1984. He survives her, as do three stepchildren and six stepgrandchildren.

Ms. Previn's other albums include "Mary C. Brown and the Hollywood Sign" (1973), about an actress who jumps to her death from the famous sign overlooking Los Angeles; "Live at Carnegie Hall" (1973); "Dory Previn" (1975); and "We're Children of Coincidence and Harpo Marx" (1976).

Ms. Previn and Mr. Previn reconciled in the 1980s and remained friends. (He had divorced Ms. Farrow in 1979.) In 1995 they collaborated on "The Magic Number," a composition for soprano and orchestra by Mr. Previn; Ms. Previn — who went by Dory Previn Shannon then, using her mother's maiden name — wrote the text. The work had its premiere in 1997 at Lincoln Center in New York.

Ms. Previn came to loathe the idea that she was known more for their breakup than for her music. The pain and grief, however, were the foundation of her art. In the hospital after her breakdown, she was encouraged to write down her feelings, and they emerged as poems.

"I was always afraid to write music," she said in 1970. "I wouldn't have presumed to with a musician like André around the house. But I play a little guitar. So I started working them out on the guitar, thinking I could interest some singer in recording them, and that's how all these songs were born."

— BY BRUCE WEBER

GARY CARTER

The 'Kid' Who Loved Baseball

APRIL 8, 1954 · FEB. 16, 2012

GARY CARTER, the slugging catcher who entered the Hall of Fame as a Montreal Expo, helped propel the Mets to their dramatic 1986 World Series championship and endeared himself to players and fans as Kid, for the sheer joy he took in playing baseball, died on Feb. 16 in West Palm Beach, Fla., less than nine months after learning he had brain cancer. He was 57.

Carter played with intensity and flair, hitting 324 home runs and punctuating many of the ones he hit at Shea Stadium with arm-flailing curtain calls emblematic of the Mets' swagger in the middle and late 1980s. In his 19 seasons in the major leagues, all but two of them with the Expos or the Mets, he was an 11-time All-Star and was twice named the most valuable player in the All-Star Game.

Carter's exuberance complemented his

prowess at the plate. Curly-haired and with a ready smile, he was loved by the fans, first in Montreal and then in New York.

"I am certainly happy that I don't have to run for election against Gary Carter," Pierre Elliott Trudeau said when he was prime minister of Canada.

Carter excited Shea Stadium fans in his first game as a Met. After sliding into second with a double to left-center field in the 1985 season opener against the St. Louis Cardinals, he jumped up and pumped his right fist. In the 10th inning he hit a game-winning homer over the left-field fence, then pumped his arm again and again while he rounded the bases as the crowd roared. He was mobbed by his teammates at home plate, and when the fans chanted for a curtain call, he came out of the dugout waving both arms.

He was just as exuberant behind the plate. When Carter tagged a runner out at home, he'd add an exclamation point by happily holding the ball aloft. He may have led the 1986 Mets in hugging teammates.

Playing his first 11 seasons with the Expos, Carter became the face of a franchise that sometimes struggled. But the Expos' ownership chafed at his high salary and traded him to the Mets in December 1984 for four young players.

Some Expos were put off by Carter's unabashed enthusiasm. They felt he was obsessed with his image and basked in his press coverage too eagerly. They called him Camera Carter.

"He had some problems among his teammates," Andre Dawson, the Expos' future Hall of Fame outfielder, told The New York Times after Carter was traded. They "felt he was more a glory hound than a team player," Dawson said.

Carter said his reputation as a self-absorbed straight arrow burdened him.

"I carried a lot of baggage with me," he told Jeff Pearlman for his book on the 1986 Mets, "The Bad Guys Won!" (2004). "I'd go to a new team and guys were saying they wondered how I was in the clubhouse, whether I had a big head or was a team player."

The Mets teased Carter about his image, but they cared more about his power and his savvy behind the plate.

"We all disliked Gary when we played against him," said Keith Hernandez, the star first baseman who became Carter's Mets teammate. "He was just a little rah-rah varsity collegiate type, even though he didn't go to college. But I respected him as a player. And when he came to New York, I appreciated him, too."

Carter's big opening day in 1985 was the prelude to a season in which he hit a career-high 32 home runs, setting the stage for the 1986 championship year.

In his five seasons with the Mets, the right-handed-hitting Carter, a brawny 6 feet 2 inches and 205 pounds or so, added considerable pop

A CROWD FAVORITE: Gary Carter was one of the most popular baseball players of his time and basked in the admiration of his fans, much to the chagrin of his teammates, who called him "Camera Carter."

to a lineup that featured the left-handed-hitting Hernandez and Darryl Strawberry.

He had a powerful arm, he was sure-handed in blocking pitches in the dirt, and he was adept at handling pitchers, notably Dwight Gooden and Ron Darling.

"He's the heart of the pitching staff," Manager Davey Johnson once said. "We'd be lost without him."

Carter hit 24 homers and drove in 105 runs as the Mets won 108 games in 1986. His 12th-inning single drove in the winning run in a 2-1 victory over the Houston Astros in Game 5 of the National League Championship Series. The Mets won that series in six games, then faced the Boston Red Sox in the World Series.

The Red Sox took the first two games, but Carter drove in three runs in Game 3, at Fenway Park, then hit two home runs over the left-field wall in Game 4, to help the Mets tie the series at 2-2.

After the Red Sox won Game 5, Carter touched off the most memorable single-inning rally in the Mets' history. Playing at Shea, the Red Sox were leading, 5-3, in the 10th inning of Game 6 and were one out from winning a World Series for the first time since 1918. The Mets had nobody on base.

Carter kept the Mets alive with a single off reliever Calvin Schiraldi, and a pair of singles brought him home. A wild pitch allowed the tying run to score. Then, in one of baseball's most famous and crushing misplays, Mookie Wilson hit a grounder that went between the legs of Red Sox first baseman Bill Buckner, bringing Ray Knight home with the winning run.

The Mets won the World Series two nights later.

"Nothing will ever replace the moment when Jesse Orosco struck out Marty Barrett to end Game 7, and I was able to go out and jump in his arms," Carter said when he was elected to the Hall of Fame. "That was my biggest thrill."

Gary Edmund Carter was born on April 8, 1954, in Culver City, Calif., near Los Angeles. He was both an infielder and a star quarterback at Sunny Hills High School in Fullerton, Calif. He planned to play football at U.C.L.A. but pursued baseball instead when he was selected by the Expos in the third round of the 1972 draft.

The Expos switched Carter to catcher, and he made his debut for them in September 1974. Playing the outfield as well as catching in 1975, he was selected to the National League All-Star team and was the runner-up in the voting for National League rookie of the year. Carter became a full-time catcher in 1977.

The Expos reached the N.L. Championship Series in 1981, losing to the Los Angeles Dodgers. But by 1984 they were floundering, and they sent Carter to the Mets after the season.

After four solid years with the Mets, Carter was hampered by injuries. He played in only 50 games in 1989, when he hit .183, and was released after the season. He played for the Giants and the Dodgers, then ended his career back with the Expos in 1992.

In addition to his 324 home runs, Carter drove in 1,225 runs and had a career batting average of .262. His 298 home runs while in games as a catcher put him at No. 7 on the career list; Mike Piazza, the former Met, is No. 1, having hit 396 of his 427 homers while catching.

With the Expos Carter won three consecutive Gold Glove awards, from 1980-82. He caught in 2,056 games, placing him No. 4 among major league catchers.

When Carter was elected to the Hall of Fame in 2003, the Hall's management decided he would go in as an Expo rather than as a Met. Carter said he was happy with that but wondered aloud if he could be shown on the plaque wearing a "split" hat, one side representing the Expos, the other the Mets.

After his playing days, Carter was a roving minor league instructor for the Mets, a broadcaster for the Florida Marlins, a manager in the Mets' minor league system and with the independent Long Island Ducks, and most recently the coach at Palm Beach Atlantic University.

Because of his illness, his coaching duties had been taken over by his assistants, but he visited his team on Feb. 2 when Palm Beach Atlantic opened its season against Lynn University in Jupiter, Fla. His daughter Kimmy Bloemers is the softball coach at the university.

She said that after his cancer was diagnosed in May 2011, Carter underwent chemotherapy and radiation treatments, but that new tumors were discovered in January. He is also survived by his wife, Sandy, as well as a son, another daughter and three grandchildren.

When closing out his career in a second stint with the Expos (who left Montreal in 2005 and became the Washington Nationals), Carter, at 38, reflected on being known as the perennial Kid.

"Everybody calls me that," he told The Times. "Even our rookie catcher, Tim Laker, calls me that. I got that nickname my first spring training camp with the Expos in 1974. Tim Foli, Ken Singleton and Mike Jorgensen started calling me Kid because I was trying to win every sprint. I was trying to hit every pitch out of the park."

— By Richard Goldstein

ANTHONY SHADID

Dateline: A Region Torn

SEPT. 26, 1968 - FEB. 16, 2012

ANTHONY SHADID, a two-time Pulitzer Prize-winning foreign correspondent whose dispatches for The New York Times, The Washington Post, The Boston Globe and The Associated Press covered nearly two decades of Middle East conflict and turmoil, died on Feb. 16 while on a reporting assignment in Syria. He was 43 and lived in Beirut.

Mr. Shadid, who had asthma and was apparently allergic to horses, died during an asthma attack while he and Tyler Hicks, a Times photographer, were leaving Syria, guided by smugglers using horses to carry the journalists' bags. Mr. Shadid, who carried asthma medication, had been walking behind the horses when he collapsed. Mr. Hicks tried but failed to revive him with cardiopulmonary resuscitation. They were 45 minutes from safety, Mr. Hicks said.

The two had been inside Syria for a week, gathering information on the Free Syrian Army and other armed elements of the resistance to the government of President Bashar al-Assad. By then Syrian military forces had been engaged in a harsh repression of the political opposition for almost a year.

Jill Abramson, the executive editor of The Times, announced Mr. Shadid's death in an e-mail to the news staff, writing, "Anthony died as he lived — determined to bear witness to the transformation sweeping the Middle East and to testify to the suffering of people caught between government oppression and opposition forces."

The Syria undertaking, which Mr. Shadid had arranged through a network of smugglers, was fraught with dangers, not the least of which was discovery by the pro-government authorities, who exerted tight control over foreign journalists' activities and had not been told of the Times assignment.

Entering the country required traveling at night to a mountainous area in Turkey. There the Times journalists crossed into Idlib Province in Syria by pulling apart the wires of a barbed-wire fence and squeezing through them. Guides on horseback met them on the other side. Mr. Shadid had an asthma attack that night, a precursor to the fatal one.

His work in the region had long entailed great peril. In 2002, as a correspondent for The Globe, he was shot in the shoulder while walking on a street in Ramallah, in the Israeli-occupied

A WITNESS TO MIDDLE EAST HISTORY: Anthony Shadid, seated, interviewing the residents of a Cairo neighborhood during the Egyptian revolution in 2011.

West Bank. During the protests in Cairo that led to the fall of President Hosni Mubarak in 2011, he was hounded by the police; at one point, during a raid, he had to hide the computers used by Times reporters.

The same year, Mr. Shadid, Mr. Hicks and two other Times journalists, Stephen Farrell and Lynsey Addario, were arrested by pro-government militias during the conflict in Libya, held for about a week and beaten before being released. Their driver, Mohammad Shaglouf, died.

And later that year, as the Syrian authorities denounced him for his coverage and as his family was being stalked by Syrian agents in Lebanon, Mr. Shadid nonetheless stole across the border on a motorcycle to interview Syrian protesters who had defied bullets and torture to return to the streets.

On his last visit to Syria, he and Mr. Hicks were guided by civilian fighters. "They, too, are risking their lives to tell the world what is happening to their country," Mr. Hicks wrote in an account in The Times published after Mr. Shadid's death. "Almost all of them have been jailed and tortured." He added: "It was clear that they understood the importance of having Anthony there."

At one point the two men were present when a fire fight broke out against Syrian tanks. On another occasion, however, Mr. Hicks encountered Mr. Shadid in a carpeted room full of fighters singing and playing traditional music.

"Directly across from me, amid cigarette smoke and sitting among them, was Anthony with a huge smile on his face," Mr. Hicks wrote. "This was exactly the kind of connection that made him most happy as a reporter; his great warmth and intelligence were part of what made him the most important journalist covering the Arab world. He put his arms out and said gleefully, 'Tyler, look at this!' "

Mr. Shadid's interest in the Middle East had been long and passionate, first because of his Lebanese-American heritage and later because of what he saw there firsthand. He spent most of his professional life covering the region for a succession of news organizations, centering much of his reporting on ordinary people who had been forced to pay an extraordinary price for living in the region — or belonging to the religion, ethnic group or social class — that they did.

"He had such a profound and sophisticated understanding of the region," said Martin Baron, the editor of The Boston Globe, for whom Mr. Shadid once worked. "More than anything, his effort to connect foreign coverage with real people on the ground, and to understand their lives, is what made his work so special. It wasn't just a matter of diplomacy; it was a matter of people, and how their lives were so dramatically affected by world events."

Mr. Shadid was born in Oklahoma City on Sept. 26, 1968, the son of Rhonda and Buddy Shadid. The younger Mr. Shadid, who became fluent in Arabic only as an adult, earned a bachelor's degree in political science and journalism from the University of Wisconsin in 1990. He reported from Cairo for The A.P. before moving to The Globe in 2001. He was with The Washington Post from 2003 until 2009 as the Islamic affairs correspondent and Baghdad bureau chief.

It was with The Post that he earned his two Pulitzer Prizes, both for international reporting, the first in 2004 for his coverage of the invasion and occupation of Iraq and the second in 2010, again for his Iraq coverage.

He was also a Pulitzer finalist in 2007 for his reporting from Lebanon. And three days after his death the George Polk Awards in Journalism honored him posthumously with a special award "for extraordinary valor for his work in the Middle East." Mr. Shadid had won a Polk in 2003.

With his reputation as an intrepid reporter, a keen observer, an insightful analyst and a gifted writer, his hiring by The Times, on Dec. 31, 2009, was considered a coup for the newspaper. The Times appointed him Baghdad bureau chief and in 2011 posted him to Beirut.

His first marriage ended in divorce. Survivors include his second wife, the journalist Nada Bakri, as well as a son, a daughter, a sister, a brother and his parents.

He was the author of three books, "Legacy of the Prophet: Despots, Democrats and the New Politics of Islam" (2001); "Night Draws Near: Iraq's People in the Shadow of America's War" (2005); and "House of Stone: A Memoir of Home, Family, and a Lost Middle East," which was published a week after his death.

In a front-page article for The Times in 2011, Mr. Shadid, reporting from Tunisia amid the Arab Spring, displayed his combination of authority, acumen and style.

"The idealism of the revolts in Egypt and Tunisia, where the power of the street revealed the frailty of authority, revived an Arab world anticipating change," he wrote. "But Libya's unfinished revolution, as inspiring as it is unsettling, illustrates how perilous that change has become as it unfolds in this phase of the Arab Spring.

"Though the rebels' flag has gone up in Tripoli," he continued, "their leadership is fractured and opaque; the intentions and influence of Islamists in their ranks are uncertain; Col. Muammar el-Qaddafi remains at large in a flight reminiscent of Saddam Hussein's; and foreigners have been involved in the fight in the kind of intervention that has long been toxic to the Arab world." He added, "Not to mention, of course, that a lot of young men have a lot of guns."

— BY RICK GLADSTONE AND MARGALIT FOX

JOE THOMPSON

Old-Time Fiddling Rollicked Again

DEC. 9, 1918 - FEB. 20, 2012

"I GOT THE NAME OF BEING A PRETTY GOOD FIDDLE PLAYER," Joe Thompson once said. "I even been to Carnegie Hall playing fiddle."

He also played at the Kennedy Center in Washington and at folk festivals from coast to coast, including one at the Smithsonian. The National Endowment for the Arts awarded him a National Heritage Fellowship. And he is credited with helping to keep alive an African-American musical tradition — the black string band — that predates the blues and influenced country music and bluegrass.

Yet until 1973, when he was in his mid-50s, not many people outside North Carolina had ever heard him play.

Mr. Thompson often said death would come when "the good Lord sends the morning train"; the train arrived on Feb. 20, in Burlington, N.C., at a nursing home. He was 93.

Mr. Thompson was born not far from there, in north-central North Carolina, and one of his earliest memories was of squirming on the floor as his father played the fiddle. His father had learned the instrument from his own father, a slave, and taught Joe in turn. Joe Thompson made the strings for his first fiddle from screen-door wires, and by the time he was 7, he was playing a fiddle — a real one this time — at dances while propped on a wooden chair, his feet not yet reaching the floor.

Later on he and his brother Nate and a first cousin, Odell Thompson, formed a string band, with Nate and Odell on banjos. Well into their teens they played their music — something like square dance music, only more rhythmic — all over North Carolina.

"People loved to see us come," Mr. Thompson told American Legacy magazine in 2008. "Every year we would shuck corn and strip tobacco, then hoop it up with a big dance."

Then came World War II, and Mr. Thompson entered the Army, serving in a segregated unit in Europe driving a bulldozer. After the war, fiddling became less and less a part of his life. By the postwar years, black string bands were a local hobby at most. Mr. Thompson bought a four-room house on an unpaved country road and began a 38-year stint working in a furniture factory.

That was where he was in 1973, running a rip saw, when Kip Lornell, then a graduate student in ethnomusicology, decided to check out rumors that some masters of the old-time string-band music were still around. Stopping by Mr. Thompson's house, he heard him and his cousin play — his brother had moved to Philadelphia by then — and urged them to look into performing at folk music festivals that were springing up.

They did, and soon they were invited to perform across the country, from Massachusetts to Washington State. They played in Australia, too. In 1989 they recorded "Old-Time Music from the North Carolina Piedmont" for the Global Village label. The musical folklorist Alan Lomax included the three Thompsons in his American Patchwork documentary film series. And in 1990 Joe and Odell Thompson were onstage at Carnegie Hall as part of its Folk Masters program.

Mr. Thompson was in fine fettle. "Holding his bow about five inches from the end, Joe Thompson draws a scratchy, rakish tone from his fiddle, full of higher overtones," Jon Pareles wrote of the performance in The New York Times. "He breaks melodies into short phrases and often adds double-stops that suggest modal harmonies."

After Odell Thompson died in a car accident in 1994, Joe almost quit. But he went on to record a solo album, "Family Tradition," on the Rounder label in 1999. He received the National Endowment for the Arts fellowship in 2007 and performed that year at the Kennedy Center for the Performing Arts in Washington.

String-band music, which combines fiddle, banjo and sometimes other instruments, owes much to African-American traditions. Banjos originally came from Africa, and though violins are European in origin, slaves were taught to play them for their masters as early as the 17th century. Paul F. Wells, a former president of the Society for American Music, wrote in the Black Music Research Journal that slaves were most likely the earliest musicians to combine violin and banjo.

Both whites and blacks — sometimes separately, sometimes together, as in Mr. Thompson's Piedmont region — created string-band music in the 19th century. The white bands tended to play at square dances and the black bands at their own dances, called "frolics."

But there were differences. Black fiddlers played in a style that was more rhythmic, syncopated and African in character. They called the tunes "Negro jigs." As music became more commonly recorded in the 1920s, the black string-band tradition faded. Black music was veering toward the blues, while white string bands were categorized as "hillbilly," playing what is acknowledged to be the precursor of today's bluegrass and country music. The influence of black string bands on white country musicians slipped from memory.

As if this slight wasn't enough, Mr. Thompson complained in a 2004 interview with a North Carolina newspaper that when Elvis Presley started singing the blues, "people thought that was white people's music, too."

"That messes black people up," he said.

Joseph Aquilla Thompson was born on Dec. 9, 1918, on a farm near Mebane, N.C., a town where he lived most of his life. Mr. Thompson had a stroke in 2001 that hurt his fiddling but not his strong singing voice, said his friend Larry Vellani, a musician.

Mr. Thompson's first wife, the former Hallie Evans, died in 1987. He is survived by his wife, the former Pauline McAdoo Mebane, as well as two sons, four stepchildren, eight grandchildren, 14 great-grandchildren and five great-great-grandchildren.

The Thompsons may have been the last black string band still active, said Wayne Martin, folklife director for the North Carolina Arts Council. But Mr. Thompson planted a seed for the future. In 2005, three young musicians started coming to his house every Thursday to learn the old ways. They formed a band, the Carolina Chocolate Drops, "mostly as a tribute to Joe," they said. Their 2010 album, "Genuine Negro Jig," won a Grammy for best traditional folk album.

"He lived long enough for people to get what it was he had to share," Mr. Vellani said.

— BY DOUGLAS MARTIN

BARNEY ROSSET

The First Amendment Prefaced Every Book

MAY 28, 1922 - FEB. 21, 2012

BARNEY ROSSET, the provocative publisher who helped change the course of publishing in the United States by bringing masters like Samuel Beckett to Americans' attention under his Grove Press imprint and winning celebrated First Amendment slugfests against censorship, died on Feb. 21 in Manhattan. He was 89.

Over a long career Mr. Rosset championed Beat poets, French Surrealists, German Expressionists and dramatists of the absurd, helping to bring them to prominence. Besides publishing Beckett, he brought early exposure to European writers like Eugène Ionesco and Jean Genet and gave intellectual ammunition to the New Left by publishing Che Guevara, Ho Chi Minh and "The Autobiography of Malcolm X."

Most of all, beginning in high school, when he published a mimeographed journal titled "The Anti-Everything," Mr. Rosset, slightly built and sometimes irascible, savored a fight.

He defied censors in the 1960s by publishing D. H. Lawrence's "Lady Chatterley's Lover" and Henry Miller's "Tropic of Cancer," ultimately winning legal victories that opened the door to sexually provocative language and subject matter in literature published in the United States. He did the same thing on movie screens by importing the sexually frank Swedish film "I Am Curious (Yellow)."

Mr. Rosset called Grove "a breach in the dam of American Puritanism."

Beyond being sued scores of times, he received death threats. Grove's office in Greenwich Village was bombed. In 2008 the National Book Foundation honored him as "a tenacious champion for writers who were struggling to be read in America."

Other mentions were less lofty. Life magazine in 1969 titled an article about him "The Old Smut Peddler." That same year a cover illustration for The Saturday Evening Post showed him climbing out of a sewer.

A publisher stood up to the censors, and won.

Mr. Rosset was hardly the only publisher to take risks, lasso avant-garde authors or print titillating material. But few so completely relied on seat-of-the-pants judgment as he did. Colleagues said he had "a whim of steel."

"He does everything by impulse and then figures out afterward whether he's made a smart move or was just kidding," Life said.

Simply put, Mr. Rosset liked what he liked. In an interview with Newsweek in 2008, he said he printed erotica because it "excited me."

In 1957 he helped usher in a new counterculture when he began the literary journal

Evergreen Review, originally a quarterly. (It later became a bimonthly and then a glossy monthly.) The Review, published until 1973, sparkled with writers like Beckett, who had a story and poem in the first issue, and Allen Ginsberg, whose poem "Howl" appeared in the second. There were also lascivious comic strips.

Barnet Lee Rosset Jr. was born into wealth in Chicago on May 28, 1922. His father owned banks, and though the elder Mr. Rosset had conservative views, he sent his son to the liberal Francis W. Parker School. The school was so progressive, Mr. Rosset told The New York Times in 2008, that teachers arranged for students to sleep with one another.

"I'm half-Jewish and half-Irish," he told The Associated Press in 1998, "and my mother and grandfather spoke Gaelic. From an early age my feelings made the I.R.A. look pretty conservative. I grew up hating fascism, hating racism."

He called his 17th year his happiest. He was class president, football star, holder of a state track record and, he said, boyfriend of the school's best-looking girl. He circulated a petition demanding that John Dillinger be pardoned. In 1940 he went to Swarthmore College, which he disliked because class attendance was compulsory. After a year he transferred to the University of Chicago for a quarter, then to the University of California, Los Angeles. A few months later he joined the Army and served in a photographic unit in China. After the war he earned a bachelor's degree in philosophy at the University of Chicago. He joined the Communist Party but soon rejected it, he said, after visiting Eastern Europe.

PROVOCATEUR: Barney Rosset introduced controversial works to American readers.

Initially interested in film, he spent $250,000 of his family's fortune in New York to produce a documentary, "Strange Victory," about the prejudice that black veterans faced when they returned from World War II. The film was poorly received, and afterward he headed for Paris with Joan Mitchell, a former high school classmate who became an admired Abstract Expressionist painter. They married in 1949 and returned to New York, where he studied literature at the New School for Social Research, earning another bachelor's degree in 1952.

Told that a small press on Grove Street in Greenwich Village was for sale, he bought it in 1951 for $3,000. Almost from the beginning his goal was to publish Miller's "Tropic of Cancer," an autobiographical, sexually explicit novel that had been published in Paris in 1934 and long been banned in the United States.

But he decided first to publish "Lady Chatterley's Lover," which had originally appeared in Italy in 1928. He theorized that though it was also banned in the United States, it commanded greater respect than Miller's book.

Arthur E. Summerfield, the postmaster general, lived up to Mr. Rosset's expectations and barred the book from the mails — Grove's means of distribution — in June 1959, calling it "smutty." But a federal judge in Manhattan lifted the ban, ruling that the book had redeeming merit. The reasoning pleased Mr. Rosset less than the result: as a foe of censorship he was an absolutist.

"If you have freedom of speech, you have freedom of speech," he said.

He faced a new round of censorship after buying the rights to "Tropic of Cancer" for $50,000 in 1961, the agreement having been struck by Miller and Mr. Rosset over a game of table tennis. Mr. Summerfield again imposed a ban but lifted it before it could be challenged in court.

Nevertheless, the book was attacked in more than 60 legal cases seeking to ban it in 21 states, and Mr. Rosset was arrested and taken before a Brooklyn grand jury, which decided against an indictment. Grove won the dispute in 1964 when the United States Supreme Court reversed a Florida ban, bringing all the cases to a halt. Grove sold 100,000 hardcover and one million paperback copies of "Cancer" in the first year.

In 1962 Grove released "Naked Lunch" by William S. Burroughs, a series of druggy, sexually explicit vignettes first published in Paris in 1959. Mr. Rosset had already printed 100,000 copies and kept them under wraps while the "Cancer" case was still in the courts. Almost immediately a Boston court found "Naked Lunch" without social merit and banned it. The Massachusetts Supreme Judicial Court reversed that judgment in 1966.

Many more Grove books proved controversial. One was "Story of O," a novel of love and sexual domination, by Anne Desclos writing under the name Pauline Réage. But lawsuits dwindled. It was the film "I Am Curious (Yellow)," the rights to which Mr. Rosset bought in 1968, that sparked the next firestorm. He saw it as an exploration of class struggle, he said, but its huge audiences were clearly attracted by the nudity and staged sexual intercourse.

When a theater refused to show "I Am Curious," Mr. Rosset bought the theater. He then sold it back after showing the movie. The authorities in 10 states banned the film entirely.

After Maryland's highest court ruled that the film was obscene, the matter went to the Supreme Court. In 1971 it split, 4-to-4, on whether the film should be banned everywhere. Justice William O. Douglas had recused himself, fearing that the publication of an excerpt from one of his books in Evergreen Review could be perceived as a conflict of interest. The deadlock meant the Maryland ruling would stand, although it had no weight as precedent. By that time Grove had made $15 million from the film, doubling the company's revenues.

There were run-ins over other films. Ruling on a suit by the State of Massachusetts, a Superior Court judge in 1968 banned further showings of another Grove release, "Titicut Follies," Frederick Wiseman's harrowing film about the abuse of patients at Bridgewater State Hospital.

There were triumphant moments, like Mr. Rosset's late-night Champagne session in Paris with Beckett in 1953 that led to his acquiring the American publishing rights to "Waiting for Godot." The printed version of the play sold more than 2.5 million copies in the United States. Beckett was just one winner of the Nobel Prize in Literature published by Grove; others included Harold Pinter and Kenzaburo Oe.

At Grove's peak, in the late 1960s, Mr. Rosset ran what he called "a self-contained mini-conglomerate" from a seven-story building on Mercer Street. Mr. Rosset was adept at spotting potential best sellers. "Games People Play: The Basic Handbook of Transactional Analysis," by Eric Berne, spent two years atop the Times best-seller list and has sold more than five million copies.

But he also made mistakes. Mr. Rosset turned down J. R. R. Tolkien's "Lord of the Rings," saying he "couldn't understand a word," and a planned trilogy of films based on short works by Beckett, Ionesco and Pinter was never completed, though it did lead in 1965 to an unusual art-house film, "Film," starring Buster Keaton with a script by Beckett.

In 1967 Mr. Rosset sold a third of the common stock of Grove to the public, retaining the rest himself. As a businessman he stumbled when he diversified into other fields, including real estate, film distribution and Off Broadway theater programs modeled on Playbill.

Mr. Rosset courted controversy, publishing "Lady Chatterly's Lover," "Tropic of Capricorn" and importing "I Am Curious (Yellow)."

A violent blow occurred on July 26, 1968, when a fragmentation grenade, thrown through a second-story window, exploded in the Grove offices, then on University Place. The offices were empty, and no one was hurt. Exiles opposed to Fidel Castro took responsibility, angry that the Evergreen Review had published excerpts of "The Bolivian Diary," by Che Guevara, the former aide to Mr. Castro who had been executed by Bolivian troops less than a year before.

To Mr. Rosset, things turned decidedly against him in 1970 when employees tried to unionize several departments, including the editorial staff. He was accused of sexism, and some said his publications were demeaning to women. When protesters took over the office, Mr. Rosset called in the police. The union proposal was voted down.

Mr. Rosset sold Grove in 1985 to Ann Getty, the oil heiress, and George Weidenfeld, a British publisher. Part of the deal was that he would remain in charge. But the new owners fired him a year later. He sued, contending that the dismissal had violated the sales contract. The dispute was settled out of court.

After leaving Grove, Mr. Rosset published Evergreen Review online and books under a new imprint, Foxrock Books. After discovering a trove of suppressed 19th-century erotic books, including "My Secret Life," he started Blue Moon Books, which published those as well as newer titles. He also took up painting and filled a wall of his Manhattan apartment with a mural. Grove's backlist was acquired by Atlantic Monthly Press in 1993. The combined entity today is Grove/Atlantic.

After his marriage to Ms. Mitchell ended in divorce, Mr. Rosset married four more times. His subsequent marriages to Hannelore Eckert, Cristina Agnini and Elisabeth Krug also ended in divorce. He is survived by his fifth wife, the former Astrid Myers, as well as two sons, two daughters, four grandchildren and four stepgrandchildren. He died after a double-heart-valve replacement.

Algonquin Books plans to release an autobiography Mr. Rosset was writing, tentatively titled "The Subject Was Left-Handed." A documentary film about his career, titled "Obscene" and directed by Neil Ortenberg and Daniel O'Connor, was released in 2008.

Mr. Rosset liked to tell the story of how he had responded to a Chicago prosecutor who suggested that he had published "Tropic of Cancer" only for the money. He whipped out a paper he had written on Miller while at Swarthmore (the grade was a B-) to demonstrate his long interest in the author. He won the case.

"I remember leaving the courtroom and somehow getting lost going home," he told The Times in 2008. "It was snowing. But I was so happy that I thought, 'If I fall down and die right here, it will be fine.'"

— By Douglas Martin

MARIE COLVIN

Witness to War to the Last

JAN. 12, 1956 - FEB. 22, 2012

O N FEB. 22, during a terrifying two minutes, 11 rockets slammed into a single apartment building in the Baba Amr neighborhood of Homs, the rebellious city in Syria that had been besieged by government forces for 19 days. When the barrage stopped, at least 22 bodies were recovered.

Among them was a 6-year-old boy and two foreign journalists, Marie Colvin, 56, an American-born war correspondent working for The Sunday Times of London, and Rémi Ochlik, 28, a French freelance photojournalist. They had been among the few outsiders able to reach Homs, having secretly crossed the border from Lebanon at great personal risk in defiance of a government determined to hide its repression from the world.

RISKY ASSIGNMENTS: Marie Colvin covered important stories in the most dangerous of places.

Syrian activists said the building had been targeted because it housed their media center. The satellite transmitters on the roof had probably been spotted by Syrian reconnaissance aircraft, they said.

Ms. Colvin had recognized the significance of the story unfolding in Homs. The problem was how to get at it. She had been hoping for an official visa to visit Syria's capital, Damascus, but with none forthcoming, she decided to sneak over the border despite strong misgivings about her safety. At the time, Homs was suffering a constant battering from government tanks and heavy artillery.

"I cannot remember any story where the security situation was potentially this bad, except maybe Chechnya," Ms. Colvin told a reporter for The New York Times over dinner on her last night in Beirut, a week before she was killed.

In her first dispatch from Homs, in The Sunday Times of London, she described the dangers in merely reaching her destination. Her welcoming party was ecstatic that a foreign reporter had braved the odds to reach them.

"So desperate were they that they bundled me into an open truck and drove at speed with the headlights on, everyone standing in the back shouting, 'Allahu akbar!' — God is the greatest," she wrote. "Inevitably, the Syrian Army opened fire."

She then transferred into a small car, which was also fired upon as it speeded into a row of abandoned buildings for cover. But she found her story.

She described a "widows' basement" crammed with women cowering in the only shelter they could find in a city where there is only sugar and water to feed a newborn baby.

"Among the 300 huddling in this wood factory cellar in the besieged district of Baba Amr is 20-year-old Noor, who lost her husband and her home to the shells and rockets," Ms. Colvin wrote, etching in stark detail how the woman's husband and brother died when they went out into the streets to forage for food. Telephones and electricity had been cut off.

"Few homes have diesel for the tin stoves they rely on for heat in the coldest winter that anyone can remember," Ms. Colvin wrote. "Freezing rain fills potholes, and snow drifts in through windows empty of glass. No shops are open, so families are sharing what they have with relatives and neighbors." She added, "Fearing the snipers' merciless eyes, families resorted last week to throwing bread across rooftops, or breaking through communal walls to pass unseen."

Mr. Ochlik, the photographer who died alongside her, had received a World Press Photo award for his work in Libya the previous year. Their deaths came six days after that of Anthony Shadid, a reporter for The New York Times, who had a fatal asthma attack in Syria after a week of reporting there. (See page 222.)

Ms. Colvin was intimately familiar with risk. She had worn a black eye patch since losing an eye while crossing battle lines in Sri Lanka in 2001. She was known for angling to get into places that others were desperate to escape. The list of wars she covered over 25 years or so ringed the globe — the Balkans, the Middle East, Somalia, Afghanistan, Southeast Asia and East Timor. In one of her last journalistic coups, she and two other reporters were granted an audience with Col. Muammar el-Qaddafi as Libya went up in flames.

"Nothing seemed to deter her," John Witherow, editor of The Sunday Times, said in a note to the newspaper's staff.

Committed to documenting the conflict, especially the horrors visited on civilians,

Ms. Colvin found a particular sense of purpose in the Arab world.

"We can and do make a difference in exposing the horrors of war and especially the atrocities that befall civilians," Ms. Colvin said in a speech in London in 2011 honoring correspondents killed in the line of work. But she acknowledged the risks. "We always have to ask ourselves whether the level of risk is worth the story," she said. "What is bravery, and what is bravado?"

Marie Catherine Colvin was born on Jan. 12, 1956, and grew up in Oyster Bay, on Long Island. After spending a year in Brazil on a student-exchange program while attending Oyster Bay High School, she enrolled at Yale. She graduated in 1978 with a degree in anthropology. In college she took a journalism course with the Pulitzer Prize-winning writer John Hersey. After Yale, she worked briefly for a labor union in Manhattan before being hired by United Press International in New Jersey. U.P.I. sent her to Washington and later to Paris. At 30, she was recruited by The Sunday Times to report from the Middle East.

Her mother, Rosemarie Colvin, of East Norwich, Long Island — survivors also include two brothers — said the last time she heard her daughter's voice was on television, when she was interviewed on CNN hours before her death. She said it would have been pointless to try to dissuade her daughter from going into conflict zones.

"There was no saying, 'Don't do this,'" her mother said. "This is who she was, absolutely who she was, and what she believed in: cover the story, not just have pictures of it, but bring it to life in the deepest way you could."

— BY ROD NORDLAND,
NEIL MACFARQUHAR AND JAMES BARRON;
NOAH ROSENBERG, MAYY EL SHEIKH AND
HWAIDA SAAD CONTRIBUTED REPORTING.

WILLIAM HAMILTON

Is God Dead? He Had an Answer

MARCH 9, 1924 - FEB. 28, 2012

ILLIAM HAMILTON was a tenured professor of church history at a small divinity school in Rochester, N. Y., in April 1966 when Time magazine created a sensation with a cover article featuring some of the ideas he had been writing about for years in journals read mainly by ministers and theologians.

In large red type against a black background, Time boiled those ideas down to three words: "Is God Dead?" It became one of the magazine's most famous covers, and it upended Dr. Hamilton's quiet life as an academic theologian.

The article, appearing in the season of Easter and Passover, gave a primer on the history of the war between religious and secular ideas in Western culture going back to Copernicus. It quoted Billy Graham and Simone de Beauvoir as exemplars of the two sides, and it introduced the world to Dr. Hamilton as the leader of a new school of religious thinking it called the "Death of God Movement."

Dr. Hamilton became the target of death threats in the year after the article was published. He left his job, feeling ostracized. And he spent a good deal of the rest of his life — he died on Feb. 28 at 87 — adding air quotes with his fingers around the word God, which was what he had meant when he referred to "the death of God," he said.

But the article was basically accurate about his views. He believed that the concept of God had run its course in human history. Civilization now operated according to secular principles. And, he said, churches should, too, by helping people learn to care for one another unconditionally, without illusions about heavenly rewards.

For better or worse, it was not something he would have said out loud at the Third Presbyterian Church in Rochester, where he and his family attended services for many years until he started meeting icy silences after the Time article appeared.

Whether Jesus was divine or not, he said, didn't matter so much as whether people followed his teachings.

To him it was a scholarly idea, written for scholarly journals, intended to address the big theological question of the postwar era: how to reconcile the notion of an all-powerful God with an overwhelmingly secular and often brutal modern life. The question was being explored from every angle by theologians, who were as likely to quote Camus, Nietzsche and Kierkegaard as they were the Bible.

The "Death of God" thinking had attracted attention the year before, when Dr. Hamilton and Thomas J. J. Altizer, a religion professor at Emory University in Atlanta, published "Radical Theology and the Death of God," a collection of their essays.

Reviewing the book for The New York Times, Edward B. Fiske described it as an open challenge to the ideas of Karl Barth, the Swiss theologian whose conservative "neo-Orthodox" ideas had dominated Christian thinking in the 20th century. A Times article reported, "Many theologians who challenge the conclusions of the radical theologies nevertheless admit that they must be taken seriously."

Time magazine ran an article about the subject on its religion page. But there had been no big stir.

The cover article caused a big stir.

"What does your dad mean, 'God is dead'" Dr. Hamilton's son Donald recalled being asked in the schoolyard in the spring of 1966, when he was 12. "I don't know" was his reply.

Time's coverage "was a complete surprise to these guys," said Terrence W. Tilley, chairman of the theology department at Fordham University, referring to Dr. Hamilton, Dr. Altizer and others identified in the article as members of the "Death of God" group. "Academic theologians, exploring radical ideas in uncharted territory, generally do not expect to see their ideas on the cover of Time magazine."

Dr. Hamilton contended that many people had misunderstood him. He was not an atheist, he said, in the way that the evolutionary biologist and author Richard Dawkins is. He considered himself a follower of Christ, but whether Jesus was the son of God or not, he said, did not matter so much as whether people followed his teachings.

"The 'death of God' is a metaphor," he told the newspaper The Oregonian in 2007. "We

BLASPHEMOUS?: William Hamilton received a storm of criticism, even death threats, after Time magazine featured his ideas on "the death of God" in a cover story.

needed to redefine Christianity as a possibility without the presence of God."

Loretta Lynn, the country music star, would have none of it. She voiced her feelings in the title song of her 1968 album "Who Says God Is Dead!" "That's stupid and mighty low," she sang. "I like to meet 'em face to face and tell 'em it's not so."

Though Dr. Hamilton held a tenured professorship at Colgate-Rochester Divinity School, the intense displeasure he felt from trustees and fellow faculty members led him to accept a job offer in 1967 from New College, a non-traditional institution in Sarasota, Fla. He was named dean of arts and letters at Portland State University in Oregon in 1970 and taught there until his retirement in 1986. He died of congestive heart failure at his home in Portland, his son Donald said.

Traditionalists dismissed his ideas as blasphemous, and many liberal theologians criticized his work as inconsistent and confusing. How could he say God was dead and call himself a Christian? But some theologians, including Ellen T. Charry of Princeton Theological

Seminary, maintain that the call to action inherent in "Death of God" ideas stirred an interest in social justice among liberal Christians and influenced the liberation theology movement of the 1960s and '70s.

William Hughes Hamilton III was born on March 9, 1924, in Evanston, Ill., one of two children of William Hughes Hamilton II, a windmill engineer, and the former Helen Anderson. He graduated from Oberlin College in Ohio. After serving in the Navy during World War II, he studied at Union Theological Seminary in New York and received his Ph.D. at the University of St. Andrews in Scotland.

Besides his son Donald, he is survived by his wife, the former Mary Jean Golden, as well as two other sons, two daughters and eight grandchildren.

Dr. Hamilton's later writing remained below the radar of the press, focusing on the presence and absence of God in the works of Herman Melville, Emily Dickinson and Shakespeare. But in the end, he told The Oregonian, he never regretted the hubbub his theological work had caused, however misunderstood his ideas may have been.

"The 'death of God' enabled me to understand the world," he said. "Looking back, I wouldn't have gone in any other direction. I faced all my worries and questions about death long ago."

— BY PAUL VITELLO

ANNA LOU DEHAVENON

A Plane Crashed, and a Life Pivoted

NOV. 24, 1926 - FEB. 28, 2012

ANNA LOU DEHAVENON, an urban anthropologist, was documenting the lives of women living in a Bronx homeless shelter in the 1980s when she had an epiphany.

She had just determined that the median age of women at the shelter was 26, and that the median number of children of the women was 2, when she suddenly remembered the day her own life was turned upside down — when she, too, was 26 and the mother of two.

It was Oct. 29, 1953, the day her husband, William Kapell, one of his generation's most brilliant pianists, died in a plane crash at the age of 31. He was returning to the United States from a tour of Australia when the plane struck King's Mountain south of San Francisco, killing all 19 on board.

Mr. Kapell, who had spent a small fortune transporting his chosen pianos to concerts, left his widow little. And she, having dropped her own career as a promising pianist to raise a family, found herself with no income and no college degree. If she wasn't exactly homeless, she was the closest thing to it.

At the Bronx shelter, Dr. Dehavenon saw how much she had in common with the women she was studying, and how her own experience had motivated her choice of career.

"I'm thinking, my God, that's one of the reasons I'm so concerned," she said in an interview with The New York Times in 2005. "Freud would have had a wonderful time with it. Subconsciously, my own experience fed into it."

With help, she rebuilt her life and went on to earn a Ph.D. in anthropology, becoming a respected authority on poverty, hunger and homelessness in New York City and beyond. She died at 85 on Feb. 28 at a nursing home in Greenport, on Long Island.

Dr. Dehavenon's influence came from the strength of the statistics and empirical observations she collected as an urban anthropologist doing studies for private social welfare groups. Her reports were read closely by government agencies, judicial officials and the news media, and her research influenced a 1979 landmark ruling that affirmed a right to shelter in New York City.

She was as much an advocate as she was an observer. One organization she started was called the Action Research Project on Hunger.

"Are people starving?" Dr. Dehavenon asked rhetorically in 1988. "I don't really use that kind of language. We can't ever see hunger, because it's a subjective experience. But we can build a case inferring that people here are suffering from hunger, and that's what we've done."

Starting in 1978, Dr. Dehavenon produced annual studies on hunger for the East Harlem Interfaith Welfare Committee, an alliance of seven religious, voluntary organizations she

'WE CAN'T SEE HUNGER':
Anna Lou Dehavenon's observations and reports on the homeless were read closely by government agencies and led to a 1979 landmark ruling.

helped form. She had been raised a Presbyterian and embraced Buddhism.

Using social science research techniques, Dr. Dehavenon found that more and more Harlem residents went hungry each year, some of them relying on what they could steal, others sifting through garbage to feed their families.

She traced the causes to cuts in federal assistance and an eagerness by New York City officials to bump people from public assistance rolls. She titled her 1985 report "The Tyranny of Indifference."

Dr. Dehavenon focused increasingly on homelessness as the problem surged in the 1980s. Her analyses contributed to the litigation in a class-action suit brought by the Legal Aid Society on behalf of a group of homeless families. It led to the ruling, by a State Supreme Court justice, ordering New York City to provide shelter to all homeless families.

"In the society's court papers, she recounted her weekly observations of case after case of families who had been left without shelter," said Jane Bock, senior staff attorney for the society's Homeless Rights Project. Dr. Dehavenon's expert testimony about families living in filth led to contempt rulings against the city, Ms. Bock said.

When the Community Service Society presented Dr. Dehavenon with its highest award in 1990, it said, "Her research has been instrumental in forcing critical changes in social policy in New York City."

Rebecca Ann Lou Melson was born on Nov. 24, 1926, in Bellingham, Wash., and soon showed a gift for the piano. After two years at Reed College in Portland, Ore., she moved to Chicago to study at DePaul University with Sergei Tarnovsky, who had taught Vladimir

Horowitz in Russia. She met Mr. Kapell when he performed in Chicago, and they married in 1948.

After Mr. Kapell's death, family friends helped her find an apartment. She met Gaston T. de Havenon, an art dealer, and married him in 1955. (She adopted a slightly different rendering of the surname.) They had two children, and with his two children from an earlier marriage and her two with Mr. Kapell, she acted as mother for six. She divorced Mr. de Havenon in 1974, having grown bored with being a homemaker, she told The Times.

At 40, she started taking classes at Columbia University's School of General Studies. One teacher, the anthropologist Marvin Harris, who was known for finding practical explanations for human behavior, had students videotape the behavior of a range of people, from garbage collectors to the Macy's Santa Claus.

Ms. Dehavenon continued to use videotape in her doctoral studies of hunger, recording the behavior of families, in some cases as they ran out of food. She spoke of being moved by an unemployed father in East Harlem who had borrowed $10 from his sister and spent three days comparing prices before buying a Thanksgiving turkey.

After receiving her doctorate in 1978, she taught on and off at both the Mount Sinai School of Medicine in Manhattan and the Albert Einstein College of Medicine in the Bronx throughout her career. She is survived by three daughters, two sons, a stepson and 10 grandchildren.

Dr. Dehavenon strove to keep Mr. Kapell's memory alive by helping to publish his diaries and issue new recordings of his music. In one instance, by a circuitous route, she unexpectedly received CD copies of some forgotten acetate-disc recordings of Mr. Kapell's last concerts, performed in Australia in 1953. A Melbourne department store salesman, who had since died, had recorded them from radio broadcasts.

The found music led to the release in 2008 of the two-disc album "Kapell Rediscovered: The Australian Broadcasts," by Sony BMG Masterworks.

In a 2004 radio interview in Australia, Dr. Dehavenon said she still got goose flesh when she heard Mr. Kapell's music. There are times, she said, "when music can speak but words can't speak."

— BY DOUGLAS MARTIN

DAVY JONES

Monkees Heartthrob

DEC. 30, 1945 - FEB. 29, 2012

DAVY JONES, a singer and, by long-held public consensus, the handsomest and most popular of the Monkees, the collectively young, longhaired, wildly famous and preternaturally buoyant pop group of the 1960s and afterward, died on Feb. 29 in Indiantown, Fla. He was 66.

Created in 1966, the Monkees — Mr. Jones, Micky Dolenz, Michael Nesmith and Peter Tork — sold millions of records. Its recording of "Daydream Believer," by John Stewart, became a No. 1 single, as did its recording of "Last Train to Clarksville," by Tommy Boyce and Bobby Hart, and its cover of Neil Diamond's "I'm a Believer."

Though the Monkees officially lasted only until the early '70s, they reconvened sporadically for decades. For much of that time Mr. Jones also toured as a solo singer-songwriter; among his last performances was one on Feb. 18 at B. B. King Blues Club & Grill in Manhattan.

COVER BOY: Before joining the Monkees and becoming a teen idol, Davy Jones appeared on television and on stage, notably in the long-running British soap "Coronation Street" and in the musical "Oliver!"

For all the Monkees' chart-topping acclaim, the group never pretended to be anything other than what it was: a smoke-and-mirrors incarnation of a pop group reminiscent of that mop-topped one from Liverpool, created for a benignly psychedelic American TV sitcom.

Broadcast on NBC, "The Monkees" lasted just two seasons, from September 1966 to March 1968, and featured Messrs. Jones, Dolenz, Nesmith and Tork as members of a free-wheeling, fun-loving, beach-house-dwelling, up-and-coming pop group. The show won two Emmys in 1967: for outstanding comedy series and for outstanding directorial achievement (given to James Frawley) in comedy.

To this day, its theme song is hard-wired into the baby-boomer brain:

Hey, hey, we're the Monkees, and people say we monkey around. But we're too busy singing to put anybody down.

While the four did much of their own singing, they were relatively unbusy playing. Though each played an instrument — growing more proficient with time — most of the instrumentals on their albums were supplied by studio musicians. (On one album, "Headquarters," released in 1967, the Monkees played their instruments themselves.)

The group's critical reception was not unsurpassed. In 1967, in an article about one of the Monkees' relatively rare live concerts of the period, at Forest Hills Stadium in Queens, The New York Times said:

"Frequently during the performance, sound that resembled the lowing of a sick cow hovered over the stadium. This turned out to be one of those horns often heard at Shea Stadium during baseball games. It didn't seem to hurt the musical evening."

But the critics could not dim the profuse enthusiasm of fans, who were overwhelmingly young, female and shrieking — tweeners before the word was applied to that demographic.

This adulation (and, in later years, nostalgia) kept the Monkees going, in various incarnations, on and off for decades. Last year three-quarters of the group, absent Mr. Nesmith, briefly toured Britain and the United States before cutting the tour short because of unspecified internal dissension.

The only actual Englishman of the four, Mr. Jones was inclined to elicit the loudest shrieks of all. An index of his appeal was his guest appearance on a memorable episode of "The Brady Bunch" from 1971 entitled "Getting Davy Jones." In it, Mr. Jones, playing himself, saves Marcia, the family's eldest daughter, from social ruin by attending her prom.

Television and the stage were actually Mr. Jones's original vocations.

David Thomas Jones was born on Dec. 30, 1945, in Manchester, England. A child actor, he appeared on "Coronation Street," the British soap opera that went on the air in 1960 and is still running, and in the police drama "Z Cars." After his mother's death when he was a teenager, he abandoned acting. Slight of build — he stood not much more than 5 feet tall in his prime — he began to train as a jockey.

Lured back into the theater a few years later, he played the Artful Dodger in the West End musical "Oliver!" When the production moved to Broadway in 1963, he reprised the role (billed as David Jones), earning a Tony nomination as best featured actor in a musical.

Appearing with the cast of "Oliver!" on "The Ed Sullivan Show," Mr. Jones had a transformative moment. After the cast sang, he heard wild cheering. But alas it was not for them: it was for the Beatles, also booked on the show that day.

"I thought: Is that what happens when you're a pop singer?" Mr. Jones told The Palm Beach Post in 2004. "I want to be part of that!"

His work on Broadway led to guest roles on a few mid-'60s television shows, including "Ben Casey" and "The Farmer's Daughter." He was signed to a contract with Columbia Pictures/Screen Gems Television, which produced "The Monkees."

Mr. Jones, who had homes in Hollywood, Fla., and Beavertown, Pa., spent his later years touring; acting occasionally on television shows like "My Two Dads" and "Boy Meets World"; raising horses; and recording, including the well-received solo album "Just Me" (2001), which featured his original songs. He appeared to have died of a heart attack, his publicist, Helen Kensick, said.

Whatever Monkeedom still attached to him (and it was considerable) did not dismay him.

"People ask me if I ever get sick of playing 'Daydream Believer' or whatever," he told The Chicago Daily Herald, a suburban newspaper, in 2006. "But I don't look at it that way. Do they ask if Tony Bennett is tired of 'I Left My Heart in San Francisco'?"

Mr. Jones's first marriage, to Linda Haines, ended in divorce, as did his second, to Anita Pollinger. His survivors include his third wife, Jessica Pacheco; two daughters from his first marriage; two daughters from his second marriage; three sisters; and three grandchildren.

The other three members of the Monkees also survive.

Perhaps Mr. Jones's most enduring legacy takes the form of a name. The name belongs to another English musician, who burst on the scene some years after the Monkees. This man, too, had been born David Jones. But thanks to the Monkees' renown, he knew he would have to adopt another name entirely if he was to have the hope of a career.

So he called himself David Bowie.

— BY MARGALIT FOX

ANDREW BREITBART

'Bulldog for the Conservative Cause'

FEB. 1, 1969 - MARCH 1, 2012

ANDREW BREITBART, a conservative blogger and activist who built a national media persona by putting undercover video and damaging photos on the Internet to bring discredit and disgrace to his liberal targets, died on March 1 in Los Angeles. He was 43.

His father-in-law, the actor Orson Bean, said Mr. Breitbart collapsed on a sidewalk near his home, apparently of a heart attack, while taking a walk shortly after midnight. Paramedics were unable to revive him, and the Los Angeles coroner's office later said that he had died of heart failure.

Mr. Breitbart was as polarizing as he was popular. On the political right he was hailed in the same breath with Rush Limbaugh and Matt Drudge as a truth-teller who exposed bias and corruption. On the left, he was derided by many as a provocateur who played fast and loose with the facts to further his agenda.

Among his biggest coups was the resignation of Anthony D. Weiner from the House of Representatives. The episode began when someone in Mr. Breitbart's network of tipsters and fans e-mailed him sexually explicit photos that Mr. Weiner, a liberal Democrat from New York, had taken of himself and sent to women online. Mr. Breitbart published some of the photos on his Web site, BigGovernment .com, igniting a firestorm that reached to the highest levels of Congress and solidifying his status as a conservative force in his own right.

After his death, many of the luminaries he looked up to as a young man paid homage. Mr. Limbaugh called him "an indefatigable bulldog for the conservative cause."

Mr. Breitbart was one of the most aggressive and controversial users of blogs to disseminate political information and rumors. His video methods in particular were new in conservative media. Indeed, he was to online video what Mr. Limbaugh was to radio and Mr. Drudge to the Internet.

Mr. Breitbart worked with Mr. Drudge early in his career, helping him staff The Drudge Report. But another media star, Arianna Huffington, gave Mr. Breitbart his biggest break. She hired him in 1997 when she was a conservative commentator in need of research help, giving him the title of director of research and what he described in his book "Righteous Indignation" as a "bizarre and cloistered office" in her Los Angeles home.

It did not take long for Ms. Huffington to see his value as a tireless employee. He struck up a friendship with her and her mother, who came to regard him as almost a son of her own.

"She would say, 'Andrew, you've got to sleep, got to stop,'" Ms. Huffington said in an interview. "You could sort of see the destructive side of his incredible passion for whatever he believed in at the time. It was all-consuming."

Mr. Breitbart was instrumental in helping Ms. Huffington create an early Web presence with a site called Arianna Online. After he left her for The Drudge Report, she reached out to him again. He wrote that he got a call from her one day in 2004. "Do you have any ideas for a Web site?" he quoted her as asking.

Mr. Breitbart went to work with Ms. Huffington and her business partners Kenneth Lerer and Jonah Peretti for the next seven months creating the now heavily trafficked news site The Huffington Post.

Andrew James Breitbart was born on Feb. 1, 1969, in Los Angeles, a month before Gerry and Arlene Breitbart adopted him. He grew up in the exclusive Brentwood section of Los Angeles, an experience he called disjointing.

"Even though it was very much a keep-up-with-the-Joneses enclave, my parents seemed oblivious to all that," he wrote. "When the first sushi restaurant popped up in our neighborhood in the early 1980s, we had meat loaf that night."

RIGHT-WING HERO: Andrew Breitbart, the conservative head of BigGovernment.com, was one of the first to expose the sexual scandal involving Representative Anthony Weiner.

He was a graduate of Tulane University, having majored in American studies.

Although he described his parents as Republican, he said they were not overtly political. "They came from the Silent Generation," he said.

Silent Mr. Breitbart was not. As a conservative commentator he appeared often on cable television shoutfests. He seemed to thrive on conflict.

In 2009, Mr. Breitbart started the first in a series of "Big" blogs with names like Big Journalism, Big Hollywood and Big Government. They gave him a prominent online perch of his own from which to attack liberal causes and figures.

One target, in 2009, was the community organizing group Acorn. A young conservative activist named James O'Keefe had come to Mr. Breitbart with undercover video of Acorn workers apparently offering advice on how to evade taxes and conceal child prostitution. In videotaping the encounter, Mr. O'Keefe and a companion had posed as a pimp and a prostitute. Mr. Breitbart eagerly published the tapes, and they went viral. In response, Congress ended grants to Acorn, and federal agencies severed ties with the group.

Mr. Breitbart earned a reputation for being selective with the facts. In an infamous case in 2010, he helped instigate the firing of an Agriculture Department official, Shirley Sherrod, by publishing a heavily edited video clip of her speaking at an N.A.A.C.P. event. Her comments, as edited, suggested that she had discriminated against a white farmer more than 20 years ago.

In the full video, however, she could be heard saying that she had eventually helped the farmer and had learned from the experience — that all people must overcome their prejudices. At Mr. Breitbart's death, she was suing him for defamation.

Many on the left, like the liberal Web site Media Matters, portrayed Mr. Breitbart as a caricature, an image he abetted in some respects. There was an element of performance in what he did, whether his behavior seemed crude or playful. He was often profane, and it was not uncommon to find him in rumpled shirts and torn jeans.

But there were other sides to him. He supported gay rights and once served on the board of GOProud, a conservative organization dedicated to gay and lesbian causes. His friends described him as a deeply committed father to his four children and a loyal husband to his wife, Susie — all of whom survive him.

And while he often railed against what he called corrupt mainstream media, he also knew that he needed them to further his own legitimacy. When he released the Weiner photos, he partnered with ABC News because, he said, he knew it would lend an imprimatur of authority.

He was true to his reputation right up until he died. At 11:25 p.m., perhaps within an hour of his death, he sent out a Twitter message to someone who had taken issue with one of his comments. Mr. Breitbart had referred to him using a vulgarity "cause I thought you were being intentionally disingenuous," he wrote. "If not I apologize."

— BY JEREMY W. PETERS;
IAN LOVETT, BRIAN STELTER AND
DANIEL E. SLOTNIK CONTRIBUTED REPORTING.

JAMES Q. WILSON

Crime and the Importance of Fixing a Window

MAY 27, 1931 - MARCH 2, 2012

JAMES Q. WILSON, a wide-ranging social scientist whose "broken windows" theory of law enforcement laid the groundwork for crime reduction programs in New York, Los Angeles and other cities, died on March 2 in Boston. He was 80.

Mr. Wilson, who taught government at Harvard for more than 20 years, wrote disquisitions about politics, the family, virtue and vice, and the nature of bureaucracies that steered intellectual trend and sometimes countered them. But he was best known for his research on the behavior of police officers and lawbreakers.

Probably his most influential theory holds that when the police emphasize the maintenance of order — addressing less-threatening disturbances to urban life like street-corner drug dealing, graffiti and subway turnstile-jumping — rather than concentrating on the piecemeal pursuit of rapists, murderers and carjackers, the rate of serious crime goes down.

Such a strategy became a cornerstone of the "quality of life" crime-reduction program in the 1990s of Mayor Rudolph W. Giuliani of New York and his first police commissioner, William J. Bratton.

During Mr. Giuliani's two terms in office, from 1994 through 2001, the rate of violent felonies plunged, enhancing the mayor's reputation as a crime-fighter — he had been a prosecutor — and increasing his popularity. Mr. Bratton left New York to become commissioner in Los Angeles, where crime also fell.

But Mr. Wilson's theory and its application have had their critics. Some accused Mr. Giuliani and Mr. Bratton of waging an overly aggressive campaign against panhandlers and the so-called squeegee men, who confronted motorists. And some researchers have questioned the efficacy of the program, saying that other factors, including the waning of the crack epidemic, were more responsible for the declining crime rate than the "broken windows" approach. The theory was first espoused by Mr. Wilson and George L. Kelling, a criminologist who had studied foot patrols in Newark, in an article in 1982 in The Atlantic.

The approach is psychologically based. It proceeds from the presumption, supported by research, that residents' perceptions of the safety of their neighborhood is based not on whether there is a high rate of crime but on whether the neighborhood appears to be well tended — that is, whether its residents hold it in mutual regard, uphold the locally accepted obligations of civility and outwardly disdain the flouting of them.

In Mr. Wilson's metaphor — Mr. Kelling gave Mr. Wilson credit for it — when a window is broken and someone fixes it, that is a sign that disorder will not be tolerated. But "one unrepaired broken window," they wrote, "is a signal that no one cares, and so breaking more windows costs nothing."

> Mr. Wilson's most influential theory held that when the police maintain everyday order in a neighborhood, crime goes down.

The authors argued that acts of criminality are fostered by such an "untended" environment, and that the solution is to tend it by being intolerant of the smallest illegalities. The wish "to 'decriminalize' disreputable behavior that 'harms no one' — and thus remove the ultimate sanction the police can employ to maintain neighborhood order — is, we think, a mistake," Mr. Wilson and Mr. Kelling wrote. "Arresting a single drunk or a single vagrant who has harmed no identifiable person seems unjust, and in a sense it is. But failing to do anything about a score of drunks or a hundred vagrants may destroy an entire community."

They added: "A particular rule that seems to make sense in the individual case makes no sense when it is made a universal rule and applied to all cases. It makes no sense because it fails to take into account the connection between one broken window left untended and a thousand broken windows."

Mr. Bratton said in an interview after Mr. Wilson's death that he had become interested in the "broken windows" theory independently, when he was working in Boston, where residents living in high-crime areas told him that what they worried about most was prostitution and graffiti.

"The importance of what Wilson and Kelling wrote was the emphasis not only on crime committed against people but the emphasis on crimes committed against the community, neighborhoods," Mr. Bratton said.

James Quinn Wilson was born on May 27, 1931, in Denver, and grew up mostly in Long Beach, Calif. His father, Claude, was a salesman; his mother, Marie, a homemaker.

He graduated from the University of Redlands in the San Bernardino Valley, east of Los Angeles, then served in the Navy during the Korean War (not in combat). He pursued advanced degrees at the University of Chicago, where he earned an M.A. and a Ph.D. in political science.

He arrived at Harvard in 1961. He later taught at the University of California, Los Angeles, and at Pepperdine University.

Mr. Wilson, who lived in North Andover, Mass., for his last three years after more than 20 years in Southern California, met his wife, the former Roberta Evans, in high school; they married in 1952. She survives him, along with a son, a daughter, a sister and five grandchildren. He died of complications of leukemia.

Mr. Wilson's first book, "Negro Politics" (1960), was among the first serious sociological analyses of the role of blacks in urban politics.

He continued to explore individual behavior and its relationship to institutions and to society as a whole in several books and dozens of magazine articles.

In "Bureaucracy: What Government Agencies Do and Why They Do It" (1989), he analyzed the inner workings of agencies like the Federal Bureau of Investigation as well as prisons and schools, pointing out the general disconnect between the people at the top who make the policies and the people at the bottom who do the work.

Most of his writing, however, was devoted to crime. An early book, "The Varieties of Police Behavior," led to an invitation to serve on President Lyndon B. Johnson's Commission on Crime and the Administration of Justice. Mr. Wilson was an avowed conservative, arguing, for example, that strict punishment for criminals, including the death penalty, has a deterrent effect on crime.

But even his critics acknowledged that he was less an ideologue than he was a scientist; he supported the war in Iraq and wrote that marriage should be defined by the union of one man and one woman, but he dismissed suspicions about Darwin's theory of evolution.

"I know my political ideas affect what I write," he acknowledged in a 1998 interview in The New York Times, "but I've tried to follow the facts wherever they land. Every topic I've written about begins as a question. How do police departments behave? Why do bureaucracies function the way they do? What moral intuitions do people have? How do courts make their decisions? What do blacks want from the political system?

"I can honestly say I didn't know the answers to those questions when I began looking into them."

—By Bruce Weber

WILLIAM HEIRENS

The 'Lipstick Killer' Who Terrified Chicago

NOV. 15, 1928 - MARCH 5, 2012

WILLIAM HEIRENS, the notorious "Lipstick Killer" who in 1946 confessed to three horrific murders in Chicago and then spent the rest of his life — more than 65 years — in prison as questions about his guilt lingered, was found dead on March 5 in the Dixon Correctional Center in Dixon, Ill. He was 83.

He was pronounced dead at the University of Illinois at Chicago Medical Center. He was known to have had diabetes.

Mr. Heirens' notoriety stemmed from the separate killings of two women, Josephine Ross and Frances Brown, in 1945. At the scene of the second, the Brown murder, someone had used lipstick to scrawl on a wall: "For heaven's sake catch me before I kill more. I cannot control myself."

The reports of a "lipstick killer" terrified Chicago as the press took note of other unsolved murders of women. Then, on Jan. 7, 1946, about two weeks after the Brown murder, a 6-year-old girl named Suzanne Degnan was discovered missing from her bedroom at her North Side home. A ladder was found outside the window. The police later determined that the killer had strangled her and taken the body to the basement of a nearby building, where it was dismembered. Her head was found in a sewer; other body parts were found scattered about the neighborhood.

The newspapers called the killing the crime of the century, and though the police questioned a parade of suspects, there was no arrest.

Almost six months later, Mr. Heirens (pronounced HIGH-rens), a 17-year-old student at the University of Chicago, was apprehended at the scene of a burglary in the girl's neighborhood.

'I CONFESSED TO LIVE': William Heirens recanted his confession to three horrific murders but was never acquitted. He served one of the nation's longest prison terms.

The police charged him with her murder after determining that his fingerprints were on a $20,000 ransom note that had been left behind at the girl's home.

While he was in custody, The Chicago Tribune, citing what it called "unimpeachable sources," reported that Mr. Heirens had confessed to the Degnan murder. Four other Chicago newspapers published similar articles, basing them on The Tribune's account. The outcry against him mounted.

Mr. Heirens, who said he was beaten and given "truth serum" in jail, disputed the newspaper accounts, saying he was about to sign a confession in exchange for one life term but rebelled at "being forced to lie to save myself." Prosecutors then charged him with the Brown and Ross murders, saying they had incriminating physical evidence against him, including crime-scene fingerprints and a handwriting analysis. Offered three consecutive life terms in exchange for a guilty plea, he accepted, on the advice of his lawyers. Later he said he had done so only to avoid a death sentence if he had gone to trial.

"I confessed to live," he said.

When he did confess, his memory seemed ragged. Time after time during the plea bargaining, prosecutors brought up details from The Tribune article, which he then incorporated into his testimony. Mr. Heirens recanted his confession soon afterward and maintained his innocence for the rest of his life. He questioned the validity of the fingerprints and other evidence, as did public interest lawyers who supported him, but he was denied parole or clemency numerous times.

In one clemency petition in 2002, his lawyers from the Northwestern University Center on Wrongful Convictions said there was more "prosecutorial misconduct, incompetent defense counsel, unprecedented prejudicial pretrial publicity, junk science, probably false confessions and mistaken eyewitness identification" in the Heirens case than in "any other case we have studied."

But others could not ignore his detailed admissions of guilt, even if he had retracted them. "He is the yardstick by which all evil is judged," Thomas Epach, a Chicago police official, said at the 2002 clemency hearing.

Suzanne Degnan's family fought all efforts to release him. Betty Finn, Suzanne's older sister, said at the 2002 hearing, "Think of the worse nightmare that you cannot put out of your mind, you're not allowed to put out of your mind."

William George Heirens was born on Nov. 15, 1928, in Evanston, Ill. His father's flower business failed, and the family teetered on the edge of poverty. In interviews, William said that his parents had fought frequently and that he had burglarized houses to relieve the tension he felt at home. He did not try to sell the things he stole, he said.

He was placed in two Roman Catholic youth detention centers. At the second, he proved to be an excellent student, skipping his senior year of high school. He was admitted to the University of Chicago at 16, with plans to major in engineering. In interviews, Mr. Heirens said his mother had led him to believe that sex was dirty. When he kissed a girl, he said, he would burst into tears and vomit. He said one reason he broke into houses was to play with women's underwear.

In the burglary in which he was arrested, the police testified that he had aimed a gun at an officer and twice pulled the trigger, but that the weapon misfired. He was additionally convicted of assault with the intention of killing a police officer.

After Mr. Heirens went to jail, his parents and brother changed their names to Hill. He left no known survivors.

While serving one of the nation's longest prison terms, Mr. Heirens became the first prisoner in Illinois to earn a degree from a four-year college. He also managed the prison garden factory and set up several education programs. In recent years, his diabetes damaged his eyesight, and he used a wheelchair. He told The New York Times in 2002 that he had learned that prison friendships were fleeting.

"Most of them, you hear for a little while, and then they kind of fade out," he said. "Usually when they get out, they try to forget they were ever in."

— By Douglas Martin

SAMUEL GLAZER

Making Mr. Coffee

FEB. 24, 1923 - MARCH 12, 2012

AMUEL GLAZER, a co-founder of the company that gave the world Mr. Coffee, one of the first and most popular automatic drip coffee makers to appear on American kitchen counters, died on March 12 in Cleveland. He was 89.

Before Mr. Glazer and Vincent Marotta came up with the idea, the two most common ways to make a cup of coffee at home were to percolate it (smells good but can taste bitter) or to stir instant coffee in boiled water (not as good as brewed).

Good friends since high school, the two men had been partners in a series of businesses for more than 20 years, particularly real estate development, when they bought a coffee delivery company serving the Cleveland area in the late 1960s. Mr. Glazer's son, Robert, recalled in an interview that on the delivery trucks were bulky, stainless steel commercial coffee dispensers.

ON EVERY KITCHEN COUNTER: Samuel Glazer co-created the most popular automatic drip coffee maker in America. Joe DiMaggio, pictured, endorsed the brand for 14 years.

"Can we get one of these for the house?" customers would ask, he said.

It gave the partners an idea. They hired two former Westinghouse engineers, Edmund Abel and Erwin Schulze, to create a compact, stylish version of the commercial dispenser. They came up with a system in which water enters an electric heating element at the top, then trickles into the coffee grounds in a disposable paper filter before emptying into a glass pot resting on another heating element to keep it warm. To avoid the bitterness that boiling can cause, it heats the brew to only about 200 degrees.

Thus was Mr. Coffee born. Introduced in 1972, it caught on quickly. The parent company, North American Systems, sold more than a million units within three years. Although more established appliance manufacturers created their own versions, Mr. Coffee would gain and maintain about 50 percent of the market share into the late 1970s.

A large reason was the baseball legend Joe DiMaggio. He was the public face of the company for 14 years, promoting Mr. Coffee in print advertisements and television commercials. In one commercial, a voice asks of the hitting great, "You're pitching for Mr. Coffee?" In 2002, the trade publication Home Furnishings News listed Mr. Coffee among the most important home products created in the past 75 years.

Mr. Glazer and Mr. Marotta sold the company to a securities firm in an $82 million leveraged buyout in 1987, a year after it had sales of $120 million. Mr. Coffee is now a brand of the Sunbeam Corporation.

Samuel Lewis Glazer was born in Cleveland on Feb. 24, 1923, to Isador and Yetta Gross Glazer. His father died when Sam was 6, and for years Sam supported his family, first by delivering newspapers and then by selling dog food to stores and boots to steelworkers.

After serving stateside in the Army during World War II, he joined with Mr. Marotta to form a company that built garages, sold garage doors and eventually developed real estate, including homes and shopping malls in many states. The partners sold much of their property to finance the coffeemaker enterprise, which at its peak had nearly 1,000 workers.

Mr. Glazer's wife, the former Jeanne Berger, and his son are his only immediate survivors. He died of complications of leukemia.

For Mr. Glazer, who lived in Beachwood, a suburb of Cleveland, Mr. Coffee was a readily available gift. His wife said he often spent time in California, where he became friends with Johnny Carson. "Please, Sam, I don't need any more coffee machines," Mr. Carson once said.

— BY DENNIS HEVESI

JOHN DEMJANJUK

The Murder Charge Listed 27,900 Counts

APRIL 3, 1920 - MARCH 17, 2012

THE STRANGER SETTLED IN CLEVELAND after World War II with his wife and little girl. He became an autoworker and changed his first name from Ivan to John. He had two more children, became a naturalized American, lived quietly and retired. His war and the terrors of concentration camps were all but forgotten.

Decades later, the past came back to haunt John Demjanjuk. And for the rest of his life it hovered over a tortuous odyssey of denunciations by Nazi hunters and Holocaust survivors, of questions over his identity, citizenship revocations, deportation orders and eventually trials in Israel and Germany for war crimes.

He was convicted and reprieved in Israel and, steadfastly denying the accusations, was appealing a guilty verdict in Germany when he died on March 17 at a nursing home in southern Germany, his son, John Demjanjuk Jr., said. He was 91.

Even at the end of his life questions remained in a case that had always been riddled with mysteries.

Had he been, as he and his family claimed, a Ukrainian prisoner of war in Germany and Poland who made his way to America and became a victim of mistaken identity? Or had he been, as prosecutors charged, a collaborating guard who willingly participated in the killing of Jews at the Treblinka, Majdanek and Sobibor death camps?

Nazi hunters and protesters who had demonstrated outside his home for years had no doubts. Nor did the Justice Department. Mr. Demjanjuk, stripped of his citizenship in 1981, was deported to Israel, where witnesses and an identity card of "Ivan the Terrible," a sadist who had murdered thousands of Jews at Treblinka, had turned up. The photograph on the card bore a striking resemblance to Mr. Demjanjuk.

He was placed on trial, convicted in 1988 of crimes against humanity and sentenced to be hanged. But five years later, the Israeli Supreme Court overturned the conviction when new evidence showed that another Ukrainian was probably the notorious Ivan. Back in America, Mr. Demjanjuk regained his citizenship, only to have it revoked again as new allegations arose.

Deported to Germany in 2009, Mr. Demjanjuk, suffering from bone-marrow and kidney diseases, was tried in a Munich court on charges in the killing of 27,900 Jews at the Sobibor camp in German-occupied Poland in 1943. In the nearly seven decades since 250,000 people were put to death at Sobibor, no surviving witnesses, even those who had been shown photographs, could place him at the scene.

The case was largely based on testimony by relatives of victims killed in the camp and on documentary evidence: an S.S. identity card purporting to be Mr. Demjanjuk's, Nazi orders sending the man identified as Mr. Demjanjuk to work as a guard at Sobibor and other records of the era.

In May 2011, the Munich court found Mr. Demjanjuk guilty and sentenced him to five years in prison. He was credited with two years of pretrial detention, leaving three left to serve if an appeal failed. Pending the appeal, he was released from prison and transferred to a nursing home. The court said his age, infirmity and statelessness made it unlikely he would flee.

Even some relatives of the victims, who were recognized as co-complainants at the trial, said it was the proof of guilt, finally, that counted. "Whether it's three, four or five years doesn't really matter," said David van Huiden, who lost his mother, father and sister at Sobibor. "He took part. He volunteered."

In Munich, Mr. Demjanjuk was accused of participating in "the routine process of extermination" of Jews.

But Mr. Demjanjuk's son, John Jr., said that under German law, a conviction is not official until appeals are completed, and that his father's death had the effect of "voiding" the Munich verdict.

Mr. Demjanjuk died a "a victim and a survivor of Soviet and German brutality," his son said, adding, "History will show Germany used him as a scapegoat to blame helpless Ukrainian P.O.W.'s for the deeds of Nazi Germans."

Ivan Demjanjuk (pronounced (dem-YAHN-yook) was born on April 3, 1920, in Dubovye Makharintsy, a village in Ukraine, to impoverished, disabled parents. The family nearly starved in a forced famine in the early 1930s that left millions dead in Ukraine. He had only four years of schooling, and was drafted into the Soviet Army in 1941. In 1942, the Germans wounded and captured him in the Crimea. What he did for the rest of the war was the crux of the issues surrounding his later life.

After the war, Mr. Demjanjuk met Vera Bulochnik in a German camp for displaced persons. They married and in 1950, still living in camps, had a daughter. In 1952, they emigrated to the United States and settled in Cleveland. Mr. Demjanjuk, who was naturalized in 1958, became a mechanic at a Ford plant, and his wife worked in a factory. The couple had two more children before moving to the Cleveland suburb of Seven Hills in 1973.

Besides John Jr., Mr. Demjanjuk is survived by his wife, two daughters, seven grandchildren and two great-grandchildren.

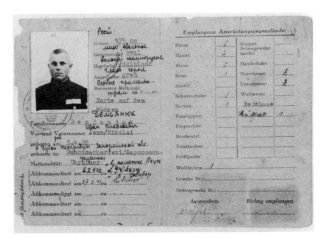

MASS MURDERER OR MISTAKEN IDENTITY?: John Demjanjuk was believed to be Ivan the Terrible, a Nazi who murdered 27,900. Evidence against him relied largely on an identity card. He died trying to clear his name.

In 1977, the Justice Department sued to revoke Mr. Demjanjuk's citizenship, saying he had lied on his immigration application to hide mass murders and other war crimes at Treblinka, the camp in Poland where 870,000 died. The accusations arose from Holocaust survivors who had identified Mr. Demjanjuk as Ivan the Terrible, a Ukrainian captured and trained by the Germans to operate gas chambers.

In 1981, after years of delays, a federal judge ruled that Mr. Demjanjuk had lied on his immigration papers and revoked his citizenship. He appealed, and the case was pending when Israel extradited him to stand trial as Ivan the Terrible. He was deported to Israel in 1986, and the trial began in 1987.

Prosecutors produced a Nazi identity card, said to be from the S.S. training camp at Trawniki, Poland, that bore what looked like Mr. Demjanjuk's photograph. It cited his name and date of birth, his father's name, and a scar like one Mr. Demjanjuk had.

Prosecutors said he had volunteered to collaborate and had been trained at Trawniki to run diesel engines that supplied carbon monoxide for gas chambers. They said he had killed thousands at Treblinka in 1942 and 1943. Treblinka survivors testified that Ivan the Terrible had also savaged Jews, breaking arms and legs with a steel pipe, cutting off ears and noses with a sword, and flogging women and children with sadistic glee.

But the defense noted that the survivors were relying on memories four decades old. It also challenged the identity card, saying the photo showed signs of having been lifted from another document, cited an incorrect height for Mr. Demjanjuk, and said its bearer had been at camps in Poland at Chelmno in 1942 and Sobibor in 1943 but did not mention Treblinka. Mr. Demjanjuk testified that he had been held as a prisoner at Chelmno for 18 months until 1944, and then in Austria until the war's end.

Found guilty and sentenced to death in 1988, he was held until 1993, when the Israeli Supreme

Court struck down his conviction, citing new evidence from former guards at Treblinka that Ivan the Terrible was another Ukrainian, Ivan Marchenko. On his citizenship application, Mr. Demjanjuk had listed his mother's maiden name as Marchenko, but contended later that he had forgotten her real maiden name and used Marchenko only because it was common in Ukraine.

Released by Israel, Mr. Demjanjuk returned to Cleveland, where a federal appeals court overturned his 1981 conviction for lying on his immigration papers, saying prosecutors had deliberately withheld evidence and committed fraud. His citizenship was restored in 1998.

But in 1999, the government again sued to strip him of citizenship, charging that he had been a Nazi guard at Majdanek and Sobibor in Poland and at Flossenbürg in Bavaria. After a trial, a court in 2002 upheld the government. An appeal confirmed the decision in 2004. In 2005, he was ordered deported to Germany, Poland or Ukraine, and the United States Supreme Court denied him a hearing in 2008.

In 2009, Germany agreed to accept Mr. Demjanjuk as a deportee to stand trial on charges that he helped kill Jews at Sobibor. His lawyers and family argued that he was too sick, but doctors concluded that he was fit enough.

The case involved 15 transport trains known to have arrived at Sobibor in 1943 from the Westerbork camp in the Netherlands, carrying 29,579 people. Mr. Demjanjuk was charged with 27,900 counts based on a theory that some must have died in transit.

"When a transport of Jews arrived, routine work was suspended and all camp personnel took part in the routine process of extermination," the indictment said. The unloading of the trains proceeded "with loud cries, blows and also shots. If people refused to come out, the Trawnikis entered the cars and forced those who hesitated, with violence, out of the train and onto the ramp."

In painful detail, witnesses like Rudie S. Cortissos recited dates when the trains arrived, the number of people aboard and the names of prisoners. Mr. Cortissos said his mother arrived on May 21, 1943, with 2,300 others, mostly Dutch Jews who were immediately sent to the gas chambers.

Defense lawyers argued that the Soviets had falsified Mr. Demjanjuk's identity card and other documents, but a judge found a clear trail of evidence showing his path from Soviet prisoner to Sobibor guard. The court rejected arguments that he had no choice but to work in the camp, and concluded that it would have been impossible for a guard there not to have been part of the Nazi death machinery.

Evidence at the trial also filled in previously unknown details of Mr. Demjanjuk's life between Sobibor and the end of the war. It showed that after Sobibor was shut down in 1943, Mr. Demjanjuk served in a Ukrainian unit that fought alongside the Germans, was captured by American forces in 1945 and was sent to the displaced persons camp where he met and married the woman who was to share his odyssey.

The Munich case might well have been the last major war crimes trial in Germany, ending an era that began in Nuremberg in 1945. As survivors and defendants have aged and died, the prosecution of Nazi-era war criminals has become increasingly rare and difficult.

And the elusiveness lies not only in the distance of the past, as Justice Meir Shamgar of the Israeli Supreme Court said in striking down Mr. Demjanjuk's conviction. "This was the proper course for judges who cannot examine the heart and the mind, but have only what their eyes see and read," he wrote. "The matter is closed — but not complete. The complete truth is not the prerogative of the human judge."

— BY ROBERT D. MCFADDEN

//////////////////////

MURRAY LENDER

An All-American Jewish English Muffin

OCT. 29, 1930 · MARCH 21, 2012

MURRAY LENDER, who with his brothers took over what started as their father's bakery in a backyard garage and built it into a business that brought the bagel (the "Jewish English muffin," as he called it) into kitchens across the country — frozen — died on March 21 in Miami. He was 81.

Murray, Marvin and Sam Lender expanded H. Lender & Sons — founded by their father, Harry — into the nation's leading distributor of packaged frozen bagels.

Lender's Bagels, now owned by the Pinnacle Foods Group, had revenue of $40.9 million in 2011 from the sale of 23.4 million six-bagel packages, according to SymphonyIRI Group, a Chicago-based market research company.

That's a long way from the several dozen a day that Harry Lender hand-rolled and baked after emigrating from Poland in 1927, setting up

BAGGED AND FROZEN: With his two brothers, Murray Lender helped boost the bagel's presence at American kitchen tables.

shop in his garage in West Haven, Conn., and delivering to local grocers.

Murray Lender was president of the company from 1974 to 1982 and chairman two years later when it was sold to Kraft Foods. Pinnacle bought the company in 2003.

To be sure, it was Harry who started the transformation when he bought a large freezer in the 1950s. By ensuring that his product would not go stale after 24 hours, he was able to start distributing it across a large swath of Connecticut. After he died in 1960, his sons pooled their resources to build a plant in West Haven. At first about 100 workers produced 120,000 dozen bagels a week, packaging them in plastic bags and shipping them to 30 states.

"The 1970s saw an unprecedented interest in all things ethnic, and Lender's frozen bagel was at the vanguard of the resurgence," The Jerusalem Post reported in 2009, adding that by the end of the decade Lender's had "reinvented the bagel as a versatile sandwich bread that could be as easily paired with peanut butter and jelly as it could be with ham and cheese."

The company eventually had two plants in the New Haven area, one in Buffalo and another in Mattoon, Ill., a prairie town 180 miles south of Chicago. That plant, built by Kraft in 1986, has a 12-foot-wide conveyor belt holding 24 bagels across, a 70-yard-long oven and an 80-foot-tall, 250-foot-long freezer. By then the bagel had become a national food, in variants from the cinnamon raisin to the green St. Patrick's Day variety.

"The vision," Mr. Lender told The New York Times in 1996, "was to really get it out of the ethnic marketplace."

Murray Isaac Lender was born in New Haven on Oct. 29, 1930, one of six children of Harry and Rose Braighter Lender. He was counting bagels in the backyard bakery before he was 11. After graduating from the Junior College of Commerce (now Quinnipiac University) in Hamden, Conn., he served two years in the Army, then went to work full time in the family business.

Mr. Lender, who lived in Aventura, Fla., died of complications of a fall. He is survived by his brother Marvin; his wife, the former Gilda Winnick; a daughter; two sons; and eight grandchildren. His brother Sam died in 2004.

After Kraft bought the company in 1984, Mr. Lender continued to work as its spokesman. "I never walked into anybody's office without a toaster under one arm and a package of bagels under the other," he said.

To those who contended that frozen bagels didn't compare with the fresh ones found at shops opening around the country, he said, "I think our bagel is the best bagel in America, but on the other hand, I've never eaten a bad bagel."

— BY DENNIS HEVESI

CHRISTINE BROOKE-ROSE

In One Book, 'to Be' Is Not to Be Found

JAN. 16, 1923 - MARCH 21, 2012

CHRISTINE BROOKE-ROSE, an English experimental writer known for wielding words with the ardor of a philologist, the fingers of a prestidigitator and the appetite of a lexivore, resulting in novels that exhilarated many critics and enervated others, died on March 21. She was 89.

Her death was announced on the Web site of her British publisher, Carcanet Press. Fittingly for a writer whose work could take artful pains to dispense with seemingly indispensable linguistic foundation stones (she once wrote an entire novel without using the verb "to be"), the "where" of Ms. Brooke-Rose's death — whether it occurred at her longtime home in the South of France or elsewhere — was unspecified.

The author of more than a dozen novels, as well as short stories, essays and criticism, Ms. Brooke-Rose was one of relatively few Britons to maintain a long association with experimental fiction. Her stylistic techniques — playful, polyglot, punning, postmodern and slyly self-referential — are more typically associated with writers of the French Nouveau Roman school.

Because she often used alternative narrative devices (including unorthodox chronology and unusual typography) to create alternative realities, her work is sometimes classified as science fiction, though much of it is beyond category. As with much postmodern fiction, her writing — organized around an unspoken compact between the author, who is unspooling the text, and the reader, who is watching it unspool — is about the act of writing itself.

Her best-known novels include four whose combined titles run to just five syllables — "Out" (1964), "Such" (1965), "Between" (1968), "Thru" (1975) — followed by a syllabic splurge: "Amalgamemnon" (1984), "Xorandor" (1986), "Verbivore" (1990) and "Textermination." In "Textermination," published in 1992, literary characters from a spate of famous pens — Austen's, Flaubert's, Pynchon's, Rushdie's — convene in a San Francisco hotel to importune readers for their continued existence.

Ms. Brooke-Rose was a linguistic escape artist. In book after book she dons self-imposed syntactic shackles, and in book after book she gleefully slips them.

In "Between," the very nature of identity is called into question by her avoidance of the verb "to be" in all its forms. In "Next" (1998), about the dispossessed in London, her characters are literal have-nots: throughout the book, she avoids the verb "to have."

In "Amalgamemnon," narrated by a literature professor about to lose her job, Ms. Brooke-Rose uses only verb forms — including future tense and subjunctive mood — that conjure conditions unobtainable in the present.

Ms. Brooke-Rose's earliest novels, published in the late 1950s, are conventional satires of manners. But as early as her third novel, "The Dear Deceit," published in 1960, she had begun to

ESCAPE ARTIST: Christine Brooke-Rose wrote an entire novel without the verb "to be."

play with narrative form. The novel opens with the death of its protagonist and, in successive chapters, works backward to his birth.

This convention has a time-honored analogue in narrative nonfiction, as when, for instance, a newspaper article begins with word of its subject's death and, only lower, reads:

Christine Frances Evelyn Brooke-Rose was born in Geneva on Jan. 16, 1923, into a French-, German- and English-speaking household. Her enigmatic English father, who left the family when she was a child and died when she was 11, had been, she later learned, an Anglican Benedictine monk and a convicted thief, though not necessarily in that order; her American-Swiss mother became a Benedictine nun after the dissolution of her marriage.

Reared in Geneva, Brussels and Britain, the young Ms. Brooke-Rose worked at Bletchley Park during the war, decrypting intercepted German messages. She earned degrees from Oxford, followed by a doctorate in medieval literature from University College London. From the late 1960s to the late '80s she taught British and American literature at the University of Paris.

Ms. Brooke-Rose was married three times. (Her second marriage was to the prominent Polish writer Jerzy Pietrkiewicz.)

Her other books include an autobiographical novel, "Remake" (1996); the story collection "Go When You See the Green Man Walking" (1970); a volume of criticism, "A ZBC of Ezra Pound" (1971); and translations of the French experimental writer Alain Robbe-Grillet.

What proved to be her last book was a novel published in 2006. It is presciently titled, in the manner of a catalog entry, "Life, End Of."

— BY MARGALIT FOX

ADRIENNE RICH

Feminism's Poet Laureate

MAY 16, 1929 - MARCH 27, 2012

ADRIENNE RICH, a poet of towering reputation and towering rage, whose work — distinguished by an unswerving progressive vision and a dazzling, empathic ferocity — brought the oppression of women and lesbians to the forefront of poetic discourse and kept it there for nearly a half-century, died on

March 27 at her home in Santa Cruz, Calif. She was 82.

Widely read, widely anthologized, widely interviewed and widely taught, Ms. Rich was for decades among the most influential writers of the feminist movement and one of the best-known American public intellectuals. She wrote two dozen volumes of poetry and more than a half-dozen of prose; the poetry alone has sold nearly 800,000 copies, according to W. W. Norton & Company, her publisher since the mid-1960s.

THE MIGHTIER PEN: Triply marginalized, Adrienne Rich used fearless poetry to combat societal domination. She declined the National Medal of Arts for the cause.

Triply marginalized — as a woman, a lesbian and a Jew — Ms. Rich was concerned in her poetry, and in her many essays, with identity politics long before the term was coined.

She accomplished in verse what Betty Friedan, author of "The Feminine Mystique," did in prose. In describing the stifling minutiae that had defined women's lives for generations, both argued persuasively that women's disenfranchisement at the hands of men must end.

For Ms. Rich, the personal, the political and the poetical were indissolubly linked; her body of work can be read as a series of urgent dispatches from the front. While some critics called her poetry polemical, she remained celebrated for the unflagging intensity of her vision, and for the constant formal reinvention that kept her verse — often jagged and colloquial, sometimes purposefully shocking, always controlled in tone, diction and pacing — sounding like that of few other poets.

All this helped ensure Ms. Rich's continued relevance long after she burst genteelly onto the scene as a Radcliffe senior in the early 1950s.

Her constellation of honors includes a MacArthur Foundation "genius" grant in 1994 and a National Book Award for poetry in 1974 for "Diving Into the Wreck." That volume, published in 1973, is considered her masterwork.

In the title poem, Ms. Rich uses the metaphor of a dive into dark, unfathomable waters to plumb the depths of women's experience:

I am here, the mermaid whose dark hair
streams black, the merman in his armored
*   body*
We circle silently about the wreck
we dive into the hold.

. . .

We are, I am, you are
by cowardice or courage
the one who find our way
back to the scene
carrying a knife, a camera
a book of myths
in which
our names do not appear.

Ms. Rich was far too seasoned a campaigner to think that verse alone could change entrenched social institutions. "Poetry is not a healing lotion, an emotional massage, a kind of linguistic aromatherapy," she said in an acceptance speech to the National Book Foundation in 2006, on receiving its medal for distinguished contribution to American letters. "Neither is it a blueprint, nor an instruction manual, nor a billboard."

But at the same time, as she made resoundingly clear in interviews, in public lectures and in her work, Ms. Rich saw poetry as a keen-edged beacon by which women's lives — and women's consciousness — could be illuminated.

She was never supposed to have turned out as she did.

Adrienne Cecile Rich was born in Baltimore on May 16, 1929. Her father, Arnold Rice Rich, a doctor and assimilated Jew, was an authority on tuberculosis who taught at Johns Hopkins University. Her mother, Helen Gravely Jones Rich, a Christian, was a pianist and composer who, cleaving to social norms of the day, forsook her career to marry and have children. Adrienne was baptized and confirmed in the Episcopal Church.

Theirs was a bookish household, and Adrienne, as she said afterward, was groomed by her father to be a literary prodigy. He encouraged her to write poetry when she was still a child, and she steeped herself in the poets in his library — all men, she later ruefully observed. But those men gave her the formalist grounding that let her make her mark when she was still very young.

When Ms. Rich was in her last year at Radcliffe (she received a bachelor's degree in English there in 1951), W. H. Auden chose her first collection, "A Change of World," for publication in the Yale Younger Poets series, a signal honor. Released in 1951, the book, with its sober mien, dutiful meter and scrupulous rhymes, was praised by reviewers for its impeccable command of form.

She had learned the lessons of her father's library well, or so it seemed. For even in this volume Ms. Rich had begun, with subtle subversion, to push against a time-honored thematic constraint — the proscription on making poetry out of the soul-numbing dailiness of women's lives.

A poem in the collection, "Aunt Jennifer's Tigers," depicting a woman at her needlework and reprinted here in full, is concerned with precisely this:

Aunt Jennifer's tigers prance across a screen,
Bright topaz denizens of a world of green.
They do not fear the men beneath the tree;
They pace in sleek chivalric certainty.

Aunt Jennifer's fingers fluttering through her
*   wool*
Find even the ivory needle hard to pull.
The massive weight of Uncle's wedding band
Sits heavily upon Aunt Jennifer's hand.

When Aunt is dead, her terrified hands will lie
Still ringed with ordeals she was mastered by.
The tigers in the panel that she made
Will go on prancing, proud and unafraid.

Once mastered, poetry's formalist rigors gave Ms. Rich something to rebel against, and by her third collection, "Snapshots of a Daughter-in-Law," published by Harper & Row, she had pretty well exploded them. That volume appeared in 1963, a watershed moment in women's letters: "The Feminine Mystique" was also published that year.

In the collection's title poem, Ms. Rich chronicles the pulverizing onus of traditional married life. It opens this way:

You, once a belle in Shreveport,
with henna-colored hair, skin like a
peachbud,
still have your dresses copied from that time,
. . .
Your mind now, mouldering like
wedding-cake,
heavy with useless experience, rich
with suspicion, rumor, fantasy,
crumbling to pieces under the knife-edge
of mere fact. In the prime of your life.

Though the book horrified some critics, it sealed Ms. Rich's national reputation.

She knew the strain of domestic duty firsthand. In 1953 Ms. Rich had married a Harvard economist, Alfred Haskell Conrad, and by the time she was 30 she was the mother of three small boys. When Professor Conrad took a job at the City College of New York, the family moved to New York City, where Ms. Rich became active in the civil rights and antiwar movements.

By 1970, partly because she had begun, inwardly, to acknowledge her erotic love of women, Ms. Rich and her husband had grown estranged. That autumn, he died of a gunshot wound to the head; the death was ruled a suicide. To the end of her life, Ms. Rich rarely spoke of it.

Ms. Rich effectively came out as a lesbian in 1976, with the publication of "Twenty-One Love Poems," whose subject matter — sexual love between women — was still considered disarming and dangerous. In the years that followed her poetry and prose ranged over her increasing self-identification as a Jewish woman, the Holocaust and the struggles of black women.

Ms. Rich's other volumes of poetry include "The Dream of a Common Language" (1978), "A Wild Patience Has Taken Me This Far" (1981), "The Fact of a Doorframe" (1984), "An Atlas of the Difficult World" (1991) and, most recently, "Tonight No Poetry Will Serve," published in 2011.

Her prose includes the essay collections "On Lies, Secrets, and Silence" (1979); "Blood, Bread, and Poetry" (1986); an influential essay, "Compulsory Heterosexuality and Lesbian Existence," published as a slender volume in 1981; and the nonfiction book "Of Woman Born" (1976), which examines the institution of motherhood as a socio-historic construct.

For Ms. Rich, the getting of literary awards was itself a political act to be reckoned with. On sharing the National Book Award for poetry in 1974 (the other recipient that year was Allen Ginsberg), she declined to accept it on her own behalf. Instead, she appeared onstage with two of that year's finalists, the poets Audre Lorde and Alice Walker; the three of them accepted the award on behalf of all women.

In 1997, in a widely reported act, Ms. Rich declined the National Medal of Arts, the United States government's highest award bestowed upon artists. In a letter to Jane Alexander, then chairwoman of the National Endowment for the Arts, which administers the award, she expressed her dismay, amid the "increasingly brutal impact of racial and economic injustice," that the government had chosen to honor "a few token artists while the people at large are so dishonored."

Art, Ms. Rich added, "means nothing if it simply decorates the dinner table of power which holds it hostage."

Ms. Rich's other laurels — and these she did accept — include the Bollingen Prize for Poetry, the Academy of American Poets Fellowship and the Ruth Lilly Poetry Prize.

She taught widely, including at Columbia, Brandeis, Rutgers, Cornell and Stanford Universities.

Ms. Rich died of complications of rheumatoid arthritis, with which she had lived for most of her adult life. Her survivors include her partner of more than 30 years, the writer Michelle Cliff; three sons from her marriage to Professor Conrad; a sister; and two grandchildren.

For all her verbal prowess, for all her prolific output, Ms. Rich retained a dexterous command of the plain, pithy utterance. In a 1984 speech she summed up her reason for writing — and, by loud unspoken implication, her reason for being — in just seven words.

What she and her sisters-in-arms were fighting to achieve, she said, was simply this: "the creation of a society without domination."

— By Margalit Fox

\\\\\\\\\\\\\\\\\\\\\\\\\\\

HILTON KRAMER

Holding Aloft the High Art Banner

MARCH 25, 1928 · MARCH 27, 2012

Hilton Kramer, whose clear, incisive style and combative temperament made him one of the most influential critics of his era and a passionate defender of high art against the claims of popular culture, died on March 27 in Harpswell, Me. He was 84.

Admired for his intellectual range and feared for his imperious judgments, Mr. Kramer emerged as a critic in the early 1950s and joined The New York Times in 1965, a period when the tenets of high Modernism were being questioned and increasingly attacked. He saw himself not simply as a critic offering informed opinion on this or that artist but also as a warrior upholding the values that made civilized life worthwhile.

This stance became more marked as political art and its advocates came to the fore to ignite the culture wars of the early 1980s, a struggle in which Mr. Kramer took a leading role in 1982 as the founding editor of The New Criterion, where he was also a frequent contributor.

In its pages, Mr. Kramer took dead aim at a long list of targets: creeping populism at leading art museums; the incursion of politics into artistic production and curatorial decision-making;

the fecklessness, as he saw it, of the National Endowment for the Arts; and the decline of intellectual standards in the culture at large.

A resolute high Modernist, he was out of sympathy with many of the aesthetic waves that came after the great achievements of the New York School, notably Pop ("a very great disaster"), Conceptual art ("scrapbook art") and postmodernism ("modernism with a sneer, a giggle, modernism without any animating faith in the nobility and pertinence of its cultural mandate").

At the same time, he made it his mission to bring underappreciated artists to public attention and open up the history of 20th-century American art to include figures like David Smith, Milton Avery and Arthur Dove, about whom he wrote with insight and affection. Some of his best criticism was devoted to artists who had up until then been regarded as footnotes.

CULTURE WARRIOR: Hilton Kramer's intellectual criticism ardently defended high art.

"Nothing gives me more pleasure," he wrote in a 1999 catalog essay for the painter Bert Carpenter, "than to discover unfamiliar work of significant quality and intelligence."

Roger Kimball, editor and publisher of The New Criterion, said of Mr. Kramer: "As a critic of culture, he had a broad range. He wrote on everything from novels and poetry to dance and philosophy, but it was as an art critic that he was best known. His chief virtue was independence. He called it as he saw it — an increasingly rare virtue in today's culture."

Hilton Kramer was born on March 25, 1928, in Gloucester, Mass. As a boy he gravitated toward the local artists' colony and spent long hours in Boston's art museums.

After earning a bachelor's degree in English at Syracuse University in 1950, he studied literature and philosophy at Columbia, the New School for Social Research and Harvard.

While studying Dante and Shakespeare at the Indiana University School of Letters in the summer of 1952, he struck up an acquaintance with Philip Rahv, the editor of Partisan Review, who encouraged his critical ambitions.

Art, by pure chance, provided his entry point — specifically Harold Rosenberg's essay on action painting, published in Art News in December 1952.

Mr. Kramer regarded it, he later said, as "intellectually fraudulent."

"By defining Abstract Expressionist painting as a psychological event, it denied the aesthetic efficacy of painting itself and attempted to remove art from the only sphere in which it can be truly experienced, which is the aesthetic sphere," Mr. Kramer said in an interview on the occasion of receiving a medal from the National Endowment for the Humanities in 2004. "It reduced the art object itself to the status of a psychological datum."

He wrote a rebuttal to Mr. Rosenberg and submitted it to Partisan Review, which published it in 1953. The magazine's enormous prestige established him as an important art critic overnight, giving him, as he recalled in a 1996 essay, "a ticket to a career I wasn't yet certain I wanted." He was invited to write regular art reviews for Arts Digest, a fortnightly. Clement Greenberg, the most powerful critic of the day, asked him to write on art for Commentary.

In 1955, Arts Digest became a monthly magazine, Arts. Mr. Kramer, who was hired as its managing editor and became its chief editor in 1961, turned it into one of the most highly respected art journals in the United States. He also wrote art criticism for The New Republic and The Nation.

He married the former Esta Teich, a former assistant editor at Arts, in 1964. She is his only immediate survivor. Mr. Kramer died of heart failure. He had developed a rare blood disease and had moved to an assisted living facility in Harpswell. He and his wife lived nearby in southern Maine, in Damariscotta.

Mr. Kramer became art-news editor of The New York Times in 1965 and in January 1974 succeeded John Canaday as the newspaper's chief art critic. He was a prolific, forceful critic at a time when the art world was undergoing sweeping stylistic and institutional changes. Pop Art, Minimalism and the myriad tendencies grouped under the term postmodernism asserted their claims after the heady days of Abstract Expressionism. Museums, eager to capitalize on the public's growing appetite for modern art and enticed by the box-office success of blockbuster exhibitions, took a more populist approach to the kinds of shows they mounted and the way they presented them.

Mr. Kramer made it his mission to uphold the high standards of Modernism. In often withering prose, he made life miserable for curators and museum directors who, in his opinion, let down the side by exhibiting trendy or fashionably political art.

The Whitney Museum of American Art, in particular, felt the full force of his scorn every time it raised the curtain on a new biennial, whose roster generally favored installation, video and performance art, usually with a political message and an emphasis on gender and ethnic identity.

Mr. Kramer would have none of it. "The Whitney curatorial staff has amply demonstrated its weakness for funky, kinky, kitschy claptrap in recent years," he wrote in a review of the 1975 Biennial, "and there is the inevitable abundance of this rubbish in the current show."

Two years later, he threw his hands up in despair. The biennials, he wrote, "seem to be governed by a positive hostility toward — a really visceral distaste for — anything that might conceivably engage the eye in a significant or pleasurable visual experience."

Mr. Kramer was impassioned in his praise when art met his high expectations. "He was a high Modernist, but he embraced a rather diverse lot that ran the gamut from Richard Pousette-Dart to Pollock to Matisse to the Russian constructivists," Mr. Kimball said.

He could surprise. Julian Schnabel, precisely the sort of artist one would have expected him to eviscerate, won qualified praise. In reviewing one of Mr. Schnabel's first shows, in 1981, Mr. Kramer said he could be "a painter of remarkable powers." He would later greet with enthusiasm, at least initially, the work of the highly eccentric Norwegian figurative painter Odd Nerdrum.

"He really had a good grasp of Modernism — maybe too good a grasp, because he tended to ignore other things," the critic Donald Kuspit said of Mr. Kramer. "I admired his seriousness, although I think he became more and more frustrated with the scene, the focus on emerging artists at the expense of mature artists."

In 1982, Mr. Kramer left The Times to edit The New Criterion, a monthly journal of culture and ideas created to take a contrarian view of multiculturalism, ethnic and gender politics, and other currents coming into prominence in the arts, as well as a neoconservative take on cultural politics generally.

He plunged into acrimonious debate on cultural politics, staking out a conservative position in attacks on the artists and programs financed by the National Endowment for the Arts and the National Endowment for the Humanities, and revisiting the political debates of the McCarthy era and the 1960s.

In his mind, the battle lines were clearly drawn "in this age of irony and institutionalized subversion."

On the one side was postmodernism, "a revolt against the basic traditions of Western civilization." On the other, Modernism, whose ideals he characterized as "the discipline of truthfulness, the rigor of honesty."

In the 1990s he wrote Times Watch, a column in The New York Post devoted to criticism of what he regarded as liberal bias in The New York Times. He later broadened his focus and renamed the column Media Watch. At the same time, he wrote a weekly art column for The New York Observer.

Many of his essays on art and politics were republished in four collections, "The Age of the Avant-Garde: An Art Chronicle of 1956-1972" (1973); "The Revenge of the Philistines: Art and Culture, 1972-1984" (1985), "The Twilight of the Intellectuals: Culture and Politics in the Era of the Cold War" (1999); and "The Triumph of Modernism: The Art World, 1985-2005" (2006).

Mr. Kramer remained unfazed by the furor his criticism aroused and professed to be somewhat puzzled at his reputation. "I'm really not very angry at all," he told New York magazine in 1984. "I am appalled at times; astonished, disappointed, anxious, worried. I think of myself as judicious."

— By WILLIAM GRIMES

HARRY CREWS

The Man Who Ate a Car, and Other Tales

JUNE 7, 1935 · MARCH 28, 2012

Harry Crews, whose novels out-Gothic Southern Gothic by conjuring a world of hard-drinking, punch-throwing, snake-oil-selling characters whose physical, mental, social and sexual deviations render them somehow entirely normal and eminently sympathetic, died on March 28

at his home in Gainesville, Fla. He was 76.

A Georgia-born Rabelais, Mr. Crews was renowned for darkly comic, bitingly satirical, grotesquely populated and almost preternaturally violent novels.

Though his books captivated many reviewers, they were not the stuff of best-seller lists, in part because they bewildered some readers and repelled others. But they attracted a cadre of fans so fiercely devoted that the phrase "cult following" seems inadequate to describe their ardor.

Mr. Crews came to wide notice with his first novel, "The Gospel Singer," published in 1968. The book, about a traveling evangelist who meets a lurid fate in a Georgia town, features characters of the sort that would people his dozen later novels: sideshow freaks, an escaped lunatic and a sociopath or two.

"You don't intend to make a career out of midgets, do you?" Mr. Crews's wife asked him early in his writing life.

Indeed he did. Besides midgets, later novels feature a 600-pound man who consumes titanic quantities of the diet drink Metrecal ("Naked in Garden Hills," 1969); a woman who sings tenderly to her dead husband's skull ("Scar Lover," 1992); and, perhaps most famously, a man who eats an automobile — a 1971 Ford Maverick, to be exact — four ounces in a sitting ("Car," 1972).

Alcohol loomed large in Mr. Crews's body of work, as it did for many years in his corporeal body. Once, on assignment for a magazine in Alaska — he wrote regular essays for Playboy and Esquire in the 1970s — he awoke after a liquid night to find himself in possession of a tattoo (a "hinge" inside his elbow) that he did not have before.

Despite their teeming decadence, or more likely because of it, Mr. Crews's novels betray a fundamental empathy, chronicling his characters' search for meaning in a dissolute, end-stage world. His ability to spin out a dark, glittering thread from this tangle of souls gave him a singular voice that could make his prose riveting.

"A Feast of Snakes" (1976), which concerns a town's obsessive annual ritual — a rattlesnake rodeo — and is considered by many critics to be his finest novel, opens this way:

"She felt the snake between her breasts, felt him there, and loved him there, coiled, the deep tumescent S held rigid, ready to strike. She loved the way the snake looked sewn onto her V-neck letter sweater, his hard diamondback pattern shining in the sun. It was unseasonably hot, almost sixty degrees, for early November in Mystic, Georgia, and she could smell the light musk of her own sweat. She liked the sweat, liked the way it felt, slick as oil, in all the joints of her body, her bones, in the firm sliding muscles, tensed and locked now, ready to spring — to strike — when the band behind her fired up the school song: 'Fight On Deadly Rattlers of Old Mystic High.'"

Mr. Crews was renowned for darkly comic, bitingly satirical, grotesquely populated and almost preternaturally violent novels of the South.

To critics who taxed him with sensationalism, Mr. Crews — a plainspoken ex-Marine, ex-boxer, ex-bouncer and ex-barker — replied, in effect, that it took decadence to lampoon decadence. His actual replies are largely unprintable.

What was clear from his interviews, and grew clearer still with the publication of his acclaimed memoir, "A Childhood: The Biography of a Place" (1978), was that for freakish drama, deep tragedy and the blackest of black comedy, anything in Mr. Crews's fiction was resoundingly eclipsed by the facts of his own life.

Harry Eugene Crews was born on June 7, 1935, in Alma, Ga., a rural community near the Okefenokee Swamp where, he later wrote, "there wasn't enough cash money in the county to close up a dead man's eyes." There was rarely enough to eat; local people supplemented their diet with clay for the minerals it contained.

His father, Ray, a tenant farmer, died before Harry was 2. Not long afterward his mother, Myrtice, married Ray's brother, a violent alcoholic.

"We lived on a series of tenant farms," Mr. Crews told The New York Times in 1978. "The kinds of places where you could lay awake at night and look through the roof and see the stars and you could fish for chickens through the big wide cracks in the floor by tying a piece of tobacco twine to a fish hook."

Young Harry loved stories, but there were few books to be had. Instead, his narrative gifts took root in the Sears, Roebuck catalog. "Things were so awful in the house that I'd fantasize about the people in the catalog," he said in the same interview. "They all looked so good and clean and perfect, and then I'd write little stories about them."

When Harry was about 5, an illness, possibly polio, paralyzed his legs for a time, causing them to fold up behind him in unremitting spasm. A parade of family, faith healers and the merely curious passed before his sickbed, gawking, he later said, as if he were something in a carnival.

About a year later, recovered from his illness, he fell into a cauldron of scalding water used to slough the skin off slaughtered hogs. It sloughed off his skin. Once more, he was bedridden.

At 17, he joined the Marine Corps, serving three years. Afterward, on the G.I. Bill, he attended the University of Florida in Gainesville, where he studied with the noted Southern novelist Andrew Lytle. He earned a bachelor's degree in literature from the university in 1960, followed by a master's in education there. Before retiring in the 1990s, Mr. Crews taught writing there for many years. He died of complications of neuropathy.

In early 1960 Mr. Crews married a classmate, Sally Ellis. They divorced at the end of 1961 but remarried the next year. They had two sons, one of whom died in a drowning accident at 4. The couple divorced again in 1972. Mr. Crews is survived by a son, a brother and a grandson.

His other books include the novels "The Hawk Is Dying" (1973), "The Gypsy's Curse" (1974), "The Knockout Artist" (1988) and "Celebration" (1998), as well as essay and short-story collections.

For many years, as Mr. Crews openly discussed in interviews, alcohol was his anesthetic of choice. He stopped drinking in the late 1980s.

"I had an ex-wife and I had an ex-kid and I had an ex-dog and I had an ex-house and I'm an ex-drunk," he told The Times in 2006. "I've supported whores and dopers and drunks and bartenders. Thank God I don't do that anymore."

— By MARGALIT FOX

LOU GOLDSTEIN

Simon Says, Read This Obit

SEPT. 8, 1921 - APRIL 2, 2012

Lou GOLDSTEIN was the consummate tummler, one of a zany species of entertainer who kept them laughing, or tried to, long ago in the borscht belt hotels of the Catskills.

A tummler (pronounced TOOM-ler) — the title comes from a Yiddish word for someone who stirs up tumult or excitement — was a jack-of-all-trades social director who was supposed to entertain hotel guests as they sat by the pool, say, or headed for bingo by telling jokes, singing songs and performing a shtick that might better be described as slapshtick.

Perhaps the classic illustration was given by Mel Brooks, himself a former tummler.

"A tummler wakes up the Jews when they fall asleep around the pool after lunch," Mr. Brooks said. "One of the things I had to do as the pool tummler was, I used to do an act. I wore a derby and an alpaca coat, and I would carry two rock-laden cardboard suitcases and go to the edge of the diving board and say, 'Business is no good!' and jump off."

But Mr. Goldstein was more than a tummler. He was also famous as an impresario of Simon Says, a commanding figure (in a manner of speaking) in a game beloved by children and not a few adults. His act appeared on national television and in sports arenas (at halftime).

He died on April 2 at the age of 90 and had lived in Liberty, N.Y., at the southern edge of his beloved Catskill Mountains.

Mr. Goldstein, a slender six-footer, performed his antics at Grossinger's, perhaps the premier Catskills resort, from 1948 until the hotel closed in 1986. He'd hold absurd exercise classes. He'd have a circle of grown men don silly hats and maneuver them onto one another's heads using only one hand, the object being to keep the hats from tumbling to the ground. He'd tell jokes during pauses in a diving exhibition, or tell stories on tours of the Grossinger's grounds and kitchens (one for meat and one for dairy).

"He used to joke that the tour was 45 minutes and all downhill," said Douglas Lyons, 64, a lawyer and son of the columnist Leonard Lyons. The younger Mr. Lyons went to Grossinger's every summer from the time he was a baby until 1980, and Mr. Goldstein, he said, was the annual highlight.

In addition to Mr. Brooks, world-class comedians like Danny Kaye, Sid Caesar and Red Buttons put in summers as tummlers, according to "The Haunted Smile: The Story of Jewish Comedians in America," by Lawrence J. Epstein. Mr. Goldstein did stand-up routines as well, more than a few with borrowed jokes. There was the one about the mother whose son excitedly announces that he has been picked for the part of the Jewish husband in a school play. The mother replies, "You tell the teacher you want a speaking part."

But his forte became the Simon Says routines. (He spelled it Simon Sez.) Contestants stayed in the game as long as they did only what Simon told them to do, of course, and Mr. Goldstein, with a rapid-fire delivery, was masterly at tricking them into doing what Simon had actually kept mum about.

As his renown spread, he began performing the act on "Wide World of Sports," "The Mike Douglas Show," ABC's "Superstars" and other television shows, sometimes with sports celebrities like Reggie Jackson. He carried his act to professional basketball games, cruise ships and corporate and charity events like the Special Olympics.

"Simon says, move to your right," he would tell a group, or, "Simon says, jump up in the air," then whisper to a too-satisfied participant, "By the way, what's your name?" When the person answered, Mr. Goldstein would reply in a mock gruff voice. "You're out!"

Corny as it was, there was something about his patter, with its grumpy Yiddish inflection, that charmed.

"They watched him more than listened to him, and if you watched him he would do the opposite and you would be out," his wife, Jackie Horner, said.

For his talents, Mr. Goldstein earned $600 a week and room and board at a hotel whose Jewish dishes were legendary for both their taste and their size. At one point the singer Eddie Fisher was his roommate.

Mr. Goldstein, the son of a tailor, was born on Sept. 8, 1921, in a small town outside Warsaw. The family emigrated when he was 5 and settled in the Williamsburg section of Brooklyn.

He was a basketball standout at Eastern District High School in Brooklyn and Long Island University. When the Catskill hotels started basketball tournaments to entertain guests, Grossinger's recruited him. And when he proved adept at other forms of entertainment, the hotel signed him up as its tummler.

Ms. Horner, who was a consultant and something of an inspiration for "Dirty Dancing," the 1987 film about a mountain resort not too different from Grossinger's, said she and

BORSCHT BELT IMPRESARIO: Lou Goldstein, left, leading a game of "Simon Says" at Grossinger's, the popular Catskills resort, in 1985.

Mr. Goldstein met when she came there as a dance instructor. They married at Grossinger's in 1960 and lived at the hotel, in Liberty, for the many years they worked there. They stayed on in the town afterward.

Ms. Horner, her husband's only immediate survivor, has always enjoyed repeating some of Mr. Goldstein's tummler jokes, like the one about the wife who tells her husband after a bitter argument that when he dies she's going to dance on his grave. The husband goes to his lawyer the next day and asks for a new clause in his will. He wants to be buried at sea.

— By JOSEPH BERGER

\\\\\\\\\\\\\\\\\\\\\\\\\

ELIZABETH CATLETT

The Black Experience in Clay and Stone

APRIL 15, 1915 · APRIL 2, 2012

ELIZABETH CATLETT, whose abstracted sculptures of the human form reflected her deep concern with the African-American experience and the struggle for civil rights, died in her sleep on April 2 at her home in Cuernavaca, Mexico, where she had lived since the late 1940s. She was 96.

In creating smoothly modeled clay, wood and stone sculptures and vigorous woodcuts and linocuts, Ms. Catlett drew on her experience as an African-American woman who had come of age at a time of widespread segregation and had felt its sting. But her art had other influences, including pre-Columbian sculpture, Henry Moore's sensuous reclining nudes and Diego Rivera's political murals.

Her best-known works depict black women as strong, maternal figures. In one early sculpture, "Mother and Child" (1939), a young woman with close-cropped hair and features resembling a Gabon mask cradles a child against her shoulder. It won first prize in sculpture at the American Negro Exposition in Chicago. In "Bather" (2009), a similar-looking subject flexes her triceps in a gesture of vitality and confidence.

Her work did not exclude men; "Invisible Man," her 15-foot-high bronze memorial to the author Ralph Ellison, can be seen in Riverside Park in Manhattan, at 150th Street.

Her art was often presented in major surveys in the United States, among them "Two Centuries of Black American Art" at the Los Angeles County Museum of Art in 1976. Her posters of Harriet Tubman, Angela Davis, Malcolm X and other figures were widely distributed.

Alice Elizabeth Catlett was born on April 15, 1915, in Washington, the youngest of three children. Her mother, the former Mary Carson, was a truant officer; her father, John, who died before she was born, had taught at Tuskegee University and in the local public school system.

Ms. Catlett became an educator, too. After graduating cum laude from Howard University in 1935, she taught high school in Durham, N.C.

Howard hadn't been her first choice. She had won a scholarship to the Carnegie Institute of Technology, in Pittsburgh, but the college refused to allow her to matriculate when it learned she was black. So she entered historically black Howard, with one semester's worth of tuition saved by her mother. She earned scholarships to cover the rest.

An interest in the painter Grant Wood led her to pursue an M.F.A. at the University of Iowa, where Wood was teaching. There she focused on stone carvings rooted in her own experience — sensitive portraits of African-American women and children.

EQUAL PARTS: Elizabeth Catlett's art balanced abstraction and realism.

After graduating she moved to New Orleans to teach at Dillard University, another historically black institution. There she organized a trip to the Delgado Museum of Art so that her students could see a Picasso exhibition. But this was no ordinary school trip; the museum was officially off-limits to blacks, so Ms. Catlett arranged to visit on a day when it was closed to the public.

While on a summer break from Dillard, she met the artist Charles White in Chicago. They married in 1941 and divorced five years later.

She left New Orleans for New York to study with the Russian-born sculptor Ossip Zadkine. Mr. Zadkine, who spent his formative years in Montparnasse alongside Modigliani and Brancusi, nudged her work in a more abstract direction. During this time, the early 1940s, Ms. Catlett also worked in adult education at the George Washington Carver School in Harlem, a program that nurtured the photographer Roy DeCarava, among others.

In 1946 Ms. Catlett traveled to Mexico on a fellowship. There she married the artist Francisco Mora and accepted an invitation to work at Taller de Gráfica Popular (TGP), a workshop in Mexico City for murals and graphic arts. The TGP inspired her to reach out to the broadest possible audience, which often meant balancing abstraction with figuration.

"I learned how you use your art for the service of people, struggling people, to whom only realism is meaningful," she later said.

Like other artists and activists, Ms. Catlett felt the political tensions of the McCarthy years. The TGP was thought to have ties to the Communist Party; Ms. Catlett never joined the party, but Mr. White, her first husband, had been a member, and she was closely watched by the United States Embassy.

In 1949 she was arrested, along with other expatriates, during a railroad workers' strike in Mexico City. Eventually she gave up her American citizenship and was declared an undesirable alien by the State Department. In 1971 she had to obtain a special visa to attend the opening of her one-woman show at the Studio Museum in Harlem.

Ms. Catlett continued to teach even after becoming a successful artist. In 1958 she became the first female professor of sculpture and head of the sculpture department at the National Autonomous University of Mexico's School of Fine Arts in Mexico City. She retired to Cuernavaca, about 35 miles southwest of Mexico City, in 1975.

Ms. Catlett's art is in museums around the world, including the Museum of Modern Art and the Metropolitan Museum of Art in

New York; the High Museum in Atlanta; the Museum of Modern Art in Mexico City; and the National Museum of Prague. In 2003, the International Sculpture Center gave her a lifetime achievement award.

Mr. Mora, her husband, died in 2002. She is survived by three sons, 10 grandchildren and six great-grandchildren.

In 1998, the Neuberger Museum of Art at Purchase College in Westchester County exhibited a 50-year retrospective of Ms. Catlett's sculpture. The critic Michael Brenson wrote in the show's catalog, "Ms. Catlett's sculptures communicate a deeply human image of African-Americans while appealing to values and virtues that encourage a sense of common humanity." He also singled out the "fluid, sensual surfaces" of her sculptures, which he said "seem to welcome not just the embrace of light but also the caress of the viewer's hand."

In his review of that show for The New York Times, Ken Johnson wrote that Ms. Catlett "gives wood and stone a melting, almost erotic luminosity." But he also found her iconography "generic and clichéd."

Last year, the Bronx Museum mounted "Stargazers: Elizabeth Catlett in Conversation With 21 Contemporary Artists," an exhibition that placed her sculptures, prints and drawings in the company of works by Ellen Gallagher, Kalup Linzy, Wangechi Mutu and others at the forefront of the contemporary art scene.

In her own words, Ms. Catlett was more concerned with the social dimension of her art than its novelty or originality. As she told a former student, the artist and art historian Samella S. Lewis, "I have always wanted my art to service my people — to reflect us, to relate to us, to stimulate us, to make us aware of our potential."

— BY KAREN ROSENBERG

MIKE WALLACE

On '60 Minutes,' a Weekly Grilling

MAY 9, 1918 - APRIL 7, 2012

MIKE WALLACE, the CBS reporter who became one of America's best-known broadcast journalists as an interrogator of the famous and infamous on "60 Minutes," died on April 7 in New Canaan, Conn., where he had lived in recent years. He was 93.

A reporter with the presence of a performer, Mr. Wallace went head to head with chiefs of state, celebrities and con artists for more than 50 years, living for that moment when "you forget the lights, the cameras, everything else, and you're really talking to each other," he said in a 2006 interview videotaped for the New York Times online feature "The Last Word."

Mr. Wallace created enough of those moments to become a paragon of television journalism in the heyday of network news. His success often lay in the questions he hurled, not the answers he received.

"Perjury," he said, in his staccato style, to President Richard M. Nixon's right-hand man, John D. Ehrlichman, while interviewing him during the Watergate affair. "Plans to audit tax returns for political retaliation. Theft of psychiatric records. Spying by undercover agents. Conspiracy to obstruct justice. All of this by the law-and-order administration of Richard Nixon."

Mr. Ehrlichman paused and said, "Is there a question in there somewhere?"

IN GOOD COMPANY: Mike Wallace, second from right, with the producer Don Hewitt and two fellow "60 Minutes" correspondents, Morely Safer and Dan Rather. It was just one of the many news shows he'd work on at CBS.

No, Mr. Wallace later conceded. But it was riveting television.

Both the style and the substance of his work drew criticism. CBS paid Nixon's chief of staff H. R. Haldeman $100,000 for exclusive, if inconclusive, interviews with Mr. Wallace in 1975. Critics called it checkbook journalism, and Mr. Wallace later conceded that it had been "a bad idea."

For a 1976 report on Medicaid fraud, the show's producers set up a simulated health clinic in Chicago. Was the use of deceit to expose deceit justified? Hidden cameras and ambush interviews were all part of the game, Mr. Wallace said, though he abandoned those techniques in later years, when they became clichés and no longer good television.

Some subjects were unfazed by Mr. Wallace's blunt methods and unblinking stare. Interviewing the Ayatollah Ruhollah Khomeini, the Iranian leader, in 1979, Mr. Wallace remarked that President Anwar el-Sadat of Egypt had called Mr. Khomeini —

"forgive me, his words, not mine — a lunatic." The translator blanched, but the Ayatollah responded calmly, calling Sadat a heretic.

"Forgive me" was a favorite Wallace phrase, the caress before the garrote. "As soon as you hear that," he said in the Times interview, "you realize the nasty question's about to come." As he grilled his subjects, he said, he walked "a fine line between sadism and intellectual curiosity."

Mr. Wallace invented his hard-boiled persona on an interview program called "Night Beat," which was broadcast weeknights at 11 on the New York affiliate of the short-lived DuMont television network beginning in 1956.

"We had lighting that was warts-and-all close-ups," he remembered. The camera closed in tighter and tighter on the guests. The smoke from Mr. Wallace's cigarette swirled between him and his quarry. Sweat beaded on his subjects' brows.

"I was asking tough questions," he said. "And I had found my bliss." He had become Mike Wallace.

"All of a sudden," he said, "I was no longer anonymous." In the words of Michael J. Arlen, The New Yorker's television critic, Mr. Wallace had become "the fiery prosecutor, the righteous and wrathful D.A. determined to rid Gotham City of its undesirables."

"Night Beat" moved to ABC in 1957 as a half-hour, coast-to-coast, prime-time program, renamed "The Mike Wallace Interview." ABC, then the perennial loser among the major networks, promoted him as "the Terrible Torquemada of the TV Inquisition."

ABC canceled "The Mike Wallace Interview" in 1958 and Mr. Wallace's career path meandered afterward. He had done entertainment shows and quiz shows and cigarette commercials. He had acted onstage. But now he resolved to become a real journalist after a harrowing journey to recover the body of his firstborn son, Peter, who died at 19 in a mountain-climbing accident in Greece in 1962.

"He was going to be a writer," Mr. Wallace said in the Times interview. "And so I said, 'I'm going to do something that would make Peter proud.'"

He set his sights on CBS News and joined the network as a special correspondent. He was soon anchoring "The CBS Morning News With Mike Wallace" and reporting from Vietnam. Then he caught the eye of Richard Nixon.

Running for president, Nixon offered Mr. Wallace a job as his press secretary shortly before the 1968 primaries began. "I thought very, very seriously about it," Mr. Wallace said. "I regarded him with great respect. He was savvy, smart, hard working."

But Mr. Wallace turned Nixon down, saying he had no desire to put a happy face on bad news for a living. Only months later, "60 Minutes" made its debut, at 10 p.m. on Tuesday, Sept. 24, 1968.

It was something new on the air: a "newsmagazine," usually three substantial pieces of about 15 minutes each — a near-eternity on television. Mr. Wallace and Harry Reasoner were the first co-hosts, one fierce, one folksy.

The show was the brainchild of Don Hewitt, a producer who was "in bad odor at CBS News at the time," Mr. Wallace said in the interview.

"He was unpredictable, difficult to work with, genius notions, a genuine adventurer, if you will, in television news at that time." Mr. Hewitt died in 2009.

The show, which moved to Sunday nights at 7 in 1975, was slow to catch on. Meanwhile Mr. Wallace fought his fellow correspondents for stories and airtime and developed, as he put it, the "not necessarily undeserved reputation" for being prickly — he used a stronger word — and for "stealing stories from my colleagues," who came to include Morley Safer, Ed Bradley, Dan Rather and Diane Sawyer in the 1970s and early '80s.

"This was just competition," he said. "Get the story. Get it first."

Mr. Wallace and his teams of producers — who researched, reported and wrote the stories — took on American Nazis and nuclear power plants through his patented brand of exposé.

The time was ripe for investigative television journalism. Watergate and its seamy sideshows had made muckraking a respectable trade. By the late 1970s, "60 Minutes" was the top-rated show on Sundays. Five different years it was the No. 1 show on television, a feat matched only by the sitcoms "All in the Family" and "The Cosby Show." In 1977, it began a 23-year run in the top 10. No show of any kind has matched that.

Mr. Wallace was rich and famous and a powerful figure in television news when his life took a stressful turn in 1982. That year he anchored a "CBS Reports" documentary called "The Uncounted Enemy: A Vietnam Deception." It led to a $120 million libel suit filed by Gen. William C. Westmoreland, the commander of American troops in Vietnam from 1964 to 1968. At issue was the show's assertion that General Westmoreland had deliberately falsified the "order of battle," the estimate of the strength of the enemy.

The question turned on a decision that American military commanders made in 1967. The uniformed military said the enemy was no more than 300,000 strong, but intelligence analysts said the number could be half a million or more. If the analysts were correct, then there was no "light at the end of the tunnel," the optimistic phrase General Westmoreland had used.

Documents declassified after the cold war showed that the general's top aide had cited reasons of politics and public relations for insisting on the lower figure. The military was "stonewalling, obviously under orders" from General Westmoreland, a senior Central Intelligence Agency analyst cabled his headquarters; the "predetermined total" was "fixed on publicrelations grounds," the analyst said. The C.I.A. officially accepted the military's invented figure of 299,000 enemy forces or fewer.

The documentary asserted that rather than a politically expedient lie, the struggle revealed a vast conspiracy to suppress the truth. The key theorist for that case, Sam Adams, a former C.I.A. analyst, was not only interviewed for the documentary but also received a consultant's fee of $25,000. The program had arrived at something close to the truth, but it had used questionable means to reach it.

After more than two years General Westmoreland abandoned his suit, CBS lost some of its reputation, and Mr. Wallace had a nervous breakdown.

He said at the time that he feared "the lawyers for the other side would employ the same techniques against me that I had employed on television." Already on antidepressants, which gave him tremors, he had a waking nightmare sitting through the trial.

"I could see myself up there on the stand, six feet away from the jury, with my hands shaking, and dying to drink water," he said in the Times interview. He imagined the jury thinking, "Well, that son of a bitch is obviously guilty as hell."

He attempted suicide. "I was so low that I wanted to exit," Mr. Wallace said. "And I took a bunch of pills, and they were sleeping pills. And at least they would put me to sleep, and maybe I wouldn't wake up, and that was fine."

Later in life he discussed his depression and advocated psychiatric and psychopharmaceutical treatment.

A paragon of television journalism in the heyday of network news.

The despair and anger he felt over the documentary were outdone 13 years later when, as he put it in a memoir, "the corporate management of CBS emasculated a '60 Minutes' documentary I had done just as we were preparing to put it on the air."

The cutting involved a damning interview with Jeffrey Wigand, a chemist who had been director of research at Brown & Williamson, the tobacco company. Mr. Wigand said on camera that the nation's tobacco executives had been lying when they swore under oath before Congress that they believed nicotine was not addictive. Among many complicating factors, one of those executives was the son of Laurence A. Tisch, the chairman of CBS at the time. The full interview was eventually broadcast in 1996.

Mr. Wallace remained bitter at Mr. Tisch's stewardship, which ended when he sold CBS in

1995, after dismissing many employees and dismantling some of its parts.

"We thought that he would be happy to be the inheritor of all of the — forgive me — glory of CBS and CBS News," Mr. Wallace said. "And the glory was not as attractive to him as money. He began to tear apart CBS News." Mr. Tisch died in 2003.

Mr. Wallace officially retired from "60 Minutes" in 2006, after a 38-year run, at the age of 88. A few months later he was back on the program with an exclusive interview with the president of Iran, Mahmoud Ahmadinejad. He won his 21st Emmy for the interview.

And he kept working. Only weeks before his 2008 bypass surgery, he interviewed the baseball star Roger Clemens as accusations swirled that Mr. Clemens had used performance-enhancing drugs. It was Mr. Wallace's last appearance on television, CBS said.

Myron Leon Wallace was born in Brookline, Mass., on May 9, 1918, one of four children of Friedan and Zina Wallik, who had come to the United States from a Russian shtetl before the turn of the 20th century. (Friedan became Frank and Wallik became Wallace in the American melting pot.) His father started as a wholesale grocer and became an insurance broker.

Myron came out of Brookline High School with a B-minus average and worked his way through the University of Michigan, graduating in 1939. (Decades later he was deeply involved in two national programs for journalists based at the university: the Livingston Awards, given to talented reporters under 35, and the Knight-Wallace fellowships, a sabbatical for midcareer reporters; its seminars are held at Wallace House, which he purchased for the programs.)

After he graduated from college, Mr. Wallace went almost immediately into radio, starting at $20 a week at a station with the call letters WOOD-WASH in Grand Rapids, Mich. (It was jointly owned by a furniture trade association, a lumber company and a laundry.) He went on to Detroit and Chicago stations as narrator and actor on shows like "The Lone Ranger," taking "Mike" as his broadcast name.

In 1943 he enlisted in the Navy, did a tour of duty in the Pacific and wound up as a lieutenant junior grade in charge of radio entertainment at the Great Lakes Naval Training Station.

Mr. Wallace married his first wife, Norma Kaphan, in 1940; they were divorced in 1948. Besides Peter, who died in the mountain-climbing accident, they had a second son, Chris Wallace, the television journalist now at Fox News.

Mr. Wallace and his second wife, Buff Cobb, an actress, were married in 1949 and took to the air together in a talk show called "Mike and Buff," which appeared first on radio and then television. "We overdid the controversy pattern of the program," she said after their divorce in 1954. "You get into a habit of bickering a little, and you carry it over into your personal lives." Ms. Cobb died in 2010.

His marriage to his third wife, Lorraine Perigord, which lasted 28 years, ended with her departure for Fiji. His fourth wife, Mary Yates, was the widow of one of his best friends — his "Night Beat" producer, Ted Yates, who died in 1967 while on assignment for NBC News during the 1967 Arab-Israeli war.

Besides his wife and his son Chris, Mr. Wallace is survived by a stepdaughter, two stepsons, seven grandchildren and four great grandchildren.

Mr. Wallace and Ms. Yates were married in 1986 and lived for a time in a Park Avenue duplex in Manhattan and in a bay-front house on Martha's Vineyard, where their social circle included the novelist William Styron and the humorist Art Buchwald.

All three men "suffered depression simultaneously," Mr. Wallace said in an interview in 2006, "so we walked around in the rain together on Martha's Vineyard and consoled each other," adding, "We named ourselves the Blues Brothers." Mr. Styron died in 2006 and Mr. Buchwald in 2007.

Mr. Wallace said that Ms. Yates had saved his life when he came close to suicide before they married, and that their marriage had saved him afterward.

He died at a care facility in New Canaan. Mr. Wallace had a long history of cardiac care, receiving a pacemaker more than 20 years ago and undergoing triple bypass heart surgery in January 2008.

He had known since he was a child that he wanted to be on the air, he said. He felt it was his calling. He said he wanted people to ask: "Who's this guy, Myron Wallace?"

— By Tim Weiner

JONATHAN FRID

Vampire of the Afternoon

DEC. 2, 1924 · APRIL 14, 2012

Jonathan Frid, a Shakespearean actor who found unexpected — and by his own account unwanted — celebrity as the vampire Barnabas Collins on the sanguinary soap opera "Dark Shadows," died on April 14 in Hamilton, Ontario. He was 87.

Though the befanged Mr. Frid was the acknowledged public face of "Dark Shadows" — his likeness was on comic books, board games, trading cards and many other artifacts — Barnabas did not make his first appearance until more than 200 episodes into the run. The character was conceived as a short-term addition to the cast, and early on the threat of the stake loomed large.

Broadcast on weekday afternoons on ABC, "Dark Shadows" began in 1966 as a conventional soap opera (with Gothic overtones), centering on the Collins family and their creaky manse in Maine.

The next year, with ratings slipping, the show's executive producer, Dan Curtis, chose to inject an element of the supernatural. Enter Barnabas, a brooding, lovelorn, eternally 175-year-old representative of the undead. Today TV vampires are legion, but such a character was an unusual contrivance then.

The ratings shot up, and not only among the traditional soap-opera demographic of stay-at-home women. With its breathtakingly low-rent production values and equally breathtakingly purple dialogue, "Dark Shadows" induced a generation of high school and college students to cut class to revel in its unintended high camp. The producers shelved the stake.

Swirling cape, haunted eyes and fierce eyebrows notwithstanding, Barnabas, as portrayed by Mr. Frid, was no regulation-issue vampire. An 18th-century man — he had been entombed in the Collins family crypt

— he struggled to comes to terms with the 20th-century world.

He was a vulnerable vampire, who pined for his lost love, Josette. (She had leaped to her death in 1795.) He was racked with guilt over his thirst for blood, and Mr. Frid played him as a man in the grip of a compulsion he devoutly wished to shake.

Mr. Frid starred in almost 600 episodes, from April 18, 1967, to April 2, 1971, when the show went off the air. (It remains perennially undead on DVD.) Along with several castmates, he made a cameo appearance in Tim Burton's feature film "Dark Shadows," released in May 2012, with Johnny Depp playing Barnabas.

Mr. Frid received nearly 6,000 fan letters a week. "I wish you'd bite ME on the neck," read one, from a woman in Illinois.

Others contained snapshots of the letter-writers' necks — and everything on down — laid bare.

All this, Mr. Frid said in 1968, was exquisitely ironic in that "the other vampires we've had on the show were much more voluptuous biters than I am."

It was also an exquisitely unimagined career path for a stage actor trained at the Yale School of Drama and the Royal Academy of Dramatic Art in London. Mr. Frid, as he made plain in interviews, was as conflicted about his calling as Barnabas was about his own.

The son of a prosperous construction executive, John Herbert Frid was born in Hamilton on Dec. 2, 1924; he changed his given name to Jonathan early in his stage career.

After service in the Royal Canadian Navy in World War II, Mr. Frid received a bachelor's degree from McMaster University in Hamilton;

GOTHIC GROUNDBREAKER:
Jonathan Frid played the first popular TV vampire.

he later moved to London, where he studied at the Royal Academy and appeared in repertory theater. In 1957, he earned a master's degree in directing from Yale.

Mr. Frid spent his early career acting in North American regional theater, appearing at the Williamstown Theater Festival in Massachusetts and the American Shakespeare Festival in Stratford, Conn. On Broadway, he played Richard Scroop, Archbishop of York, in "Henry IV, Part 2" in 1960.

Long after "Dark Shadows" ended, Barnabas remained an albatross. Mr. Frid reprised the role in the 1970 feature film "House of Dark Shadows"; the few other screen roles that came his way also tended toward the ghoulish. He starred opposite Shelley Winters in the 1973 TV movie "The Devil's Daughter," about Satanism; the next year he played a horror writer in "Seizure," Oliver Stone's first feature.

Returning to the stage, Mr. Frid played Jonathan Brewster — a role originated by Boris Karloff — in a 1986 Broadway revival of the macabre comedy "Arsenic and Old Lace."

Mr. Frid, who died of complications of a fall, lived in Ancaster, Ontario, and left no immediate survivors.

As critical as he was of "Dark Shadows," Mr. Frid was equally critical of his performance in it.

"I'd get this long-lost look on my face," he told The Hamilton Spectator in 2000. "'Where is my love? Where is my love?,' it seemed to say. Actually, it was me thinking: 'Where the hell is the teleprompter? And what's my next line?'"

— By MARGALIT FOX

DICK CLARK

The Ambassador of Rock 'n' Roll

NOV. 30, 1929 - APRIL 18, 2012

DICK CLARK, the perpetually youthful-looking television host whose long-running daytime song-and-dance fest, "American Bandstand," did as much as anyone or anything to advance the influence of teenagers and rock 'n' roll on American culture, died on April 18 in Santa Monica, Calif. He was 82.

Mr. Clark had a heart attack in the morning at Saint John's Health Center after entering the hospital the night before for an outpatient procedure. He had a stroke in 2004 shortly before he was to appear on the annual televised New Year's Eve party he had produced since 1972 and hosted for most of that time. He returned a year later, and though he spoke haltingly, he continued to make brief appearances on the show, including New Year's Eve 2011.

With the boyish good looks of a bound-for-success junior executive and a ubiquitous on-camera presence, Mr. Clark was among the most recognizable faces in the world, even if what he was most famous for — spinning records and jabbering with teenagers — was on the insubstantial side. In addition to "American Bandstand" and "New Year's Rockin' Eve," he hosted innumerable awards shows, comedy specials, series based on TV outtakes and the game show "$10,000 Pyramid" (which lasted long enough to see the stakes ratcheted up to $100,000). He also made guest appearances on dramatic and comedy series, usually playing himself.

But he was as much a businessman as a television personality. "I get enormous pleasure and excitement sitting in on conferences with accountants, tax experts and lawyers," he said in an interview with The New York Times in 1961. He was especially deft at packaging entertainment products for television.

Starting in the 1960s, Mr. Clark built an entertainment empire on the shoulders of "Bandstand," producing other music shows like "Where the Action Is" and "It's Happening." He expanded into game shows, awards shows, comedy specials and series, talk shows, children's programming, reality programming, and movies. His umbrella company, Dick Clark Productions, has produced thousands of hours of television; it also has a licensing arm and has owned or operated restaurants and theaters like the Dick Clark American Bandstand Theater in Branson, Mo.

None of it would have been possible without "American Bandstand," a show that earned immediate popularity, had remarkable longevity and became a cultural touchstone for the baby-boomer generation. It helped give rise to the Top 40 radio format and helped make rock 'n' roll a palatable product for visual media — not just television but also the movies. It was influential enough that ABC broadcast a 40th-anniversary special in 1992, three years after the show went off the air, and a 50th-anniversary special 10 years later. Mr. Clark, who had long since been popularly known as "the world's oldest teen-ager," was the host of both tributes, of course.

"American Bandstand" was broadcast nationally, originally from Philadelphia, from 1957 to 1989, offering a stage to generations of performers, from Ritchie Valens to Luther Vandross; from the Monkees to Madonna; from Little Anthony and the Imperials to Los Lobos; from Dusty Springfield to Buffalo Springfield to Rick Springfield (many of them lip-syncing their recently recorded hits). Mr. Clark was around for it all.

"It meant everything to do Dick's show," Paul Anka said in a telephone interview after Mr. Clark's death. "This was a time when there was no youth culture — he created it. And the impact of the show on people was enormous. You knew that once you went down to Philadelphia to see Dick, and you went on the show, your song went from nowhere to the Top 10."

"American Bandstand's" influence began waning in 1963, when it changed from a week-day to a weekly format, appearing on Saturday afternoons, and moved its base of operations to Los Angeles the next year. As the psychedelic era took hold in the late 1960s, and rock 'n' roll fragmented into subgenres, the show no longer commanded a central role in the pop music scene.

Though the show was criticized for sani-tizing rock 'n' roll, at heart a sexualized and rebellious music, it was on the leading edge of integrating the dance floor; much of the music, after all, was being made by black performers.

"I can remember, a vivid recollection, the first time ever in my life I talked to a black teen-ager on national television; it was in what we called the rate-a-record portion of 'Bandstand,'" Mr. Clark recalled. "It was the first time in a hundred years I got sweaty palms."

He was afraid of a backlash from Southern television affiliates, he said, but that didn't

AMERICA'S FAVORITE EMCEE: With "American Bandstand," Dick Clark went from local radio personality to popular television host, becoming a media mogul along the way.

happen, and more blacks began appearing on the show. As time went on, the show's will-ingness to bridge the racial divide, which had gone almost entirely unacknowledged by net-work programming, became starkly apparent, "providing American television broadcasting with the most visible ongoing image of ethnic diversity until the 1970s," in the words of an essay about the program on the Web site of the Chicago-based Museum of Broadcast Communications.

"We didn't do it because we were do-gooders, or liberals," Mr. Clark said. "It was just a thing we thought we ought to do. It was naïve."

The right man at the right time, Mr. Clark was a radio personality in Philadelphia in 1956 when he succeeded the fired host of what was then a local television show called "Bandstand." By the following October, the show was being broadcast on ABC nationwide with a new name, "American Bandstand," and for the next several years it was seen every weekday afternoon by as many as 20 million viewers, most of them not yet out of high school. All were eager to watch a few dozen of their peers dance chastely to the latest recordings of pop hits, show off new steps like the twist, the pony and the Watusi, and rate the new records in brief interviews.

"It's got a good beat and you can dance to it" became a national catchphrase.

Handsome and glib, Dick Clark was the young's music-savvy older brother, and from that position of authority he presided over a grassroots revolution in American culture in the late 1950s and early '60s. "American Bandstand" was the first show to make use of the new technology, television, to spread the gospel of rock 'n' roll. In its early years it introduced a national audience to teen idols like Fabian and Connie Francis, first-generation rockers like Bill Haley and Jerry Lee Lewis, and singing groups like the Everly Brothers. Even more, it helped persuade broadcasters and advertisers of the power of teenagers to steer popular taste.

"At that moment in time, the world realized that kids might rule the world," Mr. Clark said. "They had their own music, their own fashion, their own money."

By early 1958, "American Bandstand" was so big a hit that network executives installed a new show in a concert format in its Saturday night lineup, calling it "The Dick Clark Show." In June, ABC sent it on the road to broadcast from a number of cities. In October, when "The Dick Clark Show" originated from Atlanta, both black and white teenagers were in the audience — making it one of the first racially integrated rock concerts — and with National Guard troops present, it weathered threats from the Ku Klux Klan. The nighttime show lasted until 1960.

In spite of his success, Mr. Clark, who never hid his desire for wealth, had not been getting rich as a network employee. But he had been investing, shrewdly and voluminously, in the businesses that "American Bandstand" supported: talent management, music publishing, record distribution and merchandising, among others. His bank account ballooned.

His finances were dealt a blow, however, and his clean-cut image was tarnished when Congress convened hearings into payola, the record company practice of bribing disc jockeys to play their records on the air. In late 1959, with the hearings pending, ABC insisted that Mr. Clark divest himself of all his record-related businesses, which he did. He was called to testify before the House Special Subcommittee on Legislative Oversight in April 1960, and though he denied ever taking money to play records, he acknowledged a number of actions that exposed what many in Congress considered a too-cozy relationship between the music industry and D.J.s, Mr. Clark in particular.

For an investment of $125 in one record company, for example, Mr. Clark received $31,700 in salary and stock profits over two years. He admitted that some songs and records may have been given to his publishing and distribution companies because of his affiliation with "American Bandstand." He also acknowledged accepting a ring and a fur stole from a record manufacturer.

Mr. Clark, who was never charged with a crime, said that having to comply with the network's divestiture request cost him millions.

"I never took any money to play records," Mr. Clark said in his 1999 Archive of American Television interview. "I made money other ways. Horizontally, vertically, every which way you can think of, I made money from that show."

Mr. Clark made millions as a producer or executive producer for more than 50 years, shepherding projects onto the airwaves that even he acknowledged were more diverting than ennobling: awards shows like the Golden Globes, the Academy of Country Music Awards and the American Music Awards; omnibus shows like "TV's Bloopers & Practical Jokes," featuring collections of clips; and television-movie biographies and dramas that targeted devotees of camp, kitsch or B-list celebrities.

He excelled in signing up top acts for his shows, and had to be especially creative on his New Year's Eve show. Top acts often had lucrative bookings that night, so Mr. Clark worked around that by taping the dance party portion of the show at a Los Angeles studio in August.

"You would go out there and see all these people in their New Year's Eve outfits getting a smoke outside in 100-degree heat," said Ted Harbert, then an ABC program executive and now chairman of NBC Broadcasting. "That's how he got the stars to turn up on a New Year's Eve show. He taped them in August. It was genius."

"It's got a good beat and you can dance to it" became a national catchphrase.

Mr. Clark wasn't high-minded about his work. "I've always dealt with light, frivolous things that didn't really count; I'm not ashamed of that," he said in an interview for the Archive of American Television. "There's no redeeming cultural value whatsoever to 'Bloopers,' but it's been on for 20 years." He added: "It's a piece of fluff. I've been a fluffmeister for a long time."

Richard Wagstaff Clark was born on Nov. 30, 1929, in Bronxville, N.Y., and grew up nearby in Mount Vernon, the second son of Richard A. and Julia Clark. His father was a salesman who commuted to New York City until he was hired to manage a radio station in upstate New York, in Utica. The older brother, Bradley, was killed in World War II, and young

Dick, who idolized "Brad," a high school athlete, was devastated and depressed afterward, his father once said in an interview.

As a boy, Dick listened often to the radio, and at 13 he went to see a live radio broadcast starring Jimmy Durante and Garry Moore. From then on, he wanted to be in broadcasting. His first job, at 17, was in the mailroom of his father's station. He often said he learned the most important lesson of his career from listening to Arthur Godfrey.

"I emulated him," Mr. Clark said. "I loved him, I adored him, because he had the ability to communicate to one person who was listening or watching. Most people would say, in a stentorian voice, 'Good evening, everyone.' Everyone? Godfrey knew there was only one person listening at a time."

Mr. Clark studied business administration at Syracuse University, where he was a disc jockey on the student radio station. After graduating he worked briefly as an announcer for his father's station before getting a job in television, at WKTV in Utica, as a news announcer.

In 1952 WFIL in Philadelphia gave him his own radio show, "Dick Clark's Caravan of Music," an easy-listening afternoon program. A few months later, the station's television affiliate began an afternoon show called "Bandstand," with Bob Horn and Lee Stewart. At first it showed films of musical performances for studio audiences, Mr. Clark recalled, but it evolved into a dance show when teenagers, bored with the films, started dancing to the music. As the show grew more popular, the station changed the name of Mr. Clark's radio show to "Bandstand" as well, even though his playlist remained uncontroversial fare for a relatively small middle-aged afternoon audience.

It was in the summer of 1956 that Mr. Horn, by then the show's sole host, was fired and the station turned to young Dick Clark.

"I was 26 years old, looked the part, knew the music, was very comfortable on television," Mr. Clark recalled. "They said, 'Do you want it?' And I said, 'Oh, man, do I want it!'"

Mr. Clark's first two marriages ended in divorce. He is survived by his wife, Kari Wigton, as well as a daughter, two sons and three grandchildren.

He won five Emmy Awards, including a Daytime Emmy lifetime achievement award in 1994, and in 1993 was inducted into the Television Hall of Fame and the Rock and Roll Hall of Fame. He owed his success, he said, to knowing the mind of the broad audience.

"My greatest asset in life," he said, "was I never lost touch with hot dogs, hamburgers, going to the fair and hanging out at the mall."

— By Bruce Weber;
Bill Carter and Ben Sisario
contributed reporting.

LEVON HELM

Deep-Rooted Music in the Age of Rock

MAY 26, 1940 - APRIL 19, 2012

Levon Helm, who helped forge a deep-rooted American music as the drummer and singer for the Band, one of the most admired groups in rock history, died on April 19 in Manhattan. He was 71.

His death, at Memorial Sloan-Kettering Cancer Center, was from complica-tions of cancer, a spokeswoman for Vanguard Records said. He had recorded several albums for the label.

In Mr. Helm's drumming, muscle, swing, economy and finesse were inseparably merged. His voice held the bluesy, weathered and resilient essence of his Arkansas upbringing in the Mississippi Delta.

Mr. Helm was the American linchpin of the otherwise Canadian group that became Bob Dylan's backup band and then the Band. Its own songs, largely written by the Band's guitarist, Jaime Robbie Robertson, and pianist, Richard Manuel, spring from roadhouse, church, backwoods, river and farm; they are rock-ribbed with history and tradition yet hauntingly surreal.

After the Band broke up in 1976, Mr. Helm continued to perform at every opportunity, working with a partly reunited Band and leading his own groups. He also acted in films, notably "Coal Miner's Daughter" (1980). In the 2000s he became a roots-music patriarch, turning his barn in Woodstock, N.Y. — it had been a recording studio since 1975 — into the home of eclectic concerts called Midnight Rambles, which led to tours and Grammy-winning albums.

Mr. Helm gave his drums a muffled, bottom-heavy sound that placed them in the foundation of the arrangements, and his tom-toms were tuned so that their pitch would bend downward as the tone faded. Mr. Helm didn't call attention to himself. Three bass-drum thumps at the start of one of the Band's anthems, "The Weight," were all that he needed to establish the song's gravity.

His playing served the song. In "The Shape I'm In," he juxtaposed Memphis soul, New Orleans rumba and military tattoo. But while it was tersely responsive to the music, the drumming also had an improvisational feel.

In the Band, lead vocals changed from song to song and sometimes within songs, and harmonies were elaborately communal. But particularly when lyrics turned to myths and tall tales of the American South — like "The Night They Drove Old Dixie Down," "Ophelia" and "Rag Mama Rag" — the lead went to Mr. Helm, with his Arkansas twang and a voice that could sound desperate, ornery and amused at the same time.

In a 1984 interview with Modern Drummer magazine, Mr. Helm described the "right ingredients" for his work in music and film as "life and breath, heart and soul."

A ROCK LEGEND, ON THE DRUMS AND THE MIC: Levon Helm, the drummer for the Band, sang lead on many of the group's songs, a true rarity in rock or any other genre.

Mark Lavon Helm was born on May 26, 1940, in Elaine, Ark., the son of a cotton farmer with land near Turkey Scratch, Ark. In his 1993 autobiography, "This Wheel's on Fire: Levon Helm and the Story of the Band," written with Stephen Davis, Mr. Helm said he was part Chickasaw Indian through his paternal grandmother. He grew up hearing live bluegrass, Delta blues, country and the beginnings of rock 'n' roll; Memphis was just across the river.

His father gave him a guitar when he was 9, and he soon started performing: in a duo with his sister Linda and in a high school rock 'n' roll band, the Jungle Bush Beaters. He also played drums in the Marvell High School band.

Mr. Helm was in 11th grade when the Arkansas-born rockabilly singer Ronnie Hawkins hired him as a drummer. He traveled with Mr. Hawkins to Canada, where the shows paid better, and Mr. Hawkins settled there and formed a band. Ronnie Hawkins and the Hawks played six nights a week in Ontario and had a number of hit singles, like "Mary Lou." They performed on Dick Clark's TV show "American Bandstand." (Mr. Clark's obituary is on page 275.)

By 1961 Mr. Hawkins had assembled the lineup that would become the Band: Mr. Helm, Mr. Robertson, Mr. Manuel, Rick Danko on bass and Garth Hudson on organ. "He knew what musicians had the fire," Mr. Helm said of Mr. Hawkins. The others had trouble pronouncing Lavon, so Mr. Helm began calling himself Levon.

In 1963, weary of Mr. Hawkins's discipline, the five Hawks started their own bar-band career as Levon and the Hawks. The blues singer John Hammond Jr. heard them in Toronto and brought Mr. Robertson, Mr. Hudson and Mr. Helm into the studio in 1964 to back him on the album "So Many Roads."

Bob Dylan had famously brought an electric band to the 1965 Newport Folk Festival, and after its members had made other commitments, he hired Mr. Robertson and Mr. Helm for a summer tour. At their first rehearsals, Mr. Helm recalled, his reaction to Mr. Dylan was, "I couldn't believe how many words this guy had in his music, or how he remembered them all." Before playing their first show, at Forest Hills Tennis Stadium in Queens, N.Y., Mr. Dylan told the band, "Just keep playing, no matter how weird it gets."

They polarized the audience — those wanting to hear only Dylan's folk music booed — and while a subsequent concert at the Hollywood Bowl was better received, another band member, the keyboardist Al Kooper, chose to leave. At that point Mr. Helm told Albert Grossman, Mr. Dylan's manager, "Take us all or don't take anybody." The Hawks became Mr. Dylan's band.

They backed Mr. Dylan on a studio single, "Can You Please Crawl Out Your Window?," and toured with him through the fall, still getting booed. Mr. Helm quit the band late in 1965. "I wasn't made to be booed," he wrote.

Mr. Dylan's motorcycle accident in 1966 ended his touring with the Hawks. While he recuperated in Woodstock, the Hawks, who were on retainer, rented a big pink house in a neighboring town, West Saugerties, for $125 a month. For most of 1967 the Hawks, with Mr. Manuel playing drums, worked five days a week on music: writing songs with and without Mr. Dylan, playing them at his home and at the house they called Big Pink, and recording them on a two-track tape recorder in the basement. Songs sent to Mr. Dylan's publisher were soon bootlegged.

In the winter of 1967, the band summoned Mr. Helm to rejoin them. With Mr. Manuel on drums, Mr. Helm picked up the mandolin, though he would soon return to drums.

Mr. Grossman got the Hawks their own recording contract with Capitol in February 1968, initially as the Crackers, a name Capitol didn't like. There was no band name on the LP label or front cover of "Music From Big Pink," the group's debut album, which simply had a painting by Mr. Dylan on the front. (The songs had been written at Big Pink but recorded in professional studios.) The LP label listed all the musicians' names, while inside the double-fold cover the musicians were listed under the words "The Band." "The name of the group is just our Christian names," Mr. Robertson insisted in an interview. But the band became the Band.

Released on July 1, 1968, a year after the Beatles' "Sgt. Pepper's Lonely Hearts Club Band," "Music From Big Pink" was "rebelling against the rebellion," Mr. Helm wrote. There were no elaborate studio confections, no psychedelic jams, no gimmicks; the music was stately and homespun, with a deliberately old-time tone behind the enigmatic lyrics. Sales were modest, but the album's influence was huge, leading musicians like Eric Clapton and the Grateful Dead back toward concision. The Band was inducted into the Rock and Roll Hall of Fame in 1994.

Adding to its mystique, the Band didn't tour until 1969 because Mr. Danko broke his neck in an auto accident. It made its concert debut as the Band at Winterland in San Francisco in April 1969.

By then, the Band was well into recording its second album, simply titled "The Band," which would include the group's only Top 30 single, "Up on Cripple Creek." The album was universally hailed, and the Band played a summer of huge pop festivals, backing Mr. Dylan at the Isle of Wight and performing in August at Woodstock. In 1970, Mr. Helm and the songwriter Libby Titus had a daughter, Amy Helm, now a member of the band Ollabelle; she survives him, along with his wife since 1981, the former Sandra Dodd, and two grandchildren.

The Band would never match its two initial LP masterpieces. By the time the group started recording its 1970 album, "Stage Fright," members were drinking heavily and using heroin, and there were disputes over songwriting credits and publishing royalties, of which Mr. Robertson had by far the greatest share. The collaborative spirit of the first two albums was disappearing. But the Band's career had momentum; it produced several more studio albums, toured internationally, and released a live album, "Rock of Ages," which reached the Top 10 in 1972. In 1973, the Band, the Grateful Dead and the Allman Brothers were the triple bill for the Watkins Glen festival, which drew 600,000 people to upstate New York — larger than Woodstock. In 1974, the Band made an album with Mr. Dylan, "Planet Waves," and toured with him, resulting in another live album, "Before the Flood." "The Basement Tapes," a collection of songs with and without Mr. Dylan from the Big Pink era, was released in 1975.

In September 1976, Mr. Robertson decided to declare the end of the Band's touring career with a grand finale: "The Last Waltz," an all-star concert at Winterland on Thanksgiving 1976. Recorded for an album, it was also filmed by Martin Scorsese and released under the same title. Mr. Helm hated the film, believing that it glorified Mr. Robertson and slighted the rest of the Band. After "The Last Waltz," the original Band lineup returned to the studio for one last album, the desultory "Islands," which completed its Capitol contract.

By then, Mr. Helm had embarked on a solo career. He also branched out into acting, playing Loretta Lynn's father in "Coal Miner's Daughter" and appearing in "The Right Stuff" and "The Dollmaker," a television movie with Jane Fonda.

But Mr. Helm wanted above all to be a working musician. In the early 1980s he toured with his fellow Band members, minus Mr. Robertson. They were on the road in 1986 when Mr. Manuel committed suicide at 42 in a Florida motel room. But Mr. Helm, Mr. Danko and Mr. Hudson continued to work together as the Band, with additional musicians and songwriters, releasing three albums during the 1990s. Mr. Danko died in 1999 at 56.

Meanwhile, Mr. Helm's barn studio became a hub for musicians from Woodstock and beyond, often with Mr. Helm and Mr. Hudson sitting in. Mr. Helm, a heavy smoker, contracted throat cancer in the late 1990s, and for months he could not speak above a whisper. A tumor was removed from his vocal cords, and he underwent 28 radiation treatments. Medical bills threatened him with the loss of his home. Partly to raise money, he began hosting the Midnight Rambles at his barn in 2004. More house parties than concerts, they featured unannounced guest stars and a band of his own that delved into Americana as well as the Band catalog.

His voice strengthened, and the core of his Midnight Ramble bands became a touring and recording group; it performed in 2009 at the 40th anniversary of the Woodstock Festival on its site in Bethel, N.Y., although Mr. Helm was unable to sing that night. Mr. Helm's 2007 and 2009 studio albums, "Dirt Farmer" and "Electric Dirt," won Grammy Awards, as did his 2011 "Ramble at the Ryman," recorded live in Nashville and broadcast on PBS.

Nearly to the end, Mr. Helm spent his life on the bandstand. "If it doesn't come from your heart," he wrote, "music just doesn't work."

— BY JON PARELES

CHARLES COLSON

Dirty Tricks Led to Prison, and a Rebirth

OCT. 16, 1931 - APRIL 21, 2012

CHARLES W. COLSON, who as a political saboteur for President Richard M. Nixon masterminded some of the dirty tricks that led to the president's downfall, then emerged from prison to become an important evangelical leader, saying he had been "born again," died on April 21

in Falls Church, Va. He was 80.

The cause was complications of a brain hemorrhage, according to Prison Fellowship Ministries, which Mr. Colson founded in Lansdowne, Va. He had brain surgery to remove a clot after becoming ill on March 30 while speaking at a conference.

Mr. Colson went to prison after pleading guilty to obstructing justice in one of the criminal plots that undid the Nixon administration. After having what he called his religious awakening behind bars, he spent much of the rest of his life ministering to prisoners, preaching the Gospels and forging a coalition of Republican politicians, evangelical church leaders and Roman Catholic conservatives that has had a pronounced influence on American politics.

It was a remarkable reversal.

Mr. Colson was a 38-year-old Washington lawyer when he joined the Nixon White House as a special counsel in November 1969. He quickly caught the president's eye. His "instinct for the political jugular and his ability to get things done made him a lightning rod for my own frustrations," Nixon wrote in "RN: The Memoirs of Richard Nixon." In 1970, the president made him his "political point man" for "imaginative dirty tricks."

"When I complained to Colson, I felt confident that something would be done," Nixon wrote. "I was rarely disappointed."

Mr. Colson and his colleagues "started vying for favor on Nixon's dark side," Bryce N. Harlow, a former counselor to the president, said in an oral history. "Colson started talking about trampling his grandmother's grave for Nixon and showing he was as mean as they come."

As the president's re-election campaign geared up in 1971, "everybody went macho," Mr. Harlow said. "It was the 'in' thing to swagger and threaten."

Few played political hardball more fiercely than Mr. Colson. When a deluded janitor from Milwaukee shot Gov. George C. Wallace of Alabama on the presidential campaign trail in Maryland in May 1972, Nixon asked about the suspect's politics. Mr. Colson replied, "Well, he's going to be a left-winger by the time we get through." He proposed a political frame-up: planting leftist pamphlets in the would-be killer's apartment. "Good," the president said, as recorded on a White House tape. "Keep at that."

Mr. Colson hired E. Howard Hunt, a veteran covert operator for the Central Intelligence Agency, to spy on the president's opponents. Their plots became part of the cascade of high crimes and misdemeanors known as the Watergate affair.

Their efforts began to unravel after Mr. Hunt and five other C.I.A. and F.B.I. veterans were arrested in June 1972 after a botched burglary and wiretapping operation at Democratic National Committee headquarters at the Watergate office complex in Washington. To this day, no one knows whether Nixon authorized the break-in or precisely what the burglars wanted.

"When I write my memoirs," Mr. Colson told Mr. Hunt in a November 1972 telephone conversation, "I'm going to say that the Watergate was brilliantly conceived as an escapade that would divert the Democrats' attention from the real issues, and therefore permit us to win a landslide that we probably wouldn't have won otherwise." The two men laughed.

That month, Nixon won that landslide. On election night, the president watched the returns with Mr. Colson and the White House chief of staff, H. R. Haldeman. "I couldn't feel any sense of jubilation," Mr. Colson said in a 1992 television interview. "Here we were, supposedly winning, and it was more like we'd lost."

He continued, "The attitude was, 'Well, we showed them, we got even with our enemies and we beat them,' instead of 'We've been given a wonderful mandate to rule over the next four years.' We were reduced to our petty worst on the night of what should have been our greatest triumph."

The Watergate operation and the dirty tricks campaign surrounding it led to the criminal indictments and convictions of most of Nixon's closest aides. On June 21, 1974, Mr. Colson was sentenced to prison and fined $5,000. Nixon resigned seven weeks later after one of his secretly recorded White House tapes made clear that he had tried to use the C.I.A. to obstruct the federal investigation of the break-in.

Mr. Colson served seven months after pleading guilty to obstructing justice in the case of Daniel Ellsberg, a former National Security Council consultant who leaked the Pentagon Papers, a secret history of the Vietnam War, to The New York Times. In July 1971, a few weeks after the papers were published, Mr. Colson approved Mr. Hunt's proposal to steal files from the office of Mr. Ellsberg's psychiatrist. The aim was "to destroy his public image and credibility," Mr. Hunt wrote.

"I went to prison, voluntarily," Mr. Colson said in 2005. "I deserved it."

He announced upon emerging that he would devote the rest of his life to religious work. In 1976, he founded Prison Fellowship Ministries, which delivers a Christian message of redemption to thousands of prison inmates and their families. In 1983, he established Justice Fellowship, which calls itself the nation's largest religion-based criminal justice reform group. In 1993, he won the $1 million Templeton Prize for Progress in Religion, and donated it to his ministries.

By the end of the 1990s, Mr. Colson had become a leading voice in the evangelical political movement, with books and a syndicated radio broadcast. He helped form a conservative coalition of leaders from the Republican Party, the Protestant evangelical community and the Catholic Church. The Catholics and the evangelicals, once combatants over issues of religious doctrine, now joined forces in fights over abortion rights and religious freedom, among other issues.

Mr. Colson also reached out to the Rev. Richard John Neuhaus, a Catholic theologian who edited the journal First Things and who had warned of a coming tide of secularism in his book "The Naked Public Square." They inaugurated a theological dialogue that resulted in the publication of the document "Evangelicals and Catholics Together" in 1994.

Mr. Colson said the manifesto drew hate mail from evangelicals and cost the Prison Fellowship a million dollars in donations. But in pushing for religion-based policies in government, the initiative cleared the path for a political and cultural alliance that has reshaped the political debate in America, adding fuel to a rightward turn in the Republican Party and a rising conservative grassroots movement.

In 2000, Mr. Colson was a resident of Florida when Gov. Jeb Bush restored his rights to practice law, vote and serve on a jury — all of them having been lost with his federal felony conviction. "I think it's time to move on," Mr. Bush said at the time. "I know him. He's a great guy."

With that, Mr. Colson re-entered the political arena. In January 2001, six days after President George W. Bush's inauguration, a Wall Street Journal editorial praised Mr. Colson's prison work as "a model for Bush's ideas about faith-based funding."

When he went to the White House to state his case for religious faith as a basis for foreign and domestic policies, Mr. Colson found himself pushing on an open door. "You don't have to tell me," he said President Bush told him. "I'd still be drinking if it weren't for what Christ did in my life. I know faith-based works."

In 2006, a federal judge ruled that a religion-based program operated by a Prison Fellowship

NIXON'S POINT MAN: Charles Colson during his 1974 trial during the Watergate affair. He would serve seven months after pleading guilty to obstructing justice.

affiliate in Iowa had violated the constitutional separation of church and state. By using tax money for a religious program that gave special privileges to inmates who embraced evangelical Christianity, the state had established a congregation and given its leaders "authority to control the spiritual, emotional, and physical lives of hundreds of Iowa inmates," the judge said.

Mr. Colson blasted the ruling, and Prison Fellowship appealed it. But in December 2007, a federal appeals court upheld the decision.

By then, Mr. Colson had stepped down as chairman of the group to devote himself to writing and speaking for his causes. In 2008, President Bush awarded him the Presidential Citizens Medal.

Charles Wendell Colson — friends called him Chuck — was born on Oct. 16, 1931, in Boston, the only child of Wendell B. and Inez Ducrow Colson, His father was a struggling lawyer; his mother, nicknamed Dizzy, was an exuberant spendthrift.

He grew up at 15 different addresses in and around the city and attended eight schools. He got his first taste of politics as a Republican teenage volunteer in Robert F. Bradford's unsuccessful re-election campaign for governor of Massachusetts. It was where he learned "all the tricks," he said, including "planting misleading stories in the press, voting tombstones, and spying on the opposition in every possible way."

He graduated from Browne & Nichols, a private school in Cambridge, in 1949, and went to Brown University with a scholarship from the Navy Reserve Officer Training Program. After graduating in 1953, he married his college sweetheart, Nancy Billings, and joined the Marines.

In 1956, Mr. Colson went to Washington as an administrative assistant to Senator Leverett Saltonstall, a Massachusetts Republican. He met Nixon, who was then vice president, and became, in his words, a lifelong "Nixon fanatic." The two men "understood each other," Mr. Colson wrote in "Born Again," his memoir. They were "prideful men seeking that most elusive goal of all — acceptance and the respect of those who had spurned us."

After obtaining a law degree from George Washington University in 1959, Mr. Colson became partner in a Washington law firm and practiced politics on the side, with an eye to a Nixon presidency. He was crushed when his candidate lost the 1960 election by a whisker to Senator John F. Kennedy.

A sympathetic biography, "Charles W. Colson: A Life Redeemed" (2005), by Jonathan Aitken, depicts him in these years as a hard-drinking, chain-smoking, amoral man with three young children and a failing marriage. He divorced his first wife and married Patricia Ann Hughes in 1964.

She, the three children and five grandchildren are among Mr. Colson's survivors. He lived in Leesburg, Va., and Naples, Fla.

In 1973, while looking for work after leaving the White House and fearing that he was going to wind up in jail, Mr. Colson got into his car and found himself in the grip of the spiritual crisis that led to his conversion. "This so-called White House hatchet man, ex-Marine captain, was crying too hard to get the keys into the ignition," he remembered. "I sat there for a long time that night deeply convicted of my own sin."

— BY TIM WEINER; LAURIE GOODSTEIN CONTRIBUTED REPORTING.

FRED HAKIM

Mustard, Relish and Some Times Square History

AUG. 19, 1928 - APRIL 25, 2012

FRED HAKIM'S family owned a hole-in-the-wall, last-of-its-kind hot-dog counter in Times Square when New York decided to revitalize the area in the 1990s by condemning dozens of establishments like it. It was a seven-seat, 250-square-foot piece of Edward Hopper streetscape at 229-31 West

42nd Street, which Mr. Hakim's father had opened in 1941 and wryly named the Grand Luncheonette.

Mr. Hakim (pronounced HAY-kim) tried to keep the place open as a sort of living museum of the golden age of hawkers and honky-tonks in Times Square. But the city had other ideas, and after a two-year fight, he was evicted on Oct. 19, 1997.

He died on April 25 at age 83.

Mr. Hakim seemed stumped by the economics of the Times Square redevelopment. In conversations with family members, and in interviews with the reporters who crowded his joint in its last days, he often asked, "Where are the people who just want a hot dog and a knish?"

Working for his father from age 13, Mr. Hakim was witness to a New Yorker's version of the history of the world. From the counter, he saw bobby-soxers rounding the corner to swoon over Frank Sinatra at the Paramount. He watched the crowds flood the street like a dam burst on V-E Day, May 8, 1945, which also marked the end of the wartime brownout, when the lights in Times Square — the billboards, the marquees, the windows in every building that had been dark for three years — blazed once again.

He met a world of shoeshine men, longshoremen, sailors, drug dealers, prostitutes and policemen in the gritty years. "He called it a symbiotic relationship," his son Mark said. "You depended on each other, and no one was in anybody's business."

THE LAST OF HIS KIND: Fred Hakim, left, and his son at their 42nd Street diner in 1997. From his seven-seat restaurant, Mr. Hakim witnessed the transformation of Times Square.

Unlike his father, who had owned several hot-dog counters in Times Square at various times, Fred Hakim never fully depended on the Grand Luncheonette for his living. He worked there seven days a week, sometimes 20 hours on a weekend, but he also taught physical education and coached the handball team at Murry Bergtraum High School in Lower Manhattan.

Still, though Mr. Hakim liked teaching, the luncheonette was his calling. "He loved the people there," his son said. "The regular people, the shady people with rolls of dollar bills they peeled off. They were all his friends."

Peter Sillen, an independent filmmaker, made a short documentary about the Grand Luncheonette in 1997, casting it as an emblem of the larger battle, since lost, to preserve some of the earthy character of Times Square.

Mr. Hakim comes across in the film as gentle ("Be right with you, young man"), authoritative ("Hot dogs, hot dogs! Git y'hot dogs hee-ah!") and wise ("A knish? It's potatoes," he explains to an off-camera customer. "Potatoes inside, outside, every side").

Fred Hakim was born on Aug. 19, 1928, in the Bronx, one of three children of Albert and Luna Hakim. He earned bachelor's and master's degrees in education from the City University of New York.

Besides his son Mark, Mr. Hakim is survived by his wife, Jane; three other children; a sister; a brother; and three grandchildren.

Mr. Hakim lamented the closing of the Grand Luncheonette, but it turned out to be one of the luckiest days of his life.

If not for the eviction, he told his family and friends, he would have most likely been behind the counter when the building collapsed less than six weeks later, burying the luncheonette under tons of rubble. Demolition work next door, and a bit of wind, were the probable causes.

"He used to say what a blessing it was," Mark Hakim said. "Being made to close the business at 69" — Mr. Hakim's father, Albert, had worked into his 80s — "was very hard for him. He hoped to work till he was 90. But losing that fight was the best thing he ever did."

— By Paul Vitello

////////////////////////////

AMARILLO SLIM

Thomas Austin Preston Jr. Was a Gambling Man

DEC. 31, 1928 · APRIL 29, 2012

A MARILLO SLIM, the pencil-slender, cornpone-spouting Texan who became poker's first superstar by overpowering opponents with charm, cunning and preternatural coolness, died on April 29 in Amarillo, Tex. He was 83.

After honing his gambling skills as a pool hall hustler and illegal bookmaker, Thomas Austin Preston Jr. turned his attention to poker in the 1960s, when it was played mainly on kitchen tables and in smoky backrooms and Las Vegas casinos. With his cowboy hat and boots, Texas drawl and country wit, he became the public face of poker as he won major titles at a time when the game was rising to a multibillion-dollar mainstream business, first on television and then on the Internet.

"Slim used his name and face to promote poker in a way it had never been done before, and without Amarillo Slim, the poker world would likely not exist in the way we know it today," Poker Player News said in its obituary.

Amarillo Slim won five times in World Series of Poker events, was elected to at least four gambling halls of fame and played poker with Presidents Lyndon B. Johnson and Richard M. Nixon, the drug lord Pablo Escobar and the magazine publisher Larry Flynt, who dropped $1.7 million.

His wagers that had nothing to do with poker garnered just as much attention. He once bet the 1939 Wimbledon tennis champion Bobby Riggs that he could beat him at table tennis as long as he, Amarillo Slim, picked the rackets; he then showed up with iron skillets — with which he had spent months practicing.

He then bet a syndicate of Tennessee gamblers that he could beat a world table tennis champion. The champion practiced with a skillet, only to find that Amarillo Slim had changed weapons. He showed up with a pair of empty Coke bottles, and won handily.

He said he won $300,000 from Willie Nelson playing dominoes. He bet on which sugar cube a fly would land on.

Amarillo Slim's gift for colorful patois was legendary. When asked if he could bluff his way to victory with a bad hand, he said, "Is fat meat greasy?" He then offered the thought that most people who play poker "don't have the guts of an earthworm."

He was just as uncharitable to individual opponents. One "couldn't track an elephant through four feet of snow"; another "had as good a chance of beating me as getting a French kiss out of the Statue of Liberty."

He liked to say that he had been so skinny as a child, he had to get out of the bathtub before he pulled the plug. As an adult, he was 6 feet 4 inches and 170 pounds.

Thomas Preston was born in Johnson, Ark., on New Year's Eve 1928. His family moved to Turkey, Tex., nine months later. His father was a car salesman, and the family moved frequently between Arkansas and Amarillo. His memory could astound: he memorized the United States Constitution and could remember a license plate 15 years later.

After picking up snooker, the billiards game popularized by the British, he was soon hustling in pool halls in the Mexican part of Amarillo. In 1945, he enlisted in the Navy and entertained sailors with pool exhibitions. He said he made $100,000 from a bookmaking business he ran while in the Navy. After returning to Amarillo, he said, he grew bored and enlisted in the Army. Stationed in Europe, he

POKER'S SUPERSTAR: Amarillo Slim was one of the greatest players of all time.

developed a large black-market business that included selling thousands of Mickey Mouse watches to Russian soldiers.

Mr. Preston spent most of the 1950s hustling pool. Some stories have it that he adopted his pseudonym after playing matches with Minnesota Fats. He enhanced his hustles by learning to play the bumpkin.

Eventually, his reputation at pool spread so widely that Amarillo Slim thought he had to switch businesses, so he turned to engaging in illegal bookmaking in the winter and traveling around Texas in the summer playing poker. When the World Series of Poker was first played in Las Vegas in 1970, he was there. The handful of competitors played his favorite game, hold

'em. He ultimately won more than $500,000 in tournament play and was inducted into the Poker Hall of Fame in 1992.

He was free with advice. Poker players, he said, should concentrate on their opponents more than on the cards, watching their eyes and ignoring their words. (His giant Stetson obscured his own eyes.) Most critical, he advised, was to be able to quit a loser.

Amarillo Slim's reputation was tarnished in 2003 when he was accused of touching a granddaughter inappropriately and charged with multiple counts of indecency to a child, a felony. In a deal with prosecutors, he pleaded guilty to misdemeanor assault charges. But he professed his innocence, saying he had accepted the plea deal to protect his family from the embarrassment of a public trial.

His marriage to Helen E. Byler ended in divorce. Mr. Preston, who died of colon cancer, is survived by two sons, a daughter, seven grandchildren and three great-grandchildren.

Younger poker players more scientific about the game have eclipsed Amarillo Slim, but none beat his pithiness.

"I like you, son," he once said, "but I'll put a rattlesnake in your pocket and ask you for a match."

— By Douglas Martin

ADAM YAUCH

Beastie Boy

AUG. 5, 1964 · MAY 4, 2012

ADAM YAUCH, a rapper and founder of the pioneering and immensely successful hip-hop group the Beastie Boys, died on May 4 in Manhattan at 47. He had been treated for cancer of the salivary gland for the last three years.

With a scratchy voice that grew scratchier through the years, Mr. Yauch rapped as MCA in the Beastie Boys, who were inducted into the Rock and Roll Hall of Fame only weeks earlier. They were vanguard white rappers who gave many listeners their first exposure to hip-hop in the 1980s and helped extend the art of sampling, gaining the respect of their African-American peers.

While many hip-hop careers are brief, the Beastie Boys appealed to successive generations, making multimillion-selling albums into the 2000s, all the while growing up without losing their sense of humor or their ear for a party beat. *"I burn the competition like a flame thrower/My rhymes they age like wine as I get older,"* Mr. Yauch rapped on the Beastie Boys' 2011 album, "Hot Sauce Committee Part Two."

Mr. Yauch (pronounced yowk) was a major factor in the Beastie Boys' evolution from testosterone-driven pranksters to sonic experimenters and socially conscious rappers. The Beastie Boys became an institution (and keepers of old-school hip-hop memories) — one that could have arisen only amid the artistic, social and accidental connections of New York City.

In the history of hip-hop, the Beastie Boys were both improbable and perhaps inevitable: appreciators, popularizers and extrapolators of a culture they weren't born into.

"The Beasties opened hip-hop music up to the suburbs," said Rick Rubin, who produced the group's 1986 debut album, in an interview with The Plain Dealer of Cleveland. "As crazy as they were, they seemed safe to Middle America, in a way black artists hadn't been up to that time."

The Beastie Boys started their major-label career with two pivotal albums: "Licensed to Ill" (1986), a cornerstone of rap-rock that became the first hip-hop album to top the Billboard chart, and "Paul's Boutique" (1989), a wildly eclectic, sample-based production that became a template for experimental hip-hop.

The Beasties brand expanded well beyond music: with their own magazine and record label, Grand Royal; with Mr. Yauch's social activism promoting Tibetan rights; and with work in film. Mr. Yauch (calling himself Nathanial Hörnblowér) directed Beastie Boys videos and started Oscilloscope Laboratories, an independent film production and distribution company.

BRINGING HIP-HOP TO THE SUBURBS: Adam Yauch, left, a founder of the Beastie Boys, helped introduce rap music to a larger audience.

When they started rapping in 1983, the Beastie Boys — Mr. Yauch, Adam Horovitz (Ad-Rock) and Mike Diamond (Mike D) — were greeted by some hip-hop purists as a novelty act. They were Jewish bohemians, not ghetto survivors; they were jokers, not battlers. Yet the Beastie Boys recorded for a bastion of New York hip-hop, the Def Jam label, and they toured alongside Run-D.M.C. and LL Cool J.

They went on to win admiration and influence with productions that kept coming up with surprises — including, eventually, the rappers' playing instruments again — and with rhymes that would mingle humor, boasting and a growing idealism. Even when the Beastie Boys were treated as a joke, it was a joke they would be in on for decades.

Adam Nathaniel Yauch was born on Aug. 5, 1964, in Brooklyn. Playing bass, he and Mr. Diamond started the Beastie Boys in 1981 as a hard-core punk band. The group's original drummer, Kate Schellenbach, has said, "Whereas other bands, just as awful as the Beastie Boys, would actually believe they were good, for Mike and Adam the whole point was to be terrible and admit it."

That group broke up after releasing an eight-song, seven-inch EP, "Polly Wog Stew." The Beastie Boys reappeared in 1983 with Mr. Horovitz on guitar, and made "Cooky Puss," a 12-inch single of prank phone call recordings over a rock guitar riff and hip-hop scratching. The group had been listening to New York hip-hop since the late 1970s.

The Beasties started rapping as a joke, Mr. Yauch once said, but then found that audiences liked it better than their punk-rock. Mr. Rubin, then a student at New York University, joined the group as a disc jockey. He also brought them to the attention of Russell Simmons, the manager of Run-D.M.C. and other leading hip-hop acts. He added the Beasties to his roster.

When Mr. Rubin and Mr. Simmons started Def Jam, the Beastie Boys were one of the label's first signings: catalog number DJ 002, in 1984, was the Beastie Boys' single "Rock Hard." The following year the Beastie Boys toured with Madonna, to the confusion of pop audiences.

But with the 1986 release of "Licensed to Ill," hip-hop pushed its way onto rock radio. The songs blasted rock guitar riffs from bands like AC/DC and Led Zeppelin behind the Beastie Boys' cartoon-voiced rhymes about girls, drunken escapades, vandalism and guns. "(You Gotta) Fight for Your Right (To Party!)" became a Top 10 single, and "Licensed to Ill" sold more than nine million copies in the United States. The group toured with a stage set including caged go-go dancers and a 20-foot hydraulic penis.

The Beasties parted ways with Mr. Rubin and Def Jam amid a lawsuit over royalties. On "Paul's Boutique," their first album for Capitol, they worked with the Dust Brothers production team. The results were innovative, densely packed tracks with quick-cut elements of rock, funk, jazz and more; the rappers shared the lyrics so thoroughly that all three might rap a word or two in a single line. The album sold two million copies, and musicians inside and outside hip-hop have called it a landmark.

The Beastie Boys expanded their ambitions as tastemakers in 1992 by starting a label, Grand Royal, in association with Capitol. The label released music by At the Drive-In, Sean Lennon, Atari Teenage Riot and Jimmy Eat World. They also started Grand Royal magazine, which delved into fashion and movies as well as music. But those efforts lost money and shut down in 2001.

With their album "Check Your Head" in 1992, the Beastie Boys began featuring their own instruments. (Their instrumental album, "The Mix-Up," in 2007, won a Grammy Award.)

While the Beastie Boys' music continued to offer a crunching, squealing good time during the 1990s, the rhymes it carried grew more mature. Vandalism was replaced by constructive thoughts, and offhand sexism was replaced by explicit respect for women. After travels in Tibet and Nepal, Mr. Yauch became a practicing Tibetan Buddhist. On the Beastie Boys' 1994 album, "Ill Communication," he rapped "Bodhisattva Vow," a version of a pledge taken by Buddhists, over a hip-hop drumbeat mixed with the deep chanting of Buddhist monks. The Beasties brought Buddhist monks to perform ceremonies at the 1994 Lollapalooza Festival.

In 1994 Mr. Yauch started the nonprofit Milarepa Fund, which presented an international series of Tibetan Freedom Concerts to raise awareness of Chinese control of Tibet. The first one, in 1996, drew more than 100,000 people to Golden Gate Park in San Francisco.

In 1998 Mr. Yauch married Dechen Wangdu, who survives him, as do his parents and a daughter.

Yet the Beastie Boys never grew overly serious. Mr. Yauch directed Beastie Boys videos with a deft touch for slapstick and retro references. He also directed a 2006 documentary made from footage shot by Beasties fans, and a 2008 basketball documentary, "Gunnin' for That No. 1 Spot."

With Oscilloscope Laboratories, Mr. Yauch moved into film distribution and production. Its first releases, small indie films and documentaries, were modest in critical reception and box office, but the company quickly scaled up.

In 2009 Oscilloscope drew recognition for Oren Moverman's military drama "The Messenger," which drew Oscar nominations for best original screenplay and best supporting actor (Woody Harrelson). Another Oscar nomination, for the documentary "Exit Through the Gift Shop," followed.

Oscilloscope has continued to release films that often do not shy away from difficult topics, like a Columbine-style killing in "We Need to Talk About Kevin" and the documentary "If a Tree Falls: A Story of the Earth Liberation Front." In his brief film career, Mr. Yauch earned a reputation for nurturing films and filmmakers that others wouldn't touch.

After his cancer diagnosis in 2009, Mr. Yauch underwent extensive treatment. He was eventually able to participate in the recording of "Hot Sauce Committee Part Two," which is full of songs celebrating the sound and bygone figures of the 1980s New York City — uptown and downtown — that had nurtured the Beastie Boys.

— *By Jon Pareles*

ROBERT DE LA ROCHEFOUCAULD

The Saboteur Who Posed as a Nun

SEPT. 16, 1923 - MAY 8, 2012

ROBERT DE LA ROCHEFOUCAULD belonged to one of the oldest families of the French nobility, whose members included François de La Rochefoucauld, the author of a classic 17th-century book of maxims. For 30 years he was the mayor of Ouzouer-sur-Trézée, an idyllic canal town in the Loire Valley, and he used the aristocratic title of count.

But he is best remembered as a courageous and celebrated saboteur who fought for the honor of France in World War II as a secret agent with the British.

His exploits were legend, involving an eclectic and decidedly resourceful collection of tools in the service of sabotage and escape, including loaves of bread, a stolen limousine, the leg of a table, a bicycle and a nun's habit — not to mention the more established accouterments of espionage like parachutes, explosives and a submarine.

And perhaps befitting a man whose wartime adventures were accomplished out of the public eye, the news of his death, on May 8, in Ouzouer-sur-Trézée, emerged slowly, first announced by his family in the French newspaper Le Figaro and then reported late in June in the British press. He was 88.

Robert Jean-Marie de La Rochefoucauld (pronounced ROASH-foo-coe) was born on Sept. 16, 1923, in Paris, one of 10 children in a family living in a fashionable area near the Eiffel Tower. He attended private schools in Switzerland and in Austria. When he was 15, on a class trip, he visited Hitler's retreat at Berchtesgaden in the Bavarian Alps and received a pat on the cheek from Hitler himself.

Two years later, Hitler's army invaded France, and Count de La Rochefoucauld's father was taken prisoner. The count became a follower of Charles de Gaulle, who was assembling Free French forces in England, and one day a postal worker tipped him off to a letter he had seen that denounced him to the Gestapo.

With the help of the French resistance, Count de La Rochefoucauld took a pseudonym and fled to Spain in 1942 with two downed British airmen, who were also being sheltered by the underground. He hoped to go on to England and link up with de Gaulle's movement.

The Spanish authorities interned the three men, but the British secured their freedom and were so impressed with Count de La Rochefoucauld's boldness and ingenuity that they asked him to join the Special Operations Executive, the clandestine unit known as the S.O.E., which Prime Minister Winston Churchill created in 1940 to "set Europe ablaze," as he put it, by working with resistance groups on the German-occupied Continent.

Count de La Rochefoucauld fought for France using explosives, a table leg, a loaf of bread, a bicycle and a stolen limousine, among other things.

Count de La Rochefoucauld was an asset to the British in another way. As their ambassador in Spain told him: "The courage and skill of British agents is without equal. It is just that their French accents are appalling."

The British flew Count de La Rochefoucauld to England, where they trained him to jump out of airplanes, set off explosives and kill a man quickly using only his hands. They parachuted him into France in June 1943. There, he destroyed an electric substation and blew up railroad tracks at Avallon but was captured and condemned to death by the Nazis.

While being taken for execution, he jumped from the back of his captors' truck, dodged

bullets, then ran through the streets, winding up outside a German headquarters, where he spotted a limousine flying a swastika flag, its driver nearby, the keys in the ignition. He drove off in the car and then caught a train to Paris, hiding in one of its bathrooms.

"When we arrived in Paris, I felt drunk with freedom," the British newspaper The Telegraph quoted him as saying.

The S.O.E. later evacuated him to England by submarine, but in May 1944 he parachuted back into France. Dressed as a workman, he smuggled explosives into a huge German munitions plant near Bordeaux, hiding them in hollowed-out loaves of bread. He set off the explosives on May 20 and fled on a bicycle, but was caught by the Germans once more.

In his cell he feigned an epileptic seizure, and when a guard opened the door Count de La Rochefoucauld hit him over the head with a table leg and then broke his neck. He took the guard's uniform and pistol, shot two other guards, and escaped. Desperate to avoid recapture, he contacted a French underground worker whose sister was a nun. He donned her habit and walked unobtrusively to the home of a more senior agent, who hid him.

The S.O.E. was disbanded in 1946. As an officer in the postwar French military, Count de La Rochefoucauld trained French troops in the Indochina war and the Suez campaign, in which the French joined Britain and Israel against Egypt over control of the Suez Canal. He later pursued international business ventures.

The count was the mayor of Ouzouer-sur-Trézée from 1966 to 1996. His memoir, "La Liberté, C'est Mon Plaisir, 1940-1946," was published in 2002. He is survived by his wife, Bernadette, as well as a son and three daughters.

In 1997 he testified on behalf of Maurice Papon, who was being tried on charges of deporting French Jews to their deaths in Nazi concentration camps while Mr. Papon was an official with France's wartime collaborationist Vichy government. He told the court that Mr. Papon had risked his life to help the Resistance and the Allies.

Mr. Papon was convicted of complicity in Nazi crimes against humanity but fled to Switzerland while appealing. He was arrested at a Gstaad hotel, where he had registered as Robert Rochefoucauld. One of Mr. Papon's lawyers said later that Count de La Rochefoucauld had given his passport to Mr. Papon.

Mr. Papon was returned to France and served less than three years of his sentence before being released. He died in 2007.

Count de La Rochefoucauld was a knight in the French Legion of Honor and a recipient of France's Medal of Resistance, and he was decorated for bravery by the British. At his death he was believed to have been one of the last living Frenchmen of Churchill's S.O.E.

— By Richard Goldstein

MAURICE SENDAK

The Wild and Wonderful Things of Childhood

JUNE 10, 1928 - MAY 8, 2012

MAURICE SENDAK, widely considered the most important children's book artist of the 20th century, who wrenched the picture book out of the safe, sanitized world of the nursery and plunged it into the dark, terrifying and hauntingly beautiful recesses of the human psyche, died on May 8

in Danbury, Conn. He was 83.

Roundly praised, intermittently censored and occasionally eaten, Mr. Sendak's books were essential ingredients of childhood for the generation born after 1960 or thereabouts, and in turn for their children. He was known in particular for more than a dozen picture books he wrote and illustrated himself, most famously "Where the Wild Things Are," which was simultaneously genre-breaking and career-making when it was published by Harper & Row in 1963.

Mr. Sendak's work was the subject of critical studies and major exhibitions; in the second half of his career, he was also renowned as a designer of theatrical sets. His art graced the writing of other eminent authors for children and adults, including Hans Christian Andersen, Leo Tolstoy, Herman Melville, William Blake and Isaac Bashevis Singer.

In book after book, Mr. Sendak upended the staid, centuries-old tradition of American children's literature, in which young heroes and heroines were typically well scrubbed and even better behaved; nothing really bad ever happened for very long; and everything was tied up at the end in a neat, moralistic bow.

Mr. Sendak's characters, by contrast, are headstrong, bossy, even obnoxious. (In his 1962 story "Pierre," "I don't care!" is the response of the small eponymous hero to absolutely everything.) His pictures are often unsettling. His plots are fraught with rupture: children are kidnapped, parents disappear, a dog lights out from her comfortable home.

A largely self-taught illustrator, Mr. Sendak was at his finest a shtetl Blake, portraying a luminous world, at once lovely and dreadful, suspended between wakefulness and dreaming. In so doing, he was able to convey both the propulsive abandon and the pervasive melancholy of children's interior lives.

His visual style could range from intricately crosshatched scenes that recalled 19th-century prints to airy watercolors reminiscent of Chagall to bold, bulbous figures inspired by the comic books he loved all his life, with outsize feet that the page could scarcely contain. He never did learn to draw feet, he often said.

In 1964, the American Library Association awarded Mr. Sendak the Caldecott Medal, considered the Pulitzer Prize of children's book illustration, for "Where the Wild Things Are." In simple, incantatory language, the book told the story of Max, a naughty boy who rages at his mother and is sent to his room without supper. A pocket Odysseus, Max promptly sets sail:

And he sailed off through night and day
and in and out of weeks
and almost over a year
to where the wild things are.

There, Max leads the creatures in a frenzied rumpus before sailing home, anger spent, to find his supper waiting.

As portrayed by Mr. Sendak, the wild things are deliciously grotesque: huge, snaggletoothed, exquisitely hirsute and glowering maniacally. He always maintained he was drawing his relatives — who, in his memory at least, had hovered like a pack of middle-aged gargoyles above the childhood sickbed to which he was often confined.

PICTURE BOOKS, BOTH LOVELY AND DREADFUL: Maurice Sendak was one of the most renowned children's book writers and illustrators of the 20th century.

Maurice Bernard Sendak was born in Brooklyn on June 10, 1928; his father, Philip, worked in the garment district of Manhattan. Family photographs show the infant Maurice, or Murray as he was then known, as a plump, round-faced, slanting-eyed, droopy-lidded, arching-browed creature — looking, in other words, exactly like a baby in a Maurice Sendak illustration. Mr. Sendak adored drawing babies, in all their fleshy petulance.

A frail child beset by a seemingly endless parade of illnesses, Mr. Sendak was reared, he said afterward, in a world of looming terrors: the Depression; World War II; the Holocaust, in which many of his European relatives perished, and the seemingly infinite vulnerability of children to danger. He experienced the kidnapping of the Lindbergh baby in 1932 as a personal torment: if that fair-haired, blue-eyed princeling could not be kept safe, what certain peril lay in store for him, little Murray Sendak, in his humble apartment in Bensonhurst?

An image from the Lindbergh crime scene — a ladder leaning against the side of a house — would find its way into "Outside Over There" (1981), in which a baby is carried off by goblins.

As Mr. Sendak grew up — lower class, Jewish, gay — he felt permanently shunted to the margins of things. "All I wanted was to be straight so my parents could be happy," he told The New York Times in a 2008 interview. "They never, never, never knew."

His lifelong melancholia showed in his work, in picture books like "We Are All in the Dumps With Jack and Guy" (1993), a parable about homeless children in the age of AIDS. It showed in his habits. He could be dyspeptic and solitary, working in his white clapboard home in Ridgefield, deep in the Connecticut countryside, with only Mozart, Melville, Mickey Mouse and his dogs for company.

It showed in his everyday interactions with people, especially those blind to the seriousness of his enterprise. "A woman came up to me the other day and said, 'You're the kiddie-book man!'" Mr. Sendak told Vanity Fair in 2011. "I wanted to kill her."

But Mr. Sendak could also be warm and forthright, if not quite gregarious. He was a man of many enthusiasms — for music, art, literature, argument and the essential rightness of children's perceptions of the world around them. He was also a mentor to a generation of younger writers and illustrators for children, several of whom, including Arthur Yorinks, Richard Egielski and Paul O. Zelinsky, went on to prominent careers of their own.

As far back as he could remember, Mr. Sendak had loved to draw. That and looking out the window had helped him pass the long hours in bed. While he was still in high school — at Lafayette in Brooklyn — he worked part time for All-American Comics, filling in backgrounds

for book versions of the "Mutt and Jeff" comic strip. His first professional illustrations were for a physics textbook, "Atomics for the Millions," published in 1947.

In 1948, at 20, he took a job building window displays for F. A. O. Schwarz. Through the store's children's book buyer, he was introduced to Ursula Nordstrom, the distinguished editor of children's books at Harper & Row. The meeting, the start of a long, fruitful collaboration, led to Mr. Sendak's first children's book commission: illustrating "The Wonderful Farm," by Marcel Aymé, published in 1951.

Under Ms. Nordstrom's guidance, Mr. Sendak illustrated books by other well-known children's authors, including several by Ruth Krauss, notably "A Hole Is to Dig" (1952), and Else Holmelund Minarik's "Little Bear" series. The first title that he wrote and illustrated himself, "Kenny's Window," published in 1956, was a moody, dreamlike story about a lonely boy's inner life.

Mr. Sendak's books were often a window on his own experience. "Higglety Pigglety Pop! Or, There Must Be More to Life" (1967) was a valentine to Jennie, his beloved Sealyham terrier, who died shortly before the book was published.

At the start of the story, Jennie, who has everything a dog could want — including "a round pillow upstairs and a square pillow downstairs" — packs her bags and sets off on her own, pining for adventure. She finds it on the stage of the World Mother Goose Theatre, where she becomes a leading lady. Every day, and twice on Saturdays, Jennie, who looks rather like a mop herself, eats a mop made out of salami. This makes her very happy.

"Hello," Jennie writes in a satisfyingly articulate letter to her master. "As you probably noticed, I went away forever. I am very experienced now and very famous. I am even a star. ... I get plenty to drink too, so don't worry."

By contrast, the huge, flat, brightly colored illustrations of "In the Night Kitchen" (1970), the story of a boy's journey through a fantastic nocturnal cityscape, are a tribute to the New York of Mr. Sendak's childhood, recalling the 1930s films and comic books he adored all his life. (The three bakers who toil in the night kitchen are the spit and image of Oliver Hardy.)

Mr. Sendak's later books could be much darker. "Brundibar" (2003), with text by the playwright Tony Kushner, is a picture book based on an opera performed by the children of the Theresienstadt concentration camp. The opera, also called "Brundibar," had been composed in 1938 by Hans Krasa, a Czech Jew who died in Auschwitz.

Reviewing the book in The New York Times Book Review, the novelist and children's book author Gregory Maguire called it "a capering picture book crammed with melodramatic menace and comedy both low and grand." He added: "In a career that spans 50 years and counting, as Sendak's does, there are bound to be lesser works. 'Brundibar' is not lesser than anything."

With Mr. Kushner, Mr. Sendak collaborated on a stage version of the opera, performed in 2006 at the New Victory Theater in New York.

In September 2011, a new picture book by Mr. Sendak, "Bumble-Ardy" — the first in 30 years for which he produced both text and illustrations — was issued by HarperCollins Publishers. The book, which spent five weeks on the New York Times children's best-seller list, tells the not-altogether-lighthearted story of an orphaned pig (his parents are eaten) who gives himself a riotous birthday party.

A posthumous picture book, "My Brother's Book" — a poem written and illustrated by Mr. Sendak and inspired by his love for his late brother, Jack — was scheduled to be published in early 2013.

Despite its wild popularity, Mr. Sendak's work was not always well received. Some early reviews of "Where the Wild Things Are" expressed puzzlement and outright unease. Writing in Ladies' Home Journal, the psychologist Bruno Bettelheim took Mr. Sendak to task for punishing Max:

"The basic anxiety of the child is desertion," Mr. Bettelheim wrote. "To be sent to bed alone is one desertion, and without food is the second desertion." (Mr. Bettelheim admitted that he had not actually read the book.)

"In the Night Kitchen," which depicts its young hero, Mickey, in the nude, prompted many school librarians to bowdlerize the book by drawing a diaper over Mickey's nether region.

But these were minority responses. Mr. Sendak's other awards include the Hans Christian Andersen Award for Illustration, the Laura Ingalls Wilder Award and, in 1996, the National Medal of the Arts, presented by President Bill Clinton. Twenty-two of his titles have been named New York Times best illustrated books of the year.

Many of Mr. Sendak's books had second lives on stage and screen. Among the most notable adaptations are the operas "Where the Wild Things Are" and "Higglety Pigglety Pop!" by the British composer Oliver Knussen, and Carole King's "Really Rosie," a musical version of "The Sign on Rosie's Door," which appeared on television as an animated special in 1975 and on the Off Broadway stage in 1980.

In 2009, a feature film version of "Where the Wild Things Are" — part live action, part animated — by the director Spike Jonze opened to favorable notices. In the 1970s, Mr. Sendak began designing sets and costumes for adaptations of his own work and, eventually, the work of others. His first venture was Mr. Knussen's "Wild Things," for which Mr. Sendak also wrote the libretto. Performed in a scaled-down version in Brussels in 1980, the opera had its full premiere four years later, to great acclaim, staged in London by the Glyndebourne Touring Opera.

With the theater director Frank Corsaro, he also created sets for several venerable operas, among them Mozart's "Magic Flute," performed by the Houston Grand Opera in 1980.

Mr. Sendak died of complications of a recent stroke. His companion of a half-century, Eugene Glynn, a psychiatrist who specialized in the treatment of young people, died in 2007. No immediate family members survive.

Though he understood children deeply, Mr. Sendak by no means valorized them unconditionally. "Dear Mr. Sun Deck ..." he could drone with affected boredom, imitating the semiliterate forced-march school letter-writing projects of which he was the frequent, if dubious, beneficiary.

But he cherished the letters that individual children sent him unbidden, which burst with the sparks that his work had ignited.

"Dear Mr. Sendak," read one, from an 8-year-old boy. "How much does it cost to get to where the wild things are? If it is not expensive, my sister and I would like to spend the summer there."

— BY MARGALIT FOX

DONNA SUMMER

The Queen of Disco, but More Than That

DEC. 31, 1948 - MAY 17, 2012

D ONNA SUMMER, the singer and songwriter whose hit recordings captured both the giddy hedonism of the 1970s disco era and the feisty female solidarity of the early 1980s, died of cancer on May 17 at her home in Naples, Fla. She was 63.

With her doe eyes, cascade of hair and sinuous dance moves, Ms. Summer was the queen of disco — the music's glamorous public face — as well as an idol with a substantial gay following. Her voice, airy and ethereal or brightly assertive, sailed over dance floors and leapt from radios from the mid-'70s well into the '80s.

She riffled through styles as diverse as funk, electronica, rock and torch song as she piled up 14 Top 10 singles in the United States, among them "Love to Love You Baby," "Bad Girls," "Hot Stuff," "Last Dance" and "She Works

Hard for the Money." In the late '70s she had three double albums in a row that reached No. 1, and each sold more than a million copies.

Her combination of a church-rooted voice and up-to-the-minute dance beats was a template for 1970s disco, and with her producers Giorgio Moroder and Pete Bellotte she pioneered electronic dance music with the synthesizer pulse of "I Feel Love" in 1977, a sound that pervades 21st-century pop. Her own recordings have been sampled by Beyoncé, the Pet Shop Boys, Justice and Nas.

Ms. Summer won Grammy Awards for dance music, R&B, rock and gospel. Her recorded catalog spans the orgasmic moans of her first hit, "Love to Love You Baby," the streetwalker chronicle of "Bad Girls," the feminist moxie of "She Works Hard for the Money" and the religious devotion of "Forgive Me," a gospel song that earned her another Grammy.

Through it all, Ms. Summer's voice held on to an optimistic spirit and a determination to flourish, winning loyal fans. In 2009 she performed in Oslo at the concert honoring the Nobel Peace Prize awarded to President Barack Obama. After her death, the president released a statement, saying, "Her voice was unforgettable, and the music industry has lost a legend far too soon."

In his own statement, Jon Landau, the chairman of the nominating committee at the Rock and Roll Hall of Fame, said it was unfortunate that the hall had never inducted her. "There is absolutely no doubt that the extraordinary Donna Summer belongs in the Rock and Roll Hall of Fame," Mr. Landau wrote. "Regrettably, despite being nominated on a number of occasions, our voting group has failed to recognize her — an error I can only hope is finally and permanently rectified next year."

LaDonna Adrian Gaines was born Dec. 31, 1948, in the Dorchester neighborhood of Boston, one of seven children. She grew up singing in church and decided in her teens to make music her career. In the late 1960s she joined the Munich company of the rock musical "Hair" and relocated to Germany, where she became fluent in German and worked as a

ICON OF AN ERA: Donna Summer epitomized the hedonistic glamour of 1970s disco music.

studio vocalist, in musical theater and briefly as a member of the Viennese Folk Opera. She married an Austrian actor, Hellmuth Sommer, in 1972, and after they divorced she kept his name but changed the spelling. She had already recorded her first single under the name Donna Gaines, an unsuccessful remake in 1971 of the Jaynetts' "Sally Go 'Round the Roses."

Her work as a backup singer brought her to the attention of Mr. Moroder and Mr. Bellotte. Her 1974 debut album with them, "Lady of the Night," was released only in Europe. But with "Love to Love You Baby" in 1975, Ms. Summer became a sensation. She said she recorded that song's breathy, moaning vocals lying on her back on the studio floor with the lights out, thinking about how Marilyn Monroe might coo its words.

The American label Casablanca signed her after hearing the song in its initial European version, titled "Love to Love You," and asked her to extend it for disco play. The resulting 17-minute single contains more than 20 simulated orgasms and became an international hit, reaching No. 2 on the American pop chart. Ms. Summer quickly released two more albums, "A Love Trilogy" and "Four Seasons of Love," a concept album tracing a romance over the course of a year.

But she was increasingly uncomfortable being promoted as a sex goddess. "I'm not just sex, sex, sex," she told Ebony magazine in 1977. "I would never want to be a one-dimensional person like that."

She became so depressed that in late 1976 she attempted suicide, she wrote in her 2003 autobiography, "Ordinary Girl: The Journey," written with Marc Eliot. She began taking medication for depression and seeking consolation in religion, becoming a born-again Christian in 1979.

"I Remember Yesterday," one of two albums Ms. Summer released in 1977, revolved around the concept of mixing disco with the sounds of previous decades. But it was a song representing the future, "I Feel Love," that would make the most impact. Its all-electronic arrangement was a startling new sound for a pop song, and its contrast of human voice versus synthetic backdrop would echo through countless club hits in its wake.

Ms. Summer was still demonstrating her versatility. She followed up with an orchestral album, "Once Upon a Time," a set of songs telling a Cinderella story, and then a live album in 1978, "Live and More," which yielded a hit with a version of "MacArthur Park." That was the first of four No. 1 singles she would have in a year, followed by "Hot Stuff," "Bad Girls" and a duet with Barbra Streisand, "No More Tears (Enough Is Enough)." Ms. Summer won her first Grammy Award — for best R&B vocal performance, female — with "Last Dance," a song by Paul Jabara. It was introduced on the soundtrack to the 1978 movie "Thank God It's Friday" and has ended many a wedding party ever since.

Disco as a fad was peaking, and Ms. Summer strove to outlast it. Her 1979 double album, "Bad Girls," put some rock guitar into songs like "Hot Stuff"; it won a Grammy for best rock vocal performance, female. Her first collection of hits, "On the Radio: Greatest Hits Volumes 1 and 2," also reached No. 1 in 1979, and the newly recorded title song was a Top 10 single.

Another hit from 1979, "Heaven Knows," reached No. 4 on the pop chart, with personal repercussions. Ms. Summer recorded it with the group Brooklyn Dreams, and she married its

co-founder, Bruce Sudano, in 1980. He survives her, along with three daughters, four grandchildren, a brother and four sisters.

"On the Radio" was Ms. Summer's last album for Casablanca. As disco receded, she moved to Geffen Records, seeking to hold her broader pop audience. She tried new wave rock on "The Wanderer" in 1981, then switched to the R&B produced by Quincy Jones for "Donna Summer" in 1982. But she would reach her 1980s commercial peak with "She Works Hard for the Money" in 1983, collaborating with the producer Michael Omartian. It was her last Top 10 album, and amid its gleaming pop productions it included "He's a Rebel," an indirect Christian rock song — "He's a rebel, written up in the lamb's book of life" — that won a Grammy for best inspirational performance.

Ms. Summer grew uncomfortable with being promoted as a sex goddess.

Ms. Summer's career waned in the mid-1980s. Pop fans paid little attention to two albums from that period, and she alienated gay fans when she was quoted as having described AIDS as divine punishment for an immoral lifestyle. Though she denied making that statement, many gay listeners boycotted her music, and by the time she had reconciled with gay organizations, her hitmaking streak was broken. Her last Top 10 hit, "This Time I Know It's for Real," was in 1989.

But she continued to record and perform. She and Mr. Sudano moved to Nashville (they had homes there and in Florida) and wrote songs together, including a No. 1 country single for Dolly Parton, "Starting Over Again." A 1997 remix of a song Ms. Summer recorded in 1992 with Mr. Moroder, "Carry On," won her the first Grammy given for best dance music. Well into the 2000s, she continued to appear on the dance-music charts: three songs from her last studio album, "Crayons," in 2008, reached No. 1 on that chart, as did her final single, "To Paris With Love," in 2010.

"This music will always be with us," Ms. Summer told The New York Times in 2003. "I mean, whether they call it disco music or hip-hop or bebop or flip-flop, whatever they're going to call it, I think music to dance to will always be with us."

— By Jon Pareles

〰〰〰〰〰〰〰〰

DIETRICH FISCHER-DIESKAU

'One of the Most Remarkable Voices in History'

MAY 28, 1925 - MAY 18, 2012

D IETRICH FISCHER-DIESKAU, the German baritone whose beautiful voice and mastery of technique made him the 20th century's pre-eminent interpreter of art songs, died on May 18 at his home in Bavaria. He was 86.

Mr. Fischer-Dieskau was by virtual acclamation one of the world's great singers, from the 1940s to his official retirement in 1992, and an influential teacher and orchestra conductor for many years thereafter.

He was also a formidable industry, making hundreds of recordings that pretty much set the modern standard for performances of lieder, the musical settings of poems first popular in the 18th and 19th centuries. His output included the many hundreds of Schubert songs appropriate for the male voice, the songs and song cycles of Schumann and Brahms, and those of later composers like Mahler, Shostakovich and Hugo Wolf. He won two Grammy Awards, in 1971 for Schubert lieder and in 1973 for Brahms's "Schöne Magelone."

Mr. Fischer-Dieskau (pronounced FEE-shur-DEES-cow) had sufficient power for the concert hall and for substantial roles in his parallel career as a star of European opera houses. But he was essentially a lyrical, introspective singer whose effect on listeners was not to nail them to their seat backs, but rather to draw them into the very heart of song.

The pianist Gerald Moore, who accompanied many great artists of the postwar decades, said Mr. Fischer-Dieskau had a flawless sense of rhythm and "one of the most remarkable voices in history — honeyed and suavely expressive." Onstage he projected a masculine sensitivity informed by a cultivated upbringing and by dispiriting losses in World War II: the destruction of his family home, the death of his feeble brother in a Nazi institution, induction into the Wehrmacht when he had scarcely begun his voice studies at the Berlin Conservatory.

His performances eluded easy description. Where reviewers could get the essence of a

Pavarotti appearance in a phrase (the glories of a true Italian tenor!), a Fischer-Dieskau recital was akin to a magic show, with seamless shifts in dynamics and infinite shadings of coloration and character.

He had the good luck to age well, too. In 1988, at 62, he sang an all-Schumann program at Carnegie Hall, where people overflowed onto the stage to hear him.

Mr. Fischer-Dieskau described in his memoir "Reverberations" (1989) how his affinity for lieder had been formed in childhood. "I was won over to poetry at an early age," he wrote. "I have been in its thrall all my life because I was made to read it, because it gave me pleasure, and because I eventually came to understand what I was reading."

He discerned, he said, that "music and poetry have a common domain, from which they draw inspiration and in which they operate: the landscape of the soul."

Albert Dietrich Fischer was born in Berlin on May 28, 1925, the youngest of three sons of Albert

Fischer, a classical scholar and secondary school principal with relatively liberal ideas about education reform, and his young second wife, Theodora Klingelhoffer, a schoolteacher. (In 1934 Dr. Fischer added the hyphenated "Dieskau" to the family name; his mother had been a von Dieskau, descended from the Kammerherr von Dieskau, for whom J. S. Bach wrote the "Peasant Cantata.")

Family members knew Dietrich, as he was called, as a shy, private child who nonetheless liked to entertain. He put on puppet shows in which he voiced all the parts, sometimes for an audience of one: his physically and mentally disabled brother, Martin, with whom he shared a room.

Before adolescence Dietrich was inducted into a Hitler Youth group where, he recalled years later, he was appalled by the officiousness as well as by the brutality. His father died when he was 12. And he had just finished secondary school and one semester at the Berlin Conservatory when, in 1943, he was drafted into the Wehrmacht and assigned to care for army horses on the Russian front. He kept a diary there, calling it his "attempt at preserving an inner life in chaotic surroundings."

"Poems by Morgenstern," one entry read. "It is a good idea to learn them by heart, to have something to fall back on."

"Lots of cold, lots of slush and even more storms," read another. "Every day horses die for lack of food."

It was in Russia that he heard that his mother had been forced to send his brother to an institution outside Berlin. "Soon," he wrote later, "the Nazis did to him what they always did with cases like his: they starved him to death as quickly as possible."

And then his mother's apartment in Lichterfelde was bombed. Granted

"AKIN TO A MAGIC SHOW": Dietrich Fischer-Dieskau, right, performs with the pianist Gerald Moore, circa 1965.

home leave to help her, he found that all that remained of their possessions could be moved to a friend's apartment in a handcart. But as early as his second day home, he and his mother began seeking out "theater, concerts, a lot of other music — defying the irrational world."

Instead of returning to the disastrous campaign in Russia, he was diverted to Italy, along with thousands of other German soldiers. There, on May 5, 1945, just three days before the Allies accepted the German surrender, he was captured and imprisoned. It turned out to be a musical opportunity: soon the Americans were sending him around to entertain other P.O.W.'s from the back of a truck. The problem was, they were so pleased with this arrangement that they kept him until June 1947. He was among the last Germans to be repatriated.

Still, he was only 22 when he returned for further study at the Berlin Conservatory. He didn't stay long. Called to substitute for an indisposed baritone in Brahms's "German Requiem," he became famous practically overnight. As he said, "I passed my final exam in the concert hall."

Because of his youth, Mr. Fischer-Dieskau had been in no position to make his own choices in the 1930s and '40s, so he didn't encounter the questions about Nazi ties that hung over many a prominent German artist after the war. (The soprano Elisabeth Schwarzkopf, his frequent musical collaborator, repeatedly denied that she had joined the Nazi Party until confronted with evidence in 1983. "It was akin to joining a union," she said in an explanatory letter to The Times, "and exactly for the same reason: to have a job.")

Mr. Fischer-Dieskau gave his first professional lieder recital in Leipzig in the fall of 1947. Success followed success, with lieder performances in Britain and other European countries, beginning in 1949. He first toured the United States in 1955, choosing for his New York debut

to sing Schubert's demanding "Winterreise" cycle without intermission.

He had made his opera debut in 1948, singing Posa in Verdi's "Don Carlos" at Berlin's Städtische Oper (later renamed the Deutsche Oper), where he was hired as principal lyric baritone. He also sang regularly at the Bavarian State Opera in Munich and appeared frequently in the opera houses of Vienna, Covent Garden, Salzburg and Bayreuth.

Versatility was not the least of Mr. Fischer-Dieskau's assets. He tackled everything from Papageno in "The Magic Flute" — who knew that a goofy bird catcher could have immaculate diction? — to heavier parts like Wotan in "Das Rheingold" and Wolfram in "Tannhäuser." He recorded more than three dozen operatic roles, Italian as well as German, along with oratorios, Bach cantatas and works of many modern composers, including Benjamin Britten, whose "War Requiem" he sang at its premiere in 1962.

Mr. Fischer-Dieskau was married in 1949 to his sweetheart from his student days, the cellist Irmgard Poppen. They had three sons: Matthias, who became a stage designer; Martin, a conductor; and Manuel, a cellist. Ms. Poppen did not live to see them grow: she died of complications after Manuel's birth in 1963. For her husband it was a profound, disorienting loss.

He was married again, to the actress Ruth Leuwerik, from 1965 to 1967, and again, to Christina Pugel-Schule, the daughter of an American voice teacher, from 1968 to 1975.

His fourth marriage, in 1977, to the Hungarian soprano Julia Varady, was a rewarding match. Like the many artists who studied with him more formally, Ms. Varady found him to be a kindly, constructive and totally unsparing mentor.

Mr. Fischer-Dieskau's insistence on getting things right comes through vividly in scenes of him at rehearsal or conducting master class. In a video widely circulated at the time, showing him coaching a young Christine Schäfer, Ms. Schäfer is singing beautifully, or so it would seem to your average mortal, yet the smiling maestro interrupts time and again to suggest something better. And it isn't merely that he is invariably correct; it's also that when he rises to sing just a few illustrative notes, the studio is instantly a stage, and he illuminates it with what seems to be an inner light.

Even better is a documentary by Bruno Monsaingeon, "Dietrich Fischer-Dieskau: Autumn Journey," with archival and up-to-date footage.

Besides making music, he wrote about it: insightful, accessible books about the lives and music of great composers, including Schubert and Schumann. He was a widely exhibited painter, too, known especially for his portraits.

Mr. Fischer-Dieskau retired from opera in 1978. He continued giving song recitals through the end of 1992 and then, on New Year's Day 1993, announced that he would sing onstage no more.

Of the many tributes he received over the decades, perhaps none was more heartfelt than that of the British music critic John Amis:

"Providence gives to some singers a beautiful voice, to some musical artistry, to some (let us face it) neither, but to Fischer-Dieskau Providence has given both. The result is a miracle, and that is just about all there is to be said about it." Mr. Amis continued, "Having used a few superlatives and described the program, there is nothing else to do but write 'finis,' go home, and thank one's stars for having had the good luck to be present."

— BY DANIEL LEWIS

EUGENE POLLEY

He Handed the World the Remote

NOV. 29, 1915 - MAY 20, 2012

EUGENE POLLEY, an inventor whose best-known creation has fostered blissful sloth, caused decades of domestic discord and forever altered the way consumers watch television, died on May 20 in Downers Grove, Ill. Mr. Polley, the inventor of the wireless television remote control, was 96.

His death was announced by the Zenith Electronics Corporation, where Mr. Polley began his career in the stockroom before rising through the engineering ranks to invent the device, called the Flash-Matic, in 1955.

"Just think!," an advertisement breathlessly proclaimed that year. "Without budging from your easy chair you can turn your new Zenith Flash-Matic set on, off, or change channels. You can even shut off annoying commercials while the picture remains on the screen."

The Flash-Matic remote, which worked like a flashlight, was shaped like a snub-nosed revolver. The shape was a considered choice on Mr. Polley's part, as he explained in 2000, letting viewers in the age of ubiquitous

TV westerns "shoot out" commercials.

Flash-Matic made the TV audience less captive, though also less active. For the first time, viewers could comfortably exercise dominion over sound and image without simultaneously exercising the body on the march between couch and dial.

(The "dial" was a round thing with numbers on it — all the way up to 13 — by which viewers changed the channel through the direct application of fingers and wrist. One did not so much surf channels in those days as ride their gentle swells with all due deliberateness.)

As Mr. Polley, by then 86, proudly told an interviewer in 2002: "The flush toilet may have been the most civilized invention ever devised, but the remote control is the next most important. It's almost as important as sex."

For his invention, Mr. Polley received a thousand-dollar bonus. But his device was soon supplanted by a more efficient, more enduring and far better-selling one, developed by a Zenith colleague, Robert Adler.

News accounts over the years have often described Mr. Adler erroneously as the TV remote's sole inventor. Mr. Polley, a plainspoken man who seemed to avail himself of his own internal mute button only rarely, was largely relegated to the margins of history, a condition that rankled.

"Not only did I not get credit for doing anything," he told The Chicago Tribune in 2006, "I got a kick in the rear end."

Eugene Theodore Polley was born in Chicago on Nov. 29, 1915. (He disliked the name Theodore and adopted his confirmation name, Joseph, as his middle name.) His father, a bootlegger, abandoned the family when Gene was about 10.

The young Mr. Polley studied at the City Colleges of Chicago and the Armour Institute of Technology (now the Illinois Institute of

THE DAWN OF CHANNEL SURFING: A 1955 advertisement for Eugene Polley's Flash-Matic, the first wireless TV remote.

Technology), but lacked the money to complete a degree. At 20 he joined the Zenith Radio Company, as it was then known, as a stock boy earning 40 cents an hour.

Mechanically adept, he worked his way into the engineering department. During World War II Mr. Polley, on loan from Zenith, worked for the United States military on bomb fuses and ship-detecting radar.

After the war, as TV sets began to colonize American homes, Zenith's president, Eugene F. McDonald, faced a quandary. Mr. McDonald, who held a utopian view of the new medium, was certain that viewers would revolt en masse against television commercials, by his lights a growing scourge.

But until that halcyon day arrived, Mr. McDonald knew, he needed to offer consumers a stopgap, and he enlisted the company's engineers to make it.

The first TV remote, called Lazy Bones, was introduced by Zenith in 1950. It had one profound drawback, however: a cable snaking from the remote to the set, over which users were inclined to trip.

Mr. McDonald enlisted Mr. Polley to build a wireless remote, and the Flash-Matic was born. The hand-held device emitted a visible beam of light, which consumers could point at a compatible TV set.

The new, purpose-built sets had a photo cell embedded in each corner of the screen; the viewer activated the cell by "shooting" it with the remote. One cell changed the channel up, another changed the channel down, a third muted the sound, and the fourth turned the set on and off.

The device proved popular: during its first and only year of existence, 30,000 Flash-Matic sets were sold.

But there were difficulties. Because the system was light-activated, sunlight hitting the TV screen could cause the channels to change in spontaneous roulette. Viewers also had trouble remembering which corner of the screen controlled which function.

Mr. Adler improved Mr. Polley's device by making it responsive to sound instead of light. His remote, called Space Command, used inaudible, high-frequency sound waves to control the set. It, too, had problems — it could be set off by the sound of jangling keys or rattling coins — but was deemed enough of an improvement on its predecessor to be brought to market in 1956.

From that year to the early 1980s, when infrared remotes became standard, more than nine million sets controlled by Space Command technology were sold.

Mr. Polley, a longtime resident of Lombard, Ill., had lived most recently in Glen Ellyn, Ill. He is survived by a son and a grandson. His wife, the former Blanche Wiley, died before him, as did a daughter.

With other colleagues, Mr. Adler and Mr. Polley represented Zenith when it was given a special Emmy Award in 1997 for its development of wireless remotes.

Mr. Adler died in 2007. Zenith has said publicly that it considers him and Mr. Polley the joint inventors of the device.

Mr. Polley begged to differ.

"A father has to be present at conception," he said in a 2002 interview. "And if you're not, you're not that father."

— BY MARGALIT FOX

ROBIN GIBB

Bee Gee

DEC. 22, 1949 - MAY 20, 2012

ROBIN GIBB, one of the three singing brothers of the Bee Gees, the long-running Anglo-Australian pop group whose chirping falsettos and hook-laden disco hits like "Jive Talkin'" and "You Should Be Dancing" shot them to worldwide fame in the 1970s, died on May 20 in London. He was 62.

The cause was complications of cancer and intestinal surgery, his family said in a statement.

Cancer had spread from his colon to his liver, and in the weeks before his death he was in a coma for a while. He was the third Gibb brother to die. His fraternal twin and fellow Bee Gee, Maurice Gibb, died of complications of a twisted intestine in 2003 at 53. The youngest brother, Andy, who had a successful solo career, was 30 when he died of heart failure in 1988.

With brilliant smiles, polished funk and adenoidal close harmonies, the Bee Gees — Barry, Robin and Maurice Gibb — were disco's ambassadors to Middle America in the 1970s, embodying the peacocked look of the time in their open-chested leisure suits and gold medallions.

They sold well over 100 million albums and had six consecutive No. 1 singles from 1977 to 1979. They were also inextricably tied to the disco era's defining movie, "Saturday Night Fever," a showcase for their music that included the hit "Stayin' Alive," its propulsive beat in step with the strut of the film's star, John Travolta.

But the group, whose first record came out in 1963, had a history that preceded its disco hits, starting with upbeat ditties inspired by the Everly Brothers and the Beatles, then with lachrymose ballads like "How Can You Mend a Broken Heart."

Barry, the oldest brother, was the dominant Bee Gee for most of the group's existence. But the lead singer for many of the early hits was Robin, whose breaking voice, gaunt frame and gloomy eyes were well suited to convey adolescent fragility. "I Started a Joke" (with the second line, "Which started the whole world crying"), "I've Gotta Get a Message to You," "Massachusetts" and other heavy-hearted songs brought the Bee Gees to the top of the charts as one of the British Invasion's most musically conservative groups.

"While other guys, like Ray Davies of the Kinks, were writing about social problems, we were writing about emotions," Robin Gibb told

a British newspaper last year. "They were something boys didn't write about then because it was seen as a bit soft. But people love songs that melt your heart."

Robin Hugh Gibb and his twin, Maurice, were born on Dec. 22, 1949, on the Isle of Man, a British dependency in the Irish Sea. (Barry was born there in 1946.) The boys largely grew up in Manchester, England, where the family lived on the edge of poverty. Their father, Hugh, a drummer and bandleader, encouraged his sons to sing. Their mother, Barbara, was also a singer.

According to Bee Gees lore, the boys' first performance, in the mid-1950s, was unplanned. They had been scheduled to perform as a lip-synching act at a movie theater in Manchester when the record broke, forcing them to sing for real.

The family moved to Australia in 1958, and before long the brothers, performing as the Bee Gees — for Brothers Gibb — began scoring local hits and appearing on television. They left for London in early 1967 and within weeks had signed with Robert Stigwood, the impresario who guided them in their peak years.

The band's first single in Britain, "New York Mining Disaster 1941," was released in April 1967 and reached the Top 20.

In performance, Robin and Maurice usually played second fiddle to Barry, and Robin's taciturn manner was part of his public persona. On "The Barry Gibb Talk Show," a recurring skit on "Saturday Night Live," Barry, played by Jimmy Fallon, would repeatedly ask Robin, played by Justin Timberlake, if he had anything to add to his talks with congressmen and Supreme Court justices. "No," Robin would reply softly. "No, I don't."

But in private Robin was far from dull. He and his wife, Dwina Murphy, who survives him, lived in a 12th-century former monastery in

Oxfordshire that he had restored and filled with statues of Buddha and suits of armor. In Miami, his mansion was open to celebrities and politicians like Tony Blair.

Robin briefly left the group in 1969 and tried out a solo career. After he rejoined his brothers, they scored their first No. 1 in the United States with "How Can You Mend a Broken Heart" in 1971. But with harder rock taking over, the Bee Gees' popularity ebbed, reaching bottom in 1974 with a series of supper-club gigs in England to pay off tax debts.

At that point their label, Atlantic, sent the brothers to Miami for musical experimentation. There, with the 1975 album "Main Course," they reinvented the Bee Gees' sound with Latin and funk rhythms, electronic keyboards and vocals that owed a debt to Philadelphia soul. It brought the band its first hits in years: "Nights on Broadway" and "Jive Talkin'," which went to No. 1.

From there it moved further toward disco. The soundtrack to "Saturday Night Fever," in 1977 — with "You Should Be Dancing," "How Deep Is Your Love?," "Stayin' Alive" and "Night Fever," all No. 1's — became the biggest-selling album ever. (It was overtaken by Michael Jackson's "Thriller" in 1984.)

For many listeners, the Gibbs were the face of disco. Even "Sesame Street" got caught up in the trend, with Robin singing on the disco-themed album "Sesame Street Fever." It went gold.

The Bee Gees' 1979 album, "Spirits Having Flown," produced three more No. 1 singles, "Too Much Heaven," "Tragedy" and "Love You Inside Out." Then, in 1980, the band filed a $200 million lawsuit against Mr. Stigwood, saying he had swindled them out of royalties. Mr. Stigwood countersued for defamation and breach of contract. They settled out of court and publicly reconciled.

In the '80s the band's popularity waned in the United States but remained strong abroad. Robin released three solo albums, with limited success. The Bee Gees returned with some moderate hits in the late 1990s and were inducted into the Rock and Roll Hall of Fame in 1997. With his brothers, Mr. Gibb won six Grammys.

In addition to his wife and his brother Barry, Robin Gibb, who lived in Thame, Oxfordshire, England, is survived by two sons, two daughters, a sister and his mother. An earlier marriage ended in divorce.

Mr. Gibb had recently been working on a classical piece, "The Titanic Requiem," with his son Robin-John, who is known as R. J. It had its premiere in London on April 10, played by the Royal Philharmonic Orchestra, but Robin was too ill to attend.

DISCO'S AMBASSADORS: Robin Gibb, center, and his brothers, Barry, left, and Maurice, brought "Stayin' Alive" and other Bee Gees hits from Britain to Middle America.

Despite the Bee Gees' close association with disco, the Gibb brothers had long insisted that they had no stake in the genre. They had simply written songs that suited their voices and caught their fancy, they said.

"We always thought we were writing R&B grooves, what they called blue-eyed soul," Robin said in 2010. "We never heard the word disco; we just wrote groove songs we could harmonize strongly to, and with great melodies."

"The fact you could dance to them," he added, "we never thought about."

— BY BEN SISARIO

\\\\\\\\\\\\\\\\\\\\\\\\\\\\\\

DOC WATSON

He Didn't Need to See the Guitar to Master It

MARCH 3, 1923 · MAY 29, 2012

DOC WATSON, the guitarist and folk singer whose flat-picking style elevated the acoustic guitar to solo status in bluegrass and country music, and whose interpretations of traditional American music profoundly influenced generations of folk and rock guitarists, died on

May 29 in Winston-Salem, N.C. He was 89.

Mr. Watson, who had been blind since he was a baby, came to national attention during the folk music revival of the early 1960s, when he injected a note of authenticity into a movement awash in protest songs and bland renditions of traditional tunes. In a sweetly resonant, slightly husky baritone, he sang old hymns, ballads and country blues he had learned growing up in the northwestern corner of North Carolina, which has produced fiddlers, banjo pickers and folk singers for generations.

His mountain music came as a revelation to the folk audience, as did his virtuoso guitar playing. Unlike most country and bluegrass musicians, who thought of the guitar as a secondary instrument for providing rhythmic backup, Mr. Watson executed the kind of flashy, rapid-fire melodies normally played by a fiddle or a banjo. His style influenced a generation of young musicians learning to play the

guitar as folk music achieved national popularity.

"He is single-handedly responsible for the extraordinary increase in acoustic flat-picking and fingerpicking guitar performance," said Ralph Rinzler, the folklorist who discovered Mr. Watson in 1960. "His flat-picking style has no precedent in earlier country music history."

Arthel Lane Watson was born in Stoney Fork, N.C., the sixth of nine children, on March 3, 1923. His father, General Dixon Watson, was a farmer and day laborer who led the singing at the local Baptist church. His mother, Annie, sang old-time ballads while doing household chores and at night sang the children to sleep.

When Mr. Watson was still an infant an eye infection left him blind, and the few years of formal schooling he received were at the Raleigh School for the Blind. His musical training, typical for the region, began in early childhood. At the age of 5 or 6 he received his first harmonica as a Christmas gift, and at 11 his father made him a fretless banjo with a head made from the skin of a family cat that had just died.

Mr. Watson dropped out of school in the seventh grade and began working for his father, who helped him get past his disability. "I would not have been worth the salt that went in my bread if my dad hadn't put me at the end of a crosscut saw to show me that there was not a reason in the world that I couldn't pull my own weight and help to do my part in some of the hard work," he told Frets magazine in 1979.

By then, he had moved beyond the banjo. His father, hearing him plucking chords on a borrowed guitar, promised to buy him his own guitar if he could teach himself a song by the end of the day. The boy taught himself the Carter Family's "When the Roses Bloom in Dixieland," and a week later he was the proud owner of a $12 Stella guitar.

Mr. Watson initially employed a thumb-picking style, in which the thumb establishes a bass line on the lower strings while the rest of the fingers pick out a melody or chords. That soon changed.

"I began listening to Jimmie Rodgers recordings seriously and I figured, 'Hey, he must be doing that with one of them straight picks,'" he told Dirty Linen magazine in 1995. "So I got me one and began to work at it. Then I began to learn the Jimmie Rodgers licks on the guitar, then all at once I began to figure out, 'Hey, I could play that Carter stuff a lot better with a flat pick.'"

To pay for a new Martin guitar bought on the installment plan, Mr. Watson played for tips at a cab stand in Lenoir, N.C. Before long he was appearing at amateur contests and fiddlers' conventions. One day, as he prepared to play for a radio show being broadcast from a furniture store, the announcer decided that the young guitarist needed a snappier name and appealed to the audience for suggestions. A woman yelled out, "Doc!," and the name stuck. (Last year, a

AN INFLUENTIAL STYLE: Doc Watson brought the acoustic guitar to the forefront of bluegrass and country music during the folk music revival of the 1960s.

life-size statue of Mr. Watson was dedicated in Boone, N.C., at another spot where he had once played for tips to support his family. At his request the inscription read, "Just One of the People.")

In 1947 he married Rosa Lee Carlton, the daughter of a local fiddler. The couple's first child, Merle, took up the guitar and began performing with his father in 1964. Their partnership, which produced 20 albums, ended with Merle Watson's death at 36 in a tractor accident in Lenoir in 1985. Mr. Watson, who lived in Deep Gap, N.C., is survived by his wife, a daughter, a brother, two grandchildren and several great-grandchildren.

In 1953, Mr. Watson began playing electric guitar with a country dance band, Jack Williams and the Country Gentlemen. The band usually played without a fiddle, so Mr. Watson learned how to play lead fiddle parts on the guitar, often complicated melodies executed at top speed.

This technique, which he carried over to the acoustic guitar, became a hallmark, exemplified by his much imitated version of "Black Mountain Rag."

In 1960 Mr. Rinzler, the folklorist, was attending a fiddlers' convention in Union Grove, N.C., when he encountered Clarence Ashley, an old-time folk musician better known as Tom Ashley, whom he persuaded to sit for a recording session. Mr. Ashley put together a group of top local musicians that included Mr. Watson on banjo and guitar. Impressed, Mr. Rinzler went to Mr. Watson's home and recorded him with family members, including his father-in-law, Gaither Carlton.

A year later Mr. Watson, Mr. Ashley and several other musicians gave a concert at P.S. 41 in Greenwich Village sponsored by the Friends of Old Time Music. The performance led to appearances at colleges and folk festivals and a solo career for Mr. Watson, who became a star attraction at clubs like Gerdes Folk City and an audience favorite for his folksy, humorous banter onstage. He was invited to appear at the Newport Folk Festival in 1963 and 1964. In 1963 he performed at Town Hall in Manhattan with the bluegrass pioneer Bill Monroe.

In the meantime Folkways released "Old Time Music at Clarence Ashley's" and "The Watson Family," and Vanguard released Mr. Watson's first solo album, "Doc Watson." His recordings for Folkways and Vanguard in the 1960s are regarded as classics.

Despite his image, Mr. Watson was not a folk-music purist. Even as a child he absorbed big-band jazz and the guitar playing of Django Reinhardt, whose records he heard at school. "I can't be put in a box," he told Fred Metting, the author of "The Life, Work, and Music of the American Folk Artist Doc Watson" (2006). "I play traditional music and whatever else I'm drawn to."

His catholic tastes expressed themselves on albums like "Good Deal!" (1968), recorded in Nashville with mainstream country musicians; "Docabilly" (1995), a return to the kind of rock 'n' roll he had played in the 1950s; and the eclectic "Memories" (1975), which included "field hollers, black blues, sacred music, mountain music, gospel, rhythm and blues, even traces of jazz," the critic Chet Flippo wrote in his liner notes.

Folk audiences, however, saw Mr. Watson as a direct conduit to the roots music of Appalachia, which he played with conviction. "To me the old-time fiddling, the old-time ballads — there never was anything prettier and there never will be," he said.

Mr. Watson found touring hard to bear. "For a green country man not really used to the city, it was a scary thing to come to New York and wonder, 'Will that guy meet me there at the bus station, and will the bus driver help me change buses?' and all that stuff, people not knowing you're blind and stepping on your feet," he told The Washington Post. "It's scary, the road is."

In 1964 Merle Watson, then 15, joined him as a rhythm guitarist and eased most of the burdens of the road from his father's shoulders. The two performed together for 20 years, receiving Grammy Awards for the albums "Then and Now" in 1974, "Two Days in November" in 1975 and "Big Sandy/Leather Britches" in 1980. A sampling of their work was collected on "Watson Country: Doc and Merle Watson" (1996).

Waning interest in folk music slowed Mr. Watson's career in the late 1960s, but in 1972 he was invited to contribute to "Will the Circle Be Unbroken," an album that paired the Nitty Gritty Dirt Band with country artists like Maybelle Carter, Merle Travis (Merle Watson's namesake) and Earl Scruggs. The record's success brought Mr. Watson a new audience, and he and Merle toured constantly until Merle's death.

Mr. Watson returned to the road a week after the funeral. Merle, he said, had appeared to him in a dream and urged him to carry on. In his son's honor, he helped found an annual music festival in Wilkesboro, N.C., now known as Merlefest.

In the post-Merle period, Mr. Watson won Grammys for the albums "Riding the Midnight Train" in 1987, "On Praying Ground" in 1991 and "Legacy" in 2003. His fingers were dexterous well into old age, as he showed on the track "Whiskey Before Breakfast," recorded with the guitarist Bryan Sutton, which won a Grammy for best country instrumental performance in 2007. In concerts he was often joined on guitar by his grandson Richard, Merle's son.

In 1997, President Bill Clinton presented Mr. Watson with the National Medal of Arts at the White House. "There may not be a serious, committed baby boomer alive who didn't at some point in his or her youth try to spend a few minutes at least trying to learn to pick a guitar like Doc Watson," Mr. Clinton said.

Quiet and unassuming offstage, Mr. Watson played down his virtuoso guitar playing as nothing more than "country pickin'." He told interviewers that had he not been blind, he would have become an auto mechanic and been just as happy.

"He wants to be remembered as a pretty good old boy," said the guitarist Jack Lawrence, who had played with Mr. Watson since the early 1980s. "He doesn't put the fact that he plays the guitar as more than a skill."

— By WILLIAM GRIMES

JACK TWYMAN

In the Friendship Hall of Fame, Too

MAY 21, 1934 - MAY 30, 2012

Jack Twyman was a Hall of Fame basketball player who once scored 59 points in an N.B.A. game. In 1959-60 he and Wilt Chamberlain became the first players to average more than 30 points a game in a season. He later became an analyst for the N.B.A. game of the week on ABC and a food company executive

who pocketed more than $3 million when he sold the company in 1996.

But Twyman's greatest fame came from simply helping out a friend. After his Cincinnati Royals teammate Maurice Stokes had a paralyzing brain injury in the final regular-season game

in 1958, Twyman learned that Stokes was nearly destitute.

So he became Stokes's legal guardian. He helped him get workers' compensation; raised hundreds of thousands of dollars to pay for medical care, partly through organizing an annual charity game of basketball superstars; and helped him learn to communicate by blinking his eyes to denote individual letters.

And for decades Twyman pressed the Naismith Memorial Basketball Hall of Fame in Springfield, Mass., to induct Stokes, a power forward who once grabbed 38 rebounds in a game. When the Hall of Fame finally did so, in 2004, 21 years after Twyman's induction, Twyman accepted the award for his friend.

Twyman, who was 78, died of cancer in Cincinnati on May 30, more than 40 years after Stokes died of a heart attack at 36.

On March 12, 1958, the Royals were playing their season finale, against the Minneapolis Lakers. Stokes went over the shoulder of an opponent and hit his head on the floor so hard that he was knocked out. In those days, teams had no trainers, much less doctors, and scant knowledge of head injuries. Once revived, he continued to play.

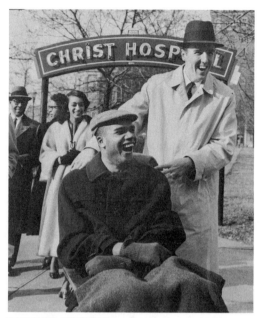

TEAMMATE, GUARDIAN: Maurice Stokes, left, and Jack Twyman, leaving the hospital for the first time since Mr. Stokes's injury.

Three days later, Stokes, who was 24, went into a coma. When he came out of it, he could not move or talk. The diagnosis was brain damage. Stokes, whose family lived in Pittsburgh, had to stay in Cincinnati to be eligible for workers' compensation.

"Maurice was on his own," Twyman told The New York Post in 2008. "Something had to be done and someone had to do it. I was the only one there, so I became that someone."

Twyman always insisted that any teammate would have done the same. Others saw something special. On the occasion of Stokes's death in 1970, the sports columnist Arthur Daley of The New York Times wrote that

he saw "nobility and grandeur" in Twyman's actions, likening him to the biblical good Samaritan.

"What gives it a quality of extra warmth," he wrote, "is the pigmentation of the two principals." Stokes was black, Twyman white.

John Kennedy Twyman, the son of a steel company foreman, was born in Pittsburgh on May 21, 1934, and grew up playing against Stokes in summer leagues. Twyman went to the University of Cincinnati and Stokes to St. Francis College (now University) in Loretto, Pa. Their teams met in the 1955 National Invitation Tournament.

Both were genuine stars. Stokes, at 6 feet 7 inches and 232 pounds, was the N.B.A. rookie of the year in 1956. The next year he set a league rebounding record, and he became a three-time All-Star. The Boston Celtics star Bob Cousy called him "the first great, athletic power forward."

Twyman was a skinny 6-6 forward who in 11 seasons with the Royals (now the Sacramento Kings) was a six-time All-Star.

He shot 45 percent over his career, and when he retired in 1966 he had scored 15,840 points. In their record-setting season of averaging more than 30 points a game, Chamberlain averaged 37.6, Twyman 31.2. Twyman's 59-point game came with the Royals against the Minneapolis Lakers on Jan. 15, 1960.

Twyman sometimes worried that his wife and family might become upset over the amount of time he devoted to Stokes over 12 years, but his daughter Lisa Bessone said in an interview that they had come to look forward to Stokes's Sunday visits from the hospital. Twyman's wife of 57 years, the former Carole Frey, became, with her husband, a co-trustee of the Maurice Stokes Foundation, which was set up to defray Stokes's hospital costs but grew to help other needy N.B.A. veterans as well.

The charity basketball tournament they began at Kutsher's Hotel in the Catskills drew stars like Bill Russell, Oscar Robertson and, of course, Chamberlain.

Twyman, who had an insurance business even while playing basketball, was an analyst for "The NBA on ABC" in the late 1960s and early '70s, working with Chris Schenkel. In the moments before Game 7 of the 1970 N.B.A. championship between the Knicks and the Los Angeles Lakers, Twyman saw the injured Knicks center Willis Reed limping toward the Madison Square Garden court. "I think we see Willis coming out," he told viewers.

Reed's appearance is credited with inspiring the Knicks to their 113-99 victory over the Lakers.

From 1972 to 1996, Twyman was chairman and chief executive of Super Food Services, a food wholesaler based in Dayton, Ohio. During the 1980s, he quintupled its earnings.

In addition to his daughter, Twyman is survived by his wife as well as a son, two other daughters and 14 grandchildren.

Years after Stokes's accident, when he had recovered enough finger flexibility to type, his first message was: "Dear Jack, How can I ever thank you?"

Twyman shrugged this off, saying that whenever he felt down, he "selfishly" visited the always cheerful Stokes. "He never failed to pump me up," he said.

— By Douglas Martin

ROSA GUY

Her Young Readers, She Said, Were Too Old for Fairy Tales

SEPT. 1, 1922 - JUNE 3, 2012

Rosa Guy, a Caribbean-born writer known for her unflinchingly direct novels for young people about black life in urban America, died on June 3 at her home in Manhattan. She was 89.

Ms. Guy (her surname rhymes with "key") was widely considered one of the 20th century's most distinguished writers for young adults. She addressed subjects that had remained largely unexplored in fiction for teenagers when she began her career four decades ago.

The themes to which she returned repeatedly in these books — and in several well-received novels for adults — included race, class, poverty, sexuality and simmering tensions between American blacks and Afro-Caribbean immigrants newly arrived in the United States.

"She's never afraid of the truth," the writer Maya Angelou, a friend of more than 50 years, said in a telephone interview after Ms. Guy's death. "Some writers dress the truth in a kind of elegant language, so it doesn't seem quite so blatant, so harsh, so raw. But Rosa was not afraid of that."

Of her books for young adults, the best known was a trilogy of novels, "The Friends" (1973), "Ruby" (1976) and "Edith Jackson" (1978). The books drew partly on Ms. Guy's experience as a young immigrant from Trinidad, coming of age in New York without money, parents or stability.

"The Friends" centers on the sometimes wary alliance between two teenage schoolmates: Phyllisia Cathy, an educated West Indian immigrant, and Edith Jackson, a poor, street-smart African-American born and reared in Harlem.

The second book in the trilogy features Phyllisia's sister, Ruby, who embarks on a lesbian relationship with another girl — a taboo subject in children's literature then. The third returns to Edith, now in a foster home and pregnant, who must choose between having the baby and having an abortion.

Reviewing "The Friends" in The New York Times Book Review in 1973, the novelist Alice Walker described it as a "heart-slammer," adding: "This book is called a 'juvenile.' So be a juvenile while you read it. Rosa Guy will give you back a large part of the memory of those years that you've been missing."

Ms. Guy's novels for adults include "My Love, My Love: Or, the Peasant Girl" (1985), a Caribbean-inflected reworking of Hans Christian Andersen's story "The Little Mermaid."

In Andersen's story, a mermaid's love for a prince is doomed by her inability to survive on land. In Ms. Guy's retelling, a Creole peasant woman falls in love with a wealthy man but finds she cannot transcend his family's class prejudice.

The novel was made into a musical, "Once on This Island," with book and lyrics by Lynn Ahrens and music by Stephen Flaherty. Directed by Graciela Daniele, it played for more than a year on Broadway in 1990 and 1991 and was nominated for eight Tony Awards.

BLEAK BUT HOPEFUL:
Rosa Guy's fiction for young adults dealt with difficult themes and harsh truths.

Ms. Guy's own childhood was like something from a fairy tale, though not the kind suffused with light. Rosa Cuthbert was born in Diego Martin, Trinidad, on Sept. 1, 1922. At 7, Rosa arrived in Harlem with her 10-year-old sister, Ameze, to join their parents, who had moved to New York to seek a better life.

Their mother died two years later, "leaving us," Ms. Guy said in a 1965 interview, "with a tyrant of a father, who was terrified at the prospect of raising two girls in the corrupting influence of the big-city life."

He soon married a well-to-do woman, and for a brief halcyon period, Ms. Guy recounted, the girls "were swept from abject poverty to a situation where we were being taken to picnics on the weekend in a chauffeur-driven car."

The marriage foundered, and the girls resumed life with their father, whose behavior was increasingly erratic. By the time Rosa was 14, he too had died. To support herself and her sister — Ameze was too frail for the task — Rosa left school for factory work in the garment district.

The sisters were eventually shunted through a series of orphanages and foster homes. Hearing the personal narratives of the children she met there, Ms. Guy said, made her realize that her vocation lay in storytelling.

Before turning to writing, she studied acting at the American Negro Theater, a Harlem-based group of the 1940s where Sidney Poitier and Harry Belafonte received early training. With John Oliver Killens and others, Ms. Guy founded the Harlem Writers Guild in 1950.

Ms. Guy was a passionate participant in midcentury black nationalist organizations, and in more traditional civil rights groups. Her first book, "Bird at My Window," a critically praised novel for adults published in 1966, told the story of a gifted young black man crushed by systemic poverty and violence.

An early marriage, to Warner Guy, ended in divorce; they had a son who died in 1995. Ms. Guy's survivors include five grandchildren and eight great-grandchildren. She died of cancer.

Among her other books are "Children of Longing" (1971), a nonfiction volume of interviews with African-American youth she compiled after the assassinations of Malcolm X and the Rev. Dr. Martin Luther King Jr.; a trilogy of young-adult novels featuring Imamu Jones, an inquisitive adolescent boy; several picture books; and the adult novel "A Measure of Time" (1983), about a self-made woman's rise amid the Harlem Renaissance.

For all their surface bleakness, Ms. Guy's books were far from hopeless. Characters often rose above their circumstances through new-found self-awareness and, in particular, through the capacity to forge durable bonds with others.

"She loved to write about love," Ms. Angelou said. "If you thought a situation called for a kind of mournfulness, she was the one to laugh and turn music on and dance."

— By Margalit Fox

RAY BRADBURY

The Poet Laureate of Science Fiction

AUG. 22, 1920 - JUNE 5, 2012

R AY Bradbury, whose imaginative and lyrical evocations of the future in his masterly, immensely popular science fiction reflected both the optimism and the anxieties of his own postwar America, died on June 5 in Los Angeles. He was 91.

By many estimations Mr. Bradbury was the writer most responsible for bringing modern science fiction into the literary mainstream. His name would appear near the top of any list of major science fiction writers of the 20th century, beside those of Isaac Asimov, Arthur C. Clarke, Robert A. Heinlein and the Polish author Stanislaw Lem. His books are still being taught in schools, where many a reader has been introduced to them half a century after they first appeared. Many have said that his stories fired their own imaginations.

More than eight million copies of his books have been sold in 36 languages. They include the short-story collections "The Martian Chronicles," "The Illustrated Man" and "The Golden Apples of the Sun," and the novels "Fahrenheit 451" and "Something Wicked This Way Comes."

Though none of his works won a Pulitzer Prize, Mr. Bradbury received a Pulitzer cita-tion in 2007 "for his distinguished, prolific and deeply influential career as an unmatched author of science fiction and fantasy."

It was a career that stretched across 70 years, to the last weeks of his life. The New Yorker published an autobiographical essay by Mr. Bradbury in its June 4, 2012, double issue devoted to science fiction. There he recalled his "hungry imagination" as a boy in Illinois.

"It was one frenzy after one elation after one enthusiasm after one hysteria after another," he wrote, noting, "You rarely have such fevers later in life that fill your entire day with emotion."

Mr. Bradbury sold his first story to a maga-zine called Super Science Stories in his early 20s. By 30 he had made his reputation with "The

Martian Chronicles," a collection of thematically linked stories published in 1950.

The book celebrated the romance of space travel while condemning the social abuses that modern technology had made possible, and its impact was immediate and lasting. Critics who had dismissed science fiction as adolescent prattle praised "Chronicles" as stylishly written morality tales set in a future that seemed just around the corner.

Mr. Bradbury was hardly the first writer to represent science and technology as a mixed bag of blessings and abominations. The advent of the atomic bomb in 1945 left many Americans deeply ambivalent toward science. The same "super science" that had ended World War II now appeared to threaten the very existence of civilization. Science fiction writers, who were accustomed to thinking about the role of science in society, had trenchant things to say about the nuclear threat.

But the audience for science fiction, published mostly in pulp magazines, was small and insignificant. Mr. Bradbury looked to a larger audience: the readers of mass-circulation magazines like Mademoiselle and The Saturday Evening Post. These readers had no patience for the technical jargon of the science fiction pulps. So he eliminated the jargon; he packaged his troubling speculations about the future in an appealing blend of cozy colloquialisms and poetic metaphors.

Though his books became a staple of high school and college English courses, Mr. Bradbury himself disdained formal education. He went so far as to attribute his success as a writer to his never having gone to college.

Instead, he read everything he could get his hands on: Edgar Allan Poe, Jules Verne, H. G. Wells, Edgar Rice Burroughs, Thomas Wolfe, Ernest Hemingway. He paid homage to them in 1971 in the essay "How Instead of Being Educated in College, I Was Graduated From Libraries." (Late in life he helped raise money for public libraries in Southern California.)

Mr. Bradbury referred to himself as an "idea writer," by which he meant something quite different from erudite or scholarly. "I have fun with ideas; I play with them," he said. "I'm not a serious person, and I don't like serious people. I don't see myself as a philosopher. That's awfully boring."

"My goal," he added, "is to entertain myself and others."

He described his method of composition as "word association," often triggered by a favorite line of poetry.

Mr. Bradbury's passion for books found expression in his dystopian novel "Fahrenheit 451," published in 1953. But he drew his primary inspiration from his childhood. He boasted that he had total recall of his earliest years, including the moment of his birth. Readers had no reason to doubt him. As for the protagonists of his stories, no matter how far they journeyed from home, they learned that they could never escape the past.

In his best stories and in his autobiographical novel, "Dandelion Wine" (1957), he gave voice to both the joys and fears of childhood, as well as its wonders.

"Dandelion Wine" begins before dawn on the first day of summer. From a window, Douglas Spaulding, 12, looks out upon his town, "covered over with darkness and at ease in bed." He has a task to perform.

"One night each week he was allowed to leave his father, his mother, and his younger brother Tom asleep in their small house next door and run here, up the dark spiral stairs to his grandparents' cupola," Mr. Bradbury writes, "and in this sorcerer's tower sleep with thunders and visions, to wake before the crystal jingle of milk bottles and perform his ritual magic.

"He stood at the open window in the dark, took a deep breath and exhaled. The streetlights, like candles on a black cake, went out. He exhaled again and again and the stars began to vanish."

Now he begins to point his finger — "There, and there. Now over here, and here . . ." — and lights come on, and the town begins to stir.

"Clock alarms tinkled faintly. The courthouse clock boomed. Birds leaped from trees like a net thrown by his hand, singing. Douglas, conducting an orchestra, pointed to the eastern sky.

"The sun began to rise.

"He folded his arms and smiled a magician's smile. Yes, sir, he thought, everyone jumps, everyone runs when I yell. It'll be a fine season.

"He gave the town a last snap of his fingers.

"Doors slammed open; people stepped out.

"Summer 1928 began."

Raymond Douglas Bradbury was born on Aug. 22, 1920, in Waukegan, Ill., a small city whose charms, befitting a Norman Rockwell painting, he evoked in his depiction of the fictional Green Town in "Dandelion Wine" and "Something Wicked This Way Comes," and in the fatally alluring fantasies of the astronauts in "The Martian Chronicles." His father, Leonard, a lineman with the electric company, numbered among his ancestors a woman who was tried as a witch in Salem, Mass.

An unathletic child who suffered from bad dreams, Ray relished the tales of the Brothers Grimm and the Oz stories of L. Frank Baum, which his mother, the former Esther Moberg, read to him. An aunt took him to his first stage plays, dressed him in monster costumes for Halloween and introduced him to Poe's stories.

UNCERTAIN FUTURE: Ray Bradbury's fiction reflected postwar American anxieties.

He discovered the science fiction pulps and began collecting the comic-strip adventures of Buck Rogers and Flash Gordon. The impetus to become a writer was supplied by a carnival magician named Mr. Electrico, who engaged the boy, then 12, in a conversation that touched on immortality.

In 1934 young Ray, his parents and his older brother, Leonard, moved to Los Angeles. (Another brother and a sister had died young.) Ray became a movie buff, sneaking into theaters as often as nine times a week by his count. Encouraged by a high school English teacher and the professional writers he met at the Los Angeles chapter of the Science Fiction League, he began an enduring routine of turning out at least a thousand words a day on his typewriter.

His first big success came in 1947 with the short story "Homecoming," narrated by a boy who feels like an outsider at a family reunion of witches, vampires and werewolves because he lacks supernatural powers. The story, plucked from the pile of unsolicited manuscripts at Mademoiselle by a young editor named Truman Capote, earned Mr. Bradbury an O. Henry Award as one of the best American short stories of the year.

With 26 other stories in a similar vein, "Homecoming" appeared in Mr. Bradbury's first book, "Dark Carnival," published by a small specialty press in 1947. That same year he married Marguerite Susan McClure, whom he had met in a Los Angeles bookstore.

Having written himself "down out of the attic," as he later put it, Mr. Bradbury focused on science fiction. In a burst of creativity from 1946 to 1950, he produced most of the stories later collected in "The Martian Chronicles" and "The Illustrated Man" and the novella that would form the basis of "Fahrenheit 451."

While science fiction purists complained about Mr. Bradbury's cavalier attitude toward scientific facts — he gave his fictional Mars an impossibly breathable atmosphere — the literary establishment waxed enthusiastic. The novelist Christopher Isherwood greeted Mr. Bradbury as "a very great and unusual talent," and one of Mr. Bradbury's heroes, Aldous Huxley, hailed him as a poet. In 1954, the National Institute of Arts and Letters honored Mr. Bradbury for "his contributions to American literature," in particular the novel "Fahrenheit 451."

Mr. Bradbury was one of the few science fiction authors on school reading lists.

"The Martian Chronicles" was pieced together from 26 stories, only a few of which were written with the book in mind. The patchwork narrative, spanning the years 1999 to 2026, depicts a series of expeditions to Mars and their aftermath. The native Martians, who can read minds, resist the early arrivals from Earth, but are finally no match for them and their advanced technology as the humans proceed to destroy the remains of an ancient civilization.

Parallels to the fate of American Indian cultures are pushed to the point of parody; the Martians are finally wiped out by an epidemic of chickenpox. When nuclear war destroys Earth, the descendants of the human colonists realize that they have become the Martians, with a second chance to create a just society.

"Fahrenheit 451" is perhaps his most successful book-length narrative. An indictment of authoritarianism, it portrays a book-burning America of the near future, its central character a so-called fireman, whose job is to light the bonfires. (The title refers to the temperature at which paper ignites.) Some critics compared it favorably to George Orwell's "1984." François Truffaut adapted the book for a well-received movie in 1966 starring Oskar Werner and Julie Christie.

As Mr. Bradbury's reputation grew, he found new outlets for his talents. He wrote the screenplay for John Huston's 1956 film version of "Moby-Dick," scripts for the television series "Alfred Hitchcock Presents" and collections of poetry and plays.

In the mid-1980s he was the on-camera host of "Ray Bradbury Theater," a cable series that featured dramatizations of his short stories.

While Mr. Bradbury championed the space program as an adventure that humanity dared not shirk, he was content to restrict his own adventures to the realm of imagination. He lived in the same house in Los Angeles for more than 50 years, rearing four daughters with his wife, Marguerite, who died in 2003. For many years he refused to travel by plane, preferring trains, and he never learned to drive.

In 2004, President George W. Bush and the first lady, Laura Bush, presented Mr. Bradbury with the National Medal of Arts. Mr. Bradbury is survived by his four daughters and eight grandchildren.

Though the sedentary writing life appealed to him most, he was not reclusive. He developed a flair for public speaking on the national lecture circuit, where he talked about his struggle to reconcile his mixed feelings about modern life, a theme that animated much of his fiction and won him a large and sympathetic audience.

And he talked about the future, perhaps his favorite subject, describing how it both attracted and repelled him, leaving him filled with apprehension and hope.

— By GERALD JONAS

HENRY HILL

Goodfella

JUNE 11, 1943 - JUNE 12, 2012

H ENRY HILL, an associate in the Luchese organized-crime family whose decision to turn federal informer, and subsequent itinerant life in and out of the federal witness protection program, inspired Martin Scorsese's acclaimed film "Goodfellas," died on June 12 in Los Angeles. He was

69 and had lived openly in Topanga, Calif., in recent years.

He had previously lived, far less openly, in Seattle; Cincinnati; Omaha; Butte, Mont.; and Independence, Ky., among many other places; as well as in the United States Penitentiary in Lewisburg, Pa.

His death, in a hospital, came after a series of health problems that included heart disease and the toll of years of heavy smoking, his fiancée, Lisa Caserta, said.

A native New Yorker of half-Irish, half-Sicilian parentage, Mr. Hill was involved with the Luchese family, considered the most powerful of the city's original five Mafia families, from his youth in the 1950s until 1980.

That year, arrested on drug-trafficking charges and facing the prospect of a long prison term, to say nothing of possible execution by his former bosses, Mr. Hill became a government witness against his past associates. His testimony in multiple trials helped send dozens of people to prison.

THE INFORMANT: Henry Hill left the mob to become a government witness.

In Mr. Scorsese's movie, released in 1990 and currently ranked 92nd on the American Film Institute's list of the top 100 pictures, Mr. Hill is played by Ray Liotta. The film was based on Nicholas Pileggi's best-selling biography, "Wiseguy: Life in a Mafia Family," published in 1985. Mr. Hill enjoyed "Goodfellas" immensely, telling Premiere magazine, "Had I the opportunity to direct the film myself — if I knew anything about directing — I don't think I could have done a better job."

Mr. Hill wrote several books of his own, including "The Wiseguy Cookbook" (2002; with Priscilla Davis), a collection of recipes and reminiscences that includes a disquisition on the problems of finding authentic pecorino Siciliano in the flyspecks on the map to which Mr. Hill was frequently consigned.

A garrulous figure to whom the anonymity of the witness protection program was anathema — he was expelled from the program in 1987 for relentless misbehavior that included drug possession — Mr. Hill took part in several headline-making crimes during his underworld days.

Chief among them was the Lufthansa heist of 1978, in which he and confederates robbed the airline's cargo terminal at Kennedy International Airport of $5 million in cash and nearly $1 million in jewels.

At the time, the heist was widely described as the most lucrative cash robbery in the United States. Mr. Hill, who was not prosecuted in the case, testified against other participants.

In the late 1970s, Mr. Hill was involved in a point-shaving scandal at Boston College, in which basketball players were bribed to fix games.

Although Mr. Hill said in interviews — and he gave a lot of them — that he had never killed anyone, by his own admission he knew, quite literally, where a great many bodies were buried.

"I was present when people got murdered," he told The Advocate of Stamford, Conn., in 2010. "I dug a lot of holes."

After leaving witness protection, Mr. Hill lived in comparative safety: most of those he feared were either dead or in prison. But given his former line of work, he remained suitably wary, moving often and adopting disguises as needed.

"If I go to the racetrack, I put a hat and glasses on, and I take my teeth out," he told the British newspaper The Independent in 2001. "You can't recognize me, trust me."

Mr. Hill was a frequent guest on television talk shows, including Geraldo Rivera's, and on Howard Stern's radio show. He also started a Web site, goodfellahenry.com, on which he sold memorabilia and dispensed practical advice on subjects like "Best Ways to Hide a Corpse."

But beneath Mr. Hill's surface charm and ready self-justification lay a lifelong addiction to drugs and alcohol and, family members have said, a flash-flood propensity for violence.

Henry Hill was born in Manhattan on June 11, 1943, and raised in Brooklyn. His father, an electrician who worked on the construction of the World Trade Center, deplored the local Mafiosi and tried to impress on his son the need for a suitable vocation.

"I actually wanted to be a priest," Henry Hill told The Chicago Tribune in 1986. "But that didn't work out."

He was soon seduced, he said, by the flash and dazzle of the neighborhood wiseguys, with their sleek cars, glinting rings and glittering women. At about 12, he began work as an errand boy at a local mob-run cab stand and pizzeria, where he refined his budding love of cooking. By 13 he was catering some of Brooklyn's biggest permanent floating craps games.

He joined the Army at 17 and soon had a tidy sideline in surplus mess-hall steaks, which he sold to restaurants near his base at Fort Bragg, in North Carolina.

He was discharged several years later, he wrote, when he started a brawl and, after the sheriff arrived, elected to steal the sheriff's car. He returned to Brooklyn and the mob, becoming a protégé of Paul Vario, a capo in the Luchese organization.

Mr. Hill's portfolio included arson, numbers running, truck hijacking, loan sharking, assault and dealing cocaine and heroin. In the 1970s, he served four years in Lewisburg on an extortion charge.

Mr. Hill's behavior, often intensified by drugs and alcohol, could be highly erratic. In "On the Run: A Mafia Childhood," a joint memoir published in 2004, his son Gregg (who was 13 when the family went underground) and his daughter, Gina (who was 11), recounted their father's hair-trigger temper.

"On my 17th birthday, he beat me within an inch of my life and then took a butcher knife to a picture of me," Gina Hill, promoting the book on Fox News, told Greta Van Susteren.

Mr. Hill's marriage to his first wife, Karen (portrayed by Lorraine Bracco in "Goodfellas"), ended in divorce. He is survived by their children, both of whom have long lived under other names. Also surviving is a son from his marriage (possibly a common-law union) to his second wife, Kelly; a brother; four sisters; and four grandchildren.

For all Mr. Hill's celebrity as an erstwhile criminal, he was never entirely rehabilitated. In 2005, while working as a chef in North Platte, Neb., he pleaded no contest to attempted possession of methamphetamine and, in a plea agreement, was sentenced to 180 days in jail.

Later that year, he was sentenced to another 180 days, to be served concurrently, for threatening his wife, Kelly, and another man with a knife.

He yearned, he sometimes said, to be other than what he was. "I wish I could be more like normal people — like these people here," he told The Yakima Herald-Republic of Washington in 2003, indicating passers-by in Leavenworth, Wash., his hometown of the moment. "I don't know how."

But Mr. Hill did manage to find time for ordinary pleasures. As he often said, he never missed an episode of "The Sopranos."

— BY MARGALIT FOX

RODNEY G. KING

The World Watched His Beating, and Heard His Plea

APRIL 2, 1965 · JUNE 17, 2012

RODNEY G. KING, whose 1991 videotaped beating by the Los Angeles police became a symbol of the nation's continuing racial tensions and subsequently led to a week of deadly race riots after the officers were acquitted, was found dead on June 17 in a swimming pool at the home he shared with his fiancée in

Rialto, Calif. He was 47.

There was no evidence of foul play, the Rialto police said.

Mr. King, whose life was a roller coaster of drug and alcohol abuse, multiple arrests and unwanted celebrity, pleaded for calm during the 1992 riots. More than 55 people were killed and 600 buildings destroyed in the violence.

In a phrase that became part of American culture, he asked at a news conference, "Can we all get along?"

"People look at me like I should have been like Malcolm X or Martin Luther King or Rosa Parks," he told The Los Angeles Times in April. "I should have seen life like that and stay out of trouble, and don't do this and don't do that. But it's hard to live up to some people's expectations."

Mr. King published a memoir in April detailing his struggles, saying in several interviews that he had not been able to find steady work.

He said he had once blamed politicians and lawyers "for taking a battered and confused addict and trying to make him into a symbol for civil rights." But he was unable to escape that role. After his death, the Rev. Al Sharpton said in a statement, "History will record that it was Rodney King's beating and his actions that made America deal with the excessive misconduct of law enforcement."

Mr. King came to embrace the role, saying his beating had enabled others to succeed and "made the world a better place."

"Obama, he wouldn't have been in office without what happened to me and a lot of black people before me," he told The Los Angeles Times. "He would never have been in that situation, no doubt in my mind. He would get there eventually, but it would have been a lot longer. So I am glad for what I went through. It opened the doors for a lot of people."

Though Mr. King wrote in his memoir that he still drank and used drugs occasionally, he insisted that, with his fiancée, Cynthia Kelley, who had been a juror in a civil suit he filed against the City of Los Angeles, he was on the road to reclaiming his life.

"I realize I will always be the poster child for police brutality," he said, "but I can try to use that as a positive force for healing and restraint."

Mr. King was essentially broke, he said, though he had received an advance for his book, "The Riot Within: My Journey from Rebellion to Redemption," published to coincide with the 20th anniversary of the riots.

He still walked with a limp, and several of his scars were visible. His best outlets for relaxation, he said, were fishing and swimming.

The police in Rialto, 50 miles east of Los Angeles, said they received a 911 call from

RELUCTANT SYMBOL: Rodney G. King came to represent the nation's racial troubles.

Ms. Kelley at 5:25 a.m. on June 17 reporting that she had found Mr. King in the pool that he had built himself. (He had inscribed in two tiles the date of his beating and that of the start of the riots.) Emergency personnel tried to resuscitate him, but he was pronounced dead at the hospital at 6:11 a.m.

The police said that Mr. King had been at the pool throughout the early morning and that he had been talking to Ms. Kelley, who was in the house. Neighbors reported hearing music, talking and crying before there was a splash. Afterward, a pair of sandals was still sitting next to the pool, visible from a neighbor's backyard.

On the night when the police beating occurred, March 3, 1991, Mr. King was out on parole on a 1989 robbery conviction. He was driving about 100 miles per hour when he and two passengers were pulled over by the Los Angeles police. After he tried to escape on foot — afraid, he said later, that he would be in violation of his parole — he was caught by officers. Mr. King, who was 6 feet 3, was struck with batons and kicked dozens of times, and hit with Tasers.

"It felt like I was an inch from death," he said in interviews.

Video of the beating, recorded by George Holliday, who lived in an apartment building nearby, was broadcast on television repeatedly, inflaming anger and starkly illustrating what many said had been a pattern of aggression and abuse by the Los Angeles police toward blacks and Hispanics. After a public outcry, four officers were brought to trial.

Many people thought the video alone would lead to convictions. But on April 29, 1992, a jury in Simi Valley, Calif., which included no black jurors, acquitted three of the officers, and a mistrial was declared for the fourth.

The verdict touched off riots in South Los Angeles, among the worst in the nation's history, resulting in damage estimated at $1 billion.

The four white officers charged with beating Mr. King — Stacey Koon, Theodore Briseno, Timothy Wind and Laurence Powell — were indicted in the summer of 1992 on federal civil rights charges. Officers Koon and Powell were convicted and sentenced to two years in prison, and Mr. King was awarded $3.8 million in damages.

The Los Angeles police chief, Daryl Gates, resigned under pressure amid criticism that officers had been slow to respond to the riots. He died of cancer in 2010.

Mr. King spent much of the money he received on legal fees. He also bought cars and houses, including the modest one in which he lived, and invested in a rap music label called Straight Alta-Pazz, which failed.

But much of his life was consumed by tabloid drama. He spent the subsequent years in and out of jail and rehabilitation centers, mostly for drug and alcohol abuse. He was arrested multiple times for driving under the influence, and spent short periods in prison in the late 1990s for assaulting his former wife and his daughter. In recent years he had appeared on the television shows "Celebrity Rehab" and "Sober House" on VH1.

Rodney Glen King was born on April 2, 1965, in Sacramento, the youngest of five children. He grew up in Altadena, near Pasadena, raised by his mother, Odessa King, and an alcoholic father, Ronald King, who died at 42.

Mr. King was married twice. Besides Ms. Kelley, survivors include three daughters.

In an interview in April, Mr. King said he understood how posterity would view him.

"It's taken years to get used to the situation I'm in in life and the weight it holds. One of the cops in the jail said: 'You know what? People are going to know who you are when you're dead and gone. A hundred years from now, people still going to be talking about you.' It's scary, but at the same time it's a blessing."

— BY JENNIFER MEDINA; IAN LOVETT CONTRIBUTED REPORTING FROM RIALTO, CALIF., AND WHITNEY BOYD AND MICHAEL SCHWIRTZ FROM NEW YORK.

LEROY NEIMAN

Bon Vivant With a Vivid Brush

JUNE 8, 1921 - JUNE 20, 2012

LeRoy Neiman, whose brilliantly colored, impressionistic sketches of sporting events and the international high life made him one of the most popular artists in the United States, died on June 20 in Manhattan. He was 91.

Mr. Neiman's kinetic, quickly executed paintings and drawings, many of them published in Playboy, offered his fans gaudily colored visual reports on heavyweight boxing matches, Super Bowl games and Olympic contests, as well as social panoramas like the horse races at Deauville, France, and the Cannes Film Festival.

Quite consciously, he cast himself in the mold of French Impressionists like Toulouse-Lautrec, Renoir and Degas, chroniclers of public life who found rich social material at racetracks, dance halls and cafes.

Mr. Neiman often painted or sketched on live television. With the camera recording his progress at the sketchpad or easel, he interpreted the drama of Olympic Games and Super Bowls for an audience of millions.

When Bobby Fischer and Boris Spassky faced off in Reykjavik, Iceland, to decide the world chess championship, Mr. Neiman was there, sketching. He was on hand to capture Federico Fellini directing "8 1/2" and the Kirov Ballet performing in the Soviet Union.

In popularity, Mr. Neiman rivaled American favorites like Norman Rockwell, Grandma Moses and Andrew Wyeth. A prolific one-man industry, he generated hundreds of paintings, drawings, watercolors, limited-edition serigraph prints and coffee-table books yearly, earning gross annual revenue in the tens of millions of dollars.

Although he exhibited constantly and his work was included in the collections of dozens of museums around the world, critical respect eluded him. Mainstream art critics either ignored him completely or, if forced to consider his work, dismissed it with contempt as garish and superficial — magazine illustration with pretensions. Mr. Neiman professed not to care.

"Maybe the critics are right," he told American Artist magazine in 1995. "But what am I supposed to do about it — stop painting, change my work completely? I go back into the studio, and there I am at the easel again. I enjoy what I'm doing and feel good working. Other thoughts are just crowded out."

His image suggested an artist well beyond the reach of criticism. A dandy and bon vivant, he cut an arresting figure with his luxuriant ear-to-ear mustache, white suits, flashy hats and Cuban cigars. "He quite intentionally invented himself as a flamboyant artist not unlike Salvador Dalí, in much the same way that I became Mr. Playboy in the late '50s," Hugh Hefner told Cigar Aficionado magazine in 1995.

LeRoy Runquist was born on June 8, 1921, in St. Paul. His father, a railroad worker, deserted the family when LeRoy was quite young, and the boy took the surname of his stepfather.

He showed a flair for art at an early age. While attending a local Roman Catholic school, he impressed schoolmates by drawing ink tattoos on their arms during recess.

As a teenager, he earned money doing illustrations for local grocery stores. "I'd sketch a turkey, a cow, a fish, with the prices," he told Cigar Aficionado. "And then I had the good sense to draw the guy who owned the store. This gave me tremendous power as a kid."

After being drafted into the Army in 1942, he served as a cook in Europe and in his spare time painted risqué murals on the walls of kitchens and mess halls. The Army's Special Services Division, recognizing his talent, put him to work painting stage sets for Red Cross shows when he was stationed in Germany after the war.

On leaving the military, Mr. Neiman studied briefly at the St. Paul School of Art (now the Minnesota Museum of American Art) before enrolling in the School of the Art Institute of Chicago, where, after four years of study, he taught figure drawing and fashion illustration throughout the 1950s.

When the janitor of the apartment building next door to his threw out half-empty cans of enamel house paint, Mr. Neiman found his métier. Experimenting with the new medium, he embraced a rapid style of applying paint to canvas imposed by the free-flowing quality of the house paint.

While doing freelance fashion illustration for the Carson Pirie Scott department store in Chicago in the early 1950s, he became friendly with Mr. Hefner, a copywriter there who was on the verge of publishing the first issue of a men's magazine.

In 1954, after five issues of Playboy had appeared, Mr. Neiman ran into Mr. Hefner and invited him to his apartment to see his paintings of boxers, strip clubs and restaurants. Mr. Hefner, impressed, showed the work to Playboy's art director, Art Paul, who commissioned an illustration for "Black Country," a story by Charles Beaumont about a jazz musician.

Thus began a relationship that endured for more than 50 years and established Mr. Neiman's reputation.

In 1955, when Mr. Hefner decided that the party-jokes page needed visual interest, Mr. Neiman came up with the Femlin, a curvaceous brunette who cavorted across the page in thigh-high stockings, high-heeled shoes, opera gloves and nothing else. She appeared in every issue of the magazine thereafter.

Three years later, Mr. Neiman devised a running feature, "Man at His Leisure." For the next 15 years, he went on assignment to glamour spots around the world, sending back visual reports on subjects as varied as the races at Royal Ascot, the dining room of the Tour d'Argent in Paris, the nude beaches of the Dalmatian coast, the running of the bulls at Pamplona, and Carnaby Street in swinging London. He later produced more than 100 paintings and 2 murals for 18 of the Playboy clubs that opened around the world.

"MAN AT HIS LEISURE": Leroy Neiman's paintings captured glamorous locales and exhilarating sporting events like the Olympics and the Super Bowl.

"Playboy made the good life a reality for me and made it the subject matter of my paintings — not affluence and luxury as such, but joie de vivre itself," Mr. Neiman told V.I.P. magazine in 1962.

Working in the same copywriting department at Carson Pirie Scott as Mr. Hefner was Janet Byrne, a student at the Art Institute. She and Mr. Neiman married in 1957. She survives him.

A prolific artist, he generated dozens of paintings each year that routinely commanded five-figure prices. When Christie's auctioned off the Playboy archives in 2003, his 1969 painting "Man at His Leisure: Le Mans" sold for $107,550. Sales of the signed, limited-edition print versions of his paintings, published in editions of 250 to 500, became a lucrative business in itself after Knoedler Publishing, a wholesale operation, was created in 1975 to publish and distribute his serigraphs, etchings, books and posters.

Mr. Neiman's most famous images came from the world of sports. His long association with the Olympics began with the Winter Games in Squaw Valley in 1960, and he went on to cover the games, on live television, in Munich in 1972, Montreal in 1976, Lake Placid in 1980, and Sarajevo and Los Angeles in 1984, using watercolor, ink or felt-tip marker to produce images with the dispatch of a courtroom sketch artist. At the 1978 and 1979 Super Bowls, he used a computerized electronic pen to portray the action for CBS.

Although he was best known for scenes filled with people and incident, he also painted many portraits. Athletes predominated, with Muhammad Ali and Joe Namath among his more famous subjects, but he also painted Leonard Bernstein, the ballet dancer Suzanne Farrell, the poet Marianne Moore and Sylvester Stallone, who gave Mr. Neiman cameo roles in three "Rocky" films.

His many books included "LeRoy Neiman: Art and Life Style," "Horses," "Winners: My Thirty Years in Sports," "Big-Time Golf," "LeRoy Neiman on Safari" and "Leroy Neiman: Five Decades." In 1995, he donated $6 million to Columbia University's School of the Arts to endow the LeRoy Neiman Center for Print Studies.

His memoir, "All Told: My Art and Life Among Athletes, Playboys, Bunnies and Provocateurs," was published 15 days before his death.

—BY WILLIAM GRIMES

ANNA J. SCHWARTZ

Follow the Money Supply, the Economist Said

NOV. 11, 1915 - JUNE 21, 2012

ANNA J. SCHWARTZ, a research economist who wrote monumental works on American financial history in collaboration with the Nobel laureate Milton Friedman while remaining largely in his shadow, died on June 21 at her home in Manhattan. She was 96.

Mrs. Schwartz, who earned her Ph.D. in economics at the age of 48 and dispensed policy appraisals well into her 90s, was often called the "high priestess of monetarism," upholding the view that the size and turnover of the money supply largely determines the pace of inflation and economic activity.

The Friedman-Schwartz collaboration "A Monetary History of the United States, 1867-1960," a book of nearly 900 pages published in 1963, is considered a classic. Ben S. Bernanke, the Federal Reserve chairman, called it "the leading and most persuasive explanation of the worst economic disaster in American history."

The authors concluded that policy failures by the Fed, which largely controls the money supply, were a root cause of the Depression.

Mr. Bernanke acknowledged as much when he spoke at a 90th birthday celebration for Mr. Friedman in 2002. "I would like to say to Milton and Anna: Regarding the Great Depression, you're right, we did it," he said. "We're very sorry, but thanks to you we won't do it again."

Mrs. Schwartz was the co-author of much of the work that led to Mr. Friedman's Nobel in economic science in 1976. Her supporters thought the prize might have justly been awarded jointly.

"Anna did all of the work, and I got most of the recognition," Mr. Friedman said on one occasion.

After Mr. Friedman's death in 2006, Mrs. Schwartz "became the standard-bearer" of Friedman monetarism, said Michael D. Bordo, a professor of economics at Rutgers University and for decades a Schwartz collaborator himself. Though "not a deep theorist," he said, Mrs. Schwartz was "probably the best woman economist of the 20th century."

During the financial collapse that began in 2008, she was one of the few economists with a firsthand recollection of the Depression. After praising early moves by Mr. Bernanke, she wrote, at age 93, in July 2009, a bitingly critical Op-Ed article in The New York Times opposing the reappointment of the Fed chairman who had been so influenced by her work.

She contended that Mr. Bernanke had erred in producing "extreme ease" in monetary policy and in failing to warn investors that new financial instruments were difficult to price.

Mrs. Schwartz also held that the government had been a bigger contributor to the crisis than had been widely realized. By her measure, the government had oversold the benefits of homeownership, pushing Fannie Mae and Freddie Mac, the government-backed mortgage finance giants, to lend freely to lower-income borrowers and fostering exceptionally low mortgage rates.

A leading financial historian, Mrs. Schwartz was also an expert on the monetary and banking statistics of Britain and the United States. Besides her collaborations, she had a large body of work in her own name.

Her most visible public role was in 1981, when she agreed to be executive director of the 17-member United States Gold Commission, a Washington panel that was charged with recommending the future role of gold in the nation's monetary system.

With little interest in a return to any form of gold standard, she and most other members of the panel, consisting mainly of political appointees, limited their recommendations to urging the government to mint gold coins.

Mrs. Schwartz was born Anna Jacobson on Nov. 11, 1915, in the Bronx, the third of five children of Hillel Jacobson and the former Pauline Shainmark, Jewish immigrants from Eastern Europe.

She was drawn to economics while still at Walton High School in the Bronx — "I found it more exciting than literature or foreign languages," she said — and graduated from Barnard College at 18.

She worked for the Agriculture Department in 1936, the year she married Isaac Schwartz, whom she had met at a Hebrew summer camp. The couple raised four children. Mr. Schwartz, who was the financial officer for a Manhattan import company and had earned a master's degree in classics from Columbia, died in 1999.

Mrs. Schwartz is survived by two daughters, two sons, seven grandchildren and six great-grandchildren.

After five years at Columbia University's

Social Science Research Council, Mrs. Schwartz joined the National Bureau of Economic Research in New York in 1941 and continued to work there for more than 70 years. But she maintained her ties to Columbia, earning a Ph.D. there in her middle years.

It was at the National Bureau, a private, nonpartisan research organization that has been the nation's semiofficial arbiter of business cycles, that Mrs. Schwartz met Mr. Friedman and his wife, Rose Director Friedman, who was also an economist. Rose Friedman had heard from mutual friends that the Schwartzes might have a baby carriage to lend.

"THE HIGH PRIESTESS OF MONETARISM": Anna J. Schwartz was an influential research economist, a leading financial historian, and an expert on the Great Depression.

Arthur F. Burns, the president of the National Bureau and a future chairman of the Federal Reserve, suggested that Mrs. Schwartz and Mr. Friedman work together.

The two of them — she in New York and he at the University of Chicago — formed a close relationship based on exchanges of drafts and ideas by mail. "I'll write something and send it to him, and he'll criticize it, and he'll do the reverse," she told a reporter for The Times in 1970 on the publication of their second major work, "Monetary Statistics of the United States: Estimates, Sources, Methods." "The wonderful thing about this relationship is that neither of us takes offense if the other says it's no good."

Mrs. Schwartz did take offense, however, when Paul Krugman, an economist and an Op-Ed columnist for The Times, attacked the Friedman legacy in an article in The New York Review of Books in 2007.

She responded angrily that Mr. Krugman had mischaracterized the work and made "inaccurate forays into economic history" by attributing the Depression to a liquidity trap, in which monetary policy fails to stimulate the economy by either lowering interest rates or expanding the money supply.

"She went ballistic," Mr. Bordo said.

Even after breaking a hip in 2009 and having a stroke, Mrs. Schwartz, by then using a wheelchair, collaborated with Mr. Bordo and Owen Humpage, an economist at the Cleveland Fed, on a project tracing the history of governmental intervention in currency markets. "Anna never stopped," Mr. Bordo said.

She often spoke about her successful collaboration with Mr. Friedman on their "Monetary History of the United States," expressing elation that they had taken on an economic establishment that had little regard for theories based on the importance of money.

Decades afterward, writing in The Cato Journal, a publication of the Cato Institute, the conservative public policy research organization, she quoted Wordsworth:

"Bliss was it in that dawn to be alive,
But to be young was very heaven!"

— By Robert D. Hershey Jr.

NORA EPHRON

Wit, Wisdom and a Hollywood Touch

MAY 19, 1941 · JUNE 26, 2012

Nora Ephron, an essayist and humorist in the Dorothy Parker mold (only smarter and funnier, some said) who became one of her era's most successful screenwriters and filmmakers, making romantic comedy hits like "Sleepless in Seattle" and "When Harry Met Sally ... ," died on June 26

in Manhattan. She was 71.

The cause was pneumonia brought on by acute myeloid leukemia, a condition she had kept from all but a few intimates.

In a commencement address she delivered in 1996 at Wellesley College, her alma mater, Ms. Ephron recalled that women of her generation weren't expected to do much of anything. But she wound up having several successful careers, many of them simultaneously.

She was a journalist, a blogger, an essayist, a novelist, a playwright, an Oscar-nominated screenwriter and a movie director — a rarity in a film industry whose directorial ranks were and continue to be dominated by men. Her later box-office successes included "You've Got Mail" and "Julie & Julia." By the end of her life, though remaining remarkably youthful looking, she had even become something of a philosopher about age and its indignities.

"Why do people write books that say it's better to be older than to be younger?" she wrote in "I Feel Bad About

"HOW CAN I MAKE THIS MORE FUN?": Nora Ephron's work exhibited a good dose of humor and honesty.

My Neck," her 2006 best-selling collection of essays. "It's not better. Even if you have all your marbles, you're constantly reaching for the name of the person you met the day before yesterday."

Nora Ephron was born on May 19, 1941, on the Upper West Side of Manhattan, the eldest of four sisters, all of whom became writers. That was no surprise; writing was the family business. Her father, Henry, and her mother, the former Phoebe Wolkind, were Hollywood screenwriters who wrote, among other films, "Carousel," "There's No Business Like Show Business" and "Captain Newman, M.D."

"Everything is copy," her mother once said, and she and her husband proved it by turning the college-age Nora into a character in a play, later a movie, "Take Her, She's Mine." The lesson was not lost on Ms. Ephron. She seldom wrote about her own children but could make sparkling copy out of almost anything else: the wrinkles on her neck, her apartment, cabbage strudel, Teflon pans and the tastelessness of egg-white omelets.

She turned her painful breakup with her second husband, the Watergate journalist Carl Bernstein, into a best-selling novel, "Heartburn," which she then recycled into a successful movie starring Jack Nicholson as a philandering husband and Meryl Streep as a quick-witted version of Ms. Ephron.

When Ms. Ephron was 4, her parents moved from New York to Beverly Hills, Calif., where she grew up, graduating from Beverly Hills High School in 1958. At Wellesley, in Massachusetts, she began writing for the school newspaper, and in the summer of 1961 she was a summer intern in the Kennedy White House. Perhaps her greatest accomplishment there, she said, was rescuing the speaker of the house, Sam Rayburn, from a men's room in which he had inadvertently locked himself. In an essay in 2003, she said she was probably the only intern that President John F. Kennedy had never hit on.

After graduation from college in 1962, she moved to New York, a city she adored, intent on becoming a journalist. Her first job was as a mail girl at Newsweek. (There were no mail boys, she later pointed out.) Soon she was contributing to a parody of The New York Post put out during the 1962 newspaper strike. Her piece of it earned her a tryout at The Post, where the publisher, Dorothy Schiff, remarked: "If they can parody The Post, they can write for it. Hire them."

Ms. Ephron stayed at The Post for five years, covering stories like the Beatles, the Star of India robbery at the American Museum of Natural History, and a pair of hooded seals at the Coney Island aquarium that refused to mate.

"The Post was a terrible newspaper in the era I worked there," she wrote. But the experience taught her to write short and to write around a subject, she added, since the kinds of people she was assigned to cover were never going to give her much interview time.

In the late 1960s Ms. Ephron turned to magazine journalism, at Esquire and New York mostly. She quickly made a name for herself by writing frank, funny personal essays — about the smallness of her breasts, for example — and tart, sharply observed profiles of people like Ayn Rand, Helen Gurley Brown and the composer and best-selling poet Rod McKuen. Some of these articles were controversial. In one, she criticized Betty Friedan for conducting a "thoroughly irrational" feud with another feminist leader, Gloria Steinem; in another, she discharged a withering assessment of Women's Wear Daily.

But all her articles were characterized by humor and honesty, written in a clear, direct, understated style marked by an impeccable sense of when to deploy the punchline. (Many of her articles were assembled in the collections "Wallflower at the Orgy," "Crazy Salad" and "Scribble Scribble.")

Ms. Ephron made as much fun of herself as of anyone else. She was labeled a practitioner of the New Journalism, with its embrace of novelistic devices in the name of reaching a deeper truth, but she always denied the connection. "I am not a new journalist, whatever that is," she wrote. "I just sit here at the typewriter and bang away at the old forms."

Ms. Ephron got into the movie business more or less by accident after her marriage to Mr. Bernstein in 1976. He and Bob Woodward, his partner in the Watergate investigation, were unhappy with William Goldman's script for the movie version of their book "All the President's Men," so Mr. Bernstein and Ms. Ephron took a stab at rewriting it. Their version was ultimately not used, but it was a useful learning experience, she said, and it brought her to the attention of Hollywood.

Her first screenplay, written with her friend Alice Arlen, was for "Silkwood," a 1983 film based on the life of Karen Silkwood, who died under suspicious circumstances while investigating abuses at a plutonium plant where she had worked. Ms. Arlen was in film school then, and Ms. Ephron had scant experience writing for anything other than the page. But Mike Nichols, who directed the movie (which starred Ms. Streep and Kurt Russell), said that the script made an immediate impression on him. He and Ms. Ephron had become friends when she visited him on the set of "Catch-22."

Best-selling books, box-office hits: a one-woman industry.

"I think that was the beginning of her openly falling in love with the movies," Mr. Nichols said in an interview, "and she and Alice came along with 'Silkwood' when I hadn't made a movie in seven years. I couldn't find anything that grabbed me." He added: "Nora was so funny and so interesting that you didn't notice that she was also necessary."

Ms. Ephron followed "Silkwood" three years later with a screenplay adaptation of her own novel "Heartburn," which was also directed by Mr. Nichols. But it was her script for "When Harry Met Sally . . . ," which became a hit Rob Reiner movie in 1989 starring Billy Crystal and Meg Ryan, that established Ms. Ephron's gift for romantic comedy and for delayed but happy endings that reconcile couples who are clearly meant for each other but don't know it.

"When Harry Met Sally . . ." is probably best remembered for Ms. Ryan's table-pounding faked-orgasm scene with Mr. Crystal in Katz's Delicatessen on the Lower East Side of New York City, prompting a middle-aged woman

(played by Mr. Reiner's mother, Estelle Reiner) sitting nearby to remark to her waiter, indelibly, "I'll have what she's having."

The scene wouldn't have gotten past the Hollywood censors of the past, but in many other respects Ms. Ephron's films are old-fashioned movies, only in a brand-new guise. Her 1998 hit, "You've Got Mail," for example, which she both wrote (with her sister Delia) and directed, is partly a remake of the old Ernst Lubitsch film 'The Shop Around the Corner."

Ms. Ephron began directing because she knew from her parents' example how powerless screenwriters are (at the end of their careers both became alcoholics) and because, as she said in her Wellesley address, Hollywood had never been very interested in making movies by or about women. She once wrote, "One of the best things about directing movies, as opposed to merely writing them, is that there's no confusion about who's to blame: you are."

Mr. Nichols said he had encouraged her to direct. "I knew she would be able to do it," he recalled. "Not only did she have a complete comprehension of the process of making a movie — she simply soaked that up — but she had all the ancillary skills, the people skills, all the hundreds of things that are useful when you're making a movie."

Her first effort at directing, "This Is My Life" (1992), with a screenplay by Ms. Ephron and her sister Delia, based on a novel by Meg Wolitzer about a single mother trying to become a standup comedian, was a dud. But Ms. Ephron redeemed herself in 1993 with "Sleepless in Seattle" (she shared the screenwriting credits), which brought Tom Hanks and Meg Ryan together so winningly that they were cast again in "You've Got Mail."

Among the other movies Ms. Ephron wrote and directed were "Lucky Numbers" (2000), "Bewitched" (2005) and, her last, "Julie & Julia"

(2009), in which Ms. Streep played Julia Child.

She and Ms. Streep had been friends since they worked on "Silkwood" together. "Nora just looked at every situation and cocked her head and thought, 'Hmmmm, how can I make this more fun?'" Ms. Streep wrote in an email.

Ms. Ephron earned three Oscar nominations for best screenplay, for "Silkwood," "Sleepless in Seattle" and "When Harry Met Sally . . . " But in all her moviemaking years she never gave up writing in other forms. Two essay collections, "I Feel Bad About My Neck: And Other Reflections on Being a Woman" (2006) and "I Remember Nothing" (2010), were both best sellers. With her sister Delia she wrote a play, "Love, Loss, and What I Wore," about women and their wardrobes (once calling it "'The Vagina Monologues' without the vaginas"), and by herself she wrote "Imaginary Friends," a play, produced in 2002, about the literary and personal quarrel between Lillian Hellman and Mary McCarthy.

She also became an enthusiastic blogger for The Huffington Post, writing on subjects like the Las Vegas mogul Steve Wynn's accidentally putting a hole in a Picasso he owned and Ryan O'Neal's failing to recognize his own daughter and making a pass at her.

Several years ago, Ms. Ephron learned that she had myelodysplastic syndrome, a pre-leukemic condition, but she mostly kept the illness a secret and continued to lead a busy, sociable life.

"She had this thing about not wanting to whine," the writer Sally Quinn said. "She didn't like self-pity. It was always, you know, 'Suck it up.'"

Ms. Ephron's first marriage, to the writer Dan Greenburg, ended in divorce, as did her

HAPPY ENDINGS: Nora Ephron on the set of "This is My Life," her directorial debut. She would go on to write and direct some of the most beloved romantic comedies of the 1980s and '90s.

marriage to Mr. Bernstein. In 1987 she married Nicholas Pileggi, the author of the books "Wiseguy" and "Casino." (Her contribution to "Not Quite What I Was Planning: Six-Word Memoirs by Writers Famous and Obscure," edited by Larry Smith and Rachel Fershleiser, reads: "Secret to life, marry an Italian.") He survives her, along with two sons and her sisters Delia Ephron; Amy Ephron, who is also a screenwriter; and Hallie Ephron, a journalist and novelist.

In person Ms. Ephron — small and fine-boned with high cheeks and a toothy smile — had the same understated, though no less witty, style that she brought to the page.

"Sitting at a table with Nora was like being in a Nora Ephron movie," Ms. Quinn said. "She was brilliant and funny."

She was also fussy about her hair and made a point of having it professionally blow-dried twice a week. "It's cheaper by far than psychoanalysis and much more uplifting," Ms. Ephron said.

Another friend, Robert Gottlieb, who had edited her books since the 1970s, said her death would be "terrible for her readers and her movie audience and her colleagues." But "the private Nora was even more remarkable," he added, saying she was "always there for you with a full heart plus the crucial dose of the reality principle."

Ms. Streep called her a "stalwart."

"You could call on her for anything: doctors, restaurants, recipes, speeches, or just a few jokes, and we all did it, constantly," she wrote in her email. "She was an expert in all the departments of living well."

The producer Scott Rudin recalled that less than two weeks before her death, at Weill Cornell Medical College and New York-Presbyterian Hospital, he had a long phone session with her while she was undergoing treatment, going over notes for a pilot she was writing for a TV series

about a bank compliance officer. Afterward she told him, "If I could just get a hairdresser in here, we could have a meeting."

Ms. Ephron's collection "I Remember Nothing" concludes with two lists, one of things she says she won't miss and one of things she will. Among the "won't miss" items are dry skin, Clarence Thomas, the sound of the vacuum cleaner, and discussion panels on "Women in Film." The other list, of the things she will miss, begins with "my kids" and "Nick" and ends this way:

"Taking a bath
Coming over the bridge to Manhattan
Pie."

— BY CHARLES MCGRATH; PAUL VITELLO
CONTRIBUTED REPORTING.

DORIS SAMS

A Star in the League of Their Own

FEB. 2, 1927 - JUNE 28, 2012

DORIS SAMS, who pitched a perfect game and set a single-season home run record in the women's professional baseball world of the 1940s and '50s that inspired the movie "A League of Their Own," died on June 28 in Knoxville, Tenn. She was 85.

Sams was one of the leading players in the All-American Girls Professional Baseball League. Founded in 1943 by Phil Wrigley, the owner of the Chicago Cubs, the league was meant to provide evening entertainment in Midwestern towns and keep interest in baseball alive when the majors were losing most of their players to military service in World War II.

The women's league, which survived into 1954, was largely forgotten until the 1992 Hollywood comedy with Madonna and Geena Davis on the field and Tom Hanks as the profane manager who drove one of his players to tears before exclaiming in bewilderment, "There's no crying in baseball!"

The real women's pro game featured spirited and highly competitive athletes who were often managed by former major leaguers and who played through their many abrasions, or "strawberries," from sliding in their short-skirted uniforms.

"We had a lot of girls who could play and who really understood the game, and the managers appreciated that," Sams told The St. Louis Post-Dispatch in 1989.

Playing for Michigan's Muskegon Lassies and their successor franchise, the Kalamazoo Lassies, from 1946 to 1953, Sams, who was 5 feet 9 inches and wore glasses, pitched underhand, sidearm and overhand, as the rules governing deliveries evolved.

She hit a league-record 12 home runs in 1952, playing in 109 games; she hit better than .300 in each of her last four seasons; threw out many runners playing the outfield when she was not pitching; and was elected the league's player of the year in 1947 and 1949.

ALL-AMERICAN GIRL:
Doris Sams, a women's league star, in her Muskegon Lassies uniform.

She once outdueled Lois Florreich of the Rockford Peaches through 22 innings, winning by 1-0, as she remembered it, in a game that had been tied after the scheduled seven innings as the short game of a doubleheader.

"After that, I told my manager: 'I don't want to pitch any more seven-inning games. They're too long,'" Sue Macy quoted Sams saying in her league history "A Whole New Ball Game" (1993).

Sams pitched her perfect game in August 1947, retiring all 27 batters for the Fort Wayne Daisies in a 2-0 victory, then threw a no-hitter the next year against the Springfield Sallies.

She credited her fielders with several dazzling plays in that perfect game.

"That last pitch, a girl just about drove down my throat," she told The New York Times in 1988 when the Baseball Hall of Fame in Cooperstown, N.Y., unveiled a permanent exhibition devoted to women's baseball. "It ricocheted off my knee, almost tore off my kneecap, and the shortstop made a great stop and threw her out."

Doris Jane Sams was born in Knoxville on Feb. 2, 1927. A grandfather and her father, Robert, played semipro baseball, and she joined with two older brothers in playing baseball as a youngster. By 11, she was playing fast-pitch softball on a team with much older girls. She also won a regional marbles tournament and was a Knoxville city badminton champion before turning to pro baseball after a tryout in 1946.

She was soon a star and shared the covers of Dell publishing's 1948 major league yearbook with Ted Williams — he on the front, she on the back. She estimated that she was paid about $4,000 a season.

After retiring from baseball, Sams held an office job with the Knoxville Utilities Board. She died of complications of Alzheimer's disease. Never marrying, she left no immediate survivors.

The Hall of Fame displayed one of Sams's player-of-the-year trophies along with her Louisville Slugger bat when it opened its permanent exhibition on women in baseball.

In her interview with The Post-Dispatch, Sams said that a mannequin of Babe Ruth was on display near the women's exhibit.

"I look over to the right and see Babe Ruth," she said. "I look over on the left and see Ted Williams. Then I look in the mirror and say, 'What are you doing here?' It's all so unbelievable. I never ever dreamed our league would get this kind of recognition."

— BY RICHARD GOLDSTEIN

YITZHAK SHAMIR

From the Underground to the Pinnacle in Israel

OCT. 22, 1915 - JUNE 30, 2012

YITZHAK SHAMIR, who emerged from the militant wing of a Jewish militia and served as Israel's prime minister longer than anyone but David Ben-Gurion, promoting a muscular Zionism and expansive settlement in the occupied West Bank and Gaza Strip, died on June 30 at a nursing home in Tel Aviv. He was 96.

A native of Poland whose family was wiped out in the Holocaust, Mr. Shamir was part of a group of right-wing Israeli politicians led by Menachem Begin, who rose to power in the 1970s during the decline of the more left-wing Labor Party, which was viewed as corrupt and disdainful of the public.

Stubborn and laconic, Mr. Shamir embodied his government's policy of patient, determined, unyielding opposition to territorial concessions. Many of his friends and colleagues ascribed his character to his years in the underground in the 1940s, when he sent Jewish fighters out to kill British officers, whom he saw as occupiers. He was a wanted man then; to the British rulers of the Palestine mandate, he was a terrorist, an assassin. He appeared in public only at night, disguised as a Hasidic rabbi. Still, he said, they were "the best years of my life."

His wife, Shulamit, once said that in the underground she and her husband had learned not to talk about their work for fear of being overheard. It was a habit he apparently never lost.

Mr. Shamir was not blessed with a sharp wit, a warm manner or much oratorical talent. Most often he answered questions with a shrug and an air of weary wisdom, as if to say: "This is so clear. Why do you even ask?"

In 1988, at a meeting of the political party Herut, he sat slumped on a sofa, gazing at the floor as party stalwarts heaped praises on him. Afterward he said: "I like all those people, they're nice people. But this is not my style, not my language. This kind of meeting is the modern picture, but I don't belong to it."

Rather than bend to them, Mr. Shamir simply outlasted his political opponents, who were usually more willing to say what was on their minds and more likely to get in trouble for it. To Mr. Shamir, victory came from strength, patience and cunning, not compromise.

"If he wants something, it may take a long time, but he'll never let go," Avi Pazner, his media adviser, once remarked.

Prime Minister Begin appointed Mr. Shamir foreign minister in 1980. When Mr. Begin suddenly retired in 1983, Mr. Shamir became a compromise candidate to replace him, alternating in the post with Shimon Peres for one four-year term. Mr. Shamir won his own term in 1988. He entered the political opposition when Yitzhak Rabin of the Labor Party was elected prime minister in 1992. Mr. Shamir retired from politics a few years later, at 81.

As prime minister, Mr. Shamir promoted Jewish settlement in the West Bank and the

Gaza Strip, which Israel conquered in 1967. The Jewish population in the occupied territories increased by nearly 30 percent while he was in office. He also encouraged the immigration of tens of thousands of Soviet Jews to Israel, an influx that changed the country's demographic character.

Mr. Shamir was in office during the so-called intifada, the Palestinian uprising against Israeli control that began in December 1987. He and his defense minister, Mr. Rabin, deployed thousands of Israeli troops throughout the occupied territories to quash the rebellion. They failed, and year after year of violence and death on both sides brought condemnation from around the world.

An Israeli inquiry found that when Mr. Shamir heard reports that Palestinians had been slaughtered in refugee camps, he all but ignored them.

The fighting also deepened divisions between Israel's two political camps: leftists, who believed in making concessions to bring peace, and those in the right wing, who, in Mr. Shamir's words, believed that "Israel's days without Jerusalem, Judea and Samaria and the Gaza Strip are gone and will not return."

As the intifada dragged on, the death toll climbed from dozens to hundreds. Israel's isolation increased, until the rebellion was overshadowed in 1991 by the first Persian Gulf war. During that war, at the request of the United States, Prime Minister Shamir held Israel back from attacking Iraq, even as Iraqi Scud missiles

fell on Tel Aviv. For that he won new favor in Washington and promises of financial aid from the United States to help with the settlement of new Israeli citizens from the Soviet Union.

Then, in the fall of 1991, under pressure from President George H. W. Bush and Secretary of State James A. Baker III, Mr. Shamir agreed to represent Israel at the Middle East peace conference in Madrid, Israel's first summit meeting with the Arab states. There he was as unyielding as ever, denouncing Syria at one point as having "the dubious honor of being one of the most oppressive, tyrannical regimes in the world."

Yitzhak Shamir was born on Oct. 22, 1915, to Shlomo and Perla Penina Yezernitzky in a Polish town under Russian control. He immigrated to the Palestine mandate when he was 20 and selected Shamir as his Hebrew surname. The word means thorn or sharp point.

Members of his family who remained in Poland died in the Holocaust; his father was killed by Poles whom the family had regarded as friends. Memories of the Holocaust colored his opinions for the rest of his life.

In the British-ruled Palestine mandate, Mr. Shamir worked at first as a bookkeeper and a construction worker. But after Arabs attacked Jewish settlers and the British in 1936, he joined the Irgun Zvai Leumi, the underground Jewish defense league. In 1940, the Irgun's most militant members formed the Lehi, or Stern Gang, named for its first leader, Abraham Stern.

After the British police killed Mr. Stern in 1942, Mr. Shamir became one of the group's top commanders. Under his leadership it began a campaign of what it called personal terror, assassinating top British military and government officers, often gunning them down in the street.

To the Jewish public, and even to the other Jewish underground groups, Mr. Shamir's gang was "lacking even a spark of humanity and Jewish conscience," Israel Rokach, the mayor of

Tel Aviv, said in 1944 after Stern Gang gunmen shot three British police officers on the streets of his city.

Years later, however, Mr. Shamir contended that it had been more humane to assassinate specific military or political figures than to attack military installations and possibly kill innocent people, as the other underground groups did. Besides, he once said, "a man who goes forth to take the life of another whom he does not know must believe only one thing: that by his act he will change the course of history."

Several histories of the period have asserted that Mr. Shamir masterminded a failed attempt to kill the British high commissioner, Sir Harold MacMichael, and the killing in Cairo of Britain's minister of state for the Middle East, Lord Moyne. When Mr. Shamir was asked about these episodes in later years, his denials held a certain evasive tone.

It was during his time in the underground, he wrote in his autobiography, "Summing Up," that he met Shulamit Levy, who was his courier and confidante. The couple married in 1944, meeting at a location in Jerusalem and gathering

people off the street as witnesses, their daughter, Gilada Diamant, said. After a hasty ceremony in deep cover, each departed immediately for a separate city.

Shulamit Shamir died in 2011. In addition to his daughter, Mr. Shamir is survived by a son, five grandchildren and seven great-grandchildren. Mr. Shamir had Alzheimer's disease in his last years.

For a brief period after World War II, the three major Jewish underground groups cooperated — until the bombing of the King David Hotel in Jerusalem on July 22, 1946. Scores of people were killed, and Mr. Shamir was among those arrested and exiled to an internment camp in Eritrea. But he escaped a few months later and took refuge in France. He arrived in the newly independent Israel in May 1948.

Mr. Shamir was a pariah of sorts to the new Labor government of Israel, which regarded him as a terrorist. Rebuffed in his efforts to work in the government, he drifted from one small job to another until 1955, when he finally found a government agency that appreciated his past: the Mossad, Israel's intelligence service. He became its top agent in France before returning to Israel and spending several years in business.

He joined Mr. Begin's Herut Party in 1970 and was elected to Parliament in December 1973. When the Likud, or unity, bloc, which absorbed Herut, won power in 1977, Mr. Shamir was elected speaker. And when President Anwar el-Sadat of Egypt visited Jerusalem in November 1977, Mr. Shamir and Israel's president, Ephraim Katzir, escorted him to the speaker's rostrum for his speech. But the next year, when the Parliament voted on the Camp David accords, which set out the terms for peace with Egypt, Mr. Shamir abstained.

ZIONIST STALWART: Yitzhak Shamir at a 1984 solidarity meeting for Soviet Jews. As prime minister, he encouraged the immigration of tens of thousands of Soviet Jews to Israel.

In 1979, when Moshe Dayan resigned as foreign minister, Mr. Begin proposed appointing Mr. Shamir to replace him. Yechiel Kadishai, chief of the prime minister's office under Mr. Begin, recalled that Mr. Shamir was chosen because the prime minister did not want or need a powerful figure high in his cabinet.

"Begin had already established himself," Mr. Kadishai said. "But by 1980, he wanted no competitors for power and selected Shamir because he was not so known in political circles."

The liberal members of Mr. Begin's coalition objected, so Mr. Begin named himself foreign minister until 1980, when Mr. Shamir finally took the post. The Labor Party, considering Mr. Shamir an extremist, saw his appointment as a mistake.

His political opponents said his laconic nature played into his handling of the massacres at the Sabra and Shatila refugee camps in West Beirut in September 1982, during Israel's war in Lebanon.

On the evening of Sept. 16, Lebanese Christian militiamen known as Phalangists entered the camps and began killing hundreds of Palestinian men, women and children while the Israeli Army, largely unaware of the killings, stood guard at the gates.

The next morning in Tel Aviv, Ze'ev Schiff, a prominent Israeli journalist, received a call from a military official, who told him about the slaughter. He rushed to the office of his friend Mordechai Zipori, the minister of communications, and told him what he had heard. Mr. Zipori called the foreign minister, Mr. Shamir.

Mr. Shamir was scheduled to meet with military and intelligence officials shortly, so with some urgency Mr. Zipori told him to ask about the report he had received that the Phalangists "are carrying out a slaughter."

Mr. Zipori remembered that Mr. Shamir promised to look into the report. But according to an Israeli government inquiry, Mr. Shamir merely asked Foreign Ministry officers to see "whether any new reports had arrived from Beirut." When the meeting ended, Mr. Shamir "left for his home and took no additional action," the report said.

Years later, Mr. Shamir said: "You know, in those times of the Lebanese war, every day something happened. And from the first glance of it, it seemed like just another detail of what was going on every day. But after 24 hours, it became clear it was not a normal event."

Mr. Shamir was not the only Israeli official who failed to act, but the commission found it "difficult to find a justification" for his decision not to make "any attempt to check whether there was anything in what he heard."

When Mr. Begin retired in 1983, Mr. Shamir was designated his successor largely because of his position in the Foreign Ministry.

Even many in his own party thought Mr. Shamir would lose the election. And even after he took office, many saw this low-key, colorless man as a caretaker. In some ways he was. Asked once what he intended to do in his second full term in office, he said he had no plans except to "keep things as they are."

"With our long, bitter experience," he added, "we have to think twice before we do something."

— BY JOEL BRINKLEY; ETHAN BRONNER AND JODI RUDOREN CONTRIBUTED REPORTING.

ANDY GRIFFITH

America's Aw-Shucks Sheriff

JUNE 1, 1926 - JULY 3, 2012

ANDY GRIFFITH, an actor whose folksy Southern manner charmed audiences for more than 50 years on Broadway, in movies, on albums and especially on television, as the small-town sheriff in the long-running situation comedy that bore his name, died on July 3 at his home on Roanoke Island in

North Carolina. He was 86.

Mr. Griffith had already been a star on Broadway, in "No Time for Sergeants," and in Hollywood, in Elia Kazan's film "A Face in the Crowd," when "The Andy Griffith Show" made its debut in the fall of 1960. And in the 1980s and '90s he returned to the television spotlight as a cagey defense lawyer in the title role of the courtroom drama "Matlock."

But his fame was never as great as it was in the 1960s, when for eight years he was Andy Taylor, the sagacious sheriff of the make-believe town of Mayberry, N.C. Every week he rode herd on a collection of eccentrics, among them his high-strung deputy, Barney Fife, and the simple-minded gas station attendant Gomer Pyle. At home, as a widower, Andy raised a young son, Opie, often taking him fishing.

"The Andy Griffith Show," seen on Monday nights on CBS, was No. 4 in the Nielsen ratings its first year and never fell below the Top 10. After the run ended with Episode No. 249, the show lived on in spinoff series, endless reruns and even Sunday school classes organized around its rustic moral lessons.

The show imagined a reassuring world of fishin' holes, ice cream socials and rock-hard family values during a decade that grew progressively tumultuous. Racial unrest was sweeping the South and beyond in the real world while altogether bypassing gentle Mayberry. The show's vision of rural simplicity (captured in its familiar theme song, whistled over the opening credits) was part of a TV trend that began with "The Real McCoys" on ABC in 1957 and extended to "The Beverly Hillbillies," "Petticoat Junction," "Green Acres" and "Hee Haw."

But by the late 1960s, the younger viewers networks prized were spurning corn pone, and Mr. Griffith had decided to leave after the 1966-67 season to make movies. With a lucrative offer, CBS persuaded him to do one more season, and "The Andy Griffith Show" became the No. 1 series in the 1967-68 season. But, like Mr. Griffith, the times were moving on. "Rowan & Martin's Laugh-In," with its one-liners about drugs and Vietnam, and "The Mod Squad," about an integrated trio of undercover officers, were grabbing a new audience.

Still, the characters in "Andy Griffith" — Barney (Don Knotts), Gomer (Jim Nabors), Opie (Ron Howard, who went on to fame as a movie director), Aunt Bee (Frances Bavier) and the rest — have lived on, in reruns and online.

Andy Griffith was more complex than Andy Taylor, though the show was based on his hometown, Mount Airy, N.C. Before he fetched up in Mayberry, Mr. Griffith was known for bringing authenticity to dark roles, beginning in 1957 with the lead in "A Face in the Crowd," the story of a rough-hewn television personality who, in the clutches of his city-slicker handlers, becomes something of a megalomaniac.

From the 1970s to the '90s, Mr. Griffith starred in no fewer than six movies with the words "murder" or "kill" in their titles. In 1983, in "Murder in Coweta County," he played a chillingly wicked man who remains stone cold even as he is strapped into the electric chair.

Sheriff Taylor aside, Mr. Griffith was no happy rustic; he enjoyed life in Hollywood and knew his way around a wine list. His career was tightly controlled by a personal manager, Richard O. Linke.

"If there is ever a question about something, I will do what he wants me to do," Mr. Griffith told The New York Times Magazine in 1970. "Had it not been for him, I would have gone down the toilet."

Far from the gregarious Andy Taylor, Mr. Griffith was a loner and a worrier. He once hit a door in anger, and for two episodes of "The Andy Griffith Show" he had a bandaged hand — explained on the show as an injury Andy had received while apprehending criminals.

But the show's 35 million viewers would have been reassured to learn that even at the peak of his popularity, Mr. Griffith drove a Ford station wagon and bought his suits off the rack. He said his favorite honor was having a stretch of a North Carolina highway named after him in 2002. (That was before President George W. Bush presented him with the Presidential Medal of Freedom in 2005.)

> Far from the gregarious Andy Taylor, Mr. Griffith was a loner and a worrier. He once hit a door in anger, and for two episodes of his show he had a bandaged hand.

He was also gratified to find his character ranked No. 8 on TV Guide's list of the "50 Greatest TV Dads of All Time" in 2004. (Bill Cosby's Dr. Cliff Huxtable was No. 1.) But one honor denied him was an Emmy Award: he was nominated only once, for his role in the TV movie "Murder in Texas." "The Andy Griffith Show" itself, though nominated three times, also never won an Emmy, but Mr. Knotts did — five times — for his performance as Deputy Fife, and so did Ms. Bavier, once, as Andy's aunt.

Andy Samuel Griffith was born in Mount Airy on June 1, 1926, the only child of Carl

Lee Griffith and the former Geneva Nann Nunn. His father was a foreman at a furniture factory. Mr. Griffith described his childhood as happy, but said he never forgot the pain he felt when someone called him "white trash."

After seeing the trombonist Jack Teagarden in the 1941 film "Birth of the Blues," he bought a trombone from Sears, Roebuck & Company and wheedled lessons out of a local pastor. The pastor later recommended him to the University of North Carolina, where he won a music degree and married Barbara Edwards.

He moved on to singing, and for a while he hoped to be an opera singer. He tried teaching music and phonetics in a high school but left after three frustrating years. "First day, I'd tell the class all I knew," he told The Saturday Evening Post in 1964, "and there was nothin' left to say for the rest o' the semester."

In spare moments Mr. Griffith and his wife put together an act in which he posed as a country preacher and told jokes (one was about putting frogs in the baptismal water) while she danced. They played local civic clubs.

In 1953, performing for an insurance convention, Mr. Griffith, in his bumpkin preacher persona, told a comic first-person tale about attending a college football game and trying to figure out what was going on. Some 500 discs of the monologue were pressed under the title "What It Was, Was Football," and it became a hit on local radio. Mr. Linke, then with Capitol Records, scurried to North Carolina to acquire the rights and sign Mr. Griffith.

Mr. Linke was soon guiding him onto television and nightclub stages. But Mr. Griffith's big

MAYBERRY MAN: Andy Griffith, center, was best known as the small-town sheriff on "The Andy Griffith Show." His costars on the beloved series were Don Knotts, left, and Jim Nabors.

break came on Broadway, in 1955, when he was cast in "No Time for Sergeants" as a mountain yokel drafted into the Air Force, a role he had played on television, on "Playhouse 90." The play was a hit, running for almost two years, and he reprised the role for the 1958 film version.

His first movie role, in "A Face in the Crowd," was more complicated. The character, Larry Rhodes, known as Lonesome, is a vagrant who is discovered playing the guitar in an Arkansas jail and then groomed to become a beloved television star, only to be undone by his dark side. Mr. Griffith was so consumed by the stormy character that it affected his marriage.

"I'll tell you the truth," he told the Times magazine. "You play an egomaniac and paranoid all day and it's hard to turn it off at bedtime. We went through a nightmare."

In 1959, Mr. Griffith returned to Broadway in the musical comedy "Destry Rides Again" in a role that had been played in films by

Tom Mix, James Stewart, Joel McCrea and Audie Murphy. Though reviews were mixed, Newsday declared, "There isn't a more likable personality around than Andy Griffith."

The pilot of "The Andy Griffith Show," in February 1960, was actually an episode of "The Danny Thomas Show," in which Mr. Thomas, as Danny Williams, is arrested by a sheriff for running a stop sign while driving through Mayberry.

Danny baits the sheriff, calling him "hayseed" and "Clem."

"The name ain't Clem," Mr. Griffith responds. "It's Andy, Sheriff Andy Taylor!"

Sheldon Leonard, producer of Mr. Thomas's show, had decided to build a sitcom around Mr. Griffith after seeing him in "Destry." Mr. Griffith negotiated for 50 percent ownership, which gave him a large say in the show's development.

Critical to the show's success was the casting of Mr. Knotts as the inept but lovable Barney Fife. So was the simple but appealing formula: characters would confront a problem, then resolve it by exercising honesty or some other virtue.

When Mr. Knotts left the show in 1965, a year after Mr. Nabors did, Mr. Griffith became "nervous" about its future, he said. Indeed, some critics and viewers said the show in its later years lacked the sparkle it had once possessed. But its ratings never tottered.

Still, after the 1967-68 season, Mr. Griffith had had enough and left the show. But he did produce a kind of sequel series for the following season, "Mayberry R.F.D.," with Ken Berry starring as a widowed farmer alongside many of the characters from "Andy Griffith." It ran three seasons.

Mr. Griffith's acting career stalled afterward, despite a five-year deal with Universal Pictures. He said he was not offered roles he wanted to play. Returning to television in 1970, he starred in two short-lived shows, "The Headmaster" and "The New Andy Griffith Show."

Then came a raft of made-for-TV movies. One, "Diary of a Perfect Murder," served as the pilot for "Matlock," presenting Mr. Griffith in a new guise as a rumpled lawyer. The show's run, from 1986 to 1995, exceeded that of "The Andy Griffith Show."

Mr. Griffith continued to play occasional movie and television parts, including that of an 80-something widower who rediscovers romance, and sex, in a nursing home in "Play the Game."

He never lost his singing voice. In 1996 he recorded a gospel album, "I Love to Tell the Story: 25 Timeless Hymns," which won a Grammy.

In 2010 he showed a political side when he extolled President Barack Obama's health care legislation in a television commercial for it. Republican politicians and conservative talk show hosts leapt on him, and Jon Stewart made boisterous fun of the brouhaha on "The Daily Show."

Mr. Griffith's marriage to Barbara Edwards, in 1949, ended in divorce in 1972. An eight-year marriage to the Greek actress Solica Cassuto ended in divorce in 1981. In 1983, he married Cindi Knight, who survives him, as does a daughter. A son from that marriage died in 1996.

To viewers, Mr. Griffith's portrayal of the sheriff seemed so effortless, they presumed he was just playing himself. He was not, he insisted; he was always acting. But he took that misimpression as a compliment to his artistry.

"You're supposed to believe in the character," he said. "You're not supposed to think, 'Gee, Andy's acting up a storm.'"

— BY DOUGLAS MARTIN

JIMMY BIVINS

The Might-Have-Been Champion

DEC. 6, 1919 · JULY 4, 2012

J IMMY BIVINS, a heavyweight boxer who in the 1940s and '50s beat eight future world champions but who, to his lasting regret, never got a shot at the title himself, died on July 4 in a Cleveland nursing home. He was 92.

If prizefighting adds up to a montage of cruelty and courage, fame and fear, Bivins's life was representative. He realized the power of his fists early on, and then glimpsed the heights to which they could carry him. But bad luck, bad timing and perhaps bad people thwarted him, and near the end of his life he was a neglected shell of the warrior he had been.

From 1942 to 1946, Bivins plowed through the heavyweight and light-heavyweight divisions, going undefeated before losing to Jersey Joe Walcott in February 1946. Between 1940 and 1955, he beat a parade of fighters who would go on to become champions, among them Gus Lesnevich, Joey Maxim, Ezzard Charles and Archie Moore.

Playing the villain and sticking his tongue out at opponents, Bivins became one of boxing's big attractions, a scrappy, crouching slugger with a stinging left jab. At one point he was a top title contender in both the light-heavyweight and heavyweight divisions. Joe Louis was among many in the sport who were puzzled that Bivins was not given a chance to be a champion.

"I can't understand why he hasn't gotten further than he has," Louis said in an interview with The New York Times in 1948.

Bivins did not say much at the time, but in 1999, speaking with The Plain Dealer of Cleveland, he mentioned a conversation with "this mob guy from New York." The man said Bivins "should play ball with him." To Bivins, the message was clear — that he should be willing to throw fights when told to.

"Shoot, I told him I wasn't a ballplayer; I'm a fighter," Bivins said.

For a man who never wore a championship belt, Bivins, known as the Cleveland Spider-Man, left a lasting impression. In 1997, Boxing Digest named him the No. 16 light-heavyweight of all time; in 2002, Ring Magazine ranked him No. 6 in the same category. He was inducted into the International Boxing Hall of Fame in 1999.

All that eased his disappointment but did not erase it. "The only thing is, I fought my heart out and didn't get no pay," he told The Plain Dealer in 1994. "Now, guys go for two rounds and come out a millionaire. They couldn't wipe my nose. That's the way the fight game is."

Though he fought Louis in a six-round exhibition match in 1948 and again in a 10-round, nonchampionship fight in 1951, Bivins lived the rest of his life regretting never fighting him for the title. "All I wanted was a chance," Bivins said. "I deserved a chance."

James Louis Bivins was born in Dry Branch, Ga., on Dec. 6, 1919. His family moved north to Cleveland three years later. His first sport was track, and when young people made fun of him for his dedication to his school work, he would run away, he said. One day he stopped in his tracks and this time faced his tormentors. "I beat the stew out of them," he said.

After his sister Viola married a boxer, Bivins went with him to a recreation center to try the sport. His father took him to see the legendary Jack Johnson put on an exhibition. And when his friend and fellow track runner Jesse Owens told him that he should make boxing his sport because it paid better, Bivins was persuaded. (In the 1936 Olympics, Owens achieved the glory that would elude Bivins.)

ONCE A WARRIOR: Jimmy Bevins was one of boxing's biggest stars in the 1940s and '50s.

Though only 5 feet 9 inches, Bivins had a 79-inch reach, and in 1937 he won the Cleveland Golden Gloves novice featherweight championship. Two years later, he won as a welterweight. He made his professional debut as a middleweight in January 1940 and won $25 by knocking out his opponent in the first round. By the end of 1942, he was the No. 1 contender in the light-heavyweight division.

But all titles were frozen until the end of World War II. In February 1943, Bivins beat Anton Christoforidis to become the temporary light-heavyweight champion until fighters in the military returned to competition. Later that year, the National Boxing Association ranked Bivins second or third among the contenders for Louis's heavyweight crown.

Louis was in the Army at the time. In 1944, Bivins, too, joined the Army.

By February 1945, Bivins had been honorably discharged and was fighting again. One of his most memorable postwar fights was against Moore, in August 1945. He knocked Moore down six times en route to a knockout victory. But he began to lose more often.

Bivins retired in 1953 before trying to make a comeback in two fights in 1955. His lifetime record was 86 wins, 25 losses and one draw. He knocked out 31 opponents and was knocked out five times.

In his retirement, Bivins drove trucks delivering bakery goods, potato chips and pretzels, and he coached youths in boxing. He made a tradition of cooking Sunday dinners for them, always ending with homemade cobbler and ice cream. His third wife, Elizabeth, died in 1995.

Bivins dropped out of sight and was largely forgotten until 1998, when the police discovered him living in the squalid attic of his daughter's house, wrapped in a urine-soaked blanket. His 110-pound frame was covered with bedsores, and he had severed a piece of his right middle finger trying to pry open a can of beans with a knife. The injury required a partial amputation.

His son-in-law, Darrell Banks, was convicted of elder abuse. As part of his plea, the case against Bivins's daughter, Josetta Banks, was dismissed. She survives him, as do five grandchildren and numerous great- and great-great-grandchildren. He had three sisters and two brothers, all of whom have died.

During his last years, his sister Maria Bivins Baskin cared for him. He liked to play checkers, making up his own rules.

— BY DOUGLAS MARTIN

ERNEST BORGNINE

Forever Marty and McHale

JAN. 24, 1917 · JULY 8, 2012

ERNEST BORGNINE, the rough-hewn actor who seemed destined for tough-guy characters but who won an Academy Award for embodying the gentlest of souls, a lonely Bronx butcher, in the 1955 film "Marty," died on July 8 in Los Angeles. He was 95.

Mr. Borgnine, who later starred on "McHale's Navy" on television, made his first big impression in films at age 37, appearing in "From Here to Eternity" (1953) as Fatso Judson, the sadistic stockade sergeant who beats Frank Sinatra's character, Private Maggio, to death. But Paddy Chayefsky, who wrote "Marty" as a television play starring Rod Steiger, and Delbert Mann, who directed it, saw something beyond brutality in Mr. Borgnine and offered him the title role when it was made into a feature film.

The 1950s had emerged as the decade of the common man, with Willy Loman of "Death of a Salesman" on Broadway and the bus driver Ralph Kramden ("The Honeymooners") and the factory worker Chester Riley ("The Life of Riley") on television. Mr. Borgnine's Marty Pilletti, a 34-year-old blue-collar bachelor who still lives with his mother, fit right in, showing the tender side of the average, unglamorous guy next door.

Marty's awakening, as he unexpectedly falls in love, was described by Bosley Crowther in The New York Times as "a beautiful blend of the crude and the strangely gentle and sensitive in a monosyllabic man."

Mr. Borgnine received the Oscar for best actor for "Marty." For the same performance he also received a Golden Globe and awards from the New York Film Critics Circle, the National Board of Review and the British Academy of Film and Television Arts.

Mr. Borgnine won even wider fame as the star of the ABC sitcom "McHale's Navy" (1962-66), originating the role of an irreverent con man of a PT boat skipper. (The cast also included a young Tim Conway.) He wrote in his autobiography, "Ernie" (2008), that he had initially turned down the role, saying he had no interest in a television series, but changed his mind after a boy came to his door selling candy. The boy said he knew who James Arness of "Gunsmoke" was, and he knew who Richard Boone of "Have Gun, Will Travel" was, but Ernest Borgnine? He had never heard of him.

Over a career of more than six decades, the burly, big-voiced Mr. Borgnine was never able to escape typecasting completely, at least in films. Although he did another Chayefsky screenplay, starring with Bette Davis as a working-class father of the bride in "The Catered Affair" (1956), and even appeared in a musical, "The Best Things in Life Are Free" (1956), playing a Broadway showman, the vast majority of his characters were villains.

Military roles continued to beckon. One of his best known was as Lee Marvin's commanding officer in "The Dirty Dozen" (1967), about hardened prisoners on a World War II commando mission. He also starred in three television-movie sequels.

He worked in virtually every genre. Filmmakers cast him as a gangster, even in satirical movies like "Spike of Bensonhurst" (1988). He was in westerns like Sam Peckinpah's blood-soaked classic "The Wild Bunch" (1969) and crime dramas like "Bad Day at Black Rock" (1955).

He played gruff police officers, like his character in the disaster blockbuster "The Poseidon Adventure" (1972), and bosses from hell, as in the horror movie "Willard" (1971). Twice he played a manager of gladiators, in "Demetrius and the Gladiators" (1954) and in the 1984 miniseries "The Last Days of Pompeii."

Mr. Borgnine's menacing features seemed to disappear when he flashed his trademark

SHOWING HIS TENDER SIDE: Ernest Borgnine, here with co-star Betsy Blair, won an Academy Award for playing the title role in the 1955 film "Marty."

gaptoothed smile, and later in life he began to find good-guy roles, like the helpful taxi driver in "Escape From New York" (1981) and the title role in "A Grandpa for Christmas," a 2007 television movie.

"McHale's Navy" and the 1964 film inspired by it were his most notable forays into comedy, but in 1999 he began doing the voice of a recurring character, the elderly ex-superhero Mermaidman, in the animated series "SpongeBob SquarePants." He continued to play that role until last year.

He began his career on the stage, but unlike many actors who had done the same, Mr. Borgnine professed to have no burning desire to return there. "Once you create a character for the stage, you become like a machine," he told The Washington Post in 1969. In films, he said, "you're always creating something new."

Ermes Effron Borgnino was born on Jan. 24, 1917, in Hamden, Conn., near New Haven. His father was a railroad brakeman. His mother was said to be the daughter of a count, Paolo Boselli, an adviser to King Victor Emmanuel of Italy.

The boy spent several years of his childhood in Italy, where his mother returned during a long separation from her husband. But they returned to Connecticut, and he graduated from high school there.

He joined the Navy at 18 and served for 10 years. During World War II he was a gunner's mate. After the war he considered factory jobs, but his mother suggested that he try acting. Her reasoning, he reported, was, "You've always liked making a damned fool of yourself."

He studied at the Randall School of Drama in Hartford, then moved to Virginia, where he became a member of the Barter Theater in Abingdon and worked his way up from painting scenery to playing the Gentleman Caller in "The Glass Menagerie."

In the late 1940s he headed for New York, where by 1952 he was appearing on Broadway as a bodyguard in the comic fantasy "Mrs. McThing," starring Helen Hayes. He had already made his movie debut playing a Chinese shopkeeper in the 1951 adventure "China Corsair."

Mr. Borgnine never retired from acting. In the 1980s he starred in another television series, the adventure drama "Airwolf," playing a helicopter pilot. He took a supporting role as a bubbly doorman in the 1990s sitcom "The Single Guy." His last film appearance was in "The Man Who Shook the Hand of Vicente Fernandez," not yet released at his death, in which he plays an elderly man who becomes a celebrity to Latino employees at the nursing home where he lives. On television, he was in the series finale of "ER" in 2009 and appeared in a cable film, "Love's Christmas Journey," last year.

His other films included "The Vikings" (1958); "Ice Station Zebra" (1968); "Gattaca" (1997); and "Hoover" (2000), in which he played J. Edgar Hoover.

Mr. Borgnine, who lived in Beverly Hills, was married five times. In 1949 he married Rhoda Kemins, whom he had met when they were both in the Navy. They had a daughter but divorced in 1958. On New Year's Eve 1959 he

and the Mexican-born actress Katy Jurado were married; they divorced in 1962.

His third marriage was his most notorious because of its brevity. He and the Broadway musical star Ethel Merman married in late June 1964 but split up in early August. Mr. Borgnine later contended that Ms. Merman had left because she was upset that on an international honeymoon trip he was recognized and she wasn't.

In 1965 he married Donna Rancourt; they had two children before divorcing in 1972. In 1973 he married for the fifth and last time, to Tova Traesnaes, who under the name Tova Borgnine became a cosmetics entrepreneur.

She survives him, as do a son and two daughters, a stepson, six grandchildren and a sister.

Asked about his acting methods in 1973, Mr. Borgnine told The Times: "No Stanislavsky. I don't chart out the life histories of the people I play. If I did, I'd be in trouble. I work with my heart and my head, and naturally emotions follow."

Sometimes he prayed, he said, or just reflected on character-appropriate thoughts. "If none of that works," he added, "I think to myself of the money I'm making."

—By Anita Gates

\\\\\\\\\\\\\\\\\\\\\\\\\\\\

MARION CUNNINGHAM

The Food That Matters Most1 Is on the Kitchen Table

FEB. 11, 1922 - JULY 11, 2012

MARION CUNNINGHAM, a former California homemaker who overcame agoraphobia later in life to become one of America's most famous and enthusiastic advocates of home cooking, died on July 11 in Walnut Creek, Calif. She was 90.

"More than anyone else, she gave legitimacy to home cooking," Michael Bauer, the executive food editor of The San Francisco Chronicle, said of Mrs. Cunningham. "She took what many people would say was housewife food and really gave it respect by force of her own personality."

Mrs. Cunningham's most enduring trait may have been her ability to make even novice cooks feel as if they could accomplish something in the kitchen. She took many of them under her wing and drew from them for her popular book "Learning to Cook."

She loved to go to the supermarket and peer into the baskets of startled strangers, whom she would then interview about their cooking skills. Preserving the family supper table was one of her causes.

"No one is cooking at home anymore, so we are losing all the wonderful lessons we learn at the dinner table," she said in an interview in 2002.

It was a theme she focused on in the preface to "The Fannie Farmer Cookbook," the classic American volume that she was hired to revise in the late 1970s.

"Too many families seldom sit down together; it's gobble and go," she wrote, "eating food on the run, reheating it in relays in the microwave as one dashes off to a committee meeting, another to basketball practice. As a result we are losing an important value. Food is more than fodder. It is an act of giving and receiving because the experience at table is a communal sharing; talk begins to flow, feelings are expressed, and a sense of well-being takes over."

Marion Enwright was born in Los Angeles on Feb. 11, 1922, to Joseph Enwright and the former Maryann Spelta. She grew up, in her words, as a Southern California beach girl. A high school graduate, she did not go to college.

In 1942 she married Robert Cunningham, a medical malpractice lawyer, and moved to San

SAVIOR OF THE FAMILY DINNER: An advocate for home cooking, Marion Cunningham counted celebrity chefs and renowned food writers as friends.

Diego, where he was serving in the Marines. At a time when men were in short supply for many civilian jobs, she worked in a gas station. They eventually settled in Walnut Creek, Calif., outside Oakland.

Mrs. Cunningham spent the first half of her adult life mostly raising her children, a boy and a girl — who survive her — and tending to the family's ranch home. For much of that time she struggled with agoraphobia, a fear of open and public places. It was so intense at times that she could barely cross the Bay Bridge to San Francisco.

She also developed a drinking problem, and once she stopped, she became known for her love of a good cup of black coffee — sometimes ordered when everyone else was drinking Champagne.

Prompted by a friend's invitation in 1972 to go to Oregon to attend cooking classes led by the renowned food writer James Beard, Mrs. Cunningham overcame her phobia and headed out of the state for the first time.

Mr. Beard took to this tall, blue-eyed home-maker, and for the next 11 years she was his assistant, helping him establish cooking classes in the Bay Area. The job gave her a ringside seat to a period in American cooking when regional food, organic produce and a new way of cooking and eating were just becoming part of the culinary dialogue. Her association with Mr. Beard also gave her the big break of her career, in the late 1970s, when he passed her name to Judith Jones, the well-known New York culinary editor, who was looking for someone to rewrite "The Fannie Farmer Cookbook."

That project led to seven more cookbooks; her own television show, "Cunningham & Company," which ran for more than 70 episodes, sometimes on the Food Network; and a longstanding cooking column for The Chronicle.

In 1989 she and a friend started the Baker's Dozen, an informal group of San Francisco bakers. It grew to more than 200 members and led to another cookbook.

Like many others, Ruth Reichl, the author and former restaurant critic for The New York Times, came to regard Mrs. Cunningham as a mother figure.

"She was the glue that held the nascent food movement together," Ms. Reichl said, "the touchstone, the person you checked in with to find out who was doing what all over the country."

"Food is more than fodder. It is an act of giving and receiving because the experience at table is a communal sharing."

Mrs. Cunningham bought a Jaguar with her first royalty check from "The Breakfast Book," one of her most enduring cookbooks. The Jaguar became identified with her, and she would drive it to a different Bay Area restaurant almost every night, sometimes logging 2,500 miles a month.

Along the way she collected a passel of friends who changed how America cooked and ate; among them was her close friend Chuck Williams, whose kitchenware company, Williams-Sonoma, was just getting started.

One of the people she discovered was a young Alice Waters, who was cooking organic and local food at a little restaurant in Berkeley, Calif., called Chez Panisse. Mrs. Cunningham took Mr. Beard to the restaurant in 1974, and he put it on the culinary map, marking the beginnings of California cuisine and the modern organic movement. "She was always my biggest cheerleader," Ms. Waters once said.

Mrs. Cunningham, who had Alzheimer's disease, had been living in an assisted-care home in Walnut Creek at her death.

Plain-spoken and quick with a quip or a gentle jab, she could cut through the puffery of fancy chefs and food writers. Once, after a food author spent the day watching her make pie crust, taking meticulous notes on how many times she cut and stirred, she called Ms. Reichl.

"He really is crazy, dear, don't you think?" Ms. Reichl recalled her saying. "Nobody could make a decent crust following those directions."

Mrs. Cunningham's humor extended to her cookbooks. In one passage from "The Fannie Farmer Cookbook," on how to crack fresh coconut, she suggested throwing it on a hard surface, preferably a concrete patio.

"That's how monkeys do it," she wrote, "and they are professionals."

— By Kim Severson

MARVIN TRAUB

The Barnum of Bloomingdale's

APRIL 14, 1925 - JULY 11, 2012

M ARVIN S. TRAUB, the retailing impresario who transformed Bloomingdale's from a stodgy Upper East Side family department store into a trendsetting international showcase of style and showmanship in the 1970s and '80s, died on July 11 at his home in Manhattan. He was 87.

One of the most creative retailers of his era, Mr. Traub made Bloomingdale's synonymous with luxury, introduced many of the world's best-known clothing designers and created a national chain that acquired a reputation for status-conscious merchandising and chic interior moods.

At his flagship store, at 59th Street and Lexington Avenue in Manhattan — a block-square emporium that stood hard by the rumble of Third Avenue elevated trains until 1955 — he staged promotional events with the dazzle of a Broadway opening.

As if Bloomingdale's had its own foreign policy, he saluted China, Italy, France, Portugal, Ireland and Israel with lavish productions that featured not only traditional furnishings, clothing and gourmet foods but also displays of artifacts from antiquity, glittering dinner parties and guest lists that included ambassadors, business titans, movie stars, presidents' wives and sometimes royalty.

Jacqueline Kennedy, Lady Bird Johnson and Betty Ford were patrons. During America's Bicentennial celebrations in 1976, Mr. Traub escorted Queen Elizabeth II and Prince Philip through crowds of gawking shoppers as the royal couple took in Wedgwood china, winter sportswear reminiscent of Britain's hunting gear and reproductions of English antique furniture.

For "India: The Ultimate Fantasy," in 1978, Mr. Traub deployed life-size papier-mâché elephants and camels in primary colors, wooden temple carvings, silk banners waving from the ceilings, and kohl-eyed Indian women, who mingled in their saris and bangles with patrons in musk-scented halls overflowing with Indian jewelry, accessories, apparel and home furnishings.

When Mr. Traub decided to build a new restaurant in the flagship store in 1979, he created Le Train Bleu, a reproduction of the 70-foot dining car that once made the Lyons-Marseille-Monte Carlo run in style: mahogany paneling with green channel-quilted trim, beveled mirrors, Victorian lamps and brass luggage racks — to hold shopping bags, of course — all tucked into the sixth-floor housewares department.

In 1980, "Come to China at Bloomingdale's," a six-week pageant Mr. Traub negotiated in Beijing like a treaty, featured an entire Cantonese farmhouse, a Chinese garden pavilion and 20 exquisite robes from 1763 to 1908 that had never been seen outside the Forbidden City. He filled 14 branch stores in the Northeast with enough food, fashions and filigree for 11 million shoppers.

In 1984, his $20 million "Fête de France" was a cornucopia of chocolate by Mazet de Montargis; oils, herbs and pâtés from Provence; the fashion creations of 25 designers; replicas of silver from the liner Normandie; and sculptures from the Georges Pompidou Center in Paris. It began with a dinner for 1,600 people who paid $200 each to talk at one another above a crush of shoulders and satin.

"We are not only in competition with other stores, but with the Guggenheim and the Met," Mr. Traub once explained.

Grace Mirabella, Vogue's editor in chief in the 1970s and '80s, anointed him "the Sol Hurok of retailing," a reference to the great impresario who brought the Bolshoi Ballet to America.

Marvin Stuart Traub was born in Manhattan on April 14, 1925, the only child of Sam and Bea Traub. His father was a corset company executive, and his mother was a senior saleswoman at Bonwit Teller; her customers included Rose Kennedy, Marlene Dietrich and Mary Martin.

Marvin attended Peekskill Military Academy in upstate New York. After a year at Harvard, he was drafted into the wartime Army as an infantry private and was wounded in France in 1944. A bullet shattered his right thighbone. A year of surgery and convalescence followed, and he was mustered out with his leg in a brace and seriously shortened. He eventually overcame his handicap through therapy and a built-up shoe, and became an able golfer, skier and jogger.

Returning to Harvard to study government, he graduated with high honors in 1947.

In 1948, Mr. Traub married Lee Laufer. The couple had a daughter and two sons, including James Traub, a journalist who writes frequently for The New York Times. They survive him, as do four grandchildren.

"LIKE NO OTHER STORE": As chairman and chief executive, Marvin Traub helped turn Bloomingdale's into an international retail destination with creative merchandising and imaginative displays.

After earning a master's degree from Harvard Business School, Mr. Traub joined Bloomingdale's in 1950, starting at the bottom, in charge of the bargain basement. When business was slow, he and a colleague put on coats and pretended to be customers reveling in merchandise at the bargain tables. After attracting a crowd, he recalled, "we would quietly slip back to our offices."

Demolition of the Third Avenue El in 1955-56 changed the East Side landscape, clearing the way for luxury high-rise apartment buildings and a wealthier clientele, and Mr. Traub climbed the executive ranks, becoming president in 1969 and chairman and chief executive in 1978.

He also became a celebrity-about-town, featured in newspapers and on television at fund-raising affairs and Bloomingdale's promotions with the rich and famous: Gov. Hugh L. Carey, Ethel Kennedy and Senator George McGovern, as well as designers like Ralph Lauren, Perry Ellis, Donna Karan, Calvin Klein and, from Europe, Yves Saint Laurent and Giorgio Armani.

Another promotional hit was Bloomingdale's designer shopping bags, which became self-advertising souvenirs. A 1961 design by the artist Jonah Kinigstein was based on French tarot cards in red, black and white. The iconic Brown Bag by Massimo Vignelli was introduced in 1973. Michaele Vollbracht's 1975 bag, featuring a woman's stark face and the artist's signature, was a sensation, not least because the store name was omitted, a kind of reverse chic: it carried no advertising, but everyone knew it was Bloomingdale's.

While appealing to affluent buyers, Bloomingdale's did not ignore the less well-off; it also carried goods for bargain hunters, who could brag that they bought it at Bloomingdale's. "People assume wrongly," Mr. Traub said, "that because we are unique, everything we sell is high-priced or whimsical. We could not have a business of this size without a broader base."

In the boom times of the 1980s, Mr. Traub added branches on the East Coast and in Florida, Texas and California. Princess Yasmin Khan, Robert De Niro, Barbra Streisand and Faye Dunaway had charge cards. Long before Old Navy T-shirts, women wore panties marked "Bloomies."

But by the late '80s, sales were soft, and Bloomingdale's and other department stores were under pressure from factory outlets and lower-price chains like Gap and Target. The Campeau Corporation acquired Bloomingdale's and its 17-store chain in 1988 when it bought the parent company, Federated Department Stores. In early 1990, after unsuccessful efforts by Mr. Traub and others to buy Bloomingdale's, Campeau filed for bankruptcy.

Bloomingdale's survived, but in 1991 Mr. Traub retired and began a new career as a consultant, founding Marvin Traub Associates in 1992. He acquired clients like Ralph Lauren, American Express and the Jones Apparel Group and began a joint consulting venture with Financo, a retail-focused investment firm.

Mr. Traub co-wrote two books, whose titles echo his promotional theme for the place he had long run: "Like No Other Store: The Bloomingdale's Legend and the Revolution in American Marketing," a memoir and retailing history written with Tom Teicholz and published in 1993; and, in 2008, another memoir, written with Lisa Marsh, "Marvin Traub: Like No Other Career."

— BY ROBERT D. McFADDEN

FLORENCE WAREN

She in the Spotlight, Nazis in the Dark

MARCH 28, 1917 - JULY 12, 2012

EVEN IN THE DEPTHS OF WAR IN OCCUPIED FRANCE, Florence Waren and Frederic Apcar — or "Florence et Frederic," as they were billed — dazzled Paris, he in tails, she in jeweled gowns with flowers in her hair, the two of them gliding and swirling across the stage as one of the most famous ballroom-dance teams in Europe.

In old black-and-white photographs, Ms. Waren, then in her early 20s, is often airborne, seemingly weightless in Mr. Apcar's arms. At times they shared the stage with Édith Piaf and Maurice Chevalier. And on many nights Nazi officers were in the audience, applauding lustily.

But what the members of the Wehrmacht did not know was that Ms. Waren was, as she later described it, "hiding in the spotlight."

Ms. Waren — Florence Rigal at the time — was a Jew in disguise, performing in a Nazi-held city where Jews lived under constant threat. She was a lawbreaker, hiding other Jews in her apartment, risking her own deportation to a concentration camp. And she was a smuggler, helping to supply guns to the French Resistance.

"I think she was very scared," her son, Mark Waren, said in a telephone interview. "But I don't think it was something she thought much about. It was simply what one did."

Ms. Waren died on July 12 at her home in Manhattan, her son said. She was 95. She had eluded capture during the war and had come to New York not long afterward, to dance at the Copacabana with Mr. Apcar. She went on to carve out a career on stage and in television and to lead the dance and theater department at City College in New York, even though she had never finished high school in her native South Africa.

Ms. Waren was a dancer at the Bal Tabarin Music Hall in Paris and had not yet met Mr. Apcar when the Germans occupied France in 1940. Jews were ordered to register with the police, but an owner of the music hall urged her not to. She took his advice, and her heritage went undetected. But because, as a South African, she was a British citizen, the Nazis considered her an enemy alien, and in late 1940 she was among several thousand people, mostly Britons, who were arrested and

interned for months in a louse-infested prison in Besançon.

After her release, she resumed dancing at the Bal Tabarin, which had become a favorite destination of German officers, and teamed up with Mr. Apcar. Briefly, they were lovers. They moved in glamorous circles, with Ms. Piaf, Mr. Chevalier and another immensely popular singer, Charles Trenet.

Ms. Waren had friends in the Resistance and began to help them, hiding and transporting guns, hiding Jews in her apartment or helping them find their way from one safe house to another. After performing in Germany in a camp for French prisoners of war, she carried home a suitcase full of their letters to relatives, an act for which she could have been arrested.

In a documentary film by her son, "Dancing Lessons," Ms. Waren, still graceful and elegant at 86, described a time during the war when she noticed a French policeman following her. When he caught up with her on a bridge over the Seine, he told her not to be afraid, but also not to speak or even turn her head to look at him.

"You have some people in your apartment," he said. Her landlady had informed the police that Ms. Waren was hiding two Jewish sisters there, he said. The apartment was going to be searched, he warned her.

"You must get them out," the policeman said. "Tonight."

That night, Ms. Waren escorted the sisters through the dark streets to a convent. Across the street, she said, Nazis were raiding an orphanage, throwing Jewish children out of high windows.

Near the end of the occupation in 1944, Mr. Apcar was told that Ms. Waren was going to be arrested, so he rented a house in the suburbs to hide her and several other Jewish performers. One morning, American soldiers drove up in a tank and asked directions to Paris. Soon,

Ms. Waren and Mr. Apcar set out for Paris, too, to watch the liberation.

After the war, the French government declared Ms. Waren a "privileged resident."

She was born Sadie Rigal in Johannesburg on March 28, 1917, one of seven children. Her father was a traveling salesman for a department store. Her mother, who had been a teacher in New York, had a breakdown after the death of her youngest son during an influenza epidemic in 1919 and was committed to a mental hospital in South Africa. Mr. Rigal raised the family alone.

A childhood event shaped Ms. Waren's life: seeing the Ballets Russes, one of the world's greatest ballet companies. She dreamed of becoming a dancer and began taking lessons. She became good enough to win competitions, and in 1938, at 21, she left Johannesburg for Europe, hoping for a career in ballet. She studied in England and Paris, with renowned — and stern — teachers from Russia. When one struck her in the calf with a cane, she snatched the cane and broke it, then had to buy the teacher a new one before being allowed back in class.

Soon she was hired by the Bal Tabarin and began dancing in revues there, elaborate shows with dozens of dancers in fancy costumes (or none at all). She changed her first name to Florence. In 1939 she was offered her dream job — a place in the Ballet Russe de Monte Carlo, a descendant of the company that had inspired her in the first place. But World War II broke out before she could join the troupe.

In 1948, she and Mr. Apcar were performing in New York at the Copacabana when she met Stanley Waren, an actor, director and teacher. On their first date, they went to a delicatessen and got into such a furious argument that they were thrown out, Mr. Waren said. They were married in 1949, and Ms. Waren decided to leave the dance act. Mr. Apcar was said to have been devastated, but Ms. Waren agreed to train a replacement.

She was a lawbreaker, hiding other Jews in her apartment, risking her own deportation to a concentration camp. And she was a smuggler, helping to supply guns to the French Resistance.

In New York, she began a new career, appearing in plays and on television, on the Ed Sullivan and Kate Smith shows. Mr. Apcar died in 2008 in Las Vegas, after a long career producing shows at the Dunes hotel and casino.

Ms. Waren also worked with her husband — she as choreographer, he as director — on shows in Africa, Taiwan and China. From 1973 to 1983 she was a professor of theater and dance at City College, leading the department for part of that time. She was also a dance panelist on the New York State Council on the Arts.

Besides her son and her husband, a granddaughter survives her.

"She led a rather adventurous life," Stanley Waren said. "Wherever she went, she somehow became part of the scene, and people helped her and she helped them. She didn't want anything from anybody except to work. She was really one of those natural-born performers who loved what she was doing."

— By DENISE GRADY

\\\\\\\\\\\\\\\\\\\\\\\\\\\\\\\\

KITTY WELLS

A Song About Women Rang True About Men

AUG. 30, 1919 - JULY 16, 2012

K ITTY WELLS, who was on the verge of quitting music to be a homemaker when she recorded a hit in 1952 that struck a chord with women and began opening doors for them in country music, died on July 16 at her home in Madison, Tenn. She was 92.

Ms. Wells was an unlikely and unassuming pioneer. When she recorded "It Wasn't God Who Made Honky Tonk Angels," she was a 33-year-old wife and mother intending to retire from the business to devote herself to her family full time. The only reason she made the record, she told the weekly newspaper Nashville Scene in 1999, was to collect the union-scale wage ($125) that the session would bring.

"I wasn't expecting it to make a hit," she said. "I just thought it was another song."

But Ms. Wells's record proved to be much more than just "another song." It was a rejoinder to Hank Thompson's No. 1 hit "Wild Side of Life," a brooding lament in which the singer blames a woman he picks up in a bar for breaking up his marriage, and it became her signature song.

"Honky Tonk Angels" resonated with women who had been irked, if not outraged, by Mr. Thompson's record, which called into question their morals and their increasing social and sexual freedom. At a time when divorce rates were rising and sexual mores changing in postwar America, the song, with lyrics by J. D. Miller, resounded like a protofeminist anthem.

"As I sit here tonight, the jukebox playin'/ The tune about the wild side of life," Ms. Wells sings, she reflects on married men pretending to be single and causing "many a good girl to go wrong." She continues:

It's a shame that all the blame is on us women
It's not true that only you men feel the same
From the start most every heart that's ever broken
Was because there always was a man to blame.

The NBC radio network banned Ms. Wells's record, deeming it "suggestive," and the Grand Ole Opry would not let her perform it on their show. The Opry eventually relented, however, in part because of the song's popularity and Ms. Wells's nonthreatening image.

Ms. Wells "sang of 'Honky Tonk Angels,' but no one would have ever mistaken her for one," Mary A. Bufwack and Robert K. Oermann wrote in the book "Finding Her Voice: Women in Country Music, 1800-2000."

"She was always proper, always dignified," they added. "She dressed in prewar gingham instead of pantsuits, flamboyant Western garb or satin costumes."

Sung in a gospel-inflected moan and backed by a crying steel guitar, Ms. Wells's record spent six weeks at the top of the country charts and crossed over to the pop Top 40. The song's success not only made her the biggest female country music star of the postwar era; it also persuaded record executives in Nashville to offer recording contracts to other women. (Music labels had not thought female singers were worth the investment.)

Ms. Wells became a model for generations of women in country music, from Loretta Lynn and Dolly Parton to Iris DeMent. The renowned song publisher Fred Rose anointed her the Queen of Country Music.

HONKY TONK ANGEL: Kitty Wells's 1952 hit became a protofeminist anthem.

Muriel Ellen Deason was born in Nashville on Aug. 30, 1919. Her father, a brakeman for the Tennessee Central Railroad, played guitar and sang folk songs after the fashion of Jimmie Rodgers. Ms. Wells grew up listening to the Grand Ole Opry and singing gospel music.

She learned to play the guitar at 14 and made her singing debut on the radio in 1936. She married Johnnie Wright the following year and worked briefly in a group with her new husband and his sister. When Mr. Wright and Jack Anglin formed the singing duo Johnny and Jack in the late 1930s, Ms. Wells, at that point performing under her married name, was the featured "girl singer" in their show.

She appeared on some of the biggest radio hoedowns of the day, including "Louisiana Hayride" and the weekly Grand Ole Opry broadcast. Under the name the Little Rag Doll she worked as a disc jockey, playing records and selling quilt pieces on KWKH in Shreveport, La. Mr. Wright suggested that she adopt the stage name Kitty Wells, drawn from an old folk ballad made popular by the Pickard Family.

Ms. Wells recorded for RCA Victor in 1949, but all her major hits were made after that for the Decca label and produced by Owen Bradley. Several of her early records were duets with country stars like Red Foley and Webb Pierce. During her 27-year recording career she placed 84 singles on the country charts, 38 of them in the Top 10.

In 1968 she had her own syndicated television show, and in 1974 she made a country-rock album with members of the Allman Brothers and the Marshall Tucker Band. She was elected to the Country Music Hall of Fame in 1976.

Family was important to Ms. Wells and her husband. Early on they incorporated their children into their touring revue. They also recorded with them.

Ms. Wells, who died after having a stroke, is survived by a son, a daughter, eight grandchildren, 12 great-grandchildren and five great-great-grandchildren. Another daughter died in 2009. Mr. Wright, her husband of more than 70 years, died in 2011.

In 1991 the National Academy of Recording Arts and Sciences presented Ms. Wells with a lifetime achievement award. At the time, only two other performers in country music, Hank Williams and Roy Acuff, had received that honor.

— By Bill Friskics-Warren

BILL STAUB

Building a Better Treadmill

NOV. 3, 1915 - JULY 19, 2012

BEFORE PERSONAL TRAINERS AND PADDLEBOARD YOGA, before "Just Do It," Bill Staub read a book that changed his life. It was called "Aerobics," published in 1968, and it declared that a better life was rooted in better cardiovascular health.

"It said if you can run a mile in eight minutes, you'll always be in the upper echelon of fitness," Mr. Staub's son Thomas recalled.

So Mr. Staub started running — and soon made his way to the workshop at Besco, the manufacturing company he owned in Clifton, N.J. While employees on one side of the building made fuel nozzles for airplane engines and wing weights for helicopters, he was on the other side making early versions of a device that the book argued had the potential to get many more Americans exercising — and on their way to that eight-minute mile.

The device was a treadmill, and the author of the book, Dr. Kenneth H. Cooper, presumed it would never be affordable for home use.

"He took away a lot of the excuses people had not to exercise . . . I don't know how long he exercised for himself, but I know he didn't die early."

Mr. Staub proved otherwise. His earliest models, built under the brand name PaceMaster, had wooden rollers and a simple on-off switch near the floor. They were more rudimentary than the ones doctors had started using in the 1950s for stress tests, but they were also much cheaper, as little as $399 in the 1970s.

"He was the pioneer for the use of the treadmill in the home," Dr. Cooper said of Mr. Staub. "He took away a lot of the excuses people had not to exercise. They don't have to worry about the weather, safety or whatever may be. I don't know how long he exercised for himself, but I know he didn't die early."

Mr. Staub died on July 19 at his home in Clifton. He was 96. His sons say he was walking on one of his treadmills as little as two months before his death.

By the mid-1980s the company he formed to manufacture them, Aerobics Inc., was selling 2,000 treadmills a year to a nation increasingly eager to work up a sweat in the rec room. By the mid-90s, sales reached 35,000 a year. Innovation became essential as competition increased. Newer machines could be customized for different speeds, for warm-ups and cool-downs, and to replicate hilly or flat conditions.

Early on, Mr. Staub's son Gerald designed

an on-off switch that could be mounted on the handlebars. His father was perplexed.

"My father said, 'Well, why would you want to do that?' " Thomas Staub said. "My brother said, 'To make it easier for people.' And my dad said, 'But it's an exercise device.' "

The brothers bought Aerobics from their father in the late 1990s, then sold it to a private equity firm, which moved production overseas. The private equity firm filed for bankruptcy in 2010. With the help of an investor, the brothers tried to restart Aerobics, but it closed for good in the fall of 2011.

Dr. Cooper, who is 81 and was among the doctors who monitored President George W. Bush's health, said treadmills in general had a promising future. He pointed to a recent study suggesting that elderly people who maintain a faster gait live longer. "The next step is to use it to increase longevity," Dr. Cooper said of

treadmills. He runs Cooper Aerobics, which has two fitness centers in Texas.

William Edward Staub was born in Philadelphia on Nov. 3, 1915. (The initials in the company name Besco stood for Bill Edward Staub Corporation.) In addition to his sons Thomas and Gerald, his survivors include two other sons, two daughters, a sister, 21 grandchildren and 14 great-grandchildren. His wife, Dorothy, died in 2007. Another daughter died in 1977.

Mr. Staub was a man of routine. He counted calories and did not invite disruptions to his daily diet, which started with tea and toast in the morning.

"If he felt he was gaining any weight at all, he would cut back immediately," Thomas Staub said. "He controlled his life, and it gave him the results he was looking for."

— By WILLIAM YARDLEY

SYLVIA WOODS

Her Soul Food Became the Heart of Harlem

FEB. 2, 1926 - JULY 19, 2012

SYLVIA WOODS, whose namesake Harlem soul-food restaurant became a New York City landmark, frequented by local and national politicians, celebrities and tourists, epicures and ordinary people from the neighborhood, died on July 19 at her home in Westchester County, N.Y. She was 86.

Her death came only a few hours before she was to receive an award from Mayor Michael R. Bloomberg of New York at a reception at Gracie Mansion commemorating the 50th anniversary of Sylvia's Restaurant. There was a moment of silence before the award

presentation; a family friend accepted it on Ms. Woods's behalf.

If Aretha Franklin is the Queen of Soul, Ms. Woods was, by unofficial acclamation, the Queen of Soul Food. A woman who had not set foot in a restaurant until her 20s — forbidden territory for a young black growing up in the Jim Crow South — she went on to create the culinary anchor and de facto social center of Harlem, serving ribs, hot cakes, corn bread, collard greens and fried chicken to the likes of Roberta Flack, Quincy Jones, Diana Ross, Muhammad Ali, Bill Clinton, Jack Kemp, Robert F. Kennedy and, besides Mr. Bloomberg, Mayors Edward I. Koch and David N. Dinkins.

"There has never been a major figure in our community that did not have to come by way of Sylvia's," the Rev. Al Sharpton said. Whenever black leaders needed a place to meet to address a crisis, he said, there was never any question where that meeting would be.

A HARLEM INSTITUTION: Luminaries and locals broke bread at Sylvia and Herbert Woods's restaurant.

"Sylvia never took sides," Mr. Sharpton added. "It was understood, when you walked past the doors of Sylvia's, that your differences were left outside, and we'd have a family meeting inside. She wouldn't let us fuss and fight. She would say, 'Y'all go sit down and have something to eat, and let's talk about it.'"

Ms. Woods opened her establishment on Aug. 1, 1962, starting with six booths and 15 stools in modest quarters on Lenox Avenue near 127th Street. Over time, Sylvia's expanded to seat more than 250. It is now the cornerstone of a commercial empire that includes a catering service and banquet hall and a nationally distributed line of prepared foods. Cookbooks celebrate its cuisine.

As the restaurant expanded, so did its renown. Spike Lee used it as a location for his 1991 film "Jungle Fever." Today, busloads of tourists from as far away as Japan routinely descend on the place — to the consternation of many Harlem residents, who say the restaurant has lost some of its appeal since it became a sightseeing attraction and a magnet for the well-heeled.

"It was a neighborhood joint," said Max Vesterhalt, a regular at Sylvia's. "Then it started to become famous around the world."

The daughter of a farming couple, Van and Julia Pressley, Sylvia Pressley was born in Hemingway, S.C., on Feb. 2, 1926; her father died when she was a baby.

The first thing she cooked as a girl, she recalled, was a pot of rice on the family's wood stove. But the rice burned after Sylvia ran out to play and left it to cook on its own, a fact she withheld from her mother. A switching ensued.

"I got punished," Ms. Woods told The Post and Courier of Charleston, S.C., in 1999, "but not for burning it — for telling a lie."

Sylvia met her future husband, Herbert Deward Woods, when she was 11 and he was 12 and both were working in the fields, picking beans under the blazing sun.

As a teenager, Sylvia moved to New York to join her mother, who had gone there for work. She found work herself, in a hat factory in Queens. In 1944, she married Mr. Woods, who had come North for her.

In the 1950s, Ms. Woods began work as a waitress at Johnson's Luncheonette in Harlem;

because she had grown up poor in the Jim Crow era, the day she first set foot in the place was the first time she had been inside a restaurant anywhere.

In 1962, with help from her mother, who mortgaged the family farm, Ms. Woods bought the luncheonette and renamed it Sylvia's. Three decades ago, Gael Greene, the food critic of New York magazine, wrote a laudatory article on Sylvia's, sealing the restaurant's success.

Ms. Woods, known for her effusive warmth in greeting customers, ran the business until her retirement at 80.

"I keep pressing on," she told The New York Times in 1994. "I can't give up. I've been struggling too long to stop now."

Ms. Woods had been treated for Alzheimer's disease in her last years. Mr. Woods, her self-effacing but stalwart husband and partner in the venture, died in 2001. Survivors include two sons, two daughters, 18 grandchildren, five great-grandchildren and two great-great-grandchildren.

Her recipes survive in the restaurant's kitchen and in the cookbooks "Sylvia's Soul Food: Recipes From Harlem's World Famous Restaurant," which she wrote with Christopher Styler and published in 1992, and "Sylvia's Family Soul Food Cookbook: From Hemingway, South Carolina, to Harlem," from 1999, written with Melissa Clark.

At Ms. Woods's funeral, at the Abyssinian Baptist Church in Harlem, former President Clinton, who has an office in Harlem, was one of several luminaries who spoke.

"When I moved to Harlem, Sylvia made me feel welcome and at home," he said. "When people came to see me from all over America and the world and wanted to know what Harlem was like, I sent them to Sylvia's."

The restaurant's chefs trailed in last for the service, and each touched the coffin to a round of applause.

The restaurant's enduring appeal, Ms. Woods learned firsthand, rested in large part with the time-honored conservatism of its cooking. In the 1990s, in deference to an increasingly health-conscious public, Ms. Woods chose to supplement the menu with lighter fare.

"We had lots of salads and stuff," she told The Philadelphia Daily News in 1999. "And it went to waste. When people come here, they got in their mind what they want."

— BY MARGALIT FOX;
KIA GREGORY CONTRIBUTED REPORTING.

HERBERT VOGEL

Just Two Ordinary People Collecting Masterworks

AUG. 16, 1922 - JULY 22, 2012

NEW YORK CITY TEEMS with questionable urban legends. But the one about the postal clerk and his wife, a Brooklyn librarian, scrimping to amass an astounding collection of modern art, cramming all 5,000 pieces in a rent-controlled one-bedroom apartment, and then donating the lot of it to museums and galleries in all 50 states, happens to be true. The National Gallery of Art in Washington will attest to it.

Indeed, it was the museum that announced that the former clerk, Herbert Vogel, had died, on July 22, in a Manhattan nursing home at the age of 89, some 32 years after he had retired from the Postal Service but not, to be sure, from art collecting.

When he and his wife, Dorothy, gave thousands of artworks to the National Gallery in 1992, its director then, J. Carter Brown, called their collection "a work of art in itself."

So were the lives of the couple informally known as Dorothy and Herbert (in that order, Mr. Vogel insisted). They bought their first piece of art — a small crushed-metal sculpture by John Chamberlain — in 1962, shortly after their wedding. Realizing that their own efforts at making art were not up to the standards of Mr. Chamberlain and other artists they admired, they began buying others' artworks. Starting slowly, they bought what they liked (and what they could afford on two civil-service incomes), with only one stipulation: they had to be able to carry their choice home.

Finding room for the art in their small apartment on Manhattan's Upper East Side was no problem, as long as they didn't mind donating their closets to art, getting rid of the sofa and tripping over paintings. But Mrs. Vogel did not — repeat, did not — keep art in her oven. "We didn't set out to live bizarrely," she said in an interview with The New York Times in 1992.

Manet, Renoir and Corot liked to wander in and around the mountains of art, as cats are wont to do. There were five others, all with similarly illustrious names. Twenty exotic turtles completed the scene.

The Vogel collection became a guidepost for a school of art that followed Abstract Expressionism's long reign: Minimal Art.

Minimal works tended to be austere in their examination of monochromatic surfaces and essential forms, and, not surprising, they were nowhere near as popular as another genre on the rise, Pop Art, which drew its colorful imagery from consumer products.

The Vogels also took advantage of a buyers' market for conceptual art, in which the image is an idea. One conceptual piece in their collection involved a few inches of frayed rope with a nail through it; another was a black cardboard square with the definition of the word "nothing" printed on it in white.

The Vogels' style was to approach the young and often unknown artists who were making the new art, befriend them, and buy from them directly, bypassing the galleries. Some in the art world characterized that practice as cheating the system. The Vogels bought on credit and were known to be slow to pay. They had no car, took no vacations and ate TV dinners. A night out was dinner at the neighborhood Chinese restaurant. Sometimes they did cat-sitting in exchange for art.

In the 2008 documentary "Herb & Dorothy" (not "Dorothy & Herb," as Mr. Vogel might have preferred), the director, Megumi Sasaki, had her camera operators focus on Mr. Vogel's eyes as they lit up when he liked something.

The Vogels developed a pattern of buying artists' works made over a period of years, the better to capture their evolving careers. Artists appreciated that.

"They passionately collect some artists, and they collect them from the beginning, before gallery or critical interest," the artist Christo told The Miami Herald in 1989. He was a favorite of the Vogels before he became famous for his monumental works of environmental art.

The Vogels also collected works by Sol LeWitt, Robert Mangold, Richard Tuttle, Donald Judd and Chuck Close, among others.

In recent years they added Andy Goldsworthy, James Siena and Pat Steir to their roster.

Speaking to Newsday in 1992, Mr. Close, who helped develop the painting style called photorealism, said of the Vogels, "You knew when you were selling them something it was becoming part of an important collection."

Herbert Vogel was born in Manhattan on Aug. 16, 1922. After dropping out of school he worked in garment-industry sweatshops. But as he told Smithsonian magazine in 1992, "I knew there was another world out there, and somehow I'd find it for myself."

THE VOGEL COLLECTION: Herbert Vogel, a postal worker, and his wife, Dorothy, collected thousands of modern artworks in their rent-controlled, one-bedroom apartment.

His interest in art began percolating after he had finished a stint in the Army and begun visiting the Metropolitan Museum of Art, where he encountered Old Master paintings. That led him to contemporary art, and contemporary art led him to the Cedar Bar, the fabled artists' hangout in Greenwich Village, where he listened in awe as Mark Rothko, Franz Kline and David Smith held forth.

"I was nothing — a postal clerk," he told The Times. "But I respected the artists, and they sort of respected me. They would talk until 3, 4 in the morning, and I would be one of the people who just listened. I just remember it very vividly. I never even asked a question."

In 1960 he met Dorothy Faye Hoffman at a resort in the Poconos. On their first date, art did not come up. On subsequent dates, as they went to the movies and watched the presidential election returns together (Senator John F. Kennedy won), they fell in love. After their honeymoon in Washington, where they visited the National Gallery, they took classes in painting. The classes helped them realize that they would rather hang other artists' work on their walls.

"I wasn't bad," Mrs. Vogel told Newsday. "I didn't like Herbie's paintings, actually."

She and a sister survive him.

In 1992, five full-size moving vans were needed to move their art to the National Gallery, where they were soon feted by William H. Rehnquist, the chief justice of the United States, and the banker David Rockefeller. In 2008, the gallery announced that it would help the Vogels carry out their plan to give 50 artworks to one museum in each of the 50 states. The couple liked to work with the National Gallery because it had never sold a painting and admission was free.

Mr. Vogel's highest annual salary at the post office was $23,000 before taxes, he told The Associated Press in 1992. He acknowledged that he and his wife could have been multimillion-aires if they had chosen to sell their collection rather than donate it.

"But we weren't concerned about that aspect," he said.

— BY DOUGLAS MARTIN

SALLY RIDE

A Ceiling in Space Was Shattered

MAY 26, 1951 - JULY 23, 2012

ALLY RIDE, the first American woman to fly in space, died on July 23 at her home in San Diego. She was 61.

The cause was pancreatic cancer, according to Sally Ride Science, an educational company she founded in 2001. Her death took many by surprise; she

had not talked about her illness publicly, in keeping with her long insistence on protecting her privacy. Indeed, only on her death was it publicly learned that she and another woman had been partners for 27 years, a revelation that set off wide public discussion.

Dr. Ride, a physicist who was accepted into the space program in 1978 after she answered a newspaper ad for astronauts, flew on the shuttle Challenger on June 18, 1983, and on a second mission in 1984. At 32, she was the youngest American in space.

And after the Challenger exploded over Florida in 1986 and the Columbia crashed on re-entry over Texas in 2003, killing all on board in each case, Dr. Ride was the only person to sit on both commissions convened to investigate the catastrophes.

Dr. Ride was finishing studies at Stanford University and looking for a job when she saw NASA's advertisement. Holding degrees in physics and astrophysics (and also English), she looked at the qualifications and said, "I'm one of those people,"

RIDE, SALLY RIDE: Sally Ride made history as the first American woman in space.

she told The New York Times in 1982.

She applied, and made the cut.

"The women's movement had already paved the way, I think, for my coming," she said.

By the time she began studying laser physics at Stanford, women had already broken through into the physics department, once a boys' club. And when she applied to the space program, NASA had already made a commitment to admit women.

But there were still rough spots. Speaking to reporters before the first shuttle flight, Dr. Ride — chosen in part because she was known for keeping her cool under stress — politely endured a barrage of questions focused on her sex: Would spaceflight affect her reproductive organs? Did she plan to have children? Would she wear a bra or makeup in space? Did she cry on the job? How would she deal with menstruation in space?

The CBS News reporter Diane Sawyer asked her to demonstrate a newly installed privacy curtain around the shuttle's toilet. On "The Tonight Show," Johnny Carson joked that the shuttle flight would be delayed because Dr. Ride had to find a purse to match her shoes.

At a NASA news conference, Dr. Ride said: "It's too bad this is such a big deal. It's too bad our society isn't further along."

The Soviets had already sent two women into space. When one came aboard a space station, a male cosmonaut welcomed her by saying the kitchen and an apron were all ready for her.

In her early days at NASA, Dr. Ride trained in parachute jumping, water survival, weightlessness and the huge G-forces of a rocket launch. She learned to fly a jet plane. She also switched from physics to engineering and helped in the development of a robotic arm for the space shuttle. The Challenger commander, Robert L. Crippen, chose her for the 1983 mission in part because of her expertise with the device. She was part of a crew of five that spent about six days in space, during which she used the arm to deploy and retrieve a satellite.

At Cape Canaveral, many in the crowd of 250,000 that watched the launching wore T-shirts that said, "Ride, Sally Ride" — from the lyrics of the song "Mustang Sally."

The next day, Gloria Steinem, editor of Ms. magazine at the time, said, "Millions of little girls are going to sit by their television sets and see they can be astronauts, heroes, explorers and scientists."

When the shuttle landed, Dr. Ride told reporters, "I'm sure it was the most fun that I'll ever have in my life."

Her next mission, in 1984, lasted about eight days. She was on the roster for another shuttle flight before the Challenger blew up on Jan. 28, 1986, 73 seconds after taking off from Cape Canaveral. The program was immediately suspended, and she retired the next year.

As a member of the panel appointed by President Ronald Reagan to investigate the accident, Ms. Ride gained a reputation for asking tough questions. The panel learned from testimony and other evidence that there had been signs of trouble on earlier Challenger flights, but that they had been dismissed as not critical. Dr. Ride told a colleague that it was difficult not to be angered by the findings.

> Johnny Carson joked that the launch was delayed — Dr. Ride had to find a purse to match her shoes.

One witness was Roger Boisjoly, an engineer who had worked for the company that made the shuttle's rocket boosters. He had been shunned by colleagues for revealing that he had warned his bosses and NASA that the boosters' seals, called O-rings, could fail in cold weather. The Challenger had taken off on a cold morning.

After his testimony, the normally reticent Dr. Ride publicly hugged him. She was the only panelist to offer him support. Mr. Boisjoly, who died in January (see page 182), said her gesture had helped sustain him during a troubled time.

In 2003, after sitting on a shuttle-disaster panel for the second time, Dr. Ride said in an interview with The Times that part of the problem at NASA was that people had forgotten some of the lessons learned from the Challenger accident. The panel had months earlier expressed its conviction that the disintegration of the shuttle Columbia was triggered when a chunk of foam insulation fell off the external fuel tank and gashed the leading edge of the wing.

But she also said: "I flew the shuttle twice. It got me home twice. I like the shuttle."

In 1987, Dr. Ride led a study team that wrote a report advising NASA on the future of the space program. The team recommended an outpost on the Moon, but said that Mars should still be the "ultimate objective." In the report, Dr. Ride wrote that a lunar outpost would combine "adventure, science, technology and perhaps the seeds of enterprise." She noted darkly that the United States had "lost leadership" to the Soviet Union in a number of aspects of space exploration.

Retiring from NASA that year, she became a science fellow at the Center for International Security and Arms Control at Stanford. In 1989, she became a professor of physics and director of the California Space Institute at the University of California, San Diego.

She also developed a passion for trying to interest young people in science, math and technology. She wrote six science books for children, including one that explained how to make a sandwich in space. (She advised eating it fast, before it floated away.) She started Sally Ride Science, she said, to "make science and engineering cool again." The company provides science-oriented school programs, materials and teacher training.

Steadfastly guarding her privacy, Dr. Ride rejected most offers for product endorsements, memoirs and movies, and her reticence lasted to the end. NASA had kept her illness secret at her request. When her company's Web site revealed after her death that she and Tam O'Shaughnessy, a psychology professor who is the chief operating officer of Sally Ride Science, had been partners since 1985, some commentators called it a posthumous "coming out"; others saw the disclosure as an invasion of the privacy she had long maintained. Some gay rights organizations adopted her posthumously as a heroine; but their critics countered that she had never identified herself with their cause. Some news organizations were

accused of playing down the relationship; others, of "outing" her.

In 1983, writing in The Washington Post, Susan Okie, a journalist and longtime friend, described Dr. Ride as elusive and enigmatic, protective of her emotions. She quoted Dr. Ride's younger sister, the Rev. Karen Scott, a Presbyterian minister, as saying, " 'Closeness' is not a word that is often used to describe relationships in our family." Their mother told Dr. Okie that Dr. Ride always needed to be in control.

"During college and graduate school," Dr. Okie wrote of Dr. Ride, "I had to interrogate her to find out what was happening in her personal life."

Sally Kristen Ride was born on May 26, 1951, in Encino, part of Los Angeles. Her father was a political science professor at Santa Monica College, and her mother worked as a volunteer counselor at a women's correctional facility. Both parents were elders in the Presbyterian Church.

Dr. Ride gravitated toward math and science from an early age. She was strong-willed and athletic, and became so obsessed with playing football in the street that her parents pushed her into tennis lessons because it was a safer sport. She was soon playing in tournaments.

Dr. Ride attended Westlake School for Girls, a prep school in Los Angeles. Dr. Okie was her schoolmate, and wrote that she and Dr. Ride, both on scholarship, felt out of place among the actors' daughters and "Bel Air belles" at the school. Dr. Ride called herself an underachiever there, though she acknowledged that she did not have to work hard for good grades. If she was bored in class, she said, she would refuse to feign interest.

But it was at Westlake that Dr. Ride found a mentor and friend in Elizabeth Mommaerts, a science teacher whom she described as "logic personified." Dr. Mommaerts would invite

Dr. Ride and other students to her home to sample French food and wine and to hear stories about her life in Europe.

(In graduate school, Dr. Ride was devastated to learn that Dr. Mommaerts had committed suicide. When she was chosen to be an astronaut, the one person she wanted most to call was Dr. Mommaerts, she told Dr. Okie. "And I can't," she said.)

After graduating from high school in 1968, Dr. Ride attended Swarthmore College in Pennsylvania but quit after three semesters. She was homesick for California and was considering a career in tennis. Back home, she practiced tennis incessantly, but science also continued to have a hold on her, and she began taking physics courses at the University of California, Los Angeles.

Her tennis ambitions took her to Stanford, where she enrolled as a junior in 1970. She became the tennis team's No. 1 women's singles player and was nationally ranked. In the summer she taught at tennis camps, and at one of them she met Billie Jean King, who urged her to quit college and become a professional tennis player.

Years later, when a child asked her what had made her decide to be a scientist instead of a tennis player, she laughed and said, "A bad forehand."

At Stanford she received bachelor's degrees in physics and English in 1973 (her specialty was Shakespeare), a master's degree in physics in 1975 and a Ph.D. in astrophysics in 1978. Her graduate work involved X-ray astronomy and free-electron lasers.

One of her enduring concerns was encouraging young people, girls in particular, to embrace the sciences. She bridled at the persistence of stereotypes about girls and science and math — the idea, for example, that girls had innately less ability or interest in those subjects, or that they would be unpopular if they excelled in

them. She thought peer pressure, especially in middle school, began driving girls away from the sciences.

Through her company, Sally Ride Science, she set up science programs all over the country for both boys and girls. But some have been tailored specifically to appeal to girls — science festivals, science camps, science clubs — to help them find mentors, role models and one another.

"It's no secret that I've been reluctant to use my name for things," she said. "I haven't written my memoirs or let the television movie be made about my life. But this is something I'm very willing to put my name behind."

Dr. Ride married a fellow astronaut, Steven Hawley, in 1982. They divorced in 1987. Besides

A HISTORIC FLIGHT: As part of a crew of five, Sally Ride spent six days on the shuttle Challenger during her 1983 mission to space.

Dr. O'Shaughnessy, Dr. Ride is survived by her sister, Ms. Scott, and her mother.

Dr. Ride was the co-author of several books on science, some written with Dr. O'Shaughnessy.

President Barack Obama said in a statement that Dr. Ride had been "a national hero and a powerful role model.

"She inspired generations of young girls to reach for the stars and later fought tirelessly to help them get there by advocating for a greater focus on science and math in our schools," he said. "Sally's life showed us that there are no limits to what we can achieve."

But Dr. Ride told interviewers that what drove her was not the desire to become famous or to make history as the first woman in space. All she wanted to do was fly, she said, to soar into space, float around weightless inside the shuttle, look out at the heavens and gaze back at Earth. In photographs of her afloat in the space-ship, she is grinning, as if she had at long last reached the place where she was meant to be.

— BY DENISE GRADY

\\\\\\\\\\\\\\\\\\\\\\\\\\\\\\\\\\\\

GORE VIDAL

As He Himself Might Have Said, There Will Never Be Another

OCT. 3, 1925 · JULY 31, 2012

Gore Vidal, the elegant, acerbic all-around man of letters who presided with a certain relish over what he declared to be the end of American civilization, died on July 31 at his home in the Hollywood Hills section of Los Angeles, where he moved in 2003 after years of living in Ravello, Italy. He was 86.

Mr. Vidal was, at the end of his life, an Augustan figure who believed himself to be the last of a breed, and he was probably right. Few American writers have been more versatile or gotten more mileage from their talent. He published some 25 novels, two memoirs and several volumes of stylish, magisterial essays. He also wrote plays, television dramas and screen-plays. For a while he was even a contract writer at MGM. And he could always be counted on for a spur-of-the-moment aphorism, put-down or sharply worded critique of American foreign policy.

Perhaps more than any other American writer except Norman Mailer or Truman Capote, Mr. Vidal took great pleasure in being a public figure. He twice ran for office — in 1960, when he was the Democratic Congressional candidate for the 29th District in upstate New York, and in 1982, when he campaigned in California for a seat in the Senate — and though he lost both times, he often conducted himself as a sort of unelected shadow president. He once said, "There is not one human problem that could not be solved if people would simply do as I advise."

Mr. Vidal was an occasional actor, appearing in animated form on "The Simpsons" and "Family Guy," in the movie version of his own play "The Best Man," and in the Tim Robbins movie "Bob Roberts," in which he played an aging, epicene version of himself. He was a more-than-occasional guest on talk shows, where his poise, wit, good looks and charm made him such a regular that Johnny Carson offered him a spot as a guest host of "The Tonight Show."

Television was a natural medium for Mr. Vidal, who in person was often as cool and detached as he was in his prose. "Gore is a man without an unconscious," his friend the Italian writer Italo Calvino once said. Mr. Vidal said of himself: "I'm exactly as I appear. There is no warm, lovable person inside. Beneath my cold exterior, once you break the ice, you find cold water."

Mr. Vidal loved conspiracy theories of all sorts, especially the ones he imagined himself at the center of, and he was a famous feuder; he engaged in celebrated on-screen wrangles with Mailer, Capote and William F. Buckley Jr. Mr. Vidal did not lightly suffer fools — a category that for him comprised a vast swath of humanity, elected officials particularly — and he was not a sentimentalist or a romantic. "Love is not my bag," he said.

By the time he was 25, he had already had more than 1,000 sexual encounters with both men and women, he boasted in his memoir "Palimpsest." Mr. Vidal tended toward what he called "same-sex sex," but frequently declared that human beings were inherently bisexual, and that labels like gay (a term he disliked) or straight were arbitrary and unhelpful. For 53 years, he had a live-in companion, Howard Austen, a former advertising executive, but the secret of their relationship was that they did not sleep together, Mr. Vidal said.

He sometimes claimed to be a populist — in theory, anyway — but he was not convincing as one. Both by temperament and by birth he was an aristocrat.

A Child on the Senate Floor

Eugene Luther Gore Vidal Jr. was born on Oct. 3, 1925, at the United States Military Academy at West Point, where his father, Eugene, had been an All-American football player and a track star and had returned as a flying instructor and assistant football coach. An aviation pioneer, Eugene Vidal Sr. went on to found three airlines, including one that became T.W.A. He was director of the Bureau of Air Commerce under President Franklin D. Roosevelt. Mr. Vidal's mother, Nina, was an actress and socialite and the daughter of Thomas Pryor Gore, a Democratic senator from Oklahoma.

Mr. Vidal's television clashes with Mailer and Buckley were legendary.

Mr. Vidal, who once said he had grown up in "the House of Atreus," detested his mother, whom he frequently described as a bullying, self-pitying alcoholic. She and Mr. Vidal's father divorced in 1935, and she married Hugh D. Auchincloss, the stepfather of Jacqueline Kennedy Onassis — a connection that Mr. Vidal never tired of bringing up.

After his mother's remarriage, Mr. Vidal lived with her at Merrywood, the Auchincloss family estate in Virginia, but his fondest memories were of the years the family spent at his maternal grandfather's sprawling home in the Rock Creek Park neighborhood of Washington.

He loved to read to his grandfather, who was blind, and sometimes accompanied him onto the Senate floor. Mr. Vidal's lifelong interest in politics began to stir back then, and from his grandfather, an America Firster, he probably also inherited his unwavering isolationist beliefs.

Mr. Vidal attended St. Albans School in Washington, where he lopped off his Christian names and became simply Gore Vidal, which he considered more literary-sounding. Though he shunned sports himself, he formed an intense romantic and sexual friendship — the most important of his life, he later said — with Jimmie Trimble, one of the school's best athletes.

AN EARLY SUCCESS: Gore Vidal quickly became a glamorous young literary figure.

Trimble was his "ideal brother," his "other half," Mr. Vidal said, the only person with whom he ever felt wholeness. Jimmie's premature death at Iwo Jima in World War II at once sealed off their relationship in a glow of A. E. Housman-like early perfection, and seemingly made it impossible for Mr. Vidal ever to feel the same way about anyone else.

After leaving St. Albans in 1939, Mr. Vidal spent a year at the Los Alamos Ranch School in New Mexico before enrolling at Phillips Exeter Academy in New Hampshire. He contributed stories and poems to the Exeter literary magazine, but he was an indifferent student who excelled mostly at debating. A classmate, the writer John Knowles, later used him as the model for Brinker Hadley, the know-it-all conspiracy theorist in "A Separate Peace," his Exeter-based novel.

Mr. Vidal graduated from Exeter at 17 — only by cheating on virtually every math exam, he admitted — and enlisted in the Army, becoming first mate on a freight supply ship in the Aleutian Islands. He began work on "Williwaw," a novel set on a troopship and published in 1946, while he was an associate editor at the publishing company E. P. Dutton, a job he soon gave up. Written in a pared-down, Hemingway-like style, "Williwaw" (the title is a meteorological term for a sudden wind out of the mountains) won some admiring reviews but gave little clue to the kind of writer Mr. Vidal would become. Neither did his second book, "In a Yellow Wood" (1947), about a brokerage clerk and his wartime Italian mistress. Mr. Vidal later said it was so bad, he couldn't bear to reread it. He nevertheless became a glamorous young literary figure, pursued by Anaïs Nin and courted by Christopher Isherwood and Tennessee Williams.

In 1948 Mr. Vidal published "The City and the Pillar," which was dedicated to J. T. (Jimmie Trimble). It is what would now be called a coming-out story, about a handsome, athletic young Virginia man who gradually discovers that he is homosexual. By today's standards it is tame and discreet, but at the time it caused a scandal and was denounced as corrupt and pornographic. Mr. Vidal went on to claim that the literary and critical establishment, The New York Times especially, had blacklisted him because of the book, and he may have been right. He had such trouble getting subsequent novels reviewed that he turned to writing mysteries under the pseudonym Edgar Box and then, for a time, gave up novel-writing altogether. To make a living he concentrated on writing for television, then for the stage and the movies.

POLITICS ONSTAGE, AND FOR REAL

Work was plentiful. He wrote for most of the shows that presented hourlong original dramas in the 1950s, including "Studio One," "Philco Television Playhouse" and "Goodyear Playhouse." He became so adept, he could knock off an adaptation in a weekend and an original play in a week or two. He turned "Visit to a Small Planet," his 1955 television drama about an alien who comes to Earth to study the art of war, into a Broadway play. His most successful play was "The Best Man," about two contenders for the presidential nomination. It ran for 520 performances on Broadway before it, too, became a well-received film, in 1964, with a cast headed by Henry Fonda and a screenplay by Mr. Vidal. It was revived on Broadway in 2000 and was revived there again in 2012 as "Gore Vidal's The Best Man."

Mr. Vidal's reputation as a script doctor was such that in 1956 MGM hired him as a contract writer; among other projects, he helped rewrite the screenplay of "Ben-Hur," though he was denied an official credit. He also wrote the screenplay for the movie adaptation of his friend Tennessee Williams's play "Suddenly, Last Summer."

By the end of the '50s, though, Mr. Vidal, at last financially secure, had wearied of Hollywood and turned to politics. He had purchased Edgewater, a Greek Revival mansion in Dutchess County, N.Y., and it became his headquarters for his 1960 run for Congress. He was encouraged by Eleanor Roosevelt, a neighbor who had become a friend and adviser.

The 29th Congressional District was a Republican stronghold, and though Mr. Vidal, running as Eugene Gore on a platform that included taxing the wealthy, lost, he received more votes in running for the seat than any Democrat in 50 years. He liked to point out that he did better in the district than the Democratic presidential candidate that year, John F. Kennedy.

Mr. Vidal also returned to writing novels in the 1960s and published three books in fairly quick succession: "Julian" (1964), "Washington, D.C." (1967) and "Myra Breckinridge" (1968). "Julian," which some critics still consider Mr. Vidal's best, was a painstakingly researched historical novel about the fourth-century Roman emperor who tried to convert Christians back to paganism. (Mr. Vidal himself never had much use for religion, Christianity especially, which he once called "intrinsically funny.") "Washington, D.C." was a political novel set in the 1940s. "Myra Breckinridge," Mr. Vidal's own favorite among his books, was a campy black comedy about a male homosexual who has sexual reassignment surgery. (A 1970 film version, with Raquel Welch and Mae West, proved to be a disaster.)

Perhaps without intending it, Mr. Vidal had set a pattern. In the years to come he found his greatest successes with historical novels, notably what became known as his American Chronicles: "Washington, D.C.," "Burr" (1973), "1876" (1976), "Lincoln" (1984), "Empire" (1987), "Hollywood" (1990) and "The Golden Age" (2000).

He turned out to have a gift for this kind of writing. These novels were learned and scrupulously based on fact, but also witty and contemporary-feeling, full of gossip and shrewd asides. Harold Bloom wrote that Mr. Vidal's imagination of American politics "is so powerful as to compel awe." Writing in The Times, Christopher Lehmann-Haupt said, "Mr. Vidal gives us an interpretation of our early history that says in effect that all the old verities were never much to begin with."

But Mr. Vidal also persisted in writing books like "Myron" (1974), a sequel to "Myra," and "Live From Golgotha: The Gospel According to

Gore Vidal" (1992). Both were clearly meant as provocations. "Live From Golgotha," for example, rewrites the Gospels, with Saint Paul as a huckster and pederast and Jesus a buffoon. John Rechy said of it in The Los Angeles Times Book Review, "If God exists and Jesus is his son, then Gore Vidal is going to hell."

In the opinion of many critics, though, Mr. Vidal's ultimate reputation is apt to rest less on his novels than on his essays, many of them written for The New York Review of Books. His collection "The Second American Revolution" won the National Book Critics Circle Award for criticism in 1982. About a later collection, "United States: Essays 1952-1992," R. W. B. Lewis wrote in The New York Times Book Review that Vidal the essayist was "so good that we cannot do without him," adding, "He is a treasure of state."

Mr. Vidal's essays were literary, resurrecting the works of forgotten writers like Dawn Powell and William Dean Howells, and also political, taking on issues like sexuality and cultural mores. The form suited him ideally: he could be learned, funny, stylish, show-offy and incisive all at once. Even Jason Epstein, Mr. Vidal's longtime editor at Random House, once admitted that he preferred the essays to the novels, calling Mr. Vidal "an American version of Montaigne."

"I always thought about Gore that he was not really a novelist," Mr. Epstein wrote, "that he had too much ego to be a writer of fiction because he couldn't subordinate himself to other people the way you have to as a novelist."

VIDAL VS. BUCKLEY (AND MAILER)

Success did not mellow Mr. Vidal. In 1968, while covering the Democratic National Convention on television, he called William F. Buckley a "crypto-Nazi." Buckley responded by calling Mr. Vidal a "queer," and the two were

in court for years. In a 1971 essay he compared Norman Mailer to Charles Manson, and a few months later Mailer head-butted him in the green room while the two were waiting to appear on "The Dick Cavett Show." They then took their quarrel on the air in a memorable exchange that ended with Mr. Cavett's telling Mailer to take a piece of paper on the table in front of them and "fold it five ways and put it where the moon don't shine." In 1975 he sued Truman Capote for libel after Capote wrote that Mr. Vidal had been thrown out of the Kennedy White House. Mr. Vidal won a grudging apology.

Mr. Vidal said of himself: "I'm exactly as I appear. There is no warm, lovable person inside. Beneath my cold exterior, once you break the ice, you find cold water."

Some of his political positions were similarly quarrelsome and provocative. Mr. Vidal was an outspoken critic of Israel's treatment of the Palestinians, and once called Norman Podhoretz, the editor of Commentary, and his wife, the journalist Midge Decter, "Israeli fifth columnists." In the 1990s he wrote sympathetically about Timothy McVeigh, who was executed for the Oklahoma City bombing. And after the Sept. 11 terrorist attacks, he wrote an essay for Vanity Fair arguing that America had brought the attacks upon itself by maintaining imperialist foreign policies. In another essay, for The Independent, he compared the attacks to the Japanese raid on Pearl Harbor, arguing that both Presidents Franklin D. Roosevelt and George W. Bush knew of them in advance and exploited them to advance their agendas.

As for literature, it was more or less over, he declared more than once, and he had reached a point where he no longer much cared. He became a sort of connoisseur of decline, in fact. America is "rotting away at a funereal pace," he told The Times of London in 2009. "We'll have a military dictatorship pretty soon, on the basis that nobody else can hold everything together."

In 2003 Mr. Vidal and his companion, Mr. Austen, who was ill, left their cliffside Italian villa La Rondinaia (the Swallow's Nest) on the Gulf of Salerno and moved to the Hollywood Hills to be closer to Cedars-Sinai Medical Center. Mr. Austen died that year, and in "Point to Point Navigation," his second volume of memoirs, Mr. Vidal recalled that Mr. Austen asked from his deathbed, "Didn't it go by awfully fast?"

"Of course it had," Mr. Vidal wrote. "We had been too happy and the gods cannot bear

MAN OF LETTERS: Few writers were as prodigious as Gore Vidal.

the happiness of mortals." Mr. Austen was buried in Washington in a plot Mr. Vidal had purchased in Rock Creek Cemetery. The gravestone was already inscribed with their names side by side.

Mr. Vidal died of complications of pneumonia, his nephew Burr Steers said. Mr. Vidal's survivors also include a sister.

After Mr. Austen's death, Mr. Vidal lived alone in declining health himself. He was increasingly troubled by a knee injury he suffered in the war, and used a wheelchair to get around.

In November 2009 he made a rare public appearance to attend the National Book Awards in New York, where he was given a lifetime achievement award. He had evidently not prepared any remarks, and instead delivered a meandering impromptu speech that was sometimes funny and sometimes a little hard to follow. At one point he even seemed to speak fondly of Buckley, his old nemesis. It sounded like a summing up.

"Such fun, such fun," he said.

— BY CHARLES MCGRATH

INDEXES

GENERAL INDEX

SPECIALTY INDEX

PHOTOGRAPHY CREDITS

COVER (clockwise from upper left): Associated Press, Australian War Memorial/Associated Press, Richard Saker/Rex USA, Jeff Kravitz/Film Magic/Getty Images, Justin Sullivan/Getty Images, Associated Press, Korea News Service/Associated Press, Photofest.

ASSOCIATED PRESS: p. 1, p. 33, p. 43, p. 53, p. 60, p. 66, p. 75, p. 83, p. 101, p. 114, p. 116, p. 121, p. 155, p. 163, p. 183, p. 195, p. 202, p. 218, p. 220, p. 274, p. 276, p. 285, p. 287, p. 320, p. 322, p. 340, p. 347, p. 351, p. 366, p. 369, p. 375, Australian War Memorial p. 10, Bettmann/Corbis p. 133, p. 245, p. 314, p. 367, Sidney Corrallo/Agencia Estado p. 140, CTK Photo p. 165, Dapd p. 63, Betty Skelton Erde p. 31, Korea News Agency p. 158, LG Electronics p. 306, Ed Ou for The New York Times p. 223, Ted Soqui/Corbis p. 325, The Dallas Morning News p. 124, The Knoxville News Sentinel p. 337, The Oregonian/Ross William Hamilton p. 234, Writer Pictures p. 231, Burney Yeargin/Ebony Collection p. 189.

SUZANNE DeCHILLO: p. 265.

GETTY IMAGES: Richard E. Aaron/Redferns p. 17, Erich Auerbach p. 303, Authenticated News p. 269, B. Bennett p. 104, Andrew Burton p. 241, Jerry Cooke/Time Life Pictures p. 372, Don Cravens/Time Life Pictures

p. 71, Mark Cunningham p. 196, Robert Doisneau/Gamma-Rapho p. 118, Evening Standard p. 95, Sid Fields/NY Daily News Archive p. 252, Foto24/Gallo Images p. 91, James Fraher/Redferns p. 29, David Gahr p. 311, Ernst Haas/Hutlon Archive p. 170, Harry Hamburg/NY Daily News p. 168, Ethan Hill/Contour p. 228, James Keyser/Time Life Pictures p. 296, Keystone-France/Gamma-Keystone p. 85, Jeff Kravitz/Film Magic p. 49, Bob Landry/Time Life Pictures p. 161, Andrew Lepley p. 267, Neil Liefer/Sports Illustrated p. 328, Steve Liss/Time Life Pictures p. 69, Fred W. McDarrah p. 259, Richard Meek/Sports Illustrated p. 144, Michael Ochs Archives p. 19, p. 55, p. 187, p. 205, p. 238, p. 300, p. 359, Mondadori p. 349, Sydney O'Meara p. 309, Dennis Oulds/Ted West/Leonard Burt/Central Press/Hulton Archive p. 112, Joe Raedle p. 98, Ebet Roberts p. 280, Ebet Roberts/Redferns p. 212, p. 291, Adalberto Roque/AFP p. 80, Astrid Stawiarz p. 332, Terrence Donovan Archive p. 139, The Washington Post p. 22, Time Life Pictures p. 8, p. 214, John Torgovnik/Edit p. 148.

MAGNUM PHOTOS: © Eve Arnold, Photo by Robert Penn p. 179.

NEWSCOM: Brigitte Hellgoth/akg-images p. 35, LaPresse/Zuma Press p. 38, Pete Marovich/Zuma Press p. 107, Marijaan Murat/EPA p. 250, Rockefeller University p. 57.

PHOTOFEST: p. 127, p. 199, ABC p. 274, CBS p. 344, Liane Enkelis/The Living Century p. 181, NBC p. 135, Ralph Nelson/Columbia Pictures p. 191, Twentieth Century-Fox Film Corporation p. 335.

REUTERS: Larry Downing p. 78, Korea-Unification/School p. 157, Stringer p. 4.

REX USA: Michael Burnett/Associated New p. 210.

© SCOTT MARKEWITZ PHOTOGRAPHY, INC.: p. 108.

THE NEW YORK TIMES: p. 27, Monica Almeida p. 289, Neal Boenzi p. 255, Fred R. Conrad p. 174, p. 184, p. 354, p. 365, Tyrone Dukes p. 81, Mark Mahaney p. 152, Jack Manning p. 7, Andrea Mohin p. 146, Ozier Muhammad p. 352, Librado Romero p. 142, Nancy Siesel p. 94, George Tames p. 130, Dilip Vishwanat p. 51, Ruby Washington p. 236, Jim Wilson p. 12, p. 317, Damon Winter p. 216, Teresa Zabala p. 331.

COURTESY PHOTOS: Carcanet p. 254, © Aaron Litvinoff p. 47, © Shakespeare and Company Paris Archive 1979-1980 p. 150, Michael Spengler p. 136, The Estate of Budd Hopkins p. 15, The Keith Tantlinger Family p. 25, The René Morel Family p. 110, © Ziggy and Friends, Inc. Distributed by Universal Click p. 40.

PERMISSIONS

ACKNOWLEDGMENTS

A BOOK, like this, of many parts requires many hands to pull it together — those of writers, editors, photographers, photo editors, designers and more — and it's all for the better when they've done it before. So it was for many who helped produce this book, the second annual compilation of New York Times

obituaries under the Workman banner: it was their second go-round. But they didn't simply repeat themselves. They brought new energy and ideas and a fresh look to the project.

Again the team was composed of two squads: one at Workman, the other at The Times. The Workman group was led by Maisie Tivnan, whose sound and creative guidance was again invaluable. Her assistant, Justin Krasner, deftly shepherded much of the book through its production stages. New to the project was Judit Bodnar, the production editor, and Sarah Smith who, along with Orlando Adiao, created a lively, inviting new design for the book. The photo editor, Michael Dimascio, gathered another thoughtful selection of striking pictures. And again Merrill Perlman, a former Times editor, brought her deep knowledge of language and Times style to the task of copy editing all these thousands of words.

At The Times, my colleagues on the obituary desk and elsewhere in the newsroom contributed to this book mainly by doing their jobs so well in creating a consistently fine obituary section for the newspaper over the 12 months this book covers. The reporters are too numerous to be listed here (see their bylines throughout these pages), but gratitude must be extended to them first. It was their painstaking research, resourceful

reporting and artful writing that, if you'll pardon the expression, brought their subjects to life.

Joining me on the obits desk were two editors, Jack Kadden and Peter Keepnews, who had the good judgment and imagination to recognize the significance of many of the unsung people portrayed here, and then to generate and help shape the obituaries about them. And behind them was the desk's news assistant, Daniel E. Slotnik, who helped with the reporting for many of these obits and, for good measure, wrote a couple himself. Meanwhile Phyllis Colazzo plumbed the Times's photo archives and came up with treasures in helping to illustrate this book. A word of thanks as well to Alex Ward, the editorial director of book projects for The Times and, for all of us, the chief navigator between two worlds — book publishing and newspapering.

Finally, another sincere thank you to those on the outside who helped us in the challenging task of summing up the lives of hundreds of people we had never met. Husbands and wives, sons and daughters, companions and friends, colleagues and associates — all were essential to our work, providing facts, sharing memories and contributing insights as we ventured to tell the stories of the ones they had lost.

—WILLIAM MCDONALD